INTERNATIONAL UNION
FOR CONSERVATION
OF NATURE AND NATURAL
RESOURCES

THE
IUCN MAMMAL
RED DATA BOOK
PART 1

PART I: Threatened mammalian
taxa of the Americas and the
Australasian zoogeographic
region (excluding Cetacea)

Compiled by
JANE THORNBACK

and

MARTIN JENKINS

of the
IUCN CONSERVATION
MONITORING CENTRE

with the help and advice
of the Species Survival Commission
of IUCN and other experts
throughout the world.

Prepared with the financial
assistance of

THE WORLD WILDLIFE FUND

and

THE UNITED NATIONS
ENVIRONMENT PROGRAMME

Published by IUCN,
Gland, Switzerland, 1982
(IUCN Conservation
Monitoring Centre,
219(c) Huntingdon Road,
Cambridge CB3 0DL, U.K.)

IUCN

IUCN (International Union for Conservation of Nature and Natural Resources) is a network of governments, nongovernmental organizations (NGOs), scientists and other conservation experts, joined together to promote the protection and sustainable use of living resources.

Founded in 1948, IUCN has more than 450 member governments and NGOs in over 100 countries. Its six Commissions consist of more than 700 experts on threatened species, protected areas, ecology, environmental planning, environmental policy, law and administration, and environmental education.

IUCN

- monitors the status of ecosystems and species throughout the world;
- plans conservation action, both at the strategic level through the World Conservation Strategy and the programme level through its programme of conservation for sustainable development;
- promotes such action by governments, intergovernmental bodies and nongovernmental organizations;
- provides assistance and advice necessary for the achievement of such action.

ISBN No. 2-88032-600-1

Cover drawing of a Jaguar (*Panthera onca*) by Sarah Anne Hughes

Printed by Unwin Brothers Limited,
The Gresham Press, Old Woking, Surrey, U.K.

PREAMBLE

IUCN has always had as one of its principal functions the gathering of data on species and habitats under threat, so that action can be taken. It has, over the years, initiated and solicited information throughout the world. For species, this has been mainly through the Specialist Groups of the Species Survival Commission (SSC) or particular contracted individuals.

It was recognised some while ago that to handle and put to best advantage the amount of data being received, together with the requirement to present information in many different ways and to insure that action programmes be developed rapidly, there was a need for a full-time Monitoring Centre to be set up. This has now been possible with the moral and financial support of the United Nations Environment Programme (UNEP) and the World Wildlife Fund (WWF), for which I am most grateful.

It has been my pleasure and privilege to help create this Centre and watch it quickly grow. It is now coming to the production stage, having had to collate sufficiently all the previous scattered information. This, as all researchers know, is a most frustrating task; working hard but having little to show for one's efforts. We now see the beginnings of not just a whole new generation of the Red Data Books, but a computer-held data base with much wider information available. In time this will allow many different outputs for many different purposes as well as updated information on single or groups of sheets; either geographic or taxonomically arranged as needed.

The present work is the result of this activity, involving the sustained attention of the compiler, support from the Centre's administrative staff and guidance from the Species Survival Commission's Specialist Group members and consultants. As will be evident from the Introduction, we rely heavily on the assistance and support of our own expert associates to ensure that our data is of the highest quality. May I count on your help?

I would like to express my thanks and congratulations to all those who have contributed towards this work; in particular Jane Thornback who has compiled it, Martin Jenkins who assisted her, Carol Hovenden who was responsible for handling the text storage and processing equipment, and Tony Mence, the Centre's manager.

G. Ll. Lucas
Chairman
Species Survival Commission

September 1981

CONTENTS

The IUCN Mammal Red Data Book was published in 1966, as the first volume in what has become the authoritative international register of threatened species. Volumes on birds, amphibians and reptiles, fish and plants have followed, and a volume on invertebrates is in progress.

The Red Data Book provides reliable data in synoptic form on species threatened throughout their range; it does not deal with taxa threatened within the boundaries of one nation but which are relatively abundant elsewhere. This reference work is the instrument of the Species Survival Commission (SSC) of the International Union for Conservation of Nature and Natural Resources (IUCN). The SSC, one of six Commissions of IUCN, was established in 1949, and is concerned primarily with action to prevent the extinction of species, and to preserve viable wild populations in their native habitats. Information on the status of species is vital to, and forms the basis of, this work.

To establish its data base with respect to mammals, the SSC concentrated initially on the revision and expansion of two works published in the 1940s by the American Committee for International Wildlife Protection - 'Extinct and Vanishing Mammals of the Old World' published in 1942, and its companion volume, 'Extinct and Vanishing Mammals of the New World' published in 1945. By the early 1960s the information so far collected had been stored on data cards amalgamated into a loose-leaved book. Sir Peter Scott, then Chairman of the SSC, had the idea of publishing this information as a Red Data Book series aimed at drawing public attention to the global threats to species in order to gain support, funds, and most important, action in the fight to save them.

The first volume - Mammalia - appeared in 1966 and was compiled by Noel Simon who continued the task until the end of 1971. In 1972 a major revision was undertaken by Harry A. Goodwin and Colin Holloway of the IUCN Secretariat; new and revised sheets were then issued in 1973, 1974, and 1976, with Holloway as the chief compiler. A further edition in 1978 was compiled by Jane Thornback.

Prior to 1978 editions of the Red Data Book were compiled on a part time basis, relying heavily on voluntary assistance from the SSC's global network of wildlife experts. The books were loose-leaf in format, a single sheet being assigned to a single taxon, and different colours used to designate the degree of threat: red for Endangered, yellow for Vulnerable, white for Rare, grey for Indeterminate.

This edition is a breakaway from that traditional format and has followed the example set by the IUCN Plant Red Data Book, published in 1978, which was the first to be published as a bound volume. Although a loose-leaf system was ideal for the private individual, many institutions found it difficult to maintain, for instance pages were easily removed, revisions were difficult to incorporate and the indexing system required a certain taxonomic knowledge to comprehend.

These factors led to the decision to change to a bound format and, for the Mammal volume, covering at present over 320 taxa, this necessitated a split into two parts if the information was to be published whilst still current. Since a geographic split seemed the most sensible, this edition incorporates those threatened mammalian taxa to be found in the Americas and the Australasian zoogeographic region (essentially Australia, New Zealand and the island of New Guinea). Threatened taxa of Africa, Europe and Asia will be detailed in subsequent editions, as will the Cetacea which are here excluded. Currently four species - the Wolf (Canis lupus), the Polar Bear (Ursus maritimus), the Brown and Grizzly Bear (Ursus arctos) and the Dugong (Dugong dugon) occur in several

i

zoogeographic regions. Information concerning their entire ranges will be given in each edition.

As well as having a new published format, the actual compilation of all Red Data Books has changed markedly since 1979. This has been necessitated by the accelerating threats to species survival. Virtually everywhere the major threat to wild species is loss of habitat to a rapidly increasing human population requiring more space to build villages and cities and to grow food; and invading and disturbing once remote areas in the pursuit of both renewable resources such as timber, and non-renewable resources such as oil and minerals in the race for industrial prizes. The majority of species have not been recognized as having any role to play in a modern world in which much of the population is striving against poverty, whilst the rest makes ever-increasing demands on its resources.

The World Conservation Strategy*, published in 1980, succinctly articulated the rationale for species conservation and absorbed it into the concept of conservation for development.

Living resource conservation for sustainable development was seen to have three specific objectives:
to maintain essential ecological processes and life support systems (such as soil regeneration and protection, the recycling of nutrients, and the cleansing of waters), on which human survival and development depend;
to preserve genetic diversity (the range of genetic material found in the world's organisms), on which depend the breeding programmes necessary for the protection and improvement of cultivated plants and domesticated animals, as well as much scientific advance, technical innovation, and the security of the many industries that use living resources;
to ensure the sustainable utilization of species and ecosystems (notably fish and other wildlife, forests and grazing lands), which support millions of rural communities as well as major industries.

The increasing threats to species survival and the urgent need for conservation action thus made it essential that the updating of the Red Data Books be accelerated, that full-time staff be employed, and that modern methods of data collection, storage and processing be used. In response, IUCN in 1979 established the Species Conservation Monitoring Unit (SCMU) in Cambridge, England. This Unit, when joined at the end of 1980 by the International Council for Bird Preservation (ICBP) which compiles the Bird Red Data Book, brought together under one roof the compilation of all animal Red Data Books. At the same time IUCN's Wildlife Trade Monitoring Unit (WTMU) (formerly known as TRAFFIC) moved in to share the Cambridge premises. The enlarged operation demanded a new name, thus the IUCN's Conservation Monitoring Centre (CMC) came into existence as an umbrella title. The Centre also embraces IUCN's

---

* World Conservation Strategy: Living Resource Conservation Strategy for Sustainable Development. Prepared by IUCN with advice, cooperation and financial assistance of the United Nations Environment Programme (UNEP) and the World Wildlife Fund (WWF) and in collaboration with the Food and Agriculture Organization of the United Nations (FAO) and the United Nations Educational, Scientific and Cultural Organisation (UNESCO).

Threatened Plants Committee (TPC) which compiles the Plant Red Data Book and is located at The Royal Botanic Gardens, Kew, England, and IUCN's Protected Areas Data Unit (PADU), established in 1981, also based at Kew. The latter is an instrument of IUCN's Commission on National Parks and Protected Areas (CNPPA) and compiles and maintains up-to-date lists of the world's protected areas. Some of this information is published in the United Nations List of National Parks and Equivalent Reserves and The World Directory of National Parks and other Protected Areas. PADU will assess the coverage by protected areas of each biogeographical province on land as identified by Udvardy, and biophysical province at sea. CNPPA will then be able to identify gaps in the world-wide system of reserves and thus focus its attention on the establishment of protected areas where they are most required. Initially PADU plans to produce volumes on each of the eight biogeographical realms.

All sections of the Centre have word-processing facilities which have greatly increased the efficiency of data compilation, and a computer has been installed at Kew to store and process the data base that is emerging.

The establishment of a data base incorporating animal and plant status, wildlife trade, and protected area data is now the principal aim of the Centre. Close collaboration will also be maintained with IUCN's Environmental Law Centre in Bonn, Germany, which provides legislative data, and with the Global Environment Monitoring System (GEMS) of the United Nations Environment Programme (UNEP).

Red Data Books are seen as but one output of this data base. Data will also be made available to, for instance, national and regional endangered species programmes, conservation funding agencies, and conventions such as the 1973 Convention on International Trade in Endangered Species of Wild Fauna and Flora (CITES), and the 1979 Convention on Conservation of Migratory Species of Wild Animals. Already the Centre has provided the European Economic Community (EEC) with draft lists, and detailed data sheets, of threatened mammals (excluding bats and cetacea), amphibians and reptiles, and plants, within its boundaries.

The information will, in addition, be used by the SSC to produce and update its programme of Action to Prevent Extinction (APX) and this will provide an input into the overall IUCN and World Wildlife Fund programmes and will assist them in their task of screening project proposals submitted for funding.

More importantly the availability of species, habitat and protected area information in the same data system will at last allow species conservation to take on a strategic aspect; reserves can be planned in areas where the maximum benefit to the maintenance of species diversity will accrue. Such information will be available to, for instance, development banks and technical assistance agencies so that the problems and needs of species conservation can be incorporated into land use and development planning at an early stage.

A single data base will allow the processing of data and the chance for strategic conservation to take over from the opportunistic 'fire brigade' conservation of the past. At last, land use planning will be able to take into account species' needs.

The years ahead bring with them great challenges in the environmental debate. In the case of wildlife conservation it is essential that the arguments, efforts and action be based on the most accurate and up-to-date information available. With the establishment of the Conservation Monitoring Centre, IUCN hopes to provide that essential data base.

Jane Thornback
Compiler, IUCN Mammal RDB
September, 1981.

The list of 155 mammals inhabiting the Americas and the Australasian zoogeographic region included in this publication is derived from previous editions of the Mammal Red Data Book, supplemented and refined by reference to the United States Endangered Species List, the status reports of the Committee on the Status of Endangered Wildlife in Canada (COSEWIC), the Official List of Endangered Australian Vertebrate Fauna, the appendices of the 1973 Convention on International Trade in Endangered Species of Wild Fauna and Flora (CITES), and information from government wildlife departments, non-governmental organizations, and scientists and naturalists, many of whom belong to the Specialist Groups of the Species Survival Commission of IUCN. It is best described as the list of known threatened mammals; it would be wrong to assume that all threatened mammals are included as undoubtedly there are many taxa, particularly among the bats and rodents, which are threatened but about which nothing is known.

The information presented on each taxon has been gathered by literature searches and correspondence. The literature search identifies and reviews the major field studies of the past and thus gives an indication of the degree of knowledge of the taxon and also of the gaps in that knowledge. It also identifies those individuals who are most familiar with the animal and who are therefore likely to be of assistance both in corrobating the information and in signposting possible new sources of data.

However a data sheet based solely on a literature search would in most cases fail to provide the necessary information vital to conservation action. This is for two reasons: first, for many species, particularly in Central and South America, what little information is known about the status of an animal frequently never reaches the scientific or popular literature. It may be written up in reports with a small circulation e.g. governmental reports, WWF or United Nations reports, or it may never be written up at all but simply be the knowledge an experienced scientist or naturalist has developed after long experience and awareness of an area and/or a species. Second, reports appearing in scientific journals or popular natural history magazines are usually based on field work conducted several years previously. A data sheet to be of maximum benefit to conservation action must however be as up to date as possible. Thus information must be actively sought and this is done by correspondence. Two types of person or institution are approached: those familiar with the general status of wildlife in a particular area or country and those who are studying or have studied one taxon in particular.

Over the years the Mammal Red Data Book has amassed an extensive network of correspondents; these comprise institutions, particularly government departments and wildlife societies, many of which are members of IUCN, and scientists and naturalists, many of whom belong to the SSC Specialist Groups. For example, Specialist Groups exist for Australian Mammals, Insectivores, Bats, Primates, Edentates, Lagomorphs, Rodents, the Wolf (Canis lupus), the Polar Bear (Ursus maritimus), Mustelids and Viverrids, Otters, Cats, Marine Mammals, Tapirs, Pigs and Peccaries, South American Camelids, Deer and Caprinae. Thus every taxon, except Pronghorns, listed in this publication has a group of specialists who are requested by IUCN to suggest and coordinate conservation action for it. Other correspondents have been located from the literature, by attendance at conferences, and from a review of projects funded and/or administered by institutions such as IUCN and the World Wildlife Fund, the New York Zoological Society, the Fauna and Flora Preservation Society, Michigan State University, the Smithsonian Institution, United Nations agencies especially FAO, UNEP, UNESCO, and national overseas aid agencies.

Thus a typical line of enquiry for a species endemic to a country would entail a literature search and compilation of a draft data sheet, then correspondence with the relevant government departments, local natural history, wildlife or conservation societies, the relevant IUCN/SSC Specialist Group, and any field workers known to be studying, or to have recently studied, the species in the wild. Not only does this approach lead to the most current data available but also serves as a cross-check that the best sources of information have indeed been identified. If the species is wide-ranging then the process is repeated for each country within its range. The limits of time and personnel dictate that within any one revision of the Mammal Red Data Book only a certain number of 'sweeps of the net' for information can be undertaken. Thus on some data sheets mention is made that concerning a particular item e.g. legal protection, no data have yet been located. Obviously work such as this by its very nature is in a continous state of review, thus it is hoped that the next revision will have filled in any lacunae.

Several data sheets in this publication have been researched and written by an expert on that particular taxon, the RDB compiler editing the draft. For example George Heinsohn, the spokesman on Dugongs (Dugong dugon) on the IUCN Marine Mammal Committee, researched and wrote the Dugong account. Similarly Ian Stirling, Chairman of the IUCN/SSC Polar Bear Specialist Group, aided by Wendy Calvert researched and wrote the Polar Bear (Ursus maritimus) sheet. The Primate sheets have been compiled in close collaboration with Russell A. Mittermeier, Chairman of the IUCN/SSC Primate Specialist Group. The Wolf (Canis lupus) account is largely based on the many publications of the IUCN/SSC Wolf Specialist Group. Many of the sheets relevant to United States species are based on correspondence with the official government 'Recovery Teams' which have been established, for instance for the Delmarva Fox Squirrel (Sciurus niger cinereus), the Hawaiian Monk Seal (Monachus schauinslandi) and the Red Wolf (Canis rufus). Some of the Australian and New Guinea sheets are based on data sheets prepared by specialists for a symposium of threatened Australasian species held in Adelaide in 1978; recent correspondence has brought these accounts up to date.

The information derived from many of these sources has, by its very newness, never been published (and may never be) and is cited on the data sheets as 'In litt'. Acknowledgements to suppliers of data are given in the Remarks paragraph on the sheets and IUCN is greatly indebted to all those people who have willingly shared their time and knowledge. A few people have been especially helpful and are acknowledged on page xix. New information on the status of species is always most welcome and should adhere approximately to the headings outlined in the 'Inventory Report Form' on page vii.

As far as is possible, each data sheet is self explanatory and since each is designed to be self-sufficient, there is some repetition of information on many of the sheets, e.g. with regard to the 1973 Convention on International Trade in Endangered Species of Wild Fauna and Flora. The data sheets themselves are arranged phylogenetically - by Order, Family, Genus, Species, and in some cases, Subspecies.

Apologies must be made for the omission of accents from Spanish and Portuguese names which is unfortunately due to the limitations of our equipment. It is hoped to remedy this deficiency in future revisions.

INVENTORY REPORT FORM

Report to be mailed to the SCMU, 219(c) Huntingdon Rd, Cambridge, CB3 0DL, U.K.

1. Country

2. Date

3. Reporter

    Name:

    Address:

4. Taxon

    Scientific Name: Common Name:

5. Distribution

    Present: Former:
    If possible, please include a map. (Is present range preferred, or enforced habitat?)

6. Population

    Estimated numbers in the wild. Indicate .date of estimate and describe method of estimation. Are numbers increasing, decreasing or stable?

7. Habitat and Ecology

    Biome type. Elevation range. Brief notes about social structure, feeding habits and diet, reproduction (gestation, breeding season, number of young, age of sexual maturation), longevity etc.

8. Threats to Survival

    Eg. habitat destruction, over-exploitation, hybridization, natural disasters, competition for food.

9. Conservation Measures Taken

    Legal measures (international conventions, national laws); is law enforced? Protected areas - does it occur in national parks, reserves etc? If so, please list. Management programmes or research programmes in progress.

10. Conservation Measures Proposed

    Same as for 9, but measures that are needed for the conservation of the taxon.

11. Captive Breeding

    Numbers in captivity. Does it breed readily in captivity?

12. Remarks

Reference citations for description of animal. Comments about related taxa. If the above information concerns a subspecies then brief information should be given about the distribution and status of the species as a whole. Special acknowledgements etc.

13. References

Can be published papers, unpublished manuscripts, or references to correspondence (cited as In litt.).

RED DATA BOOK CATEGORIES

EXTINCT (Ex).

Species not definitely located in the wild during the past 50 years (criterion as used by CITES).

ENDANGERED (E).

Taxa in danger of extinction and whose survival is unlikely if the causal factors continue operating.

Included are taxa whose numbers have been reduced to a critical level or whose habitats have been so drastically reduced that they are deemed to be in immediate danger of extinction. Also included are taxa that are possibly already extinct but have definitely been seen in the wild in the past 50 years.

VULNERABLE (V).

Taxa believed likely to move into the 'Endangered' category in the near future if the causal factors continue operating.

Included are taxa of which most or all the populations are decreasing because of over-exploitation, extensive destruction of habitat or other environmental disturbance; taxa with populations that have been seriously depleted and whose ultimate security has not yet been assured; and taxa with populations that are still abundant but are under threat from severe adverse factors throughout their range.

RARE (R).

Taxa with small world populations that are not at present 'Endangered' or 'Vulnerable', but are at risk.

These taxa are usually localised within restricted geographical areas or habitats or are thinly scattered over a more extensive range.

INDETERMINATE (I).

Taxa known to be 'Endangered', 'Vulnerable' or 'Rare' but where there is not enough information to say which of the three categories is appropriate.

OUT OF DANGER (O).

Taxa formerly included in one of the above categories, but which are now considered relatively secure because effective conservation measures have been taken or the previous threat to their survival has been removed.

INSUFFICIENTLY KNOWN (K).

Taxa that are suspected but not definitely known to belong to any of the above categories, because of lack of information.

N.B. In practice, 'Endangered' and 'Vulnerable' categories may include, temporarily, taxa whose populations are beginning to recover as a result of remedial action, but whose recovery is insufficient to justify their transfer to another category.

145 threatened taxa are listed in this publication and include representatives of all thirteen orders of mammals excluding Cetacea which inhabit the Americas and the Australasian zoogeographic region. Of these 35 inhabit North America, 70 Central and South America, and 47 Australasia.

Virtually everywhere the major threat to wild species is destruction and disturbance of the habitats on which their existences depend. Human activities have steadily modified wilderness areas into manmade landscapes of settlement, agriculture or industry, that preclude coexistence with many wild creatures. Disturbance has resulted from increased human intrusion into remote areas for timber, oil or mineral extraction, and from the introduction of exotics into native ecosystems. Today even the apparently remotest of areas may be afflicted by the effects of pollution.

The problem of habitat loss exists in each of the three major regions addressed in this book, but it is particularly serious in the tropical forests of Central and South America where species diversity is greatest and thus where species losses can expect to be highest. For much of history these vast forests have been little disturbed, major changes essentially taking place only in the last few decades. Much forested land has now been totally cleared by timber extraction to make way for plantations, settlement, or cattle pasture, thus the forest animals which depended on them have become locally extinct. This scenario has been particularly prevalent in Central America, northwestern Colombia and southeastern Brazil.

Most tropical countries have a large and rapidly expanding rural population which usually relies for its survival on subsistence agriculture. The traditional method is that of shifting cultivation - cropping one area for a few years, then clearing another area, leaving the first one fallow to revert to scrub and forest. The fallow period lasts from 8-12 years in tropical rain forests to 20-30 years in drier areas, and during this time the forest cover enables the soil to regenerate. This is a stable, productive practice if the human population itself is stable; but if populations are growing, which nowadays they usually are, the pressure on land increases, fallow periods shorten, and the soil has no chance to regenerate. Tropical soils are notoriously infertile, the luxuriant forests they support being deceptively fragile and reliant upon complex water, nitrogen and other mineral cycles to persist. Once these forests are cut, the soil is invariably rapidly leached of minerals by the heavy rains, and deprived of the holdfast supplied by the vegetation the soil itself is washed into the nearest stream or river. The land becomes exhausted and eroded and requires all too expensive fertilizers to return to its productive capacity. Wider and wider tracts of otherwise productive forest land are thus destroyed. Species which were once able to coexist with shifting cultivation now find their habitat fragmented, islands of forest being separated by vast seas of surrounding farmland or scrub. Not only have critical habitat requirements frequently been lost but the species are also more accessible to the hunter. Once a species has been eradicated from such island habitats it can usually no longer recolonise that area, except by human reintroduction. Such depletion of forest cover has been particularly severe in the Caribbean. For example in Haiti forest cover was reduced from 80% to 9% between 1958 and 1978. Such clearance is the most immediate threat to the endemic fauna of the island.

These tropical countries tend to be economically poor, much of their populace lives at subsistence level, education standards are low and few funds have been allocated to their environment and wildlife departments. Thus even though the wealth of species diversity is greatest in the Tropics and the need for habitat conservation and wise land-use planning is greatest and will be of utmost importance to the long term economic well-being of these nations, it is here that little has yet been achieved to preserve habitats and their array of species. It is here that the international community must assist in conservation with funds, expertise and encouragement.

North America presents a somewhat different scenario. It is largely temperate in climate, species diversity is much lower and the ecosystems more resilient to modification. Thus, although vast regions such as the prairies were rapidly and almost totally transformed into agricultural areas the loss of actual species was much less than that predicted in the tropics under the same degree of environmental modification. A wealthy nation quickly developed with an educated populace who began to regret their loss of wilderness and, in response, to develop a highly sophisticated environmental control system. For wild species this culminated in the 1973 Endangered Species Act which provided legal protection and funds to enact conservation measures for the recovery of species. Also the 1972 Environmental Protection Act required that all land-use plans be subjected to an environmental impact statement which had to take into consideration the effect of the project on the taxa inhabiting the area, and if necessary, to be modified or abandoned if a taxon were found to be faced with extinction. However, even such sophisticated safeguards are all too vulnerable to the whims of a changing political climate, particularly in times of economic recession when governments wish to cut their spending programmes.

Australasia is different again. The loss and decline of species in modern times has resulted principally from the introduction of livestock and exotic animals such as rabbits and foxes which have led to modification of ecosystems, outcompeted the native fauna for forage, or predated upon them. Australia, like North America, developed to a wealthy nation early in its history and, similarly to North America, is enacting a sophisticated programme of environmental and species protection. New Guinea is still relatively little disturbed, but as yet the human population is small. Fortunately however the development, in Papua New Guinea at least, which is now occurring is being made with the awareness of the needs for environmenal protection as a companion of development. Indeed butterfly and crocodile ranching, based on wildlife management principles, are in operation, providing industry and foreign exchange for the country.

Apart from habitat destruction which is undoubtedly the major factor in species decline worldwide, the other threats are over-exploitation (both legal and illegal), the effects of introduced exotic species, hybridization, and pollution. Invariably these threats act in concert to cause the decline of species, but for the different mammalian orders represented in this publication, the importance of one or other of these threats is invariably greater.

The following comments briefly describe the main factors affecting the different mammalian groups.

Australian marsupials have been threatened chiefly by the introduction of exotics into their ecosystems. The introduced herbivores such as cattle, sheep, goats and rabbits have outcompeted the native species for forage, and in some instances have altered the floristic content of the vegetation so that it is no longer suitable for the indigenous fauna. For example, the endangered Northern Hairy-nosed Wombat, Lasiorhinus krefftii, reduced to a single colony in northeast Australia, is threatened chiefly by habitat damage caused by cattle, especially during drought. Similarly the Desert Bandicoot, Perameles eremiana, the Pig-footed Bandicoot, Chaeropus ecaudatus, the Western Barred Bandicoot,

Perameles bougainville, the Burrowing Bettong, Bettongia lesueur, and the Banded Hare-wallaby, Lagostrophus fasciatus, are all believed to have declined principally because of drastic alteration of vegetation by stock grazing and rabbits. Introduced predators, such as foxes and feral dogs and cats, have preyed on species which previously had few known enemies. For example predation is thought to have played a major role in the decline of the Crescent Nailtail Wallaby, Onychogalea lunata, last recorded in 1930 in Western Australia. Similarly the Toolache Wallaby, Macropus greyi, now extinct, was exterminated principally as a result of human persecution and predation by introduced foxes.

The threatened marsupials of New Guinea are mainly those which have apparently specialized habitat requirements and are additionally affected by overhunting as game species e.g. Goodfellow's Tree-kangaroo, Dendrolagus goodfellowi shawmayeri, Doria's Tree-kangaroo, Dendrolagus dorianus notatus, Papuan Dorcopsis, Dorcopsulus macleayi, Black Dorcopsis Wallaby, Dorcopsis atrata, Woodlark Island Cuscus, Phalanger lullulae; this also applies to the monotreme, Zaglossus bruijni.

The threatened insectivores, bats, lagomorphs and rodents tend to have very small ranges and to be subjected to habitat loss or disturbance within these limited areas. For example, the highly endangered Solenodons of Cuba and Hispaniola (Solenodon paradoxus and S. cubanus) are losing their habitat to the steady onslaught of slash-and-burn agriculture, bringing with it the increased risk of predation by domestic dogs; similarly affected is the endangered Volcano Rabbit, Romerolagus diazi, which inhabits the slopes of volcanoes surrounding Mexico City. The bats largely suffer from disturbance of their roosting and maternity sites by vandals, and cavers. Indeed the Gray Bat, Myotis grisescens, has actually been a victim of the very measures taken to preserve it: gates constructed across the entrance to its caves have raised the ambient temperature above that suitable for hibernation, resulting in a die-off of animals. The identification of threatened rodents and bats is in its infancy and those so far recognized tend to be confined to small areas in well-studied regions, e.g. the Morro Bay Kangaroo Rat, Dipodomys heermanni morroensis; Delmarva Fox Squirrel, Sciurus niger cinereus, and Vancouver Island Marmot, Marmota vancouverensis. The diverse Hutias of the Caribbean islands are threatened by habitat loss and hunting, compounded by small ranges and a slow breeding rate. Threatened Australian rodents seem to be mainly those susceptible to habitat degradation by stock-grazing and introduced herbivores such as rabbits, e.g. the Greater Stick-nest Rat, Leporillus conditor.

Primates have become threatened by habitat loss and disturbance, combined for some species with over-exploitation for the pet, zoo and biomedical industries. For example the Cotton-top Tamarin, Saguinus oedipus oedipus, now confined to remnant forest patches in northwestern Colombia, and the Central American Squirrel Monkey, Saimiri oerstedi, with a limited area in Panama and adjacent Costa Rica, were both heavily traded in the 1960s principally for the biomedical industry. The southeastern forests of Brazil possess a rich array of primate species, some endemic, and many on the brink of extinction. Very few individuals now remain in the wild and in the forest islands they inhabit they are critically endangered. For example the Golden Lion Tamarin, Leontopithecus rosalia, is now (1981) reduced to less than 100 animals and survives precariously in only two areas. It has also been a popular zoo exhibit, widely sold in the pet trade, and occasionally used for research in biomedical laboratories. Between 200 and 300 were exported annually for these purposes from 1960 to 1965.

Edentates are as yet little known but habitat loss and hunting for food seem to be emerging as possible deleterious forces.

The carnivores - the canids, bears, otters and cats have declined mainly because of hunting, either for their skins as with otters and cats, or because their predatory habits e.g. the Spectacled Bear, Tremarctos ornatus, on corn and the Maned Wolf, Chrysocyon brachyurus, on chickens, have continuously brought them into conflict with man. They are feared as dangerous to humans, e.g. Wolf (Canis lupus) (often based on myth), and hated because of predation on domestic livestock and poultry, and on the large herbivores and game birds favoured by the hunting fraternity. The human response has been to eradicate them. Sport hunting has played a minimal role. In addition, these predators tend to require large areas of land over which to hunt and populations therefore exist at low densities. It is thus easy to eradicate them from a large area by killing a seemingly small number, and their conservation, which usually entails the establishment of reserves, is difficult simply because of the extensive amount of land required to preserve a viable population.

The aquatic species, the threatened seals and sirenians, declined largely as a result of over-exploitation, principally for their hides in the case of seals and for their meat in the case of the sirenians. Where protected from disturbance and hunting populations have tended to recover.

Amongst the Artiodactyls, over-exploitation has been the principal threat. The deer and pronghorns declined largely because of uncontrolled hunting, with habitat loss being of relatively lesser importance. The tapirs have suffered from habitat loss plus hunting for food; the Chacoan Peccary, Catagonus wagneri, from hunting for meat and its hide, and the Vicuna, Vicugna vicugna, for its wool.

Many taxa, for example the Polar Bear (Ursus maritimus), the Gray Bat (Myotis grisescens), the Brush-tailed Bettong (Bettongia penicillata), the Morro Bay Kangaroo Rat (Dipodomys heermanni morroensis) and the Vicuna (Vicugna vicugna), are the subject of extensive conservation programmes intended to bring about their recovery or security in the wild. Such programmes usually focus on legal protection, the establishment of reserves, education campaigns and etho-ecological studies. They may be funded nationally e.g. in Argentina by the Fundacion vida Silvestre Argentina (FVSA) and in Brazil by the Instituto Nacional de Pesquisas de Amazonica (INPA), and/or with financial support from foreign or international agencies such as IUCN/WWF, the New York Zoological Society, or United Nations Agencies such as UNEP, FAO, UNESCO etc.

International cooperation with regard to threatened species may also be facilitated by conventions such as the 1973 Convention on International Trade in Endangered Species of Wild Fauna and Flora (CITES) which has helped to control trade in wildlife products and has undoubtedly assisted the conservation of the furbearers such as otters and cats.

Such conservation actions have had, and are having, a beneficial effect on the status of wild taxa and some are well on the way to recovery e.g. the Vicuna, Polar Bear and Fur Seals. Others, although severely endangered, at least now have a chance e.g. the Hawaiian Monk Seal, (Monachus schauinslandi), and the Argentine Pampas Deer, (Ozotoceros bezoarticus celer); thus conservation can save species.

However there is no time for complacency, the great majority of taxa listed in this publication are still declining and there are doubtless many others similarly under threat but which are as yet unrecognised. Indeed a number, for example the mammalian fauna of the Atlantic forests of southeastern Brazil, are doomed to extinction in the wild in a very short time unless major steps are taken for their survival.

Recommendations

Each Red Data sheet includes a section on 'Conservation Measures Proposed', which comprises recommendations on the action required to improve the taxon's prospects of survival. The proposals are primarily concerned with the protection of the animal and its habitat, and the elimination of threats to its survival, and/or the collection of etho-ecological data on which to base more specific and effective remedial measures.

Below is a general check-list of conservation measures for threatened species, the original of which was compiled by the Species Survival Commission in 1966/67.

1. Fact-Finding

    (1). To conduct a survey to determine
        (a) the status of the taxon;
        (b) the current threats to its survival;
        (c) the remaining habitat suitable to its needs;
        (d) the legal and enforcement situation.

    (2). To launch a research project to ascertain its ecology, the factors limiting its population growth, and the relationship between it, its habitat, and the local human population.

2. Action Proposed

    (1). Legal
        (a) to promote or prompt new legislation, or make better use of powers under existing legislation;
        (b) to promote a special international convention;
        (c) to improve law enforcement:
            (i) within national parks or reserves;
            (ii) in the country generally;
            (iii) with regard to international trade;
        (d) to add a taxon to one of the Appendices of the 1973 Convention on International Trade in Endangered Species of Wild Fauna and Flora (CITES), or to transfer it to a higher Appendix;
        (e) to improve the legal situation in any other way.

    (2). To promote the formation of a national park, nature reserve or wildlife refuge
        (a) by an official body;
        (b) by a voluntary organization.

    (3). To establish a continuing scientific presence
        (a) through a scientific research programme;
        (b) by establishing a research station;
        (c) by establishing a research foundation.

    (4). To undertake educational or public relations measures.

    (5). To encourage existing conservation effort.

    (6). To promote a programme of captive propagation
        (a) in a zoo;
        (b) in an institution designed for propagating threatened taxa;

(c)   on a site in the taxons' own habitat.

(7).   To re-establish a taxon in an area where it is either extinct or very rare
    (a)   by translocation direct from the wild;
    (b)   by release of captive bred stock;
    (c)   by increasing the food supply or living space by habitat management.

(8).   To offer bounties for successful rearing of young (chiefly applicable to birds).

(9).   To control feral or introduced animals
    (a)   predators;
    (b)   competitors for the available forage.

It is hoped that the Red Data Book will help to stimulate conservation action by individuals, by groups such as universities, schools and wildlife societies, and by governments.

However individual and group action is only likely to be effective in the long term if backed by a full and integrated range of government policies favourable to species and habitat conservation. Since governments have the capacity to be the biggest and most effective conservation agencies the following recommendations are suggested

(1).   The compilation of national threatened species lists and Red Data Books.
(2).   Legal protection afforded to species included on these lists.
(3).   The establishment of national parks and reserves for such species.
(4).   The incorporation of safeguards in future planning strategies to protect all listed species, as the major threat to many species is created by changing land use.
(5).   To stimulate, undertake or coordinate through competent organizations multidisciplinary research at national or international level concerning listed species.
(6).   To give appropriate support to scientific institutions so that they have the facilities required to breed and distribute animals to other institutions and, where appropriate, for reintroduction to the wild.
(7).   To ratify, if this has not already been done, the Convention on International Trade in Endangered Species of Wild Fauna and Flora.

Conservation must be built into planning in both the short and long term, for it is upon natural renewable resources such as forests and rangelands that humans depend and must rely for continuing employment and income.

TAXONOMIC REFERENCES

The systems of classification and nomenclature principally follow the undermentioned authors:

CABRERA, A. (1957-61). Catalogo de los mamiferos de America del Sur. Rev. del. Mus. Argent. de Cienc. Nat. 'Bernardino Rivadavia', Cienc. Zool. 4(1,2): 1-732.

CORBET, G.B. and HILL, J.E. (1980). A world list of mammalian species. British Museum (Natural History) and Cornell Univ. Press.

HALL, E.R. and KELSON, K.R. (1959). The mammals of North America. The Ronald Press Co., New York.

RIDE, W.D.L. (1970). A guide to the native mammals of Australia. Oxford Univ. Press, Melbourne.

ACKNOWLEDGEMENTS

Many, many people have assisted in the compilation of this publication and without their generous help the end result would have been a far inferior product. Wherever appropriate these people have been acknowledged on the individual data sheets and to all of them we extend our sincere thanks and gratitude. However a particular thanks must also be extended to the following people who have been particularly helpful.

Argentina	E.O. Gonzalez Ruiz
	A. Tarak
Australasian	A.A. Burbidge
zoogeographic region	J.C. Calaby
	G.G. George
	T.H. Kirkpatrick
	A.K. Lee
	A.C. Robinson
	G.W. Saunders
	G.B. Sharman
	R. Strahan
	R.M. Warneke
	C.H.S. Watts
	G.R. Wilson
	The participants of the 1978 symposium on the status of endangered Australasian wildlife who provided draft red data sheets
Brazil	M. Ayres
	R. Best
Bolivia	G. Bejarano
Chile	J. Rottmann
Colombia	J. Hernandez-Camacho
Cuba	L. Varona
Ecuador	F.I. Ortiz-Crespo
	G. Orces
	J. Black
El Salvador	J. Boursot
Peru	M. Dourojeanni Ricordi
Uruguay	E. Gudynas
	R. Praderi
	L. Caviglia Tahier
U.S.A.	R. Nowak
Polar Bear	I. Stirling
	Wendy Calvert
Dugong	G. Heinsohn
Primates	R.A. Mittermeier
	A.F. Coimbra-Filho
	A. Rylands
Hutias	C. Woods
Rodents	J. Layne
Canids	D. Macdonald

We would also especially like to thank the staff of the Mammal Section and Zoology Library of the British Museum (Natural History), and the Fauna and Flora Preservation Society for helpfulness and guidance.

As compiler of the Mammal Red Data Book I also wish to give my particular thanks to my assistant, Martin Jenkins, for his support and hard work during the compilation of this document.

(IN SYSTEMATIC ORDER)

The letter preceding each taxon refers to its status category (see page ix). Also included are seven taxa that are categorised as 'Insufficiently Known' and three categorised as 'Out of Danger'.

MONOTREMATA

TACHYGLOSSIDAE

V	Zaglossus bruijni	Long-beaked Echidna

MARSUPIALIA

MACROPODIDAE

Ex	Macropus greyi	Toolache Wallaby
E	Onychogalea fraenata	Bridled Nailtail Wallaby
Ex	Onychogalea lunata	Crescent Nailtail Wallaby
Ex	Lagorchestes asomatus	Central Hare-wallaby
R	Lagorchestes hirsutus	Rufous Hare-wallaby
Ex	Lagorchestes leporides	Eastern Hare-wallaby
R	Lagostrophus fasciatus	Banded Hare-wallaby
R	Petrogale sp. nova	Proserpine Rock-wallaby
V	Dendrolagus dorianus notatus	Doria's Tree-kangaroo
V	Dendrolagus goodfellowi shawmayeri	Goodfellow's Tree-kangaroo
R	Dorcopsis atrata	Black Dorcopsis Wallaby
R	Dorcopsulus macleayi	Papuan Dorcopsis
I	Caloprymnus campestris	Desert Rat-kangaroo
E	Bettongia penicillata	Brush-tailed Bettong
R	Bettongia lesueur	Burrowing Bettong
Ex	Potorous platyops	Broad-faced Potoroo
I	Potorous longipes	Long-footed Potoroo

PHALANGERIDAE

R	Phalanger interpositus	Stein's Cuscus
R	Phalanger lullulae	Woodlark Island Cuscus
R	Phalanger rufoniger	Black-spotted Cuscus

PETAURIDAE

E	Gymnobelideus leadbeateri	Leadbeater's Possum

VOMBATIDAE

E	Lasiorhinus krefftii	Northern Hairy-nosed Wombat

PERAMELIDAE

Ex	Chaeropus ecaudatus	Pig-footed Bandicoot
R	Echymipera clara	Clara Bandicoot
R	Perameles bougainville	Western Barred Bandicoot

Ex	_Perameles eremiana_	Desert Bandicoot

THYLACOMYIDAE

E	_Macrotis lagotis_	Greater Bilby
Ex	_Macrotis leucura_	Lesser Bilby

DASYURIDAE

I	_Antechinus apicalis_	Dibbler
I	_Phascogale calura_	Red-tailed Phascogale
K	_Sminthopsis longicaudata_	Long-tailed Dunnart
K	_Sminthopsis psammophila_	Sandhill Dunnart
I	_Sminthopsis douglasi_	Julia Creek Dunnart

MYRMECOBIIDAE

E	_Myrmecobius fasciatus_	Numbat

THYLACINIDAE

Ex	_Thylacinus cynocephalus_	Thylacine

INSECTIVORA

SOLENODONTIDAE

E	_Solenodon cubanus_	Cuban Solenodon
E	_Solenodon paradoxus_	Haitian Solenodon

CHIROPTERA

MEGADERMATIDAE

V	_Macroderma gigas_	Ghost Bat

VESPERTILIONIDAE

V	_Myotis sodalis_	Indiana Bat
E	_Myotis grisescens_	Gray Bat
I	_Lasiurus cinereus semotus_	Hawaiian Hoary Bat
I	_Plecotus townsendii ingens_	Ozark Big-eared Bat
E	_Plecotus townsendii virginianus_	Virginia Big-eared Bat

PRIMATES

CALLITRICHIDAE

E	_Callithrix flaviceps_	Buffy-headed Marmoset
V	_Callithrix argentata leucippe_	White Marmoset
E	_Callithrix aurita_	Buffy-tufted-ear Marmoset
V	_Callithrix humeralifer_	Tassel-eared Marmoset
E	_Saguinus oedipus oedipus_	Cotton-top Tamarin
I	_Saguinus bicolor_	Bare-face Tamarin
I	_Saguinus imperator_	Emperor Tamarin
V	_Saguinus leucopus_	White-footed Tamarin
E	_Leontopithecus rosalia_	Golden Lion Tamarin

E	Leontopithecus chrysomelas	Golden-headed Lion Tamarin
E	Leontopithecus chrysopygus	Golden-rumped Lion Tamarin
R	Callimico goeldii	Goeldi's Marmoset

CEBIDAE

E	Saimiri oerstedi	Central American Squirrel Monkey
V	Callicebus personatus	Masked Titi
V	Chiropotes albinasus	White-nosed Saki
E	Chiropotes satanas satanas	Southern Bearded Saki
V	Cacajao calvus	Uakari (Red and White)
V	Cacajao melanocephalus	Black-headed Uakari
I	Alouatta fusca	Brown Howler Monkey
I	Alouatta villosa	Guatemalan Howler Monkey
E	Lagothrix flavicauda	Yellow-tailed Woolly Monkey
V	Lagothrix lagothricha	Woolly Monkey
E	Brachyteles arachnoides	Woolly Spider Monkey
V	Ateles belzebuth	Long-haired Spider Monkey
I	Ateles fusciceps	Brown-headed Spider Monkey
V	Ateles geoffroyi	Geoffroy's Spider Monkey
V	Ateles paniscus	Black Spider Monkey

EDENTATA

MYRMECOPHAGIDAE

V	Myrmecophaga tridactyla	Giant Anteater

BRADYPODIDAE

E	Bradypus torquatus	Maned Sloth

DASYPODIDAE

V	Priodontes giganteus	Giant Armadillo
I	Tolypeutes tricinctus	Brazilian Three-banded Armadillo
K	Chlamyphorus truncatus	Lesser Pichi Ciego
K	Burmeisteria retusa	Greater Pichi Ciego

LAGOMORPHA

LEPORIDAE

E	Romerolagus diazi	Volcano Rabbit

RODENTIA

SCIURIDAE

E	Sciurus niger cinereus	Delmarva Fox Squirrel
E	Marmota vancouverensis	Vancouver Island Marmot
V	Cynomys parvidens	Utah Prairie Dog

HETEROMYIDAE

E	Dipodomys heermanni morroensis	Morro Bay Kangaroo Rat
R	Dipodomys elator	Texas Kangaroo Rat

CRICETIDAE

| E | Reithrodontomys raviventris | Salt-marsh Harvest Mouse |

MURIDAE

Ex	Conilurus albipes	Rabbit-eared Tree-rat
Ex	Leporillus apicalis	Lesser Stick-nest Rat
R	Leporillus conditor	Greater Stick-nest Rat
R	Microtus breweri	Beach Vole
Ex	Notomys amplus	Short-tailed Hopping-mouse
K	Notomys aquilo	Northern Hopping-mouse
Ex	Notomys longicaudatus	Long-tailed Hopping-mouse
Ex	Notomys macrotis	Big-eared Hopping-mouse
Ex	Notomys mordax	Darling Downs Hopping-mouse
I	Oryzomys argentatus	Silver Rice Rat
Ex	Pseudomys fieldi	Alice Springs Mouse
R	Pseudomys praeconis	Shark Bay Mouse
I	Pseudomys oralis	Hastings River Mouse
K	Xeromys myoides	False Water-rat
I	Zyzomys pedunculatus	Central Rock-rat

ERITHIZONTIDAE

| I | Chaetomys subspinosus | Thin-spined Porcupine |

CHINCHILLIDAE

| I | Chinchilla laniger | Long-tailed Chinchilla |
| I | Chinchilla brevicaudata | Short-tailed Chinchilla |

CAPROMYIDAE

E	Capromys angelcabrerai	Cabrera's Hutia
E	Capromys auritus	Large-eared Hutia
I	Capromys garridoi	Garrido's Hutia
I	Capromys melanurus	Bushy-tailed Hutia
E	Capromys nanus	Dwarf Hutia
E	Capromys sanfelipensis	Little Earth Hutia
I	Geocapromys brownii	Jamaican Hutia
R	Geocapromys ingrahami	Bahamian Hutia
I	Plagiodontia aedium	Hispaniolan Hutia

CARNIVORA

CANIDAE

V	Canis lupus	Wolf
E	Canis rufus	Red Wolf
K	Atelocynus microtis	Small-eared Dog
V	Chrysocyon brachyurus	Maned Wolf
V	Speothos venaticus	Bush Dog

URSIDAE

V	Tremarctos ornatus	Spectacled Bear
E	Ursus arctos nelsoni	Mexican Grizzly Bear
V	Ursus maritimus	Polar Bear

MUSTELIDAE

E	Mustela nigripes	Black-footed Ferret
V	Lutra felina	Marine Otter
V	Lutra platensis	La Plata Otter
I	Lutra provocax	Southern River Otter
V	Pteronura brasiliensis	Giant Brazilian Otter

FELIDAE

V	Felis pardalis	Ocelot
E	Felis concolor cougar	Eastern Cougar
E	Felis concolor coryi	Florida Cougar
R	Felis jacobita	Andean Cat
V	Felis tigrina	Little Spotted Cat
I	Felis yagouaroundi	Jaguarundi
V	Felis wiedii	Margay
V	Panthera onca	Jaguar

PINNIPEDIA

OTARIIDAE

O	Arctocephalus galapagoensis	Galapagos Fur Seal
V	Arctocephalus philippii	Juan Fernandez Fur Seal
V	Arctocephalus townsendi	Guadalupe Fur Seal

PHOCIDAE

E	Monachus tropicalis	Caribbean Monk Seal
E	Monachus schauinslandi	Hawaiian Monk Seal

SIRENIA

DUGONGIDAE

V	Dugong dugon	Dugong

TRICHECHIDAE

V	Trichechus manatus	Caribbean Manatee
V	Trichechus inunguis	Amazonian Manatee

PERISSODACTYLA

TAPIRIDAE

V	Tapirus pinchaque	Mountain Tapir
V	Tapirus bairdii	Central American Tapir

ARTIODACTYLA

TAYASSUIDAE

V	Catagonus wagneri	Chacoan Peccary

CAMELIDAE

V	Vicugna vicugna	Vicuna

CERVIDAE

O	Cervus elaphus nannodes	Tule Elk
R	Odocoileus virginianus clavium	Key Deer
O	Odocoileus virginianus leucurus	Columbian White-tailed Deer
R	Odocoileus hemionus cerrosensis	Cedros Island Mule Deer
E	Hippocamelus bisulcus	South Andean Huemul
V	Hippocamelus antisensis	North Andean Huemul
V	Blastocerus dichotomus	Marsh Deer
E	Ozotoceros bezoarticus celer	Argentinian Pampas Deer
I	Pudu mephistophiles	Northern Pudu

ANTILOCAPRIDAE

E	Antilocapra americana peninsularis	Lower California Pronghorn
E	Antilocapra americana sonoriensis	Sonoran Pronghorn

Countries are grouped under the zoogeographic regions first described by Wallace in 1876, the only exceptions being certain Oceanic Islands which, together with Oceans, are grouped under an additional heading.

The Australasian region includes Australia, New Zealand and the island of New Guinea, but not the smaller islands and archipelagos of the southwest Pacific.

The Nearctic region covers all of North America, including Greenland, the Aleutian Islands, and northern Mexico.

The Neotropical region includes southern Mexico, all Caribbean islands, and Central and South America (for the sake of clarity Mexico is listed only in the Nearctic region).

Oceans and Oceanic Islands are treated separately.

'Ex' following a taxon denotes that it is regarded as extinct in that country and '?' denotes the lack of confirmation of its presence.

AUSTRALASIAN REGION

AUSTRALIA

Macropus greyi	Toolache Wallaby (Ex)
Onychogalea fraenata	Bridled Nailtail Wallaby
Onychogalea lunata	Crescent Nailtail Wallaby (Ex)
Lagorchestes asomatus	Central Hare-wallaby (Ex)
Lagorchestes hirsutus	Rufous Hare-wallaby
Lagorchestes leporides	Eastern Hare-wallaby (Ex)
Lagostrophus fasciatus	Banded Hare-wallaby
Petrogale sp. nova	Proserpine Rock-wallaby
Caloprymnus campestris	Desert Rat-kangaroo
Bettongia penicillata	Brush-tailed Bettong
Bettongia lesueur	Burrowing Bettong
Potorous platyops	Broad-faced Potoroo (Ex)
Potorous longipes	Long-footed Potoroo
Gymnobelideus leadbeateri	Leadbeater's Possum
Lasiorhinus krefftii	Northern Hairy-nosed Wombat
Chaeropus ecaudatus	Pig-footed Bandicoot (Ex)
Perameles bougainville	Western Barred Bandicoot
Perameles eremiana	Desert Bandicoot (Ex)
Macrotis lagotis	Greater Bilby
Macrotis leucura	Lesser Bilby (Ex)
Antechinus apicalis	Dibbler
Phascogale calura	Red-tailed Phascogale
Sminthopsis longicaudata	Long-tailed Dunnart
Sminthopsis psammophila	Sandhill Dunnart
Sminthopsis douglasi	Julia Creek Dunnart
Myrmecobius fasciatus	Numbat
Thylacinus cynocephalus	Thylacine (Ex)
Macroderma gigas	Ghost Bat
Conilurus albipes	Rabbit-eared Tree-rat (Ex)
Leporillus apicalis	Lesser Stick-nest Rat (Ex)
Leporillus conditor	Greater Stick-nest Rat
Notomys amplus	Short-tailed Hopping-mouse (Ex)

Notomys aquilo	Northern Hopping-mouse
Notomys longicaudatus	Long-tailed Hopping-mouse (Ex)
Notomys macrotis	Big-eared Hopping-mouse (Ex)
Notomys mordax	Darling Downs Hopping-mouse (Ex)
Pseudomys fieldi	Alice Springs Mouse (Ex)
Pseudomys praeconis	Shark Bay Mouse
Pseudomys oralis	Hastings River Mouse
Xeromys myoides	False Water-rat
Zyzomys pedunculatus	Central Rock-rat
Dugong dugon	Dugong

INDONESIA (IRIAN JAYA)

Zaglossus bruijni	Long-beaked Echidna
Dendrolagus dorianus notatus	Doria's Tree-kangaroo
Phalanger interpositus	Stein's Cuscus
Phalanger rufoniger	Black-spotted Cuscus
Echymipera clara	Clara Bandicoot
Dugong dugon	Dugong

PAPUA NEW GUINEA

Zaglossus bruijni	Long-beaked Echidna
Dendrolagus dorianus notatus	Doria's Tree-kangaroo
Dendrolagus goodfellowi shawmayeri	Goodfellow's Tree-kangaroo
Dorcopsis atrata	Black Dorcopsis Wallaby
Dorcopsulus macleayi	Papuan Dorcopsis
Phalanger interpositus	Stein's Cuscus
Phalanger lullulae	Woodlark Island Cuscus
Phalanger rufoniger	Black-spotted Cuscus
Echymipera clara	Clara Bandicoot
Dugong dugon	Dugong

NEARCTIC REGION

CANADA

Marmota vancouverensis	Vancouver Island Marmot
Canis lupus	Wolf
Ursus maritimus	Polar Bear
Mustela nigripes	Black-footed Ferret (Ex)
Felis concolor cougar	Eastern Cougar

DENMARK (GREENLAND)

Canis lupus	Wolf
Ursus maritimus	Polar Bear

MEXICO

Alouatta villosa	Guatemalan Howler Monkey
Ateles geoffroyi	Geoffroy's Spider Monkey
Romerolagus diazi	Volcano Rabbit
Canis lupus	Wolf

Ursus arctos nelsoni	Mexican Grizzly Bear
Felis pardalis	Ocelot
Felis yagouaroundi	Jaguarundi
Felis wiedii	Margay
Panthera onca	Jaguar
Arctocephalus townsendi	Guadalupe Fur Seal
Trichechus manatus	Caribbean Manatee
Tapirus bairdii	Central American Tapir
Odocoileus hemionus cerrosensis	Cedros Island Mule Deer
Antilocapra americana peninsularis	Lower California Pronghorn
Antilocapra americana sonoriensis	Sonoran Pronghorn

U.S.A.

Myotis sodalis	Indiana Bat
Myotis grisescens	Gray Bat
Lasiurus cinereus semotus	Hawaiian Hoary Bat
Plecotus townsendii ingens	Ozark Big-eared Bat
Plecotus townsendii virginianus	Virginia Big-eared Bat
Sciurus niger cinereus	Delmarva Fox Squirrel
Cynomys parvidens	Utah Prairie Dog
Dipodomys heermanni morroensis	Morro Bay Kangaroo Rat
Dipodomys elator	Texas Kangaroo Rat
Reithrodontomys raviventris	Salt-marsh Harvest Mouse
Microtus breweri	Beach Vole
Oryzomys argentatus	Silver Rice Rat
Canis lupus	Wolf
Canis rufus	Red Wolf
Ursus arctos nelsoni	Mexican Grizzly Bear
Ursus maritimus	Polar Bear
Mustela nigripes	Black-footed Ferret
Felis pardalis	Ocelot
Felis concolor cougar	Eastern Cougar
Felis concolor coryi	Florida Cougar
Felis yagouaroundi	Jaguarundi
Panthera onca	Jaguar
Monachus shauinslandi	Hawaiian Monk Seal
Trichechus manatus	Caribbean Manatee
Cervus elaphus nannodes	Tule Elk
Odocoileus virginianus clavium	Key Deer
Odocoileus virginianus leucurus	Columbian White-tailed Deer
Antilocapra americana sonoriensis	Sonoran Pronghorn

NEOTROPICAL REGION

ARGENTINA

Ateles paniscus	Black Spider Monkey (?)
Myrmecophaga tridactyla	Giant Anteater
Priodontes giganteus	Giant Armadillo
Chlamyphorus truncatus	Lesser Pichi Ciego
Burmeisteria retusa	Greater Pichi Ciego
Chinchilla brevicaudata	Short-tailed Chinchilla (?)
Chrysocyon brachyurus	Maned Wolf
Speothos venaticus	Bush Dog
Tremarctos ornatus	Spectacled Bear (?)
Lutra platensis	La Plata Otter
Lutra provocax	Southern River Otter
Pteronura brasiliensis	Giant Brazilian Otter
Felis pardalis	Ocelot
Felis jacobita	Andean Cat
Felis tigrina	Little Spotted Cat
Felis yagouaroundi	Jaguarundi
Felis wiedii	Margay
Panthera onca	Jaguar
Catagonus wagneri	Chacoan Peccary
Vicugna vicugna	Vicuna
Hippocamelus bisulcus	South Andean Huemul
Hippocamelus antisensis	North Andean Huemul
Blastocerus dichotomus	Marsh Deer
Ozotoceros bezoarticus celer	Argentinian Pampas Deer

BAHAMAS

Geocapromys ingrahami	Bahamian Hutia
Trichechus manatus	Caribbean Manatee

BELIZE

Alouatta villosa	Guatemalan Howler Monkey
Ateles geoffroyi	Geoffroy's Spider Monkey
Myrmecophaga tridactyla	Giant Anteater
Felis pardalis	Ocelot
Felis yagouaroundi	Jaguarundi
Felis wiedii	Margay
Panthera onca	Jaguar
Trichechus manatus	Caribbean Manatee
Tapirus bairdii	Central American Tapir

BOLIVIA

Saguinus imperator	Emperor Tamarin
Callimico goeldii	Goeldi's Marmoset
Alouatta fusca	Brown Howler Monkey
Lagothrix lagothricha	Woolly Monkey
Ateles paniscus	Black Spider Monkey
Myrmecophaga tridactyla	Giant Anteater
Priodontes giganteus	Giant Armadillo
Burmeisteria retusa	Greater Pichi Ciego (?)
Chinchilla brevicaudata	Short-tailed Chinchilla (?)
Chrysocyon brachyurus	Maned Wolf

Speothos venaticus	Bush Dog
Lutra platensis	La Plata Otter (?)
Pteronura brasiliensis	Giant Brazilian Otter
Tremarctos ornatus	Spectacled Bear
Felis pardalis	Ocelot
Felis yagouaroundi	Jaguarundi
Felis wiedii	Margay
Felis jacobita	Andean Cat
Panthera onca	Jaguar
Catagonus wagneri	Chacoan Peccary
Vicugna vicugna	Vicuna
Hippocamelus antisensis	North Andean Huemul
Blastocerus dichotomus	Marsh Deer

BRAZIL

Callithrix flaviceps	Buffy-headed Marmoset
Callithrix argentata leucippe	White Marmoset
Callithrix aurita	Buffy-tufted-ear Marmoset
Callithrix humeralifer	Tassel-eared Marmoset
Saguinus bicolor	Bare-face Tamarin
Saguinus imperator	Emperor Tamarin
Leontopithecus rosalia	Golden Lion Tamarin
Leontopithecus chrysomelas	Golden-headed Lion Tamarin
Leontopithecus chrysopygus	Golden-rumped Lion Tamarin
Callimico goeldii	Goeldi's Marmoset
Callicebus personatus	Masked Titi
Chiropotes albinasus	White-nosed Saki
Chiropotes satanas satanas	Southern Bearded Saki
Cacajao calvus	Uakari (Red and White)
Cacajao melanocephalus	Black-headed Uakari
Alouatta fusca	Brown Howler Monkey
Lagothrix lagotricha	Woolly Monkey
Brachyteles arachnoides	Woolly Spider Monkey
Ateles belzebuth	Long-haired Spider Monkey
Ateles paniscus	Black Spider Monkey
Myrmecophaga tridactyla	Giant Anteater
Bradypus torquatus	Maned Sloth
Priodontes giganteus	Giant Armadillo
Tolypeutes tricinctus	Brazilian Three-banded Armadillo
Chaetomys subspinosus	Thin-spined Porcupine
Atelocynus microtis	Small-eared Dog
Chrysocyon brachyurus	Maned Wolf
Speothos venaticus	Bush Dog
Tremarctos ornatus	Spectacled Bear (?)
Lutra platensis	La Plata Otter
Pteronura brasiliensis	Giant Brazilian Otter
Felis pardalis	Ocelot
Felis tigrina	Little Spotted Cat
Felis yagouaroundi	Jaguarundi
Felis wiedii	Margay
Panthera onca	Jaguar
Trichechus manatus	Caribbean Manatee
Trichechus inunguis	Amazonian Manatee
Blastocerus dichotomus	Marsh Deer

CHILE

Chinchilla laniger	Long-tailed Chinchilla
Chinchilla brevicaudata	Short-tailed Chinchilla
Lutra felina	Marine Otter
Lutra provocax	Southern River Otter
Felis jacobita	Andean Cat
Arctocephalus philippii	Juan Fernandez Fur Seal
Vicugna vicugna	Vicuna
Hippocamelus bisulcus	South Andean Huemul
Hippocamelus antisensis	North Andean Huemul

COLOMBIA

Saguinus oedipus oedipus	Cotton-top Tamarin
Saguinus leucopus	White-footed Tamarin
Callimico goeldii	Goeldi's Marmoset
Cacajao calvus	Uakari (Red) (?)
Cacajao melanocephalus	Black-headed Uakari
Lagothrix lagothricha	Woolly Monkey
Ateles belzebuth	Long-haired Spider Monkey
Ateles fusciceps	Brown-headed Spider Monkey
Ateles geoffroyi	Geoffroy's Spider Monkey (?)
Myrmecophaga tridactyla	Giant Anteater
Priodontes giganteus	Giant Armadillo
Atelocynus microtis	Small-eared Dog
Speothos venaticus	Bush Dog
Tremarctos ornatus	Spectacled Bear
Pteronura brasiliensis	Giant Brazilian Otter
Felis pardalis	Ocelot
Felis tigrina	Little Spotted Cat
Felis yagouaroundi	Jaguarundi
Felis wiedii	Margay
Panthera onca	Jaguar
Trichechus manatus	Caribbean Manatee
Trichechus inunguis	Amazonian Manatee
Tapirus pinchaque	Mountain Tapir
Tapirus bairdii	Central American Tapir
Pudu mephistophiles	Northern Pudu

COSTA RICA

Saimiri oerstedi	Central American Squirrel Monkey
Ateles geoffroyi	Geoffroy's Spider Monkey
Myrmecophaga tridactyla	Giant Anteater
Felis pardalis	Ocelot
Felis tigrina	Little Spotted Cat
Felis yagouaroundi	Jaguarundi
Felis wiedii	Margay
Panthera onca	Jaguar
Trichechus manatus	Caribbean Manatee
Tapirus bairdii	Central American Tapir

CUBA

Solenodon cubanus	Cuban Solenodon
Capromys angelcabrerai	Cabrera's Hutia
Capromys auritus	Large-eared Hutia

Capromys garridoi	Garrido's Hutia
Capromys melanurus	Bushy-tailed Hutia
Capromys nanus	Dwarf Hutia
Capromys sanfelipensis	Little Earth Hutia
Trichechus manatus	Caribbean Manatee

DOMINICAN REPUBLIC

Solenodon paradoxus	Haitian Solenodon
Plagiodontia aedium	Hispaniolan Hutia
Trichechus manatus	Caribbean Manatee

ECUADOR

Callimico goeldii	Goeldi's Marmoset (?)
Lagothrix lagothricha	Woolly Monkey
Ateles belzebuth	Long-haired Spider Monkey
Ateles fusciceps	Brown-headed Spider Monkey
Myrmecophaga tridactyla	Giant Anteater (?)
Priodontes giganteus	Giant Armadillo (?)
Atelocynus microtis	Small-eared Dog
Speothos venaticus	Bush Dog
Tremarctos ornatus	Spectacled Bear
Pteronura brasiliensis	Giant Brazilian Otter
Felis pardalis	Ocelot
Felis tigrina	Little Spotted Cat
Felis yagouaroundi	Jaguarundi
Felis wiedii	Margay
Panthera onca	Jaguar
Arctocephalus galapagoensis	Galapagos Fur Seal
Trichechus inunguis	Amazonian Manatee (?)
Tapirus pinchaque	Mountain Tapir
Tapirus bairdii	Central American Tapir (?)
Pudu mephistophiles	Northern Pudu

EL SALVADOR

Ateles geoffroyi	Geoffroy's Spider Monkey
Myrmecophaga tridactyla	Giant Anteater (Ex)
Felis pardalis	Ocelot
Felis yagouaroundi	Jaguarundi
Felis wiedii	Margay
Panthera onca	Jaguar (Ex)
Tapirus bairdii	Central American Tapir (Ex)

FRENCH GUIANA

Ateles paniscus	Black Spider Monkey
Myrmecophaga tridactyla	Giant Anteater
Priodontes giganteus	Giant Armadillo
Speothos venaticus	Bush Dog
Pteronura brasiliensis	Giant Brazilian Otter
Felis pardalis	Ocelot
Felis tigrina	Little Spotted Cat
Felis yagouaroundi	Jaguarundi
Felis wiedii	Margay
Panthera onca	Jaguar
Trichechus manatus	Caribbean Manatee

GUATEMALA

Alouatta villosa	Guatemalan Howler Monkey
Ateles geoffroyi	Geoffroy's Spider Monkey
Myrmecophaga tridactyla	Giant Anteater
Felis pardalis	Ocelot
Felis yagouaroundi	Jaguarundi
Felis wiedii	Margay
Panthera onca	Jaguar
Trichechus manatus	Caribbean Manatee
Tapirus bairdii	Central American Tapir

GUYANA

Ateles paniscus	Black Spider Monkey
Myrmecophaga tridactyla	Giant Anteater
Priodontes giganteus	Giant Armadillo
Speothos venaticus	Bush Dog
Pteronura brasiliensis	Giant Brazilian Otter
Felis pardalis	Ocelot
Felis tigrina	Little Spotted Cat
Felis yagouaroundi	Jaguarundi
Felis wiedii	Margay
Panthera onca	Jaguar
Trichechus manatus	Caribbean Manatee
Trichechus inunguis	Amazonian Manatee

HAITI

Solenodon paradoxus	Haitian Solenodon
Plagiodontia aedium	Hispaniolan Hutia
Trichechus manatus	Caribbean Manatee

HONDURAS

Ateles geoffroyi	Geoffroy's Spider Monkey
Myrmecophaga tridactyla	Giant Anteater
Felis pardalis	Ocelot
Felis yagouaroundi	Jaguarundi
Felis wiedii	Margay
Panthera onca	Jaguar
Trichechus manatus	Caribbean Manatee
Tapirus bairdii	Central American Tapir

JAMAICA

Geocapromys brownii	Jamaican Hutia
Trichechus manatus	Caribbean Manatee

NICARAGUA

Ateles geoffroyi	Geoffroy's Spider Monkey
Myrmecophaga tridactyla	Giant Anteater
Felis pardalis	Ocelot
Felis tigrina	Little Spotted Cat (?)
Felis yagouaroundi	Jaguarundi
Felis wiedii	Margay
Panthera onca	Jaguar (?)

Trichechus manatus	Caribbean Manatee
Tapirus bairdii	Central American Tapir

PANAMA

Saimiri oerstedi	Central American Squirrel Monkey
Ateles fusciceps	Brown-headed Spider Monkey
Ateles geoffroyi	Geoffroy's Spider Monkey
Myrmecophaga tridactyla	Giant Anteater
Tremarctos ornatus	Spectacled Bear (?)
Speothos venaticus	Bush Dog
Felis pardalis	Ocelot
Felis tigrina	Little Spotted Cat
Felis yagouaroundi	Jaguarundi
Felis wiedii	Margay
Panthera onca	Jaguar
Trichechus manatus	Caribbean Manatee
Tapirus bairdii	Central American Tapir

PARAGUAY

Myrmecophaga tridactyla	Giant Anteater
Priodontes giganteus	Giant Armadillo
Burmeisteria retusa	Greater Pichi Ciego (?)
Chrysocyon brachyurus	Maned Wolf
Speothos venaticus	Bush Dog
Lutra platensis	La Plata Otter
Pteronura brasiliensis	Giant Brazilian Otter
Felis pardalis	Ocelot
Felis tigrina	Little Spotted Cat
Felis yagouaroundi	Jaguarundi
Felis wiedii	Margay
Panthera onca	Jaguar
Catagonus wagneri	Chacoan Peccary
Blastocerus dichotomus	Marsh Deer

PERU

Saguinus imperator	Emperor Tamarin
Callimico goeldii	Goeldi's Marmoset
Cacajao calvus	Red Uakari
Lagothrix flavicauda	Yellow-tailed Woolly Monkey
Lagothrix lagothricha	Woolly Monkey
Ateles belzebuth	Long-haired Spider Monkey
Ateles paniscus	Black Spider Monkey
Myrmecophaga tridactyla	Giant Anteater
Priodontes giganteus	Giant Armadillo
Chinchilla brevicaudata	Short-tailed Chinchilla (Ex)
Atelocynus microtis	Small-eared Dog
Chrysocyon brachyurus	Maned Wolf
Speothos venaticus	Bush Dog
Tremarctos ornatus	Spectacled Bear
Lutra felina	Marine Otter
Pteronura brasiliensis	Giant Brazilian Otter
Felis pardalis	Ocelot
Felis jacobita	Andean Cat
Felis tigrina	Little Spotted Cat (?)
Felis yagouaroundi	Jaguarundi

Felis wiedii	Margay
Panthera onca	Jaguar
Trichechus inunguis	Amazonian Manatee
Tapirus pinchaque	Mountain Tapir
Vicugna vicugna	Vicuna
Hippocamelus antisensis	North Andean Huemul
Blastocerus dichotomus	Marsh Deer
Pudu mephistophiles	Northern Pudu

SURINAME

Ateles paniscus	Black Spider Monkey
Myrmecophaga tridactyla	Giant Anteater
Priodontes giganteus	Giant Armadillo
Speothos venaticus	Bush Dog
Pteronura brasiliensis	Giant Brazilian Otter
Felis pardalis	Ocelot
Felis tigrina	Little Spotted Cat
Felis yagouaroundi	Jaguarundi
Felis wiedii	Margay
Panthera onca	Jaguar
Trichechus manatus	Caribbean Manatee

TRINIDAD AND TOBAGO

Trichechus manatus	Caribbean Manatee

URUGUAY

Chrysocyon brachyurus	Maned Wolf (Ex)
Lutra platensis	La Plata Otter
Pteronura brasiliensis	Giant Brazilian Otter
Felis wiedii	Margay
Panthera onca	Jaguar (Ex)
Blastocerus dichotomus	Marsh Deer (?)

VENEZUELA

Cacajao melanocephalus	Black-headed Uakari
Ateles belzebuth	Long-haired Spider Monkey
Ateles paniscus	Black Spider Monkey
Myrmecophaga tridactyla	Giant Anteater
Priodontes giganteus	Giant Armadillo
Atelocynus microtis	Small-eared Dog (?)
Speothos venaticus	Bush Dog
Tremarctos ornatus	Spectacled Bear
Pteronura brasiliensis	Giant Brazilian Otter
Felis pardalis	Ocelot
Felis tigrina	Little Spotted Cat
Felis yagouaroundi	Jaguarundi
Felis wiedii	Margay
Panthera onca	Jaguar
Trichechus manatus	Caribbean Manatee
Tapirus pinchaque	Mountain Tapir

OCEANS AND OCEANIC ISLANDS

EAST PACIFIC OCEAN

Arctocephalus galapagoensis	Galapagos Fur Seal
Arctocephalus philippii	Juan Fernandez Fur Seal
Arctocephalus townsendi	Guadalupe Fur Seal

NORTH PACIFIC OCEAN

Monachus schauinslandi	Hawaiian Monk Seal
Dugong dugon	Dugong

SOUTH PACIFIC OCEAN

Dugong dugon	Dugong

CARIBBEAN SEA

Monachus tropicalis	Caribbean Monk Seal
Trichechus manatus	Caribbean Manatee

ATLANTIC OCEAN

Trichechus manatus	Caribbean Manatee

Macropus parma. Parma Wallaby. A thriving population exists on Kawau Island, New Zealand, where they were introduced in the 1870s. Small populations have been discovered since the 1960s in wet sclerophyll forest, rainforest and dry sclerophyll forest in northeastern New South Wales. Its biology has been extensively studied, and although still an uncommon species, it does not appear to be immediately threatened at present.

Petrogale xanthopus. Yellow-footed Rock Wallaby. Recent surveys funded by WWF Australia have shown there to be a substantial population of this species in the Flinders Range, South Australia, with evidence of occurrence at over 170 separate sites. It also occurs in the Gawler Range in South Australia, extending into the Barrier Range in New South Wales and the Grey Range in Queensland. It is fully protected over its range and there is no evidence of a threatened status.

Wyulda squamicaudata. Scaly-tailed Possum. Occurs in the Kimberley District of northern Western Australia. The relative scarcity of records appears to be a product of the inaccessibility of its range rather than actual rarity; it is well known to local Aboriginals and there is no evidence of any major threat to the species at present.

'Planigale subtilissima'. Kimberley Planigale. Taxanomic studies have led to the view that it is a subspecies of Ingram's Planigale (**Planigale ingrami**) which as a species is not considered threatened. The Kimberley populations themselves are now known to be considerably more widespread than was originally thought.

Planigale tenuirostris. Narrow-nosed Planigale. Originally known from seven specimens from western New South Wales, it is now known to be quite common in the area and has also been collected in South Australia and Queensland. There appears to be no reason to now regard it as under threat.

Antechinomys laniger. Kultarr. Now considered to be synonymous at the specific level with the central Australian form (now **Antechinomys laniger spenceri**) which is relatively common and widespread. There is no clear evidence that the nominate form itself is particularly threatened.

'Microtus pennsylvanicus provectus'. Block Island Meadow Vole. Recent work has shown that this taxon is so similar to the mainland Meadow Vole that it cannot even be considered a marginal subspecies; moreover the population of the vole on Block Island is considered secure at present.

'Dipodomys elephantinus'. Big-eared Kangaroo Rat. This taxon is now taken as conspecific with **Dipodomys venustus**, which is not considered threatened. The 'elephantinus' phenotype itself is now known to be considerably more widespread than formerly supposed.

Euderma maculatum. Spotted Bat. Although rarely recorded, this species appears to be widely distributed in the southern United States and Northern Mexico and to occupy a considerable altitudinal range. Indications are that summer habitat consists of open, hot, treeless areas and dry canyons; this habitat is widespread within its range and there is no evidence of any threat to the species at present.

Vulpes velox hebes. Northern Kit Fox. When listed in the Red Data Book the above taxon referred to the northern subspecies of **Vulpes velox**, an animal ranging from the southern parts of the Canadian prairie provinces (Alberta, Saskatchewan, Manitoba) south through Montana, E. Wyoming, the Dakotas,

Minnesota and Iowa to the Texas Panhandle. Two subspecies were described, Vulpes velox velox and V. v. hebes. Information sought during the compilation of this revision initially led us to believe that V. v. hebes was no longer considered a valid taxon and hence it was decided to exclude the taxon from the present revision. However since then a new revision (Hall, E.R. 1981. The Mammals of North America. John Wiley and Sons, New York) has considered Kit and Swift Foxes V. velox and V. macrotis to be conspecific under the name V. velox. Ten subspecies are described, including V. v. hebes, but assigning to it a much smaller area of distribution. Within this area Kit Foxes are highly endangered, if not extinct, and thus the 'new' V. v. hebes should be included in the Red Data Book. However there was not time to so list it and hence V. v. hebes has been omitted from the current Red Data Book revision. The IUCN/SSC Canid Specialist is pursuing enquiries concerning Kit Foxes and a meeting is to be held in Canada in 1982 on Northern Swift (Kit) Fox conservation.

Ovis canadensis. Bighorn Sheep. This species was listed in the Mammal Red Data Book in 1972 as Vulnerable. However the Rocky Mountain Sheep O. c. canadensis has not been considered threatened for many decades and should not have been included in 1972. Although at that time there was some justification for including some of the other subspecies, all are now the subject of extensive management and conservation programmes, many new herds have been, and are being, established and no individual subspecies is listed or being contemplated at the present time for listing on the U.S. Endangered Species List. The Red Data Book compiler therefore felt there was no justification for including Bighorn Sheep in the Red Data Book at the present time. However anyone seeking information on this animal should contact the IUCN Species Conservation Monitoring Unit directly or else consult the Transactions of the Desert Bighorn Council which are published annually.

LONG-BEAKED ECHIDNA

VULNERABLE

Zaglossus bruijni (Peters & Doria, 1876)

Order   MONOTREMATA   Family   TACHYGLOSSIDAE

SUMMARY   Confined to humid mid-montane forests of New Guinea. Overall population is probably still relatively high, but the species is considered at risk because of a marked decline in many areas as a result of increased forest clearance and hunting pressure from the rapidly increasing human population. Although a protected species, restriction of traditional hunting practices would be extremely difficult and establishment of reserves would appear to offer the best means of conserving the species.

DISTRIBUTION   Endemic to the island of New Guinea, where inhabits the mountains of the Vogelkop, the central cordillera from western Irian Jaya to southeastern Papua, and the mountainous Huon Peninsula (4,11). Menzies has noted that its distribution appears patchy and, although some of this can doubtless partly be attributed to extirpation by man, the lack of a vernacular name for the animal in some areas with apparently suitable habitat implies that it has not existed there, at least in historical times (8). Has been reported to occur on the relatively low altitude island of Salawati, which is narrowly separated by shallow water from the coast of western New Guinea, but its presence there is doubtful (11). Fossil remains of a larger Zaglossus-like monotreme have also been found in deposits of Pleistocene age in Australia, although there are no recent records outside New Guinea (11).

POPULATION   No precise estimates available, but George and Van Deusen in 1974 calculated that if an average density of four animals per square mile (2.59. sq. km) were assumed as a conservative estimate, then the area of habitat currently available to the species would suggest a total population of about 300,000 (5,7). In the extensive central highlands of Papua New Guinea Zaglossus populations are very low and the species has been extirpated from many districts of high human population density (4,7). It is still relatively common, however, in areas of undisturbed forest remote from human habitation (5,8,10).

HABITAT AND ECOLOGY   Inhabits humid mid-montane forests at elevations of 1000-3000 m that are blanketed seasonally by cloud cover (4,10,11). Zaglossus is believed to be primarily nocturnal and forages for its food (believed to be principally ants, termites and earthworms) in the litter of the forest floor (4,10). There is some indication that the breeding season may coincide with the monsoonal summer (late November to late March) rather than winter, when the related lowland Short-beaked Echidna Tachyglossus aculeatus is thought to breed (10). Nothing else appears known of the breeding biology of Zaglossus. In Tachyglossus one egg is normally produced, rarely two or three; incubation (in the pouch) lasts about ten days with the young remaining in the pouch for up to eight weeks and remaining under maternal care for at least a further three months (10).

THREATS TO SURVIVAL   Habitat destruction and hunting. Zaglossus is considered a great delicacy and is hunted by traditional methods using specially trained dogs; it is often traded over long distances for use in ceremonial feasts (4,7). With the increasing human population, especially in the Central Highlands, it is coming under increasing hunting pressure and George in 1979 noted that it had been widely extirpated in living memory, now no longer occurring in many areas with suitable habitat (4). In the long term, however, habitat destruction is liable

1

to be of more importance than hunting. Although much habitat, especially on the northern side of the Central Cordillera is very rugged and relatively secure from logging and mining activities, forest clearance for garden cultivation is accelerating and as settlement spreads into more remote areas, formerly secure Echidna populations can be expected to come under increasing threat (4,7,10). Natural predation is thought to be of very minor importance (7).

CONSERVATION MEASURES TAKEN Zaglossus is listed in Appendix 2 of the 1973 Convention on International Trade in Endangered Species of Wild Fauna and Flora, and trade in it or its products is thus subject to monitoring by ratifying nations. Protected in Irian Jaya under the Decree of the Minister of Agriculture No.66/Kpts/UM/2/1973, and has been protected in Papua New Guinea, where it is a 'National Animal', since January 1975 (1,4,6). Protection, in Papua New Guinea at least, does not extend to traditional hunting methods and George and Van Deusen noted in 1974 that legislation to control such hunting was not feasible at present (4,17). Studies of this species in the wild to determine ecological requirements and map out distribution in more detail would be very desirable.

CONSERVATION MEASURES PROPOSED George noted in 1974 that, as control of hunting on traditional hunting grounds was not feasible, conservation plans for this species would have to involve the setting aside of large areas of suitable habitat as national parks or reserves (3). The land tenure system which operates, at least in Papua New Guinea, will make this difficult to achieve.

CAPTIVE BREEDING Although it does not appear to have ever bred in captivity, individuals have been kept alive for long periods - one lived at London Zoo for over thirty years (10). In 1979, Dallas Zoo, U.S.A. held one male, Taronga Park Zoo, Sydney, two females and London Zoo one female and two unsexed animals (9).

REMARKS For description see (2). This primitive but highly specialized egg-laying mammal is of considerable scientific interest. Until recently three species of Zaglossus were recognized, of which bruijni was thought to be the rarest, but it is now considered that all are the same species, showing considerable clinal variation, and the name bruijni has priority (11).

REFERENCES   1.   Anon. (1981). List of protected mammals in Indonesia. Appendix 3 to 1980 Indonesia CITES report. 7pp.
2.   George, G.G. (1973). 1972-1973 Annual Report of the Trustees of the Wildlife and Bird of Paradise Sanctuary, Baiyer River, Papua New Guinea.
3.   George, G.G. (1974). In litt.
4.   George, G.G. (1979). The status of endangered Papua New Guinea mammals. In Tyler, M.J. (Ed.), The Status of endangered Australasian Wildlife. Royal Zool. Soc. S. Aust.
5.   George, G.G. and Van Duesen H.M. (1974). In litt.
6.   Hudson, B. (1978). Papua New Guinea's National Animals. Wildlife Division, Papua New Guinea Department of Lands and Environment, Konedobu.
7.   IUCN. (1974). Long-beaked Echidna. Sheet code 1.1.2.1 In Red Data Book. Vol.1. Mammalia. IUCN, Switzerland.
8.   Menzies, J.I. (1976). Some thoughts on the ecology and conservation of mammals, reptiles and amphibians. In Lamb, K.P. and Gressit, J.L. (Eds) Ecology and conservation in Papua New Guinea. Wau Ecology Institute Pamphlet No.2.
9.   Olney, P.J.S. (Ed.) (1980). International Zoo Yearbook 20. Zool. Soc. London.
10. Van Deusen, H.M. (1971). Zaglossus, New Guinea's

egg-laying anteater. Fauna 2: 12-19.

11. Van Deusen, H.M. and George, G.G. (1969). Results of the Archbold Expeditions. No.90. Notes on the echidnas (Mammalia, Tachyglossidae) of New Guinea. Amer. Mus. Novitates, No. 2383.

TOOLACHE WALLABY

Macropus greyi (Waterhouse, 1846)

Order   MARSUPIALIA   Family   MACROPODIDAE

SUMMARY   Almost certainly extinct; was confined to a relatively small area of southeast Australia where it appears to have been exterminated in the 1920s, principally as a result of human persecution and predation by introduced foxes.

DISTRIBUTION   Australia. Seems to have always had a limited distribution in a small region of South Australia, southeast of Adelaide, and in the contiguous part of Victoria (1,3).

POPULATION   Almost definitely extinct; in 1975-76 an extensive survey by the South Australian National Parks and Wildlife Service failed to find any reliable evidence for the species' continued existence (3). The last known wild population, at Konetta sheep station, 42 km southeast of Robe in South Australia, was apparently exterminated by 1927 (1). It was recorded as locally numerous throughout its range in the nineteenth century and was apparently not uncommon as late as 1910 in scattered bands inland from Millicent to Kingston (4).

HABITAT AND ECOLOGY   Essentially an open country species, avoiding heavy timber and thick scrub and favouring grasslands rather than more arid regions. It showed a marked and persistent preference for certain quite restricted areas to which animals would repeatedly return if driven away. These were frequently in the 'fringe' or 'Black Rush' country, a transition zone between light sandy soils and richer loams and clays. Such regions were flat or gently undulating, becoming swampy in winter with depressions filled with Low Rush (Lepidosperma laterale), alternating with which were patches of tall, coarse grasses, especially Poa caespitosa and Themeda triandra, with clumps of Banksia marginata, B. ornata and dwarf Xanthorrhoea (1). It was notable for a greater degree of sociality than most other Macropus species but is said not to have differed greatly from them in other aspects of its biology, being probably both a grazer and browser and carrying only one pouch-young at a time (1).

THREATS TO SURVIVAL   Finlayson has given a detailed account of the extermination of the Toolache, which he attributes to human persecution for sport and furs, and to predation by the introduced fox (1). The species had a beautiful pelt which was much in demand for the fur trade, being marketed in 'very great numbers' in Melbourne sale-rooms at the turn of the century. Its great speed and open-country habitat made it a favourite object for coursing with greyhounds. Large numbers were also incidentally killed by dogs on fox-hunts (1,4). Until the early part of the century a bonus of sixpence was paid for all kangaroo and wallaby scalps obtained, thus adding further incentive for its persecution. The fox, preying principally on the young, was probably the main agent in the extirpation of the Toolache from the drier parts of its range which at that time were otherwise little disturbed by man. By 1923 the known population had been reduced to the band on Konetta sheep farm, comprising around 14 individuals, with isolated pairs probably scattered through the rest of its range in rougher 'stringy-bark' country. The precarious state of the population led to abortive attempts in 1923 and 1924 to capture some of the surviving specimens for transfer to a sanctuary on Kangaroo Island; these merely resulted in the death of four of the survivors. The attention drawn to the rarity of the species led to the last few known specimens being killed for trophies, although a female, captured by two kangaroo dogs, survived in captivity at least until 1927 (1).

CONSERVATION MEASURES TAKEN Appears on the Official List of Australian Endangered Vertebrate Fauna.

CONSERVATION MEASURES PROPOSED Immediate, effective protection of any area found to hold a population of this species.

CAPTIVE BREEDING Has been kept in captivity (1). Breeding potential was probably good.

REMARKS For description see (4).

REFERENCES
1. Finlayson, H.H. (1927). Observations on the South Australian species of the subgenus, 'Wallabia'. Trans. R. Soc. S. Aust. 51: 363-377.
2. Ride, W.D.L. (1970). A guide to the native mammals of Australia. Oxford University Press, Melbourne.
3. Robinson, A.C. (1981). In litt.
4. Troughton, E. (1941). Furred animals of Australia. Angus and Robertson Ltd. Sydney.

BRIDLED NAILTAIL WALLABY   ENDANGERED

Onychogalea fraenata (Gould, 1840)

Order   MARSUPIALIA   Family   MACROPODIDAE

SUMMARY   Only survives, as far as is known, in a small area of northern Australia where a 'reasonably-sized' population was discovered in 1973. Principal threat appears to be habitat clearance for agriculture but the recent purchase of a portion of the known range to form a reserve for the species should safeguard part of the population.

DISTRIBUTION   Australia, where the only known population at present (1980) is in an area of approx 11,200 ha northeast of Dingo in eastern central Queensland (2,6,12,15). Reports of individuals observed on the borders of the Gibralter Range National Park in New South Wales in the late 1960s and early 1970s are conflicting and subject to confirmation (1,2,3). An extensive survey by the National Parks and Wildlife Service in 1975 of the northern slopes and table-lands of New South Wales failed to locate the species (14). Formerly occurred in eastern Queensland from the Townsville region through the Darling Downs to inland New South Wales as far as the plains of the lower Murray and probably into adjacent regions of South Australia and northwest Victoria, near the junction of the Murray and Darling Rivers (6,8,11,14).

POPULATION   In 1980 was said to exist in 'reasonable' numbers within its limited range (4). The wallaby was at least locally common in inland eastern and southeastern Australia at the time of European settlement. Krefft in 1866 described it as the commonest small macropod in the region near the junction of the Murray and Darling rivers (8). By the beginning of the present century the species was apparently in decline and Le Souëf in 1923 considered it in danger of extinction although in 1930 it was reported as 'not uncommon' in some parts of southern Queensland (9,10). In 1941 Troughton observed that it was by then rare or absent over its entire former range (16). Up to 1972 the most recent specimens were from Manilla, New South Wales in 1924, the Dawson River in southeast Queensland in 1929, and an unrecorded locality, possibly in central Queensland, in 1937 (11). In 1973 the population near Dingo in Queensland was discovered (6,15).

HABITAT AND ECOLOGY   Surveys by Gordon and Lawrie have recorded the wallaby in a wide variety of shrubland and wooded habitats comprising most of the major vegetation types within its range, including regenerated open-forest and shrubland and areas with partly disturbed canopies resulting from thinning, partial clearing or fire disturbance, as well as undisturbed areas (6). Most communities are dominated by Brigalow (Acacia harpophylla) but there are also areas of Eucalypt woodland and associations dominated by other Acacia species (e.g. A. rhodoxylon and A. burrowi). Gordon and Lawrie also reported that within the region surveyed the wallabies were only recorded from those areas on more fertile soils, especially 'cracking clays', and alluvial soils, and were absent from sites on less fertile and shallower soils with apparently suitable habitat structure. They also suggest on the basis of nocturnal sightings in more open habitat that there may be at least some dependence on edge conditions in scrubland, enabling animals to forage widely in grassy Eucalyptus communities (6). Historical comments on habitat prefrence associate the species with unspecified scrub types (6). Gilbert noted that it seemed independent of water and dietary preference appeared to be for bulbous roots (6,11). Predominantly solitary and nocturnal, it tends to rest up during the day in a shallow nest scratched out beneath a tussock

7

of grass or bush and is notoriously shy and difficult to observe (7,13).

THREATS TO SURVIVAL The region where the wallaby is now found is subject to large clearing and intesive pasture development for beef cattle as part of the 'Brigalow Development Scheme' (6). Gordon and Lawrie note, however, that the original decline of the species in Queensland preceded the widespread clearing of Brigalow lands and thus cannot be attributed to this. Earlier, more patchy clearing may have been a possible cause of decline but habitat disturbance other than total clearing does not appear to affect the wallaby significantly within its present range. The decline does not appear to be correlated with the presence of introduced foxes or rabbits at high densities - within the present range, cats and rabbits were reportedly common while foxes were scarce but still present (6). They note that major extirpations of this and many other Australian terrestrial mammals appear more closely correlated with the distribution of introduced domestic grazing animals, especially sheep, than with other factors, and argue that the decline of this species in central and northern Queensland, where many other species have been as yet relatively unaffected, indicates it to be especially sensitive to such disturbance (6). Although the Dingo district has been found to be unsuitable for sheep, cattle are raised in large numbers and the success of the Brigalow Development Scheme has led to increased stocking rates and a great reduction in the size of uncleared areas that may act as reservoirs for fauna (6).

CONSERVATION MEASURES TAKEN Listed in Appendix 1 of the 1973 Convention on International Trade in Endangered Species of Wild Fauna and Flora, trade in it or its products therefore being subject to strict regulation by ratifying nations, and trade for primarily commercial purposes banned. Legally protected and in 1979 it was reported that the Queensland government had purchased about half the area known to be inhabited by the species to form a reserve (12,14); this should safeguard part of the population from further habitat destruction. Some research has been carried out on the ecology of the species and will be useful in management of the reserve (4,14). A captive breeding colony has been established by the Queensland National Parks and Wildlife Service and a study of reproductive biology was reported as underway in 1978 (15). An attempt in the late 1930s to introduce the species to Bulba Island, Lake Macquarie, New South Wales, failed (13).

CONSERVATION MEASURES PROPOSED Continued management and protection of the only presently known wild population is essential for the survival of the species. It is planned to develope a method for monitoring numbers and also to enlarge the area of the reservation (4). If surplus captive stock can be built up, the establishment of colonies in suitable protected areas should be considered. Any further wild populations which may be discovered should immediately be afforded rigorous protection.

CAPTIVE BREEDING A captive breeding colony was reported in 1978 as maintained by the Queensland National Parks and Wildlife Service (15). As far as is known no others are held in captivity.

REMARKS For description see (13). The common name is that recommended by the Australian Mammal Society. This data sheet was compiled from a draft provided in 1978 by Dr G. Gordon, Queensland National Parks and Wildlife Service.

REFERENCES 1. Anon. (1975). Bridled Nail-tailed Wallaby in New South Wales and Queensland, Australia. Tigerpaper 2(3): 26.
2. Anon. (1976). Bridled Nail-tailed Wallaby. Tigerpaper 3(1): 26.
3. Anon. (1976). More on the Bridled Nail-tailed Wallaby. Tigerpaper 3(3): 25.

4. Australian National Parks and Wildlife Service (1980). Bridled Nailtail Wallaby. Unpd. draft data sheet.

5. Collett, R. (1887). On a collection of mammals from central and northern Queensland. Zool. Jahrbucher. 2: 829-940.

6. Gordon, G. and Lawrie, B.B. (1980). The rediscovery of the Bridled Nail-tailed Wallaby Onychogalea fraenata (Gould) (Marsupialia: Macropodidae) in Queensland. Aust. Wildl. Res. 7: 339-345.

7. Gould, J. (1863). The Mammals of Australia. Taylor and Francis, London.

8. Krefft, G. (1866). On the vertebrate animals of the lower Murray and Darling, their habits, economy and geographical distribution. Trans. philos. soc. N.S.W. 1862-65. 1-33.

9. Le Souëf, A.S. (1923). The Australian native animals, how they stand today and the cause of scarcity of certain species. Aust. Zool. 3: 108-111.

10. Longman, H. (1930). The marsupials of Queensland. Mem. Queensland Mus. 10: 55-64.

11. Marlow, B.J. (1948). A survey of the marsupials of New South Wales. CSIRO Wildl. Res. 3: 71-114.

12. Poole, W.E. (1979). The status of the Australian Macropodidae. In Tyler, M.J. (Ed.), The status of endangered Australasian wildlife. Royal. Zool. Soc. S. Aust.

13. Ride, W.D.L. (1970). A guide to the native mammals of Australia. Oxford University Press, Melbourne.

14. Robertson, G. (1980). Bridled Nail-tailed Wallaby. In Endangered Animals of New South Wales. New South Wales National Parks and Wildlife Service. 41-44.

15. Smith, H.A. (1978). In litt.

16. Troughton, E. (1941). Furred animals of Australia. Angus and Robertson Ltd., Sydney.

CRESCENT NAILTAIL WALLABY   EXTINCT

Onychogalea lunata (Gould, 1840)

Order   MARSUPIALIA   Family   MACROPODIDAE

SUMMARY Extremely rare if not extinct. Last fully authenticated record, in inland Western Australia, was in 1930. Surveys are needed to discover if the species still persists and, if so, to define immediate effective protective measures.

DISTRIBUTION Australia; where formerly distributed from the southwest, east of the Darling Range, through southern and central areas as far as the Alice Springs region, the northern limit being about 23°S, and to the east of the Lake Eyre Basin (1,3,6,7). It may also have been recorded from the junction of the Murray and Darling Rivers in Victoria and New South Wales (6). Populations are now most likely to survive in inland arid regions of Western and central Australia (8).

POPULATION Unknown. If the species does still persist its numbers must be very low; the last fully accepted record is dated 1930 (8). There is a record from Western Australia in 1964, when a dead wallaby found near the Gahnda Rockhole in the Gibson Desert, apparently killed by a fox, was reportedly identified on the basis of a still greasy mandibular fragment (2); the veracity of this record has been questioned, however, and the specimen was not preserved (2). In 1979 it was reported that the Aborigines native to the Warburton region said that it was no longer found there (2). Finlayson in 1961 stated that it was still extant in central Australia east of the Warburton region and reported a specimen killed between the Tarlton and Jervois Ranges in 1956 (3).

HABITAT AND ECOLOGY In the Warburton region it inhabited areas of mulga woodland and creek country where there were River Gums (Eucalyptus camuldensis) (2). According to Gould it rested up during the day in a hollow made in soft ground beneath a thick bush and would take shelter in hollow logs or burrows when pursued (4). Little else is known of the biology of the species.

THREATS TO SURVIVAL Presumably susceptible to the same generalised threats -- exotic predators, habitat loss through conversion for agriculture and competition from introduced herbivores such as cattle, sheep and rabbits -- as have affected much of the Australian mainland fauna (1,5,6,7). Predation by feral cats and foxes has been particularly implicated in the decline of this species (3,7), though loss of habitat to cereal crops and persecution by farmers are likely to have been important factors in the Western Australian wheat-belt (1).

CONSERVATION MEASURES TAKEN Listed in Appendix 1 of the 1973 Convention on International Trade in Endangered Species of Wild Fauna and Flora, trade in it or its products therefore being subject to strict regulation by ratifying nations, and trade for primarily commercial purposes banned. Legally protected throughout its former range, and appears on the Official List of Endangered Australian Vertebrate Fauna.

CONSERVATION MEASURES PROPOSED Immediate protection of any areas found to hold populations of this species.

CAPTIVE BREEDING No captive specimens exist though breeding potential is probably good (8).

REMARKS For description see (1,6). The function of the horny growth at the end of the tail which gives the genus its name is unknown. The common name used is that recommended by the Australian Mammal Society in 1981. This data sheet was compiled from a draft provided in 1978 by Dr A.A. Burbidge, Western Australian Wildlife Research Centre.

REFERENCES
1. Anon. (1977). Crescent Nail-Tailed Wallaby Onychogalea lunata. Mammals No. 8. In Australian Endangered Species. Australian National Parks and Wildlife Service.
2. Burbidge, A.A. and Fuller, P.J. (1979). Mammals of the Warburton Region, Western Australia. Res. West Aust. Mus. 8(1): 57-73.
3. Finlayson, H.H. (1961). On Central Australian mammals Part IV. The distribution and status of Central Australian species. Rec. S. Aust. Mus. 14: 141-191.
4. Gould, J. (1863). Mammals of Australia. Taylor and Francis, London.
5. Poole, W.E. (1979). The status of the Australian Macropodidae. In Tyler, M.J. (Ed.), The status of endangered Australasian wildlife. Royal. Zool. Soc. S. Aust.
6. Ride, W.D.L. (1970). A guide to the native mammals of Australia. Oxford University Press, Melbourne.
7. Troughton, E. (1941). Furred animals of Australia. Angus and Robertson Ltd. Sydney.
8. Burbidge, A.A. (1978-81). In litt.

Lagorchestes asomatus Finlayson, 1943

Order   MARSUPIALIA   Family   MACROPODIDAE

SUMMARY Known from a single skull collected in 1931 in central Australia. The validity of the species is doubtful.

DISTRIBUTION Australia. The only known specimen is a skull collected between Mt. Farewell in the Northern Territory and Lake Mackay on the Western Australian border in 1931. It was described by Finlayson in 1943 (1).

POPULATION Unknown. Presumed extinct, and there is some doubt whether the species ever existed at all (2).

HABITAT AND ECOLOGY Unknown.

THREATS TO SURVIVAL Unknown.

CONSERVATION MEASURES TAKEN Appears on the Official List of Australian Endangered Vertebrate Fauna.

CONSERVATION MEASURES PROPOSED Effective protection of any areas found to contain populations of this animal.

CAPTIVE BREEDING None.

REMARKS There are no details of external description. The common name is that recommended by the Australian Mammal Society.

REFERENCES 1. Finlayson, H.H. (1943). A new species of Lagorchestes (Marsupialia). Trans. R. Soc. S. Aust. 67: 319-321.
            2. Kirkpatrick, T.H. (1977). In litt.

RUFOUS HARE-WALLABY

Lagorchestes hirsutus (Gould, 1844)

Order   MARSUPIALIA   Family   MACROPODIDAE

SUMMARY Known populations confined to Bernier and Dorre islands, Western Australia and two small colonies in central Australia. Changes in fire regime have been implicated as a major cause of the species' decline. Remaining populations seem secure at present (1981) but must be considered potentially at risk because of their very limited range.

DISTRIBUTION Australia where it now has a highly disjunct distribution, being apparently confined to Bernier and Dorre Islands (about 10,560 ha combined) in Shark Bay, Western Australia, and the Tanami Desert, Northern Territory, where two small colonies are known (1,6,7). Formerly inhabited arid inland regions of western and central Australia, though the limits of its range were never precisely determined (3).

POPULATION Numbers on Bernier and Dorre Island are unknown.   The population appears to flucuate there, as succeeding visits to the islands have noted different relative abundances of this and the similar Banded Hare-wallaby, Lagostrophus fasciatus, also a Red Data Book species (6,7). In 1906 the Rufous Hare-wallaby was reportedly abundant but in 1910, following several years of drought was much less so.   The 1959 expedition to the islands found it to be apparently rare whereas in 1969 it was readily observed (5,7). This may, however, simply reflect different emphasis on the two species' preferred habitats (tall scrub in the case of Lagostrophus fasciatus as opposed to more open areas in the present species) by different investigators rather than real population changes (7), though this needs further investigation and in 1981 it was reported that numbers of Lagorchestes hirsutus had recently risen dramatically in an area burnt 5 years previously (2). In 1978 the two colonies in the Tanami Desert were estimated as holding possibly as few as 6 to 10 individuals each (1). A careful search of 2300 km of apparently suitable habitat in this region failed to reveal any further colonies (1). Reportedly formerly abundant where it did occur though Finlayson in 1961 noted that its pattern of occurrence was fluctuating and discontinuous, the wide separation of individual colonies making accurate estimates of population status difficult (3). He concluded, however, that there had been a major collapse in numbers in the 1940s and 1950s, especially in the Musgrave, Mann and Tomkinson Ranges in southwest central Australia where it had been a major aboriginal food source in the 1930s (3). It apparently disappeared from much of its former range considerably earlier (8).

HABITAT AND ECOLOGY On Bernier and Dorre found in heath or open steppe association and in spinifex or porcupine grass (Triodia) areas (6,7). The colonies in the Tanami Desert are adjacent to a stock route; here the habitat is broadly described as sandplain interspersed with numerous small saltpans. Giant mounds of the termite Nasutitermes triodiae are characteristic. Ground . cover is predominantly soft spinifex, Plectrachne spp. and Triodia pungens, with Melaleuca glomerata, Acacia spp. and other shrubs. The areas around the colonies are typified by a tight mosaic of different vegetative generative stages, brought about by the deliberate lighting of 'cool' low intensity winter fires. This fire pattern is considered to produce conditions of food supply and cover essential to the animal's survival.   The centres of activity of the colonies are unburnt stands of spinifex of 0.5-0.8 sq. km, adjacent recently burnt patches are heavily used for foraging, as regrowths tends to be succulent and nutritious. Elsewhere the region is subject to extensive hot summer fires started by lightning which cause almost total destruction of vegetation and would almost certainly wipe out any colonies in their path (1). Appears exclusively vegetarian; has a ruminant-like digestion, with a stomach adapted to a high-fibre diet (2). Feeds on spinifex seeds, sedges and perennial shrubs, the exact composition depending on season (1). It is nocturnal, resting in the day in forms hidden under bushes or in spinifex clumps (1,6), in summer short burrows up to 700 mm deep may be dug (2).

THREATS TO SURVIVAL Bolton and Latz conclude from their 1978 study of the Tanami Desert population that changes in the fire regime this century may have been a principal factor in the population decline (1). Small scale, carefully controlled fire was very extensively used by nomadic Aborigines for a variety of purposes and would have resulted in large areas of habitat suitable for the species. Since the 1930s such firing has been reduced to negligible proportions with the congregation of Aborigines into settlements and missions. This has led to vegetative conditions developing which allow the establishment of wide-ranging 'hot' summer fires started by lightning. These are now common and have destroyed the Hare-wallaby's habitat over much of its range (1). The effect of introduced animals is difficult to guage. Foxes and cattle are mainly absent from the Tanami Desert and also from large areas of inland Western Australia. Feral cats are as common around the two colonies as they are elsewhere and it is thought likely that Hare-wallabies are largely able to elude them. Heavy rabbit infestations are liable to exclude the wallaby through general habitat deterioration but large areas of uninfested habitat still occur (1). The populations on Bernier and Dorre, although apparently secure at present (1981), are potentially very vulnerable to fire or the introduction of foxes, cats or rabbits (6). The vegetation on Bernier was formerly subject to damage from a feral goat population but an intensive eradication programme has alleviated this and allowed recovery of affected areas to begin (7).

CONSERVATION MEASURES TAKEN Listed in Appendix 1 of the 1973 Convention on International Trade in Endangered Species of Wild Fauna and Flora, trade in it or its products therefore being subject to strict regulation by ratifying nations, and trade for primarily commercial purposes banned. Legally protected and appears on the Official List of Endangered Australian Verbetrate Fauna. The mainland colonies are in a desert wildlife sanctuary, where habitat is managed by controlled burning (2). Bernier and Dorre Islands are class 'A' faunal reserves with strictly controlled access (1,7).

CONSERVATION MEASURES PROPOSED Continued management and protection of the areas where it occurs are essential for the species' survival. Any other areas where relict populations may be discovered should be afforded immediate protection. Reintroduction to suitable fire-managed areas using captive bred stock is planned (2).

CAPTIVE BREEDING Five specimens were collected in the Tanami Desert during 1980 to establish a captive breeding colony at the Arid Zone Research Insitute of the Northern Territory Conservation Commission at Alice Springs (4).

REMARKS For description see (8). The common name used here is that recommended by the Australian Mammal Society in 1980; the animal is also known the Western Hare-wallaby. This data sheet was compiled from a draft provided in 1978 by Dr A.A. Burbidge, Western Australian Wildlife Research Centre.

REFERENCES 1. Bolton, B.L. and Latz, P.K. (1978). The Western Hare-Wallaby, Lagorchestes hirsutus (Gould) (Macropodidae), in the Tanami Desert. Aust. Wildl. Res. 5: 285-93.

2. Burbidge, A.A. and Johnson, K.A. (no date). _Lagorchestes hirsutus_, Mala. Draft entry for 'Mammals of Australia'. Unpd. 4pp.

3. Finlayson, H.H. (1961). On Central Australian mammals Part IV. The distribution and status of Central Australian species. _Rec. S. Aust. Mus._ 14: 141-191.

4. George, G.G. (1981). In litt.

5. Prince, R.I.T. (1978). Pers. comm. to A.A. Burbidge.

6. Ride, W.D.L. and Tyndale-Biscoe, C.H. (1962). Mammals. In Fraser, A.J. (Ed.). The results of an expedition to Bernier and Dorre Islands, Shark bay, Western Australia in 1959. _West. Australian Fisheries Dept. Fauna Bull._ 2: 54-97.

7. Robinson, A.C., Robinson, J.F., Watts, C.H.S. and Baverstock, P.R. (1976). The Shark Bay Mouse _Pseudomys praeconis_ and other mammals on Bernier Island, Western Australia. _Western Australian Naturalist._ 13 (7): 149-155.

8. Troughton, E. (1941). _Furred animals of Australia._ Angus and Robertson Ltd. Sydney.

EASTERN HARE-WALLABY   EXTINCT

Lagorchestes leporides (Gould, 1841)

Order MARSUPIALIA   Family   MACROPODIDAE

SUMMARY   Almost certainly extinct. Formerly occurred in southeastern Australia where declined rapidly following European settlement, the last known specimen being taken in 1890.

DISTRIBUTION Australia, where formerly occurred in interior New South Wales, eastern South Australia and northwestern Victoria (3,4). In the 19th century Gould recorded it in the Liverpool Plains and in the vicinity of the Namoi and Gwydir Rivers. He also found it tolerably abundant on grassy plains in the region of the Murray (1). The species then apparently declined rapidly throughout its range and the last known specimen was taken in 1890, 30 miles north of Booligal, New South Wales (3).

POPULATION Probably extinct. Unrecorded for 90 years.

HABITAT AND ECOLOGY 19th century observers found it to be generally solitary and nocturnal, resting under a bush in a 'form' during the day (1,4). Gould commented on its great speed and jumping ability when pursued (1). Diet and breeding biology are unknown, though Krefft in 1865 noted that individuals lived quite well on a diet of biscuits, bread and boiled rice when kept about the camp in the bush (4)!

THREATS TO SURVIVAL The specific causes of its presumed extinction are unknown, though its former range was in a part of Australia which had already been extensively cleared and settled by the mid-19th century and it was undoubtedly affected by this and the introduction of exotic wild herbivores (principally rabbits) and predators (mostly feral cats at that time)(2).

CONSERVATION MEASURES TAKEN Appears on the Official List of Australian Endangered Vertebrate Fauna.

CONSERVATION MEASURES PROPOSED Immediate effective protection of any area found to hold a population of this species.

CAPTIVE BREEDING None.

REMARKS For description see (3).

REFERENCES   1.   Gould, J. (1863). The Mammals of Australia. Taylor and Francis, London.
2.   Ovington, D. (1978) Australian Endangered Species. Cassell, Australia.
3.   Ride, W.D.L. (1970). A guide to the native mammals of Australia. Oxford Univ. Press, Melbourne.
4.   Troughton, E. (1941). Furred animals of Australia. Angus and Robertson Ltd. Sydney.

Lagostrophus fasciatus (Péron, 1807)

Order   MARSUPIALIA   Family   MACROPODIDAE

SUMMARY Almost certainly extinct on mainland Australia but good populations survive on Bernier and Dorre Islands off Western Australia. These are, however, potentially vulnerable to introduced predators or fire. A reintroduction programme was begun on Dirk Hartog Island in 1974.

DISTRIBUTION Australia. Now confined as far as is known to Bernier and Dorre Islands (about 10,560 ha combined) in Shark Bay, Western Australia, and the nearby Dirk Hartog Island (about 62,000 ha), where a reintroduction programme was begun in 1974 (1,4). Recent records have all been confined to the southwest of Western Australia (A.A. Burbidge, In litt., 1981); an early record for South Australia is unsubstantiated by any specimen but remains of the the species have been found in deposits at an Aboriginal site on the lower Murray River (3).

POPULATION In 1959 Bernier and Dorre Islands were found to support a large, stable population; it being the most abundant species on the islands (4). Absolute population levels have not been measured but the relative numbers of this and the other two macropod species present there, the Rufous Hare-wallaby, (Lagorchestes hirsutus) and the Boodie (Bettongia lesueur) (both in the Red Data Book) have appeared to fluctuate on succeeding visits to the islands - an expedition to Bernier in 1975 did not observe the Banded Hare-wallaby at all (4,5). This may reflect different emphasis on the species' preferred habitats by different investigators rather than real changes in abundance - the 1975 expedition examined very little of the Banded Hare-wallaby's preferred tall scrub habitat (5). Numbers at present on Dirk Hartog Island following the release of animals in 1977 are unknown. The species was formerly abundant there but became extinct around 1920 (1). On the mainland it was still abundant in some localities (e.g. near Pingelly and Wagin) in the early 1900s but apparently disappeared shortly afterwards, the last mainland specimen being taken in 1906 (3). Troughton in 1941 stated that it was said to occur at that time in a few isolated localities in southern Western Australia, east of the Great Southern Railway, but there has been no confirmation of this (3,6).

HABITAT AND ECOLOGY On Bernier and Dorre the species was found to be nocturnal, sheltering during the day, often several together, under low divaricating shrubs of Acacia coriacea, Diplolaena dampieri, Pileanthus lirnacis and Eucalyptus spp. At night large numbers moved into Spinifex tussocks of the coastal sand dunes to feed, diet consisting mainly of Spinifex and Eulalia. Single pouch young were found at any time from February to August, there being little indication of a definite breeding season. There is heavy juvenile mortality - partially through predation by owls, hawks and goannas (Varanus) - but adult mortality is low, leading to an apparently stable population structure (2,4).

THREATS TO SURVIVAL Clearance of native vegetation for agriculture was undoubtedly one of the major factors in its extinction on the mainland. It may only ever have been locally abundant and its apparent dependence on thick scrub would make it especially vulnerable to bush clearing (3,6). It also appears intolerant of competition with introduced herbivores such as sheep and rabbits. On Dirk Hartog Island it rapidly disappeared from areas used for sheep grazing, persisting longest in the ungrazed northern region (1). The rapid spread of predators such as foxes and feral cats in the early 1900s would certainly have accelerated its extinction on the mainland. The populations on Bernier and Dorre, although thought to be stable at present, are potentially very vulnerable to fire or the accidental introduction of foxes, cats or rabbits (4). An intensive programme to eradicate the formerly large feral goat population on Bernier has alleviated a major threat to the ecology of the island and allowed recovery of the natural vegetation to commence in areas that had suffered damage (5).

CONSERVATION MEASURES TAKEN Listed in Appendix 1 of the 1973 Convention on International Trade in Endangered Species of Wild Fauna and Flora, trade in it or its products therefore being subject to strict regulation by ratifying nations, and trade for primarily commercial purposes banned. Appears on the Official List of Endangered Australian Vertebrate Fauna. Protected under Western Australian law and Bernier and Dorre Islands are class 'A' fauna reserves with strictly controlled access. In 1974 a programme to reintroduce the species to Dirk Hartog Island was begun with the release of 11 adults and 6 pouch young into pens on the island. These had increased to 33 adults and 3 young by December 1976 and the first release into the wild took place in May 1977 (1). A bounty system to eradicate goats on the island was began in the early 1970s with 800 killed in two years and attempts to reduce the feral cat population by poisoning were also undertaken with unknown success. The island is still used as a sheep station, though only the southern two-thirds is stocked and the number of sheep in 1972 was down to 4000, normal numbers in the past being 10,000-11,000 (1).

CONSERVATION MEASURES PROPOSED Continued protection of the islands where the wallaby occurs is an essential prerequisite for its long-term survival (4). Further reintroduction programmes to suitable areas are strongly recommended to mitigate against the possibility of the species being exterminated by any drastic changes occurring in its present very limited range.

CAPTIVE BREEDING Does not appear to be held in any zoo at present. The 1959 expedition to Bernier and Dorre Islands found them very nervous and prone to damage themselves on fencing when penned (4), though the reintroduction programme on Dirk Hartog Island has evidently had considerable breeding success with animals in enclosures (1).

REMARKS For description see (3). This data sheet was compiled from a draft provided in 1978 by Dr A.A. Burbidge, Western Australian Wildlife Research Centre, who also in 1981 kindly commented on the final draft.

REFERENCES   1.   Burbidge, A.A. and Fuller, P.J. (1979). The flora and fauna of Dirk Hartog Island, Western Australia. J.R. Soc. West. Aust. 60: 71-90.
2.   Hughes, R.D. (1965). On the age composition of a small sample of individuals from a population of the Banded Hare Wallaby, Lagostrophus fasciatus (Peron & Lesueur). Aust. J. Zool. 13: 75-95.
3.   Ride, W.D.L. (1970). A guide to the native mammals of Australia. Oxford University Press, Melbourne.
4.   Ride, W.D.L. and Tyndale-Biscoe, C.H. (1962). Mammals. In Fraser, A.J. (Ed.), The results of an expedition to Bernier and Dorre Islands, Shark bay, Western Australia in 1959. West. Australian Fisheries Dept. Fauna Bull. 2: 54-97.
5.   Robinson, A.C., Robinson, J.F., Watts, C.H.S. and Baverstock, P.R. (1976). The Shark Bay Mouse Pseudomys praeconis and other mammals on Bernier Island, Western Australia. West. Australian Naturalist. 13 (7): 149-155.
6.   Troughton, E. (1941). Furred animals of Australia. Angus and Robertson Ltd. Sydney.

PROSERPINE ROCK-WALLABY

RARE

Petrogale sp. nova

Order   MARSUPIALIA   Family   MACROPODIDAE

SUMMARY Discovered in 1976 in a small area of northeastern Australia. Surveys to determine the extent of distribution of the species and measures to conserve the known population are urgently required.

DISTRIBUTION Australia, where only known from the Proserpine area on the east Queensland coast (2). It may be a relict species of limited distribution (2).

POPULATION Total numbers unknown, though almost certainly low on account of the apparently small size of its range.

HABITAT AND ECOLOGY Occupies closed forest over rocky outcrops (2).

THREATS TO SURVIVAL At risk because of its very limited distribution.

CONSERVATION MEASURES TAKEN Legally protected (1), and appears on the Official List of Endangered Australian Vertebrate Fauna.

CONSERVATION MEASURES PROPOSED Effective protection of the limited area in which the species is presently known to occur is the most urgent requirement (1). Surveys to determine its status and extent of distribution and to formulate more detailed conservation measures are recommended.

CAPTIVE BREEDING No information.

REMARKS The species was identified in 1976 during a comprehensive study of the distribution, habitat and taxonomy of rock wallabies (Petrogale spp. and Peradorcas concinna) undertaken by Professor G.B. Sharman and colleagues at Macquarie University (1,2). On cytological criteria it appears to be most closely related to Rothschild's Rock Wallaby (Petrogale rothschildi) from the Pilbara region of Western Australia and the widespread but uncommon Yellow-footed Rock Wallaby (Petrogale xanthopus) (2).

REFERENCES   1.   Anon. (1979). New Rock-wallaby species in Queensland. Wildl. Preservation Soc. of Queensland Newsletter 69: 2.
2.   Poole, W.E. (1979). The status of the Australian Macropodidae. In Tyler, M.J. (Ed.), The status of endangered Australasian wildlife. Royal. Zool. Soc. S. Aust.

DORIA'S TREE-KANGAROO

VULNERABLE

Dendrolagus dorianus notatus Matschie, 1916

Order   MARSUPIALIA

Family   MACROPODIDAE

SUMMARY   Still fairly common in central highlands of New Guinea although subject to strong hunting pressure. Legally protected in Irian Jaya but not in Papua New Guinea; reserves are recommended as is some form of control on traditional hunting.

DISTRIBUTION   New Guinea, where found above 2400 m in the central highlands of Papua New Guinea, extending westwards to those of Irian Jaya (2).

POPULATION   Numbers unknown. Still relatively abundant but declining under hunting pressure, especially on the lower and more accessible mountain slopes (2).

HABITAT AND ECOLOGY   Montane and lower montane forest (2). Dendrolagus spp. are arboreal and predominantly nocturnal herbivores. Gestation period of the congeneric D. matschiei has been noted as 32 days in captivity with an average litter size of one (4).

THREATS TO SURVIVAL   It is very vulnerable to traditional hunting techniques using dogs. Depletion of game on the lower slopes is expected to lead to increased hunting pressure on once secure remote populations. Montane and lower montane forest in the central highlands has been, and continues to be, exploited for timber in areas where road access to a mill site is possible. However, suitable habitat still exists on ridges, mountain tops and steep slopes which would be difficult to exploit commercially and it is believed that decline due to hunting overrides that caused by habitat loss at present (2).

CONSERVATION MEASURES TAKEN   None in Papua New Guinea (2). Legally protected in Irian Jaya (6).

CONSERVATION MEASURES PROPOSED   Extension of the proposed Mt. Wilhelm National Park to include montane and lower montane forest would safeguard one population, as long as hunting within the park were controlled. Further protection of habitat on remote mountain peaks is also advocated, as is some control or restriction on traditional hunting e.g. limitation on taking females with pouch young or young at heel may be feasible (viz. restriction which already applies (1978) to taking of female Birds of Paradise in some areas). Such measures would need to be supported by an extensive public education programme and be initiated and policed at local government level (2).

CAPTIVE BREEDING   A captive breeding colony at Baiyer River Sanctuary, Papua New Guinea, although having initial difficulties was reported in 1981 as having been more successsful in recent years (3). In 1978 it held 7 males and 11 females, of which 1 male and 9 females were captive bred. 19 individuals of D. dorianus (subspecies not known) were recorded held in zoos outside Papua New Guinea, of which 7 were bred in captivity (5).

REMARKS   For description see (1). The nominate subspecies D. d. dorianus occurs in the Owen Stanley Range in southeast Papua New Guinea, apparently at lower altitudes than D. d. notatus and may be sympatric with D. goodfellowi. Its status is unknown though it is thought unlikely to be under the same pressures as D. d. notatus (2). Populations in the mid-mountain regions of the Morobe and

Southern Highlands Provinces are intermediate between $\underline{D}$. $\underline{d}$. $\underline{dorianus}$ and $\underline{D}$. $\underline{d}$. $\underline{notatus}$ and appear to occupy an intermediate altitudinal range (4). This data sheet was compiled from a draft very kindly provided in 1978 by Graeme G. George, Director of the Sir Colin MacKenzie Fauna Park, Victoria, Australia.

REFERENCES
1. George, G.G. (1977). Up a tree with kangaroos. Animal Kingdom. May 1977.
2. George, G.G. (1979). The status of endangered Papua New Guinea mammals. In Tyler, M.J. (Ed.), The Status of endangered Australasian Wildlife. Roy. Zool. Soc. S. Aust.
3. George, G.G. (1981). In litt.
4. Olds, T.J. and Collins, L.R. (1973). Breeding Matschie's Tree Kangaroo (Dendrolagus matschiei) in captivity. In Duplaix-Hall, N. (Ed.), International Zoo Yearbook 13. Zool. Soc. London.
5. Olney, P.J.S. (Ed.) (1979). International Zoo Yearbook 19. Zool. Soc. London.
6. Indonesian Directorate of Nature Conservation and Wildlife Management. (1981). Appendix 3, CITES Report, 1980.

Dendrolagus goodfellowi shawmayeri Rothschild & Dollman, 1936

Order   MARSUPIALIA   Family   MACROPODIDAE

SUMMARY Still fairly widely distributed on forested slopes in Papua New Guinea but many populations have been seriously depleted through overhunting and others are expected to suffer similarly in the future. Reserves and control of hunting are advocated.

DISTRIBUTION Papua New Guinea, where found at altitudes of 1200 to 2750 m on the northern slopes of the central cordillera and the northern and southern slopes of the Owen Stanley Range in the southeast (1).

POPULATION Numbers unknown but has declined markedly since European settlement in the central highlands where former populations in the Kratke Ranges and the Sepik-Wahgi Divide have been considerably reduced or exterminated by hunting over the past 50 years. In 1977 it was reported as still relatively common in the remote and unsettled parts of its range in the northwest and southeast but populations here were also expected to decline (1).

HABITAT AND ECOLOGY Lower montane oak (Castanopsis) and beech (Nothofagus) forest, usually on rugged terrain. This rugged habitat may not be the preferred one and it is likely that populations on more accessible, less steep slopes were exterminated prior to European settlement (1). Dendrolagus spp. are predominantly arboreal and nocturnal herbivores; gestation period of the congener D. matschiei has been measured at 32 days in captivity, with an average litter size of one (2).

THREATS TO SURVIVAL Very vulnerable to hunting and is considered a prime game species. As traditional hunting extends to more remote areas and hunting with modern weapons increases, decline of formerly secure populations is expected. Suitable habitat in rugged areas is at present in little danger from agriculture or forestry, and habitat loss is not considered to be a significant factor in the current decline (1).

CONSERVATION MEASURES TAKEN None.

CONSERVATION MEASURES PROPOSED Reservation of suitable habitat and control of hunting to manage existing populations are necesssary. Reintroduction to accessible and secure national parks would be worthwhile to generate public support for conservation and the acceptance of management programmes in traditional hunting areas (1).

CAPTIVE BREEDING A captive breeding population has been successfully established at the Baiyer River Sanctuary in the central highlands of Papua New Guinea. In 1978 this held 9 males and 12 females (4 males and 7 females bred in captivity). Outside New Guinea, 37 were reported from 13 collections in 1979, of which 12 had been bred in captivity (3).

REMARKS For description see (4). The taxonomy of the species requires clarification. The nominate form D. g. goodfellowi is only known from the type specimen collected at 2400 m on Mt. Obree in the Owen Stanley Range before 1908. This differs from the widespread D. g. shawmayeri and may be an aberrant individual; specimens from the lower parts of the Owen Stanley Range are referable to D. g. shawmayeri. D. spadix recorded from the remote lowland rainforest in the hinterland of the Gulf of Papua is probably also a subspecies of D. goodfellowi (1). Very few specimens have been collected and its status is unknown (1). This data sheet was compiled from a draft very kindly provided in 1978 by Graeme G. George, Director of the Sir Colin Mackenzie Fauna Park, Victoria, Australia.

REFERENCES   1.   George, G.G. (1979). The status of endangered Papua New Guinea mammals. In Tyler, M.J. (Ed.), The Status of endangered Australasian Wildlife. Roy. Zool. Soc. S. Aust.
2.   Olds, T.J. and Collins, L.R. (1973). Breeding Matschie's Tree Kangaroo (Dendrolagus matschiei) in captivity. In Duplaix-Hall, N. (Ed.), International Zoo Yearbook 13. Zool. Soc. London.
3.   Olney, P.J.S. (Ed.) (1979). International Zoo Yearbook 19. Zool. Soc. London.
4.   Walker, E.P. (1975). Mammals of the World. The Johns Hopkins University Press, Baltimore and London.

BLACK DORCOPSIS WALLABY   RARE

Dorcopsis atrata Van Deusen, 1957

Order   MARSUPIALIA   Family   MACROPODIDAE

SUMMARY Endemic, as far as is known, to one island off eastern Papua New
Guinea. Collected on only one occasion, in 1953; subject to hunting pressure.
Surveys needed.

DISTRIBUTION Known only from Goodenough Island (about 36 by 74 km), Milne
Bay Province, Papua New Guinea. Could possibly also occur on the neighbouring
islands of Fergusson and Normanby but this is unconfirmed (2).

POPULATION Unknown but considered rare (1). Known only from seven skins
and skulls, three skulls and 76 trophy mandibles (purchased from local hunters)
collected during the Fourth Archbold Expedition to New Guinea in 1953 (2).

HABITAT AND ECOLOGY Recorded from mid-montane forests of oaks and
Castanopsis spp. between 900 and 1600 m. Probably also ranges into more open
Nothofagus forest between 1600 and 1800 m and may move into mixed rainforest
below 900 m to feed although there was no evidence of this (2). Indications are it
may be diurnal as all specimens were obtained with dogs during the day but were
not seen during nocturnal spotlight collecting (2).

THREATS TO SURVIVAL The species is considered at risk because of its very
limited range and its size, which places it in the game species category - 90% of
all known specimens were obtained from local hunters in 1953, though the extent
of hunting pressure at present and its effect on the population is not known (1,2).
Although most of the lowland rainforest had already been converted to secondary
grassland by 1953, the montane forest which appears to be the species' prime
habitat is on rugged terrain generally unsuitable for logging (1,2).

CONSERVATION MEASURES TAKEN None.

CONSERVATION MEASURES PROPOSED A faunal survey of Goodenough to
obtain more information on distribution, present population size and trends (1).

CAPTIVE BREEDING None.

REMARKS For description see (2). The species forms an interesting link between
the mountain-dwelling Dorcopsulus and the lowland Dorcopsis species of mainland
New Guinea (1). This data sheet was compiled from a draft very kindly provided
in 1978 by Graeme G. George, Director of the Sir Colin Mackenzie Fauna Park,
Victoria, Australia.

REFERENCES   1.   George, G.G. (1979). The status of endangered Papua New
                  Guinea mammals. In Tyler, M.J. (Ed.), The Status of
                  endangered Australasian Wildlife. Roy. Zool. Soc. S. Aust.
             2.   Van Deusen, H.M. (1957). Results of the Archbold
                  Expeditions No. 76. A new species of wallaby (Genus
                  Dorcopsis) from Goodenough Island, Papua. Am. Mus. Nov.
                  1826.

PAPUAN or MACLEAY'S DORCOPSIS

Dorcopsulus macleayi Miklouho-Maclay, 1885

Order   MARSUPIALIA   Family   MACROPODIDAE

SUMMARY Confined to southern Papua New Guinea where it has been collected on very few occasions. Apparently naturally rare and expected to be susceptible to hunting and habitat destruction. Surveys are needed as the basis of effective conservation plans which should include establishment of reserves.

DISTRIBUTION Papua New Guinea, where seems confined to the southwestern slopes of the Wharton and Owen Stanley Ranges in Central Province, and the northern slopes of the southeastern extension of the Owen Stanley Range in Milne Bay Province (2).

POPULATION Numbers unknown but regarded as rare. Known only from the type series collected inland from Port Moresby by Miklouho-Maclay, before 1885, animals collected by the Archbold Expedition in Mafulu, Central Province in 1933, and three additional specimens (2).

HABITAT AND ECOLOGY Little known. Around Mafulu it was collected in lowland hill forest containing emergent Araucaria, a forest community which occurs at the upper level of the lowland rainforest zone and grades into lower montane Castanopsis forest (1).

THREATS TO SURVIVAL The wallaby's size places it in the game species category and it is thus expected to be susceptible to hunting pressure. The forest type from which it has been collected has been exploited for timber elsewhere in Papua New Guinea though lack of accessibility can limit the potential of stands (2).

CONSERVATION MEASURES TAKEN None.

CONSERVATION MEASURES PROPOSED Faunal surveys in areas of southeastern Papua New Guinea with suitable habitat to determine distribution and population size, and reservation of any areas found to hold populations. Establishment of captive breeding colonies is also advocated (2).

CAPTIVE BREEDING None. Many records of this species in zoos and museums are misidentified examples of Dorcopsis muelleri luctuosa, Thylogale bruijni and Dorcopsulus vanheurni (3).

REMARKS For description see (4). This data sheet was compiled from a draft very kindly provided in 1978 by Graeme G. George, Director of the Sir Colin MacKenzie Fauna Park, Victoria, Australia.

REFERENCES   1.   Archbold, R. and Rand, A.L. (1953). Results of the Archbold Expeditions No. 7. Summary of the 1933-34 Papuan Expedition. Bull. Am. Mus. Nat. Hist. 68(8): 555-558.
2.   George, G.G. (1979). The status of endangered Papua New Guinea mammals. In Tyler, M.J. (Ed.), The Status of endangered Australasian Wildlife. Roy. Zool. Soc. S. Aust.
3.   George, G.G. and Schürer, U. (1978). Notes on Macropods commonly misidentified in zoos. In Olney, P.J.S. (Ed.), International Yearbook 18. Zool. Soc. London.

4. Walker, E.P. (1975). <u>Mammals of the World</u>. The Johns Hopkins University Press, Baltimore and London.

Caloprymnus campestris (Gould, 1843)

Order   MARSUPIALIA   Family   MACROPODIDAE

SUMMARY Last recorded in central Australia in 1935. May still survive in remote areas. Surveys are needed to try to locate any relict populations and formulate effective conservation measures.

DISTRIBUTION Australia, where in 1932 Finlayson recorded it as occurring in a large area (about 650 by 250 km) in the eastern Lake Eyre Basin as far as Coorabulka in southwest Queensland in the north, Lake Henry in the south and Innamincka on the Barcoo in the east. Similar habitat occurred south and east of this as far as Mt. Arrowsmith in northwest New South Wales and from Lake Eyre north and west to the Musgrave Ranges. It was thought possible that the species was present in low numbers in these regions also but no definite proof was obtained (1).

POPULATION Unknown. There has been no reliable record since 1935 (2). It appears to have normally occurred in small numbers within its range, being unrecorded from 1843, when Gould first described it, to 1931 when the ending of a seven year drought led to a marked temporary increase in this and other mammal species in the region. Finlayson, collecting in 1931, obtained most specimens from two small flats lying east and west of the Cooncheri sandhill, where he described it as numerous at the time (2).

HABITAT AND ECOLOGY At Cooncheri found in areas of transition between gibber plains and loamy flats with sparse shrub cover of Kochia, Atriplex, Bassia, Eremophila and occasional clumps of Hakea ivoryi (1). Apparently principally nocturnal, solitary and herbivorous, feeding mainly on the green parts of plants. It constructed a shallow 'form' either under a salt-bush, or in the open in which case it was loosely thatched over with leaves and twigs. Pouch young at various stages of development were found from June to December (1).

THREATS TO SURVIVAL Unknown though would presumably be vulnerable to introduced predators, especially foxes and feral cats, and habitat alteration through cattle grazing and the effects of rabbits.

CONSERVATION MEASURES TAKEN Listed in Appendix 1 of the 1973 Convention on International Trade in Endangered Species of Wild Fauna and Flora, trade in it or its products therefore being subject to strict regulation by ratifying nations, and trade for primarily commercial purposes banned. Legally protected, and appears on the Official List of Endangered Australian Vertebrate Fauna.

CONSERVATION MEASURES PROPOSED Surveys within its former range to try to locate any surviving populations and define protective measures for them.

CAPTIVE BREEDING None.

REMARKS For description see (1,3).

REFERENCES   1. Finlayson, H.H. (1940). Caloprymnus campestris, its recurrence and characters. Trans. R. Soc. S. Aust. 56: 148-167.
              2. Finlayson, H.H. (1961). On Central Australian mammals

Part IV. The distribution and status of Central Australian species. Rec. S. Aust. Mus. 14: 141-191.

3. Ride, W.D.L. (1970). A guide to the native mammals of Australia. Oxford University Press, Melbourne.

BRUSH-TAILED BETTONG or WOYLIE

ENDANGERED

Bettongia penicillata Gray, 1837

Order   MARSUPIALIA   Family   MACROPODIDAE

SUMMARY   Numbers and distribution drastically reduced by habitat destruction, and probably also by introduced predators.   Now confined to three areas of Eucalyptus woodland in southwest Western Australia and the Davies Creek National Park in Queensland where a population (until recently described as a separate species, Bettongia tropica), was discovered in the 1970s.   A population has also been reintroduced to St. Francis Island, Nuyts Archipelago, South Australia.   The current fire regime and fox predation are thought to be principal threats in Western Australia and changes in the former to take into account the species' habitat requirements are strongly advocated.

DISTRIBUTION   Australia where now has a highly disjunct range.   Known surviving wild populations occur in northeast Queensland and southwest Western Australia.   In the latter it is now restricted to three forest and woodland areas - Tutanning Nature Reserve, Dryandra State Forest, and Perup State Forest, east of Manjimup, where in 1975-76 there were three areas of high population density (3,5,14).   In May 1981 the species was also reintroduced to St. Francis Island, Nuyts Archipelago, South Australia where it had died out prior to 1920 when the island was farmed (13).   The Queensland population, discovered in the early 1970s, is in the Davies Creek National Park, 17 km east of Mareeba (11,17).   Until 1980 it was ascribed to a different species, Bettongia tropica, which had been described in 1966 from six museum specimens all from eastern Queensland, the most recent dated 1932 from Mt. Spurgeon, near Mareeba (20).   Serological studies have now shown that B. tropica is identical with B. penicillata, probably not being separable even at subspecific level (15,16).   The Woylie was formerly widely distributed across southern Australia from the southwest, through northern South Australia, central New South Wales and northwestern Victoria (plains of the Murray River) and into eastern Queensland (2,8,12,16,20,21).   Finlayson stated that it also occurred in the southern part of the Northern Territory, though Parker considers these records are referable to the Spectacled Hare-wallaby (Lagorchestes conspicillatus) (7,10).

POPULATION   Total numbers unknown, though in the late 1970s was reported as declining in Western Australia (5).   In 1978 the Tutanning Reserve was stated to probably hold 200-300 (2), while Christensen has stated that Perup State Forest holds the highest remaining numbers overall (5).   The status of the Davies Creek population in Queensland was reported unknown in 1978 (11); it is possible that further populations will be discovered as the interior of Queensland is surveyed in greater detail by biologists.   40 Woylies were released onto St. Francis Island, South Australia, in May 1981 (13).   Formerly very common throughout much of its range, it declined rapidly in many areas following settlement.   The last record of the species in New South Wales was in 1857, while in South Australia it was regarded as extinct by 1923 (1,21).

HABITAT AND ECOLOGY   The ecology of the Woylie has been extensively studied in Western Australia (5,6,14).   Its habitat is loosely described as dry, sclerophyll woodland or open forest with a shrub or tussock-grass understorey (5,14,17).   Christensen, who studied the species in the Perup State Forest in the Tone-Perup forest blocks, comprised principally of Jarrah (Eucalyptus marginata) or Wandoo (E. wandoo), concluded that edaphic factors and scrub cover were of prime importance in limiting the species' present distribution (5).   He found that

Woolies preferred well drained sites with deep sandy soil in areas more variable in topography than the typical Perup association. They avoided areas with massive laterite and heavier soils and the broad shallow valleys typical of the Perup. They were also absent from very open areas and those with very dense ground cover. He estimated that ideal cover density for the Woylie may be between 50 and 80% associated with 20 to 40% bare ground in the vicinity of the nesting areas (5). Individuals exhibit large overlapping home ranges (averaging 35 and 27 ha for males and 23 and 20 ha for females at Tutanning and Perup State Forest respectively). They are nocturnal, resting during the day in nests contructed over shallow depressions dug in low, dense clumped vegetation (5,6,14). The nesting area is about 2 ha. in extent and individuals may have 3-4 nests in use at any one time; males are mutually aggressive and highly territorial in their nesting areas though these may show slight overlap with those of females (5). Breeding occurs continually throughout the year. A single young is usual and remains in the pouch for about 100 days after which it remains with the mother for a further month or so. Another young is born as soon as the previous offspring leaves the pouch (5,14). Both sexes are mature at the end of the first year (14). Subterranean fungi constitute a very high proportion of the diet of the populations studied, being apparently somewhat more important in the Perup region than at Tutanning; the remainder of the diet appears to consist mainly of seeds (including wheat) and tubers (5,14).

THREATS TO SURVIVAL   The present decline is thought to be associated with habitat changes, principally a decrease in shrub cover brought about by changes in the fire regime and leading to increased predation by foxes and possibly also a deterioration in the Woylie's food supply. Former natural conditions of periodic, high intensity fires led to the maintenance of a dense shrub layer; in Wandoo woodland, the principal habitat in Dryandra State Forest and at Tutanning the shrub understorey species are largely short-lived leguminous 'fire-weeds' (e.g. Acacia pulchella, Gastrolobium oxylobioides, G. calcycinum and Dryandra nobilis) which require hot fires for germination. Current management practices often involve the use of frequent, low intensity deliberate burns. These destroy undergrowth but do not promote germination of replacement plants and leave insufficient time for regeneration, leading to a reduction of cover and the eventual disappearance of many understorey species. The process is aided by the spread of introduced grasses encouraged by fertiliser drift from adjacent farmlands which also encourage more frequent cool fires. The more open habitat then created is thought likely to expose Woylies to greatly increased predation pressure. Woylies themselves are well adapted to wild-fires, as they do not panic during a fire, tending to double back and shelter in unburnt patches and showing high fidelity to their home ranges (5). An actual decrease of understorey cover appears to be of somewhat less importance in the Perup association, at least in the short term, as rainfall is higher than at Tutanning or Dryandra, regeneration being thus more rapid and largely from fire-resistant rootstock species (5). However here also 'fire-weeds' are decreasing and this may be of importance through their presumed mediation of the nitrogen cycle; it has been noted that legumes are dominant understorey species in all the best Woylie areas of the Perup (Gastrolobium in low lying areas and Bossiaea ornata on the ridges), and the decrease of these, leading to a probable decrease in nitrogen fixation and subsequent deterioration in food supply, may be a contributary factor in the Woylie's decline. The importance of fire in sporocarp formation of the fungi which constitute much of the Woylie's diet also needs to be investigated (5). It has been suggested that the high fluoroacetate content of plants such as Gastrolobium may in fact have helped protect Woylies in areas where they still occur. Foxes are very susceptible to fluoroacetates and it is possible they may be poisoned if they eat a Woylie which has been feeding on plants containing them, thus decreasing predation pressure on the population (3). However this remains to be demonstrated (4). Foxes are not believed to have reached the Davies Creek region in Queensland (3).

CONSERVATION MEASURES TAKEN Bettongia penicillata and 'B. tropica' are listed in Appendix 1 of the 1973 Convention on International Trade in Endangered Species of Wild Fauna and Flora, trade in them or their products therefore being subject to strict regulation by ratifying nations, and trade for primarily commercial purposes banned. Legally protected and both appear on the Official List of Endangered Australian Vertebrate Fauna. The Western Australian populations are in State Forests or reserves, however Tutanning Nature Reserve is considered only marginally adequate for the long term survival of the species (2). The Queensland population occurs in the Davies Creek National Park and St. Francis Island in the Nuyts Archipelago is managed as a conservation area by the South Australian National Parks and Wildlife Service (11,13,17). In 1980 it was reported that in Western Australia habitat management consisted mainly of poisoning programmes for the eradication of foxes and control of wildfires (though see above) (3). Programmes to re-establish Woylies in areas where they have become extinct are also in progress; their outcome is expected to depend in large measure on the success of attempts to control the fox (3).

CONSERVATION MEASURES PROPOSED Continuation of reintroduction and management programmes. It seems likely that, in Western Australia at least, modification of the present fire regime and effective control of fox numbers will be the most important factors in the conservation of the species. Any further populations discovered (most likely in Queensland) should immediately be afforded full protection.

CAPTIVE BREEDING Breeds well in captivity (19). In 1979, 64 were reported as held in 8 collections, over 54 of these having been bred in captivity, with a total of 15 reared in 6 zoos in 1978 (9).

REMARKS For description see (2,12). Dr. A.A. Burbidge of the Western Australian Dept. of Fisheries and Wildlife kindly commented on a draft of this data sheet in May 1981.

REFERENCES
1. Anon. (1973). Additional protection for rare fauna. State Wildlife Authority News Service (West. Australia) 4(2): 31-33.
2. Anon. (1978). Brush-tailed Rat Kangaroo, Woylie, Brush-tailed Bettong, Kangaroo Rat. Bettongia penicillata. Mammals No.13. In Australian Endangered Species. Australian National Park and Wildlife Service.
3. Anon. (1980). Have poisonous plants helped save some of our native wildlife from extinction? State Wildlife Authority News Service (West. Aust.) 10(1): 10-12.
4. Burbidge, A.A. (1981). In litt.
5. Christensen, P.G.S. (1980). The biology of Bettongia penicillata Gray 1837 and Macropus eugenii (Desmaret 1817) in relation to fire. Forest Dept. of Western Australia Bull No.91.
6. Christensen, P. and Leftwick, T. (1980). Observations on nest-building habits of the Brush-tailed Rat Kangaroo or Woylie (Bettongia penicillata). J. R. Soc. West. Aust. 63(2): 33-38.
7. Finlayson, H.H. (1958). On Central Australian mammals (with notice of related species from adjacent tracts). Part III. The Potoroinae. Rec. S. Aust. Mus. 13: 235-302.
8. King, D.R., Oliver, A.J. and Mead, R.J. (1978). The adaptation of some Western Australian mammals to food

plants containing fluoroacetate. Aust. J. Zool. 26(4):
699-712.

9. Olney, P.J.S. (Ed.) (1980). International Zoo Yearbook 20.
    Zool. Soc. London.

10. Parker, S.A. (1973). An annotated checklist of the native
    land mammals of the Northern Territory. Rec. S. Aust.
    Mus. 16(11): 1-57.

11. Poole, W.E. (1979). The status of the Australian
    Macropodidae In Tyler, M.J. (Ed.), The status of endangered
    Australasian wildlife. Royal Zool. Soc. S. Aust.

12. Ride, W.D.L. (1970). A guide to the native mammals of
    Australia. Oxford University Press, Melbourne.

13. Robinson, A.C. (1981). In litt.

14. Sampson, J.C. (1971). The biology of Bettongia penicillata
    Gray, 1837. Unpublished Doctoral thesis, University of
    Western Australia.

15. Saunders, G.W. (1981). In litt.

16. Sharman, G.B., Murtagh, C.E., Johnson, P.M., and Weaver,
    C.M. (1980). The chromosomes of the rat-kangaroo
    attributable to Bettongia tropica (Marsupialia:
    Macropodidae). Aust. J. Zool. 28: 59-63.

17. Smith, H.A. (1978). In litt.

18. Troughton, E. (1941). Furred animals of Australia. Angus
    and Robertson Ltd., Sydney.

19. Viola, S. (1977). Observations on the Brush-tailed Bettong
    (Bettongia penicillata) at the New York Zoological Park.
    International Zoo Yearbook 17: 156-157.

20. Wakefield, N.A. (1967). Some taxonomic revision in the
    Australian Marsupial genus Bettongia (Macropodidae) with
    description of a new species. Vict. Nat., Melb. 84: 8-22.

21. Wood Jones, F. (1923-25). The mammals of South
    Australia. The Government Printer, Adelaide.

BURROWING BETTONG or BOODIE   RARE

Bettongia lesueur (Quoy & Gaimard, 1824)

Order   MARSUPIALIA   Family   MACROPODIDAE

SUMMARY Now apparently confined to four islands off the Western Australian coast, having been once very widely distributed in Australia. Decline on the mainland attributed to a combination of competition from rabbits, pastoralisation and introduced predators. Populations on the islands appear stable but must be considered at risk because of their limited range.

DISTRIBUTION Australia, where now (1981) known with certainty only from Bernier and Dorre Islands (approx. 10,560 ha combined) and Barrow Island (25 km by 11 km) off Western Australia and recently reported on Boodie Island in an island chain adjacent to Barrow (1,2,3,7,8). May still survive as remnant populations in parts of its mainland range. In 1973 Parker noted that there had been no authenticated record of the species in the Northern Territory since the 1930s, but stated that it possibly persisted in the Lake Amadeus - Lake Mackay regions and in the Elkedra - Sandover River - Plenty River area (5). Finlayson in 1959 also considered it might survive in southwest Western Australia (4), though this has not been confirmed. He additionally reported that Wood Jones had attempted to establish a colony in a sanctuary at Flinders Chase on Kangaroo Island in 1924 and stated that reports from a ranger there indicated they were still present and increasing slowly (4). More recent information on this appears to be lacking. ·Formerly one of the most widely distributed of the Australian macropods, ranging through much of Western Australia from Dampier Land southwards, South Australia, the Northern Territory (south of 20°S) and western New South Wales (4,6,10). Apparently absent from the northeast part of the continent, including most of Queensland and eastern New South Wales though this may merely reflect a dearth of detailed recording from these parts (4).

POPULATION Total numbers unknown. The populations on Bernier, Dorre and Barrow Island appear to be stable. In 1959 the Boodie was found to be relatively common on Bernier and Dorre and a 1975 visit to Bernier found burrows attributed to the species scattered sparsely throughout (7,8). It was also abundant on Barrow in 1969, though apparently commoner in the north than in the south (2). Status on Boodie Island is unknown.

HABITAT AND ECOLOGY Formerly occupied a wide range of habitats and climatic regions (1,4,10). Finlayson notes that its colonies and warrens were found in grassy and herbaceous loam flats within major hill ranges, in open mulga and ironwood parks skirting the ranges and in sandridge areas where its warrens were usually on slight elevations (4). On Barrow most burrows are beneath Triodia (Spinifex) tussocks, especially in the deeper soil of the valley floors (2). Behaviour has been studied in a captive population at Canberra (9). Boodies are the only truly burrowing macropods, often occupying large, interconnecting warrens. Males defend groups of females rather than particular territories although females do appear to form territories from which other females are excluded (9). Gestation period is very short (21 days) and the young leave the pouch after approx. 115 days with sexual maturity attained at about 280 days. Copulation often follows birth of the previous young almost immediately and the resulting embryo is delayed in development until the joey leves the pouch (11). On Bernier and Dorre breeding was principally in April and May with possibly a second peak in November and December, while Finlayson reported that in central Australia breeding occurred over the greater part of the year (4,11).

THREATS TO SURVIVAL Present populations seem secure as long as the islands are kept free of introduced species, especially rabbits, foxes and feral cats. The Boodie's burrows are thought to be largely fireproof and thus it is not as vulnerable to this threat as the other mammals on the islands (7). The vegetation, on Barrow Island at least, is thought to be fire-climax and recovers readily after fire. A construction and development programme by the West Australian Petroleum Pty Ltd. initiated in 1966 and reported as nearing completion in 1969 caused some destruction of habitat on Barrow and recovery of vegetation after this form of disturbance was apparently much slower (2). The exact causes of decline on the mainland are unknown but a variety of factors was probably contributary, mainly habitat alteration by introduced rabbits and domestic stock and predation by introduced foxes and feral cats. Rabbits are often regarded as of primary importance as they occupied the Boodie's burrows and directly competed with them for food, though Finlayson has observed that the two co-existed in central Australia for 60 years, up until the spread of the fox and the time that the region underwent a marked increase in pastoralisation (1,4,10). Large numbers were also poisoned as pests in cultivated regions of southern Australia and the comparatively low reproductive rate (a maximum of three young per female per annum) probably meant that populations were slow to recover from such attacks, allowing the faster-breeding rabbit to become dominant (10).

CONSERVATION MEASURES TAKEN Listed in Appendix 1 of the 1973 Convention on International Trade in Endangered Species of Wild Fauna and Flora, trade in it or its products therefore being subject to strict regulation by ratifying nations, and trade for primarily commercial purposes banned. Legally protected and appears on the Official List of Endangered Australian Vertebrate Fauna. Bernier and Dorre Islands are Class 'A' faunal reserves with strictly controlled access. A programme to eradicate the feral goat population on Bernier had been largely successful by 1975 and allowed recovery to start of those parts of the vegetation that had suffered damage (8).

CONSERVATION MEASURES PROPOSED Continued protection of the islands where the Boodie still occurs is vital for its continued survival. Burbidge and Main (1969) made recommendations to minimise the environmental impact of the mining activity on Barrow, including minimising the number of roads, tracks and excavation sites for road and well fill-in, and recommending the ripping up of abandoned roads and well sites to allow re-establishment of natural vegetation (2). It is not knonw to what extent these have been complied with. The re-establishment of colonies in suitable habitat on the mainland or on other islands from captive bred stock is recommended as part of a long-term conservation plan (1). Any areas found to contain relict colonies of this species should be afforded immediate protection.

CAPTIVE BREEDING Captive breeding groups have been maintained at Canberra and Perth (1,9,11). Close confinement of the females initially led to a high (over 70%) juvenile mortality but this was overcome by releasing the animals into large paddocks (11). There are not known to be any in captivity at present (1981) (Graeme G. George, In litt., 1981).

REMARKS For description see (1,6). Another commonly used name for the species is Lesueur's Rat-kangaroo. Bernier and Dorre Islands also hold populations of four other Red Data Book mammals: the Banded Hare-wallaby (Lagostrophus fasciatus), Rufous Hare-wallaby (Lagorchestes hirsutus), Western Barred Bandicoot (Perameles bougainville) and Shark Bay Mouse (Pseudomys praeconis). This data sheet was compiled from a draft provided in 1978 by Dr A.A. Burbidge, Western Australian Wildlife Research Centre, to whom we are very grateful.

REFERENCES

1. Anon. (1977). Boodie, Tungoo, Lesueur's Rat-Kangaroo, Burrowing Rat-Kangaroo. *Bettongia lesueur*. Mammals No.4 In Australian Endangered Species. Australian National Parks and Wildlife Service.

2. Burbidge, A.A. and Main, A.R. (1971). Report on a visit of inspection to Barrow Island. November, 1969. Dept. Fish and Fauna West. Aust. Report 8.

3. Butler, W.H. (1975). Additions to the fauna of Barrow Island, W.A. West. Aust. Nat. 13: 78-80.

4. Finlayson, H.H. (1958). On Central Australian mammals (with notice of related species from adjacent tracts). Part III. The Potoroinae. Rec. S. Aust. Mus. 13: 235-302.

5. Parker, S.A. (1973). An annotated checklist of the native land mammals of the Northern Territory. Rec. S. Aust. Mus. 16(11): 1-57.

6. Ride, W.D.L. (1970). A guide to the native mammals of Australia. Oxford University Press, Melbourne.

7. Ride, W.D.L. and Tyndale-Biscoe, C.H. (1962). Mammals. In Fraser, A.J. (Ed.). The results of an expedition to Bernier and Dorre Islands, Shark bay, Western Australia in 1959. West. Australian Fisheries Dept. Fauna Bull. 2: 54-97.

8. Robinson, A.C., Robinson, J.F., Watts, C.H.S. and Baverstock, P.R. (1976). The Shark Bay Mouse *Pseudomys praeconis* and other mammals on Bernier Island, Western Australia. West. Australian Naturalist. 13 (7): 149-155.

9. Stodart, E. (1966). Observations on the behaviour of the marsupial *Bettongia lesueuri* (Quoy and Gaimard) in an enclosure. C.S.I.R.O. Wildl. Res. 11: 91-101.

10. Troughton, E. (1941). Furred animals of Australia. Angus and Robertson Ltd. Sydney.

11. Tyndale-Biscoe, C.H. (1968). Reproduction and post-natal development in the marsupial *Bettongia lesueur* (Quoy and Gaimard). Aust. J. Zool. 16, 577-602.

12. Wood Jones, F. (1923-25). The Mammals of South Australia. The Government Printer, Adelaide.

Potorous platyops (Gould, 1844)

Order   MARSUPIALIA   Family   MACROPODIDAE

SUMMARY Probably extinct. Last known specimens are dated 1875 and a recent intensive search failed to find the species, though it could conceivably survive in densely-wooded parts of southwestern Australia. If so, any population found should be afforded immediate habitat protection.

DISTRIBUTION Australia. Only known localities were in southwestern Western Australia where it was first collected in 1842-3 by Gilbert in the vicinity of Goomalling and King George Sound. Four were subsequently collected by Masters around King George Sound and at the Pallinup River. The most recent known specimens are five received from dealers by the National Museum of Victoria in 1874 and 1875. Their location is given as Western Australia (6). A specimen received by London Zoo in 1908 from the Margaret River near Busselton in the extreme southwest was claimed to be of this species but was probably a misidentified juvenile Quokka (Setonix brachyurus) (2). The range appears to have contracted greatly even prior to European times as the species is known from sub-fossil bone deposits on the southern edge of the Nullarbor plain in Western Australia, Kangaroo Island in South Australia, and Aboriginal occupational deposits (ca. 1800 BC) on the lower Murray River (3,4,7).

POPULATION Unknown; probably extinct (2,5,6). In 1977 it was reported that a recent intensive search for the species conducted by the Western Australian Department of Fisheries and Wildlife had failed to locate it, though in the same year there were reports of a small mammal seen by loggers clear-felling in the Shannon Basin which may have been this species or the western subspecies of the Long-nosed Potoroo (Potorous tridactylus gilberti) which has also not been collected since the last century (8).

HABITAT AND ECOLOGY Nothing appears to be known of its ecology. Studies in Tasmania of the congeneric Potorous tridactylus apicalis indicate that Potoroos are strictly nocturnal and dependent on dense vegetation for cover and forage (4). They appear to be relatively long-lived for small mammals (up to seven years for P. t. apicalis in the wild) and can breed twice a year, though only one young is produced at a time (4).

THREATS TO SURVIVAL Unknown, though was doubtless susceptible to habitat destruction through logging and conversion to agriculture, and to the effects of introduced predators (principally feral cats at that time).

CONSERVATION MEASURES TAKEN Legally protected, and appears on the Official List of Australian Endangered Vertebrate Fauna.

CONSERVATION MEASURES PROPOSED Immediate effective protection of any population which may be found.

REMARKS For description see (6).

REFERENCES   1.   Burbidge, A.A. (1977). In litt.
              2.   Calaby, J.H. (1971). The current status of Australian Macropodidae. Aust. Zool. 16: 17-29.
              3.   Finlayson H.H. (1938). On a new species of Potorous

(Marsupialia) from a cave deposit on Kangaroo Island, South Australia. Trans. R. Soc. S. Aust. 62: 132-40.

4. Lundleius, E.L. (1963). Vertebrate remains from the Nullarbor Caves, Western Australia. J. Proc. R. Soc. W. Aust. 46: 75-80.

5. Poole, W.E. (1979). The status of the Australian Macropodidae. In Tyler, M.J. (Ed.), The status of endangered Australasian wildlife. Royal. Zool. Soc. S. Aust.

6. Ride, W.D.L. (1970). A guide to the native mammals of Australia. Oxford Univ. Press, Melbourne.

7. Wakefield, N.A. (1964). Mammal Remains. Appendix 1 to Archaeological excavation of Rock Shelter No.6. Fromm's Landing, South Australia. By D.J. Mulvaney, G. H. Lawton, and C.R. Twidale. Proc. R. Soc. Vic. 77: 494-98.

8. Anon. (1977). The elusive Potoroo. Oryx 14(2): 119.

LONG-FOOTED POTOROO

Potorous longipes Seebeck & Johnston, 1980

Order MARSUPIALIA   Family MACROPODIDAE

SUMMARY Described in 1980 and known from only 9 wild specimens. Appears to have a very limited distribution in southeastern Australia and known collecting sites are threatened by future timber extraction. Protection of these sites is strongly recommended. Has bred in captivity.

DISTRIBUTION Southeastern Australia, where collected in eastern Gippsland, Victoria, although actual range is unknown (1,2). Recent specimens have been collected from sites within 60 km of each other north and east of Orbost, Victoria, with an early specimen (1900) from the vicinity of Rosedale some 165 km to the southwest (2). Suitable habitat was reported in 1980 as apparently covering much of east Gippsland and southeastern New South Wales (1).

POPULATION Unknown although has been designated 'Rare' (1). Nine individuals have been recorded up to 1981, all except one since 1967, with six from one site, at Bellbird 32 km east of Orbost, the most recent an unsexed roadkill in December 1980 (1,2,3). The two other recent records are one in 1967 26 km southwest of Bonang and one in 1968 on the Bonang Highway probably near Sardine Creek, about 40 km south of Bonang (1,2). Sightings, believed to be of this species, reported by wildlife officials in areas north of Bellbird awaited confirmation as of October 1981 (3).

HABITAT AND ECOLOGY Recorded from open forest of mixed eucalyptus species associated with a sparse to dense understorey of sclerophyllous shrubs, and a dense field layer of wiregrass, ferns and sedge growing on friable clayey soils. Annual rainfall is 1100-1200 mm (1). Terrestrial, it obtains food by excavating characteristic conical pits with its front feet. Diet is probably similar to that of Potorous tridactylus but differences in cranial morphology between the two may reflect some differences in the diet. Breeding probably occurs throughout the year with a single young produced (1).

THREATS TO SURVIVAL Forests adjoining the recent collecting sites will be subject to timber extraction in the future under existing land tenure (1). The effect of introduced predators, mainly foxes and feral cats, is unknown.

CONSERVATION MEASURES TAKEN None. The Croajingalong National Park lies 20 km southeast of Bellbird Creek, the type locality, but contains little similar habitat (1). A recommendation to include the species on the Official List of Endangered Australian Vertebrate Fauna was made to the Council of Nature Conservation Ministers (CONCOM) in July 1981 (3).

CONSERVATION MEASURES PROPOSED Further survey work on the species is tentatively planned (3). Protection of habitat where the species is known to occur is strongly advocated.

CAPTIVE BREEDING As of October 1981 there are three adults (one male and two females) at the Sir Colin MacKenzie Fauna Park, Healesville, Victoria. Four young have so far been born, of which two died of unknown causes at four to six weeks of age (3).

REMARKS For description see (1,2). The species was described in 1980 and is distinguished from the similar P. tridactylus on the basis of its large size (about 15% heavier than the largest P. tridactylus recorded, and 100% heavier than P. tridactylus from Victoria), relatively much longer hind feet, differences in cranial morphology, the presence of 24 chromosomes in both sexes (c.f. P. tridactylus with 12 in the female and 13 in the male), and electrophoretic differences in blood proteins (2). It is not known if the two species are sympatric though they have been collected within 10 km of each other and in essentially similar habitat (1,2). John H. Seebeck of the Arthur Rylah Institute for Environmental Research, Heidelberg, Victoria, kindly commented on the data sheet in 1981.

REFERENCES 1. Seebeck, J.H. (1980). Long-footed Potoroo. Draft entry for 'Mammals of Australia'.
2. Seebeck, J.H. and Johnston, P.G. (1980). Potorous longipes (Marsupialia: Macropodidae); a new species from eastern Victoria. Aust. J. Zool. 28: 119-134.
3. Seebeck, J.H. (1981). In litt.

STEIN'S CUSCUS   RARE

Phalanger interpositus Stein, 1933

Order MARSUPIALIA   Family   PHALANGERIDAE

SUMMARY Scattered distribution in a narrow altitudinal band along the northern slopes of the central cordillera in New Guinea. Appears to be a relict form potentially very vulnerable to hunting and habitat destruction. Surveys are needed to more accurately determine distribution and to provide the basis for a conservation plan which should include establishment of reserves.

DISTRIBUTION New Guinea. Collected from widely scattered localities: Yapen (Yobi) Island, Geelvink Bay and Weyland Mountains, northwest New Guinea (Irian Jaya); the Baiyer River - Jimi River region and Kratke Ranges on the north slopes of the central highlands of Papua New Guinea; and from the southeast mountains of Papua (1).

POPULATION Recorded as an uncommon animal in the Baiyer River area; otherwise known only from a small number of museum specimens collected at widely scattered localities (1).

HABITAT AND ECOLOGY Apparently confined to mid-mountain oak (Lithocarpus) forests in a narrow altitudinal band around 1200-1500 m; this is above the range of the common congeneric Phalanger orientalis and below that of P. carmelitae (1). This species is very little known though other cuscuses are predominantly arboreal, nocturnal, fruit and leaf eaters, well adapted to a highly fibrous diet (2).

THREATS TO SURVIVAL Stein's Cuscus is considered a relict form occupying a narrow ecological zone between those of two much more successful congeners by which is possibly being naturally outcompeted. This natural rarity makes it potentially very vulnerable to habitat alteration and to hunting - cuscuses in general are highly sought-after game species. Much suitable mid-mountain forest has been cleared for traditional agriculture in the central highland valleys and the cuscus is not known to have occurred in recent times in these now heavily populated parts. Known localities are along the northern slopes of the central cordillera which tend to be rugged and relatively undisturbed, although increasing human population pressure elsewhere leading to resettlement in these areas is likely to adversely affect this species in the future (1).

CONSERVATION MEASURES TAKEN Phalanger orientalis (normally taken to include P. interpositus) is listed on Appendix 2 of the 1973 Convention on International Trade in Endangered Species of Wild Fauna and Flora, and trade in it or its products is thus subject to monitoring by ratifying nations. Phalanger orientalis is legally protected in Irian Jaya (4).

CONSERVATION MEASURES PROPOSED Faunal surveys within the animal's known altitudinal range to accurately determine distribution, and the establishment of suitable reserves.

CAPTIVE BREEDING Has been kept in captivity at the Baiyer River Sanctuary, Papua New Guinea. Captive breeding of this group of cuscuses has not been very successful in the past (1).

REMARKS For description of genus see (3). P. interpositus has for many years

47

been regarded as a synomyn of P. orientalis, as its pelage is superficially very similar, but it is now considered to be more closely related to the high altitude P. carmelitae (1). This data sheet was compiled from a draft very kindly provided in 1978 by Graeme G. George, Director of the Sir Colin MacKenzie Fauna Park, Victoria, Australia.

REFERENCES   1.   George, G.G. (1979). The status of endangered Papua New Guinea mammals. In Tyler, M.J. (Ed.), The Status of endangered Australasian Wildlife. Roy. Zool. Soc. S. Aust.
2.   Menzies, J.M. (1972). Notes on a hand-reared Spotted Cuscus, Phalanger maculatus. In Lucas, J. and Duplaix-Hall, N. (Eds), International Zoo Yearbook 12. Zool. Soc. London.
3.   Walker, E.P. (1975). Mammals of the World. The Johns Hopkins University Press, Baltimore and London.
4.   Indonesian Directorate of Nature Conservation and Wildlife Management. (1981). Appendix 3, CITES Report, 1980.

WOODLARK ISLAND CUSCUS

RARE

Phalanger lullulae Thomas, 1896.

Order   MARSUPIALIA

Family   PHALANGERIDAE

SUMMARY Endemic to Woodlark Island, Milne Bay Province, Papua New Guinea where it may be rare, and is expected to come under hunting pressure. Most of the island is suitable for logging or agriculture and is not formally protected. Surveys are needed as the basis for conservation plans.

DISTRIBUTION Endemic to Woodlark Island (about 60 by 25km), Milne Bay Province, Papua New Guinea (1,2).

POPULATION Unknown but probably rare. Has been collected only twice; most recently in 1953 when four specimens were obtained by the Fifth Archbold Expedition (1,2). Four others were collected by Albert Meek in 1896 (2).

HABITAT AND ECOLOGY Little known. About half of Woodlark Island was reported in 1978 as occupied by primary rain forest (making it one of the prime lowland areas for this habitat in the entire South Pacific (4)), the remainder by secondary forest, (much of it old and well-established (1)), and small areas of grassland (2). The cuscus is assumed to be similar to other Phalanger spp. in being predominantly arboreal, nocturnal and herbivorous, eating leaves, shoots and fruits (3).

THREATS TO SURVIVAL Apparently a relict form with a very limited distribution and is expected to come under hunting pressure, as all cuscuses are game animals in Papua New Guinea (2). The human population of Woodlark Island was reported as still low in 1977 but is expected to increase (4). Part of the forest on the island is considered to have potential for commercial logging and the remainder is topographically suitable for agriculture (5).

CONSERVATION MEASURES TAKEN Phalanger orientalis (normally taken to include P. lullulae) is included in Appendix 2 of the 1973 Convention on International Trade in Endangered Species of Wild Fauna and Flora, therefore any trade in it or its products is subject to regulation and monitoring by ratifying nations.

CONSERVATION MEASURES PROPOSED Surveys to determine ecology and population size. Restriction of forestry development to the level necessary to satisfy local needs only, restriction of agriculture to areas already denuded of forest (2), and establishment of suitable rainforest reserves. Captive breeding and relocation to other islands would be desirable (2).

CAPTIVE BREEDING None.

REMARKS For description see (1). It has usually been regarded as a spotted subspecies of the Common Cuscus Phalanger orientalis. On cranial and dental morphology it is intermediate between P. orientalis and the montane species P. interpositus (also a 'Rare' species) and P. carmelitae (2). This data sheet was compiled from a draft very kindly provided in 1978 by Graeme G. George, Director of the Sir Colin MacKenzie Fauna Park, Victoria, Australia.

REFERENCES   1.   Brass, L.J. (1959). Results of the Archbold Expeditions No.79. Summary of the Fifth Archbold Expedition to New

Guinea. Bull. Am. Mus. Nat. Hist. 118(1): 59-60.

2. George, G.G. (1979). The status of endangered Papua New Guinea mammals. In Tyler, M.J. (Ed.), The Status of endangered Australasian Wildlife. Roy. Zool. Soc. S. Aust.

3. Menzies, J.M. (1972). Notes on a hand-reared Spotted Cuscus, Phalanger maculatus. In Lucas, J. and Duplaix-Hall, N. (Eds), International Zoo Yearbook 12. Zool. Soc. London.

4. Pyle, R.M and Hughes, S.A. (1981). Pers. comm.

5. Ward, R.G. and Lea, D.A.M. (1970). An Atlas of Papua New Guinea. Univ. Papua New Guinea, Port Moresby.

BLACK-SPOTTED CUSCUS

RARE

Phalanger rufoniger Zimara, 1937

Order   MARSUPIALIA

Family   PHALANGERIDAE

SUMMARY A little known species from the lowlands of northern New Guinea. Appears to be naturally rare and expected to be susceptible to hunting and habitat loss. Surveys are needed as the basis of conservation plans.

DISTRIBUTION New Guinea where recorded from scattered localities in the northern lowlands from the Vogelkop Peninsula (Irian Jaya) in the northwest to the Huan Peninsula (Papua New Guinea) in the northeast (1).

POPULATION Known only from 18 museum specimens from scattered localities within its range, most of which have gone unrecognised until recently (1). Occasional pieces of fur appear in the head-dress of Papua New Guinea Highlanders traded from the Sepik River Basin (1). No information on any extant population, but as the large cuscuses (Phalanger spp.) are conspicuous and frequently hunted, the paucity of records of this species indicates that it is actually rare (1).

HABITAT AND ECOLOGY Virtually unknown, although appears to be a lowland rainforest species (1). Other cuscuses are predominantly nocturnal, arboreal herbivores feeding on shoots, fruits and leaves and well adapted to a highly fibrous diet (2).

THREATS TO SURVIVAL Competition with the more successful races of P. maculatus probably contributes to its natural rarity (1). All cuscuses are sought-after game and this species is thus expected to come under hunting pressure. Much lowland rainforest in Papua New Guinea is destined for once-only logging and conversion to agriculture, although it is not known if P. rufoniger occurs in areas currently proposed for exploitation (1). However there is also no evidence that it occurs in disturbed habitat, unlike the much commoner Spotted Cuscus (P. maculatus), with which it is sympatric, and it may require primary rainforest (1). It may possibly occupy hill forest above the altitudinal range of P. maculatus, which would afford it some protection from habitat destruction in rugged terrain unsuitable for gardening or timber extraction (1).

CONSERVATION MEASURES TAKEN None in Papua New Guinea (1); legally protected in Irian Jaya (4).

CONSERVATION MEASURES PROPOSED Surveys to determine distribution, population size and habitat requirements, particularly to discover whether it occurs in areas earmarked for exploitation (1).

CAPTIVE BREEDING No information.

REMARKS Until recently the species has been known only from three recorded specimens and was named P. atrimaculatus (1); for description (as P. atrimaculatus) see (3). This data sheet was compiled from a draft very kindly provided in 1978 by Graeme G. George, Director of the Sir Colin MacKenzie Fauna Park, Victoria, Australia.

REFERENCES   1.   George, G.G. (1979). The status of endangered Papua New Guinea mammals. In Tyler, M.J. (Ed.), The Status of endangered Australasian Wildlife. Roy. Zool. Soc. S. Aust.

2. Menzies, J.M. (1972). Notes on a hand-reared spotted Cuscus, Phalanger maculatus. In Lucas, J. and Duplaix-Hall, N. (Eds), International Zoo Yearbook 12. Zool. Soc. London.

3. Tate, G.H.H. (1945). Results of the Archbold Expeditions No.52. The Marsupial Genus Phalanger. Am. Mus. Nov. 1283.

4. Indonesian Directorate of Nature Conservation and Wildlife Management. (1981). Appendix 3, CITES Report, 1980.

LEADBEATER'S POSSUM

ENDANGERED

Gymnobelideus leadbeateri McCoy, 1867

Order   MARSUPIALIA

Family   PETAURIDAE

SUMMARY   Confined to scattered populations in a small area of southeastern Victoria. Believed extinct until rediscovered in 1961, the species appears to have highly specific habitat requirements and could be potentially at considerable risk from clear-felling of the eucalypt forests in which it lives. Most of the species' range appears to be in areas scheduled for logging, though conservation recommendations have been approved which should take its requirements into account in management of some sites. Most concern is felt at present (1981) in areas which were severely damaged by fire in the 1930s and where adequate forest regeneration does not appear to be taking place and close monitoring of all known populations is strongly recommended.

DISTRIBUTION   Southeastern Victoria, Australia. In surveys carried out since 1961, the possum has been recorded in numerous discrete localities at altitudes of 500-1500 m within its total range which seems to comprise over 2000 sq. km of mountain forest in an arc extending from Mt Torbreck through Mt Margaret, Mt Donna Buang, Starling Hill and Mt Whitelaw to Mt Baw Baw (3). Since 1978 the known distribution has been extended westward to the Toolangi - Mt St. Leonard area north of Healesville (11). Originally known from only five specimens, all collected in Victoria between 1867 and 1909, three of them from the Bass River valley, South Gippsland, and one from the edge of the Koo-wee-rup swamp near Tynong, Victoria. These areas have since been extensively cleared and drained. The fifth specimen was collected at Mt Wills in northeast Victoria in 1909 (2,8). The species was not recorded again until 1961 when it was rediscovered by H.E. Wilkinson in the Cumberland Valley in the highlands of southeast Victoria, 18 km southeast of Marysville. This is about 170 km WSW of the 1909 Mt Wills locality (8), and some 65 km NNE of the earlier Bass River and Koo-wee-rup records.

POPULATION   Numbers unknown. In a few localities of no great size it is moderately common with local densities of about 3 animals per ha (6). The absence of records from 1909 to 1961 could simply reflect lack of effective searching but it has been argued that there may have been a real increase in numbers in response to extensive forest regeneration following bush fires in 1939. If it is responding to seral changes in tall Eucalypt forests then it may under natural conditions have population peaks interspersed with periods of low numbers (9). However, clear felling would almost certainly disrupt such cycles and several known populations have been destroyed in recent years by forest clearance (3).

HABITAT AND ECOLOGY   Mature montane forest where the dominant canopy species are Mountain Ash (*Eucalyptus regnans*), Shining Gum (*E. nitens*) and Alpine Ash (*E. delegatensis*). Critical characteristics of the habitat appear to be the presence of large mature living or dead Mountain Ash trees over 150 years old containing hollows, and a dense understorey of shrubs and saplings (6). Nests up to 30 cm diameter are constructed in the hollows and are used by small family groups of 2-8 individuals, usually comprising one breeding female, one or more mature males and one or more generations of offspring. These nests are of great importance for insulation and energy conservation during winter when food supply is low (6). The species is nocturnal and arboreal with a diet of insects and sap (5).

THREATS TO SURVIVAL   The animal's apparently highly specific habitat requirements place it potentially at great risk from habitat destruction through forest clearance or inappropriate management. Eucalypts of the appropriate species less than 150 years old seldom contain suitable hollows which are essential for the possum and the animal has not yet been found in regrowth forest unless some old trees have been retained and suitable understorey is present. Its entire known distribution, apart from water catchment areas, was in 1978 reported as within an Australian paper manufacturer's concession and scheduled to be progressively clear-felled (3). Following clear-felling the forest was to be harvested at intervals of less than 100 years, probably less than 80 years; this would eliminate trees with hollows (3). The approval by the Victoria Government of management recommendations (see below) should have helped alleviate this problem in ensuring, in some areas at least, that the possum's habitat requirements are taken into consideration during logging. Most concern is now felt in areas where trees were killed by the fires of 1939; these trees are now rotten inside and are falling to the ground, and regrowth here does not provide the necessary habitat (i.e. hollows for nests) (12). The extent of this problem is not at present (1981) known (12). Several large areas of suitable habitat are included in proclaimed water-catchments. Manangement policy was formerly against the extraction of timber from these catchments and they appeared to offer a secure haven for the possums. However these policies were reported in 1978 as changing and it was feared that the value of the catchment areas for the possum might be seriously impaired (3). More recent information on this is lacking.

CONSERVATION MEASURES TAKEN Protected by Victorian legislation against unauthorised capture, possession or deliberate destruction under the Game Act 1958 and the Wildlife Act 1975. In March 1979 the Victorian Government approved recommendations made by the Victorian Land Conservation Council that conservation of the species be provided for in two areas of forest; one to be designated 'Special Management for Hardwood and Wildlife' in which ... 'the conservation of Leadbeater's Possum ... should be provided for in Forest's Commission management prescriptions, which should be submitted to the Fisheries and Wildlife Division for agreement'; the other is recommended for hardwood production with the provision that 'The conservation of Leadbeater's Possum ... should be provided for in management prescriptions, in agreement with the Fisheries and Wildlife Division' (1,3,12). A study on the species in the wild was completed in 1980 (6,12).

CONSERVATION MEASURES PROPOSED See previous section. At least one area of suitable forest needs to be set aside as a reserve for this possum, where its conservation does not have to be compromised by or subordinated to other objectives. Additional studies are needed to determine more precisely the habitat requirements and ecology of the species as a basis for sound conservation measures.

CAPTIVE BREEDING A captive breeding colony is maintained in a private collection under the supervision of the Victoria Fisheries and Wildlife Division derived from three females and three males caught at widely separated localities between July 1971 and April 1972. Between November 1973 and December 1980, breeding of the original stock and their offspring to the third generation has yielded 26 captive-bred animals. As of May 1981 the stock consists of five wild-caught and 19 captive-bred individuals but limited space and an imbalanced sex ratio limits the number of breeding pairs to three. The colony is to be moved in the near future to a specially constructed facility at Melbourne Zoological Gardens where breeding will be expanded by the introduction of further wild-caught males. It is anticipated that surplus stock will become available to establish colonies at other Australian Zoos (12). Additionally two males and a female are held at the Sir Colin MacKenzie Fauna Park, Healesville, Australia (10,11).

REMARKS For description of animal see (2,4,7). The SSC is indebted to the following for assistance in the compilation of the original of this data sheet in 1978: D. Hanson, J. Nelson, A. Smith, Joan Dixon, R. Warneke, K. Norris, K. King, J. Hampton and the Ministry for Conservation, Victoria. Graeme G. George of the Sir Colin MacKenzie Fauna Park, Healesville, and Robert Warneke of the Arthur Rylah Insitute for Environmental Research, Heidelberg, Victoria, also kindly provided additional comments in 1981.

REFERENCES
1. Anon. (1977). Final recommendations, Melbourne Study Area. Land Conservation Council, Victoria.
2. Brazenor, C.W. (1962). Rediscovery of a rare Australian possum. Proc. Zool. Soc. London 139(3): 529-531.
3. Mammal Survey Group of Victoria. (1978). In litt.
4. Ride, W.D.L. (1970). A guide to the native mammals of Australia. Oxford Univ. Press, Melbourne.
5. Ryan, R.M. (1963). Feeding habits of Leadbeater's possum. Victorian Naturalist 79: 275.
6. Smith, A. (1978). On the trail of the rare Leadbeater's Possum. Habitat (Australia) 6(6): 3-5.
7. Walker, E.P. (1975). Mammals of the World. The Johns Hopkins Univ. Press, Baltimore and London.
8. Wilkinson, H.E. (1961). The rediscovery of Leadbeater's Possum, Gymnobelideus leadbeateri McCoy. Victorian Naturalist 78: 97-102.
9. Winter, J.W. (1979). The status of endangered Australian Phalangeridae, Petauridae, Burramyidae, Tarsipedidae and the Koala. In Tyler, M.J. (Ed.), The status of endangered Australasian wildlife. Roy. Zool. soc. S. Aust.
10. Olney, P.J.S. (Ed.) (1980). International Zoo Yearbook 20. Zool. Soc. London.
11. George, G.G. (1981). In litt.
12. Warneke, R. (1981). In litt.

NORTHERN HAIRY-NOSED WOMBAT

ENDANGERED

Lasiorhinus krefftii (Owen, 1972)

Order   MARSUPIALIA

Family   VOMBATIDAE

SUMMARY   Confined, as far as is known, to a single colony in northeast Australia, part of which is in a national park. Habitat is very sensitive to damage by cattle, especially during droughts, and this has been a major threat to the colony. From 1981 onwards, however, no cattle grazing will be allowed in the colony area though the species continues to remain at risk because of its small numbers and very limited range.

DISTRIBUTION   Australia.   The only known surviving population is in an area of about 15.5 sq. km on Epping Forest and Waltham Stations, approximately 130 km northwest of Clermont in mid-eastern Queensland (1,3). Formerly also recorded from two other widely separated localities in the semi-arid interior of eastern Australia: one, at Deniliquin, southern New South Wales was discovered in 1884 and exterminated by 1909; the second on Bullamon Station on the Moonie River, southern Queensland, is known only from the original three specimens collected there before 1891 although there were unconfirmed sightings of wombats over a relatively extensive area there in the early 1960s and they may thus possibly still survive (1,3,5,7).

POPULATION   Not known precisely.   The Epping Forest and Waltham population is a single colony living in a system of just over 100 burrows, 60-70 of which normally show signs of occupation (1,3). The number of animals to a burrow, or burrows per animal, is unknown, though a report in 1979 stated that fewer than 40 individuals remained (4). In historic times the colony has withdrawn from about one quarter of its former range as estimated from abandoned and degraded outlying warrens (1,3).

HABITAT AND ECOLOGY   Most of the occupied burrows at Epping Forest and Waltham are situated in semi-arid woodland (mixed Ecalyptus/Acacia) on the sides of a shallow sandy lens about 100 m wide in a clay plain. Burrow entrances are strengthened by roots of Bauhinia spp. and Bonoree (Heterodendron oleifolium) (1,3,6). Studies of the more widespread congeneric Lasiorhinus latifrons have shown that the genus is physiologically and behaviourally well adapted to an arid environment, remaining underground where the air is relatively humid during the day and concentrating waste products to lose a minimum of water in excretion (11,16). They are entirely vegetarian and can exist on very low protein, high fibre diets, possibly re-using waste urea, although abundant food is required at critical times of year for ovulation and lactation and they are very selective feeders in winter and spring (4,11). L. latifrons normally produces one young in late summer (11), and L. krefftii is probably similar.

THREATS TO SURVIVAL   L. krefftii has a relict distribution and was almost certainly already rare at the time of European settlement. Its present restriction to a small and compact population makes it highly vulnerable to environmental disturbance. Vegetation around the colony was reported in 1978 as relatively stable, although was subject to low intensity cattle grazing, occasional bushfires and small scale clearing (1,3). It was however noted that cattle damage could be much more serious during droughts and in late 1979 the wombats were said to be threatened by competition for food and damage caused by the cattle (4). Permits have allowed cattle grazing within the National Park (see below) as well as in that part of the colony area outside Park boundaries (3,12); however these were issued to May 1981 only and have not been renewed (7).

CONSERVATION MEASURES TAKEN Listed in Appendix 1 of the 1973 Convention on International Trade in Endangered Species of Wild Fauna and Flora as Lasiorhinus gillespiei (see remarks), trade in it or its products therefore being subject to strict regulation by ratifying nations, and trade for primarily commercial purposes banned. Totally protected under the Fauna Conservation Act of 1952 (6) and the Queensland Fauna Conservation Act of 1974 and is on the Official List of Australian Endangered Vertebrate Fauna. In addition an area of 2633 ha was declared the Epping Forest National Park in late 1971 to protect part of the colony (1,2), and in 1980, with the help of a grant from WWF-Autralia, a fence was constructed to exclude cattle from the whole colony area (7,12). This and the cessation of cattle grazing from May 1981 should alleviate the most immediate threat. There is no evidence of any hunting or trade in the species (5).

CONSERVATION MEASURES PROPOSED It is noted that similarly sized and isolated colonies of the Southern Hairy-nosed Wombat (L. latifrons) can remain viable in times of drought if protected from undue competition from livestock and rabbits, the latter being absent from the Epping Forest area (1). A single colony will however always remain vulnerable to disease or other catastrophe and it may be desirable after studying the biology of the species to establish additional colonies in suitable areas (6). In 1981 WWF-Australia was approached to fund a project to study the species, the work to be carried out by the Queensland National Parks and Wildlife Service (7,12). Should colonies be found elsewhere protection would be required against habitat destruction from pastoral development and competition by livestock for food.

CAPTIVE BREEDING No specimens of L. krefftii are known to have been kept in captivity.

REMARKS For description see (2,9,10). The Epping Forest and Deniliquin populations were originally known as Lasiorhinus barnardi, that from Moonie River as L. gillespiei. These have now been shown to be conspecific, and distinct from the Southern Hairy-nosed Wombat, L. latifrons, and the name L. krefftii has been resurrected as an available senior synonym (5,8). The common name is that recommended by the Australian Mammal Society. Dr. T.H. Kirkpatrick of the Queensland National Parks and Wildlife Service very kindly commented on this data sheet.

REFERENCES 1. Aitken, P. (1979). The status of endangered Australian wombats, bandicoots and the marsupial mole. In Tyler, M.J. (Ed.), The status of endangered Australasian wildlife. Royal. Zool. Soc. S. Aust.
2. Anon. (1977). Queensland Hairy-nosed Wombat, Mammals No.5 In Australian Endangered Species. Australian National Parks and Wildlife Service.
3. Anon. (1978). Going! Going! Wildlife in Australia 15(4): 131-132.
4. Anon. (1979). Cattle grazing threatens survival of rare wombat. The Times, Dec 18. 1979. No. 60,503. P.6.
5. Anon. (1980). Submission to CITES Secretariat on Lasiorhinus krefftii. Unpd. 3pp.
6. IUCN. (1972). Queensland Hairy-nosed Wombat. Sheet Code 2.11.2.1. In Red Data Book Vol. 1 Mammalia. IUCN, Switzerland.
7. Kirkpatrick, T.H. (1977-81). In litt.
8. Kirsch, J.A.W. and Calaby, J.H. (1977). The species of living marsupials, an annotated list. In Stonehouse, B. and

Gilmore, D. (Eds), Biology of Marsupials. MacMillan, Melbourne.

9. Longman, H.A. (1939). A Central Queensland wombat. Mem. Quld. Mus. 11: 282-7.

10. Ride, W.D.L. (1970). A guide to the native mammals of Australia. Oxford University Press, Melbourne.

11. Wells, R.T. (1978). Field observation of the hairy-nosed wombat Lasiorhinus latifrons (Owen). Aust. Wildl. Res. 5(3): 299-304.

12. WWF Australia. (1980-81). Project 29. Conservation measures for the Queensland Hairy-nosed Wombat. WWF Australia Newsletter. 4: 1-2.; 6: 6.

PIG-FOOTED BANDICOOT

EXTINCT

Chaeropus ecaudatus (Ogilby, 1838)

Order   MARSUPIALIA   Family   PERAMELIDAE

SUMMARY Probably extinct. Last recorded as seen by Aborigines in the 1920s. If rediscovered the location should be given immediate and effective protection.

DISTRIBUTION Australia, where formerly recorded from a few widely scattered localities in semi-arid areas between Alice Springs in the Northern Territory (about 21°S), the Gawler Ranges in South Australia, Northam in Western Australia, and the Murray - Darling river junction in New South Wales (3,5). Whether the distribution was restricted to isolated pockets within this range or was more continuous is unknown (1).

POPULATION Unknown; probably extinct. The only confirmed specimen this century was one collected on the west bank of North Lake Eyre in 1907 (4,5). The most recent unconfirmed records are of one killed but not preserved between Miller's Creek and Coward Springs southwest of Lake Eyre in 1920, recorded by Wood-Jones, and a skin seen by A.S. Le Souef in 1927 at Rawlinna in South Australia (5). The Pitjanjarra Aborigines told Finlayson that it had persisted in the Musgrave Ranges until about 1926 (2).

HABITAT AND ECOLOGY Spinifex grasslands, saltbush, acacia or mallee shrublands, or plains with humid or semi-arid woodlands. Predominantly nocturnal, though Wood Jones stated it was more diurnal than most bandicoots, and constructed nests of dry grass in open burrows 30 cm long (4,5,6,7). He also recorded it as omnivorous though Krefft considered it to be largely vegetarian and noted that it, unlike other bandicoots, did not attack rodents in captivity (6,7). Breeding was thought to occur mainly in winter (May-July) and two young seemed to be the norm (5,6).

THREATS TO SURVIVAL Specific reasons for decline are unknown, though vegetation throughout much of its range has been drastically altered by stock grazing, rabbits and feral goats in settled areas and, to a lesser extent, by rabbits elsewhere. The entire range is also infested with introduced foxes and feral cats (1).

CONSERVATION MEASURES TAKEN Listed in Appendix 1 of the 1973 Convention on International Trade in Endangered Species of Wild Fauna and Flora, trade in it or its products therefore being subject to strict regulation by ratifying nations, and trade for primarily commercial purposes banned. Totally protected by legislation, and appears on the Official List of Endangered Australian Vertebrate Fauna. Some national and state reserves occur within its former range.

CONSERVATION MEASURES PROPOSED Surveys beyond the areas of current pastoral exploitation to locate any relict colonies. Any areas found to hold populations of this species should be afforded immediate protection.

CAPTIVE BREEDING None.

REMARKS For description see (5,6,7). Contrary to its specific name it does in fact have quite a long tail. This data sheet was compiled from a draft provided in 1978 by Mr. Peter Aitken, Curator of Mammals, South Australian Museum.

REFERENCES

1. Aitken, P. (1979). The status of endangered Australian wombats, bandicoots and the Marsupial Mole. In Tyler, M.J. (Ed.), The status of endangered Australasian wildlife. Royal. Zool. Soc. S. Aust.

2. Finlayson, H.H. (1961). On Central Australian mammals Part IV. The distribution and status of Central Australian species. Rec. S. Aust. Mus. 14: 141-191.

3. Frith, H.J. (1973). Wildlife Conservation. Angus and Robertson, Sydney.

4. McKenzie, J. (1907). In litt. Unpd.

5. Ride, W.D.L. (1970). A guide to the native mammals of Australia. Oxford University Press, Melbourne.

6. Troughton, E. (1941). Furred animals of Australia. Angus and Robertson Ltd. Sydney.

7. Wood Jones, F. (1923-25). The mammals of South Australia. The Government Printer, Adelaide.

CLARA or WHITE-LIPPED BANDICOOT   RARE

Echymipera clara Stein, 1932

Order   MARSUPIALIA   Family   PERAMELIDAE

SUMMARY Lowland rainforest in New Guinea north of the central cordillera. A relict species and apparently naturally rare. Considered potentially vulnerable to hunting and habitat loss. Surveys needed as the basis for a conservation plan.

DISTRIBUTION New Guinea where it is widely though sparsely distributed. All specimens have been collected north of the central cordillera: from Yapen (Yobi) Island, Geelvink Bay, the Idenburg River basin and Djayapura in Irian Jaya, and from the drainage basins of the Sepik and Ramu Rivers in northern Papua New Guinea (1,2). It is considered likely that the range extends into the drainage basins of the Mamberamo and Rouffer Rivers between Yapen and the Idenburg River in Irian Jaya (2).

POPULATION Unknown but apparently rare. Known from a total of 31 museum specimens, the first collected in 1931 (1,2). The 15 specimens collected from Papua New Guinea are all trophy skulls and mandibles purchased from villagers and represent a very small percentage of the total numbers of bandicoots (mainly Echymipera kalubu and E. rufescens) collected by hunters in these areas (1).

HABITAT AND ECOLOGY Lowland rainforest below about 1200 m. According to local inhabitants it is terrestrial and nocturnal and part of its diet consists of the fruits of a Ficus sp. and a Pandanus sp. Exhibits relatively massive dentition development, especially of the canine; this would be necessary to feed on Pandanus fruits but could also indicate more carnivorous habits (1,2).

THREATS TO SURVIVAL Appears to be a relict form which is naturally rare, probably because of competition from its more successful and abundant congeners. This natural rarity will make it particularly vulnerable to hunting which is carried out with bows and arrows or trained dogs (12). Much of its known range is currently inaccessible to commercial logging but is subject to disturbance by traditional agricultural practices (1). Although secondary rainforest rapidly re-establishes there is no evidence that E. clara (unlike E. kalubu and E. rufescens) occurs in disturbed areas and it may require primary rainforest (1).

CONSERVATION MEASURES TAKEN None in Papua New Guinea (1). Not protected in Irian Jaya (4).

CONSERVATION MEASURES PROPOSED Surveys to determine accurately the distribution, status and ecology are required as the basis of an effective conservation plan (1).

REMARKS For description see (3). This data sheet was compiled from a draft very kindly provided in 1978 by Graeme G. George, Director of the Sir Colin Mackenzie Fauna Park, Victoria, Australia.

REFERENCES   1. George, G.G. (1979). The status of endangered Papua New Guinea mammals. In Tyler, M.J. (Ed.), The Status of endangered Australasian Wildlife. Roy. Zool. Soc. S. Aust.
          2. Van Deusen, H.M. (1966). Range and habit of the bandicoot, Echymipera clara, in New Guinea. J. Mammal. 47(4): 721-723.

3. Walker, E.P. (1975). <u>Mammals of the World</u>. The Johns Hopkins University Press, Baltimore and London.
4. Indonesian Directorate of Nature Conservation and Wildlife Management. (1981). Appendix 3, CITES Report, 1980.

WESTERN BARRED BANDICOOT or MARL   RARE

Perameles bougainville Quoy & Gaimard, 1824

Order   MARSUPIALIA   Family   PERAMELIDAE

SUMMARY   Now apparently confined to Bernier and Dorre Islands off Western Australia, being unrecorded on the Australian mainland since 1922. Population appears stable but must be considered potentially at risk due to its limited range.

DISTRIBUTION   Australia; only known populations are now on Bernier and Dorre Islands (about 10,560 ha combined) in Shark Bay, Western Australia (1,4,5). Formerly occurred across a broad belt of arid to semi-arid territory in southern Australia from the islands in Shark Bay through central South Australia, along the length of the Murray River in northwestern Victoria to the Liverpool Plains in eastern New South Wales; probably now extinct on the mainland (1,2).

POPULATION   The 1959 expedition to Bernier and Dorre described it as extremely common on Bernier and probably as abundant on Dorre (4). It was still present in 1975 but no estimates of abundance were given (5). Elsewhere it was said to have been common along the length of the Murray River around 1857 but to have become extinct there shortly afterwards, the last known specimen from New South Wales being taken in 1867 near the Murray-Darling river junction. The last museum specimen from mainland Western Australia was from Onslow in 1909, and from South Australia at Ooldea in 1922 (1,4,7), though Troughton in 1942 stated it still survived at that time in sub-desert western South Australia (6).

HABITAT AND ECOLOGY   On Bernier and Dorre Islands it inhabits typical sandhill vegetation and open steppe associations (4,5). On the mainland occurred on plains and sand-ridges with woodland, shrubland or heath (1). Reported as extremely active and pugnacious, showing very high intra-specific aggression, and are presumed solitary though Troughton stated that in Western Australia they were normally found in pairs in nests (6). Nocturnal, and thought to feed principally on insects, bulbous roots and other plant matter though in captivity small rodents are also taken (6). Breeding has been recorded from May to August with litters of two, sometimes three. Females on Bernier had one or two pouch young (4,5,6).

THREATS TO SURVIVAL   The exact reasons for its decline are unknown, but vegetation throughout its mainland range has been now either cleared for crop production or drastically altered by stock grazing, rabbits and feral goats in pastoral areas and, to a lesser extent, by rabbits elsewhere. Its entire mainland range is also infested with such introduced predators as foxes, feral cats and, at its eastern end, feral pigs (1). Conditions on Bernier and Dorre Islands have remained much more pristine. Sheep were apparently never introduced to Dorre, and were only temporarily introduced to Bernier at the beginning of this century. Feral goats are also absent from Dorre, although a herd estimated at 150 was reported to be causing some vegetational damage on Bernier in 1959 (4). By 1975 these had been largely eradicated and the vegetation was recovering (5). The bandicoot populations there, although regarded as stable at present, will remain potentially very vulnerable to fire or the accidental introduction of foxes, cats or rabbits (4).

CONSERVATION MEASURES TAKEN   Listed in Appendix 1 of the 1973 Convention on International Trade in Endangered Species of Wild Fauna and Flora, trade in it or its products therefore being subject to strict regulation by ratifying nations, and trade for primarily commercial purposes banned. Legally protected and Bernier and Dorre Islands are Class 'A' Fauna Conservation Reserves with strictly controlled access.

CONSERVATION MEASURES PROPOSED Continued protection of Bernier and Dorre from any form of unnecessary disturbance is vital for the survival of the species. Surveys to locate any possible relict colonies on the Australian mainland are also recommended and reintroductions to suitable areas (especially other off-shore islands) should be considered as part of a long-term conservation plan.

CAPTIVE BREEDING In 1979 one female was reported as held at Perth Zoo, Western Australia (3).

REMARKS For description see (2). Bernier and Dorre Islands also hold viable populations of four other Red Data Book species, - the Boodie (Bettongia lesueur), Banded Hare-wallaby (Lagostrophus fasciatus), Rufous Hare-wallaby (Lagorchestes hirsutus) and Shark Bay Mouse (Pseudomys praeconis). This data sheet was compiled from a draft kindly provided in 1978 by Peter Aitken, Curator of Mammals, South Australian Museum.

REFERENCES
1. Aitken, P. (1979). The status of endangered Australian wombats, bandicoots and the Marsupial Mole. In Tyler, M.J. (Ed.), The status of endangered Australasian wildlife. Royal. Zool. Soc. S. Aust.
2. Anon. (1978). Barred Bandicoot. Perameles bougainville. Mammals No.18. In Australian Endangered Species. Australian National Parks and Wildlife Service.
3. Olney, P.J.S. (Ed.) (1980). International Zoo Yearbook 20. Zool. Soc. London.
4. Ride, W.D.L. and Tyndale-Biscoe, C.H. (1962). Mammals. In Fraser, A.J. (Ed.). The results of an expedition to Bernier and Dorre Islands, Shark Bay, Western Australia in 1959. West. Aust. Fish. Dept. Fauna Bull. 2: 54-97.
5. Robinson, A.C., Robinson, J.F., Watts, C.H.S. and Baverstock, P.R. (1976). The Shark Bay Mouse Pseudomys praeconis and other mammals on Bernier Island, Western Australia. West. Aust. Naturalist. 13 (7): 149-155.
6. Troughton, E. (1941). Furred animals of Australia. Angus and Robertson Ltd. Sydney.
7. Wakefield, N.A. (1966). Mammals of the Blandowski Expedition to northwestern Victoria, 1856-1857. Proc. R. Soc. Vict. 79(2): 371-391.

DESERT BANDICOOT   EXTINCT

Perameles eremiana Spencer, 1897

Order   MARSUPIALIA   Family   PERAMELIDAE

SUMMARY   Last definitely recorded in inland Western Australia in 1931. Probably extinct, though extensive surveys may show it to survive in remote areas. Any relict colonies discovered should be afforded immediate protection.

DISTRIBUTION   Australia. Formerly occurred across an arid belt of central Australia joining Alice Springs and Charlotte Waters, Northern Territory, in the east and the Rawlinson and McIllwrath Ranges, Western Australia, in the west. The last museum specimen was taken at Gahnda, Western Australia, in 1931 (1).

POPULATION   Unknown; may well be extinct. Reports suggest that it was once plentiful throughout much of its range and according to Finlayson it had been fairly numerous in southwestern central Australia as late as 1932-35, though then became extremely rare or absent there (2,3). He stated in 1961 that it survived in the Tanami Desert region, though Parker considers that the only (vague) reports from there are referable to the Golden Bandicoot (Isoodon auratus), (2,4).

HABITAT AND ECOLOGY   Occurred on both sand plain and sand-ridge desert with Spinifex grassland (1). Nocturnal, resting by day in a shallow hole scooped out of the surface and thatched over with grass (6). Diet presumably the same as in other Perameles, - principally invertebrates but also small mammals and some vegetable matter (5). Two young were thought to be the norm (7).

THREATS TO SURVIVAL   The exact reasons for its decline are unknown, but the vegetation in the eastern half of its range has been drastically altered by stock grazing and rabbits and, to a lesser extent, in the western half of its range by rabbits alone. Its entire range is also infested with introduced predators namely foxes and feral domestic cats (1).

CONSERVATION MEASURES TAKEN   Totally protected by legislation and appears on the Official List of Australian Endangered Vertebrate Fauna. Parts of the western edge of the range are on Aboriginal reserves with limited public access.

CONSERVATION MEASURES PROPOSED   Surveys, particularly in the western part of the range, to locate any possible relict colonies and define protective measures for them.

CAPTIVE BREEDING   None.

REMARKS   For description see (5,7). Systematic research is required to determine whether this is a valid species or merely an eremian race of the Lesser Barred Bandicoot, Perameles bougainville, itself a Red Data Book species. This data sheet was compiled from a draft provided in 1978 by Mr Peter Aitken, Curator of Mammals, South Australian Museum.

REFERENCES   1.   Aitken, P. (1979). The status of endangered Australasian wombats, bandicoots and the marsupial mole. In Tyler, M.J. (Ed.), The status of endangered Australasian wildlife. Royal. Zool. Soc. S. Aust.
              2.   Finlayson, H.H. (1961). On Central Australian mammals

Part IV. The distribution and status of Central Australian species. Rec. S. Aust. Mus. 14: 141-191.

3.   Glauert, L. (1933). The distribution of the marsupials in Western Australia. J. Roy. Soc. W. Aust. XIX: 23.

4.   Parker, S.A. (1973). An annotated checklist of the native land mammals of the Northern Territory. Rec. S. Aust. Mus. 16(11): 1-57.

5.   Ride, W.D.L. (1970). A guide to the native mammals of Australia. Oxford University Press, Melbourne.

6.   Spencer, B. (1897). Description of two New Species of Marsupials from Central Australia. Proc. Roy. Soc. Vict. IX (N.S.): 6-11.

7.   Troughton, E. (1941). Furred animals of Australia. Angus and Robertson Ltd. Sydney.

GREATER BILBY, DALGYTE, or
GREATER RABBIT-EARED BANDICOOT

Macrotis lagotis (Reid, 1837)

Order MARSUPIALIA   Family   THYLACOMYIDAE

SUMMARY Formerly widely distributed in Australia but now severely reduced in
numbers and distribution, surviving only in small remote colonies. Decline mainly
ascribed to predation by foxes and habitat destruction by cattle and rabbits, and
in some parts of its range at least, the decline continues. Some colonies are in a
desert wildlife sanctuary but more extensive habitat protection is urgently needed.

DISTRIBUTION Australia; where now largely confined to the central Northern
Territory within an area roughly bounded by Renner Springs in the north, Delmore
Downs in the east, the MacDonnell Ranges in the south and Tanami in the west
(1,9). Four small outlying populations are also known, one in southwestern
Queensland between Boulia and Betoota and three in Western Australia at
Dampier Land, around the Edgar Range, and in the Warburton region where main
strongholds were reported in 1979 as to the north and northwest of Warburton, the
west of the Jameson Range, and south of the Cavanagh Range (1,2,4,9,10).
Possibly also still survives in the Great Sandy Desert of Western Australia but
surveys are needed to confirm this (9). Formerly extremely widely distributed in
mainland Australia south of 18°S and west of the Great Dividing Range,
apparently except central Queensland and most of Victoria (1,9). It seems to have
disappeared from New South Wales and southern South Australia rather suddenly
around 1900 and from the southwest and northern South Australia in the 1930s
(9,11).

POPULATION No figures are available but it is now very rare in comparison with
its former abundance and in 1978 was reported as apparently still declining, at
least in Western Australia (6). Density where it does occur is apparently very low
- Watts in the late 1960s discovered only 7 colonies, each estimated to hold an
average of 3 individuals, in over 540 sq. km of suitable habitat around Yuendumu
in the Northern Territory (9).

HABITAT AND ECOLOGY Recorded from a wide range of desert and sub-desert
habitat, including Melaleuca and Mulga shrubland and spinifex grassland, wherever
the ground is soft enough to burrow in and is not subject to waterlogging (8,9).
Watts, who studied the species in the Northern Territory, described colonies of
7-30 burrows covering a usually elongate area of up to 16 ha apparently normally
occupied by an adult pair and any offspring of the year. Burrows could be large
and complex, up to 2 metres deep, and were normally in open areas or along
water-courses (9). Diet has been reported as omnivorous, though in the population
studied by Watts it consisted mainly of underground tap roots, bulbs (especially
Cyperus bulbosus) and fungi (Endogone), along with unidentified seeds and fruit
and some insect matter (1,2,9). In Warburton the termites Hamitermes rubriceps
and Eutermes tumuli were the principal food source (8). Wood Jones noted
breeding from March to May and litter size of 1 to 3, usually 2 (11).

THREATS TO SURVIVAL The spread of the fox from the early 1900s onwards has
been implicated as the principal cause of the Greater Bilby's disappearance from
much of its former range as it persisted in many areas well after European
settlement and the establishment of the feral cat (9). Wood Jones recorded that
very large numbers were killed for pelts in South Australia and that the trade
continued at least until 1923. Great numbers were also killed for sport at that

time. This would doubtless have contributed to its decline in heavily populated regions (11). Habitat alteration by rabbits has also been stated to have been an important factor and rabbits are uncommon in most of the present range (9). However where they are present and cattle are absent the Greater Bilby still survives in reasonable numbers (7). It has thus been suggested that the depletion of food supplies by grazing cattle which occur in about three quarters of its present range accounts for the low population density in such areas, although it can evidently survive in areas completely given over to pastoralization as in southwestern Queensland (7,10).

CONSERVATION MEASURES TAKEN Listed in Appendix 1 of the 1973 Convention on International Trade in Endangered Species of Wild Fauna and Flora, trade in it or its products therefore being subject to strict regulation by ratifying nations, and trade for primarily commercial purposes banned. Totally protected by legislation and appears on the Official list of Endangered Australian Vertebrate Fauna. Part of its Northern Territory range is protected from cattle in the Tanami Desert Wildlife Sanctuary. It has been observed that the species is generally of great interest to and specifically protected by the sparse human population within its present range (5).

CONSERVATION MEASURES PROPOSED Additional reserves for the species are urgently required to protect habitat from further depredation by domestic stock, along with regular monitoring of all presently known populations and surveys to locate any further colonies, especially in the Great Sandy Desert, Western Australia.

CAPTIVE BREEDING In 1981 one male and two females were held in captivity at Perth Zoo, Western Australia and a small colony was also being maintained at the Arid Zone Research Institute of the Northern Territory Conservation Commission at Alice Springs. The University of New South Wales had a captive breeding group from 1969 to 1977. Only males were born, however, and the colony died out (Graeme G, George, In litt., 1981).

REMARKS For description see (2,11). This is the largest Australian bandicoot (2). The genus Macrotis is often included in the family Peramelidae. This data sheet was compiled from a draft kindly provided in 1978 by Mr Peter Aitken, Curator of Mammals, South Australian Museum.

REFERENCES
1. Aitken, P. (1979). The status of endangered Australasian wombats, bandicoots and the Marsupial Mole. In Tyler, M.J. (Ed.), The status of endangered Australasian wildlife. Royal. Zool. Soc. S. Aust.
2. Anon. (1976). Rabbit-eared Bandicoot, Bilby, Dalgite. Mammals No.1 In Australian Endangered Species. Australian National Parks and Wildlife Service.
3. Burbidge, A.F. and Fuller, P.J. (1979). Mammals of the Warburton Region, Western Australia. Rec. West. Aust. Mus. 8(1): 57-73.
4. Dent, M.K. (1972). Bilbies of Boulia. Mount Isa Mines Magazine: 12-16.
5. Kirkpatrick T.H. (1977). In litt.
6. Kitchener, D. (1978). In litt. to P. Aitken.
7. Newsome, A.E. (1971). Competition between wildlife and domestic livestock. Aust. Vet. J. 47: 577-586.
8. Smyth, D.R. and Philpott, C.M. (1968). A field study of the Rabbit Bandicoot. Trans. R. Soc. S. Aust. 92: 3-14.
9. Watts, C.H.S. (1969). Distribution and habits of the Rabbit Bandicoot. Trans. R. Soc. S. Aust. 93: 135-141.

10. Watts, C.H.S. and Aslin, H. (1974). Notes on the small mammals of north-eastern south Australia and south-western Queensland. Trans. R. Soc. S. Aust. 98 (2): 61-99.

11. Wood Jones, F. (1923-25). The Mammals of South Australia. The Government Printer, Adelaide.

LESSER BILBY, YALLARA or LESSER RABBIT-EARED BANDICOOT

EXTINCT

Macrotis leucura (Thomas, 1887)

Order   MARSUPIALIA   Family   THYLACOMYIDAE

SUMMARY   Probably extinct, being unrecorded alive in its former range in central Australia since 1931. Surveys are needed to determine whether relict populations still survive and, if so, to define effective conservation measures.

DISTRIBUTION   Australia. Formerly the northern half of the Lake Eyre Basin, central Australia. Very little information on its distribution is available, the species only having been collected six times in historic times, the first of these from an unknown locality (1). Subsequent specimens have been five from 65 km northwest of Charlotte Waters, Northern Territory in 1895; three from near Barrow Creek, N.T. in 1901; one from Mungerani, South Australia, in 1924; 12 from Cooncheri, South Australia in 1931; and a skull of undetermined age from an eagle's nest 23 km south-southeast of Steele Gap, N.T. in 1967 (1,4).

POPULATION   Unknown. It must now be extremely rare if not extinct, having not been recorded alive since 1931 when according to Finlayson it was plentiful in the Cooncheri district and was at that time evidently a widespread and well-known animal (2).

HABITAT AND ECOLOGY   Recorded from sandridge desert with spinifex grassland (1,2). Nocturnal and probably solitary, in common with most other bandicoots, and dug twisting burrows up to 3m deep in sloping dune faces (2). Diet was recorded as mainly rodents and some seeds (2). Two young at once appeared to be the norm (2,5).

THREATS TO SURVIVAL   The exact causes for the decline are unknown. Even now the vegetation in the main part of its range has been relatively unmodified by cattle grazing or rabbits so it seems likely that the principle cause was invasion by introduced predators, namely feral cats in the nineteenth century and foxes during the first decade of the twentieth (1).

CONSERVATION MEASURES TAKEN   Listed in Appendix 1 of the 1973 Convention on International Trade in Endangered Species of Wild Fauna and Flora, trade in it or its products therefore being subject to strict regulation by ratifying nations, and trade for primarily commercial purposes banned. Protected by legislation throughout its former range and appears on the Official List of Australian Endangered Vertebrate Fauna. Pastoral exploitation is excluded from that part of the range covered by the Simpson Desert National Park.

CONSERVATION MEASURES PROPOSED   Surveys, particularly in the Simpson Desert, to locate and define protective measures for any possible relict colonies.

CAPTIVE BREEDING   None.

REMARKS   For description see (2,4). The validity of this species has been questioned - it is allegedly virtually sympatric with the very similar Macrotis lagotis, itself an 'Endangered' species (3). The name 'Lesser Bilby' is that recommended by the Australian Mammal Society. This data sheet was compiled from a draft provided in 1978 by Peter Aitken, Curator of Mammals, South Australian Museum.

REFERENCES   1. Aitken, P. (1979). The status of endangered Australasian wombats, bandicoots and the marsupial mole. In Tyler, M.J. (Ed.), The status of endangered Australasian wildlife. Royal. Zool. Soc. S. Aust.

2. Finlayson, H.H. (1935). On mammals from the Lake Eyre Basin. Pt II. The Peramelidae. Trans. R. Soc. S. Aust. 59: 227-236.

3. Kirkpatrick, T.H. (1977). In litt.

4. Ride, W.D.L. (1970). A guide to the native mammals of Australia. Oxford University Press, Melbourne.

5. Troughton, E. (1941). Furred animals of Australia. Angus and Robertson Ltd. Sydney.

Antechinus apicalis (Grey, 1842)

Order   MARSUPIALIA   Family   DASYURIDAE

SUMMARY Rediscovered in 1967 after more than 80 years when it was presumed extinct; has been recorded since then in only two areas of southwestern Western Australia. None have now (1981) been found since 1976 despite intensive searches in known and likely localities. Habitat has been determined in only one of the areas and is extremely limited in extent and potentially very vulnerable to fire. A survey was underway in 1981 to try to locate any surviving populations, which if found should be given immediate effective protection.

DISTRIBUTION Australia, where has been collected this century (since 1967) only in two very limited areas on the south coast of southwestern Western Australia, at Cheyne Beach and about 225 km northeast at Jerdacuttup (7,8). At the former it has only been recorded from a 10 ha area of thick woodland, despite intensive trapping efforts in surrounding uncleared land (7,8). Records at Jerdacuttup are of a male caught by a cat on a farm in January 1976 and of another found dead on a farm 10 km northeast of this in December 1976 (8). However intensive searches in 1977, 1978 and 1981 in uncleared land in this vicinity have failed to find it (8,9); the species had been thought most likely to occur in a 900 ha area, formerly Government Requirements Reserve No.28110, roughly equidistant (ca. 6 km) from the two sites where the specimens were found and which contained areas of apparently suitable habitat (8). Searches in apparently suitable habitat in Stokes and Fitzgerald River National Parks since 1976 have also been unsuccessful (9). Formerly known from a much wider area; according to Gilbert it was universally distributed over the colony of Western Australia in the first half of the 19th century, with specific records from the Victoria Plains, Albany, Moore River and Salt River (3,5) The National Museum of Victoria has 22 specimens from Western Australia probably collected between 1875 and 1884 (3). Lundelius recorded it as fossil remains from caves along the west coast as far south as Yanchep, then inland to Albany, skirting the high rainfall area of the southwest corner, it being unknown from remains in the Margaret River caves (2,3,5). There are two specimens in the Queensland Museum recorded by Thomas in 1888 as from Rockhampton, Queensland, and Gould in 1863 also reported it from South Australia (1,3). For map of old and modern records in Western Australia see (9).

POPULATION Unknown; none have now (1981) been recorded since 1976 despite intensive searches by Dr Patricia Woolley in known and likely localities (9). Only 11 specimens have been obtained in the wild this century, all since 1967 when the first four individuals recorded since the 1880s were trapped at Cheyne Beach (8). Of the remainder, two were from Jerdacuttup (see above) and the rest also from Cheyne Beach with two in 1975 and three in 1976 (8). This represents a very low trapping success rate. Since 1977 searches have been made by examination of prey hairs in predator (mainly fox and cat) scats, as well as by conventional trapping techniques - Dibbler hair is very distinctive and should be easily recognisable (9,10). Up to July 1981, over 700 scats had been examined from Cheyne Beach, Jerdacuttup, Fitzgerald River and Stokes National Parks; the failure to record Dibbler remains in any of these, along with the failure to trap any, is taken to indicate that the species is genuinely very rare (9).

HABITAT AND ECOLOGY Found at Cheyne Beach in a 10 ha area of very dense vegetation dominated by Banksia spp. to a height of 2.5 m. Ground litter was very thick and the area had not been burnt for many years (7,8). It is thought likely the

Dibbler may be dependent on such a vegetation type as it was not trapped in adjacent areas of recently burnt lower and less dense vegetation (7,8). Observations on captive specimens indicate that breeding is seasonal, taking place once a year, with mating in March and April and gestation of between 44 and 53 days (6). A litter of seven was recorded, with young dependent on the mother for approx. 4 months after birth and sexual maturity attained in 10-11 months (6). Gilbert in the 19th century described the nest, which was built on the ground below overhanging Xanthorrhoea (5). Appears to be predominantly crepuscular and diet insectivorous though nectar from Banksia and Eucalyptus flowers is readily taken in captivity (3,4,5,6).

THREATS TO SURVIVAL The species is expected to be very vulnerable to disturbance, particularly to fire (8). The known distribution at Cheyne Beach was apparently confined to a very small area in close proximity to a fishing settlement and camping area (8); the evident decline and possible extinction of the population there may be due to habitat loss - by February 1981 many of the older, larger Banksia shrubs had died and much of the vegetation in the area where most Dibblers were originally caught had been destroyed by the surveying of a road and the clearing of firebreaks around the recently established reserve there (9). Adjacent areas of vegetation had grown up and by then constituted apparently suitable habitat but no Dibblers were trapped in them (9). At Jerdacuttup the area where Dibblers had been thought most likely to occur (Govt. Requirements Reserve No. 28110) is to be released for agriculture in December 1981. The area was intensively surveyed in January 1981, following a one-year suspension of release of the land, but no Dibblers were found (9). The reasons for the original decrease in range are unknown though bush-clearing for agriculture and the introduction of predators such as foxes and feral cats are likely to have been important.

CONSERVATION MEASURES TAKEN Legally protected. The habitat at Cheyne Beach was reported in 1980 as having been recently incorported into a 75 ha reserve, but the proximity of the camping site means the area will remain at considerable risk to fire (10). Fitzgerald River National Park lies between Cheyne Beach and Jerdacuttup and contains areas of vegetation very similar to known Dibbler habitat, although intensive attempts to trap them here in 1977-78 failed (8). In 1981 an ongoing project funded by WWF Australia and led by Dr Patricia Woolley was attempting to locate further Dibbler populations; to date this has been unsuccessful (see above) (9,10).

CONSERVATION MEASURES PROPOSED Protection of any populations which may be discovered by the survey. Fire prevention measures would be of particular importance, if it is discovered that Dibblers are indeed dependent on habitat which has not been recently burnt.

CAPTIVE BREEDING One of the individuals captured in 1967 gave birth to seven young shortly afterwards and all were successfully raised to maturity. Mating was observed in these but no young were produced and the colony died out. Individuals do, however, seem to be relatively easy to maintain in captivity (6).

REMARKS For description see (4). This data sheet was compiled from a draft provided in 1978 by Dr Michael Archer, Department of Zoology, University of New South Wales and Dr Patricia Woolley, Dept. of Zoology, La Trobe University, Victoria, kindly provided information and commented on the sheet in 1981.

REFERENCES 1. Archer, M. (1979). The status of Australian dasyurids, thylacinids and myrmecobiids. In Tyler, M.J. (Ed.), The status of endangered Australasian wildlife. Royal Zool. Soc. South Aust.

2. Lundeluis, E. (1957). Additions to the knowledge of the ranges of Western Australian mammals. W. Aust. Naturalist. 10(5): 103-111.

3. Morcombe, M.K. (1967). Rediscovery after 83 years of the Dibbler. Antechinus apicalis. W. Aust. Naturalist 10 (5): 103-11.

4. Ride, W.D.L. (1970). A guide to the native mammals of Australia. Oxford University Press, Melbourne.

5. Wagstaff, R. and Rutherford, R. (1955). Letters from Knowsley Hall, Lancashire. Northwest. Naturalist. March 1955: 11-22.

6. Woolley, P. (1971). Observations on the reproductive biology of the Dibbler, Antechinus apicalis (Marsupialia: Dasyuridae). J. R. Soc. West. Aust. 54(4): 99-107.

7. Woolley, P. (1977). In search of the Dibbler, Antechinus apicalis (Marsupialia: Dasyuridae) J. R. Soc. West Aust. 59(4): 111-117.

8. Woolley, P. (1980). Further searches for the Dibbler, Antechinus apicalis (Marsupialia: Dasyuridae). J. R. Soc. West. Aust. 63(2): 47-52.

9. Woolley, P. and Valente, A. (1981). The Dibbler, Antechinus apicalis (Marsupialia: Dasyuridae): Failure to locate populations in four regions in the south of Western Australia. In prep.

10. World Wildlife Fund Australia. (1980-81). Project 5. A further attempt to locate populations of the Dibbler. WWF Australia Newsletter 4: 5., 7: 4.

RED-TAILED PHASCOGALE   INDETERMINATE

Phascogale calura Gould, 1844

Order   MARSUPIALIA   Family   DASYURIDAE

SUMMARY Formerly widely distributed in southern Australia; now confined to a few isolated populations in reserves and State Forest in southwest Western Australia. Causes of the decline are unknown as apparently suitable habitat is still widespread in its former range; predation by feral cats has been implicated as a possible factor. Surveys and studies are needed to determine ecological requirements and the present status of the species so that detailed conservation plans can be drawn up.

DISTRIBUTION   Now confined to southwestern Western Australia (2,11,12). Surveys in the Western Australian wheatbelt in the 1970s recorded it in the following reserves 150 to 250 km southwest of Perth: Bendering (5119 ha), West Bendering (1602 ha), Yornaning (247 ha) and Dongolocking (1061 ha) (4,5,7,8). It also reportedly occurs in Dryandra State Forest and Tutanning Nature Reserve (1,5). Formerly also existed in southwestern New South Wales, northern Victoria, the Murray region of South Australia (there being one nineteenth century record from Adelaide), and the central Northern Territory where one was taken at Alice Springs in 1894 (2,6,10,11,13). In 1941 Troughton observed that the range already seemed to have contracted to the extreme southwest (13).

POPULATION Unknown, though appears to be moderately abundant in the limited areas where it now occurs; 21 were trapped during surveys at Yornaning in 1975 (5). There are indications that it may never have been particularly common, as it represents a small but fairly constant fraction of Dasyurid remains in caves such as those on the Nullarbor plains in Western Australia (1,2,9).

HABITAT AND ECOLOGY A skilful climber and appears to show a preference for vegetation of trees, mallees or tall shrubs which allow easy passage through the foliage; other than this there is no indication of strong habitat selectivity (8). At Bendering and West Bendering, canopy cover in regions occupied by the species varied from sparse to dense and leaf litter was absent to moderately abundant (8). At Yornaning there was some indication of a preference for Causuarina huegeliana woodland, with Wandoo (Eucalyptus wandoo) also apparently important here and at Tutanning (5). Diet, from examination of stomach contents, appears predominantly insectivorous, though some individuals also contained bird feathers or mammalian hairs (5,8). Females apparently gave birth in early spring and were still suckling in September (8).

THREATS TO SURVIVAL The very marked contraction of range and its apparent present restriction to a few small areas, some of which may not be subject to an appropriate management regime, are considered to place the species at risk (1,2,3,12). The precise causes of the decline are unkown. Apparently suitable habitat is still reportedly widespread within its former range (1,2); predation by feral cats and possibly foxes has been implicated as a possible factor (1,2). It is noteworthy that the very similar Brush-tailed Phascogale (Phascogale tapoatafa) is still common and widespread (11).

CONSERVATION MEASURES TAKEN Legally protected; present in several reserves and in Dryandra State Forest (see above).

CONSERVATION MEASURES PROPOSED There is an urgent need for studies to identify factors affecting populations; in particular to determine the causes of the range contraction. Once the species' requirements have been determined, management plans for existing populations can be formulated. The possibility of reintroduction to suitable areas should be considered. Many reserves, especially those in the wheatbelt, are now isolated by large areas of agricultural land and are extremely unlikely to be naturally recolonised by species which have died out; this applies especially to small animals such as the Phascogale (7).

CAPTIVE BREEDING None.

REMARKS For description see (11). This data sheet was compiled from a draft provided in 1978 by Dr Michael Archer, Department of Zoology, University of New South Wales.

REFERENCES 1. Archer, M. (1981). In litt.
2. Archer, M. (1979). The status of Australian dasyurids, thylacinids and myrmecobiids. In Tyler, M.J. (Ed.), The status of endangered Australasian wildlife. Royal Zool. Soc. S. Aust.
3. Calaby, J.H. (1981). In litt.
4. Chapman, A., Dell, J., Kitchener, D.J. and Muir, B.G. (1978). Biological survey of the Western Australian wheatbelt. Part 5: Dongolocking Nature Reserve. Rec. West. Aust. Mus. Suppl. No. 6.
5. Dell, J., Harold, G., Kitchener, D.J., Morris, K.D. and Muir, B.G. (1979). Biological survey of the Western Australian wheatbelt. Part 7: Yornaning Nature Reserve. Rec. West. Aust. Mus. Suppl. No. 8.
6. Kitchener, D.J., Chapman, A., Dell, J. and Muir, B.G. (1977). Biological survey of the Western Australian wheatbelt. Part 3: Vertebrate fauna of Bendering and West Bendering Nature Reserves. Rec. West. Aust. Mus. Suppl. No. 5.
6. Finlayson, H.H. (1961). On central Australian mammals, - Part IV: the distribution and status of central Australian species. Rec. S. Aust. Mus. 14 (1): 141-191.
7. Kitchener, D.J., Chapman, A. and Muir, G.B. (1980). The conservation value for mammals of reserves in the Western Australian wheatbelt. Biol. Cons. 18: 179-207.
9. Lundelius, E.L. Jr. (1963). Vertebrate remains from the Nullarbor caves, Western Australia. J. Proc. R. Soc. West. Aust. 46: 75-80.
10. Parker, S.A. (1973). An annotated checklist of the native land mammals of the Northern Territory. Rec. S. Aust. Mus. 16(11): 1-57.
11. Ride, W.D.L. (1970). A guide to the native mammals of Australia. Oxford University Press, Melbourne.
12. Strahan, R. (1981). In litt.
13. Troughton, E. (1941). Furred animals of Australia. Angus asnd Robertson Ltd., Sydney.

Sminthopsis longicaudata Spencer, 1909

Order   MARSUPIALIA   Family   DASYURIDAE

SUMMARY   Known from only five specimens collected in Western Australia, the most recent in 1975. Studies are needed to determine status, distribution and population trends, and to formulate any necessary conservation plans.

DISTRIBUTION   Western Australia; exact distribution unknown. Only five specimens have ever been collected, the first (in 1908) and two subsequently from the Pilbara - Marble Bar region (approx. 21°20'S, 118°16'E), the most recent in 1974 approx 6 km east of Miss Gibson Hill (26°51'S, 126°23'E) in the Baker Lake area of the Gibson Desert (2,3,5). The origin of the other specimen is unknown (5).

POPULATION   Unknown. The small number of recorded specimens implies rarity but as little biological surveying has been carried out in large areas of inland Western Australia its true status and any population trends remain unknown (2,3). Its relative rarity in fossil records from, for example, Cape Range Caves in northwestern Western Australia does however suggest the species has alway been at least uncommon (3,4).

HABITAT AND ECOLOGY   The 1975 specimen was obtained in an area of low hummock grassland of *Triodia* and *Plectrachne* spp. with occasional emergent *Hakea lorea* and *Acacia* spp. (3). Other than this nothing is known of the ecology of the species. *Sminthopsis* are small, active predators, apparently principally insectivorous although birds and lizards may be taken, individual species showing markedly different dietary preferences (5). Nothing is known of the breeding biology of S. longicaudata.

THREATS TO SURVIVAL   Probably naturally rare. Archer has discussed the status and apparent decline of many of the Dasyurid marsupials. It is possible that the recent succession of years with good rains (since 1974) may have favoured introduced predators such as cats and foxes and disadvantaged native species of small Dasyurids such as S. longicaudata which are better able to cope with physiological stress in bad years (2). It is also possible that some Australian species undergo oscillations of population size and geographic range in synchrony with long term climatic changes. To test this however a much better Pleistocene-Recent mammal record than is currently available is required (2). The habitat in large areas of arid inland Western Australia is still relatively unmodified by pastoralisation or introduced herbivores.

CONSERVATION MEASURES TAKEN   Listed in Appendix 1 of the 1973 Convention on International Trade in Endangered Species of Wild Fauna and Flora, trade in it or its products therefore being subject to strict regulation by ratifying nations, and trade for primarily commercial purposes banned. Legally protected in Western Australia. The 1975 specimen was taken within the proposed 10,529 sq. km Baker Lake Reserve (2).

CONSERVATION MEASURES PROPOSED   Detailed study to determine the distribution and status of this species should be carried out, in particular investigation of the Pilbara region to discover if the species still exists there. Any populations found should be afforded protection. Effective control of introduced predators, particularly foxes and feral cats, would be highly desirable.

CAPTIVE BREEDING None are known to have been kept in captivity.

REMARKS For description see (4). This data sheet was compiled from a draft kindly provided in 1978 by Dr Michael Archer, Department of Zoology, University of New South Wales.

REFERENCES
1. Anon. (1973). Additional protection for rare fauna. State Wildlife Authority News Service (West. Australia) 4(2): 31-33.
2. Archer, M. (1979). The status of Australian dasyurids, thylacinids and myrmecobiids In Tyler, M.J. (Ed.), The status of endangered Australasian wildlife. Royal Zool. Soc. S. Aust.
3. Burbidge, A.A., McKenzie, N.L., Chapman A. and Lambert, P.M. (1976). The wildlife of some existing and proposed reserve in the Great Victoria and Gibson Desert, Western Australia. Wildl. Res. Bull. West. Aust. 5: 1-16.
4. Kendrick, G. and Porter, J.K. (1973). Remains of a Thylacine (Marsupialia: Dasyuroidea) and other fauna from caves in the Cape Range, Western Australia. J. Proc. R. Soc. West Aust. 56: 116-112.
5. Ride, W.D.L. (1970). A guide to the native mammals of Australia. Oxford University Press, Melbourne.

SANDHILL DUNNART

Sminthopsis psammophila Spencer, 1895

Order   MARSUPIALIA   Family   DASYURIDAE

SUMMARY   Two populations were discovered in southern Australia in 1969. Prior to this the only known specimen was the type, collected in 1894 in the Northern Territory. Indications suggest it may have somewhat specific ecological requirements and thus be sensitive to habitat clearance for agriculture. A population may exist in the Hambidge Conservation Park. Status surveys and studies of this species in the wild are needed.

DISTRIBUTION   Australia. Exact range unknown. In 1969 five specimens were captured at two sites on the Eyre Peninsula, Southern Australia (11): one from the Hundred of Mamblyn and four from a site 80 km southeast in the Hundred of Boonderoo (1). The type specimen was collected at Lake Amadeus in the Northern Territory, 1000 km northwest of the above populations, by the Horn Expedition in 1894 (3). The only other record is of remains found in owl pellets in a cave at Ayers Rock, Northern Territory, reported in 1973 (3).

POPULATION   The paucity of records suggests that it is, and may always have been, rare (2), though further collecting may show it to be more common and widespread than is supposed - apparently suitable habitat is reported as very abundant in central Australia and the Eyre Peninsula and Northern Territory localities are widely separate.

HABITAT AND ECOLOGY   The Eyre Peninsula sites were both of similar habitat and topography, consisting of roughly parallel sand-dunes, 3-6 m high separated by wide valleys. Ground cover was sparse. Mallees (Eucalyptus spp.) were the predominant vegetation type on the valley flats but became more heavily mixed with Broombrush (Melaleuca uncinata) and other herbaceous and ephemeral plants on the dunes; semi-open areas of Porcupine Grass (Triodia lanata) occurred intermittently on the dune slopes (1). Annual rainfall was 30-36 cm (1). The Lake Amadeus specimen was taken from sandhill Porcupine Grass country with groves of Desert Oak (Casuarina decaisneana). Sminthopsis species in general are small, active and predominantly nocturnal predators, feeding principally on invertebrates, though small vertebrates are sometimes taken (4). Nothing is known of the breeding biology of this species.

THREATS TO SURVIVAL   Bush clearance for cereal growing is proceeding rapidly at both sites where the species is known on the Eyre Peninsula (1,2). The fact that the species has only been encountered in Porcupine Grass and brush-wood dune systems implies that its ecological requirements may be somewhat specific and thus it may be relatively intolerant of habitat disturbance. The effect of introduced predators, namely foxes and cats, is unknown.

CONSERVATION MEASURES TAKEN   Included in Appendix 1 of the 1973 Convention on International Trade in Endangered Species of Wild Fauna and Flora, trade in it or its products therefore being subject to strict regulation by ratifying nations, and trade for primarily commercial purposes banned. Protected under South Australian Legislation. The specimens from Boonderoo were collected in an area immediately adjacent to the 37,847 ha Hambidge Conservation Park where the topography and vegetation are essentially the same as the collecting site and it is thought likely that the species occurs there though this has yet to be demonstrated (1,2).

CONSERVATION MEASURES PROPOSED If the species is shown to occur in the Hambidge Conservation Park then suitable management should ensure its survival there. Meanwhile, immediate acquisition of the Boonderoo collecting site and any other uncleared areas near the park is recommended, as are surveys to determine the full extent of the species' distribution. Any other populations discovered should be afforded immediate protection from habitat disturbance.

CAPTIVE BREEDING As far as is known it has never been kept in captivity.

REMARKS For description see (1,4). This is the largest Sminthopsis (1). This data sheet was compiled from a draft kindly provided by Dr Michael Archer, Department of Zoology, University of New South Wales.

REFERENCES
1. Aitken, P. (1971). Rediscovery of the large Desert Sminthopsis (Sminthopsis psammophila Spencer) on Eyre Peninsula, South Australia. Vict. Nat. 88: 103-111.
2. Archer, M. (1979). The status of Australian dasyurids, thylacinids and myrmecobiids In Tyler, M.J. (Ed.), The status of endangered Australasian wildlife. Royal Zool. Soc. S. Aust.
3. Parker, S.A. (1973). An annotated checklist of the native land mammals of the Northern Territory. Rec. S. Aust. Mus. 16(11): 1-57.
4. Ride, W.D.L. (1970). A guide to the native mammals of Australia. Oxford University Press, Melbourne.

Sminthopsis douglasi Archer, 1979

Order   MARSUPIALIA   Family   DASYURIDAE

SUMMARY   A recently described species, known from only four specimens collected from a small area in northeastern Australia. The presumed range is in an area almost entirely given over to livestock grazing and the species is thus likely to be at considerable risk from habitat destruction.

DISTRIBUTION   North-central Queensland, Australia. Has been collected only from the vicinity of Julia Creek and Richmond, both in the watershed of the Cloncurry River (1,2,3).

POPULATION   Unknown, though appears to be rare (1,2). Only four specimens are known, the most recent collected around 1972 (1). The holotype was collected at Julia Creek in 1931, though was not recognised as a distinct species until the 1970s; the other two specimens are a male from Wyangarie Station, Richmond, collected before 1963, and a female from Julia Creek believed collected around 1933 (3).

HABITAT AND ECOLOGY   Unknown. The precise localities of the collecting sites are unknown, though the area in general has low annual rainfall (444-459 mm) (1,2,3). The species has a markedly fattened tail (3), which may be an adaptation to an unpredictable or sparse food supply. One of the females had six juveniles in the pouch, though the date of birth is unknown (3).

THREATS TO SURVIVAL   The species appears to have a very limited range in a region almost entirely cleared for grazing; it is thus expected to be at considerable risk from habitat destruction (1,2).

CONSERVATION MEASURES TAKEN   Legally protected in Queensland (1).

CONSERVATION MEASURES PROPOSED   Surveys are needed to determine the localities and status of any surviving populations; suitably sized tracts of land should then be set aside for their protection (1).

CAPTIVE BREEDING   None.

REMARKS   For description see (3). This is the second largest Sminthopsis. This data sheet was compiled from a draft provided in 1978 by Dr Michael Archer, Department of Zoology, University of New South Wales.

REFERENCES   1.   Archer, M. (1978). In litt.
              2.   Archer, M. (1979). The status of Australian dasyurids, thylacinids and myrmecobiids. In Tyler, M.J. (Ed.), The status of endangered Australasian wildlife. Royal Zool. Soc. S. Aust.
              3.   Archer, M. (1979). Two new species of Sminthopsis Thomas, (Dasyuridae: Marsupiala) from Northern Australia, S. butleri and S. douglasi. Aust. Zoologist 20(2): 327-345.

Myrmecobius fasciatus Waterhouse, 1836

Order   MARSUPIALIA   Family   MYRMECOBIIDAE

SUMMARY   Apparently confined to Eucalypt woodland in southwest Western
Australia though may conceivably still persist in arid inland regions further east.
A survey in 1979 showed that a very marked decline in numbers had taken place in
the 1970s and several former populations inhabiting reserves seemed to have
disappeared. A research programme was underway in 1981 aimed at providing
management data to conserve the species.

DISTRIBUTION   Now appears confined to southwestern Western Australia where
a survey from 1954 to 1956 found it to occur in a region bounded by York in the
north, Manjimup in the west and Ongerup in the east (5). Indications from a
survey in 1979 were that the range had considerably contracted since the 1950s,
though in 1973 there were unconfirmed reports of the species at Dragon Rocks
near Hyden, northeast of Ongerup, which would represent an eastward extension
of the known range in that part of Western Australia (3,7). Formerly widely but
sparsely distributed throughout southern Australia, probably in a continuous belt
from the southwest through Laverton and the Warburton Ranges in Western
Australia and the Everard Range in northern South Australia, into southwest New
South Wales, where the last specimen was recorded in 1857 (2,9). The only record
outside Western Australia this century is one from the Everard Ranges reported
by Finlayson (6). The eastern form is normally ascribed to a separate subspecies,
M. fasciatus rufus, but only appears to have differed from the nominate race in
pelage colour and is thought to have intergraded with it somewhere in the
Kalgoorlie district in Western Australia (1,5).

POPULATION   Unknown, though reported to have drastically declined since the
mid 1970s (1). Population density, even in optimal habitat, appears to be low.
Calaby in 1954-56 recorded a maximum of five animals along a 6.4 km transect in
his study area at Dryandra (5). M. f. rufus may be extinct; the most recent record
is from the Warburton Ranges registered in the Western Australian Museum in
1950 (5). The Aborigines from this region were reported in 1979 as not having seen
it for 25 years (4).

HABITAT AND ECOLOGY   Open woodland dominated by Eucalyptus species
susceptible to termite attack, and associated with an open shrub understorey and
large numbers of hollow logs (1,5). Now principally occurs in Wandoo (Eucalyptus
wandoo) forests which are heavily infested with the termite Coptotermes
acinaciformis, and have an underbrush of Poison Shrub (Gastrolobium
microcarpum) (1,5). The termite constitutes a primary food source and also
creates the hollow logs which are important for shelter. Contrary to earlier
reports the Numbat is also found in the much more extensive Jarrah (Eucalyptus
marginata) forests despite the lower abundance of termites (Jarrah having some
resistance to termite attack), as well as in Wandoo pockets within the Jarrah, and
in hilly areas with laterite soils where Powder-bark (E. accedens) is dominant
(3,5). Diet consists of any termite species available, apparently eaten roughly in
proportion to their actual abundance, and a small quantity of predatory ants which
are believed to be ingested accidentally when they invade termite galleries being
excavated by the Numbat. Apparently almost exclusively diurnal, Numbats rest
in hollow logs at night and sometimes construct rough nests of bark, leaves and
grass. Burrows are occasionally dug. Breeding in southwest Australia seems to be
seasonal with up to four young normally born between January and April or May

THREATS TO SURVIVAL The reasons for the overall population decline and very marked contraction of range over the present century are not understood in detail though are likely to involve a combination of habitat alteration and predation by introduced foxes and feral cats. Changes in the fire regime leading to a transition to unsuitable habitat types in parts of the Numbat's present range, have been implicated in the continued decline. Formerly, infrequent wildfires of high intensity occurred which allowed the accumulation of deep leaf litter and also led to a dense shrub understorey, often of plant species such as the leguminous Gastrolobium spp. which require hot fires for seed germination. Current management practices in some areas include the use of frequent, low intensity deliberate burns. These destroy much of the leaf litter and do not allow sufficient time for shrub-layer regeneration, especially inhibiting fire-dependent plants such as Gastrolobium, and leading to a much more open habitat which may be unsuitable for Numbats (1). The marked recent decline, however, is thought likely to be mainly due to a prolonged drought and an increase in fox numbers (1). Calaby in 1960 considered, however, that the role of predators had been overemphasised, as foxes and cats were abundant in all areas where the Numbat was still fairly common (5).

CONSERVATION MEASURES TAKEN Legally protected. It is present in a number of mostly small nature reserves although much of the present range is in State Forest (3,5). In 1979 a six-month study in Western Australia demarcated the present range and estimated the population size (3).

CONSERVATION MEASURES PROPOSED The Western Australian Department of Fisheries and Wildlife has commenced (1981) a research programme aimed at conserving the species and providing management data for reserves and State Forest (3). If a captive breeding colony can be established, reintroduction to areas formerly occupied should be considered (1). Calaby notes that it can survive well in bush blocks left when areas are cleared, as long as sufficient hollow logs are available, thus the number of potential reintroduction sites should be considerable (5).

CAPTIVE BREEDING Does not appear to have ever bred in captivity. Its highly specialised diet makes captive maintenance very difficult, though a female was kept at Taronga Park, Sydney, for some years up to 1979 (1,8).

REMARKS For description see (1,9). This data sheet was compiled from a draft provided in 1978 by Dr. Michael Archer, Dept. of Zoology, University of New South Wales and Dr. A.A. Burbidge of the Western Australia Dept. of Fisheries and Wildlife kindly commented on the sheet.

REFERENCES
1. Anon. (1979). Our diminishing heritage - the Numbat. State Wildl. Authority New Service (West. Aust.) 9 (2): 40-41.
2. Archer, M. (1979). The status of Australian dasyurids, thylacinids and myrmecobiids. In Tyler, M.J. (Ed.), The status of endangered Australasian wildlife. Royal Zool. Soc. S. Aust.
3. Burbidge, A.A. (1981). In litt.
4. Burbidge, A.A. and Fuller, P.J. (1979). Mammals of the Warburton Region, Western Australia. Rec. West. Aust. Mus. 8(1): 57-73.
5. Calaby, J.H. (1960). Observation on the Banded Ant-eater Myrmecobius f. fasciatus. Waterhouse (Marsupialia), with particular reference to its food habits. Proc. Zool. Soc. Lond. 135(2): 183-207.

6. Finlayson, H.H. (1961). On Central Australian mammals Part IV. The distribution and status of Central Australian species. Rec. S. Aust. Mus. 14: 141-191.

7. McKenzie, N.L., Burbidge, A.A. and Marchant, N.G. (1973). Results of a biological survey of a proposed wildlife sanctuary at Dragon Rocks, near Hyden, Western Australia. Dept. Fish. Fauna, West. Aust. Report No. 12.

8. Olney, P.J.S. (Ed.) (1980). International Zoo Yearbook 20. Zool. Soc. London.

9. Ride, W.D.L. (1970). A guide to the native mammals of Australia. Oxford University Press, Melbourne.

THYLACINE

EXTINCT

Thylacinus cynocephalus (Harris, 1808)

Order   MARSUPIALIA   Family   THYLACINIDAE

SUMMARY   May possibly still exist in Tasmania. Once moderately abundant and widespread on the island, it was hunted to extinction over most of its range by the early 1900s. The last recorded specimen was taken in 1933, since when numerous sightings have been reported though no definite proof of its survival obtained. Rigorously protected by law and large areas of habitat where it may still survive are protected.

DISTRIBUTION   Once widespread over mainland Australia and New Guinea but has only been recorded alive in Tasmania in historic times (4,6,10,13). A Thylacine humerus associated with bones dated at 0 ± 80 BP from a cave deposit in the Napier Range in northwestern Western Australia is the most recent mainland record (4). All other documented non-Tasmanian records are of remains over 2500 years old (4). On Tasmania was apparently formerly scattered throughout, though probably never plentiful in the wet southwestern region (6). Reported sightings since the 1930s are not confined to any one part of Tasmania but are widespread with concentrations in the northeast and northwest (12).

POPULATION   Unknown, may be extinct. The last specimen taken in the wild was collected in 1933 in the Florentine Valley and died in the Hobart Zoo in 1936 (9,12). Since then there have been many reports, some considered reasonably reliable, of sightings scattered throughout Tasmania, though despite extensive expeditions to search for the species in 1938, 1945-46, 1963-64 1973, 1980-81 and numerous other smaller-scale attempts, no absolutely unequivocal evidence for its continued existence has yet been produced (3,11,12,13). Reports of the species have increased, however, since the early 1960s and some authorities believe that it may be slowly recovering in numbers (10). A lair was reported on the west coast in 1966 though the most recent date of occupancy does not appear known (7,10). In the 19th century it was common enough on Tasmania to be considered a pest by sheep farmers and analysis of bounty records shows there to have been good populations in the Central Highlands, Eastern Ranges and the northeast (6). Numbers appear to have dropped dramatically around 1905, probably for a variety of reasons (see below), though small numbers were trapped until the 1930s (6,11).

HABITAT AND ECOLOGY   Preferred habitat appears to have been savannah woodland or open sclerophyll forests with nearby rocky outcrops, though also occurred in most other habitats in Tasmania (5,6,10). Predominantly nocturnal, resting up in a lair (often a cave) during the day and was apparently solitary, although there are reports of hunting in pairs or occasionally in small family groups (14). Exclusively carnivorous, its natural food appears to have been wallabies and smaller marsupials, rats, birds and possibly lizards (14). Following European settlement large numbers of sheep and poultry were also taken. Three or four young were produced and there is evidence of an extended breeding season though bounty records indicate most were born from May to August (6,10).

THREATS TO SURVIVAL   Human persecution appears to have been the principal cause of the decline in Tasmania (5,6,10,11,12,13). Because of its sheep and poultry killing habits it was hunted intensively and a bounty system was initiated by the Van Diemen's Land Company as early as 1840. This was taken over by the Government in 1888 and between then and 1909 2,184 Thylacines were officially recorded as killed, though the total number was certainly considerably higher (6).

The sudden drop in the number of bounties claimed around 1905, following many years of intense persecution, suggests that human predation was the critical factor, though a disease which attacked most of the Tasmanian Dasyurids at that time may also have been important (6,8). Competition and super-predation by introduced European dogs has also been suggested as a contributing factor - it is widely held that competition with the dingo, which was introduced to Australia during the Pleistocene, was responsible for its extinction on the mainland (4).

CONSERVATION MEASURES TAKEN Listed in Appendix 1 of the 1973 Convention on International Trade in Endangered Species of Wild Fauna and Flora, trade in it or its products therefore being subject to strict regulation by ratifying nations, and trade for primarily commercial purposes banned. Fully protected by law since 1936 with especially heavy penalties for killing under any circumstances (1,2,12). The Thylacine is on the Official List of Endangered Australian Vertebrate Fauna. In 1966 a 647,000 ha region of southwest Tasmania between Low Rocky Cape, Sprent, Kallista and South West Cape was proclaimed a game reserve. Cats, dogs and guns are prohibited in the region (1). This is one of the areas where it is believed most likely to have survived. It could also conceivably occur in two national parks - Lake St. Clair (134,680 ha) and Frenchman's Gap (10,279 ha) (8). The Tasmania National Parks and Wildlife Service investigates all claimed sightings of the species (2), and with funding from WWF-Australia has gathered and analysed available information on the species (12). It is carrying out an ongoing field survey in conjunction with the University of Tasmania using infra-red automatically triggered cameras, though as of August 1981 no evidence of the species' survival has been obtained (15).

CONSERVATION MEASURES PROPOSED Once the species has been demonstrated to survive, detailed conservation plans can be drawn up.

CAPTIVE BREEDING Does not appear to have ever bred in captivity, although individuals were exhibited in several zoos in the first part of the century (11).

REMARKS For description see (1,10). This is the largest modern marsupial carnivore (10). This data sheet was compiled from a draft provided in 1978 by Dr Michael Archer, Department of Zoology, University of New South Wales, and Ian Eberhard of the Tasmanian National Parks and Wildlife Service kindly commented on the final draft.

REFERENCES
1. Anon. (1966). Thylacine. IUCN Bulletin New Series 20: 4.
2. Anon. (1978). Thylacine. Mammals No.9. In Australian Endangered Species. Australian National Parks and Wildlife Service.
3. Anon. (1979). Submission to CITES Secretariat. Unpd. 4pp.
4. Archer, M. (1974). New information about the Quaternary distribution of the Thylacine (Marsupialia, Thylacinidae) in Australia. J. Proc. R. Soc. West. Aust. 57: 43-50.
5. Archer, M. (1979). The status of Australian dasyurids, thylacinids and myrmecobiids. In Tyler, M.J. (Ed.), The status of endangered Australasian wildlife. Royal Zool. Soc. S. Aust.
6. Guiler, E.R. (1961). The former distribution and decline of the Thylacine. Aust. J. Sci. 23(7): 207-210.
7. Guiler, E.R. (1966). Pers. comm. to IUCN.
8. IUCN. (1972). Thylacine. Sheet Code 2.14.11. Red Data Book Vol. 1, Mammalia. IUCN, Switzerland.
9. Pearse, R. (1976). Thylacines in Tasmania. (Abstract). Bull. Aust. Mamm. Soc. 3: 58.
10. Ride, W.D.L. (1970). A guide to the native mammals of

Australia. Oxford Univ. Press, Melbourne.

11. Sayles, J. (1980). Stalking the Tasmanian Tiger. Animal Kingdom 82 (6): 35-40.

12. Smith, S.J. (1981). The Tasmanian Tiger - 1980. WWF - Nat. Parks and Wildl. Service, Tasmania.

13. Stivens, D. (1973). The Thylacine Mystery. Animal Kingdom 76 (3): 18-23

14. Troughton, E. (1941). Furred animals of Australia. Angus and Robertson Ltd., Sydney.

15. WWF-Australia. (1981). Project progress. Project 3: the Thylacine quest. WWF-Australia Newsletter 6: 4.

Solenodon cubanus Peters, 1861

Order   INSECTIVORA   Family   SOLENODONTIDAE

SUMMARY   Endemic to Cuba where it now only occurs in Oriente Province. Everywhere rare, and numbers believed to be declining and range contracting, mainly because of deforestation, although harassment by feral cats has also contributed. Legally protected. Two reserves have been established for its protection, and a third is under consideration. Continuing protection in the wild is essential to its survival.

DISTRIBUTION   Eastern Cuba where now confined to northeast, west central and southwest Oriente Province. Surveys in the mid 1970s have confirmed that in northeast Oriente it still occurs in the mountains to the west of Toa Baracoa, in the southwest in the Sierra Maestra mountain range, and in scattered localities in west central Oriente around Bayamo, the type locality (5,10,11,12,13,14,15). Pleistocene or Sub-Recent remains have been found in cave deposits in Pinar del Rio Province in western Cuba (10), and it was known to occur in Sierra del Escambray in Las Villas Province in south-central Cuba until the mid-19th century (10,11).

POPULATION   Numbers unknown but everywhere rare (5,10,13,14), Varona in 1981 reported that numbers were declining, and its range contracting slowly (10). In 1974, 14 individuals were counted on the western heights of Sierra Maestra (10,12).

HABITAT AND ECOLOGY   Dense, humid, primary montane forests (5,13.16). Shelters in burrows or caves, seemingly in family groups (10,15). Solenodons are terrestrial and primarily nocturnal, feeding on vertebrates, and invertebrates such as snails (2,3,9,15) and obtaining their food by rooting in the ground with their snouts and tearing into rotten logs and trees with their foreclaws (15,17). One to two offspring is the norm (9).

THREATS TO SURVIVAL   Deforestation has been the principal cause of decline (5,10), although feral cats may also have contributed (16). Some authors attributed decline to dogs and mongooses (1,5,17) but neither occur in the Solenodon's habitat (10,16). Varona in 1976/77 reported that local farmers always knew where Solenodons could be found, although prior to the 1970s they had not tried to capture them, partly because the meat is inedible and partly because the habitat is difficult to penetrate. However because of increased scientific interest in Solenodons the farmers have been 'trying to capture almiquis so as to see their names and photographs on television and in newspapers and magazines' (13). However specimens captured in 1976 and 1980 were re-released in the areas where they were caught (10,13,14).

CONSERVATION MEASURES TAKEN   Legally protected in Cuba and efforts are being made to ensure that protection is enforced. A new law, No. 21-79, has forbidden all hunting throughout the year in certain areas that are important for wildlife (16). The Cuban Academy of Sciences has established the Jaguani and the Cupeyal reserves for fauna and flora in the montane forest of northeastern Oriente Province, near Toa Baracoa, where both the Solenodon and the Ivory-billed Woodpecker (Campephilus principalis bairdii) occur. A third reserve in this area is planned at Duaba Arriba (10). IUCN/WWF Project 1268 aimed to investigate the status of the Haitian and Cuban Solenodons; Dr. Walter Poduschka,

Chairman of the IUCN/SSC Insectivore Specialist Group therefore visited Hispaniola in 1976, but was unable to obtain permission to visit Cuba (8).

CONSERVATION MEASURES PROPOSED Continuation of surveys in selected areas of the Solenodon's range to ascertain its distribution and ecology, as a basis for the establishment of further reserves or other action to ensure its survival.

CAPTIVE BREEDING In 1974-75 a male and two females were captured near Baracoa. The male died in April 1975, one year after capture; by March 1976 the females were still alive and kept in Havana Zoo where they were being studied by the Vertebrate Department of the Institute of Zoology (10,13); by March 1981 one of the females still lived (10). There are no records of this species ever having bred in captivity. Canas Alcober decribes his experience of taking care of two captive Almiquis in the 1950s (5), and Bridges mentions a specimen kept at Philadelphia Zoological Garden from December 1886 to July 1892 (4).

REMARKS For description of animal see (1,3,5,6,11,15,17); for photograph see (16). In 1925 Cabrera put the species in the genus Atopogale, however it is now usually placed in the genus Solenodon along with the Haitian Solenodon, Solenodon paradoxus, with Atopogale retained as the subgenus. Barbour describes two species of Solenodons on Cuba, based on colouration (3). However Varona points out that colouration is extremely variable and that probably only one species exists (10,11,15). Insectivores are considered the most primitive and oldest true mammals; the genus Solenodon is one of the most basic of the recent insectivores and its survival is therefore of fundamental interest to mammalian science (8).

This data sheet was compiled with the assistance of Dr Luis S. Varona of Havana, Cuba.

REFERENCES
1. Allen, G.M. (1942). Extinct and Vanishing Mammals of the Western Hemisphere with the marine species of all the Oceans. Spec. Publ. Amer. Comm. Int. Wildlife Protection. No.11.
2. Allen, J.A. (1908). Notes on Solenodon paradoxus Brandt. Bull. Amer. Mus. Nat. Hist. 24: 505-517.
3. Barbour, T. (1944). The Solenodons of Cuba. Proc. New Engl. Zool. Club 23: 1-8.
4. Bridges, W. (1936). The Haitian Solenodon. Bull. New York Zool. Soc. 39 (1): 13-18.
5. Canas Alcober, R. (1971). The last Almiquis (Solenodon cubanus) in captivity. Zool. Garten N.F., Leipzig 40 (1-2): 1-3.
6. McDowell, S.B. Jr., (1958). The Greater Antillean Insectivores. Bull. Am. Mus. Nat. Hist. 115 (3): 113-214.
7. Peters, W.H.C. (1861). Notes in Mber. K. preuss. Akad Wiss. Berlin. 169.
8. Poduschka, W. (1977). Project 1268. Solenodon - Cuba, Haiti and Dominican Republic. World Wildlife Yearbook 1976-77: 197-198. WWF, Switzerland.
9. Poduschka, W. (1977-81). In litt.
10. Varona, L.S. (1969-1981). In litt.
11. Varona, L.S. (1974). Catalogo de los mamiferos vivientes y extinguidos de las Antillas. Academia de Ciencias de Cuba.
12. Varona, L.S. (1974). The Cuban Solenodon. Oryx 12 (5): 542.
13. Varona, L.S. (1976). The present status of the Almiqui Solenodon (Atopogale) cubana. Unpd. Report. 3pp.
14. Varona, L.S. (1977). Cuban Solenodon surveyed. Oryx 14 (1): 7.

15. Varona, L.S. (1980). Mamíferos de Cuba. Editorial Gente Nueva, Havana, Cuba.
16. Varona, L.S. (1980). Protection in Cuba. Oryx 15(3): 282-284.
17. Walker, E.P. (1975). Mammals of the World. The Johns Hopkins University Press, Baltimore and London.

Solenodon paradoxus (Brandt, 1833)

Order   INSECTIVORA   Family   SOLENODONTIDAE

SUMMARY   Endemic to the island of Hispaniola in the Caribbean. Numbers unknown. Range contracting and numbers declining primarily because of land development and deforestation caused by a rapidly expanding human population. Protected by law in the Dominican Republic, but enforcement is difficult. Secure reserves are essential for the Solenodon's survival.

DISTRIBUTION   Dominican Republic and Haiti (Caribbean island of Hispaniola). There is no palaeontological or recent evidence of the existence of this species elsewhere. In the Dominican Republic it now only survives in areas relatively undisturbed by man (9,10,11). In Haiti, it survived throughout the southern peninsula into the 20th century, but seems to have been confined to the extreme western end of it since the 1940s (10,16,18).

POPULATION   Total numbers unknown but described as declining drastically in the Dominican Republic (9) and in imminent danger of extinction in Haiti (17,18). In 1975, Woods made an extensive search of all regions of the southern peninsula of Haiti but failed to locate any breeding populations and found only two dead animals (16,17); between April 1979 and December 1980 he found the bones of a further 15 animals (18).

HABITAT AND ECOLOGY   The essential feature of the Solenodon's habitat is that it contains crevices in coralline limestone covered with dense brush or woodland (2,9,14). This cover can vary from rainforest at 3000 m down to semi-arid woodland or even scrub at low altitudes (9,10). Solenodons shelter in burrows, caves, hollow trees and logs. They are terrestrial and primarily nocturnal, feeding on vertebrates and on invertebrates such as snails and obtaining their food by rooting in the ground with their snouts and tearing into rotten logs and trees with their foreclaws (2,9,14,15). One or two offspring is the norm (9)

THREATS TO SURVIVAL   Decline is chiefly attributed to land development and deforestation caused by a rapidly expanding human population. Even the remotest areas are now being occupied by squatters, who burn down the vegetation to start plantations and who, with their dogs, are predators of the Solenodon (6,9,10,11,18).

CONSERVATION MEASURES TAKEN   Protected by law in the Dominican Republic and although there are shortcomings in local enforcement, prohibition of export is effective. As yet no reserves for the species have been set aside in either country (9,10). However, resulting from an IUCN/WWF survey in the Dominican Republic by Walter Poduschka in 1976, a conference in 1977, and another visit by Dr Poduschka in 1978, negotiations were undertaken to try and establish at least one conservation area (9,12,13) but by 1981 this had not yet been achieved.

CONSERVATION MEASURES PROPOSED   Legal protection in Haiti. Stricter enforcement of the law at local level in the Dominican Republic. In Haiti, Charles Woods has undertaken surveys of Solenodon and the Haitian Hutia (Plagiodontia aedium), as a result of which he has been able to give the Government details of several areas that would be suitable for conservation of these species (17); there is no doubt that establishment of secure reserves is essential for the Solenodon's survival (9,10,11,18). It is also essential that captive breeding groups be established (11).

CAPTIVE BREEDING Several animals are held at Santo Domingo Zoo, Dominican Republic, and several have been held in captivity in the past (4).

REMARKS For description of animal see (1,2,3,5,7,14,15). Mohr studied this Solenodon in great detail (8). Insectivores are considered the most primitive and oldest true mammals; the genus Solenodon is one of the most basic of the recent insectivores and its survival is therefore of fundamental interest to mammalian science (11). This data sheet was compiled with the assistance of Mr. Charles A. Woods and Dr. Walter Poduschka, Chairman of the IUCN/SSC Insectivore Specialist Group.

REFERENCES 1. Allen, G.M. (1942). Extinct and Vanishing Mammals of the Western Hemisphere with the marine species of all the Oceans. Amer. Comm. Int. Wild Life Protection, Spec. Publ.
2. Allen, J.A. (1908). Notes on Solenodon paradoxus Brandt. Bull Amer. Mus. Nat. Hist. 24: 505-517.
3. Brandt, J.F. (1833). De Solenodonte, novo mammalium insectivorum genere. Mem. Acad. Sci. St. Petersbourg Ser. 6. (2): 459-478.
4. Bridges, W. (1936). The Haitian Solenodon. Bull. New York Zool. Soc. 39 (1): 13-18.
5. Dobson, G.E. (1882). A Monograph of the Insectivora. Systematic and Anatomical. Part 1. Including the families Erinaceidae, Centetidae and Solenodontidae. van Voorst, London.
6. Johnson, M.L. (1969). In litt.
7. McDowell, S.B. Jr. (1958). The Greater Antillean Insectivores. Bull. Am. Mus. Nat. Hist. 115 (3): 113-214.
8. Mohr, E. Biologische Beobachtungen an Solenodon paradoxus Brandt. Zool. Anz. 113: 177-188 (1936); 116; 65-76 (1936); 117: 223-241 (1937); 122: 132-143 (1938); 126: 94-95 (1939); 141: 264-268 (1943).
9. Poduschka, W. (1977-81). In litt.
10. Poduschka, W. (1977). Die Überlebenschancen des Schlitzrüsslers. Säugetierschutz Zt. fur Theriophylaxe 5: 3-9.
11. Poduschka, W. (1977). Project 1268. Solenodon - Cuba, Haiti and Dominican Republic. World Wildlife Yearbook 1976-77: 197-198. WWF, Switzerland.
12. Poduschka, W. (1978). Solenodon in Cuba, Dominican Rep. and Haiti - Conservation Measures. Report to IUCN/WWF.
13. Poduschka, W. (1979). Project 1538. Solenodon in Cuba, Dominican Republic and Haiti - Conservation. World Wildlife Yearbook 1978-79: 174. WWF, Switzerland.
14. Verrill, A.H. (1907). Notes on the habits and external characters of the Solenodon of San Domingo (Solenodon paradoxus). Amer. J. of Sci. 24: 55-57.
15. Walker, E.P. (1975). Mammals of the World. The Johns Hopkins Univ. Press. Baltimore and London.
16. Woods, C.A. (1976). Solenodon paradoxus in southern Haiti. J. Mammal. 57(3): 591-592.
17. Woods, C.A. (1977). In litt.
18. Woods, C.A. (1981). Last endemic mammals in Hispaniola. Oryx 16(2): 146-152.

GHOST BAT or AUSTRALIAN FALSE VAMPIRE   VULNERABLE

Macroderma gigas (Dobson, 1880)

Order   CHIROPTERA   Family   MEGADERMATIDAE

___

SUMMARY   Occurs in northern Australia.   Several thousand are thought to survive but decline in distibution and size of existing colonies is being accelerated by disturbance and quarrying. Protected by law. A research project was in progress in 1977 and a national park, protecting one important cave, is proposed.

DISTRIBUTION   Northern Australia where has a scattered distribution north of 28°S in Western Australia, Northern territory and Queensland (1,2,3,9). Douglas, who studied the species in Western Australia in the 1960s, recorded it mainly in the Pilbara region, southwest of Port Hedland, and the Kimberley District with a few isolated records in inland areas further south (1). Subfossil remains have been found as far south as 34°S and are common in, for example, coastal areas immediately north of Perth where the animal no longer occurs. This contraction in range appears to have occurred well before European settlement (1,10).

POPULATION   Exact numbers unknown but several thousand probably survive, primarily in the north. One colony apparently declined from 450 in 1960 to 150 in 1976 (7). Immense guano deposits, containing bones of this species only, indicate sites where very large colonies used to exist during the late Pleistocene (1,10).

HABITAT AND ECOLOGY   Exclusively nocturnal, roosting in caves, rock clefts and abandoned mine-shafts during the day. Diet is predominantly carnivorous, and in captivity a great variety of preferably live food was taken, including mice, small bats, birds, lizards, small snakes and large insects. Fruit was taken sparingly and only when animal food was not available. Mouse (Mus musculus), Budgerigar (Melospsicattus undulatus) and Owlet-nightjar (Aegotheles cristatus) remains were the commonest identified at feeding sites in the Pilbara. Females are believed to give birth to a single young, probably congregating in maternity colonies during the breeding season, which appeared to be in late October to early November in the Pilbara region and somewhat earlier in the far north (1).

THREATS TO SURVIVAL   The species appears to be very nervous and easily disturbed in its roosts and as remoter parts of northern Australia are increasingly settled, such disturbance can be expected to increase - in 1977 it was reported that a new road passed beside one of the largest colonies and it is thought that vandalism will almost cetainly become a problem with increasing tourism in areas where the bat is most abundant (4). Some roosts are threatened by open-cut limestone quarrying destroying caves (6); however in the Pilbara region the bats apparently make use of the very large number of abandoned mineworkings scattered through the hills (1). The species is likely to be most sensitive to disturbance at maternity sites. The causes of the original contraction in range are not understood, though may possibly be a result of changes in conditions during the Pleistocene and Recent, leading to a transition in southern areas from open savanna to dense woodland which was less suitable for hunting in (1).

CONSERVATION MEASURES TAKEN   The Ghost Bat is protected by law from being collected or killed but the law is not effectively enforced (4). Habitat generally is not protected, but a few localities where it has been recorded in small numbers are in reserves. A two-year research project into the bat's ecology was reported in 1977 as being undertaken near Rockhampton, Queensland (4).

CONSERVATION MEASURES PROPOSED The Queensland Government was reported in 1978 as planning to set up a national park incorporating the important Johannsen's Cave (4). However, other important colonies of M. gigas in the same region continue to be threatened by quarrying. Adequate protection and management of all maternity roosts is required (4). Most important are roosts around Rockhampton, in Arnhemland, Kimberley and Pilbara (SSW of Port Hedland) (4). Further research is needed to identify critical habitat for the species.

CAPTIVE BREEDING In 1979 there were two males and one female (one male captive bred) held at Perth Zoo, Western Australia (8).

REMARKS For description of animal see (10,11). E. Hamilton-Smith supplied much of the information on which this data sheet is based. This species is the only Australian member of a family (Megadermatidae) which occurs otherwise in Asia and Africa (10).

REFERENCES
1. Douglas, A.M. (1967). The natural history of the Ghost Bat, Macroderma gigas (Microchiroptera, Megadermatidae) in Western Australia. W. Aust. Nat. 10(6): 125-138.
2. Finlayson, H.H. (1958). 'Recurrence' of Macroderma gigas Dobson. Nature (London) 181: 923.
3. Finlayson, H.H. (1961). On Central Australian Mammals, IV, The distribution and status of Central Australian species. Rec. S. Aust. Mus. 14(1): 141-191.
4. Hamilton-Smith, E. (1977). In litt.
5. Hamilton-Smith, E. (1979). Endangered and threatened Chiroptera of Australia and the Pacific region. In Tyler, M.J. (Ed.), The status of endangered Australasian wildlife. Roy. Zool. Soc. S. Aust.
6. Hamilton-Smith, E. and Champion, R. (1976). Mount Etna and the Caves. Univ. of Queensland Speleological Soc., Brisbane.
7. McKean, J.L. and Price, W.J. (1967). Notes on some Chiroptera from Queensland, Australia. Mammalia 31: 101-119.
8. Olney, P.J.S. (Ed.) (1980). International Zoo Yearbook 20. Zool. Soc. London.
9. Parker, S.A. (1973). An annotated checklist of the native land mammals of the Northern Territory. Rec. S. Aust. Mus. 16(11): 1-57.
10. Ride, W.D.L. (1970). A guide to the native mammals of Australia. Oxford Univ. Press, Melbourne.
11. Walker, E.P. (1975). Mammals of the World. The Johns Hopkins Univ. Press, Baltimore and London.

INDIANA BAT   VULNERABLE

Myotis sodalis (Miller & Allen, 1928)

Order   CHIROPTERA   Family VESPERTILIONIDAE

SUMMARY Widely distributed in the eastern United States. Known population declined by 28% in 15 years (1960-1975) because of human disturbance and altered microclimate in caves where bats concentrate for hibernation. With proper protection and reclamation of caves numbers should be able to build up again to 1960 levels. Listed as endangered on the U.S. Endangered Species List; some 'Critical Habitat' has been legally determined with some caves purchased by the government and protected from disturbance. A Recovery Team has been appointed and a Recovery Plan drafted, though this still needs revision and implementation.

DISTRIBUTION Eastern United States; from New Hampshire in the northeast to Iowa and eastern Oklahoma in the west, and southeast to the Florida Panhandle (1,3,4,5,6,8,10,11,12). Their winter range is much smaller, being restricted primarily to Alabama, Tennessee, Kentucky, Indiana, Missouri, and West Virginia (12). Overall distribution is virtually unchanged though some hibernating sites have been abandoned (1). Most of the population is in two large demes; one occupies Missouri in winter, Missouri and Iowa in summer; the other occupies Indiana and Kentucky both winter and summer and western Ohio and southwestern Michigan in summer only (8). For map see (12).

POPULATION Estimated in 1978 at 509,000 following the discovery of wintering populations in two caves in Indiana (12,16). Prior to this the estimated total was 460,000, this representing a 28% decline in 15 years in the known population from the 1960 estimate of approximately 640,000 (8). Catastrophic drowning of 300,000 in one cave in 1937 suggests that the earlier population exceeded one million (4,8,12). Biggest reduction was in Kentucky, from about 209,800 to 55,800. A small decrease in Missouri was attributed to yearly variation in winter weather (8). The fact that the great majority of the population hibernates in relatively few caves makes the species particularly vulnerable to disturbance (8,12,14).

HABITAT AND ECOLOGY Hibernates in caves and mines with a stable, cool temperature. Preferred sites in the midwest have midwinter air temperature of +4 to +8°C, while the acceptable range including suboptimal sites is -3 to +17°C (11). Relatively few caves are suitable, i.e. have configurations that trap cold air masses below entrances. Suitable sites can house up to 100,000 individuals and ten hibernacula out of 63 house approx. 91% of the known population. Traditional winter roosts have high survival value and bats return year after year, using the same locations within caves (8); Clawson et al. have shown that there appear to be two hibernating strategies, with most bats forming large clusters in the coldest parts of the caves, these tending to be near the entrances, and some remaining in warmer, normally deeper areas, forming smaller and more active clusters. The latter apparently trade off warmer temperatures and thereby greater average fat expenditure during hibernation for freedom from disturbance and disaster which is likely to affect those groups nearer cave mouths (3). The bats may migrate up to 483 km between winter and summer homes (11). During summer, females form small nursery colonies in tree hollows and the space under loose bark of dead trees; they give birth to one young in late June or early July, having stored sperm overwinter from autumnn mating and forage principally in the foliage of riparian and floodplain trees near the maternity sites (10). Major summering sites of males are unknown, though they have been observed foraging in densely forested areas, mostly on hills and floodplain ridges, and are believed to roost primarily in caves with small groups known to summer around hibernacula (17). Diet, in females and juveniles at least, consists principally of small soft-bodied flying insects, mainly Diptera (12).

THREATS TO SURVIVAL Human disturbance. The bats' winter supply of fat is depleted prematurely when human visits to caves cause repeated arousal and when roost temperatures are warmed by restricted air flow through entrances that are modified to control human access; this can lead to considerable mortality as the fat reserves cannot be replenished until spring. At one cave excessive disturbance caused loss of 60,000 bats and at least 80,000 were lost in three caves in which temperatures warmed up because of intentionally blocked entrances. In some cases gates intended to protect the bats from disturbance have led to the loss of populations by altering the cave microclimate. Natural disasters such as flooding and rockfalls are important agents of winter mortality and can thus impede recovery, as does the species' low reproductive rate, although survival in undisturbed populations is generally high (8). Clawson et al. consider that the two hibernating strategies (see above) may be a guard against extinction of populations as the smaller, active clusters will be less affected by disturbance although they will presumably be similarly vulnerable to changes in the overall cave microclimate (3). The amount of apparently suitable summer habitat is very large and losses appear to be minor, though the actual extent of destruction of riparian habitat by impoundment and channelization is unknown and wholesale clearing of waterside woodland could be potentially a severe threat (10).

CONSERVATION MEASURES TAKEN Listed as endangered on the U.S. Endangered Species List and therefore protected in all states of its former and present range (13). A Recovery Team exists and a Recovery Plan has been drafted (2,14). Certain caves and mines have been given legal status as 'Critical Habitat' (15), requiring that all Federal Agencies ensure that actions authorized, funded or carried out by them do not result in the destruction or adverse modification of this habitat. Most of the important hibernacula (including the largest, in southern Indiana, with an estimated 100,000 bats) are on state or federal property and therefore receive some degree of protection, with public access often strictly controlled (14).

CONSERVATION MEASURES PROPOSED Implementation of the Recovery Plan (14), which principally entails effective protection and management of winter habitat; this should enable the species to increase to at least 765,000 individuals. Specifically, no more than one human visit per winter should come within the hearing range of hibernating bats, and structures for control of visitor access should be of a type that does not constrict entrances or passages. Thermally modified caves which are now unsuitable for bats should be reclaimed by removing or modifying structures that restrict air flow, and land managers should be trained in techniques for preserving the solitude and microclimates of caves. In 1979 it was reported that public acquisition of several caves on private land, including four in Missouri and one in West Virginia, was being sought (12). The recommendations of the Recovery Plan, if carried out, should afford protection to 99% of the population. The need has also been stressed for the recognition of summer habitat as necessary for survival and for planning to avoid or compensate for serious losses of such habitat (5,12,14). Any conservation plan should also entail a public education and information programme (12,14).

CAPTIVE BREEDING No information.

REMARKS For description of animal see (1,11). The SSC is indebted to Dr. S.R. Humphrey for much of the information on which this data sheet is based and to

Mr. J.T. Brady, Team Leader of the Indiana/Gray Bat Recovery Team who in January 1981 reviewed the sheet.

REFERENCES
1. Barbour, R.W. and Davis, W.H. (1969). Bats of America. Univ. Press of Kentucky, Lexington. 286 pp.
2. Brady, J.T. (1981). In litt.
3. Clawson, R.L., La Val, R.K., La Val, M.L. and Caire, W. (1980). Clustering behaviour of hibernating Myotis sodalis in Missouri. J. Mammal. 61(2): 245-253.
4. Hall, J.S. (1962). A life history and taxonomic study of the Indiana bat, Myotis sodalis. Reading Publ. Mus. and Art Gallery Sci. Publ. 12: 1-68.
5. Harvey, M.J. (1980). Status of the endangered bats, Myotis sodalis, M. grisescens and Plecotus townsendii ingens in the southern Ozarks. In Wilson, D.E. and Gardner, A.L. (Eds), Proc. 5th Int. Bat Research Conference. Texas Tech. Press, Lubbock, Texas.
7. Humphrey, S.R. (1977). In litt.
8. Humphrey, S.R. (1978). Status, winter habitat and management of the endangered Indiana bat, Myotis sodalis. Florida Sci. 41: 65-76.
9. Humphrey, S.R. and Cope, J.B. (1977). Survival rates of the endangered Indiana bat, Myotis sodalis. J. Mammal. 58(1): 32-36.
10. Humphrey, S.R., Richter, A.R. and Cope, J.B. (1977). Summer habitat and ecology of the endangered Indiana Bat, Myotis sodalis. J. Mammal. 58(3): 334-346.
11. Layne, J.N. (Ed.), Rare and endangered biota of Florida. Vol. I. Mammals. Univ. Presses of Florida.
12. National Fish and Wildlife Laboratory, Gainesville (1980). The Indiana Bat. FWS/OBS-80/01.23. In Selected Vertebrate Endangered Species of the Seacoast of the United States. Biological Services Programme. Fish and Wildlife Service. U.S. Department of the Interior.
13. United States Congress (1973). Public Law 93-204, 93rd Congress, S. 1983 December 28 1973. U.S. Government Printing Office, Washington, DC., 21 pp.
14. U.S. Fish and Wildlife Service. (1975). Recovery Plan for the Indiana Bat. 34 pp.
15. U.S. Dept. of Interior. (1976). Determination of critical habitat for American Crocodile, California Condor, Indiana Bat, and Florida Manatee. Federal Register 41(187): 41914-41916.
16. Richter, A.R., Seerley, D.A., Cope, J.B., and Keith, J.H. (1978). A newly discovered concentration of hibernating Indiana Bat, Myotis sodalis, in southern Indiana. J. Mammal. 59: 191.
17. LaVal, R.K., Clawson, R.L., LaVal, M.L. and Caire, W. (1977). Foraging behavior and nocturnal activity patterns of Missouri bats, with emphasis on the endangered species Myotis grisescens and Myotis sodalis. J. Mammal. 58: 592-599.

GRAY BAT

ENDANGERED

Myotis grisescens (Howell, 1909)

Order   CHIROPTERA

Family   VESPERTILIONIDAE

SUMMARY   Limited distribution in limestone areas of southeastern U.S.A. Possesses highly specific habitat requirements and is very intolerant of disturbance; total numbers are estimated to have now (1981) declined to less than 20% of the level in the early 1960s, mostly as a result of human disturbance of roosts, which still continues. 95% of the total population now winters in 9 caves, with over half in a single cave in northeastern Alabama. Adequate protection of these sites and the major maternity sites is essential for the species' survival. A Recovery Team has been appointed and a draft Recovery Plan produced. Listed as Endangered on the U.S. Endangered Species List.

DISTRIBUTION   Occupies a limited range in limestone karst areas of the southeastern United States (15,13). Populations are found mainly in Alabama, northern Arkansas, Kentucky, Missouri and Tennessee, but a few occur in northwestern Florida (Jackson County), Western Georgia (Clarke and Polk Cos.), southeastern Kansas (Crawford Co.), southernmost Indiana, southern and southwestern Illinois (mainly Hardin Co.), northeastern Oklahoma, northeastern Mississippi (Tishomingo Co.), western Virginia and possibly western North Carolina (5,13). Distribution within this range has always been patchy, but fragmentation and isolation of populations is increasing (5,13). For map see (5).

POPULATION   In 1980 a rough estimate of the total was 1,575,000 of which about 95% winter in nine hibernacula and over half in a single cave (5). Alabama and Tennessee, with four major hibernacula held around one million individuals; Arkansas and Kentucky had one major hibernaculum each and estimated populations of 250,000 and 25,000 respectively; Missouri, with 3 main hibernacula, held an estimated 300,000 (5). Tuttle has noted, however, that estimation of Gray Bat population size is extremely difficult and it was thought that some estimates may differ from actual numbers by as much as 25 to 50% (5,13). A census in 1976 of 22 of the most important known remaining colonies in Alabama and Tennessee revealed an average population decline of 54% since 1970, with an overall decrease of 76% compared to 'recent' maximum estimates for the caves (5,13). It was estimated that the 1976 population represented in total less than 20% of that around 20 years ago (5,13). The species was declared 'Endangered' by the U.S. Department of the Interior in 1976.

HABITAT AND ECOLOGY   The Gray Bat, with rare exception, roosts in caves all year round and has highly specific roost and habitat requirements (1,5,9,13). Fewer than 5% of available caves are believed suitable for occupation (5). Almost all colonies move seasonally from unusually warm caves (14 - 25ºC) summer to cold (6 - 11ºC) winter caves (4,5,7,9,11,13). Most winter caves (hibernacula) are deep and vertical; all have a large volume below the lowest entrance and act as cold air traps (5,11). Summer maternity colonies are in caves that act as warm air traps or that provide restricted 'rooms' or domed ceilings that trap body heat from resident individuals which in some cases may have numbered at least 250,000 at previous population levels (5,8,11). Maternity caves are nearly always less than 1 km from rivers or reservoirs, over which the bats feed (5,10). During spring and autumn transient or migratory periods a much wider variety of caves is used and at all seasons males and yearling females seem less restricted than breeding females and young to specific cave and roost types (5,9,13). Mating takes place in autumn and adult females enter hibernation immediately, with juveniles and adult males following several weeks later, most being in hibernation by early November. Adult females emerge in late March or early April, the rest between mid-April and mid-May; stored fat reserves must thus last for six or seven months (5,9,11). Sperm is stored over winter, fertilisation occurring on emergence from hibernation, and a single young is born in late May or early June (3,5,9). Growth rate of the flightless young is positively correlated with colony size, this being likely to be because increasing numbers of bats reduce the energy required by each individual for thermoregulation (5,8). Once young are flying, growth rates are inversely proportional to the distance from the roost to the nearest feeding areas (10). Females do not reproduce till they are two years old (5,9).

THREATS TO SURVIVAL   By far the most important cause of decline has been, and continues to be, disturbance to roosting sites by cavers and vandals (5,12,13). The restrictive habitat requirements of the species leads to the congregation of very large numbers in a few caves, making them very vulnerable to such disturbance, which is especially critical at maternity sites from late-May to mid-July and at hibernacula from mid-August to April (5,13). In the former, flightless young are present in the roosts and thousands may die from a single disturbance, while in the latter human activity will cause all bats within range of sound or light to rouse from hibernation leading to expenditure of fat reserves which cannot be replaced and thereby causing considerable mortality from starvation before spring (5,13). The popularity of caving ('spelunking') has increased enormously since the 1950s with a corresponding increase in the amount of disturbance (5,13). Several of the largest colonies were destroyed by cave commercialisation or by inundation following the construction of dams and reservoirs, which still continues. Other possible factors include mortality from pesticides (2), and water pollution, siltation and subsequent decline of insect populations, especially mayflies which are believed to be the major food source (5,13). The construction of badly designed gates, intended to protect the bats but leading to alteration in the cave microclimate, has also led to the loss of entire colonies, especially at maternity sites (5,12,13).

CONSERVATION MEASURES TAKEN   Listed as 'Endangered' by the U.S. Department of the Interior on 28 April 1976, and is therefore protected by law throughout its present and former range. A Recovery Team has been appointed and a detailed draft Recovery Plan for the Grey Bat was produced in December 1980 (5). By then the most important known summer cave (Souta Cave in Alabama), containing an estimated 127,000 bats had been purchased by the U.S. Fish and Wildlife Service, which was also considering other important acquisitions, including the only major hiberaculum in Kentucky, with an estimated 25,000 bats (5). Acquisition and management of other caves has been undertaken by a number of state and federal agencies, including the Tennessee Valley Authority, National Park Service, U.S. Forest Service, U.S. Army Corps of Engineers and Missouri Department of Conservation (5). Studies of ecological requirements and movement patterns have been published and others are in progress (6,7,8,9,10,11,12).

CONSERVATION MEASURES PROPOSED   The Recovery Team consider that the bat can be moved from 'Endangered' to 'Threatened' status when 90% of the major hibernacula are protected from disturbance and stable or increasing populations have been demonstrated in 75% of the associated maternity caves after a period of five years (5). This will entail the acquisition of at least some degree of control over the caves by government agencies and possibly private conservation bodies (5). Detailed suggestions have been made for the protection of known individual Gray Bat caves, including the construction of properly designed gates or fences, the erection of warning notices and regular patrols by conservation officials (all of which are already in use in some cases) (5,13). Such measures should be extended to recently abandoned caves as they are likely to be recolonised if afforded protection from disturbance (5). It is noted that, as Gray Bat usage of caves is seasonal, protection efforts should be concentrated during periods of residence (5). The importance of educating cave owners, cavers and the public at large about the needs of bats and their ecological importance has been stressed (5,13). Further studies of the effects of pesticides and water pollution, which may have caused significant local declines, should be carried out as should monitoring of other forms of habitat modification such as forest clearance, channelization and siltation (5). In particular it is recommended that activities which may affect foraging habitat within 25 km of major Gray Bat caves should be carefully examined and modified, if necessary, to protect the habitat (5). In general, however, it appears that much of the foraging habitat in the bat's major population centres (the Ozark and Appalachian regions) has not as yet been seriously modified by man's activities and it is thought that the bat should be capable of holding its own if protected from disturbance of roosts (5).

CAPTIVE BREEDING No information.

REMARKS For description of animal see (1). Dr. Merlin D. Tuttle very kindly provided the information on which this data sheet is based.

REFERENCES   1.   Barbour, R.W. and Davis, W.H. (1969). Bats of America. Univ. Press of Kentucky, Lexington. 286 pp.
2.   Clarke, D.R. Jr., Laval, R.K. and Swineford, D.M. (1978). Dieldrin-induced mortality in an endangered species, the Gray Bat (Myotis grisescens). Science 199 (4335): 1357-1359.
3.   Guthrie, M.J. and Jeffers, K.R. (1938). A cytological study of the ovaries of the bats Myotis lucifugus and Myotis grisescens. J. Morph. 62: 528-557.
4.   Hall, J.S. and Wilson, N. (1966). Seasonal populations and movements of the Gray Bat in the Kentucky area. Amer. Midland Nat. 75: 317-324.
5.   Indiana Bat/Gray Bat Recovery Team (1980). Draft Gray Bat Recovery Plan.
6.   LaVal, R.K., Clawson, R.L,. LaVal, M.L. and Claire, W. (1977). Foraging behaviour and nocturnal activity patterns of the endangered bats Myotis grisescens and Myotis sodalis in Missouri. J. Mammal. 58(4): 592-599.
7.   Myers, R.F. (1964). Ecology of three species of myotine bats in the Ozark Plateau. Ph.D. dissertation. Univ. of Missouri. 210 pp.
8.   Tuttle, M.D. (1975). Population ecology of the Gray Bat (Myotis grisescens): Factors influencing early growth and development. Occ. Pap. Mus. Nat. Hist., Univ. Kans., No. 36, pp. 1-24.
9.   Tuttle, M.D. (1976). Population ecology of the Gray Bat (Myotis grisescens): Philopatry, timing and patterns of movement, weight loss during migration, and seasonal adaptive strategies. Occ. Pap. Mus. Nat. Hist., Univ. Kans., 54: 1-38.
10. Tuttle, M.D. (1976). Population ecology of the Gray Bat (Myotis grisescens): Factors influencing growth and survival of newly volant young. Ecology 57: 587-595.
11. Tuttle, M.D. and Stevenson, D.E. (1977). An analysis of migration as a mortality factor in the Gray Bat based on public recoveries of banded bats. Amer. Midland Nat. 97: 235-240.
12. Tuttle, M.D. (1977). Gating as a means of protecting cave dwelling bats. In Aley, T. and Rhodes, D. (Eds), National

Cave Management Symposium Proceedings, 1976. Speleobooks, Albuquerque, N.M. Pp. 77-82.

13. Tuttle, M.D. (1979). Status, causes of decline, and management of endangered Gray Bats. J. Wildl. Manage. 43 (1): 1-17.

Lasiurus cinereus semotus (Peale & Beauvois, 1796)

Order   CHIROPTERA   Family   VESPERTILIONIDAE

SUMMARY   Occurs only in the Hawaiian Islands, principally on the islands of Hawaii and Kauai. No precise information exists on present status but believed threatened by habitat loss. Protected by the 1973 Endangered Species Act and occurs in the Hawaii Volcanoes National Park. Studies are needed to learn more of its distribution, status and habits.

DISTRIBUTION   U.S.A. where it is restricted to the Hawaiian Islands (2,4,5,6,7,9). Major populations occur on the islands of Hawaii and Kauai (7). It is not known whether there is regular interchange between these two, over the stepping-stone islands in between (5,7,9). Bats are occasionally reported on Oahu and Maui but it is not known whether they are resident. No specific records exist for Molokai, Lanai and all the other smaller islands (4,7,10).

POPULATION   Numbers unknown but in 1981 P. Quentin Tomich considered it to be threatened because of past habitat loss and the threat of future losses (10). However the taxon is non-social, has a scattered population, and may appear rarer than it actually is. Walker in 1981 travelled round the Hawaiian Islands and discussed the status of the bat with the State field biologists on each island (12). Most of them related that they saw the taxon only occasionally but that they had made no concerted effort to determine status and/or distribution. Bats were reported 'common enough' on Kauai at all elevations and in a variety of habitats and as such were not considered 'Endangered' there (12). (Kramer mentions that records he has collected indicate bats appear on Kauai only during the months from August to December (4)). In 1974 Tomich reported that the total was probably a few thousand (9). He mentioned that only on Hawaii had extended efforts been made to assess the taxons abundance and distribution, and the available data suggested that stable numbers had existed on the island at least since the 1940s (9).

HABITAT AND ECOLOGY   Able to utilize a variety of habitats - from natural forests to agricultural land (9). Typically solitary, tree-roosting, occasionally recorded singly from rock crevices and buildings. Has been reported from sea level to 4000 m but believed most common up to 1200 m (1,4). Baldwin noted that it apparently preferred habitats of either open or mixed character and that bats living along the coast consistently ventured out over the open ocean (1,4). The species as a whole is strongly migratory but it is not known if the Hawaiian subspecies has lost this instinct (4,5,9). Insectivorous, and in upland regions forages solitarily in woodland clearings, open land at forest edges, or small glades in parks etc. in or near towns (9). These sites seem to be used habitually. Occasionally bats are attracted to insects that come to street lights, and will also feed high in the air in the open, over pasture or sugarcane fields, especially if the air is still (9). Some summer foraging in maturing Macadamia nut (Macadamia integrifolia) plantations has been recorded (10). As weather cools bats accumulate fat, adding 20-25% to body weight, and suggesting hibernation although no record of this is known (5,9). Two young are produced, between May and July, and are carried by the mother until almost full-grown (4,9).

THREATS TO SURVIVAL   Loss of habitat, especially native forest has been, and is, probably the greatest threat, but may be compensated, at least locally, in use of the now maturing Macadamia nut orchards (10). There is no evidence that the bat is utilized or traded in, although there are occasionally rumours that it is shot for 'recreation' (9).

CONSERVATION MEASURES TAKEN Listed as an Endangered Species by the U.S. Fish and Wildlife Service, giving complete Federal as well as State of Hawaii protection, plus some habitat protection (3,11). Walker, Chief Wildlife Biologist of the Division of Forestry and Wildlife, State of Hawaii reported in 1980 that plans for study of the bat are 'low key' and no immediate management actions are comtemplated until much more is known (12). The taxon ranges sparingly throughout the Hawaii Volcanoes National Park (9).

CONSERVATION MEASURES PROPOSED Any conservation action must await studies of status and distribution. Although preservation of native forest would seem necessary for the animal's survival. Tomich notes that preservation of even small tracts of native forest of a 100 ha or so at strategically located sites could provide enough support to maintain small local populations of the bat (9).

CAPTIVE BREEDING None.

REMARKS This subspecies is smaller and more reddish that the continental form, for description see (4,5,7,9). The species as a whole also occurs in North, Central and South America. It is strongly migratory and regularly reaches the Farallon Islands off California, the Bermudas, and the Galapagos Islands (2,5,7,9). Specimens have also been captured in Iceland (7). The Hawaiian population is derived from one or more chance arrivals that flew, probably aided by strong winds, the 3500 km from the Americas, possibly tens of thousands of years ago, and in their prolonged isolation have differentiated slightly from the continental populations (4,5,7,9). This bat and the 'Endangered' Hawaiian Monk Seal (Monachus schauinslandi) were the only mammals that preceded man to Hawaii (7,9). This account was compiled with the help of Dr. P. Quentin Tomich, Ronald L. Walker, and Ernest Kosaka.

REFERENCES   1. Baldwin, P.H. (1950). Occurrence and behaviour of the Hawaiian Bat. J. Mammal. 31 (4): 455-456.
2. Hall, E.R. and Kelson, K.R. (1959). Mammals of North America. Ronald Press, New York.
3. Kosaka, E. (1980). In litt.
4. Kramer, R.J. (1971). Hawaiian Land Mammals. Charles E. Tuttle Company, Rutland, Vermont and Tokyo.
5. Tomich, P.Q. (1965). The Hoary Bat in Hawaii. The Elepaio. J. Hawaii Audubon Soc. 25(11): 85-86.
6. Tomich, P.Q. (1969). Mammals in Hawaii. Bishop Museum Press, Honolulu.
7. Tomich, P.Q. (1972). Mammals. In Armstrong, R.W. (Ed.), Atlas of Hawaii. Univ. Press of Hawaii. 222pp.
8. Tomich, P.Q. (1972). Rare and endangered fish and wildlife of the United States. US Dept. Interior Fish and Wildlife Service Resources Publ. 34.
9. Tomich, P.Q. (1974). The Hawaiian Hoary Bat: Daredevil of the Volcanoes. National Parks and Conservation Magazine 48 (2): 10-13.
10. Tomich, P.Q. (1981). In litt.
11. United States Congress. (1973). Public Law 93-205 93rd Congress, S. 1983, Dec. 28 1973. U.S. Government Printing Office Washington D.C. 21p.
12. Walker, R.L. (1980). In litt.

Plecotus townsendii ingens (Handley, 1959)

Order   CHIROPTERA   Family   VESPERTILIONIDAE

SUMMARY Known from only a few caves in the States of Arkansas, Oklahoma and Missouri, U.S.A. Numbered perhaps only in hundreds. First nursery colony was located in 1978 in Arkansas. Extremely intolerant of disturbance which causes it to desert favourite roosts. Listed as endangered on the 1973 U.S. Endangered Species List. A study was begun in 1978 in Arkansas to determine the distribution, status, and ecology of bats in the State including this species; information is required on its status in Missouri and Oklahoma. Greater protection of cave sites from disturbance is needed.

DISTRIBUTION United States, where known from caves in a few localities in northwestern and north central Arkansas, southwestern Missouri and eastern Oklahoma (2,8,9).

POPULATION Total numbers unknown. In the mid-1970s the U.S. Fish and Wildlife Service estimated the total to be less than 100 (5,10) but recent discoveries of colonies indicate it may be more abundant than previously thought (6,9). In 1981 Harvey reported that about 500 were known to occur in Arkansas, including 420 hibernating individuals in one cave (7). In 1978 the first maternity colony, comprising ca. 120 bats, was found in Marion County, north-central Arkansas (6,7,9,10). Numbers in Missouri and Oklahoma are unknown, as is the population trend. The taxon is considered endangered by the U.S. Fish and Wildlife Service (12).

HABITAT AND ECOLOGY Inhabits caves throughout the year (8,9); studies indicating a preference for relatively cold areas (4°C to 9°C) for hibernation (9). The Ozark Mountains are mainly mixed hardwood forest, and caves are numerous throughout the region (6). Usually only one young is born and that in early summer (2).

THREATS TO SURVIVAL Very intolerant of human disturbance, known to vacate caves if disturbed during hibernation (1,4,5,12,13). Loss of habitat, increased visitation of hibernacula and nursery caves, and vandalism have likely been influential in the demise of the taxon (5).

CONSERVATION MEASURES TAKEN Listed by the U.S. Fish and Wildlife Service and the Arkansas Game and Fish Commission as endangered (8,12,13). The Arkansas Game and Fish Commission and the National Park Service began in 1978 a study of the distribution, status, and ecology of endangered bats in Arkansas including this taxon. It is hoped the results of the study will lead to protection of 'Critical Habitat' for endangered bat species in the State (6). Continuing efforts to locate additional colonies are being made so that management plans can be formulated and implemented for the protection and recovery of this and other bat taxa in Arkansas (8).

CONSERVATION MEASURES PROPOSED Greater protection is advocated for caves housing hibernating and maternity colonies, and especially needed are gates at the entrances of such caves (6).

CAPTIVE BREEDING None.

REMARKS For description of animal see (1,2). The species as a whole ranges from British Columbia south to Mexico (excluding Baja California) and east to West Virginia (2) and is not considered threatened. One other subspecies, the Virginia Big-eared bat, Plecotus townsendii virginianus is listed in the IUCN Red Data Book. This account was compiled with the help of Dr. Michael J. Harvey, who has been studying the species in Arkansas.

REFERENCES
1. Barbour, R.W. and Davis, W.H. (1969). Bats of America. Univ. Press of Kentucky. Lexington.
2. Hall, E.R. and Kelson, K.R. (1959). Mammals of North America. Ronald Press, Co., New York.
3. Handley, C.O. Jr. (1959). A revision of American bats of the genera Euderma and Plecotus. Proc. U.S. Nat. Mus. 110: 95-246.
4. Harvey, M.J. (1975). Endangered Chiroptera of the southeastern United States. Proc. 29th Ann. Conf. S.E. Assoc. Game and Fish Commissioners 1975. 29: 429-433.
5. Harvey, M.J. (1976). Status of endangered bats in the eastern United States. Proc. 1976 Nat. Speleol. Soc. Ann. Convention 1976: 21-24.
6. Harvey, M.J. (1978). Status of the endangered bats Myotis sodalis, M. grisescens and Plecotus townsendii ingens in the southern Ozarks. In Wilson, D.E. and Gardner, A.L. (Eds), Proc. 5th Int. Bat. Res. Conf. Texas Tech. Press, Lubbock, Texas.
7. Harvey, M.J. (1980). In litt.
8. Harvey, M.J., Cassidy, J.J. and O'Hagan, G.G. (1979). Status of the endangered bats, Myotis sodalis, M. grisescens and Plecotus townsendii ingens, in Arkansas. Arkansas Acad. Sci. Proc. 33: 81.
9. Harvey, M.J., Kennedy, M.L. and McDaniel, V.R. (1978). Status of the endangered Ozark Big-eared bat (Plecotus townsendii ingens) in Arkansas. Arkansas Acad. Sci. Proc. 32: 89-90.
10. Sealander, J.A., Jr (1972). Rare and endangered fish and wildlife of the United States. U.S. Dept. Interior Fish and Wildlife Service Resource Publ. 34.
11. U.S.D.I. (1973). Threatened wildlife of the United States. U.S. Dept. Interior. Resource Pub. 114. 280p.
12. U.S.D.I. (1977). Two bat species proposed for endangered List. U.S. Dept. Interior, Fish and Wildlife Service New Release Dec. 2 1979.
13. U.S.D.I. (1979). Listing of Virginia and Ozark Big-eared Bats as endangered species, and critical habitat determination; final rule. Federal Register 44 (232): 69206-69208.

VIRGINIA BIG-EARED BAT

ENDANGERED

Plecotus townsendii virginianus (Handley, 1959)

Order   CHIROPTERA

Family   VESPERTILIONIDAE

SUMMARY   Cave-dwelling species found in eastern Kentucky, western Virginia and eastern West Virginia U.S.A. Less than 5000 estimated to survive in 1979 and numbers are apparently declining with many caves being abandoned. Intolerant of human disturbance. Listed as endangered under the U.S. Endangered Species Act of 1973. Protection of important cave sites vital.

DISTRIBUTION   Eastern United States, in the Appalachian region where it occurs in three separate populations centred in Lee County, eastern Kentucky, southwestern Virginia and eastern West Virginia in Pendleton and Tucker counties (3,4,6,10).

POPULATION   In late 1980 there were estimated to be about 1500 hibernating bats in Kentucky (7) with a 1979 estimate of 2500 to 3000 in West Virginia and 'no more than a few hundred' in Virginia (10). Numbers are reported to be declining (5,6,10); since the early 1960s at least five wintering colonies in West Virginia, have disappeared. Only three nursery colonies are known to remain in West Virginia and one in Kentucky, the latter containing fewer than 500 bats by 1979 (10). Listed as endangered by the U.S. Fish and Wildlife Service in 1979 (10). The taxon has a limited range and is highly susceptible to changes in its habitat, even minor disturbance or physical changes in the caves occupied may result in abandonment (10).

HABITAT AND ECOLOGY   Inhabits caves all year round and occasionally found in buildings in summer. Hibernation requires temperatures of 12°C or less (but generally above freezing) (1,5,6). Some caves may be used both summer and winter; summer colonies are usually smaller and are maternity colonies of a few to 100+ individuals (6). Usually only one young is born, in early summer (3).

THREATS TO SURVIVAL   Colonies are very intolerant of disturbance being reputedly among the wariest of bats and if disturbed will readily abandon the cave site (1,3,4,5,10). Gates placed at cave entrances to deter disturbance have been broken down and bats found dead. Loss of habitat may also be a contributory factor in decline (6).

CONSERVATION MEASURES TAKEN   In 1979 Listed as endangered on the U.S. Endangered Species List (9). Five caves in West Virginia have been determined as 'Critical Habitat', and thus all Federal Agencies are obliged by law to ensure that actions authorized, funded or carried out by them do not result in the destruction or adverse modification of this habitat. The National Speleological Society has a moratorium on visits to a cave which houses a colony of almost 1000 bats (5,9); but this has proved insufficient in preventing vandals entering the gated cave system (9).

CONSERVATION MEASURES PROPOSED   Protection from disturbance of important cave sites is the principal requirement.

CAPTIVE BREEDING   None.

REMARKS   For description of animal see (1). The species as a whole ranges from British Columbia in Canada south to Mexico (excluding Baja California) and east to West Virginia (3) and is not considered threatened. One other subspecies, the Ozark Big-eared Bat Plecotus townsendii ingens is listed in the IUCN Red Data Book. This account was compiled with the help of Dr. Michael J. Harvey.

REFERENCES

1. Barbour, R.W. and Davis, W.H. (1969). Bats of America. Univ. Press of Kentucky, Lexington.

2. Conrad, L.G. (1961). Distribution and speciation problems concerning the long-eared bat, Plecotus townsendii virginianus. D. C. Speleograph 17: 49-52.

3. Hall, E.R. and Kelson, K.R. (1959). Mammals of North America. Ronald Press Co., New York.

4. Harvey, M.J. (1976). Virginia Big-eared Bat. In Hillestad, H.O. (Ed.), Endangered and threatened vertebrates of the southeast. Tall Timbers Res. Sta. Bull.

5. Harvey, M.J. (1976). Status of endangered bats in the eastern United States. Proc. 1976 Nat. Speleol. Soc. Ann. Convention 1976: 21-24.

6. Harvey, M.J. (1976). Endangered chiroptera of the southeastern United States. Proc. 29th Ann. Conf. S.E. Assoc. Game and Fish Commissioners 1975. 29: 429-433.

7. Harvey, M.J. (1980). In litt.

8. Rippy, C.L. and Harvey, J.M. (1965). Notes on Plecotus townsendii virginianus in Kentucky. J. Mammal. 46 (3): 499.

9. U.S.D.I. (1977). Two bat species proposed for endangered list. U.S. Dept. of the Interior, Fish and Wildlife Service News Release Dec. 2 1977.

10. U.S.D.I. (1979). Listing of Virginian and Ozark Big-eared Bats as endangered species, and critical habitat determination; final rule. Federal Register 44 (232): 69206-69208.

BUFFY-HEADED MARMOSET

ENDANGERED

Callithrix flaviceps (Thomas, 1903)

Order   PRIMATES   Family   CALLITRICHIDAE

SUMMARY Endemic to a very small area of southeastern Brazil where much of the forest has already been destroyed. Numbers unknown but certainly very few. Protected in two reserves, included on the Brazilian Endangered Species List and a captive breeding programme is planned. Effectively protected reserves will be essential to its continued survival in the wild.

DISTRIBUTION Southeastern Brazil. Reduced to fragmented populations in Espirito Santo and eastern Minas Gerais (8). Its occurrence in the latter was confirmed in November 1979 when it was observed on the Fazenda Montes Claros, a private farm owned by Sr Feliciano Miguel Abdala and situated on the Caratinga - Ipanema road, 58 km from Caratinga. This record extends its known range some 125 km to the west and 115 km to the north of the two nearest Espirito Santo localities (Santa Teresa and Guacui) (4,8,14). Previously known only from a very small area in the mountains of southern Espirito Santo at altitudes over 400 m (1,2,3,4,11,13,14). For map see (4,11,14).

POPULATION Numbers unknown, but considered endangered because of extensive habitat loss (5,8,10). Mittermeier et al, based on 1979/80 surveys, report that much of its habitat has already been destroyed, and remaining groups in isolated forest patches cannot be considered viable populations (10). Highest numbers occur in the Nova Lombardia Biological Reserve in Espirito Santo (10), plus about 20, perhaps as many as 50, on the Fazenda Montes Claros (8,9,10,14). These two areas will probably be the last strongholds of the species and provided they remain effectively protected will allow the continued survival of the animal (10). Ruschi considered it to be threatened even in the mid-1950s (12).

HABITAT AND ECOLOGY Mountainous forests above 400 m (3,8). All sightings of _C. flaviceps_ in Montes Claros were in edge habitats, mainly along roads, and the animals range from the understorey at about 3 m to the upper part of the canopy at about 30 m (14). _Callithrix_ species live in monogamous family groups (8,11). Diet consists mainly of fruit, tree exudates and insects (7,8). Gestation period is 140-150 days. Normally two young are born, occasionally one or three. The male takes a major part in carrying and caring for the infants (11).

THREATS TO SURVIVAL Forest destruction throughout its very limited range has already eliminated much of its habitat (7,8,10,14). Any commercial exploitation of the animal itself would be disastrous (6). Since the 1800s the Atlantic coastal forests of eastern Brazil have suffered a tremendous increase in human population and widespread, largely uncontrolled forest destruction to make way for coffee plantations, sugar cane, cocoa, eucalyptus, cattle pasture and above all lumber extraction and charcoal production. In recent years industrial development has also taken its toll. As a result the forests have been devastated, especially during the rapid development and economic expansion from the 1960s onwards. Only a tiny fraction of the original forest cover remains (10,14).

CONSERVATION MEASURES TAKEN Listed in Appendix 1 of the 1973 Convention on International Trade in Endangered Species of Wild Fauna and Flora; trade in it between acceding nations is therefore subject to severe restriction, trade for primarily commercial purposes banned. Included on the Brazilian Endangered Species List (7,10). Protected in the Biological Reserve of Nova

Lombardia (4350 ha) and on the privately owned Fazenda Montes Claros (1000 ha); may also occur in Caparao National Park (10,435 ha) but this is unconfirmed (7,8,10). Mittermeier et al made preliminary surveys of this animal in 1979/80 as part of a general study of the status and conservation of eastern Brazilian primates (10).

CONSERVATION MEASURES PROPOSED The IUCN/SSC Primate Specialist Group made the following recommendations in 1980: i) investigate the presence of C. flaviceps in Caparao National Park; ii) conduct rescue operations to remove isolated groups from remnant tracts of forest slated for destruction; iii) establish a captive colony, iv) encourage Brazilian students to conduct ecological studies in both Nova Lombardia and Montes Claros; facilities exist at both sites and students could be supported at minimal expense (10); v) urge that the privately protected Fazenda Montes Claros be made into a National Biological Reserve or an Ecological Station so that it can be preserved into the future. (The area also contains the critically endangered Brachyteles arachnoides) (8,9,14).

CAPTIVE BREEDING As of 1980 there were none in captivity, however the Rio de Janeiro Primate Centre has experience with them and is planning a breeding programme. It is thought they will breed well in captivity (10).

REMARKS For description of animal see (3,11,14). Some authorities consider flaviceps to be a subspecies of Callithrix jacchus (4,11). This data sheet has been compiled with the assistance of Dr. R.A. Mittermeier, Chairman of the IUCN/SSC Primate Specialist Group and Dr. A.F. Coimbra-Filho.

REFERENCES 1. Coimbra-Filho, A.F. (1971). Os saguis do genero Callithrix da regiao oriental brasileira e um caso de duplo-hibridismo entre tres de suas formas (Callithricidae, Primates). Rev. Brasil Biol. 31: 377-388.
2. Coimbra-Filho, A.F. (1972). Mamiferos ameacados de extincao no Brasil. In Especies de Fauna Brasileira Ameacadas de Extincao. Academia Brasileira de Ciencias, Rio de Janeiro. Pp. 13-98.
3. Coimbra-Filho, A.F. and Mittermeier, R.A. (1973). New data on the taxonomy of the Brazilian marmosets of the genus Callithrix Erxleben, 1777. Folia Primat. 20: 241-264.
4. Hershkovitz, P. (1977). Living New World Monkeys (Platyrrhini) with an introduction to Primates, Vol.1. Univ. of Chicago Press, Chicago and London.
5. Kleiman, D.C. (1976). Meeting held: the biology and conservation of the Callitrichidae. Lab. Primate Newsletter 15(1): 5.
6. Mittermeier, R.A. (1976). Preliminary assessment of the conservation status of New World Monkeys. Unpd. Report. 6 pp.
7. Mittermeier, R.A. (1977-81). In litt.
8. Mittermeier, R.A., Coimbra-Filho, A.F. and Constable, I.D. (1980). Range extension for an endangered marmoset. Oryx 15(4): 380-383.
9. Mittermeier, R.A. and Constable, I.D. (1980). Fazenda Montes Claros and its importance for the conservation of endangered southeastern Brazilian Primates. Unpd. Report.
10. Mittermeier, R.A., Coimbra-Filho, A.F. and Constable I.D. (1980). Conservation of Eastern Brazilian Primates. WWF Project 1614. Report for the period 1979/80.
11. Napier, P.H. (1976). Catalogue of Primates in the British Museum (Natural History). Part 1: Families Callitrichidae

and Cebidae. British Museum (Natural History), London.

12. Ruschi, A. (1954). Algumas especies zoologicas e botanicas em vias de extincao no Espirito Santo. Bol. Mus. Biol. Prof. Mello Leitao, Prot. Nat. 16A: 1-45.

13. Vieira, C.C. (1955). Lista remissiva dos mamiferos do Brasil. Arq. Zool. Sao Paulo 8: 341-474.

14. Coimbra-Filho, A.F., Mittermeier, R.A. and Constable, I.D. (1981). Callithrix flaviceps (Thomas, 1903) recorded from Minas Gerais, Brazil (Callitrichidae, Primates). Rev. Brasil. Biol. 41(1): 141-147.

Callithrix argentata leucippe (Thomas, 1922)

Order   PRIMATES   Family   CALLITRICHIDAE

SUMMARY   Very restricted distribution in Brazilian Amazonia. Numbers unknown. Threatened by loss of habitat. The Trans-Amazonian Highway cuts right through its small range. Captive breeding programmes and a reserve or national park are needed.

DISTRIBUTION   Brazil. Occurs in a very small area of Brazilian Amazonia between the Rio Jamanxim and the Rio Cupari, east bank tributaries of the Rio Tapajos (2,4).

POPULATION   Total numbers unknown (6). Mittermeier reports this subspecies to be definitely 'Vulnerable' and possibly 'Endangered' (3,5,6).

HABITAT AND ECOLOGY   Tropical rainforest (6). This subspecies has been observed in small groups of two to four animals (4). Diurnal and arboreal. Callithrix species live in monogamous family groups (7). Diet consists mainly of tree exudates, fruit and insects (6). Gestation period is 140-150 days. Normally two young are born; the male does most of the carrying and caring for the infants (7).

THREATS TO SURVIVAL   Habitat loss. The small range of this subspecies is bisected by the Trans-Amazonian Highway and is being subjected to much clear-felling to make way for cattle ranches. When Mittermeier was in the area in 1973, habitat destruction was already underway; it has undoubtedly increased since then and if it continues the survival of this race will be in jeopardy (4,5,6).

CONSERVATION MEASURES TAKEN   Included in Appendix 2 of the 1973 Convention on International Trade in Endangered Species of Wild Fauna and Flora; trade in the subspecies between acceding nations is therefore subject to regulation and monitoring of its effects.

CONSERVATION MEASURES PROPOSED   A reserve or national park within the range of C. a. leucippe is essential and would also benefit Chiropotes albinasus, another Red Data Book species, as well as other primate species. The Trans-Amazonian Highway and associated development will make this difficult (6) but not necessarily impossible.

CAPTIVE BREEDING   As of March 1981 there were none in captivity; however captive breeding of C. a. argentata and C. a. melanura is successful and there is no reason to suppose this taxon should differ (6). A captive breeding programme is planned at the Rio de Janeiro Primate Centre (6).

REMARKS   For description of animal see (1,2,7). Callithrix argentata is found south of the Amazon between the Rio Tapajos and the Tocantins-Araguaia, as far as the points where the Rio Tacuari and Rio Mamore, respectively, flow along or across the border of northern and southern Bolivia (4). Two other subspecies are recognized: C. a. argentata which is found between the Rio Tapajos and the Tocantins-Araguaia, its southwestern limit the Rio Cupari, a right bank tributary of the Tapajos (1), and does not appear to be in any danger at the present time (3,5); and C. a. melanura with a large range to the south of C. a. argentata (3), inhabiting the drier and cooler region of central Brazil, to the west of the Rio

Araguaia (Mato Grosso), and also adjacent parts of Bolivia as far the Rio Beni (1); there is no information on its current status, but much of its range is uninhabited and it is probably common (3,5). Callithrix spp. appear to survive well in close proximity to man and are usually not hunted for food (4). This data sheet has been compiled with the assistance of Dr. R.A. Mittermeier, Chairman of the IUCN/SSC Primate Specialist Group.

REFERENCES   1.   Coimbra-Filho, A.F. and Mittermeier, R.A. (1973). New data on the taxonomy of the Brazilian marmosets of the genus Callithrix Erxleben, 1777. Folio primat. 20: 241-264.
2.   Hershkovitz, P. (1977). Living New World Monkeys (Platyrrhini). With an Introduction to Primates. Vol.1. The Univ. of Chicago Press, Chicago and London.
3.   Mittermeier, R.A. (1976). Preliminary assessment of the conservation status of New World monkeys. Unpd. Report. 6 pp.
4.   Mittermeier, R.A. and Coimbra-Filho, A.F. (1977). Primate Conservation in Brazilian Amazonia. In Prince Rainier and Bourne, G. (Eds), Primate Conservation. Acad. Press, New York.
5.   Mittermeier, R.A., Coimbra-Filho, A.F. and Roosmalen, M.G.M. van (1978). Callitrichids in Brazil and the Guianas: Current conservation status and potential for biomedical research. Prim. Med. 10: 20-29.
6.   Mittermeier, R.A. (1981). In litt.
7.   Napier, P.H. (1976). Catalogue of Primates in the British Museum (Natural History), Part 1: Families Callitrichidae and Cebidae. British Museum (Natural History), London.

BUFFY-TUFTED-EAR MARMOSET

ENDANGERED

Callithrix aurita (E. Geoffroy, 1812)

Order   PRIMATES   Family   CALLITRICHIDAE

SUMMARY   Southeastern Brazil, where it has an extremely small range and is considered endangered because of extensive habitat destruction. Not listed on the Brazilian Endangered Species List, and has disappeared from two national parks, perhaps because of epidemics. Thus far, the only adequately protected population located during the course of survey work has been in the privately protected Fazenda Barreiro Rico in Sao Paulo. Survival will depend on effective reserves.

DISTRIBUTION   Southeastern Brazil where it once occurred in southeastern Sao Paulo, western Rio de Janiero, and adjacent parts of Minas Gerais but has now disappeared from most of this area (6).

POPULATION   Numbers unknown. In 1980 the IUCN/SSC Primate Specialist Group considered it 'Endangered' because of extensive habitat loss (6), they believed its long term survival would depend on its status in the parks and reserves of coastal Sao Paulo, and these remain to be investigated. Populations in the two known protected areas were thought probably inadequate to ensure survival (6).

HABITAT AND ECOLOGY   Forests of Atlantic coastlands (6), at high altitudes in Rio de Janeiro; in both mountains and lowlands in Sao Paulo; and at low altitudes in Minas Gerais (1). Callithrix species live in monogamous family groups (7). Diet consists of fruit, tree exudates and insects (4). Gestation period is 140-150 days. Two young are the norm and the male plays a major part in carrying and caring for the infants (7).

THREATS TO SURVIVAL   Forest destruction has already destroyed most of its habitat. Since the 1800s the Atlantic coastal forests of eastern Brazil have suffered a tremendous increase in human population and widespread, largely uncontrolled forest destruction to make way for plantations of coffee, sugar cane, cocoa, and eucalyptus, also cattle pasture and above all lumber extraction and charcoal production. In recent years industrial development has also taken its toll. As a result the forests have been devastated, especially during the rapid development and economic expansion of the 1960s onwards. Only a tiny fraction of the original forest cover remains (5,6).

CONSERVATION MEASURES TAKEN   Listed in Appendix 1 of the 1973 Convention on International Trade in Endangered Species of Wild Fauna and Flora and traffic in it is therefore subject to severe restriction by signatory nations including a ban on trade for primarily commercial purposes. It is nevertheless, not yet included in the Brazilian endangered species list. Surveys in 1979/80 found it to occur in only two protected areas - the privately owned Fazenda Barreiro Rico in Sao Paulo, and the Estacao Experimental de Mogi-Gaucu, a tiny 50 ha forest belonging to the Institute Florestal of the State of Sao Paulo. The latter has one, possibly two, groups but is too small an area to be of any long-term significance to conservation (6). The species has apparently gone extinct in two national parks -- Serra dos Orgaos (10,000 ha) and Itatiaia (11,943 ha) -- in which it once definitely occurred. The reasons are unknown but the cause may possibly have been a series of epidemics (6). It may still exist in the Serra da Bocaina National Park on the Rio-Sao Paulo border (100,000 ha), and in the Jacupiranga and Carlos Botelho State Reserves but confirmation is needed (6).

CONSERVATION MEASURES PROPOSED Inclusion in Brazil's Endangered Species List. The IUCN/SSC Primate Specialist Group made the following recommendations in 1980: i) conduct surveys in the parks, reserves and experimental stations of Sao Paulo, especially in Serra da Bocaina N.P. and Jacupiranga and Carlos Botelho State Reserves; ii) establish a captive colony, iii) encourage a Brazilian student to conduct an ecological study at Fazenda Barreiro Rico (6).

CAPTIVE BREEDING In 1979 there were two males and two females (all captive bred) held in two zoo collections (8). Captive breeding is planned at the Rio de Janeiro Primate Centre (6). However additional captive breeding stocks are needed (6). Callithrix is an easy genus to breed in captivity (4).

REMARKS Some authorities treat C. aurita as a subspecies of Callithrix jacchus (2,7) but for distinctions see (1,3). This data sheet was compiled from information supplied by Dr. A.F. Coimbra-Filho and Dr. R.A. Mittermeier, Chairman of the IUCN/SSC Primate Specialist Group.

REFERENCES
1. Coimbra-Filho, A.F. and Mittermeier, R.A. (1973). New data on the taxonomy of the Brazilian marmosets of the genus Callithrix Erxleben, 1777. Folia primat. 20: 241-264.
2. Hershkovitz, P. (1968). Metachromism or the principle of evolutionary change in mammalian tegumentary colors. Evolution 22: 556-575.
3. Hershkovitz, P. (1977). Living New World Monkeys (Platyrrhini) with an introduction to Primates, Vol.1. Univ. of Chicago Press, Chicago and London.
4. Mittermeier, R.A. (1977-81). In litt.
5. Mittermeier, R.A., Coimbra-Filho, A.F. and van Roosmalen, M.G.M. (1977). Callitrichids in Brazil and Guianas: Conservation status and potential for biomedical research. In Marmosets in Experimental Medicine. Karger, Basel.
6. Mittermeier, R.A., Coimbra-Filho, A.F. and Constable I.D. (1980). Conservation of eastern Brazilian Primates. WWF Project 1614. Report for the period 1979/80.
7. Napier, P.H. (1976). Catalogue of Primates in the British Museum (Natural History). Part 1: Families Callitrichidae and Cebidae. British Museum (Natural History), London.
8. Olney, P.J.S. (Ed.) (1980). International Zoo Yearbook 20. Zool. Soc. London.

Callithrix humeralifer (E. Geoffroy, 1812)

Order   PRIMATES   Family   CALLITRICHIDAE

SUMMARY   The three races of this species have restricted distributions on the south bank of the Amazon between the Rios Madeira and Tapajos in Brazil, and are highly vulnerable to habitat destruction within their small ranges.   Anthony Rylands began studies on C. h. intermedius in 1978 and has reviewed the status of the whole species.   Adequately protected reserves are the main requirement for the species conservation.

DISTRIBUTION   Brazil. Between the Rio Madeira and the Rio Tapajos, south bank tributaries of the Amazon.   Of the three subspecies recognised, C. h. humeralifer occurs between the Rio Tapajos and the Rio Canuma extending south as far as Vila Braga.   The southern limit is not exactly known but is certainly not below 10°S.   C. h. chrysoleuca is found between the Rio Canuma and the Rio Madeira - Aripuana.   The southernmost record is Prainha, a short distance north of the mouth of the Rio Roosevelt on the east bank of the Rio Aripuana, but the animal may range as far as the headwaters of the Rio Canuma.   C. h. intermedius occurs between the Rio Roosevelt and the Rio Aripuana probably extending south to the headwaters of the Rios Aripuana and Guariba (1,7,9,10).   For distribution map see (1,7,10).

POPULATION   No estimates of numbers have been made.   In 1981 Rylands summarised the status of the species as: C. h. humeralifer: possibly vulnerable; C. h. chrysoleuca: vulnerable; C. h. intermedius: very restricted range of which more than half was destined for development (9).

HABITAT AND ECOLOGY   Rylands observed C. h. intermedius in dense primary forest, secondary growth, and low white sand forest.   Group size varied from 4 to 13, the larger groups comprised more than one adult pair.   Principal foods included small fruits, flowers, tree and liana exudates, insects, small frogs and lizards (7,8,10).   A pair of young are the norm after a gestation period of 140-150 days (5,7).

THREATS TO SURVIVAL   Habitat loss.   Amazonian Callithrix appear to survive well in close proximity to man and are usually not hunted for food (3).   However all three subspecies of C. humeralifer have very limited ranges so that habitat destruction could pose a major threat to their existence (2).   There has already been roadbuilding within the areas they occupy (4,7,9).   C. h. humeralifer in the north of its range is threatened by the Trombetas and Tapajos development programmes.   The region immediately west of the Rio Tapajos is threatened by development and habitat destruction along the Transamazonian Highway between Itaituba and Jacareacanga (9).   The range of C. h. chrysoleuca will be traversed by the planned Caceres - Manaus road and in the south is cut by the Transamazonian Highway.   In the north of its range near the Rio Amazonas there has already been considerable human colonisation which may increase in future due to the proximity of the Tapajos and Trombetas development programmes.   The Aripuana and Juruena development areas are close to its southern limits.   More than half the range of C. h. intermedius is covered by the Aripuana development area (9).

CONSERVATION MEASURES TAKEN   The species is listed in Appendix 2 of the 1973 Convention on International Trade in Endangered Species of Wild Fauna and Flora; so that trade in it between acceding nations is subject to regulation and monitoring of its effects. Protected by the 1967 Fauna Protection Law (4). C. h. humeralifer occurs in the Amazonia National Park, Para, but as yet there are no proposed reserves within the ranges of intermedius or chrysoleuca although it is possible that intermedius occurs in the Iqne-Aripuana Ecological Station to the south of its known range (7,8,9,10). Anthony Rylands began field studies on C. h. intermedius in May 1978 (7,8,9,10).

CONSERVATION MEASURES PROPOSED Adequately protected reserves are needed within the ranges of all three subspecies. Reserves on the Rios Canuma and upper Rio Tapajos would protect C. h. humeralifer and also the 'Vulnerable' Callithrix argentata leucippe as well as C. h. chrysoleuca. The latter would also benefit from an extension to the proposed Biological Reserve of Parintins, and from the establishment of reserves along the Transamazonica and Caceres-Manaus roadways and C. h. intermedius would be protected if reserves were sited in the region of the Serra das Oncas and at the mouths of the Rios Guariba and Roosevelt (9).

CAPTIVE BREEDING In 1979 there were three males in two zoo collections (6). Breeding colonies are to be set up in the Rio de Janeiro Primate Centre (4).

REMARKS For description of animal see (1,5,7). Anthony Rylands very kindly assisted with the compilation of this data sheet, and both he and Dr. R.A. Mittermeier, Chairman of the IUCN/SSC Primate Specialist Group commented on its final draft.

REFERENCES
1. Hershkovitz, P. (1977). Living New World Monkeys (Platyrrhini). With an Introduction to Primates Vol. 1. Univ. of Chicago Press, Chicago and London.
2. Hershkovitz, P. (1972). Notes on New World Monkeys. Int. Zoo Yb. Zool. Soc. London.
3. Mittermeier, R.A. and Coimbra-Filho, A.F. (1977). Primate conservation in Brazilian Amazonia. In Prince Rainier and Bourne, G. (Eds), Primate Conservation. Acad. Press, New York.
4. Mittermeier, R.A. (1977-81). In litt.
5. Napier, P.H. (1976). Catalogue of Primates in the British Museum (Natural History). Part 1: Families Callitrichidae and Cebidae. British Museum (Natural History), London.
6. Olney, P.J.S. (Ed.) (1980). International Zoo Yearbook 20. Zool. Soc. London.
7. Rylands, A.B. (1979). Observacoes preliminares sobre o sagui Callithrix humeralifer intermedius (Hershkovitz, 1977) em Dardanelos, Rio Aripuana, Mato Grosso. Acta Amazonica 9 (3): 589-602.
8. Rylands, A.B. (1980). In litt.
9. Rylands, A.B. (1981). Conservacao de primatas Amazonicos: Una analise de parques, reservas e propostas para conservacao na Amazonia. In Press Boleim Tecnico do Instituto Brasileiro de Desenvolvimento Florestal (IBDF).
10. Rylands, A.B. (1981). Preliminary field observations on the Marmoset, Callithrix humeralifer intermedius (Hershkovitz, 1977) at Dardanelos, Rio Aripuana, Mato Grosso. Primates 22(1): 46-59.

COTTON-TOP TAMARIN or PINCHE   ENDANGERED

Saguinus oedipus oedipus (Linnaeus, 1758)

Order   PRIMATES   Family   CALLITRICHIDAE

___

SUMMARY   Endemic to northwest Colombia. Total numbers unknown. Main threat is habitat destruction within its small range; also populations were probably seriously depleted by the animal trade between 1960 and 1975. Trade has been curbed, but loss of habitat to agriculture continues unabated. Protected by law and two reserves have been established in areas where the tamarin could occur. Total elimination of trade and the creation of properly protected reserves are urgently required to ensure its survival.

DISTRIBUTION   Northwest Colombia; between the Rio Atrato in the west, and the lower Rios Cauca and Magdalena in the east; in the Departments of Cordoba, Bolivar, Sucre, Atlantico, northwest Antioquia and northeast Choco (2,3,7). For map see (2,3). Southern limits in the Andes foothills are poorly known (13). Hershkovitz believes that the original distribution was similar to today's (5,7). However, Struhsaker et al have obtained reports of the tamarin's possible previous occurrence in areas east of the Magdalena (as yet unconfirmed (14)) and suggest that the apparent control of distribution by major rivers may only be an artifact of agricultural patterns that obscure the true former distribution, and S. oedipus may in fact be characteristic of the drier forests of all northernmost Colombia (4). Neyman has also received sightings reports from local Indians which suggest that the species' range is not continuous up to 500 m in the Andes foothills as previously thought. It seems S. oedipus may not inhabit steep riverine habitat, such as the upper River Sinu, but rather is confined to broader valleys, i.e. in forest on river-edge sedimentry deposits such as along the Manso River (4,11). This is compatable with Struhsaker et al's distributional theory and if correct is of consequence because it implies a smaller distributional area than previously assumed (11,13).

POPULATION   Total numbers unknown (3), not possible to provide an estimate since there is only limited knowledge of the state and extent of the remaining forest, much less the tamarin numbers contained in the various isolated forest remnants (3). In 1975 Neyman believed it unlikely that there were many forests large enough to maintain sufficient tamarins for a viable long-term breeding population (3).

HABITAT AND ECOLOGY   Deciduous forest in the northern part of its range to humid tropical forest in the Andes foothills (4,10,11). Altitudinal range from sea level to about 500 m (2,7). Survives well in secondary forests, and where this has recently replaced primary, some increase in numbers might even be temporarily expected (3). Average group size is unknown, but 11 groups observed by Neyman all numbered between 3 and 13 (3,10); groups appear territorial (3,10). Feeds on fruit, vines, epiphytes, insects, newly sprouting leaves or buds, leaves, leaf stems, and in one instance a frog (3,10). May also lick nectar or gather pollen or insects from certain flowers or fruits (3,10). Twins are the norm after a gestation of about 125-140 days (7).

THREATS TO SURVIVAL   Its range occupies an area that supported an extensive indigenous pre-Colombian human population, and is today a densely inhabited region. By 1966 at least 70% of the original forest cover in its original range had been replaced with pasture and farmland (3). By 1973/74 the more densely settled northern three-quarters of the area accounted for only about 5% of remaining forest, which was scattered in over 270 isolated tiny secondary forest patches. Some of these were known to lack tamarins even though they appeared to provide suitable habitat (3,4). In 1975 the future of these forest patches was described as at best uncertain, not only because wood and wildlife were constantly being extracted, but because in Colombia forested land not yielding cuttable timber is considered to be 'unexploited'. By law and custom such land may be colonised, a not uncommon event, and one which discourages private owners from maintaining naturally forested areas (3). The less accessible southern portions of the tamarin's range contain extensive forest tracts which were thought to contain the majority of remaining populations (3). However the 1973/74 studies documented widespread deforestation in the region and noted a great reduction in forest area compared to 1966, particularly in those foothills accessible by road (4). Even in remote areas such as the upper Sinu River, accessible only by river, a large proportion of riverine forest had already been cut or was secondary growth forest (11). Projected dam contruction along the Sinu in an area designated a reserve on 1976 Inderena maps will bring access by road and hasten the rate and permanency of deforestation (11,13). Neyman believed habitat destruction would continue at an even faster pace as the density of settlers increased. At best she considered it likely that any remaining forest would be reduced to tiny patches such as remain in the northern and central parts of the animal's range (3).

Capture of this tamarin for the pet trade and for biomedical research has undoubtedly taken its toll (3). Between 1968-72 nearly 14,000 Cotton-tops were imported to the U.S.A.; and it is likely that between 1960-1975 some 30,000-40,000 were exported from Colombia (2). The actual number taken from the wild is greater than these figures, since considerable mortality (3 to 33 per cent in marmosets (6)) undoubtedly occurs between capture and export, particularly as tamarins are delicate and difficult to maintain in captivity. Although the numbers exported were small compared to many other primates, they were large for an animal with such a restricted range (3).

CONSERVATION MEASURES TAKEN Saguinus oedipus including geoffroyi is listed in Appendix 1 of the 1973 Convention on International Trade in Endangered Species of Wild Fauna and Flora, so that trade in it between acceding nations is subject to strict control and trade for primarily commercial purposes banned. All exports of primates from Colombia has been banned since 1974. Prior to then a total ban on the export of Cotton-top tamarins from Colombia was in effect from 1969-1972, but in spite of the ban appreciable numbers (2500-3500 a year) entered the U.S.A. during this period (3). Regulations were amended in 1972 to allow permit holders to export 25 specimens, each, per month to satisfy the demands of biomedical research (1,2). In 1973 all export of primates from Colombia was banned, exceptions being temporarily made for scientific use until 1974 when all exports were halted (3). Two reserves have been established in areas where S. oedipus could occur (3). Patricia Neyman studied this tamarin between 1973-75 (3).

CONSERVATION MEASURES PROPOSED Several, properly protected reserves are urgently required within its range (3,9) and are considered of 'highest priority' in IUCN's Global Strategy for Primate Conservation (1981-1983). Any trade that still persists should be eliminated; other more abundant callitrichid species should be used in its place in biomedical research (3).

CAPTIVE BREEDING In 1979 there were at least 229 males, 219 females and 43 of undetermined sex held in 53 zoo collections, 224 captive bred (12).

REMARKS For description of animal see (7). Most authors consider the Panamanian tamarin a separate species S. geoffroyi (2). However both Hershkovitz and Napier consider geoffroyi to be a subspecies of S. oedipus (7,15). The generic name Oedipomidas is also sometimes used. S. o. geoffroyi is the only callitrichid endemic to Central America, its range extends from the Colombian Province of Choco north to Panama and a bordering part of Costa Rica (7); Dawson has made a study of this animal (16). It is not as yet considered threatened. Patricia Neyman who has studied S. o. oedipus very kindly assisted with the compilation of this data sheet; we are also grateful to Dr. G. Dawson for commenting about geoffroyi.

REFERENCES

1. Green, K.M. (1976). The nonhuman primate trade in Colombia. In Thorington, R.W. Jr. and Heltne, P.G. (Eds), Neotropical Primates: Field Studies and Conservation. National Acad. of Sciences, Washington D.C.

2. Hernandez-Camacho, J. and Cooper, R.W. (1976). The nonhuman primates of Colombia. In Thorington, R.W. Jr. and Heltne, P.G. (Eds), Neotropical Primates: Field Studies and Conservation. National Acad. of Sciences, Washington, D.C.

3. Neyman, P.F. (1978). Aspects of the ecology and social organization of free-ranging Cotton-top Tamarins (Saguinus oedipus), and the conservation status of the species. In Kleiman, D.G. (Ed.), The Biology and Conservation of the Callitrichidae. Smithsonian Institution Press, Washington, D.C.

4. Struhsaker, T.T., Glander, K., Chirivi, H., and Scott, N.J. (1975). A survey of primates and their habitats in Northern Colombia (May-August 1974). In Primate Censusing Studies in Peru and Colombia. Pan American Health Organisation, Washington, D.C.

5. Hershkovitz, P. (1949). Mammals of Northern Colombia. Preliminary Report No.4: Monkeys (Primates) with taxonomic revisions of some forms. Proc. U.S. Nat. Mus. 98: 323-427.

6. Thorington, R.W. Jr. (1972). Importation, breeding and mortality of New World Primates. Int. Zoo Yb 12: 18-23.

7. Hershkovitz, P. (1977). Living New World Monkeys (Platyrrhini). With an Introduction to Primates. Volume I. Univ. of Chicago Press, Chicago and London.

8. Muckenhirn, N.A. (1976). Addendum to the nonhuman primate trade in Colombia. In Thorington, R.W. Jr. and Heltne, P.G. (Eds), Neotropical Primates: Field Studies and Conservation. National Acad. of Sciences, Washington, D.C.

9. Heltne, P.G. and Thorington, R.W. Jr. (1976). Problems and potentials for primate biology and conservation in the New World. In Thorington, R.W. Jr. and Heltne, P.G. (Eds), Neotropical Primates: Field Studies and Conservation. National Acad. of Sciences, Washington, D.C.

10. Neyman, P.F. (1979). Ecology and social organization of the Cotton-top Tamarin (Saguinus oedipus). Ph.D Thesis, Univ. of California, Berkeley.

11. Neyman, P.F. (1977). Proteccion y manejo de los Primates de Sucre y Cordoba. Proyecto Primates Inderena - actividades adelantodas entre Junio y Septembre, 1977. Report to Inderena, Bogota, Colombia.

12. Olney, P.J.S. (Ed.) (1980). International Zoo Yearbook 20. Zool. Soc. London.

13. Neyman, P.F. (1981). In litt.

14. Hernandez-Camacho, J. (1981). Pers. comm.

15. Napier, P.H. (1976). Catalogue of Primates in the British Museum (Natural History) Part 1: Families Callitrichidae

and Cebidae. British Museum (Natural History), London.

16. Dawson, G.A. (1976). Behavioural ecology of the Panamanian Tamarin, _Saguinus_ _oedipus_ (Callitrichidae, Primates). Ph.D. Thesis. Michigan State Univ.

BARE-FACE TAMARIN

INDETERMINATE

Saguinus bicolor (Spix, 1823)

Order   PRIMATES

Family   CALLITRICHIDAE

SUMMARY   Restricted distribution in the State of Amazonas, Brazil. Three subspecies, of which S. b. bicolor is highly endangered by habitat destruction associated with the rapid growth of the city of Manaus. The other two subspecies are as yet poorly known. A study of the species began in 1980 with the aim of establishing reserves, captive breeding programmes and educational campaigns.

DISTRIBUTION   Northern Brazil where it occurs only in the State of Amazonas. Confined to the north bank of the Amazon, between the lower Rio Negro and the lower Rio Paru de Oeste or Cumina (= Erepecuru) (3). Three subspecies recognized: S. b. bicolor occurs in the vicinity of Manaus, between the lower Rio Negro and the lower Rio Uatuma (3). Initial surveys in 1980 recorded the animal east as far as the town of Itacoatiara and north at least 45 km along the Manaus-Boa Vista Road. It may well extend as far north as the Jauaperi and as far east as the Uatuma but as yet there has been little or no collecting or primatological field work in these areas (1,2). S. b. martinsi is found at the eastern end of the range, between the Rio Nhamunda and the Paru de Oeste; and the intermediate S. b. ochraceus in the 100-200 km wide belt of country between the other two (2,3,4). See maps in (2,3,4).

POPULATION   Numbers unknown. In 1972 Hershkovitz considered the species as a whole to be endangered (4). The 1980 surveys of S. b. bicolor indicated that this subspecies was endangered (1,2). Highest concentrations were found in the immediate vicinity of Manaus. One group occurred on the main campus of the National Amazonian Research Institute (INPA) and at least two groups (ca. 12 animals) in a 20 ha forest in the grounds of the Hotel Tropical, 15 km west of Manaus centre (2). The other two subspecies are very poorly known. Although similarly restricted in range they do not occur near major urban centres and are therefore more secure than S. b. bicolor. Until further information is available their status is considered 'Indeterminate' (2).

HABITAT AND ECOLOGY   The recent surveys encountered S. b. bicolor in groups of 5-10 animals in the 'campinarana' and primary forest near Manaus (2). However the species has also been observed in other forest types including secondary forest (7). Eats insects, fruit, small vertebrates and flowers and is arboreal and diurnal (2,6). Gestation period is 140-145 days. Twin births are usual; the male plays the major role in rearing the young (8).

THREATS TO SURVIVAL   The range of S. b. bicolor centres on Manaus, second largest city in Amazonia and growing rapidly. Consequently the animal is severely threatened by habitat destruction. By 1980 much of the forest surrounding the city had been divided into tens of thousands of small housing lots which will be cut over by 1985. Still further forest destruction will be caused by a major industrial district planned for the city outskirts (1,2). Considerable habitat alteration and deforestation is also taking place elsewhere in the range, especially along the new roads heading out of Manaus. An analysis of deforestation between 54°-66° and 0°-4°S (which includes the entire range of all three subspecies) indicated that the rate was increasing tremendously: in the two-year period 1976-1978 some 146,550 ha. of forest had disappeared compared to 205,100 ha in the entire period from colonisation to 1975 (2). A possibility also exists that the Golden-handed Tamarin (Saguinus midas midas) is invading the range of S. b.

131

bicolor and that the habitat alteration along new roads is assisting the spread (2).

CONSERVATION MEASURES TAKEN Included in Appendix 1 of the Convention on International Trade in Endangered Species of Wild Fauna and Flora, 1973, trade in the species between acceding nations being therefore subject to severe restriction, trade for primarily commercial purposes banned. As of 1980 S. b. bicolor occurred in only one protected area, the 10,000 ha Reserve Ducke located 25 km north of Manaus and belonging to INPA. José Marcio Ayres, in conjunction with INPA and the WWF - U.S. Primate Programme began studies on this species in 1980, the aims of which are to determine the precise range of S. b. bicolor, to locate the best possible areas for a large reserve (at least 10,000 ha) and to investigate the ecological relationship between this subspecies and S. m. midas (2). A poster campaign advertising the plight of this subspecies is also planned in Manaus by INPA/WWF and the Rare Animal Relief Fund (1,2). Such measures are part of a general conservation action plan for the whole species and are considered of 'highest priority' in IUCN's Global Strategy for Primate Conservation (1981-1983). Surveys of the ranges of S. b. ochraceous and S. b. martinsi to determine their status and possible threats to their survival are also planned (2).

CONSERVATION MEASURES PROPOSED Full legal protection for the species plus the establishment of well protected reserves.

CAPTIVE BREEDING A captive breeding programme is planned by the Rio de Janeiro Primate Centre (1,7), which in 1981 held a young female (7). The conservation action plan suggests that such a programme should make use of individuals captured from forest tracts already slated for destruction (2). The International Zoo Yearbook (1980) also lists a male at Sao Paulo Zoo, Brazil (9).

REMARKS For description of animal see (3,8). José Marcio Ayres and Dr. R.A. Mittermeier, Chairman of the IUCN/SCC Primate Specialist Group very kindly provided much of the information on which this data sheet is based.

REFERENCES   1. Ayres, J.M. (1981). In litt.
              2. Ayres, J.M., Mittermeier, R.A. and Constable, I.D. (1981). Distribution and status of the Brazilian Bare-Face Tamarins (Saguinus bicolor). Oryx in press.
              3. Hershkovitz, P. (1977) Living New World Monkeys (Platyrrhini). With an Introduction to Primates Vol. 1. Univ. of Chicago Press, Chicago and London.
              4. Hershkovitz, P. (1972). Notes on New World Monkeys. Int. Zoo Yb. 12: 3-12.
              5. Mittermeier, R.A. (1976). Preliminary assessment of the conservation status of New World monkeys. Unpd. Report. 6 pp.
              6. Mittermeier, R.A. and Coimbra-Filho, A.F. (1977). Primate conservation in Brazilian Amazonia. In Prince Rainier and Bourne, G. (Eds), Primate Conservation. Acad. Press, New York.
              7. Mittermeier, R.A. (1977-81). In litt.
              8. Napier, P.H. (1976). Catalogue of Primates in the British Museum (Natural History). Part 1: Families Callitrichidae and Cebidae. British Museum (Natural History), London.
              9. Olney, P.J.S. (Ed.) (1980). International Zoo Yearbook 20. Zool. Soc. London.

EMPEROR TAMARIN

INDETERMINATE

Saguinus imperator (Goeldi, 1907)

Order   PRIMATES

Family   CALLITRICHIDAE

SUMMARY   Occurs in the Amazon region of western Brazil, eastern Peru and northern Bolivia. Status and numbers unknown. Threatened by habitat destruction within its range. Protected in the Manu National Park in Peru. A survey is needed to determine its status and ecology.

DISTRIBUTION   Brazil, Peru and Bolivia in the region between the upper Rio Jurua and the Rio Madre de Dios, in particular in southwestern Brazilian Amazonia from the upper Rio Purus to the upper Rio Jurua (1,3,4,6,7,8,10).

POPULATION   No estimates, in 1981 reported to be scarce everywhere (9). Brazil: in 1981 Ayres considered it 'Vulnerable' (1). Bolivia: reported to be 'Endangered' in 1981 (2). Peru: no data on numbers or status.

HABITAT AND ECOLOGY   In eastern Peru, Gardner observed it in Amazonian lowland rainforest, away from rivers, and often 5 to 7 metres or higher in vine canopy vegetation (12). In Manu National Park it was usually observed in groups of about three (9). Saguinus spp. eat insects, fruit, small vertebrates, leaves, shoots, buds, and flowers (8). Gestation period is 140-145 days. Twin births are the usual. The male plays a major part in rearing the young (10).

THREATS TO SURVIVAL   Some habitat destruction is taking place within its range but the exent and effect is not known (9). In Brazil its range is increasingly occupied by large scale development projects (oil, rubber and agriculture etc.) (1), similarly in Bolivia where much of northwest Pando is being deforested to make way for cattle pasture (2). There is apparently some hunting in Bolivia (5).

CONSERVATION MEASURES TAKEN   Included in Appendix 2 of the Convention on International Trade in Endangered Species of Wild Fauna and Flora, 1973; trade in these animals between acceding nations is subject to regulation and monitoring of its effects. Legally protected in Peru and by the 1967 Fauna Protection Law in Brazil, though not on the Brazilian Endangered Species List (9). Not protected by law in Bolivia (5). A population exists in the Manu National Park on a tributary of the Rio Madre de Dios in southwest Peru (4, C. Freese, in litt., 1977).

CONSERVATION MEASURES PROPOSED   A survey to investigate the status and ecology of this species.

CAPTIVE BREEDING   In 1979 there were 28 males, 23 females and two of undetermined sex held in 8 zoo collections (11 captive bred) (11).

REMARKS   For description of animal see (10).

REFERENCES   1.   Ayres, J.M. (1981). In litt.
2.   Bejarano, G. (1981). In litt.
3.   Freese, C. (1975). A census of non-human primates in Peru. In Primate censusing studies in Peru and Colombia. Report to the National Acad. of Sciences on the activities of project AMRO -- 0719. Pan-American Health Organization. Pp. 17-41.
4.   Grimwood, I.R. (1969). Notes on the distribution and status

of some Peruvian mammals 1968. Spec. Pub. 21. Am. Comm. Int. Wildlife Protec. and New York Zool. Soc. Bronx, New York.

5. Hanson Love, A. (1981). In litt.

6. Heltne, P., Freese, C. and Whitesides, G. (1975). A field survey of non-human primates in Bolivia. Final report for the Pan-American Health Organization, Washington, D.C.

7. Hershkovitz, P. (1977). Living New World Monkeys (Platyrrhini). With an Introduction to Primates Vol. 1. Univ. of Chicago Press, Chicago and London.

8. Mittermeier, R.A. and Coimbra-Filho, A.F. (1977). Primate conservation in Brazilian Amazonia. In Prince Rainier and Bourne, G. (Eds), Primate Conservation. Academic Press, New York.

9. Mittermeier, R.A. (1977-81). In litt.

10. Napier, P.H. (1976). Catalogue of Primates in the British Museum (Natural History). Part 1: Families Callitrichidae and Cebidae. British Museum (Natural History), London..

11. Olney, P.J.S. (Ed.) (1980). International Zoo Yearbook 20. Zoo. Soc. London.

12. Wolfheim, J.H. (1974). The Status of Wild Primates. Unpublished Report, U.S. Fish and Wildlife Service. 908 pp.

WHITE-FOOTED TAMARIN   VULNERABLE

Saguinus leucopus (Gunther, 1876)

Order   PRIMATES   Family   CALLITRICHIDAE

SUMMARY   Restricted distribution in northern Colombia. Numbers unknown but habitat has been greatly reduced by forest clearance since the 1960s. A survey to locate a suitable reserve site is urgently needed.

DISTRIBUTION   Northern Colombia where it has a small range stretching from the confluence of the Rio Magdalena and the Rio Cauca in northern Bolivar (including Mompos Island) southwards into northeastern Antioquia (from Caceres and Valdivia on the Cauca to the Rio Nechi) and along the western bank of the middle Rio Magdalena in the Departments of Antioquia, Caldas and northern Tolima (2,6, F. Medem, in litt. 1977). For map see (2).

POPULATION   No estimates but has declined in recent years and in 1981 was considered 'Vulnerable' by the IUCN/SSC Primate Specialist Group (5).

HABITAT AND ECOLOGY   Forest, most frequently on the fringes, near streams or in secondary growth (1,2,8). Group size of 3 to 12 or more (2,8). Saguinus spp. eat insects, fruit, small vertebrates, leaves, shoots, buds and flowers (4). Gestation period is 140-145 days. Twin births are usual and the male plays a major part in rearing the young (6).

THREATS TO SURVIVAL   Its very small range has been greatly reduced by extensive forest clearance, especially since the 1960s (2).

CONSERVATION MEASURES TAKEN   Included in Appendix 1 of the Convention on International Trade in Endangered Species of Wild Fauna and Flora, 1973, trade in the species between acceding nations therefore being subject to severe restriction, trade for primarily commercial purposes banned. Protected by law in Colombia since 1969 (3). No existing parks or reserves are likely to contain a population (5).

CONSERVATION MEASURES PROPOSED   A survey to investigate the ecology of this tamarin is urgently needed as the basis for a sound approach to its conservation.

CAPTIVE BREEDING   In 1979 a pair were held at Lincoln Park Zoo, Chicago, the male being captive bred (7).

REMARKS   For description of animal see (2,6). This data sheet was compiled with the assistance of Dr. R.A. Mittermeier, Chairman of the IUCN/SSC Primate Specialist Group, and Dr. P. Neyman.

REFERENCES   1.   Bernstein, I.S., Balcaen, P., Dresdale, L., Gouzoules, H., Kavanagh, M., Patterson, T. and Neyman-Warner, P. (1976). Differential effects of forest degradation on primate populations. Primates 17(3): 401-411.
2.   Hernandez-Camacho, J. and Cooper, R.W. (1976). The non-human primates of Colombia. In Thorington, R.W. and Heltne, P.G. (Eds), Neotropical Primates: Field Studies and Conservation. National Acad. Sciences, Washington, D.C. Pp. 35-69.

3. Hernandez-Camacho, J. (1981). Pers. Comm.
4. Mittermeier, R.A. and Coimbra-Filho, A.F. (1977). Primate Conservation in Brazilian Amazonia. In Prince Rainier and Bourne, G. (Eds), Primate Conservation. Acad. Press, New York.
5. Mittermeier, R.A. (1977-81) . In litt.
6. Napier, P.H. (1976). Catalogue of Primates in the British Museum (Nat. Hist.). Part 1: Families Callitrichidae and Cebidae. British Museum (Natural History), London.
7. Olney, P.J.S. (Ed.) (1980). International Zoo Yearbook 20. Zool. Soc. London.
8. Wolfheim, J.H. (1974). The Status of Wild Primates. Unpubd. Report, U.S. Fish and Wildlife Service. 908 pp.

GOLDEN LION TAMARIN   ENDANGERED

Leontopithecus rosalia (Linnaeus, 1820)

Order   PRIMATES   Family   CALLITRICHIDAE

SUMMARY Southeast Brazil, where by 1980 the species survived only in two areas in the State of Rio de Janeiro one of the most densely inhabited parts of Brazil and which has suffered extensive forest destruction to make way for agriculture, pasture and urban devlopment. Less than 100 now survive in the wild and extinction is imminent unless the Poco d'Anta Reserve established for its protection is greatly improved. The reserve harbours few tamarins, the habitat has been greatly degraded and protection problems are severe. Captive colonies exist. Leontopithecus as a genus is highly endangered.

DISTRIBUTION Southeast Brazil. Entirely restricted to remaining forests of the Sao Joao basin in the State of Rio de Janeiro. Surveys in 1979/80 by Mittermeier et al and Green found the species to be confined to the municipalities of Silva Jardim, Casimiro de Abreu and Cabo Frio, and they were able to document its continued existence in only two areas within these regions: the 5000 ha Poco d'Anta Biological Reserve located 100 km northeast of Rio de Janerio, and along a 15 km stretch of coast south of the mouth of the Rio Sao Joao (6,10). The species has always been restricted to the low-lying coastal region of the State of Rio de Janeiro, south of the Rio Praiba. Several dubious records exist from the southern part of the State of Espirito Santo, but if the species ever occurred there, it is now definitely extinct (6,10).

POPULATION By 1980 numbered almost certainly less than 100 animals and was considered by Mittermeier et al to be 'the most endangered monkey in eastern Brazil and among the most endangered mammals in the world' (10). Green who surveyed the animal in the Poco d'Anta Reserve in June 1980 believed that the total number of Leontopithecus in the reserve did not exceed 75 animals (6,10) and, on the basis of actual sightings, was possibly as low as 20-25 (10). Actual sightings occurred on three occasions with one additional group detected by vocalization (6). Very few are believed to remain in the only other known habitat - along the coast - and virtually all this area is soon destined for deforestation (10). The only chance for its survival is in the Poco d'Anta and unless conditions improve there the species could well be extinct in the wild by 1985-90 (10).

HABITAT AND ECOLOGY Occurs in seasonal tropical forest of the Atlantic coast below 400-500 m altitude (3,4,10). Usually found between 3 and 10 m above the ground, where dense vines, epiphytes and interlacing branches provide cover for tamarins and their prey which sometimes includes small vertebrates; they are, however, primarily insectivorous and frugivorous. Group size varies from 2 to 8 with 3 or 4 the average. Gestation period is 126 to 132 days with twin births normal, although single birth and triplets have occasionally been recorded (3,4).

THREATS TO SURVIVAL Because the home of this species is one of the most densely inhabited parts of Brazil, the major cause of decline has been, and remains, forest destruction for lumber, agriculture (sugar cane, cocoa, rubber, coffee and bananas), pasture and housing. Always relatively uncommon and restricted in range, habitat loss affects the species particularly severely. The entire basin of the Rio Sao Joao (about 210,000 ha) is included in a large-scale agricultural project which aims to make it one of the major sources of farm produce for Rio de Janeiro. The municipalities most affected are precisely those which contain the last remaining populations of L. rosalia and although the project will take about 5-6 years to complete, it will ensure the destruction of what little remains of its forest habitat. The 1979/80 surveys found that the Poco d'Anta Reserve established specifically to ensure this animal's survival, was inadequately protected. Many areas had been deforested, slashed and burned, planted with pasture grass or reforested with eucalyptus. Squatters were still present and although part of the reserve had been fenced, cattle from neighbouring ranches regularly entered the reserve to find pasture, thus prohibiting the successional return of areas of abandoned pasture to forest. Thus much of the reserve was no longer suitable for the tamarin. Only about 30% of the reserve was forested (10% mature forest), a railroad and a road divided it into four sections, and a dam was being completed which would flood approximately 25% of the reserved area. A forested hill within the reserve had been levelled to provide land fill for the dam, and the continuous flow of large numbers of men and machines was sure to have a disturbing effect on all forested areas adjacent to the construction site. Only two of the six guards were able to actively patrol the reserve and the director who was based in Rio de Janeiro, 100 km away, rarely visited the place. Within the reserve, the existing Lion Tamarin population was dispersed in several forest islands and certainly could not be considered viable. The poor habitat and continued disturbance make any efforts at reintroduction highly inappropriate at the present time (1981). The coastal zone that the tamarin inhabits has already been divided into housing lots and will soon disappear (6,10). Lion Tamarins have long been popular zoo exhibits, occasionally used for research in biomedical laboratories and widely sold in the pet trade. Between 200 and 300 were exported annually for these purposes in the period 1960-1965 (4).

CONSERVATION MEASURES TAKEN   All three Leontopithecus (= Leontideus) species are included in Appendix 1 of the 1973 Convention on International Trade in Endangered Species of Wild Fauna and Flora so trade in them or their products is subject to strict regulation by ratifying nations, and trade for primarily commercial purposes is banned. Completely protected in Brazil and included on the Brazilian Endangered Species List. As already noted the Poco d' Anta Reserve established in 1974 and increased in size to 5000 ha in 1975 for the protection of L. rosalia, has greatly deteriorated (6,10). The species may also occur in a small forest reserve belonging to the Brazilian navy, but confirmation is needed (8). A study of the distribution and status of all eastern Brazilian primates was undertaken in 1979/80 by R.A. Mittermeier, A.F. Coimbra-Filho and I. Constable (10). Ken Green conducted the first census of this animal in the Poco d' Anta Reserve between June 1 and 26, 1980; in addition, he hoped to study its ecology and behaviour and to compare this with behaviour exhibited in captivity (6).

CONSERVATION MEASURES PROPOSED   Unless the Brazilian government makes a major effort to improve conditions in Poco d'Anta and to protect some of of the remaining forest south of the Rio Sao Joao, this species will become extinct in the wild before 1985-1990. The IUCN/SSC Primate Specialist Group made the following recommendations in 1980: a) Investigate the forest reserve belonging to the Brazilian navy to see if Lion Tamarins actually exist there. b) Investigate the remainder of the coastal region south of the Rio Sao Joao to see if there are any other tracts of forest sufficiently large for establishing a Lion Tamarin reserve. c) Urge the Brazilian Forestry Development Institute (IBDF) to substantially upgrade protection for the Poco d'Anta Reserve, and to initiate a large-scale habitat improvement program. Some ways in which this might be done are outlined in a report by Dr. K. Green. d) Add to the Poco d'Anta Reserve a 50 ha patch of forest continuous with it. The 1979/80 surveys found that this area included some of the best forest left in the Poco d'Anta area and harbored the only Leontopithecus group of any size (5+ individuals). e) Conduct rescue operations in any small tracts of forest that will definitely be cut down to make way for housing projects; this is especially urgent in the area south of the Rio Sao Joao (6,10).

CAPTIVE BREEDING The 1981 unofficial update of the International Studbook for L. rosalia registered 211 animals in 25 collections (8). In 1981 there were 15 individuals in the Rio de Janeiro Primate Centre (A. F. Coimbra-Filho 1981, Pers Comm.), and none were lost when the entire colony was transferred from the old Tijuca Biological Bank to the new Centre. Five Lion Tamarins from the Rio Centre have also been sent, with authorization from IBDF, to the National Zoo in Washington in order to increase genetic diversity in the U.S. colonies. This was an important step in international cooperation on behalf of these monkeys and hopefully will pave the way for future efforts. Expansion of the captive breeding effort at the Rio Primate Centre is recommended. Research has shown it is important that offspring remain with the parental group during the birth and rearing of at least one set of younger siblings so that they can learn and copy parental behaviour patterns (4).

REMARKS For description of animal see (2,7,11). L. chryosmelas and L. chrysopygus are sometimes considered subspecies of L. rosalia (3,4), but recent comparative morphological work by Dr. A. Rosenberger indicates that these animals are distinct enough to be considered full species (9). The generic name Leontideus is occasionally used. This data sheet was compiled with the assistance of Dr. A.F. Coimbra-Filho, and of Dr. R.A. Mittermeier, Chairman of the IUCN/SSC Primate Specialist Group.

REFERENCES
1. Coimbra-Filho, A.F. (1972). Mamiferos ameacados de extincao no Brasil. In Especies de Fauna Brasileira Ameacadas de Extincao. Academia Brasileira de Ciencias, Rio de Janeiro. Pp. 13-98.
2. Coimbra-Filho, A.F. and Mittermeier, R.A. (1972). The taxonomy of the genus Leontopithecus. In Bridgewater, D. (Ed.), Saving the lion marmoset. Wild Animal Propagation Trust, Wheeling, West Virginia. Pp. 7-22.
3. Coimbra-Filho, A.F. and Mittermeier, R.A. (1973). Distribution and ecology of the genus Leontopithecus Lesson, 1840 in Brazil. Primates 14(1): 47-66.
4. Coimbra-Filho, A.F., and Mittermeier, R.A. (1977). Conservation of the Brazilian Lion Tamarins (Leontopithecus rosalia). In Prince Rainier and Bourne, G. (Eds), Primate Conservation. Acad. Press, New York.
5. Coimbra-Filho, A.F., Magnanini, A. and Mittermeier, R.A. (1975). Vanishing Gold. Last chance for Brazil's lion tamarins. Animal Kingdom 78(6): 21-27.
6. Green, K.M. (1980). An assessment of the Poco das Antas Reserve, Brazil, and prospects for survival of the Golden Lion Tamarin, Leontopithecus rosalia rosalia. Unpd. Report. 19 pp.
7. Kleiman, D.G. (1981). Leontopithecus rosalia. Mammalian Species No. 148: 1-7. The American Society of Mammalogists.
8. Kleiman, D.G. (1981). 1981 International Studbook: Golden Lion Tamarin, Leontopithecus rosalia rosalia. Unofficial 1981 update. National Zool. Park, Washington D.C.
9. Mittermeier, R.A. (1977-81). In litt.
10. Mittermeier, R.A., Coimbra-Filho, A.F. and Constable, I. (1980). Conservation of Eastern Brazilian Primates. WWF Project 1614. Report for the period 1979/80.
11. Napier, P.H. (1976). Catalogue of Primates in the British Museum (Nat. Hist.). Part 1: Families Callitrichidae and Cebidae British Museum (Natural History), London.

GOLDEN-HEADED LION TAMARIN

ENDANGERED

Leontopithecus chrysomelas (Kuhl, 1820)

Order   PRIMATES

Family   CALLITRICHIDAE

SUMMARY   Endemic to southeast Brazil, where restricted to a small area in southeast Bahia State and is critically endangered. By 1980 less than 200 were believed to survive and the only protected area inhabited, the 5268 ha Una Biological Reserve had already been extensively invaded by squatters. Throughout the rest of its very small range most of the forests have disappeared to make way for plantations, pasture and urban development. Survival of the species will depend on the complete protection of a suitable reserve. A captive colony is maintained at the Rio de Janeiro Primate Centre. The first field study of this animal was conducted by Anthony Rylands in 1980. Leontopithecus as a genus is highly endangered.

DISTRIBUTION   Southeast Brazil. Restricted to the southeast of Bahia State, between the Rio das Contas (14°S) and Rio Pardo (15°30'S), its western limit apparently the Rio Gongogi headwaters (40°W), a bare 100 km from the coast. Still found in forests in the municipalities of Una, Buerarema, Itabuna and perhaps Ilheus (8,9). The report of a population discovered in 1971 in northern Espirito Santo has proved erroneous. The range has always been small and has scarcely changed since the animal was first discovered, but the forests which originally stretched unbroken from the central Bahian plateau to within a few km of the coast, are now fragmented (1,3,4,8,9).

POPULATION   In 1977 considered to number about 200 (4), and by 1981 was almost certainly less. The only protected area it occupies has already been degraded by more than half. Rylands (1980) believes that considering the rate of forest destruction since 1975, little hope can be entertained for the survival of appreciable populations of chrysomelas outside the Una Reserve, except perhaps in the coastal forest immediately to the east of Una, from Ilheus to Canavieras, where soils are unsuitable for agriculture (9). However a road is planned to link these two cities and will no doubt stimulate development (9). Away from Una small populations still survive north of Ilheus and Itabuna; Rylands did not directly observe chrysomelas there but interviews with hunters in Banco Central and Pimenteira, north of Itabuna, west of BR 101 road indicate that chrysomelas survive in small numbers (9). Mittermeier et al consider the species will be extinct in the wild by 1990 unless a suitable reserve is established (8).

HABITAT AND ECOLOGY   Inhabits Atlantic rainforest, little of which remains after development of cocoa and rubber plantations. However cocoa is grown under shade, thus in some areas large forest trees are left standing; hence to some extent the canopy is maintained even within plantations and L. chrysomelas can sometimes be observed in or near the shade trees, although how well it adapts to such habitat is not entirely known (3,4,8,9). Rylands noted that in such plantations it was always in close proximity to stands of intact forest (9). Coimbra-Filho (in Rylands 1980) maintains that Leontopithecus is unable to survive outside of tall primary forest because of its dependence on holes in tree trunks and branches as sleeping sites. Rylands' studies confirmed this belief and also revealed the apparent importance of large epiphytes as foraging sites. Both of these resources are absent from second growth forest (9). Leontopithecus are usually found between 3 and 10 m above the ground, where dense vines, epiphytes and interlacing branches provide cover for tamarins and their prey which sometimes includes small vertebrates; it is however, primarily insectivorous and frugivorous (3,4,9). Group size varies from 2 to 8 with 3 or 4 the average. Rylands estimated a home range of not more than 40 ha for the group of 5 chrysomelas he had under observation (9). Gestation period is 126 to 132 days with twin births normal, although single births and triplets have occasionally been recorded (3,4).

THREATS TO SURVIVAL   Because the home of this species is one of the most densely inhabited parts of Brazil, the major cause of decline has been forest destruction for lumber, agriculture (sugar cane, cocoa, rubber, coffee and bananas), pasture and housing. Always relatively uncommon and restricted in range, habitat loss affects it particularly severely. Surveys in 1979/80 by Mittermeier et al found L. chrysomelas to occur in an area where remaining forest was being cleared at a very rapid rate by logging and charcoal producing operations and, in areas of richer soil, was being converted to cocoa plantations and other agricultural projects (8).

CONSERVATION MEASURES TAKEN   All three Leontopithecus (= Leontideus) species are listed in Appendix I of the 1973 Convention on International Trade in Endangered Species of Wild Fauna and Flora so trade in them or their products is subject to strict regulation by ratifying nations, and trade for primarily commercial purposes banned. Completely protected by law in Brazil and included on the Brazilian endangered species list. In 1976 the Brazilian Forestry Development Institute (IBDF) purchased 5268 ha in Una as a reserve for this species and other examples of the regional fauna. However since then little has happened, the reserve covering an area of 11,400 ha was finally officially decreed in December 1980 (10), but already approx. 3000 ha has been invaded by some 600 squatters who have clear-cut large areas in the west of the reserve, and almost all the invaded sector is no longer suitable habitat for this species or any other forest animal. In May 1980 squatters were observed on the outskirts of the remaining forest (8,9). Anthony Rylands studied this species at the Lemos Maia Experimental Station in 1980 (9). A study of the distribution and status of all eastern Brazilian primates was undertaken in 1979/80 by R.A. Mittermeier, A.F. Coimbra-Filho and I. Constable (8).

CONSERVATION MEASURES PROPOSED   In 1980 the IUCN/SSC Primate Specialist Group made the following recommendations. a) The IBDF should protect that part of the Una Biological Reserve which is still intact, remove the squatters, and either excise the degraded areas or trade them for nearby tracts of forested land. The suggestion has also been made that IBDF turn over management of the reserve to CEPLAC, the Regional Cocoa Growing Authority, which is interested in research and conservation and, being on the scene, is better equipped to manage a protected area in southern Bahia. b) The 495 ha Lemos Maia Experimental Station, located on the edge of the town of Una and about 10 km from the Una Biological Reserve is suggested as an area which might be considered for designation as a wildlife reserve (8,9). c) Investigate some of the white sand forests extending about 30 km inland from Canavieras and also in the coastal region between Canavieras and Ilheus to locate possible sites for an additional reserve (much of this area has by 1981 been given over to cattle pasture). This area is not suitable for cocoa or other kinds of agriculture, but this tamarin and other primates occur in the forest. Since the future of the Una Reserve is uncertain, it would be wise to establish at least one other protected area in this faunally rich and interesting part of eastern Brazil. d) Conduct rescue operations in forests that are being clear cut to make way for alternative cocoa-growing methods and for lumber and charcoal (8).

CAPTIVE BREEDING   A captive colony is maintained at the Rio de Janiero Primate Centre and in 1981 numbered 9 animals (A.F. Coimbra-Filho 1981. Pers. comm.). Mittermeier et al recommend the expansion of this facility and the establishment of satellite colonies in other institutions. The future of captive populations depends on successful breeding from captive-born parents and control of disease outbreaks (4).

REMARKS For description of animal see (2,7). L. chrysomelas has occasionally been considered a subspecies of L. rosalia, (3,4), but recent comparative morphological work by Dr. A. Rosenberger indicates that these animals are distinct enough to be considered full species (6). The generic name Leontideus is sometimes used. This data sheet was compiled with the assistance of Anthony Rylands, Dr. A.F. Coimbra-Filho and Dr. R.A. Mittermeier, Chairman of the IUCN/SSC Primate Specialist Group.

REFERENCES 1. Coimbra-Filho, A.F. (1972). Mamiferos ameacados de extincao no Brasil. In Especies de Fauna Brasileira Ameacadas de Extincao. Academia Brasileira de Ciencias, Rio de Janeiro. Pp. 13-98.
2. Coimbra-Filho, A.F. and Mittermeier, R.A. (1972). The taxonomy of the genus Leontopithecus. In Bridgewater, D. (Ed.), Saving the lion marmoset. Wild Animal Propagation Trust, Wheeling, West Virginia. Pp. 7-22.
3. Coimbra-Filho, A.F. and Mittermeier, R.A. (1973). Distribution and ecology of the genus Leontopithecus Lesson, 1840 in Brazil. Primates 14(1): 47-66.
4. Coimbra-Filho, A.F. and Mittermeier, R.A. (1977). Conservation of the Brazilian Lion Tamarins (Leontopithecus rosalia). In Prince Rainier and Bourne, G. (Eds), Primate Conservation. Acad. Press, New York.
5. Coimbra-Filho, A.F., Magnanini, A. and Mittermeier, R.A. (1975). Vanishing Gold. Last chance for Brazil's lion tamarins. Animal Kingdom 78(6): 21-27.
6. Mittermeier, R.A. (1977-81). In litt.
7. Napier, P.H. (1976). Catalogue of Primates in the British Museum (Nat. Hist.). Part 1: Families Callitrichidae and Cebidae British Museum (Natural History), London.
8. Mittermeier, R.A., Coimbra-Filho, A.F. and Constable, I. (1980). Conservation of Eastern Brazilian Primates. WWF Project 1614. Report for the period 1979/80.
9. Rylands, A.B. (1981). The behavioural ecology of the Golden-headed Lion Tamarin, Leontopithecus rosalia chrysomelas (Callitrichidae, Primates). Interim Report. Unpd. Report.
10. Rylands, A.B. (1981). In litt.

GOLDEN-RUMPED LION TAMARIN ENDANGERED

Leontopithecus chrysopygus (Mikan, 1820)

Order PRIMATES Family CALLITRICHIDAE

SUMMARY Endemic to southeast Brazil where it is critically endangered in the wild. By 1981 could be found in only two areas, both reserves, and both in the State of Sao Paulo: Morro do Diabo which housed 4 or 5 groups and Caitetus which had one or two groups (a group is usually 3-4 animals). Inhabits a very densely populated part of Brazil and forest destruction for agriculture, pasture and urban development within its former range has been almost total. The Caitetus Reserve is well protected but there are plans to build an airport on the edge of Morro do Diabo and to flood one-eighth of it as part of a dam scheme. The survival of this animal in the wild is entirely dependent on its continued protection in the Morro do Diabo State Reserve. A captive colony is maintained at the Rio de Janeiro Primate Centre. Leontopithecus as a genus is highly endangered.

DISTRIBUTION Southeast Brazil. By 1981 restricted to two tracts of forest in the State of Sao Paulo: in the 37,156 ha Morro do Diabo State Reserve in the extreme west of the State, and the 2000 ha Caitetus Reserve in central Sao Paulo (9). Formerly, it ranged much more widely, occupying a large part of the interior of the State, from the Rio Tiete in the north to Rio Paranapanema in the south, and west to the Rio Parana (1,2,4,5,7,10).

POPULATION By 1981 less than 100 survived and on the verge of extinction (9). Surveys in 1979/80 could account for only 4-5 groups in Morro do Diabo, based mainly on reports of guards who regularly patrolled the reserve. It was not known whether this constituted a viable population but it is certainly the only real hope for the long-term survival of the species in the wild (9). The same studies indicated that the Caitetus Reserve has only one, or at most, two groups (9).

HABITAT AND ECOLOGY Inhabits riparian forest, in effect an extension of Atlantic coastal forest up the major rivers. Usually found between 3 and 10 m above ground, where dense vines, epiphytes and interlacing branches provide cover for tamarins and their prey which sometimes includes small vertebrates; they are, however, primarily insectivorous and frugivorous. Group size varies from 2 to 8 with 3 or 4 the average. Gestation period is 126 to 132 days with twin births normal, although single birth and triplets have occasionally been recorded (4,5).

THREATS TO SURVIVAL Because the home of this species is a very densely inhabited part of Brazil, the major cause of decline has been forest destruction for lumber, agriculture (sugar cane, cocoa, rubber, coffee and bananas), pasture and housing. Always relatively uncommon and restricted in range, habitat loss affects it particularly severely. In 1980 Mittermeier et al reported that plans were in progress to build an airport right on the edge of Morro do Diabo State Reserve, and that a dam which would flood about one-eighth of the reserve had been proposed for the Paranapanema River (9). The reserve is already traversed by a railroad and since 1969 bisected by a highway. Also in 1973 local farmers experimenting with defoliants (2,4,5-T and 2,4-D) destroyed many hectares of what little forest remained around the reserve. Such disturbances in the close proximity to the protected area could easily be fatal. The Caitetus Reserve contains a large population of Tufted Capuchins Cebus apella which certainly compete to some extent with the tamarins (9).

CONSERVATION MEASURES TAKEN All three Leontopithecus (= Leontideus) species are listed in Appendix 1 of the 1973 Convention on International Trade in Endangered Species of Wild Fauna and Flora so trade in them or their products is subject to strict regulation by ratifying nations, and trade for primarily commercial purposes banned. Completely protected in Brazil and included on the Brazilian Endangered Species List. The Reserves of Morro do Diabo and Caitetus are both under the jurisdiction of the Instituto Florestal of Sao Paulo State. Caitetus, which until 1977 was privately-owned, is well-protected and Morro do Diabo is regularly patrolled (9), although faces problems (see THREATS). A study of the distribution and status of all eastern Brazilian primates was undertaken in 1979/80 by R.A. Mittermeier, A.F. Coimbra-Filho and I. Constable.

CONSERVATION MEASURES PROPOSED The survival in the wild of L. chrysopygus depends mainly on effective management of the Morro do Diabo State Reserve. In 1980 the IUCN/SSC Primate Specialist Group made the following recommendations. i) Encourage the Sao Paulo government to continue protection of the Morro do Diabo and Caitetus Reserves, and to consider alternate sites for the hydroelectric project on the Rio Paranapanema and the proposed airport. ii) Encourage Brazilian students to conduct long-term ecological studies of L. chrysopygus in both reserves. In Morro do Diabo, the investigation should concentrate on the distribution of groups and dietary and habitat requirements. In Caitetus, it should pay particular attention to the relationship between the Tufted Capuchin and the Lion Tamarin. iii) If a field study in Morro do Diabo indicates that some trapping might be feasible, several individuals should be translocated from the larger reserve to Caitetus and the introduced animals carefully monitored. iv) If the hydroelectric project on the Rio Paranapanema cannot be prevented, plans should be made to translocate any L. chrysopygus that might live in the area to be flooded (9). The conservation of endangered eastern Brazilian monkeys is considered of highest priority in the IUCN/SSC Primate Specialist Group's Global Strategy for Primates (1981-1983).

CAPTIVE BREEDING The 1981 population at the Rio de Janeiro Primate Centre is 18 (A.F. Coimbra-Filho 1981, Pers. comm.), compared to six in 1973; the colony appears to be thriving, although inbreeding might eventually become a problem and thus the introduction of one or two individuals from Morro do Diabo might be desirable at some future date (9). Mittermeier et al recommend the expansion of the captive breeding facility at the Centre, and the establishment of satellite colonies in other institutions (9). The future of captive populations depends on successful breeding from captive-born parents and control of disease outbreaks (5).

REMARKS For description of animal see (3,7,9). L. chrysopygus has occasionally been considered a subspecies of L. rosalia (4,5) but recent morphological work by Dr. A. Rosenberger indicates that these animals are distinct enough to be considered full species (8). The generic name Leontideus is sometimes used. This data sheet was compiled with the assistance of Dr. A.F. Coimbra-Filho and of Dr. R.A. Mittermeier, Chairman of the IUCN/SSC Primate Specialist Group.

REFERENCES   1.   Coimbra-Filho, A.F. (1972). Mamiferos ameacados de extincao no Brasil. In Especies de Fauna Brasileira Ameacadas de Extincao. Academia Brasileira de Ciencias, Rio de Janeiro. Pp. 13-98.
2.   Coimbra-Filho, A.F. (1976). Leontopithecus rosalia chrysopygus (Mikan, 1823), o Mico-Leao do Estado de Sao Paulo (Callitrichidae - Primates). Silvic. S. Paulo 10: 1-36.
3.   Coimbra-Filho, A.F. and Mittermeier, R.A. (1972). The taxonomy of the genus Leontopithecus. In Bridgewater, D. (Ed.), Saving the Lion Marmoset. Wild Animal Propagation Trust, Wheeling, West Virginia. Pp. 7-22.
4.   Coimbra-Filho, A.F. and Mittermeier, R.A. (1973).

Distribution and ecology of the genus Leontopithecus Lesson, 1840 in Brazil. Primates 14(1): 47-66.

5. Coimbra-Filho, A.F. and Mittermeier, R.A. (1977). Conservation of the Brazilian Lion Tamarins (Leontopithecus rosalia). In Prince Rainier and Bourne, G. (Eds), Primate Conservation. Acad. Press, New York.

6. Coimbra-Filho, A.F., Magnanini, A. and Mittermeier, R.A. (1975). Vanishing Gold. Last chance for Brazil's lion tamarins. Animal Kingdom 78(6): 21-27.

7. Kleiman, D.G. (1981). Leontopithecus rosalia. Mammalian Species No. 148: 1-7. The American Society of Mammalogists.

8. Mittermeier, R.A. (1977-81). In litt.

9. Mittermeier, R.A., Coimbra-Filho, A.F. and Constable, I. (1980). Conservation of Eastern Brazilian Primates. WWF Project 1614. Report for the period 1979/80.

10. Napier, P.H. (1976). Catalogue of Primates in the British Museum (Nat. Hist.). Part 1: Families Callitrichidae and Cebidae. British Museum (Natural History), London.

GOELDI'S MARMOSET

Callimico goeldii (Thomas, 1904)

Order PRIMATES

Family CALLITRICHIDAE

SUMMARY Disjunct and very sparse distribution in the Upper Amazonian rainforests, probably because of specilized habitat requirements. Occurs at low density in localised areas. Surveys to determine suitable reserve sites are required.

DISTRIBUTION Wide but patchy distribution in the upper Amazonian region between 1°N and 13°S in Peru, northern Bolivia, southern Colombia and extreme western Brazil (9,10,12,17,18,21). Hershkovitz believes the species also occurs in Ecuador, although as yet unrecorded (10). Brazil: only in the extreme west. Recorded localities (all in the State of Acre) are the Rio Yaco; Ucuna on the Rio Xapuri about 150 km southwest of Rio Branco, and far to the west, about 150 km south of Cruzeiro do Sol, Seringal Oriente near Vila Taumaturgo on the upper Rio Jurua and the latter's tributary, the Rio Mu (17). Bolivia: extensive range in the north but patchily distributed (7,12,21). A 1978 study observed goeldii at 3 sites 20-50 km southwest of Cobija and noted its existence over large areas of the Pando Department -- both south and west of Cobija towards the Peruvian border, and east along the Rio Abuna and around Riberalta (21). Izawa (1979) records the southern limit as the Rio Ortho - Rio Manuripi (12). Peru: known from the Iquitos area (10,16,23) and the Department of Madre de Dios (6,10,16,23) where Izawa reports the southern limit to be the Rio Manu (13). Colombia: only known in the south where it has been collected in two localities between the upper Putumayo and Caqueta rivers and from a third locality in the lower Guamues River, a major southern tributary of the upper Putumayo (9). Northwesternmost collection was near La Chorrera on the Igara-Parana, a north bank tributary of the lower Putumayo (9,15). For map see (9,10).

POPULATION No estimates exist of this naturally rare, very sparsely distributed and little known species (17). Colombia: described in the mid-1970s as rare (15), poorly known (9). Peru: an 8-month survey of primate populations in Amazonian Peru conducted in 1974 concluded that Callimico was rare although might be numerous in isolated pockets (4,5). Izawa (1979) noted a 'relatively high population' along the Rio Tapiche and its tributary the Rio Blanco (12). Bolivia: the Pooks, based on their 1978 studies, suggested that considerable numbers of Callimico existed throughout the Pando region. Even so the population density was extremely low, e.g. within their study area Callimico had a density of probably 0.5-2.0 individuals per sq. km compared to 25-30 per sq. km for Saguinus labiatus and S. fuscicollis (21). They did not believe the species was in 'great immediate danger' provided trade controls into the U.S.A. and Europe were enforced (21). Both Heltne et al and Izawa noted considerable numbers along the Rio Acre (7,12). and both Izawa and the Pooks received similar information for the north bank of the Acre in Brazil (12,21).

HABITAT AND ECOLOGY Inhabits 'shabby forest' such as mixed forest, scrub, second-growth woods, bamboo forests, and forests with discontinuous canopies and well-developed scrub (9,10,12,17,18,21). In Bolivia Izawa found that all localities where Callimico existed were in well-developed bamboo (Bambusa sp.) forests or on their periphery (12), however Hernandez-Camacho reports that this preference for bamboo has not yet been confirmed for Colombia (8). The Pooks' study area in Bolivia was slightly hilly, about 250-300 m above sea-level and on the fringe of the low-lying main basin of the Amazon River (21). Except when feeding in tall fruit trees, C. goeldii have been observed to spend nearly all their time in understorey within 5 m of the ground and to often descend to the ground to collect food (9,10,15,21). Diet is mainly frugivorous and insectivorous (9,10,12,15,17,18) but small vertebrates are sometimes taken (17). In Bolivia the Pooks observed an average group size of 6, the largest group being 8 independent individuals plus one infant (21). Izawa observed a group of 11 for several months (13). There was also inconclusive evidence of more than one breeding female in a group (21). In Bolivia and Colombia C. goeldii often occurs in mixed groups with Saguinus spps. (9,12,21). Usually one young is born after a gestation period of 151-159 days (14). (A possibility exists that Callimico can give birth twice a year even in the wild (12)).

THREATS TO SURVIVAL Uncertain, but the rarity and sparse and localised distribution of the species make it particularly vulnerable to such adverse factors as habitat destruction and/or hunting (14,15). For Bolivia the Pooks reported that plans exist for extensive roadbuilding and development programmes in the Pando region, which include resettlement schemes to relieve the over-populated Altiplano region around La Paz. By 1979 some roadbuilding had already occurred (21). A threat of trapping for the export market also exists in Bolivia. The Pooks report that the rarity value of Callimico in the U.S.A. and Europe has led to greatly increased prices throughout the supply chain, giving incentive to illegal trapping. Callimico's distribution pattern of localised groups makes it particularly vulnerable to any systematic trapping programme since removal of a few groups could eliminate the species from a relatively large area (21).

CONSERVATION MEASURES TAKEN Listed in Appendix 1 of the 1973 Convention on International Trade in Endangered Species of Wild Fauna and Flora, and therefore any trade in it or its products is subject to strict regulation by ratifying nations, trade for primarily commercial purposes being banned. Included in the Brazilian Endangered Species List. Totally protected in Peru, where it is listed as 'rare', and Bolivia (21), but this is difficult to enforce. Occurs in 'fairly good numbers' in Manu National Park, Peru (16), and in the Apaya River National Park in Colombia (established 1981) (8). C. goeldii was the subject of a five-month field study by George and Gillian Pook in the Pando Dept. of northern Bolivia, from August 1978 to January 1979 (21), and by Kosei Izawa also in Pando Dept. from June 1979 to January 1980 (12).

CONSERVATION MEASURES PROPOSED Suitable reserve sites need to be located, also more information about distribution is desirable. A Biological Station is to be set up in Bolivia in the Nareuda-Tahuamanu area and will serve as a reserve for the species (1).

CAPTIVE BREEDING In 1979 at least 37 males, 39 females and 28 unsexed animals were held in 11 zoo collections, 61 of them captive bred (20). By the beginning of 1979 the colony at Jersey Zoo, Great Britain had tripled to 18 from a 1975 start of 3 pairs; two of those born in 1979 represented pure second generation Jersey captive bred stock (3). Brookfield Zoo, Chicago also houses a major colony, in 1979 they had 20 animals, 9 of them captive bred (20).

REMARKS For description of animal see (10,19). Shares features with both the Callitrichidae and Cebidae and some authors have placed it in a family of its own, the Callimiconidae (10), however opinion is divided on the subject (22). This data sheet was compiled with the assistance of Dr. Kosei Izawa and George Pook.

REFERENCES   1.   Bejarano, G. (1981). In litt.
              2.   Coimbra-Filho, A.F. (1972). Conservation and use of South American primates in Brazil. Int. Zoo Yearbook 12: 14-15.
              3.   Durrell, G. (1979). Goeldi's Monkey numbers now trebled.

Wildlife Preservation Trust Jersey Newsletter No. 34.

4. Freese, C.H., Freese, M.A. and Castro R., N. (1977). The status of Callitrichids in Peru. In Kleiman, D.G. (Ed.), *The Biology and Conservation of the Callitrichidae*. Smithsonian Institution Press, Washington, D.C.

5. Freese, C., Neville, M., Castro R. and Castro, N. (1976). The conservation status of Peruvian primates. *Lab. Primate Newsletter* 15(3): 1.

6. Grimwood, I.R. (1977). In litt.

7. Heltne, P., Freese, C. and Whitesides, G. (1975). *A field survey of non-human primate populations in Bolivia*. Final Report for the Pan-American Health Organisation, Washington, D.C., U.S.A.

8. Hernandez-Camacho, J. (1981). Pers. comm.

9. Hernandez-Camacho, J. and Cooper, R.W. (1976). The Nonhuman Primates of Colombia. In Thorington, R.W. Jr. and Heltne, P.G. (Eds), *Neotropical Primates: Field Studies and Conservation*. Nat. Acad. of Sciences, Washington D.C.

10. Hershkovitz, P. (1977). *Living New World Monkeys (Platyrrhini). With an Introduction to Primates. Vol.1*. The Univ. of Chicago Press, Chicago and London.

11. Hill, W.C.O. (1959). The anatomy of *Callimico goeldii* (Thomas), a primitive American primate. *Trans. Am. Phil. Soc.* 49: 1-116.

12. Izawa, K. (1979). Studies on peculiar distribution pattern of *Callimico*. Kyoto Univ. Overseas Research. Reports of New World Monkeys: 1-19.

13. Izawa, K. (1980). In litt.

14. Lorenz, R. (1972). Management and reproduction of the Goeldi's monkey *Callimico goeldii* (Thomas, 1904), Callimiconidae, Primates. In Bridgewater, D.D. (Ed.), *Saving the Lion Marmoset*. Proc. Wild Animal Propagation Trust. Golden Lion Marmoset Conference, Feb. 15-17, 1972. Pp. 92-109.

15. Medem, F. (1977). In litt.

16. Mittermeier, R.A. (1977-81). In litt.

17. Mittermeier, R.A. and Coimbra-Filho, A.F. (1978). Primate conservation in Brazilian Amazonia. In Prince Rainier and Bourne, G. (Eds), *Primate Conservation*. Acad. Press, New York.

18. Moynihan, M. (1976). *The New World Primates*. Princeton Univ. Press.

19. Napier, P.H. (1976). *Catalogue of Primates in the British Museum (Natural History). Part 1: Families Callitrichidae and Cebidae*. British Museum (Natural History), London.

20. Olney, P.J.S. (Ed.) (1980). *International Zoo Yearbook 20*. Zool. Soc. of London.

21. Pook, A. G. and Pook, G. (1979). A field study on the status and socio-ecology of the Goeldi's Monkey (*Callimico goeldii*) and other primates in northern Bolivia. Report for the New York Zool. Soc., Bronx Zoo, Bronx, New York.

22. Rosenberger, A.L. (1981). Systematics: the higher taxa. In Coimbra-Filho, A.F. and Mittermeier, R.A. (Eds), *Ecology and Behaviour of Neotropical Primates*. Academia Brasileira de Ciencias. Rio de Janeiro, Brazil.

23. Soini, P. (1972). The capture and commerce of live monkeys in the Amazonian region of Peru. *Int. Zoo Yearbook* 12: 26-36.

CENTRAL AMERICAN or RED-BACKED SQUIRREL MONKEY

Saimiri oerstedi (Reinhart, 1872)

Order   PRIMATES   Family   CEBIDAE

SUMMARY   Limited distribution in Panama and adjacent area of Costa Rica. Numbers unknown. Endangered by widespread habitat destruction. Trapped for export until recently. Reserves need to be established.

DISTRIBUTION   Western Panama, southern Costa Rica. Range in both countries restricted to the lowlands of the Pacific coast between about 80° and 85°W. Museum collections show that formerly the species ranged from Chiriqui, the westernmost Province of Panama, to latitude 10°N in Costa Rica. Surveys in 1968 and 1970 found that the range had become significantly smaller and limited to areas not yet cleared for agriculture because too remote or otherwise undesirable (1,2,8,11,13).

POPULATION   Numbers unknown but believed to have diminished greatly since the 1950s in both countries (1). In 1978 was considered in danger of extinction in Costa Rica (7). Freese believes the last big stronghold of the species will be the Reserva de Cuenca Corcovada (Corcovado National Biological Reserve) in southern Costa Rica (5).

HABITAT AND ECOLOGY   Little data available. Lives in forests (1) but in Panama also observed in low bushy secondary growth (4,10,13) and according to another report only occupying shrubby areas or deciduous woodland and disturbed habitats (3,13). Arboreal and diurnal and lives in troops (1). Home range in the Baldwins' study area was 0.175 sq. km and was not a defended territory. Diet is thought to consist of fruit and insects. Saimiri spp. have a short digestive tract which is better suited to an insectivorous rather than a frugivorous diet (1).

THREATS TO SURVIVAL   Habitat destruction and trapping for export in combination with its limited distribution; but deforestation, mainly through clearing for banana plantations, cattle ranches, sugar cane and rice farms, undoubtedly constitutes the major threat (1,2,5,9) and in Costa Rica, banana planting and the continual slash and burn agriculture practised locally have eliminated much suitable habitat (13). In Panama, where most shrub cover has been removed for cattle fodder, the human population is growing rapidly (31% per decade) and the implementation of an old land reform law has led to increasing pressure by the government on land-owners to make profitable use of forested lands or forfeit their holdings: as a result, between 1950 and 1960, the forest cover in the State of Chiriqui was reduced from 61% to 50% (1,2,3,13). Extensive pesticide spraying against malaria and yellow fever are also reported to have had an adverse effect on Squirrel Monkey populations in Panama: in Chiriqui the monkey is said to have been much more plentiful before spraying began. Hunting for meat is not a major factor (1,13), although in Costa Rica it is said to be threatened by capture for the pet trade (8). Animal exporters took large numbers of Saimiri, mainly during the 1950s and early 1960s and especially from all the more accessible areas until the species became too scarce to make the business profitable (1).

CONSERVATION MEASURES TAKEN   S. oerstedi is listed in Appendix 1 of the 1973 Convention on International Trade in Endangered Species of Wild Fauna and Flora, which makes trade in it between acceding nations subject to severe restriction, and trade for primarily commercial purposes banned. It has legal protection in Costa Rica, which is difficult to enforce; it is not protected at all in Panama. The Reserva de Cuenco Corcovada on the Osa Peninsula in south-eastern Costa Rica (36,000 ha, established 1976) safeguards one population (5,9).

CONSERVATION MEASURES PROPOSED Legal protection in Panama. Creation of national parks and wildlife refuges for the coastal lowland Panamanian fauna, including S. oerstedi.

CAPTIVE BREEDING In 1979 there were at least 55 animals (12 bred in captivity) held in eight zoo collections (12).

REMARKS For description of animal see (6,11). S. oerstedi is considered by some authorities to be conspecific with Saimiri sciureus. Populations in Costa Rica and Panama are geographically isolated from the nearest S. sciureus populations in South America. This data sheet was compiled with the assistance of Dr. R.A. Mittermeier, Chairman of the IUCN/SSC Primate Specialist Group.

REFERENCES
1. Baldwin, J.D. and Baldwin, J. (1972). The ecology and behaviour of Squirrel Monkeys (Saimiri oerstedi) in a natural forest in western Panama. Folia primat. 18: 161-184.
2. Baldwin, J.D. and Baldwin, J. (1976). Primate populations in Chiriqui, Panama. In Thorington, R.W. and Heltne, P.G. (Eds), Neotropical Primates: Field Studies and Conservation. National Acad. of Sciences, Washington, D.C.
3. Bennett, C.F. (1968). Human influences on the zoogeography of Panama. Ibero-Americana 51: 1-112.
4. Carpenter, C.R. (1935). Behaviour of Red Spider Monkeys in Panama. J. Mammal. 16(3): 171-180.
5. Freese, C.H. (1977). In litt.
6. Hill, W.C.O. (1962). Primates. Comparative Anatomy and Taxonomy, V Cebidae, Part B. Edinburgh Univ. Press.
7. Lopez, E. (1978). Informe sobre las actividades de la Direccion General de Recursos Pesqueros y Vida Silvestre de Costa Rica. In Morales, R., Macfarland, C., Incer, J. and Hobbs, A. (Eds), Memorias de la Primera Reunion Regional Centroamerican sobre Vida Silvestre. Matagalpa, Nicaragua 25-29 Julio 1978. Unidad de areas silvestres y cuencas del catie. 90-96.
8. Mena Moya, R.A. (1978). Fauna y Caza en Costa Rica. R.M. Costa Rica.
9. Mittermeier, R.A. (1977-81). In litt.
10. Moynihan, M. (1967). Comparative aspects of communication in New World Primates. In Morris, D. (Ed.), Primate Ethology. Aldine Publ. Co., Chicago.
11. Napier, P.H. (1976). Catalogue of Primates in the British Museum (Natural History). Part 1: Families Callitrichidae and Cebidae. British Museum (Natural History), London.
12. Olney, P.J.S. (Ed.) (1980). International Zoo Yearbook 20. Zool. Soc. London.
13. Wolfheim, J.H. (1974). The Status of Wild Primates. Unpd. Report, U.S. Fish and Wildlife Service. 908 pp.

MASKED TITI   VULNERABLE

Callicebus personatus (E. Geoffroy, 1812)

Order   PRIMATES   Family   CEBIDAE

SUMMARY   Occurs in coastal forests of eastern Brazil. Three subspecies described, two of which are considered 'Endangered' and the other 'Vulnerable' based on 1979/80 surveys. Habitat loss is the main threat and much of the forest within its range has already been cut. All three subspecies occur in protected areas but those harbouring C. p. melanochir are not well protected. Main needs are continued protection in reserves, long term ecological studies and a captive breeding programme.

DISTRIBUTION   Eastern Brazil. Ranges from the Rio Itapicuru in northern Bahia to the Rio Tiete in Sao Paulo (4). Kinzey has recently reviewed the taxonomy of the species (4). He recognises three subspecies: C. p. personatus from Espirito Santo and nearby Minas Gerais as far west as Teophilo Otoni, and the Rio Suacui; C. p. melanochir in Bahia as far south as the Rio Itaunas at the northern border of Espirito Santo; and C. p. nigrifrons in the States of Sao Paulo, Rio de Janeiro and southwestern Minas Gerais as far north as the Rio Paranaiba (4). For map see (4).

POPULATION   Mittermeier et al's 1979/80 survey of primates in southeastern Brazil concluded that C. p. personatus and C. p. melanochir were 'Endangered' and C. p. nigrifrons 'Vulnerable' (7). They described the species as fairly adaptable and possibly locally abundant but distribution was patchy and much of its habitat had already been destroyed (7). C. p. personatus populations were said to to be 'doing well' in the two Espirito Santo reserves in which they occur and the animal should continue to thrive and survive in the wild if protection remains adequate (7). C. p. melanochir was found to be either very rare or extinct in the northernmost part of its range where little or no habitat remains, but was still fairly common in remaining forested areas in southern Bahia. Nevertheless, forest destruction has increased tremendously in this area since 1975 and it is unlikely that much will remain outside the 'natural forest' cocoa plantations (cocoa is best grown under shade conditions and in some areas this is accomplished by leaving the large forest trees); however it is unclear whether this monkey is capable of adapting to such plantations (7). This subspecies will probably survive till 1990 in increasingly isolated forest patches in southern Bahia. However it will not survive over the long-term if existing protected areas are not greatly improved and new ones established soon (7). C. p. nigrifrons was the most abundant of the three subspecies and one of the few eastern Brazilian primates which still occurs in reasonable numbers outside parks and reserves. Nonetheless, habitat destruction, especially in areas such as the interior of the State of Sao Paulo, has been such that this animal has declined tremendously in the past few decades (7).

HABITAT AN ECOLOGY   Atlantic coastal forests (1). Kinzey has observed C. personatus in rather diverse habitats, from virtually primary forest (at Sooretama) to secondary forest (a grove of banana trees and Cecropia at Nova Lombardia), and from less than 100 m elevation (Sooretama) to over 1000 m elevation (Itatiaia Park). During 6 days of following a group they were observed to spend 82% of feeding time consuming fruits, 17% on leaves, and 1% on flowers (5).

THREATS TO SURVIVAL   The range of the species coincides with a very high human population density, thus habitat destruction, which is widespread and accelerating, and to a lesser extent hunting for food are serious threats.

Remaining forests are being cut down at a rapid rate for timber and charcoal production and to make way for agriculture and pasture; very little forest remains in the species' original range (6,7).

CONSERVATION MEASURES TAKEN Included in Appendix 2 of the Convention on International Trade in Endangered Species of Wild Fauna and Flora 1973; trade in the species between acceding nations therefore being subject to regulation and monitoring of its effects. Not listed on the Brazilian Endangered Species List. C. p. personatus occurs in at least two protected areas, the Sooretama and Nova Lombardia Biological Reserves, both in Espirito Santo; and possibly in the Rio Doce State Park (although the subspecific identity of the Titi in this park remains to be determined) (5,7). C. p. melanochir occurs in the Monte Pascoal National Park, and perhaps in the Una Biological Reserve in southern Bahia but neither of these areas is especially secure. One-third of Monte Pascoal was given to the Pataxos Indians in August, 1980, and poaching will undoubtedly increase in the remainder of the park unless there is a major effort to increase protection above 1980 levels. Una is overrun with squatters and probably has little future as a reserve. This subspecies also occurs in the Lemos Maia Experimental Station on the edge of Una town. C. p. nigrifrons occurs in Itatiaia National Park, Fazenda Barreiro Rico, both of which have substantial populations. Also occurs in the Mogi-Guacu Experimental Station which has only two or three groups, and is reported to exist in several high altitude resort areas (e.g. Campas de Jordao); probably still abundant in the large reserves of coastal Sao Paulo (7). A study of the distribution and status of all eastern Brazilian primates was undertaken in 1979/80 by R.A. Mittermeier, A.F. Coimbra-Filho, and I. Constable (7), and a short ecological study of a single group was conducted in the Sooretama Reserve by Dr. Warren Kinzey and co-workers in 1977 (5).

CONSERVATION MEASURES PROPOSED In 1980 the IUCN/SSC Primate Specialist Group made the following recommendations: a) Conduct rescue operations to capture Titi groups still living in forest areas slated for destruction. b) Investigate some of the white sand forest inland from Canavieras and also the coastal region between Canavieras and Ilheus to locate other potential reserve sites for C. p. melanochir and other southern Bahian monkeys. c) Investigate the parks and reserves of coastal Sao Paulo to see if C. p. nigrifrons still occurs there. d) Urge the Brazilian government to officially decree the Una Biological Reserve. e) Discuss with CEPLAC, the Regional Cocoa Growing Authority, the possibility of declaring the Lemos Maia Experimental Staion an official Wildlife Sanctuary. f) Encourage Brazilian students to conduct long term ecological studies of Titi populations in Nova Lombardia, Monte Pascoal, Itatiaia and Barreiro Rico to a detailed population survey of the Sooretama Reserve and a study of C. p. melanochir and other southern Bahian monkeys in cocoa plantations belonging to CEPLAC (7).

CAPTIVE BREEDING None are maintained in captivity at the present time (1981) but the Rio de Janeiro Primate Centre is interested in establishing colonies of all three subspecies as soon as possible (7).

REMARKS For description of animal see (2,3,4,9). Hershkovitz's monograph on Callicebus does not include a detailed review of C. personatus (2). Previously four subspecies were recognised (3). This data sheet was compiled with information supplied by Dr. A.F. Coimbra-Filho and by Dr. R.A. Mittermeier, Chairman of the IUCN/SSC Primate Specialist Group.

REFERENCES 1. Coimbra-Filho, A.F. (1977). In litt.
2. Hershkovitz, P. (1963). A systematic and zoogeographic account of the monkeys of the genus Callicebus (Cebidae) of the Amazonas and Orinoco River Basins. Mammalia 27: 1-80.

3. Hill, W.C.O. (1962). Primates. Comparative Anatomy and Taxonomy, IV Cebidae, Part A. Edinburgh Univ. Press.
4. Kinzey, W.G. (1981). Distribution of some Neotropical Primates and the model of Pleistocene forest refugia. In Prance, G.T. (Ed.), Proc. Fifth International Symposium, Association for Tropical Biology, 'The Biological Model of Diversification in the Tropics'. Caracas, Venezuela, February, 1979. Columbia Univ. Press, New York.
5. Kinzey, W. (1978). In litt. to R.A. Mittermeier.
6. Mittermeier, R.A. (1976). Primate Conservation in South and Central America -- Research Priorities and Areas. Unpd. Report. 16 pp.
7. Mittermeier, R.A., Coimbra-Filho, A.F. and Constable, I. (1980). Conservation of Eastern Brazilian Primates. WWF Project 1614. Report for the period 1979/80.
8. Napier, J.R. and Napier, P.H. (1967). A Handbook of Living Primates. Acad. Press, New York.
9. Napier, P.H. (1976). Catalogue of Primates in the British Museum (Nat. Hist.). Part 1: Families Callitrichidae and Cebidae. British Museum (Natural History), London.

Chiropotes albinasus (I. Geoffroy & Deville, 1848)

Order   PRIMATES   Family   CEBIDAE

SUMMARY Brazilian endemic, sparsely distributed over its range and decreasing in some areas. Threatened by loss of habitat and hunting. Protected by law and occurs in several reserve areas. Ecological studies were conducted by J.M. Ayres in 1979/80. More reserves and a captive breeding programme needed.

DISTRIBUTION Brazil. Occurs south of the Rio Amazonas between the Rio Xingu and the Rio Madeira at least as far south as the Rio Jiparana in Rondonia (2,4,6,8), and the upper Rios Aripuana and Roosevelt (8). Avila Pires (1974 in Rylands 1980-81) includes the whole of Rondonia south to the Rio Guapore (8).

POPULATION No estimates available. Ayres who studied the animal in 1979-80 considers it vulnerable (1). The species is sparsely distributed over its range and has now disappeared from parts of the lower Tapajos where it was collected in the 1930s (4).

HABITAT AND ECOLOGY Upland primary tropical rainforest (1,5) in unflooded areas and also sometimes in seasonally flooded forest along river banks (5). Ayres reports it to feed on the seeds of immature fruits, and on bark, fruits and flowers. Arboreal, diurnal and may live at low densities because of its specialised seedeating diet (1). One young is the norm (1).

THREATS TO SURVIVAL Habitat destruction and hunting. Its range is now traversed by the Trans-Amazonian Highway and the Cuiaba-Santarem Highway where considerable development will take place in the future (8). Already extensive clear-felling of forest has occurred to create pasture land for cattle. The development schemes of Rondonia, Aripuana and Juruena completely cover the southern part of its range (8). Colonisers following the Highways not only destroy forests but are avid hunters of monkeys, including C. albinasus, for food, particularly in the Rio Tapajos area. This saki is also hunted to bait cat traps and sometimes killed for its tail, which is used as a duster (4). Such pressures are likely to increase as the Highways make the region more accessible (5). At Dardanelos, on the Rio Aripuana in the State of Mato Grosso it is the most hunted primate after Lagothrix and is thus locally scarce (8).

CONSERVATION MEASURES TAKEN Included in Appendix 1 of the 1973 Convention on International Trade in Endangered Species of Wild Fauna and Flora, which makes it obligatory on countries ratifying the Convention to impose strict control on all trade in the species and ban trade for primarily commercial purposes. Protected by law in Brazil and on the Brazilian endangered species list, but enforcement of protective measures is difficult in remote areas. Early in 1974, a national park was created in Amazonia near Itaituba, on the west bank of the Rio Tapajos not far downstream of the Highway crossing, and includes part of the White-nosed Saki's range; it should provide some measure of protection for the species and its habitat (5). It also occurs in several other existing and proposed areas (8). J.M. Ayres has conducted ecological studies of the species.

CONSERVATION MEASURES PROPOSED More reserves are needed within its range.

CAPTIVE BREEDING In 1979, there were two males held in Cologne Zoo, Federal

Republic of Germany, and one male in Sao Paulo Zoo, Brazil (7). Captive breeding programmes are planned at the Rio de Janeiro Primate Research Centre (5).

REMARKS   For description of animal see (2,5). This data sheet was compiled with information supplied by Jose Marcio Ayres, Dr R.A. Mittermeier, Chairman of the IUCN/SSC Primate Specialist Group, and by Dr A.F. Coimbra-Filho. The latter two also reviewed the final draft of this account.

REFERENCES   1.   Ayres, J.M. (1981). In litt.
2.   Coimbra-Filho, A.F. (1972). Mamiferos ameacados de extincao no Brasil. In Especies de Fauna Brasileira Ameacadas de Extincao. Academia Brasileira de Ciencias, Rio de Janeiro. Pp. 13-98.
3.   Hill, W.C.O. (1960). Primates: Comparative Anatomy and Taxonomy, IV Cebidae, Part A. Edinburgh Univ. Press.
4.   Mittermeier, R.A. and Coimbra-Filho, A.F. (1977). Primate Conservation in Brazilian Amazonia. In Prince Rainier and Bourne, G. (Eds), Primate Conservation. Acad. Press, New York.
5.   Mittermeier, R.A. (1977-81). In litt.
6.   Napier, P.H. (1976). Catalogue of Primates in the British Museum (Nat. Hist.). Part I: Families Callitrichidae and Cebidae. British Museum (Natural History), London.
7.   Olney, P.J.S. (Ed.) (1980). International Zoo Yearbook 20. Zool. Soc. London.
8.   Rylands, A. (1980-81). Conservation of Amazonian Primates. Unpd. Report.

SOUTHERN BEARDED SAKI
or BLACK SAKI

ENDANGERED

Chiropotes satanas satanas (Hoffmannsegg, 1807)

Order   PRIMATES

Family   CEBIDAE

SUMMARY   Limited distribution in one of the most densely inhabited parts of Brazilian Amazonia where much forest destruction has already occurred. Such habitat loss, combined with a partiality for undisturbed high forest, a specialized diet, and a naturally low density cause this taxon to be classified as 'Endangered'. Adequately protected reserves and a captive breeding programme are urgently required.

DISTRIBUTION   Brazil where it occurs south of the Amazon, from the Rio Xingu (3,6,8) to the northeastern part of the State of Maranhao, (3,8) probably to the 'Zona dos Cocais de Sampaio' (1,8). Southeastern limit is probably the dry transition forest of Murca to the east of the Rio Araguaia (8), and to the south, Hill (1960) and Avila Pires (1974 in Rylands 1980-81) limit the range to the mouth of the Rio Araguaia (4,8), and Clutton-Brock and Ayres mention the limit as the transition forest of northern Mato Grosso and Goias (3).

POPULATION   No estimates. In 1981 considered endangered by both Mittermeier and Ayres because of its small range, specialised feeding behaviour and habitat preference, and the extensive habitat destruction within its range (1,2,5). Ayres who is studying the animal reported in 1977 that it was already extinct in many areas (1,8); in 1978 he and Clutton-Brock reported it to have disappeared from the 'Zona Bragantina' near Belem and to be rapidly decreasing in the southern part of its range and in areas close to the Trans Amazonian and Belem - Brasilia Highways (3). In the northeast they reported the only surviving population to be along the Guama River near Avila Araual (3). They also noted that preliminary observations suggested that population density may be naturally low - 15 per sq. km (3).

HABITAT AND ECOLOGY   Tropical rainforest principally in unflooded areas (3,7) and on river banks (3) and preferably undisturbed (5). Habits little known. Chiropotes species are specialised seedeaters but will also eat bark, fruits, flowers and leaves (2,5). Possibly live in groups ranging in size from 30+ animals. In Suriname Mittermeier observed a group of C. s. chiropotes which contained at least 30 animals (6).

THREATS TO SURVIVAL   A small range in a part of Amazonia where much deforestation for development has occurred (3). The Transamazonica (BR 230) and Belem - Brasilia Highways bisect its range, east to west and north to south respectively. The development schemes of Carajas and development in the Rio Araguaia region threaten southern populations (1,8). Ayres (1977) estimated that about one-quarter of its range is covered by 'Polamazon' development schemes. The Tucurui Hydroelectric scheme, to be finished in 1983, will eliminate a large area of its habitat on the Rio Tocantins (8). The tails of this animal are used as dusters and in 1978 were reported to be commonly sold in Belem (3). Mittermeier describes this taxon as being one of the first to disappear in the face of human colonization (5).

CONSERVATION MEASURES TAKEN   Listed in Appendix 2 of the 1973 Convention on International Trade in Endangered Species of Wild Fauna and Flora, therefore any trade in it or its products is subject to regulation and monitoring by ratifying nations. Not protected by law in Brazil (3). Although there are a number of Forest Reserves, National Forests and Indian Reserves within its range, these do not specifically protect wildlife and in some cases are already partly developed (8). J.M. Ayres has begun studies of the status and distribution of this subspecies.

CONSERVATION MEASURES PROPOSED Ayres (1977) has proposed three areas which would be suitable sites for reserves: a) to the east of the refuge area of Altamira between the Rios Tocantins and Xingu, to the north of the Transamazonica; b) to the northeast of the refuge area Bacia do Capim in the south of the Municipalities of Capitao Poco and Ourem; and c) the refuge area of Caxinduba which would incorporate part of the proposed Biological Reserve of Araraquara (1,8). The trade in tails for dusters should be eliminated (3).

CAPTIVE BREEDING In 1979 there were 3 males held in 2 collections (9).

REMARKS For description of animal see (4,7). C. satanas includes one other subspecies, C. s. chiropotes, which has a large range to the north of the mainstream of the Rios Amazonas from the Rio Negro to the Atlantic, and north to the Guianas and Venezuela. It is hunted for food along the Rios Negro and Trombetas, but very little information is available to determine its status (6), though there is no reason to suppose it is threatened (5). The only other species in the genus is C. albinasus which is listed in the IUCN Red Data Book as 'Vulnerable'.

REFERENCES   1.   Ayres, J.M. (1977). A situacao actual da ocorrencia do cuxiu preto, Chiropotes satanas satanas (Hoffmannsegg, 1807). Instituto Nacional de Pesquisas da Amazonia (INPA), Manaus, Unpd. Report. 40pp.
2.   Ayres, J.M. (1981). In litt.
3.   Clutton-Brock, T.H. and Ayres, J.M. (1978). In litt.
4.   Hill, W.C.O. (1960). Primates: Comparative Anatomy and Taxonomy, Vol. IV, Cebidae Part A. Univ. Press, Edinburgh.
5.   Mittermeier, R.A. (1977-81). In litt.
6.   Mittermeier, R.A. and Coimbra-Filho, A.F. (1977). Primate Conservation in Brazilian Amazonia. In Prince Rainier and Bourne, G. (Eds), Primate Conservation. Academic Press, New York.
7.   Napier, P.H. (1976). Catalogue of Primates in the British Museum (Natural History). Part 1: Families Callitrichidae and Cebidae. British Museum (Natural History, London.
8.   Rylands, A. (1980-81). Conservation of Amazonian Primates. Unpd. Report.
9.   Olney, P.J.S. (Ed.) (1980). International Zoo Yearbook 20. Zool. Soc. London.

UAKARI (RED AND WHITE)   VULNERABLE

Cacajao calvus (I. Geoffroy, 1847)

Order   PRIMATES   Family   CEBIDAE

SUMMARY   Two subspecies recognised: the White Uakari Cacajao calvus calvus, with a very small range and naturally rare, in upper Brazilian Amazonia where it is protected by law, and the Red Uakari Cacajao calvus rubicundus, which is vulnerable and has legal protection in Brazil and Peru, but not yet in Colombia where it also perhaps occurs. The total range of the White Uakari could and should be made into a reserve or national park. The Red Uakari still needs study to provide a basis for effective conservation.

DISTRIBUTION   Brazil, Peru and perhaps Colombia. Of the two subspecies the White Uakari C. c. calvus has an extremely small range in Brazil, being restricted to the large fluvial 'island' bordered by the Rio Solimoes (Upper Amazon), the Rio Japura, and the Rio Auati-Parana, an anastomosis between the Japura and Solimoes (8). The Red Uakari, C. c. rubicundus, occurs in the Upper Amazon region in Brazil, Peru, possibly Colombia, where Mittermeier now considers its eastern boundary may be the west bank of the Rio Purus and not as previously thought the Rio Jurua. In the west the Rio Ucayali in Peru appears to be the limit and in the north the Rio Putumayo-Ica, but this is uncertain (8,9).

POPULATION   No estimates available. In 1968 Grimwood found the Red Uakari to be rare and declining in Peru (4) and in 1981 Soini and Mittermeier considered it one of the three most endangered monkeys in Peruvian Amazonia (11). The Brazilian part of its range, especially south of the Amazon, may be its last major stronghold (9), but reliable evidence is lacking. The White Uakari, described by Bates in 1863 as 'rare in the limited district which it inhabits', still is so (1,2,4), and is considered by Mittermeier to be endangered because any adverse factor operating within its very restricted range could exterminate it very rapidly. In particular it is apparently an easy target for hunters (10).

HABITAT AND ECOLOGY   The entire known range of the White Uakari is within varzea forest (forest on the flood plain of silt-laden white-water rivers like the Rio Amazonas). Two groups of Red Uakaris encountered in a 1973 Brazilian survey were in igapo swamp forest (permanently flooded) and this is also the professed habitat in Amazonian Peru (11). All Uakaris seem to avoid the margins of larger rivers (4) and travel in large groups sometimes of more than 30 and even as many as 50 animals (9). Reported to associate with other primates including Squirrel Monkeys (Saimiri sciureus), Tufted Capuchins (Cebus apella) and White-fronted Capuchins (Cebus albifrons) (2,8). Diet is probably fruit, nuts and seeds (4).

THREATS TO SURVIVAL   When Mittermeier investigated its range in 1973 the White Uakari was rarely hunted and only occasionally shot for fish bait or human consumption; also its habitat had not been seriously disturbed (9,10). However, should hunting pressure increase or any habitat destruction occur within its limited range, it could be exterminated very rapidly (1,10). The current situation (1981) is unknown (10). The decline of the Red Uakari in Peru is attributed to hunting; it is easy to kill and its flesh is highly esteemed (4). Luscombe reported it to be greatly prized as a pet in Peru (7). 433 specimens were exported from Iquitos, Peru, between 1962 and 1968, but as far as is known none since (14).

CONSERVATION MEASURES TAKEN   This Uakari is listed in Appendix 1 of the

1973 Convention on International Trade in Endangered Species of Wild Fauna and Flora, and therefore any trade in it or its products is subject to strict regulation by ratifying nations, trade for primarily commercial purposes being banned. The Red Uakari is on the Peruvian Endangered Species List; specimens held as pets are confiscated. Both the Red and White forms are on the Endangered Species List of Brazil, and Dr. R.A. Mittermeier undertook a preliminary survey of the species in Brazil in 1973 (9).

CONSERVATION MEASURES PROPOSED The entire fluvial island that comprises the range of the White Uakari should be made a biological reserve or national park. The area has suffered little human disturbance, has high densities of a large variety of monkeys and birds, and is an excellent sample of the regional fauna (9). Surveys of the Red Uakari and further detailed study of the White Uakari are needed (10), and such a study is planned for 1982-83 as part of the IUCN/SSC's Primate Specialist Groups Global Strategy for Primate Conservation (6).

CAPTIVE BREEDING In 1979, there were eight male and 14 female Red Uakaris held in eight zoo collections and three male and four female White Uakaris in four collections (13). The Red Uakari has been breeding well for several years in the 'Monkey Jungle', Miami, Florida (7).

REMARKS For description of animal see (12). The White Uakari has a mainly white coat, the Red Uakari's being rusty red although in some parts of its range with a white admixture (9). Uakaris have a very short tail, which does not exceed one third of the length of the body (8,9,12). Cabrera (1957) and Napier (1976) regard the White and Red Uakaris as separate species Cacajao calvus and C. rubicundus (3). Hershkovitz and Mittermeier, whom we follow, regard them as conspecific (5,9). This data sheet was compiled with the assistance of Dr. R.A. Mittermeier, Chairman of the IUCN/SSC Primate Specialist Group.

REFERENCES
1. Ayres, M. (1981). In litt.
2. Bates, H.W. (1863). A Naturalist on the River Amazon. John Murray, London.
3. Cabrera, A. (1957-1961). Catalogo de los mamiferos de America del Sur. Rev. Mus. Argent. Cienc. Nat. 'Bernardino Rivadavia'. Cienc. Zool. 4(1,2): 1-731.
4. Grimwood, I.R. (1969). Notes on the distribution and status of some Peruvian mammals 1968. American Committee for International Wild Life Protection and New York Zool. Soc. Special Publication No. 21.
5. Hershkovitz, P. (1972). Notes on New World Monkeys. In Olney, P.J.S. (Ed.), International Zoo Yearbook 12. Zool. Soc. London. Pp. 3-12.
6. IUCN/SSC Primate Specialist Group. (1981). Global strategy for primate conservation, 1981-1983. Report for IUCN's Species Survival Commission.
7. Luscombe, A. (1977). In litt.
8. Mittermeier, R.A. and Coimbra-Filho, A.F. (1977). Primate conservation in Brazilian Amazonia. In Prince Rainier and Bourne, G. (Eds), Primate Conservation. Acad. Press, New York.
9. Mittermeier, R.A. (1978). The Weird Uakaris of Amazonia. Unpd. Report.
10. Mittermeier, R.A. (1977-81). In litt.
11. Mittermeier, R.A. and Soini, P. (1981). Pers. Comm.
12. Napier, P.H. (1976). Catalogue of Primates in the British Museum (Nat. Hist.). Part 1: Families Callitrichidae and

Cebidae. British Museum (Natural History), London.

13. Olney, P.J.S. (Ed.), (1980). *International Zoo Yearbook 20*. Zool. Soc. London.

14. Soini, P. (1972). The capture and commerce of live monkeys in the Amazonian region of Peru. *Int. Zoo Yb.*12: 26-36.

BLACK-HEADED UAKARI

VULNERABLE

Cacajao melanocephalus (Humboldt, 1811)

Order   PRIMATES

Family   CEBIDAE

SUMMARY   Restricted both in distribution and habitat, occurring mainly in the igapo forests of Brazilian Amazonia, though also recorded from Colombia and southern Venezuela. Total numbers unknown. Protected in Brazil and Colombia and occurs in a number of Refuge Areas.

DISTRIBUTION   Northern Brazil, southern Venezuela and Colombia. Principally found along small tributaries of the upper Rio Negro, on its left bank as far east as the Rio Araca, which joins the Rio Demini and flows into the Rio Negro opposite the township of Barcelos. The southern limit is definitely the Rio Solimoes, the western limit apparently the foot of the Cordillera Macarena, a spur of the eastern Andes some 200 km south of Bogota, Colombia. The northern limit is not definitely known but there are reliable records from the State of Amazonas in southern Venezuela (3,5,6). More specifically limits in Colombia are to the north the southern bank of the Rio Guaviare, to the southwest the Rio Yari and to the south the Rio Caqueta (2). For map see (3).

POPULATION   Total numbers unknown. In Brazil this is one of the more abundant primates along the small right bank tributaries of the Rio Negro (1,6) and the Rio Japura (1) but everywhere else it seems quite rare (6). In Venezuela it is apparently endangered (4). In Colombia local authorities consider it to be threatened on the grounds that it is rare, heavily hunted for food and restricted in choice of habitat (3,5). Overall Mittermeier classifies it as 'Vulnerable', but not presently 'Endangered' because of the remoteness of much of its Brazilian range (5).

HABITAT AND ECOLOGY   Lives primarily or exclusively in the igapo (seasonally or permanently flooded) forests of the small 'blackwater' rivers and lakes that are typical of the alluvial plains in the area bounded by the Rios Japura, Solimoes and Negro (6). All Uakaris avoid the margins of larger rivers (5) and seem to prefer the canopy of primary forest (2,3). They travel in groups of 20-40 animals (1,3,6). Diet is still poorly known but appears to be primarily or exclusively fruits and nuts (3,5).

THREATS TO SURVIVAL   Hunted for food in Colombia (3,5), but not usually in Brazilian Amazonia. Occasionally shot for use as fish, turtle or cat bait (5). Mittermeier reports that attitudes towards monkey hunting can change quickly with the influx of new settlers and/or the disappearance of more desirable game species; such a shift could have a very rapid deleterious effect on the status of the Black-headed Uakari (6). Habitat destruction does not appear to pose any immediate problem in Brazil as the igapo has little commercial value and the region as a whole has a fairly low human population (6).

CONSERVATION MEASURES TAKEN   All Cacajao species are included in Appendix 1 of the 1973 Convention on International Trade in Endangered Species of Wild Fauna and Flora, trade in them between acceding nations thus being subject to severe restriction, trade for primarily commercial purposes banned. C. melanocephalus is included in the Brazilian Endangered Species List and is protected by law in Colombia (2). It is not known to be present in any national parks or reserves. A four month survey of Cacajao spp. was undertaken by Dr. R.A. Mittermeier in 1973 (5,6). Rylands reports that in Brazil the species occurs in the Jau Refuge Area (9,10) (2,272,000 ha) decreed in September 1980 and in the Pico da Neblina (2,200,000 ha) decreed in June 1979 (10).

CONSERVATION MEASURES PROPOSED Rylands suggests that a reserve between the Rios Negro and Japura in the region of the Rios Curicuriari, Marie and Inuixi would protect populations south of the Rio Negro (10).

CAPTIVE BREEDING It has appeared in zoo collections on rare occasions but usually does not survive more than a few months (6). In 1979 Cologne Zoo had one male and Sao Paulo Zoo three males (8).

REMARKS For description of animal see (6,7). Uakaris have a very short tail which is extraordinary in strictly arboreal monkeys and unique in New World monkeys (6). It appears likely that two subspecies exist (2,3). This data sheet was compiled with the assistance of Dr. R.A. Mittermeier, Chairman of the IUCN/SSC Primate Specialist Group.

REFERENCES 1. Ayres, M. (1981). In litt.
2. Hernandez-Camacho, J. (1981). Pers. comm.
3. Hernandez-Camacho, J. and Cooper, R.W. (1976). The Nonhuman Primates of Colombia. In Thorington, R.W. Jr. and Heltne, P.G. (Eds), Neotropical Primates: Field Studies and Conservation. National Acad. of Sciences, Washington, D.C.
4. Mittermeier, R.A. (1977-81). In litt.
5. Mittermeier, R.A. and Coimbra-Filho, A.F. (1977). Primate Conservation in Brazilian Amazonia. In Prince Rainier and Bourne, G. (Eds), Primate Conservation. Acad. Press, New York.
6. Mittermeier, R.A. (1978). The Weird Uakaris of Amazonia. Unpd Report.
7. Napier, P.H. (1976). Catalogue of Primates in the British Museum (Nat. Hist.). Part 1: Families Callitrichidae and Cebidae. British Museum (Nat. Hist.), London.
8. Olney, P.J.S. (Ed.) (1980). International Zoo Yearbook 20. Zool. Soc. London.
9. Rylands, A. B. (1980-81) Conservation of Amazonian primates. Unpd. Report.
10. Rylands, A. B. (1981). Pers. Comm.

BROWN HOWLER MONKEY

Alouatta fusca (E. Geoffroy, 1812)

Order   PRIMATES   Family   CEBIDAE

SUMMARY   Inhabits eastern Brazil where it is hunted for food and affected by widespread habitat destruction. Possibly also susceptible to epidemics. Protected in some reserves but more needed. Studies aimed at its long term conservation began in 1980.

DISTRIBUTION   Eastern Brazil where it is restricted to coastal forests from Bahia at about 12°S to Rio Grande do Sul at about 30°S. Two subspecies usually recognized (6,7), but their validity still has to be determined (4). A. f. fusca once occurred north of the Rio Doce in northern Espirito Santo, southern Bahia, and adjacent parts of Minas Gerais, and in some highland areas south of the Rio Doce, but has now disappeared from most of this area (4). A. f. clamitans has a large range, occurring from the Rio Doce south through Rio de Janeiro and adjacent parts of Minas Gerais to Sao Paulo, Parana, Santa Catarina and northeastern Rio Grande do Sul (4). A third subspecies A. f. beniensis has been described from Puerto Salinas on the Rio Beni in northern Bolivia (7), but it may actually belong to a different Alouatta species (2).

POPULATION   Numbers unknown (2). The species might quite possibly be in the 'Endangered' category (3,4). In 1980 A. f. fusca (if valid) was considered highly endangered and on the verge of extinction in most of its range. The 'best' population occurred on the Fazenda Montes Claros and this might ensure its survival. However the population may consist of hybrid animals, if so, then this subspecies will almost certainly go extinct in the wild before 1990 (4). A. f. clamitans, once very abundant, was by 1980 considered 'Endangered' in southeastern Brazil. Its status in the southern states is unknown and overall the species is therefore considered 'Indeterminate' (4). However since the only two protected areas in which the species is known to occur do not together exceed 8000 ha the IUCN/SSC Primate Specialist Group believe it is a likely candidate for the 'Endangered' category (4).

HABITAT AND ECOLOGY   Recorded from undisturbed high forest; forested coastal lowlands, and in 'plains with small remnants of forest along rivers and creeks' (8). Known to be arboreal and diurnal.

THREATS TO SURVIVAL   Habitat destruction and hunting. Its size and the quality of its meat make this species a prized food item in some areas. Nonetheless, destruction of its forest habitat is the major factor in its decline (2,4). The east coast of Brazil has a dense human population, consequently habitat destruction has been widespread and recently accelerating, and remaining forests are being rapidly felled to make way for development projects, plantations, farms and even for the production of charcoal (3,4). Epidemics may also be a significant factor in its disappearance. Alouatta species in other parts of South and Central America are known to be far more susceptible to periodic epidemics e.g. of Sylvan yellow fever, than other monkeys and this may have caused its decline in Itatiaia National Park. An epidemic in a small and isolated reserve like the majority of those in eastern Brazil is likely to have disastrous effects (4).

CONSERVATION MEASURES TAKEN   The species is listed in Appendix 2 of the 1973 Convention on International Trade in Endangered Species of Wild Fauna and Flora, trade in it between acceding nations being therefore subject to regulation and monitoring of its effects. A 1979/80 survey of protected areas in southeastern Brazil made the following observations: A. f. fusca still exists in the Rio Doce State Forest Park where it is extremely rare, in the Nova Lombardia Biological Reserve in Espirito Santo which has 3 or 4 groups, and on the privately owned Fazenda Montes Claros which has at least 15 groups (4,5). However these latter two areas are south of its known southern limit and may, at least in Montes Claros, consist of hybrid animals. It is extremely rare, or already extinct, in Monte Pascoal National Park, and definitely extinct in the Biological Reserves of Una, Sooretama and Corrego do Veado, and Pau Brasil Ecological Station (4). The survey found A. f. clamitans to be thriving in the Cantareira Reserve on the outskirts of Sao Paulo city and in the privately owned Fazenda Barreiro Rico. It was however rare in the Morro do Diabo State Reserve and the Poco d'Anta Biological Reserve, extremely rare or extinct in the Itatiaia and Serra dos Orgaos National Park, and extinct in Tijuca National Park and the Caitetus Reserve (4). Espedito Cordeiro da Silva began studies in 1980 to examine the taxonomy of A. fusca to determine whether the two subspecies were valid, and also to develop a long term research programme to monitor the Cantareira and Barreiro Rico populations (4).

CONSERVATION MEASURES PROPOSED Survival will depend on adequately protected reserves. Surveys are also needed in the parks and reserves of coastal Sao Paulo, Parana, Santa Catarina and Rio Grande do Sul to determine its presence and status (4).

CAPTIVE BREEDING A captive breeding stock is to be established in the Rio de Janeiro Primate Center (2,4).

REMARKS For description of animal see (1,7). Another name for A. fusca, which is still often used, is Alouatta guariba (1,6). This data sheet was compiled from information supplied by Dr. A.F. Coimbra-Filho and by Dr. R.A. Mittermeier, Chairman of the IUCN/SSC Primate Specialist Group.

REFERENCES
1. Hill, W.C.O. (1960). Primates: Comparative Anatomy and Taxonomy. IV Cebidae. Part A. Edinbugh Univ. Press.
2. Mittermeier, R.A. (1977-81). In litt.
3. Mittermeier, R.A. (1976). Primate Conservation in South and Central America -- Research Priorities and Areas. Ms. 16 pp.
4. Mittermeier, R.A., Coimbra-Filho, A.F. and Constable I.D. (1980). Conservation of Eastern Brazilian Primates. WWF Project 1614. Report for the period 1979/80.
5. Mittermeier, R.A., Coimbra-Filho, A.F. and Constable, I.D. (1980). Range Extension for an Endangered Marmoset. Oryx 15(4): 380-383.
6. Napier, P.H. and Napier, J.H. (1967). A Handbook of Living Primates. Acad. Press, London.
7. Napier, P.H. (1976). Catalogue of Primates in the British Museum (Nat. Hist.). Part 1: Families Callitrichidae and Cebidae. British Museum (Nat. Hist.), London.
8. Wolfheim, J.H. (1974). The Status of Wild Primates. Unpd. Report, U.S. Fish and Wildlife Service. 908 pp.

GUATEMALAN or BLACK HOWLER MONKEY INDETERMINATE

Alouatta villosa (Gray, 1845)

Order PRIMATES Family CEBIDAE

SUMMARY Occurs in southern Mexico, northern Guatemala and Belize. Total numbers unknown but being depleted in Mexico by habitat destruction and hunting. Little known of its status in Guatemala and Belize, but protected in Tikal National Park, Guatemala. It used to be thought that villosa was a subspecies of Alouatta palliata, the Mantled howler, however A. villosa has been recognized as a distinct species since 1970 when Smith observed an apparent case of sympatry between it and A. palliata mexicana. Smith used the name pigra for this species because he believed that the name villosa was indeterminable. Napier (1976), however , examined the villosa material in the British Museum (Natural History), and indicated that the type specimen was from Mexico and that the name villosa therefore had priority over pigra and should be used in its place.

DISTRIBUTION Mexico, Guatemala and Belize (1,3,4): in Mexico it occurs in the States of Tabasco, Chiapas, Yucatan, Campeche (2,3), and Quintana Roo (1); in Guatemala only in the north extending into adjacent parts of Belize (2). For map see (3).

POPULATION Numbers unknown. Mittermeier reports it to be declining in the Mexican part of its range and to no longer occur in some localities where it was recorded earlier this century. Nothing is known of its status in Guatemala or Belize (1).

HABITAT AND ECOLOGY Tropical rainforest. Seems to prefer extensive, undisturbed and mesic or high plateau tropical forest (3), of which the general area it occupies contains one of the few remaining samples in Middle America. Howlers (Alouatta spp.), which are among the largest of the New World Monkeys (2) are arboreal and diurnal (1).

THREATS TO SURVIVAL Habitat destruction and hunting have brought about the decline of the species in Mexico (1). The alteration of the habitat may be responsible for the sympatry of Alouatta palliata mexicana and A. villosa in Macuspana, Tabasco, observed by Smith (3), who postulates that A. p. mexicana can survive in disturbed and secondary forest but A. villosa not. Thus recent disturbance through road construction and increased agriculture of forested areas previously inhabited by A. villosa may have allowed A. p. mexicana to move in and colonize (3).

CONSERVATION MEASURES TAKEN 'Alouatta palliata (villosa)' is included in Appendix 1 of the 1973 Convention on International Trade in Endangered Species of Wild Fauna and Flora, so that trade in it by countries which have ratified the Convention is subject to severe restriction, and trade for primarily commercial purposes is banned. However the listing needs clarification and the two would best be listed separately as A. palliata and A. villosa (= pigra). The species is afforded some protection by the Tikal National Park (57,600 ha) in northeastern Guatemala (1).

CONSERVATION MEASURES PROPOSED Surveys are needed to determine the status of this species throughout its range and especially in Mexico (1), to form the basis of a conservation plan.

CAPTIVE BREEDING None in captivity. A captive breeding programme would be desirable but howlers are difficult to keep in captivity (1).

REMARKS For description of animal see (3). The taxonomy of Central American howlers is confusing (2,3). A. villosa is sometimes referred to as A. pigra e.g. by Smith (1970) (3). It is also on occasions treated as a subspecies of A. palliata, the Mantled Howler, however Smith observed an apparent case of sympatry between two supposed races of A. palliata - mexicana and villosa (which he called pigra) - in Mexico, and on this basis elevated villosa to specific status (3). Smith used the name pigra because he believed that the name villosa was indeterminable. However Napier (1976) examined the villosa material in the British Museum (Natural History) and indicated that the type specimen was from Mexico and that the name villosa therefore had priority over pigra and should be used in its place (2). Alouatta caraya is also given the vernacular name Black Howler Monkey (2), but is a totally different species. This data sheet was compiled with information supplied by Dr. A.F. Coimbra-Filho and Dr. R.A. Mittermeier, Chairman of the IUCN/SSC Primate Specialist Group.

REFERENCES 1. Mittermeier, R.A. (1977-81). In litt.
2. Napier, P.H. (1976). Catalogue of Primates in the British Museum (Nat. Hist.). Part 1: Families Callitrichidae and Cebidae. British Museum (Natural History), London.
3. Smith, J.D. (1970). The systematic status of the Black Howler Monkey, Alouatta pigra Lawrence. J. Mammal. 51(3): 358-369.
4. Wolfheim, J.H. (1974). The Status of Wild Primates. Unpd. Report, U.S. Fish and Wildlife Service. 908 pp.

Lagothrix flavicauda (Humboldt, 1812)

Order   PRIMATES   Family   CEBIDAE

SUMMARY   Endemic to northern Peru where it has an extremeley limited range, occurring only in Amazon forest which intrudes in finger-like projections into the Andes. Believed extinct until rediscovered in 1974. Habitat destruction, hunting for food, a small range, and a slow breeding rate combine to make this an 'Endangered' species. Legally protected, and the subject of studies which by 1981 had identified two suitable reserve sites. A captive breeding programme would be desirable.

DISTRIBUTION   Northern Peru. Restricted to the forested slopes in both branches of the East Andes chain in the Dept. of Amazonas (between 5°30' and 6°30'S, 77°20' and 78°20'W) (3), and in October 1979 a small group were observed in cloud forest in the eastern part of La Libertad Dept. (9). This record extends the known range of the monkey southward some 200 km (9). Probably also survives in the Andes further north, in the Amazonas Department near the Ecuadorian border, in the mountains between the Chiriaco and Nieva rivers (between 5° and 5°30'S), in the Campanquis chain in Loreto Dept., and in the northern chain in San Martin Dept. (3). Limits of the range are not precisely known. First described by Humboldt from trimmed, flat skins used as saddle covers by Peruvian muleteers in the vicinity of Jaen, Dept. of Cajamarca. It is uncertain whether it actually occurs in that area since no other records are known; the skins could well have come from the Dept. of Amazonas, east of the Rio Maranon. Two specimens were collected in 1925 by Watkins at La Lejia (06°07'S, 77°28'W; alt. 230 m), Dept. of Amazonas, three more in 1926 by Hendee at Pucatambo (06°09'S, 77°11'W; alt 1555 m), Dept. of San Martin (1,5,7); more recently, in April/May 1974, an expedition searching for evidence of L. flavicauda's continued existence obtained four skins, three skulls, and a live specimen from Pedro Ruiz, an army engineers' outpost in the vicinity of Chachapoyas: it had originally been caught in the upper Rio Mayo area on the eastern edge of its currently known range (5,6,7). In 1976 the species was observed in the wild near Pedro Ruiz (2). Since then it has become the subject of studies (3). For map see (7).

POPULATION   Total numbers unknown, but undoubtedly declining. Leo Luna who is studying the species (1980) believes it will be extinct in the wild by 2030 unless effective reserves are established (3). Similarly Graves and O'Neill felt it 'could quickly become rare and endangered' if not protected (2). Mittermeier et al in 1977 rated the species 'Endangered' (7).

HABITAT AND ECOLOGY   Humid and very humid montane rainforest of the Amazonian type, which probably represents an intrusion of the riverine rainforest into climatically suitable areas on the eastern slope of the Andes (3,5,7,9). Data on altitudinal range varies: over 1800 m (3); 500-2500 m (7); 2400-2500 m (9); Graves and O'Neill encountered it at 1670 m (2); Watkins' specimens were from 230 m and Hendee's 1555 m (1,7). Leo Luna who began a field study of the species in 1978 found its habitat to be one of steep gorges and ravines, with trees 20-40 m high depending on the zone; the trunks being usually under 1 m diameter, except for some Cedrela spp. and Ficus spp. In the lower zones the understorey was dense with many Palmaceae species; in the most humid areas were many vines, Bromeliaceae and Orchidaceae, and in the upper zones and on top 'suro', Chusquea sp., predominated. Although the study was in the dry season it drizzled almost every day and every morning the fog crept up the mountain, making the forest humid and cold (3). Groups consisted of 4-10 adults (3) (in 1926 a troop of about 20 was seen (7,10)). Diet was observed to be mainly fruit and flowers (2,3,9) and a stomach analysis of one individual showed no insect or other animal residue (2,3). Birth rate seemed low with perhaps only one birth per year per group (3).

THREATS TO SURVIVAL   Hunting and habitat destruction within its restricted range (2,3,5,6,7,9). Leo Luna considered habitat destruction to be the worst danger. In all localities she visited the forest was being cut down, especially on the less steep slopes where humidity was high and which were the best places for Ficus spp., an important food tree. Although still on a relatively small scale cutting was bound to increase (3). Graves and O'Neill in their 1976 observations in the vicinity of Garcia noted that large sections of forest had been cleared on the lower slopes by settlers who had followed a newly opened road. At that time human disturbance above 800 m was limited to areas adjacent to the road, however the species was being increasingly hunted for food as settlers moved into its elevational range (2). Mittermeier et al, in the mid 1970s, believed it was primarily threatened by hunting for food and skins, with killing of females to obtain infants for sale as pets also a factor and that if hunting pressure continued the animals would disappear before the habitat (4,5,7). At that time hunting pressure from local people was greatly aggravated by that attributable to the army, which was constructing roads through parts of the species range and paid hunters to provide construction crews with fresh meat, regardless of whether it was derived from such threatened species as L. flavicauda and the Spectacled Bear (Tremarctos ornatus) and despite the fact that domestic animals were available (5,6,7).

CONSERVATION MEASURES TAKEN   Listed on Appendix 2 of the 1973 Convention on International Trade in Endangered Species of Wild Fauna and Flora, so that trade in it between acceding nations is subject to regulation and monitoring of its effects. Listed as 'Endangered' in Peru, thus hunting and trapping of it are illegal, but enforcement is difficult in isolated areas. Does not occur in any protected area (3). Mariella Leo Luna began field studies on this species in 1977 (3).

CONSERVATION MEASURES PROPOSED   More effective enforcement of the legal protection. Mittermeier in March 1981 reported that Leo Luna's work had identified two suitable sites for reserves - one in the Venceremos region to the north near the Rio Mayo and one in the Pajaten region to the south. The latter is also an area of great archaeological importance and its likelihood of being declared a national park is therefore enhanced. The Venceremos area should also be established a 'zona reservada' and requires additional surveys to determine the limits of the area and to learn more of the L. flavicauda populations there (4). In Leo Luna's 1980 paper she mentions that a reserve in the Dept. of Amazonas (or between it and San Martin) would also protect the Spectacled Bear, the Cock of the Rock, Rupicola peruviana, and the Spatuletail Loddigesia mirabilis. L. flavicauda is the only large mammal endemic to Peru, and as such is recommended for inclusion in a set of postage stamps depicting endangered Peruvian wildlife, being issued by the Government to stimulate interest in national wildlife resources (4,5,7).

CAPTIVE BREEDING   As of March 1981 (4) the live specimen, a juvenile male, of L. flavicauda that was obtained during the April/May 1974 expedition (5,6,7) still survived and was on public exhibition at the Museum of Natural History in Lima, where it has been joined by another juvenile male captured in September 1978; Mittermeier in 1981 reported both animals to be thriving (4). As the species has never before been publicly exhibited, some useful publicity for conservation has resulted (4). A captive breeding programme is desirable.

REMARKS   For description of animal see (1,7,8). This data sheet was compiled with the assistance of Dr. R.A. Mittermeier, Chairman of the IUCN/SSC Primate Specialist Group.

REFERENCES   1.   Fooden, J. (1963). A revision of the woolly monkeys (genus Lagothrix). J. Mammal. 44(2): 213-247.

2. Graves, G.R. and O'Neill, J.P. (1980). Notes on the Yellow-tailed Woolly Monkey (Lagothrix flavicauda) of Peru. J. Mammal. 61(2): 345-347.
3. Leo Luna, M. (1980). First field study of the Yellow-tailed Woolly Monkey. Oryx 15(4): 386-389.
4. Mittermeier, R.A. (1977-81). In litt.
5. Mittermeier, R.A., Macedo-Ruiz, H. de and Luscombe, A. (1975). A Woolly Monkey rediscovered in Peru. Oryx 13(1): 41-46.
6. Mittermeier, R.A., Macedo-Ruiz, H. de and Luscombe, A. (1975). Special report: Mystery monkey. Animal Kingdom 78(3): 2-7.
7. Mittermeier, R.A., Macedo-Ruiz, H. de, Luscombe, A. and Cassidy, J. (1977). Rediscovery and conservation of the Peruvian Yellow-tailed Woolly Monkey (Lagothrix flavicauda). In Prince Rainier and Bourne, G. (Eds), Primate Conservation. Acad. Press, New York.
8. Napier, P.H. (1976). Catalogue of Primates in the British Museum (Nat. Hist.). Part 1: Families Callitrichidae and Cebidae. British Museum (Nat. Hist.), London.
9. Parker, T.A. III and Barkley, L. J. (1981) New locality for the Yellow-tailed Woolly Monkey. Oryx 16(1): 71-72.
10. Thomas, O. (1927). A remarkable new monkey from Peru. Ann. Mag. Nat. Hist. 9 (19): 156-157.

Lagothrix lagothricha (Humboldt, 1812)

Order   PRIMATES   Family   CEBIDAE

SUMMARY   An inhabitant of the forests of northwestern South America. Four subspecies are recognized. Numbers unknown but threatened by hunting for food and for the pet trade, and because of its preference for undisturbed high forest which is fast disappearing. Tends to be the first primate to disappear following human encroachment. Legal protection, surveys, and the setting aside of reserve areas are needed.

DISTRIBUTION   Amazonian region west of the Rio Negro and Rio Tapajos in Brazil as far as the eastern slopes of the Andes in Colombia, Venezuela, Ecuador, Peru and Bolivia (1,6). Four subspecies are recognized: L. l. lagothricha from northwestern Brazil, (1,2), southern Venezuela probably west of the Rio Casiquiare (23), southeastern Colombia, extreme northern Peru and northeast Ecuador (1,2,23). The northernmost record in Colombia is from the north bank of the Rio Guaviare, above the mouth of the Rio Mapripa (1,2) and its northwestern extension meets the southeastern extension of L. l. lugens approximately at the junction of the peidmont forest with lowland rainforest. Observations of animals in the region of Florencia and the Orteguaza River Basin suggest that the gradation from one subspecies to another is gradual rather than abrupt (2). Rylands (1980-81) notes that L. l. lagothricha probably has a more restricted distribution in Brazil than was thought by Fooden who included the whole of the area between the Rios Negro and Japura. Rylands reports that local people say it does not inhabit this region and occurs only above Sao Gabriel da Cachoeira on the upper Rio Negro and its tributaries - the Rio Tiquie, Icana, Xie and Uapes in the region of Tarauaca, and on the Rio Negro in the region of Cucui. Woolly Monkeys do however, occur in the region of the Rio Japura and local people also report that it occurs north of the Rio Negro on the upper Rio Curicuriari (7). L. l. cana is found from west southwest Brazil, between the Rios Tapajos and Jurua, westward into southeastern Peru and thence northwards along the left bank of the upper Rio Ucayali to its confluence with the lower Rio Pachitea (1). It also occurs in the Pando region of Amazonian Bolivia in a small limited range in the head basin of the Rio Abuna on the frontier with Brazil (10), and in the 1960s quite likely still occurred east of a line linking Cobija and Porvenir i.e. on the right bank of the Abuna, however by 1981 it no longer occurred there (10). L. l. poeppigii inhabits the upper Amazonian region west of the Rios Jurua, Aguarico and Napo, in west northwest Brazil south of the Rio Solimoes, northeastern Peru and eastern Ecuador (1). L. l. lugens is almost entirely confined to Colombia, although a population has been reported from Venezuela and it may possibly occur in northern Ecuador (2). In Colombia Fooden describes it as occurring in the upper Rio Magdalena valley in the Department of Huila and on the eastern slope of the Cordillera Oriental from the upper Rio Caqueta to the upper Rio Arauca (1). Hernandez-Camacho and Cooper (1976) report a 'recently' discovered population in an area of dense piedmont forest in the Rio Sarare drainage in the State of Apure, adjacent to the Colombian border, in Venezuela, although Handley (1976) obtained no specimens (2,7,9). Its range continues south and west to the eastern slopes of the Andes, extending easterly to the plains along the Rio Ariari, to include the Macarena Mtns. It also occurs in southern parts of the Depts of Tolima and Cundinamarca (2). Also Hernandez-Camacho and Cooper (1976) report the discovery of two populations of Lagothrix in the upper San Jorge Valley in the Dept. of Cordoba, around San Pedro and in the Serrania de San Lucas in southeastern Bolivar. Only juvenile specimens had been obtained by the time of their paper and these seemed similar to L. l. lugens (2). These populations are continuous with known populations of L. l. lugens along the eastern slopes of the Central Andes (2). For map of Colombian distribution of the species see (2).

POPULATION In Peru, Bolivia, Colombia and Brazil, Lagothrix is severely threatened in any area occupied by man (2,3,7,8,10,11), and this is undoubtedly also true in Venezuela and Ecuador. Rylands (1980-81) reports that it is quite probable that in many areas Lagothrix is already extinct or seriously reduced in numbers, and distribution is discontinuous. The species is now probably absent from the Rio Negro in Brazil and the Rio Amazonas in Colombia. In Acre local people report that Lagothrix have disappeared east of the Rio Jurua between the Rios Valparaiso and Acuria except on the upper Rio Valparaiso (7). For Colombia, Hernandez-Camacho and Cooper (1976) describe L. lagothricha as probably the most persecuted species in the country because of hunting for its meat (2). For Peru Neville et al (1976) during surveys in Peru, found Lagothrix to be extensively hunted and requiring protection (11). In Venezuela Mondolfi (1976) describes it as very locally distributed and apparently rare (12). Hunting pressure combined with the Woolly Monkey's slow reproductive rate and its preference for undisturbed forest have placed it (and indeed the genus) in a precarious position throughout its range (3). Mittermeier (1981) considers some subspecies possibly endangered (5).

HABITAT AND ECOLOGY In Colombia Lagothrix is always found in some type of humid forest e.g. the gallery and palm (Mauritia flexuosa association) forests of the eastern plains, flooded and non-flooded primary rain forest and cloud forest as high as 3000 m; and always in primary forest, not secondary forest (2,15). Reported to travel in groups of up to 50 animals (2,3,8,11,15,16) and 60-70 even recorded (17). Diet consists primarily of fruit, supplemented by leaves, seeds, berries and some insects (2,3,15). In Colombia the palm fruits Maximiliana elegans, Mauritia flexuosa and Jessenia polycarpa are particularly favoured (23). Single births are the usual after a gestation of 225 days. There is no evidence of a breeding season (14).

THREATS TO SURVIVAL Hunting and habitat loss. Woolly monkeys are heavily hunted for their meat, which is highly esteemed (1,2,3,7,10,11,18,21), and to obtain infants for sale as pets; indeed they are the favourite monkey for both. They apparently make delightful pets and are more in demand locally than any other primate. The usual method of capture is to shoot the mother and remove the infant from her body after she falls to the ground. The infant is frequently killed as well (2,3,4,7,13). An international trade mainly for pets has also existed. Between 1968-1972 almost 13,000 were imported into the U.S.A. from Colombia, (19,20), and 16,500 were exported from Iquitos Peru between 1962 and 1971 (13). In the Amazonian region, the species is used to bait traps for spotted and other cats. These various hunting pressures, the Woolly Monkey's preference for undisturbed high forest, and its slow reproductive rate, make its status precarious throughout its range (2,3,4,7). In northern Colombia Bernstein et al (1976) reported that Lagothrix is the first to disappear following human encroachment and destruction of forests, and is usually absent from isolated forest pockets (8). Since much of the once extensive continuous forest is being reduced to disjunct remnants this has serious consequences for the species.

CONSERVATION MEASURES TAKEN Included in Appendix 2 of the 1973 Convention on International Trade in Endangered Species of Wild Fauna and Flora, trade in it between acceding nations is therefore subject to strict regulation and monitoring of its effects. Regarding protected areas: L. l. lagothricha: the refuge area of Norte Napo covers part of its range in Colombia, and in Brazil it is possible that of all the refuge areas apparently within its range only Parana has viable populations. L. l. cana: despite its wide range is poorly represented in refuge areas. In Brazil the areas of importance are the Parecis and Serra das

Oncas refuge areas in the south of its range where the animal is threatened by three development centres. The Marmelos and Purus refuge areas are also important. It does occur in the Amazonia National Park but is not common there. L. l. poeppigii has been observed in the Samiria National Reserve in Peru (11). A number of refuge areas occur within its range but only few proposed or existing reserves. Only the Eirunepe refuge area is within its Brazilian range. L. l. lugens is protected in several reserves in Colombia (2,7,18) -- the Macarena National Park, the Paramo de Tama National Park and the Amacayacu National Park (23).

CONSERVATION MEASURES PROPOSED The species should be transferred to Appendix 1 of the Convention on International Trade in Endangered Species of Wild Fauna and Flora, which would make trade in it subject to severe restriction, and prohibit trade for primarily commercial purposes. The species now needs full protection wherever it occurs and a series of thorough surveys to learn more of its ecology and to locate suitable sites for reserves (3). Rylands (1980-81) proposes the following: L. l. lagotricha: reserves should be considered on the Rio Japura and along the Colombian frontier, also a more detailed survey of its distribution in Brazil is required; L. l. cana: reserves should be considered on the Rios Purus and Jurua as well as in the development areas of Acre; and L. l. poeppigii: reserves should be considered in the area between the Rios Jurua and Javari or on the Peruvian frontier.

CAPTIVE BREEDING In 1979 there were 93 males and 133 females (58 captive bred) held in 50 zoological collections (22).

REMARKS For description of animal see (1,6). Fooden's study of the taxonomy and distribution of Lagothrix led him to describe four subspecies (as above). However, although he clearly defines the ranges of these subspecies, the change from one to another is in fact gradual. For example, in Colombia, in the region of Florencia and the Rio Orteguaza (a tributary of the Rio Caguan), the change from L. l. lagotricha to L. l. lugens is through a changing frequency of buffy brown coats to the characteristic greyish to blackish coat of L. l. lugens. Individuals of intermediate colour and those typical of one or other of the subspecies are to be observed in the same locality (2). The only other species in this genus, Lagothrix flavicauda from Peru is also listed in the IUCN Red Data Book, in the 'Endangered' category. This data sheet was compiled with the assistance of Dr. R.A. Mittermeier, Chairman of the IUCN/SSC Primate Specialist Group.

REFERENCES   1.   Fooden, J. (1963). A revision of the Woolly Monkeys (genus Lagothrix). J. Mammal. 44(2): 213-247.
2.   Hernandez-Camacho, J. and Cooper, R.W. (1976). The non-human primates of Colombia. In Thorington, R.W. Jr. and Heltne, P.G. (Eds), Neotropical Primates: Field studies and Conservation. National Acad. of Sciences, Washington, D.C.
3.   Mittermeier, R.A. and Coimbra-Filho, A.F. (1977). Primate conservation in Brazilian Amazonia. In Prince Rainier and Bourne, G. (Eds), Primate Conservation. Acad. Press, New York.
4.   Mittermeier, R.A., Macedo-Ruiz, H., Luscombe, B.A. and Cassidy, J. (1977). Rediscovery and conservation of the Peruvian Yellow-tailed Woolly Monkey (Lagothrix flavicauda). In Prince Rainier and Bourne, G. (Eds), Primate Conservation. Acad. Press, New York.
5.   Mittermeier, R.A. (1977-81). In litt.
6.   Napier, P.H. (1976). Catalogue of Primates in the British Museum (Nat. Hist.). Part 1: Families Callitrichidae and

Cebidae. British Museum (Natural History), London.

7. Rylands, A. B. (1980-81). Conservation of Amazonian Primates. Unpd. Report.

8. Bernstein, I.S., Balcaen, P., Dresdale, L., Gouzoules, H., Kavanagh, M., Patterson, T. and Neyman-Warner, P. (1976). Differential effects of forest degradation on primate populations. Primates 17(3): 401-411.

9. Handley, C.O. Jr. (1976) Mammals of the Smithsonian Venezuelan Project. Brigham Young Univ. Sci. Bull. 20 (5): 1-89.

10. Izawa, K. and Bejarano, G. (1981). Distribution ranges and patterns of nonhuman primates in western Pando, Bolivia. Reports of New World Monkeys (1981): 1-12.

11. Neville, M., Castro, N. and Marmol, A. (1976). Censusing primate populations in the reserved area of the Pacaya and Samiria Rivers, Department Loreto, Peru. Primates 17(2): 151-181.

12. Mondolfi, E. (1976). Fauna silvestre de los basques humedas de Venezuela. Asociacion Nacional para la defensa de la Naturaleza Venezuela.

13. Soini, P. (1972). The capture and commerce of live monkeys in the Amazonian region of Peru. Int. Zoo Yb. 12: 26-36.

14. Williams, L. (1967). Breeding Humboldt's Woolly Monkey Lagothrix lagothricha at Murrayton Woolly Monkey Sanctuary. Int. Zoo Yb. 7: 86-89.

15. Kavanagh, M. and Dresdale, L. (1975). Observations on the Woolly Monkey (Lagothrix lagothricha) in northern Colombia. Primates 16(3): 285-294.

16. Izawa, K. (1976). Group sizes and compositions of monkeys in the Upper Amazon Basin. Primates 17(3): 367-399.

17. Nishimura, A. and Izawa, K. (1975). The group characteristics of Woolly Monkeys (Lagothrix lagothricha) in upper Amazonian basin. Proc. 5th Int. Cong. Primat., Nagoya 1974, Karger, Basel.

18. Klein, L.L. and Klein, D.J. (1976). Neotropical primates: Aspects of habitat usage, population density, and regional distribution in La Macarena, Colombia. In Thorington R.W., Jr. and Heltne, P.G. (Eds), Neotropical Primates: Field studies and conservation. Nat. Acad. of Sciences, Washington, D.C.

19. Green, K.M. (1976). The nonhuman primate trade in Colombia. In Thorington, R.W., Jr. and Heltne, P.G. (Eds), Neotropical Primates: Field studies and conservation. Nat. Acad. of Sciences, Washington, D.C.

20. Muckenhirn, N.A. (1976). Addendum to the nonhuman primate trade in Colombia. In Thorington, R.W., Jr. and Heltne, P.G. (Eds), Neotropical Primates: Field studies and conservation. Nat. Acad. of Sciences, Washington, D.C.

21. Heltne, P.G. and Thorington, R.W. Jr. (1976). Problems and potentials for primate biology and conservation in the New World. In Thorington, R.W., Jr. and Heltne, P.G. (Eds), Neotropical Primates: Field studies and conservation. Nat. Acad. of Sciences, Washington, D.C.

22. Olney, P.J.S. (Ed.) (1980). International Zoo Yearbook 20. Zool. Soc. London.

23. Hernandez-Camacho, J. (1981). Pers. comm.

WOOLLY SPIDER MONKEY ENDANGERED

Brachyteles arachnoides (E. Geoffroy, 1806)

Order PRIMATES Family CEBIDAE

SUMMARY Sparsely distributed in southeastern Brazil, this monotypic genus is on the verge of extinction. In 1980 total numbers were estimated at only a few hundred and decreasing. Decline caused by habitat destruction and hunting. Protected by law. Viable populations are only known to occur in two privately protected reserves totalling less than 3000 ha in area and containing less than 100 animals. Survival of the species will depend on continued protection of these areas and on its status in the coastal mountains of Sao Paulo which need surveying, although are unlikely to house more than a few hundred animals. A captive breeding programme is planned at the Rio de Janeiro Primate Centre. This species requires immediate conservation action to ensure its survival.

DISTRIBUTION Southeastern Brazil. Very sparsely distributed in the States of Sao Paulo, Rio de Janeiro and Minas Gerais (2,3,6). According to P.E. Vanzolini (In litt., 1977), restricted to the eastern part of the State of Sao Paulo. Napier (1976) and Wolfheim (1974) describe the range as extending from the southern part of the State of Bahia to the State of Sao Paulo, which includes the States of Minas Gerais, Espirito Santo and Rio de Janeiro (7,12). Presumably once occurred in all Atlantic coastal forests of eastern and southeastern Brazil (9) and Hill (1962) believes it was even more widespread during the Pleistocene (4). Vieira (1944) suggests that before the destruction of the coastal forests began, Brachyteles occupied the entire region from Cabo de Sao Roque in the State of Rio Grande do Norte to Rio Grande do Sul, southernmost State in Brazil (9). Vieira (1955) lists the following as recent localities: southern Bahia (Rio Jucururu), eastern Minas Gerais (Rio Matipo), Espirito Santo (Rio Doce), Rio de Janeiro (Serra dos Orgaos, Itatiaia, Serra da Mantiqueira), and Sao Paulo (Ipanema, Itarare, Juquia, Piedade, Ubatuba, Alto da Serra) (10).

POPULATION Highly endangered and threatened with extinction; by 1981 only a few hundred still survived (6). Surveys in 1979/80 by Mittermeier et al found it to persist in only two privately protected reserves together containing less than 100 animals. They believed tiny groups totalling less than 25 individuals might survive in three other protected areas. Coastal Sao Paulo has long been considered a stronghold for the species but surveys are urgently needed to determine if this is true as the area has been subjected to intense hunting pressure and the Woolly Spider Monkey is a prime target. In any case Mittermeier et al doubt whether numbers in this area exceed a few hundred (6). In 1971 the estimated total was 3000 (1) and in 1972 2000 (2). When Prince Maximilian zu Wied explored southeastern Brazil in the early 1800s he found this species to be quite abundant and his expeditions frequently lived off Brachyteles meat (6).

HABITAT AND ECOLOGY Undisturbed high forest (3,6), including both lowland tropical and montane rainforest (7). Behaviour poorly known, as the species keeps to the crowns of the tallest trees and has never been observed on the ground. Diet, based on stomach contents of one specimen, consists of vegetable matter, including seeds, and some insects (7). Has been seen in bands of 6-12 individuals (7).

THREATS TO SURVIVAL Habitat loss and hunting. This species has always been rare and is threatened by loss of forest habitat through clearance for fuel, settlement and agriculture. Being a large edible primate, it is hunted for food

(6). Since the 1800s the Atlantic coastal forest of eastern Brazil have suffered a tremendous increase in human population and widespread, largely uncontrolled forest destruction to make way for coffee plantations, sugar cane, cocoa, eucalyptus, cattle pasture and above all lumber extraction and charcoal production. In recent years industrial development has also taken its toll. As a result the forests have been devastated, especially during the rapid development and economic expansion which began in the 1960s. Only a tiny fraction of the original forest cover remains (6).

CONSERVATION MEASURES TAKEN Included in Appendix 1 of the 1973 Convention on International Trade in Endangered Species of Wild Fauna and Flora, so that trade in it between acceding nations is subject to severe restriction, trade for primarily commercial purposes banned. Legally protected and included in the Brazilian Endangered Species List. Definitely known to occur in two privately protected areas totalling about 3000 ha, namely Fazenda Montes Claros in Minas Gerais (5,6) and Fazenda Barreiro Rico in Sao Paulo. May also still exist in the Biological Reserve of Nova Lombardia (Espirito Santo), and possibly in the National Parks of Itatiaia and Serra dos Orgaos (Rio de Janeiro), but populations are too small to have any long term conservation significance. May occur in Rio Doce State Forest Park but confirmation needed (6). A study of the distribution and status of all eastern Brazilian primates was conducted in 1979/80 by Dr. R.A. Mittermeier, Dr. A.F. Coimbra-Filho, and I. Constable (6).

CONSERVATION MEASURES PROPOSED Survival to the 1990s will depend on its status in the Sao Paulo coastal mountains and continued protection on the two fazendas in which it still definitely occurs. In particular in 1980 the IUCN/SSC Primate Specialist Group made the following recommendations: i) conduct a detailed survey of the three major parks and reserves in coastal Sao Paulo to determine whether Brachyteles still exists in the region and, if so, how it can best be protected; ii) urge the Brazilian government to take an active interest in Fazenda Montes Claros and assist them in purchasing this area and establishing it as a federal protected area; iii) encourage the owner of Fazenda Barreiro Rico to continue protecting the Woolly Spider monkey population on his land; iv) investigate several small, privately-protected forests in Minas Gerais, where remnant groups of Brachyteles are said to still occur. If populations exist, and if they do not appear to be viable over the long term, then thought should be given to translocating them to other protected areas (6).

CAPTIVE BREEDING It has never bred in captivity and in 1980 there was only one captive individual - a female at Sao Paulo Zoo (6,8). The Rio de Janeiro Primate Centre is planning a captive breeding programme (6).

REMARKS For description of animal see (4,7,11). This data sheet was compiled from information supplied by Dr. A.F. Coimbra-Filho and Dr. R.A. Mittermeier, Chairman of the IUCN/SSC Primate Specialist Group.

REFERENCES
1. Aguirre, A.C. (1971). O mono, Brachyteles arachnoides (E. Geoffroy). Acad. Brasil. Cienc. 53 pp.
2. Coimbra-Filho, A.F. (1972). Mamiferos ameacados de extincao no Brasil. In Especies de Fauna Brasileira Ameacadas de Extincao. Academia Brasileira de Ciencias, Rio de Janeiro. Pp. 13-98.
3. Coimbra-Filho, A.F. (1977). In litt.
4. Hill, W.C.O. (1962). Primates. Comparative Anatomy and Taxonomy. V. Cebidae. Part B. Edinburgh Univ. Press.
5. Mittermeier, R.A., Coimbra-Filho, A.F. and Constable, I.D. (1980). Range extension for an endangered marmoset. Oryx 15(4): 380-383.

6. Mittermeier, R.A., Coimbra-Filho, A.F. and Constable, I. (1980). Conservation of eastern Brazilian primates. WWF Project 1614. Report for the period 1979/80.
7. Napier, P.H. (1976). Catalogue of Primates in the British Museum (Nat. Hist.). Part 1: Families Callitrichidae and Cebidae. British Museum (Nat. Hist.), London.
8. Olney, P.J.S. (Ed.) (1980). International Zoo Yearbook 20. Zool. Soc. London.
9. Vieira, C.C. (1944). Os simios do Estado de Sao Paulo. Papeis Vaul. Dept. de Zool. Sec. de Agric. Sao Paulo 4(1): 1-31.
10. Vieira, C.C. (1955). Lista remissiva dos mamiferos do Brasil. Arq. Zool. Sao Paulo 8: 341-474.
11. Walker, E.P. (1975). Mammals of the World. The Johns Hopkins Univ. Press, Baltimore and London.
12. Wolfheim, J.H. (1974). The Status of Wild Primates. Unpd. Report, U.S. Fish and Wildlife Service. 908 pp.

LONG-HAIRED SPIDER MONKEY
or WHITE-BELLIED SPIDER MONKEY

VULNERABLE

Ateles belzebuth E. Geoffroy, 1806

Order   PRIMATES   Family   CEBIDAE

SUMMARY   Occurs in Peru, Ecuador, Colombia, Venezuela and Brazil. Numbers unknown. Threatened by hunting and habitat destruction. Has been the subject of an ecological investigation. More reserves and surveys needed.

DISTRIBUTION   Peru, Ecuador, Colombia, Venezuela and Brazil (5,6,8,17). Three subspecies are recognised: A. b. belzebuth occurs in lowlands near the junction of the Rio Orinoco and Rio Caura in central Venezuela south to the valley of the Rio Negro, Brazil, westward to Colombia east of the Cordillera Oriental (Mambita), Ecuador east of the crest of the Andes, and to northeastern Peru (Sarayacu) (5,8,22). In Colombia its range includes the Amazon lowlands northwards at least to the Guaviare River and also a fingerlike projection to the Macarena Mountains and the piedmont forests (locally to 1300 m) northward to the Upia River drainage in southern Boyaca Dept. The subspecific identificaton of populations occurring in the piedmont north of the Upia River to the border of the Comisaria of Arauca is not yet known (6). For map see (6). In Peru it occurs north of the Rio Amazonas and Maranon but possibly also south of the Maranon to the west of the mouth of the Rio Huallaga (20). In Brazil it occurs north of the Rio Negro although local people report it to be confined to the upper reaches of the northern tributaries entering the Rio Negro, and absent from the Rio Uapes (possibly because of the large areas of white sand forests (caatingas) in this region. A skin obtained from Boa Vista, reportedly from the Serra Mucajai, indicates its presence as far east as the Rio Branco north of the Rio Negro where it abuts the range of Ateles paniscus paniscus (20). The range of A. b. hybridus includes the eastern bank of the lower Cauca River basin in Colombia, the Departments of Magdalena and Cesar (northward to the southernmost slopes of the Santa Marta Mtns), the northernmost extension of the Perija Mtns in the Dept. of Guajira, and the middle Magdalena River region at least to the northern Depts. of Caldas and possibly formerly to northwest Cundinamarca (6,19). There are also at least two additional populations in Colombia on both flanks of the eastern Andes on the border with Venezuela; one occurs in the Catatumbo River basin of North Santander Dept. and the other in the northeastern piedmont in the Comisaria of Arauca (6). In Venezuela, Mondolfi reports it to be widely distributed in tropical forests of the Cuenca del Lago de Maracaibo; also in piedmont forests of the Serra de Perija as far as the Rio Guasare, and in the llanos of Trujillo, Merida and Tachira up to the lake. In addition, it inhabits the Andean piedmont forest in the Depts. of Barinas (Ticoporo Forest), Portuguesa (Mijagual Forest and north of Aparicion), and in the Dept. of Apure (San Camilo Forest). In the Cordillera de la Costa, where it is rare and very locally distributed, it has been observed in the Guatopo National Park (22). A. b. marginatus is endemic to Brazil occurring on the south side of the Rio Amazonas between the Rio Tapajos and Rio Tocantins, State of Para (8,17).

POPULATION   Numbers unknown. No data located for Ecuador or Venezuela. In Peru A. belzebuth is described as much rarer than the closely related A. paniscus, another Red Data Book primate (12), has disappeared from many parts of its range (5) and is suffering greatly from hunting pressure (13). In Brazil, A. b. marginatus is described by Rylands as the most severely threatened of the Brazilian Ateles (20). In Colombia A. belzebuth is considered threatened in areas where once it was very abundant e.g. gallery forest of the Cesar River Valley, where it is now absent because of forest destruction (19).

HABITAT AND ECOLOGY Forest. Reported to be partial to undisturbed high forest and survive poorly, or not at all, if this habitat is destroyed (14), although in northern Colombia Bernstein et al found that in response to logging A. belzebuth would persist, albeit in reduced numbers, if some large trees remained (1). In Colombia they are usually observed at middle or high-canopy levels, but are not uncommonly seen foraging on the ground. Diurnal and mainly frugivorous, favouring the palm Jessenia polycarpa, also Ficus insipida and the wild plum Spondias mombin (3,6,15,19). Ateles live in groups of 2-40, usually 15-20 (10,11,15,17,18), group size varying considerably with habitat and altitude (2,15). Groups tend to break into small subgroups rather than move together as a single cohesive unit (3,15). Ateles take 4-5 years to mature, have a long gestation of 226-232 days and produce a single infant only about once every 2-3 years (3).

THREATS TO SURVIVAL Hunting and habitat destruction (1,6,14). Hunting is the main cause of decline in Peru, Amazonia, and large parts of Colombia (6,14). Ateles are large and very good to eat and have therefore been subjected to heavy hunting pressure throughout most of their range, even in areas where other primates are usually not molested (3,4,5,6,8,11,12,13,14,15,18). Their size and noisy habits make them easy to locate, follow and hunt. They are also persecuted by cat hunters who use them as bait. Infants are captured for sale as pets (although Ateles are not as popular as Lagothrix and Cebus) (15). Since Ateles is a slow breeder populations can be rapidly reduced with moderate hunting pressure (4,11). Hernandez-Camacho and Cooper (1976) also mention sylvatic yellow fever as a possible cause of Ateles decline in parts of Colombia (6). The relatively small range of A. b. marginatus is bisected by the Transamazonica along which there has been considerable settlement, and by the Cuiaba-Santarem Highway, around which extensive colonization is planned for the future (20).

CONSERVATION MEASURES TAKEN Listed on Appendix 2 of the 1973 Convention on International Trade in Endangered Species of Wild Fauna and Flora, trade in it between acceding nations being therefore subject to regulation and monitoring of its effects. Completely protected by law in Peru (12). Not known whether protected by law in the rest of its range. Occurs in La Macarena National Park, Colombia (11). The range of A. b. belzebuth in Brazil is 'relatively well represented' by proposed and existing reserves as well as by two refuge areas (20). The species has been the subject of an ecological investigation (10).

CONSERVATION MEASURES PROPOSED Legal protection throughout its range and data on numbers and distribution are required as the basis of a conservation plan (14). Rylands mentions that reserves on the Colombian and Venezuelan borders would be desirable to protect populations of A. b. belzebuth (20). He also suggests the need for surveys in the region of the Pico da Neblina and in the mountains north of the Rio Negro to determine the status and habitat requirements of A. b. belzebuth (20). For A. b. marginatus, the regions of the Rio Cupari and Altamira are of especial importance regarding the conservation of the taxon. Altamira is the only refuge area known to be within its range but the monkey is already rare or extinct in much of this area. Reserves are also needed in the regions of the Rios Xingu, Tapajos and Tocantins (20).

CAPTIVE BREEDING In 1978 four were known to have been bred in captivity at four zoos (21).

REMARKS For description of animal see (6,8,17). Kellogg and Goldman (8) recognise four species of Ateles but a number of recent authors (6,7,16) have considered all Spider monkeys to be conspecific under the name A. paniscus. Dr. R.A. Mittermeier, Chairman of the IUCN/SSC Primate Specialist Group very kindly reviewed this data sheet in June 1981.

REFERENCES   1.   Bernstein, I.S., Balcaen, P., Dresdale, L., Gouzoules, H., Kavanagh, M., Patterson, T. and Neyman-Warner, P. (1976). Differential effects of forest degradation on primate populations. Primates 17: 401-411.
2.   Durham, N.M. (1971). Effects of altitude differences on group organisation of wild Black Spider Monkeys (Ateles paniscus). Proc. 3rd Int. Congr. Primatology, Zurich 1970. Vol. 3: 32-40.
3.   Eisenberg, J.F. (1976). Communication mechanisms and social integration in the Black Spider Monkey, Ateles fusciceps robustus and related species. Smithsonian Contributions to Zoology 213: 1-108.
4.   Freese, C. (1977). In litt.
5.   Grimwood, I.R. (1969). Notes on the distribution and status of some Peruvian mammals 1968. Special Publication No.21 American Committee for International Wild Life Protection and New York Zoological Society.
6.   Hernandez-Camacho, J. and Cooper, R.W. (1976). The Nonhuman Primates of Colombia. In Thorington, R.W. Jr. and Heltne, P.G. (Eds), Neotropical Primates: Field Studies and Conservation. National Academy of Sciences. Washington D.C.
7.   Hershkovitz, P. (1972). The recent mammals of the Neotropical region: a zoogeographic and ecological review. In Keast, A., Erk, F.C. and Glass, B. (Eds), Evolution, Mammals and Southern Continents. State Univ. of New York Press. Albany. 311-432.
8.   Kellogg, R. and Goldman, E.A. (1944). Review of the Spider Monkeys. Proc. U.S. Nat. Museum 96 (3186): 1-45.
9.   Klein, L.L. (1971). Observations on copulation and seasonal reproduction of two species of Spider Monkeys Ateles belzebuth and A. geoffroyi. Folia Primatologica 15 (3-4): 233-248.
10.   Klein, L.L. (1972). The ecology and social organisation of the Spider monkey, Ateles belzebuth. PhD Thesis. Univ. of California, Berkeley.
11.   Klein, L.L. and Klein, D.J. (1976). Neotropical Primates: aspects of habitat usage, population density, and regional distribution in La Macarena, Colombia. In Thorington, R.W. Jr. and Heltne, P.G. (Eds), Neotropical Primates: Field Studies and Conservation. National Academy of Sciences. Washington D.C.
12.   Luscombe, A. (1977). In litt.
13.   Macedo, H. de. (1977). In litt.
14.   Mittermeier, R.A. (1977-81). In litt.
15.   Mittermeier, R.A. and Coimbra-Filho, A.F. (1977). Primate conservation in Brazilian Amazonia. In Prince Rainier and Bourne, G.H. (Eds), Primate Conservation. Acad. Press. New York.
16.   Moynihan, M. (1970). Some behaviour patterns of Platyrrhine Monkeys. II Saguinus geoffroyi and some other tamarins. Smithson. Contrib. Zool. No. 28.
17.   Napier, P.H. (1976). Catalogue of Primates in the British Museum (Natural History). Part 1: Families Callitrichidae and Cebidae. British Museum (Natural History).
18.   Neville, M., Castro, N. and Marmol, A. (1976). Censusing primate populations in the reserved area of the Pacaya and

Samiria Rivers, Department Loreto, Peru. <u>Primates</u> 17(2): 151-181.

19. Hernandez-Camacho, J. (1981). Pers. comm.
20. Rylands, A. (1980-81). Conservation of Amazonian Primates. Unpd. Report.
21. Olney, P.J.S. (Ed.) (1980). <u>International Zoo Yearbook 20.</u> Zool. Soc. London.
22. Mondolfi, E. (1976). <u>Fauna silvestre de los bosques humedos de Venezuela.</u> Asociacion Nacional para la defensa de la Naturaleza Venezuela.

BROWN-HEADED SPIDER MONKEY

INDETERMINATE

Ateles fusciceps (Gray, 1866)

Order   PRIMATES

Family   CEBIDAE

SUMMARY   A little known species ranging from Panama through Colombia to Ecuador. Numbers unknown, but believed threatened by habitat destruction and hunting. Surveys are required to determine its status and ecology before conservation measures can be proposed.

DISTRIBUTION   Panama, Colombia and Ecuador. Two subspecies are recognised: A. f. fusciceps on the Pacific side of the cordillera of Ecuador (10,13,18) and possibly in Colombia in the Mira River Valley of Narino Dept. on the border with Ecuador (16) and A. f. rufiventris inhabiting the western cordillera of the Andes from southwestern Colombia northward on the west side of the Rio Cauca to eastern Panama (Mt. Pirre) (9,10,11,13). In Colombia Hernandez-Camacho and Cooper described the latter's (which they call Ateles paniscus robustus) distribution as the entire Pacific lowlands (except the region around Jurado in northwestern Choco Dept.); the Uraba region of northwestern Antioquia Dept., the Departments of Cordoba, Sucre, and northern Bolivar eastward to the lower Cauca River and along the western bank to south-central Antioquia (the most southerly record is from Concordia). In recent times the northernmost limit was the southern bank of the Canal del Dique in the Caragena region; however, it probably formerly occurred northward to the Pendales region, where some luxurious hygrotropophytic (adapting to seasonal changes in moisture) forest still survives (11). For map see (11).

POPULATION   No information on numbers located, but considered threatened because of hunting and habitat loss (11,15,21). A 1978 list of Panamanian threatened species listed it as vulnerable (21), and for Colombia Hernandez-Camacho and Cooper note the disappearance of Ateles from areas where it used to occur, although they don't specify which Ateles (11). No information has been located concerning its status in Ecuador.

HABITAT AND ECOLOGY   No field data available (1,5), however all Ateles species are closely related so the following comments probably also apply to A. fusciceps. Ateles inhabit forest and have been observed in evergreen, semideciduous, deciduous (7), tropical evergreen and cloud forest (14), and mangrove swamp (6). Reported to be partial to undisturbed high forest and to survive poorly, or not at all, if this habitat is destroyed (15). However some authors have recorded them in mature secondary forest (2,14) and Hernandez-Camacho and Cooper mention them occurring in remnant and degraded forest although noting a preference for more mature forest (11). A. f. rufiventris is reported as occupying the greatest range of habitat types of all the Colombian forms of Ateles, from hygrotropophytic through pluvial to cloud forest (11). Spider monkeys live in groups of 2-40, group size varying considerably with habitat and altitude (3,16). Groups tend to break up into small subgroups rather than moving together as a single cohesive unit (5,16). Diurnal and mainly frugivorous (5,11,16). Ateles take 4-5 years to mature, have a long gestation of 226-232 days and produce a single infant only about once every 2-3 years (4,5).

THREATS TO SURVIVAL   Hunting and habitat destruction (8,16,21). Ateles are large and very good to eat and have therefore been subjected to heavy hunting pressure throughout much of their range, even in areas where other primates are usually not molested (5,11,16). Their large size and nosiy habits make them easy

189

to locate, follow and hunt (11,16). Since Ateles are slow breeders, populations can be rapidly reduced with moderate hunting pressure (15).

CONSERVATION MEASURES TAKEN Listed on Appendix 2 of the 1973 Convention on International Trade in Endangered Species of Wild Fauna and Flora, trade in it between acceding nations being therefore subject to regulation and monitoring of its effects. No information located on whether protected in Ecuador, Colombia, or Panama or whether it occurs in any protected areas.

CONSERVATION MEASURES PROPOSED Legal protection is needed throughout its range if it does not already exist. Surveys are required to determine its status and ecology before conservation measures can be proposed (15).

CAPTIVE BREEDING In 1978 Washington Zoo bred 2 males and 1 female (20).

REMARKS For description of animal see (9,11,13,18). Kellogg and Goldman (13) recognise four species of Ateles but a number of recent authors (11,12,17) have considered all Spider monkeys to be conspecific under the name A. paniscus. A zone of hybridization exists in Panama between A geoffroyi panamensis and A. fusciceps rufiventris; (19). Kellogg and Goldman use the name A. f. robustus for A. f. rufiventris, Heltne and Kunkel (1975) have shown however that the latter name takes nomenclature precedence (10).

REFERENCES

1. Baldwin, L.A., Patterson, T.L. and Teleki, G. (1977). Field research on Callitrichid and Cebid Monkeys: An historical, geographical and bibliographical listing. Primates 18(2): 485-507.

2. Bernstein, I.S., Balcaen, P., Dresdale, L., Gouzoules, H., Kavanagh, M., Patterson, T. and Neyman-Warner, P. (1976). Differential effects of forest degradation on primate populations. Primates 17: 401-411.

3. Durham, N.M. (1971). Effects of altitude differences on group organisation of wild Black Spider Monkeys (Ateles paniscus). Proc. 3rd Int. Congr. Primatology, Zurich 1970. Vol. 3: 32-40.

4. Eisenberg, J.F. (1973). Reproduction in two species of Spider monkeys, Ateles fusciceps and Ateles geoffroyi. J. Mammal. 54(4): 955-957.

5. Eisenberg, J.F. (1976). Communication mechanisms and social integration in the Black Spider Monkey, Ateles fusciceps robustus and related species. Smithson. Contrib. Zool. 213: 1-108.

6. Eisenberg, J.F. and Kuehn, R.E. (1966). The behaviour of Ateles geoffroyi and related species. Smithson. Misc. Coll. 151(8): 1-63.

7. Freese, C. (1976). Censusing Aloutta palliata, Ateles geoffroyi and Cebus capucinus in the Costa Rican dry forest. In Thorington, R.W. Jr. and Heltne, P.G. (Eds), Neotropical Primates: Field Studies and Conservation. National Academy of Sciences, Washington DC.

8. Green, K.M. (1976). The nonhuman primate trade in Colombia. In Thorington, R.W. Jr. and Heltne, P.G. (Eds), Neotropical Primates: Field Studies and Conservation. National Academy of Sciences, Washington D.C.

9. Hall, E.R. and Kelson, K.R. (1959). The Mammals of North America. The Ronald Press Company.

10. Heltne, P.G. and Kunkel, L.M. (1975). Taxonomic notes on the pelage of Ateles paniscus paniscus, A. p. chamek (sensu

Kellogg and Goldman, 1944) and A. fusciceps rufiventris (=
A. f. robustus), Kellogg and Goldman, 1944. J. Med.
Primatol. 4: 83-102.

11. Hernandez-Camacho, J. and Cooper, R.W. (1976). The
Nonhuman Primates of Colombia. In Thorington, R.W. Jr.,
and Heltne, P.G. (Eds), Neotropical Primates: Field Studies
and Conservation. National Academy of Sciences,
Washington DC.

12. Hershkovitz, P. (1972). The recent mammals of the
Neotropical region: a zoogeographic and ecological review.
In Keast, A., Erk, F.C. and Glass, B. (Eds), Evolution,
Mammals and Southern Continents. State Univ. of New
York Press, Albany.

13. Kellogg, R. and Goldman, E.A. (1944). Review of the Spider
Monkeys. Proc. U.S. Nat. Museum 96(3186): 1-45

14. Leopold, A.S. (1959). Wildlife of Mexico. Univ. of
California Press, Berkeley and Los Angeles.

15. Mittermeier, R.A. (1977-81). In litt.

16. Mittermeier, R.A. and Coimbra-Filho, A.F. (1977). Primate
conservation in Brazilian Amazonia. In Prince Rainier and
Bourne, G.H. (Eds), Primate Conservation. Acad. Press.
New York.

17. Moynihan, M. (1970). Some behaviour patterns of
Platyrrhine monkeys. II Saguinus geoffroyi and some other
tamarins. Smithson. Contrib. Zool. No.28.

18. Napier, P.H. (1976). Catalogue of Primates in the British
Museum (Natural History). Part 1: Families Callitrichidae
and Cebidae. British Museum (Natural History).

19. Rossan, R.N. and Baerg, D.C. (1977). Laboratory and feral
hybridization of Ateles geoffroyi panamensis Kellogg and
Goldman 1944 and A. fusciceps robustus Allen 1914 in
Panama. Primates 18(1): 235-237.

20. Olney, P.J.S. (Ed.) (1980). International Zoo Yearbook 20.
Zool. Soc. London.

21. Vallester, E. (1978). Informe de Panama sobre la situacion
de la Fauna Silvestre. In Morales, R., Macfarland, C., Incer,
J. and Hobbs, A. (Eds), Memorias de la Primera Reunion
Regional Centroamerican sobre Vida Silvestre. Matagalpa,
Nicaragua 25-29 Julio 1978. Unidad de areas silvestres y
cuencas del catie.

GEOFFROY'S SPIDER MONKEY
or BLACK-HANDED SPIDER MONKEY

VULNERABLE

Ateles geoffroyi Kuhl, 1820

Order   PRIMATES   Family   CEBIDAE

SUMMARY   Ranges from Mexico to Panama. Numbers unknown. Threatened mainly by habitat destruction but hunting is an additional major threat in some regions. Found in several national parks and has been the subject of a number of ecological investigations. Effective legal protection is necessary throughout its range.

DISTRIBUTION   Mexico and Central America; from about 24°N in southern Tamaulipas, eastern Mexico, and 19°N in Jalisco on the west coast, through Guatemala, Belize, El Salvador, Honduras, Nicaragua and Costa Rica to the valley of the River Tuira in eastern Panama (3,11,12,13,16,17,20). Nine subspecies are usually recognised. A. g. geoffroyi from the coastal region bordering San Juan del Norte or Matina Bay, southeastern Nicaragua; probably ranging through the lowlands to the Pacific coast. A. g. vellerosus in the forests of Veracruz and eastern San Luis Potosi and southeastward through Tabasco, across the Isthmus of Tehuantepec in eastern Oaxaca, Mexico, to Honduras and El Salvador, except for the highlands of Guatemala. A. g. yucatanensis from the Yucatan Peninsula, northeastern Guatemala and probably adjoining parts of Belize; doubtless intergrading to the south with vellerosus. A. g. pan in the mountains of central Guatemala; also probably intergrading with vellerosus. A. g. frontatus from northwestern Costa Rica and extreme western and northern Nicaragua. A. g. ornatus from the eastern slope of the central cordillera of Costa Rica; probably intergrading with panamensis on the Pacific side of the central mountain range. A. g. panamensis from Panama east of the Canal Zone (Cordillera de San Blas), and west through Chiriqui to central western Costa Rica (16). However during the primate census of Chiriqui Province in 1968-70 Baldwin and Baldwin neither located nor heard reference to Ateles inhabiting the region (1). Napier considers panamensis to be a synonym of ornatus (20). A. g. azuerensis from the Azuero Peninsula, Panama; probably extinct but did occur in the deeper forests on both slopes, but known only from the western (Veraguas) side from the vicinity of Ponuga southward, possibly ranging west to Burica Peninsula on Panama-Costa Rica frontier. A. g. grisescens presumably occurring in the valley of the Rio Tuyra and probably southeastward through the Serrania del Sapo of extreme southeastern Panama and the Cordillera de Baudo of northwestern Colombia (16). For map see (13,16).

POPULATION   Numbers unknown and very little detailed information available, however the species has declined throughout much of its range mainly because forest destruction in Central America has been extensive. Mexico: del Toro reported in 1979 that no reliable population estimates existed but the species was definitely rapidly declining and was in his opinion threatened (24). In 1959 Leopold reported that constant clearing of the forests and excessive shooting would probably soon cause the Spider Monkey to become rare (17). Guatemala: in 1975-76 Cant noted that an 'adequately' sized population was protected in Tikal National Park; he observed a density of 14.2-41.6 Ateles per sq. km (average 28 per sq. km) (4). In 1973 the same park gave a density of 45 per sq. km (6). Different census techniques were used. A 1950 U.S. Fish and Wildlife survey found that Ateles had formerly occurred throughout the more humid forest regions, including the highlands, where it was recorded on several of the volcanoes, but that by 1950 it could only be found in Peten, in the lowland forest of both coasts and in the mountains of Quiche and Alta Vera Paz (30). Honduras: was not included in a 1978 threatened species list (25). Nicaragua: reported as 'Endangered' in 1978 (26). El Salvador: considered in danger of extinction in 1978 (27). Costa Rica: classified as 'Endangered' on a 1978 threatened species list (28). Freese censused the species in Santa Rosa National Park in 1971/72 and estimated a total of 110-160 animals. Outside the park the forest was rapidly being cut and Ateles was already scarce in the northwest (10). Panama: reported as 'Vulnerable' in 1978 (29). A 1935 study by Carpenter in the Coto Region of western Panama found it to be very plentiful - possibly more than 500 per sq. km (5). Mittermeier (1981) reports several subspecies to be certainly endangered, and A. g. azuerensis possibly already extinct (18). No information obtained from Belize.

HABITAT AND ECOLOGY Forest. In Costa Rica observed in evergreen, semi-deciduous and occasionally deciduous forests (10); in Mexico in tropical evergreen forest, rainforest, cloud forest (17) and mangrove-swamp (9). Leopold states that second growth forest, although not as desirable as primary forest, will sustain the species (17). In northern Colombia Bernstein et al found that the closely related Ateles belzebuth would survive in response to logging, albeit in reduced numbers, if some large trees remained (2). Social structure apparently varies with habitat (9). In the tall, evergreen forest of Panama Carpenter observed A. geoffroyi in large troops typically composed of smaller subgroups (5). Eisenberg and Kuehn found them living in small, cohesive groups in Mexican mangrove swamp (9) and in Costa Rican dry forest Freese observed both social structures (10). Diurnal and largely frugivorous (5,8,9,10,17). Ateles take 4-5 years to mature, have a long gestation of 226-232 days and produce a single infant only about once every 2-3 years (7,8).

THREATS TO SURVIVAL Habitat destruction, and hunting for food, export and the local pet trade (4,11,17,18,24). In Central America habitat destruction is more of a threat than hunting which is the main cause of Ateles decline elsewhere, although in some areas hunting for food, and occasionally sport is an important threat (18). In 1971-72 Freese reported rapid cutting and clearing of the tropical dry forest in northwestern Costa Rica (10). In southern Mexico Ateles infants are popular pets (18). Since Ateles is a slow breeder, populations can rapidly be reduced with moderate hunting pressure (18).

CONSERVATION MEASURES TAKEN A.g. panamensis and A. g. frontatus are listed on Appendix 1 of the 1973 Convention on International Trade in Endangered Species of Wild Fauna and Flora, (CITES), and therefore any trade in them or their products is subject to strict regulation by ratifying nations, and trade for primarily commercial purposes is banned. This species as a whole is listed on Appendix 2, trade in it between acceding nations being therefore subject to regulation and monitoring of its effects. Protected by law in Mexico (24); not known whether protected by law elsewhere. Known to occur in Tikal National Park, Guatemala (4,16); and various Costa Rican parks including Santa Rosa (A. g. frontatus) (10), and Corcovado (A. g. panamensis) (18,23). An introduced but free-ranging population of A. g. panamensis occurs on Barro Colorado Island, Panama (8,9,21).

CONSERVATION MEASURES PROPOSED The whole species should be listed in Appendix 1 of CITES. Legal protection throughout its range and a thorough survey of range and status in all countries is needed (18).

CAPTIVE BREEDING No information.

REMARKS For description of animal see (3,10,13,17,20). Kellogg and Goldman (10) recognise four species of Ateles but a number of recent authors (14,15,19) have considered all Spider Monkeys to be conspecific under the name A. paniscus.

A zone of hybridization exists in Panama between A. g. panamensis and A. fusciceps rufiventris (22). This data sheet was compiled with the assistance of Dr. R.A. Mittermeier, Chairman of the IUCN/SSC Primate Specialist Group.

REFERENCES

1. Baldwin, J.D. and Baldwin, J.I. (1976). Primate populations in Chiriqui, Panama. In Thorington, R.W. Jr. and Heltne, P.G. (Eds), Neotropical Primates: Field Studies and Conservation. National Academy of Sciences. Washington D.C.

2. Bernstein, I.S., Balcaen, P., Dresdale, L., Gouzoules, H., Kavanagh, M., Patterson, T. and Neyman-Warner, P. (1976). Differential effects of forest degradation on primate populations. Primates 17: 401-411.

3. Burt, W.H. and Stirton, R.A. (1961). The Mammals of El Salvador. Misc. Pub. Mus. of Zoo. Univ. of Michigan. No. 117.

4. Cant, J.G.H. (1978). Population survey of the Spider Monkey Ateles geoffroyi at Tikal, Guatemala. Primates 19(3): 525-535.

5. Carpenter, C.R. (1935). Behaviour of Red Spider Monkeys in Panama. J. Mammal. 16(3): 171-180.

6. Coelho, A.M., Bramblett, C.A., Quick, L.B. and Bramblett, S.S. (1976). Resource availability and population density in primates: a socio-bioenergetic analysis of the energy budgets of Guatemalan Howler and Spider Monkeys. Primates 17(1): 63-80.

7. Eisenberg, J.F. (1973). Reproduction in two species of Spider Monkeys, Ateles fusciceps and Ateles geoffroyi. J. Mammal. 54(4): 955-957.

8. Eisenberg, J.F. (1976). Communication mechanisms and social integration in the Black Spider Monkey, Ateles fusciceps robustus and related species. Smithsonian Contributions to Zoology 213: 1-108.

9. Eisenberg, J.F. and Kuehn, R.E. (1966). The behaviour of Ateles geoffroyi and related species. Smithsonian Misc. Collections 151(8): 1-63.

10. Freese, C. (1976). Censusing Alouatta palliata, Ateles geoffroyi, and Cebus capucinus in the Costa Rican Dry Forest. In Thorington, R.W. Jr. and Heltne, P.G. (Eds), Neotropical Primates: Field Studies and Conservation. National Acad. of Sciences. Washington D.C.

11. Goldman, E.A. (1920). Mammals of Panama. Smithsonian Misc. Coll. 69(5): 1-309.

12. Goodwin, G.G. (1946). Mammals of Costa Rica. Bull. Am. Mus. Nat. Hist. Vol. 87 Article 5.

13. Hall, E.R. and Kelson, K.R. (1959). The Mammals of North America. The Ronald Press Company, New York.

14. Hernandez-Camacho, J. and Cooper, R.W. (1976). The Nonhuman Primates of Colombia. In Thorington, R.W. Jr. and Heltne, P.G. (Eds), Neotropical Primates: Field Studies and Conservation. National Academy of Sciences. Washington D.C.

15. Hershkovitz, P. (1972). The recent mammals of the Neotropical region: A zoogeographic and ecological review. In Keast, A., Erk, F.C. and Glass, B. (Eds), Evolution, Mammals and Southern Continents. State Univ. of New York Press. Albany. 311-432.

16. Kellogg, R. and Goldman, E.A. (1944). Review of the Spider

Monkeys. Proc. U.S. Nat. Museum 96 (3186): 1-45.

17. Leopold, A.S. (1959). Wildlife of Mexico. Univ. of California Press, Berkeley and Los Angeles.
18. Mittermeier, R.A. (1977-81). In litt.
19. Moynihan, M. (1970). Some behaviour patterns of Platyrrhine Monkeys. II Saguinus geoffroyi and some other Tamarins. Smithson. Contrib. Zool. No. 28.
20. Napier, P.H. (1976). Catalogue of Primates in the British Museum (Natural History). Part 1: Families Callitrichidae and Cebidae. British Museum (Nat. Hist.) London.
21. Richard, A. (1970). A comparative study of the activity patterns and behaviour of Alouatta villosa and Ateles geoffroyi. Folia Primatol. 12(4): 241-263.
22. Rossan, R.N. and Baerg, D.C. (1977). Laboratory and feral hybridization of Ateles geoffroyi panamensis Kellogg and Goldman 1944 and A. fusciceps robustus Allen 1914 in Panama. Primates 18(1): 235-237.
23. Thornback, L.J. (1979). Pers. observation.
24. Toro, M.A. del (1979). In litt.
25. Aguilar, W. (1978). El manejo de la Vida Silvestre en Honduras. In Morales, R., Macfarland, C., Incer, J. and Hobbs, A. (Eds), Memorias de la Primera Reunion Regional Centroamerican sobre Vida Silvestre. Matagalpa, Nicaragua 25-29 Julio 1978. Unidad de areas silvestres y cuencas del catie.
26. Salas, J.B. (1978). Informe sobre las actividades que desarrolla el Departamento de Vida silvestre en Nicaragua. In Morales, R., Macfarland, C., Incer, J. and Hobbs, A. (Eds), Memorias de la Primera Reunion Regional Centroamerican sobre Vida Silvestre. Matagalpa, Nicaragua 25-29 Julio 1978. Unidad de areas silvestres y cuencas del catie.
27. Serrano, F. (1978). Informe de actividades de la Unidad de Parques Nacionales y Vida Silvestre en El Salvador. In Morales, R., Macfarland, C., Incer, J. and Hobbs, A. (Eds), Memorias de la Primera Reunion Regional Centroamerican sobre Vida Silvestre. Matagalpa, Nicaragua 25-29 Julio 1978. Unidad de areas silvestres y cuencas del catie.
28. Lopez, E. (1978). Informe sobre las actividades de la Direccion General de Recursos Pesqueros y Vida Silvestre de Costa Rica. In Morales, R., Macfarland, C., Incer, J. and Hobbs, A. (Eds), Memorias de la Primera Reunion Regional Centroamerican sobre Vida Silvestre. Matagalpa, Nicaragua 25-29 Julio 1978. Unidad de areas silvestres y cuencas del catie.
29. Vallester, E. (1978). Informé de Panama sobre la situacion de la Fauna Silvestre. In Morales, R., Macfarland, C., Incer, J. and Hobbs, A. (Eds), Memorias de la Primera Reunion Regional Centroamerican sobre Vida Silvestre. Matagalpa, Nicaragua 25-29 Julio 1978. Unidad de areas silvestres y cuencas del catie.
30. Saunders, G.B., Holloway, A.D. and Handley, C.O. (1950). A Fish and Wildlife Survey of Guatemala. U.S. Dept. Interior, Fish and Wildlife Service, Spec. Scient. Rep. Wild. No.5.

BLACK SPIDER MONKEY   VULNERABLE

Ateles paniscus (Linnaeus, 1758)

Order   PRIMATES   Family   CEBIDAE

___

SUMMARY   Brazil north to the Guianas, east to Peru and Bolivia. Numbers unknown. Threatened by hunting and habitat destruction. Needs effective legal protection throughout its range and surveys to determine the best areas for reserves.

DISTRIBUTION   Lower Amazonian Brazil north to Venezuela, Suriname, Guyana and French Guiana; east to Bolivia and Peru (7,13,18,22). Two subspecies are recognised: A. p. paniscus from the Rio Negro/Rio Branco to the Atlantic, and north to Venezuela and the Guianas (13,18,22), although neither Handley nor Mondolfi record its occurrence in Venezuela (8,19). A. p. chamek according to Kellogg and Goldman occurs in western Mato Grosso, eastern Bolivia, and northeastern Peru to the Rio Solimoes and Rio Jurua, Amazonas, Brazil (13). Napier describes its range as from Brazil, south of the Rio Japura, to Peru, east of the Rio Huallaga, extending to the southern tributaries of the Rio Madeira - Rio Beni, the Rio Guapore and the Rio Jiparana (22). Rylands (1980-81) reports it to be apparently absent south of the Rio Solimoes in the region of the lower Rio Purus, Madeira and Tapajos (26). However Ateles have been reported to occur in the northwest of the Amazonia National Park, Para, descriptions of which fit A. p. chamek (26). Local people also report it to be absent from the region south of the Rio Solimoes, opposite the Rio Negro (26). In Peru, Luscombe has observed it within 25 km of the border with Ecuador, and in the south almost into Brazil and Bolivia (14). Heltne et al (1976) are quoted by Rylands as stating that A. paniscus occurs south at least to 16°S, and possibly even further south in humid forest along the base of the Andes into Argentina, although not inhabiting the dry forest of the Chaco (26).

POPULATION   Numbers unknown. Has disappeared from many areas chiefly because of hunting, to which it is particularly susceptible. Shows little adaptability to human presence. Mittermeier reports A. p. paniscus to be still abundant in undisturbed and uninhabited areas of the interiors of French Guiana, Suriname and neighbouring parts of Brazil, and to be probably less threatened than any other Ateles (17), all of which however are considered threatened and are included in the IUCN Red Data Book. Suriname: Mittermeier (1977) considered Ateles to probably be the most vulnerable of Suriname monkeys because it exhibits little or no adaptability to human intrusion and was subject to considerable hunting pressure (16), but also added that Suriname was likely to remain a major stronghold for primates including Ateles for many years to come (16). Similarly Van Roosmalen who studied A. p. paniscus in Suriname in the late 1970s described it as 'probably the most vulnerable of the Suriname monkey species' (25). Guyana: a primate survey in 1975 rated A. paniscus as the most vulnerable of the Guyanese monkeys (21). Bolivia: a preliminary survey in 1975 of primates in five different geographical areas found A. paniscus to have been hunted to extinction over large areas and to be presently rare throughout the Cobija and probably the entire Pando region; to be the most common monkey in the Ixiamas region; to be absent from Riberalta; to perhaps occur in the San Jose de Chiquitos area, although unconfirmed; and to be uncommon in El Triunfo (9). Izawa and Bejarano who surveyed western Pando in 1978-80 similarly report A. paniscus to be almost certainly extinct between the Rios Acre and Tahuamanu because of hunting; the most recent record dating from 1975. The species is also close to extinction between the Rios Tahuamanu and Manuripi. Only to the south of the latter where few humans live and the forest is less disturbed, does this monkey occur extensively. However road construction between La Paz and Cobija via Ixiamas and Pto. Heath with its consequent disturbance will undoubtedly adversely affect Ateles populations (12). Brazil: Rylands (1980-81) describes A. p. paniscus as probably locally extinct or severely reduced in numbers wherever there is any extensive human settlement, although at present much of its range is relatively isolated (26); he considers hunting to be the main threat. He describes A. p. chamek as being also 'severely threatened' by hunting (26). Peru: Ateles have disappeared from many areas where they used to occur and are considered rare and threatened throughout Amazonian Peru (6,7,23,27), and in 1981 Mittermeier rated them endangered in the country (17).

HABITAT AND ECOLOGY Van Roosmalen, who has studied this species in the Raleighvallen-Voltzberg region of Suriname (25), notes that in this area it is confined exclusively to high forest, he observed it in high rain forest, mountain savanna forest, pina swamp forest and riverbank high forest; it infrequently entered edge habitats. It occurs primarily in the upper levels of the canopy in emergents, the understory being rarely visited and about 12 m seeming to be the lowest to which it will descend (25). Diurnal and mainly frugivorous (4,16,18), feeding primarily on mature fruit (25). Ateles appear to play an important role as dispersal agents for many plant species, and for some seem to be the only disperser (25). Spider Monkeys live in groups of usually 15-20 animals (25), group size varying considerably with habitat and altitude (2,18). Groups tend to break into small subgroups rather than move together as a single cohesive unit (4,16). Ateles take 4-5 years to mature, have a long gestation of 226-232 days and produce a single infant only about once every 2-3 (3,4) or 3-4 years (25).

THREATS TO SURVIVAL Hunting and habitat destruction. Hunting is the main cause of decline in Amazonia (6,17,27). Ateles are large and very good to eat and have therefore been subjected to heavy hunting pressure throughout most of their range, even in areas where other primates are usually not molested (4,5,6,7,8,10,13,14,15,18,23,25). Their size and noisy habits make them easy to locate, follow and hunt (16,18,25). Groups that have not previously seen humans usually perform a branchshaking/branch-dropping display rather than trying to escape, a hunter is thus able to wipe out an entire group with little effort (16,25). They are also persecuted by cat hunters who use them as bait. Infants are captured for sale as pets (although Ateles are not as popular as Lagothrix and Cebus) (18). Ateles is also largely restricted to undisturbed high forest so habitat destruction has more effect on it than on most other primate species (16,25). Since Ateles is a slow breeder, populations can rapidly be reduced with moderate hunting pressure (5,16,17,25), and it is poorly adapted to recover from exploitation (16,25).

CONSERVATION MEASURES TAKEN Listed on Appendix 2 of the 1973 Convention on International Trade in Endangered Species of Wild Fauna and Flora, trade in it between acceding nations being therefore subject to regulation and monitoring of its effects. Fully protected by law in Peru, where it is on the vulnerable species list, and in Suriname (16). In Brazil it is protected by the Fauna Protection Law but is not included on the Endangered Species List (17). Not known whether protected in any other country of its range. In Peru a 'good' population occurs in Manu National Park (5), it also occurs in several other Peruvian national parks (14,16). In Suriname it is found in Brownsberg Nature Park, and the following Nature Reserves - Raleighvallen-Voltzberg, Tafelberg, Eilerts de Haan and Sipaliwini Savanna Nature Reserve (16). Rylands also mentions its occurrence in the Wia Wia N.R., the Galibi N.R., the Brinckheuveli N.R. and the Coppename River Mouth N.R. (25). For Brazil, he notes that A. p. paniscus occurs in the Trombetas N.R. in Para, the Anavilhanas N.R. in Amazonas and the Rio Mapaoni, Amapa (25). A. p. chamek is well represented in refuge areas, but in Brazil a large part of its distribution is covered by development schemes. Proposed and existing reserves are concentrated to the east and south and further large reserves should be considered in the region of the development schemes of Acre, Aripuana, Rondonia and Juruena (25). In Bolivia it occurs in the Isiboro-Secure Reserve and the Pilan Lajas Reserve (25). In Guyana it occurs in the Kaieteur Nature Reserve (25). Van Roosmalen conducted an ecological study of the species in the late 1970s (25).

CONSERVATION MEASURES PROPOSED Legal protection and enforcement are required throughout its range. In Brazilian Amazonia, a thorough survey is needed to learn more about the status of Ateles and to find sites for the establishment of reserves (18).

CAPTIVE BREEDING In 1978 at least 6 were bred in captivity in six different zoological gardens (24).

REMARKS For description of animal see (13,22). Kellogg and Goldman (13) recognise four species of Ateles, but a number of recent authors (10,11,20) have considered all Spider Monkeys to be conspecific under the name A. paniscus. Dr. R.A. Mittermeier, Chairman of the IUCN/SSC Primate Specialist Group reviewed this data sheet in June 1981.

REFERENCES 1. Bernstein, I.S., Balcaen, P., Dresdale, L., Gouzoules, H., Kavanagh, M., Patterson, T. and Neyman-Warner, P. (1976). Differential effects of forest degradation on primate populations. Primates 17 (3): 401-411.
2. Durham, N.M. (1971). Effects of altitude differences on group organisation of wild Black Spider Monkeys (Ateles paniscus). Proc. 3rd Int. Congr. Primatology, Zurich 1970. Vol. 3: 32-40.
3. Eisenberg, J.F. (1973). Reproduction in two species of Spider Monkeys, Ateles fusciceps and Ateles geoffroyi. J. Mammal. 54 (4): 955-957.
4. Eisenberg, J.F. (1976). Communication mechanisms and social integration in the Black Spider Monkey, Ateles fusciceps robustus, and related species. Smith. Contr. Zool. 213: 1-108.
5. Freese, C. (1977). In litt.
6. Freese, C., Neville, M. and Castro, R. (1976). The conservation status of Peruvian primates. Lab. Primate Newsletter 15 (3): 1-9.
7. Grimwood, I.R. (1969). Notes on the distribution and status of some Peruvian mammals 1968. Special Publication No.21 American Committee for International Wild Life Protection and New York Zoological Society.
8. Handley, C.O. (1976). Mammals of the Smithsonian Venezuelan project. Brigham Young Univ. Sci. Bull. 20(5): 1-89.
9. Heltne, P., Freese, C. and Whitesides, G. (1976). A field survey of nonhuman primate populations in Bolivia. Unpd. Report.
10. Hernandez-Camacho, J. and Cooper, R.W. (1976). The nonhuman primates of Colombia. In Thorington, R.W. Jr. and Heltne, P.G. (Eds), Neotropical Primates: Field Studies and Conservation. National Academy of Sciences. Washington D.C.
11. Hershkovitz, P. (1972). The recent mammals of the

neotropical region: A zoogeographic and ecological review. In Keast, A., Erk, F.C. and Glass, B. (Eds), Evolution, Mammals and Southern Continents. State Univ. of New York Press. Albany. 311-432.

12. Izawa, K. and Bejarano, G. (1981). Distribution range and patterns of nonhuman primates in western Pando, Bolivia. Reports of New World Monkeys (1981). 1-12. Kyoto Univ. Primate Research Institute.

13. Kellogg, R. and Goldman, E.A. (1944). Review of the Spider Monkeys. Proc. U.S. Nat. Museum 96 (3186): 1-45.

14. Luscombe, A. (1977). In litt.

15. Macedo, H. de. (1977). In litt.

16. Mittermeier, R.A. (1977). Distribution, synecology and conservation of Surinam monkeys. PhD. Thesis. Harvard Univ., U.S.A.

17. Mittermeier, R.A. (1977-81). In litt.

18. Mittermeier, R.A. and Coimbra-Filho, A.F. (1977). Primate conservation in Brazilian Amazonia. In Prince Rainier and Bourne, G.H. (Eds), Primate Conservation. Acad. Press. New York.

19. Mondolfi, E. (1976). Fauna silvestre de los bosques humedos de Venezuela. Asociacion Nacional para la defensa de la Naturaleza Venezuela.

20. Moynihan, M. (1970). Some behaviour patterns of Platyrrhine monkeys. II Saguinus geoffroyi and some other tamarins. Smithson. Contrib. Zool. No. 28.

21. Muckenhirn, N.A., Mortensen, B.K., Vessey, S., Fraser, C.E.O. and Singh, B. (1976). Report on a primate survey in Guyana, July-October 1975. Report to Pan American Health Organization.

22. Napier, P.H. (1976). Catalogue of Primates in the British Museum (Natural History). Part 1: Families Callitrichidae and Cebidae. British Museum (Natural History).

23. Neville, M., Castro, N. and Marmol, A. (1976). Censusing primate populations in the reserved area of the Pacaya and Samiria Rivers, Department Loreto, Peru. Primates 17(2): 151-181.

24. Olney, P.J.S. (Ed.) (1980). International Zoo Yearbook 20. Zool. Soc. London.

25. Roosmalen, M.G.M. van (1980). Habitat preferences, diet, feeding strategy and social organization of the Black Spider Monkey (Ateles paniscus paniscus Linnaeus 1758) in Surinam. Rijksintituut voor Natuurbeheer - rapport 80/13, Leersum.

26. Rylands, A. (1980-81). Conservation of Amazonian Primates. Unpd. Report.

27. Soini, P. (1979). In litt.

GIANT ANTEATER   VULNERABLE

Myrmecophaga tridactyla (Linnaeus, 1758)

Order   EDENTATA   Family   MYRMECOPHAGIDAE

SUMMARY Inhabits savannas and open forest in Central and South America. In Central America has become extinct in several countries and is endangered in many others, principally because of habitat loss. In South America its status is not at all clear and although hunting is generally mentioned as a threat, whether it is so extensive as to cause the disappearance of the species over much of its range is difficult to determine. Protected by law in some countries and occurs in many protected areas. Studies are needed throughout its range to learn more of its distribution, status and ecology as the basis for conservation measures. A study is in progress (1981) in the Serra da Canastra National Park in Brazil. In 1980 the Species Survival Commission of IUCN established an Edentate Specialist Group to suggest and coordinate conservation action for this and other Edentates.

DISTRIBUTION Central and South America from Guatemala, where now extinct, to northern Argentina (8,10,14,15,17,22,25). Three subspecies are recognised: M. t. tridactyla from Venezuela and the Guianas as far as Peru, Paraguay, southern Brazil, and northern Argentina in the Provinces of Salta, Formosa, Chaco and Misiones (8,17). In Peru occurs mainly in the low selva zone of the Amazon region -- within the basins of the Rios Ucayali, Maranon and Curanja in the Department of Loreto, in the north and south of the Department of San Martin, and in the Provinces of Tingo Maria and Pachitea (Huanuco), Tarma and Jauja (Junin), Paucartambo (Cuzco), Sandia (Puno) and Manu (Madre de Dios) (15). M. t. artata occurs in Colombia and the western part of Venezuela as far as the Cordillera of Merida (8). Farther north it is replaced by the Central American subspecies M. t. centralis which once ranged from Belize near Punta Gorda southward along the Caribbean coast to Colombia and up the Pacific coast to Guatemala (17), but has now disappeared from its most northerly range.

POPULATION No surveys seem to have been conducted anywhere to determine numbers. Although the species has obviously declined in Central America because of habitat loss, its status over large areas of South America is unknown and although hunting is frequently mentioned as a threat, how much of an effect this has on populations is unclear. Only the following brief comments have been located, many of them years old. Argentina: in 1981 described as vulnerable by the Argentinian Dept. of Wildlife (13). Tarak in 1980 reported it to be very rare, and to occur with certainty only in Formosa Province where very low numbers persisted in Pilcomayo National Park (29); it has disappeared from Iguazu and Chaco National Parks (29). Erize in 1979 reported it to be very rare (12) and a 1965 report mentioned that it had disappeared from areas of human settlement and was rare (10). Brazil: status little known; in 1974 reported to be sparsely distributed in the Amazon region and usually shot on sight (9). James Shaw and Tracy Carter who are studying the species in the Serra da Canastra National Park in Brazil's eastern highlands found it to be abundant there, they estimated a density of 3-5 per sq. mile (2.59 sq. km). They believed that this abundance was due to the area's remoteness and, more recently by protection as a national park (28). Bolivia: in 1981 described as endangered mainly because of hunting (4). Grimwood reporting in 1978 said it was nowhere common in Bolivia (16). French Guiana: no recent data, in 1972 said to be uncommon (19). Paraguay: in the mid 1970s reported to be still fairly common in some areas (9,21). Peru: appears to have always been uncommon and by 1968 had disappeared from many areas where formerly known (15). In 1981 Dourojeanni stated that he believed that although the species had certainly been adversely affected by colonization, it could not be considered as especially threatened in Peru (11). Colombia: in 1970 described as vulnerable in the country as a whole although endangered along the Caribbean coast because of habitat destruction, and extinct in the upper Magdalena Valley. Also virtually absent from cultivated areas (6). Uruguay: unknown whether the species ever occurred in the country, however in 1971 it did not exist there (21).

Central America: Guatemala: no recent data, a wildlife survey in 1950 reported it to probably have been exterminated, and that if it should still occur there it would be along the Pacific coast between San Jose and the border with El Salvador (25). El Salvador: extinct (7,27) searches have failed to locate the species and last reported sighting was in the southeast in the 1920s (7). In 1978 also reported as endangered in Nicaragua (3), Costa Rica (20) and Panama (30). No data located from the rest of its range.

HABITAT AND ECOLOGY Grasslands and open forests of the humid tropical lowlands, but may venture into denser vegetation (10,15,17,18,22,24,25,31). Schaller decribes it as essentially nocturnal but has sighted it in daylight hours (26). Terrestrial, and diet consists mostly of ants and termites (2). A single young is born after a 190 day gestation, the young is carried on the back of the mother and remains with her for more than a year (2). Solitary (26) (other than females with young (2,23,31)). Has been known to live in captivity for 14 years (31).

THREATS TO SURVIVAL In Central America the main threat has undoubtedly been loss of habitat as human numbers have increased greatly and colonised once remote areas. In South America hunting seems to be the main cause of any decline. The species has little commercial value for its meat or skin but tends to be shot when encountered - for trophies, for protection of dogs and livestock which it is believed to attack, and out of curiosity for its strange appearance (4,5,6,15,19,21). Some capture for live animal dealers also occurs (9,21). Quite what effect such hunting pressure has on Myrmecophaga numbers is unknown. In some parts of its South American range habitat destruction has obviously caused its disappearance (5,6), but the extent of this threat is also unknown.

CONSERVATION MEASURES TAKEN Listed on Appendix 2 of the 1973 Convention on International Trade in Endangered Species of Wild Fauna and Flora, trade in it between acceding nations being therefore subject to regulation and monitoring of its effects. Totally protected by law in Brazil (and listed on the Brazilian Endangered Species List) (9) and French Guiana. Colombia and Peru have placed an indefinite ban on hunting and capturing the species. Its legal status in other countries is unknown. In Brazil occurs in at least ten national parks and three biological reserves (18). In Argentina occurs in the Pilcomayo National Park; in Costa Rica in the Tortuguero and Corcovada National Parks (1); in Hondurus in the Rio Platano Biosphere Reserve (32); in Peru in Manu National Park (15); in Suriname in Sipaliwini Nature Reserve; and in Paraguay it was reported as common in Defensores del Chaco National Park in 1978 (16). The species is being studied in the Serra da Canastra National Park in Brazil by James Shaw and Tracy Carter (28). In 1980 the Species Survival Commission of IUCN established an Edentate Specialist Group to recommend and coordinate conservation measures for this and other Edentates; its Chairman is Dennis A. Meritt, Jr.

CONSERVATION MEASURES PROPOSED Studies are urgently required to clarify the status of this species in much of its South American range and to learn more of its behaviour and ecology. Also required is stricter enforcement of protection against hunting and establishment of reserves in areas of known occurrence. Coimbra-Filho and Mittermeier suggest that a campaign is needed to convince rural populations of the importance of the Giant Anteater as a predator on termites and ants, and of its harmlessness to humans (9).

CAPTIVE BREEDING In 1979 at least 39 males and 44 females and nine of unknown sex were held in 49 zoo collections; nine were captive bred (23). A studbook for the species was begun in 1979; the studbook keeper is Dr. W. Bartmann, Tierpark, Dortmund, 4600 Dortmund 50, Mergelteichstr. 80, West Germany (22).

REMARKS For description of animal see (2,17,28). Dennis A. Meritt, Jr. kindly assisted with the compilation of this data sheet.

REFERENCES 1. Anon. (1976). Costa Rica's new national park. Oryx 13(4): 325.
2. Barlow, J.C. (1967). Edentates and Pholidotes. In Anderson, S. and Jones, J.K. Jr. (Eds), Recent mammals of the world: a synopsis of families. The Ronald Press Co., New York.
3. Bautista Salas, J. (1978). Informe sobre las actividades que desarrolla El Departmento de Vida Silvestre de Nicaragua. In Morales, R., Macfarland, C., Incer, J. and Hobbs, A. (Eds), Memorias de la Primera Reunion Regional Centroamericanan sobre Vida Silvestre. Matagalpa, Nicaragua 25-29 Julio 1978. Unidad de areas silvestres y cuencas del catie.
4. Bejarano, G. (1981). In litt.
5. Best, R. and Ayres, J.M. (1981). In litt.
6. Blaine, A. (1970). Report on endangered species of South America - Colombia. Information supplied by J. Hernandez-Camacho. Unpd. Report.
7. Boursot, J. (1979). In litt.
8. Cabrera, A. (1957-61). Catalogo de los mamiferos de America del Sur. Rev. del Mus. Argent. de Cienc. Nat. 'Bernardino Rivadavia', Cienc. Zool. 4(1,2): 1-732.
9. Coimbra-Filho, A.F. and Mittermeier, R.A. (1974). In litt.
10. Dennler de la Tour, G. (1965). The present situation of wildlife conservation in Argentina and the prospects for the future. Unpd. Report.
11. Dourojeanni R., M. (1981). In litt.
12. Erize, F. (1979). Protecting Argentina's wildlife. Oryx 15(2): 138-139.
13. Gonzales Ruiz, E.O. (1981). In litt.
14. Goodwin, G.C. (1946). Mammals of Costa Rica. Amer. Museum Nat. Hist. Bull. 87(5): 273-478.
15. Grimwood, I.R. (1969). Notes on the distribution and status of some Peruvian mammals, 1968. Amer. Comm. Inter. Wildlife Prot. Spec. Publ. No. 21: 1-86.
16. Grimwood, I. (1978). In litt.
17. Hall, E.R. and Kelson, K.R. (1959). The Mammals of North America. The Ronald Press Co., New York.
18. Jorge Padua, M.T., Magnanini, A. and Mittermeier, R.A. (1974). Brazil's national parks. Oryx 12(5): 452-464.
19. Leclerc, J. (1972). In litt.
20. Lopez, E. (1978). Informe sobre las actividades de la Direccion General de Recursos Pesqueros y Vida Silvestre de Costa Rica. In Morales, R., Macfarland, C., Incer, J. and Hobbs, A. (Eds), Memorias de la Primera Reunion Regional Centroamerican sobre Vida Silvestre. Matagalpa, Nicaragua 25-29 Julio 1978. Unidad de areas silvestres y cuencas del

catie.

21. Mittermeier, R.A. (1971). Notes on some endangered and potentially endangered species of South American mammals. Unpd. Report.

22. Mondolfi, E. (1976). Fauna silvestre de los bosques humedos de Venezuela. Asoc. Nacional para la defensa de la Naturaleza.

23. Olney, P.J.S. (Ed.), (1980). International Zoo Yearbook 20. Zool. Soc. London.

24. Reichart, H. (1979). In litt.

25. Saunders, G.B., Holloway, A.D. and Handley, C.O. (1950). A fish and wildlife survey of Guatemala. U.S. Dept. Interior. Fish and Wildlife Service, Spec. Scient. Rep. Wild. No. 5

26. Schaller, G.B. (1976). Report on a wildlife survey in southern Argentina and in the Emas National Park, Brazil. Unpd. Report.

27. Serrano, F. (1978). Informe de actividades de la Unidad de Parques Nacionales y Vida Silvestre en El Salvador. In Morales, R., Macfarland, C., Incer, J. and Hobbs, A. (Eds), Memorias de la Primera Reunion Regional Centroamericanan sobre Vida Silvestre. Matagalpa, Nicaragua 25-29 Julio 1978. Unidad de areas silvestres y cuencas del catie.

28. Shaw, J.H. and Carter, T.S. (1980). Giant Anteaters. Natural History 89(10): 62-67.

29. Tarak, A. (1980). Pers. Comm.

30. Vallester, E. (1978). Informe de Panama sobre la situacion de la Fauna Silvestre. In Morales, R., Macfarland, C., Incer, J. and Hobbs, A. (Eds), Memorias de la Primera Reunion Regional Centroamericanan sobre Vida Silvestre. Matagalpa, Nicaragua 25-29 Julio 1978. Unidad de areas silvestres y cuencas del catie.

31. Walker, E.P. (1975). Mammals of the World. The Johns Hopkins Univ. Press, Baltimore and London.

32. WWF. (1980). Honduras establishes first biosphere reserve in Central America. WWF Monthly Report, November 1980. Project 1645.

204

MANED SLOTH or BRAZILIAN THREE-TOED SLOTH   ENDANGERED

Bradypus torquatus (Illiger, 1811)

Order   EDENTATA   Family   BRADYPODIDAE

SUMMARY Restricted to the Atlantic coastal forests of eastern Brazil and considered endangered because of extensive deforestation which has occurred in this habitat. Protected by law, occurs in a number of protected areas and is the subject of study by Sergio Maria Vaz. An Edentate Specialist Group was established in 1980 by the Species Survival Commission of IUCN and will be suggesting and coordinating conservation measures for this and other Edentates.

DISTRIBUTION Eastern Brazil, in the States of Bahia, Espirito Santo and Rio de Janeiro (1,2,4). In Bahia it is reported to have disappeared from the area between Reconcavo de Bahia and the municipality of Ilheus (4). From Ilheus south to the State of Rio de Janeiro it occurs in fragmented populations in remaining areas of undisturbed forest, mainly in the south of Bahia, in a few forests in Espirito Santo and in the following muncipalities in the State of Rio de Janeiro: Santa Maria Magdalena, Cantagalo, Macae, Friburgo, Casimiro de Abreu, Silva Jardim, Mage and Petropolis (4).

POPULATION Numbers unknown, but considered endangered because of extensive deforestation which has occurred within its range (6,8).

HABITAT AND ECOLOGY Atlantic coastal forest (4). The Maned Sloth is arboreal (although swims well) and is reported by Meritt to feed only on leaves, birds and blossoms (7). Solitary. Gestation period is 120 to 180 days and the usual number of young is one. The life span is thought to be less than 12 years (10).

THREATS TO SURVIVAL The species inhabits an area of Brazil where extensive deforestation has occurred and is continuing (2,4,6). The east coast has a dense human population and consequently the Atlantic coastal forests have been subjected to widespread, largely uncontrolled destruction to make way for plantations of coffee, sugar cane, cocoa, and eucalyptus, also for cattle pasture and above all for lumber extraction and charcoal production. In recent years industrial development has also taken its toll. The forests have as a result been devastated, especially during the rapid development and economic expansion of the last twenty years. Only a tiny fraction of the original forest cover remains (9).

CONSERVATION MEASURES TAKEN Protected by law in Brazil and included in the Brazilian Endangered Species List (4). Occurs in the Monte Pascoal National Park and in the Biological Reserves of Corrego de Veado, Sooretama and Nova Lombardia and possibly in Serra dos Orgaos National Park (4). Since 1969 twelve individuals have been reintroduced into Tijuca National Park in the city of Rio de Janeiro (2,3). Studies are being conducted by Sergio Maria Vaz (7).

CONSERVATION MEASURES PROPOSED Field studies are needed to determine if there are other suitable areas which should be reserved to ensure the sloth's survival. Data are needed on the behaviour and ecology of the species in the wild (4).

CAPTIVE BREEDING This highly specialised animal has defied all efforts to keep it alive in captivity for more than a few months (5).

REMARKS For description of animal see (10).

REFERENCES

1. Cabrera, A. (1957-1961). Catalogo de los mamiferos de America del Sur. Vol. I and II. Revista del Museo Argentino de Ciencias Naturales "Bernardino Rivadavia", Ciencias Zoologicas, 4(1): 1-307; 4(2): 309-732. Buenos Aires.

2. Coimbra-Filho, A.F. (1972). Mamiferos ameacados de extincao no Brasil. Especies de Fauna Brasileira Ameacadas de Extincao. Academia Brasileira de Ciencias: 13-98. Rio de Janeiro, Brazil.

3. Coimbra-Filho, A.F., Aldrighi, A.D. and Ferreira Martins, H. (1974). Nova contribuicao ao restablecimento da fauna do Parque Nacional de Tijuca. Brasil Florestal 4(16): 7-25.

4. Coimbra-Filho, A.F. and Mittermeier, R.A. (1974). In litt.

5. Crandall, L.S. (1964). The management of wild mammals in captivity. The Univ. of Chicago Press, Chicago.

6. Maria Vaz, S. (1981). In litt. to D.A. Meritt Jr.

7. Meritt, D.A. Jr. (1981). In litt.

8. Mittermeier, R.A. (1981). In litt. to P. Sand.

9. Mittermeier, R.A., Coimbra-Filho, A.F. and Constable, I.D. (1980). Conservation of Eastern Brazilian Primates. WWF Project 1614. Report for the period 1979/80.

10. Walker, E.P. (1975). Mammals of the World. The Johns Hopkins Univ. Press. Baltimore and London.

GIANT ARMADILLO

VULNERABLE

Priodontes giganteus (Geoffroy, 1803)

Order EDENTATA

Family DASYPODIDAE

SUMMARY Widely distributed in eastern South America but populations have been reduced or exterminated in some areas by hunting, human settlement and agricultural development. Protected by law in most countries and occurs in a number of national parks, reserves and protected areas. Studies are urgently needed to learn more of its habitat requirements as a basis for formulating an appropriate conservation plan. In 1980 the Species Survival Commission of IUCN established an Edentate Specialist Group to suggest and coordinate conservation action for this and other Edentates.

DISTRIBUTION Eastern South America. Ranges from southeastern Venezuela, the Guianas (Guyana, Suriname and French Guiana), southern Colombia and Peruvian Amazonia through Brazil, Bolivia and Paraguay as far as Misiones, Formosa and Chaco in the far northeastern sector of Argentina (5,10,13). The boundaries of this range have probably altered little in recent decades, but the species' actual distribution is now broken and discontinous (5,15).

POPULATION Numbers unknown. Brazil: in 1981 described by Best and Ayres as vulnerable in the Amazon region because of habitat destruction and subsistence hunting, although protected by food taboos in some areas (3). Mittermeier in 1971 reported it to be very rare (16); in 1957 it was said to be observed most commonly in southwest Brazil (and in the Guianas) (6). Included in the Brazilian Endangered Species List. Suriname: described in 1979 as not in danger (18). Peru: in 1981 reported by Dourojeanni to be very low in numbers and declining because of human colonisation (8). Colombia: in 1970 its status was reported to be fast becoming critical; at the time it was relatively common on the northern Llanos but had disappeared from the western Llanos, and was relatively scarce southeast of a line drawn from Arauca to Caqueta Department (4). In 1971 Mittermeier described it as very rare (16), and in 1981 Meritt reported it to be 'not common' (15). Paraguay: Meritt who studied various other armadillos in Paraguay in 1972 reported Priodontes to be nowhere common, and that areas of population concentrations were not apparent (14). He described the status of the species to be almost certainly critical (14). In 1971 Mittermeier reported it to be very rare (16), and in 1981 Meritt described it as 'not common' (15). Argentina: described in 1981 by the Argentinian Department of Wildlife as in danger of extinction (9). Tarak in 1980 described it as rare, as did Grimwood in 1978 (11) and Mittermeier in 1971 (16). Venezuela: in 1981 Meritt reported it to be locally common with 'unstable populations' in certain areas (15). Bolivia: described by Meritt in 1981 as not uncommon in certain states, and not threatened in Bolivia (15). He reports similarly for the Guianas. No data located for Ecuador.

HABITAT AND ECOLOGY Inhabits continuous, relatively undisturbed forest and savannah (15). In Peru seems to be largely restricted to tropical forest in the low selva zone (below 500 m altitude) which does not flood (10). Usually solitary (6) and may be nocturnal if persecuted. A powerful and rapid digger, sheltering in burrows of its own construction and digging extensively for food. Diet consists of ants, termites, other insects, worms, spiders, larvae, snakes and carrion (1,20). Number of young is reported to be one (or two), the female has two mammae (20).

THREATS TO SURVIVAL The species is a highly specialised animal that seems to be intolerant of disturbance; in many areas it is becoming locally extinct under the impact of deforestation, settlement and agriculture. Construction of the Transamazonian Highway, and of other roads throughout Amazonia, is opening up large areas of previously undisturbed forest to human colonization (6,7). In Peru and Paraguay the flesh of the Armadillo is relished and it is hunted by man whenever encountered (15); the species is reported to have disappeared from the vicinity of all settlements (10).

CONSERVATION MEASURES TAKEN Listed in Appendix 1 of the 1973 Convention on International Trade in Endangered Species of Wild Fauna and Flora, and therefore any trade in it or its products is subject to strict regulation by ratifying nations, and trade for primarily commercial purposes is banned. Protected by law against hunting or capture in Argentina, Brazil (where it is included on the Endangered Species List), Colombia, Peru, northern Suriname, and Paraguay. In Brazil it is believed to occur in the national parks of Araguaia (Goias), Tocantins (Goias), Emas (Goias, Mato Grosso), Monte Pascoal (Bahia) and the Biological Reserves of Caracara (Mato Grosso) and Sooretama (Espirito Santo) (7). In Colombia, it occurs in the Sierra de la Macarena National Park and the El Tuparro Reserve and, in Peru, in the Manu National Park (10) and Pacaya National Reserve. In Suriname it occurs in all eight nature reserves (18).

CONSERVATION MEASURES PROPOSED Studies are needed to determine its habitat requirements before a sound conservation plan can be formulated. Stricter enforcement of protection against hunting is needed plus the establishment of reserves in suitable areas. Where habitat destruction is unavoidable, consideration should be given to the translocation of some animals to protected areas (7) or where such areas do not exist, to captivity for propagation efforts (15).

CAPTIVE BREEDING In 1979 5 males and 1 female where held in 4 zoological collections (17). The species has not bred in captivity (15).

REMARKS For description see (1,13,20).

REFERENCES
1. Barlow, J.C. (1967). Edentates and Pholidotes. In Anderson, S. and Jones, J.K. Jr (Eds), Recent mammals of the world: a synopsis of families. The Ronald Press Co., New York.
2. Best, R. and Ayres, M. (1981). In litt.
3. Bejarano, G. (1981). In litt.
4. Blaine, A. (1970). Report on endangered species of South America - Colombia. Information supplied by J.Hernandez-Camacho. Unpd Report.
5. Cabrera, A. (1957-1961). Catalogo de los mamiferos de America del Sur. Vol. I and II. Rev. del Mus. Argent. de Cienc. Nat. 'Bernardino Rivadavia', Cienc. Zool. 4(1,2):1-732.
6. Carvalho, C.T. (1957). Algunos mamiferos do Acre occidental. Bol. Mus. Paraense E. Goeldi, N.S. Zool. 6: 1-22.
7. Coimbra-Filho, A.F. and Mittermeier, R.A. (1974). In litt.
8. Dourojeanni R, M.J. (1981). In litt.
9. Gonzales Ruiz, E.O. (1981). In litt.
10. Grimwood, I.R. (1969). Notes on the distribution and status of some Peruvian mammals in 1968. Special Pubn. 21. Am. Comm. Int. Wildl. Protec. and New York Zool. Soc., Bronx, New York
11. Grimwood, I. (1978). In litt.
12. Guillermo Staudt, J.P. (1976). In litt.
13. Husson, A.M. (1978). The Mammals of Suriname. E.J. Brill, Leiden.

14. Meritt, D.A. Jr. (1973). Observations on the status of the Giant Armadillo. _Priodontes giganteus,_ in Paraguay. _Zoologica_ 58(3-4): 103

15. Meritt, D.A. Jr. (1981). In litt.

16. Mittermeier, R.A. (1971). Notes on some endangered and potentially endangered species of South American mammals. Unpd. Report.

17. Olney, P.J.S. (Ed.) (1980). _International Zoo Yearbook 20._ Zool. Soc. London.

18. Reichart, H. (1979). In litt.

19. Tarak, A. (1980). Pers. Comm.

20. Walker, E.P. (1975). _Mammals of the World._ The Johns Hopkins Univ. Press, Baltimore and London.

BRAZILIAN THREE-BANDED ARMADILLO INDETERMINATE

Tolypeutes tricinctus (Linnaeus, 1758)

Order   EDENTATA   Family   DASYPODIDAE

SUMMARY Endemic to Brazil. Very little known about this species, but believed threatened by exploitation for food; easily captured. Protected by law and occurs in a number of national parks. An Edentate Specialist Group established by the Species Survival Commission of IUCN in 1980 is to examine the problems of this and other Edentates with the aim of initiating and coordinating conservation measures.

DISTRIBUTION Brazil where according to Vieira it occurs in central and northeastern areas (11). However Cabrera mentions only northeastern Brazil and cites Pernambuco as the type locality (1). Carvalho (1969) observed the species in the caatingas near the Rio Sao Francisco (2). In 1958 Coimbra-Filho saw the animal in the Upper Jaguaribe region in Ceara, and Moojen encountered it in Barreiras in the State of Bahia (3,4). For map see (10).

POPULATION Numbers unknown. Believed rare and threatened by hunting for food but precise data on status lacking (4).

HABITAT AND ECOLOGY Inhabits the dry caatingas and sertoes. Large numbers of termite nests (Syntermes) are found in the caatingas near the Rio Sao Francisco and may represent an important source of food for the armadillo (2). Little is known of the habits of this species. Meritt observed the closely related Tolypeutes matacus in the wild and found it to be primarily a solitary animal, although groups of up to 12 animals could be found together in a shallow nest during the cold season, apparently to conserve heat. Its burrows were of two types: the 'home' burrow was shallow, rarely penetrating deeper than 60 cm and was up to 120 cm in length. The 'feeding' burrow was usually less than 30 cm deep and 12 cm long. Both were usually found in and around the bases of large clumps of bushes and small trees in grassy areas. Access to water was required all year round and the principal food items included worms, soft-bodied grubs, insects and carrion (6). One young is usual, and in the wild most births occur between November and January (5,7).

THREATS TO SURVIVAL In 1974 Coimbra-Filho and Mittermeier reported that hunting for food represented the principal threat. They mentioned that the species was easily captured if pursued, and was readily eaten in the Rio Sao Francisco region (3) and other areas (4).

CONSERVATION MEASURES TAKEN Legally protected in Brazil. May occur in the national parks of Sete Cidades (Piaui), Ubajara (Ceara) and in the Biologial Reserve of Serra Negra (Pernambuco) (4,9). In 1980 IUCN's Species Survival Commission established an Edentate Specialist Group to initiate conservation efforts for the Edentata; its chairman is D.A. Meritt Jr.

CONSERVATION MEASURES PROPOSED A large national park or biological reserve in the caatingas region of northeastern Brazil would protect a number of species, including Tolypeutes tricinctus. A study of the behaviour, ecology, zoogeography and taxonomy of this, and the other South American armadillos, is urgently needed (4,5).

CAPTIVE BREEDING In 1979 one specimen was kept in a zoological collection (8).

REMARKS For description of animal see (5,10,12). This armadillo can completely enclose itself by rolling into a perfect sphere (5,6,12). D.A. Meritt Jr. assisted with the compilation of this data sheet.

REFERENCES

1. Cabrera, A. (1957-1961). Catalogo de los mamiferos de America del Sur. Rev. del Mus. Argent. de Cienc. Nat. 'Bernardino Rivadavia', Cienc. Zool., 4(1,2): 1-732.

2. Carvalho, J.C. de M. (1969). Notas de viagen de um zoologo a regiao das caatingas e areas limitrofes. Bibl. de Cult., Serie A, Doc., Vol. 2, Imp. Univ. Ceara. 223 pp.

3. Coimbra-Filho, A.F. (1972). Mamiferos ameacados de extincao no Brasil. In Especies da Fauna Brasileira Ameacadas de Extincao. Academia Brasileira de Ciencias: 13-98. Rio de Janeiro.

4. Coimbra-Filho, A.F. and Mittermeier, R.A. (1974). In litt.

5. Meritt, D.A. Jr. (1971). The development of the La Plata Three-banded Armadillo, Tolypeutes matacus at Lincoln Park Zoo, Chicago. Int. Zoo Yearbook 11: 195-196.

6. Meritt, D.A. Jr. (1971). In nature the behaviour of armadillos. Johnson Fund Grant No. 1021 Report.

7. Meritt, D.A. Jr. (1976). The La Plata Three-banded Armadillo, Tolypeutes matacus in captivity. Int. Zoo Yearbook 16: 153-155.

8. Olney, P.J.S. (Ed.) (1980). International Zoo Yearbook 20. Zoological Soc. of London.

9. Padua, M.T.J., Magnanini, A. and Mittermeier, R.A. (1974). Brazil's National Parks. Oryx 12(5): 452-464.

10. Sanborn, C.C. (1930). Distribution and habits of the Three-banded Armadillo (Tolypeutes). J. Mammal. 11: 61-68.

11. Vieira, C.C. (1955). Lista remissiva dos mamiferos do Brasil. Arq. Zool. Sao Paulo 8: 341-474.

12. Walker, E.P. (1975). Mammals of the World. The Johns Hopkins Univ. Press, Baltimore and London.

13. Wetzel, R.M. (1980). Taxonomy and distribution of armadillos, Dasypodidae. In Montgomery, G.G. (Ed.), The Evolution and Ecology of Sloths, Anteaters and Armadillos (Mammalia, Xenarthra = Edentata). Smithsonian Institution Press, Washington D.C.

LESSER PICHI CIEGO
or PINK FAIRY ARMADILLO

INSUFFICIENTLY
KNOWN

Chlamyphorus truncatus Harlan, 1825

Order   EDENTATA   Family   DASYPODIDAE

SUMMARY Endemic to Argentina. Extremely elusive   Ploughing and predation
by domestic dogs have been cited as threats, however whether the species is truly
rare and whether in fact threatened is difficult to determine and necessitates
field studies to clarify its status. No conservation measures have been taken as
yet. An IUCN/SSC Edentate Specialist Group was established in 1980 and will
initiate conservation measures for this and other Edentates.

DISTRIBUTION Argentina, where it is restricted to desert areas in the central
and western regions. Formerly found along the southeastern fringes of the
pampas, the extreme north of Patagonia, in suitable areas in the Provinces of
Mendoza, San Juan, San Luis and La Pampa, extending northwards as far as
extreme southern Catamarca, eastern La Rioja and northeastern Cordoba and
southwards as far as the southern extremity of the Province of Buenos Aires
(1,5,6,7,9). In 1980 Meritt described its current range as unknown (5).

POPULATION Numbers unknown (5); in 1981 described by the Argentinian Dept.
of Wildlife as vulnerable (4). In 1972 Meritt spent 7 weeks surveying this species
in the field, the bulk of the time being spent in the Provinces of Mendoza, San
Juan, Cordoba and Buenos Aires (5). He found it to be extremely elusive, a fact
corroborated by local inhabitants of Pichi ciego habitat who although knowing the
animal were not aware of any patterns of activity, time of day, or particular
season as being the most appropriate time to locate the species (5). During over
200 hours of daylight field exploration in primary habitat Merritt did not observe
any Pichi ciegos, whereas dozens of other armadillos (Zaedyus pichi caurinus,
Dasypus septemcinctus and Tolypeutes matacus) were encountered (5), and indeed
more fossilized glyptodant remains were located than Chlamyphorus (5)! The
species is undoubtedly elusive - it is rarely seen and rarely caught, however
whether or not it is really rare is unknown; Cei (1967) commented that its holes
were quite plentiful indicating that it was not rare (3).

HABITAT AND ECOLOGY Desert areas but formerly also sub-Andean and
pampas zones. Fossorial (5,6,7), and seems to prefer dry soil that feels
uncomfortably warm to the human hand (3,6,8). Meritt's brief field study in 1972
found that its habitat in Mendoza and San Juan Provinces was harsh, dry, sparsely
populated, had little rainfall and exhibited a distinct flora and fauna (5). Soil type
was variable but in areas where signs of the species were most prevalent, sandy to
mixed sand and poor topsoil were predominant. Vegetation was sparse. Shrubs,
bushes and trees all exhibited reduced leaf size and many smaller plants were
thorny with tough bark covering the branches, particularly common were Prosopis
sp. a type of mesquite (5). Diet has been variously described as ants, insects,
roots and underground stems, worms and plant material ; Meritt also considers
that spiders, soft-bodied grubs, occasional carrion, birds eggs, small lizards and
snakes should be considered as possible food sources (2,5). Captive observations
found no evidence to suggest it ate roots or underground stems or tubers (7).
Usually described as nocturnal or crepuscular (6,8), although a captive male was
intermittently active during the day under dim white light (5,7).

THREATS TO SURVIVAL A 1945 report named ploughing as the main cause of
decline and stated that the species would only survive in areas where ploughing

was impossible and human inhabitants few. It also mentioned that predation by domestic dogs was a threat (6).

CONSERVATION MEASURES TAKEN None have yet been taken. In 1980 IUCN's Species Survival Commission established an Edentate Specialist Group under the Chairmanship of D.A. Meritt Jr. to initiate conservation efforts for these animals, and other Edentates.

CONSERVATION MEASURES PROPOSED Detailed field studies are required to learn more about this species (5) and to form the basis of a conservation plan, if needed.

CAPTIVE BREEDING Has been kept in captivity on several occasions but has never bred in captivity (5,7).

REMARKS For description of animal see (2,3,5,6,7,8,9,10). This species is the smallest of the armadillos, being only 125 to 150 mm in body length with a tail of approximately 25 mm (7,8). Cabrera and Yepes describe 3 subspecies (2). Dennis A. Meritt Jr. very kindly assisted with the compilation of this account.

REFERENCES
1. Cabrera, A. (1957-1961). Catalogo de los mamiferos de America del Sur. Vol. I and II. Revista del Museo Argentino de Ciencias Naturales "Bernardino Rivadavia", Ciencias Zoologicas, 4(1): 1-307; 4(2): 309-732. Buenos Aires.
2. Cabrera, A. and Yepes, J. (1940). Mamiferos Sud-Americanos. Compania Argentina de Editores, Buenos Aires.
3. Cei, J.M. (1967). Pichi ciego and Portulaca. Animals (London) 10(4): 176-177.
4. Gonzalez Ruiz, E.O., Director Nacional de Fauna Silvestre, Argentina. (1981). In litt.
5. Meritt, D.A. Jr. (1980). The Fairy Armadillo, Chlamyphorus truncatus, Harlan. In Montgomery, G.G. (Ed.), The Evolution and Ecology of Sloths, Anteaters, and Armadillos (Mammalia, Xenarthra = Edentata). Smithsonian Institution Press, Washington D.C.,
6. Minoprio, J.D.L. (1945). Sombre el Chlamyphorus truncatus Harlan. Act. Zool. Lilloana 3:5-58
7. Rood, J.P. (1970). Notes on the behaviour of the Pygmy Armadillo. J. Mammal. 51(1): 179.
8. Walker, E.P. (1975). Mammals of the World. The Johns Hopkins Univ. Press, Baltimore and London.
9. Wetzel, R.M. (1980). Taxonomy and distribution of armadillos, Dasypodidae. In Montgomery, G. G. (Ed.), The Evolution and Ecology of Sloths, Anteaters, and Armadillos (Mammalia, Xenarthra = Edentata). Smithsonian Institution Press, Washington D.C.

Burmeisteria retusa (Burmeister, 1863)

Order   EDENTATA   Family   DASYPODIDAE

SUMMARY   Precise distribution debatable but generally thought to occur in Argentina, Bolivia and Paraguay. Very little is known about the species and data concerning its status are contradictory. It is considered by some to be threatened by habitat loss and for museum collecting. No conservation measures have yet been taken. Studies are urgently required to learn more of its ecology, distribution and status and to suggest appropriate conservation actions which undoubtedly will include the establishment of reserves. An IUCN/SSC Edentate Specialist Group was established in 1980 to initiate conservation efforts for this and other Edentates.

DISTRIBUTION   Cabrera describes it as occurring in Argentina, Bolivia, and Paraguay (2) however doubt has been expressed as to its occurrence in Bolivia (1) and Paraguay (6). Cabrera mentions two subspecies: B. r. clorindae definitely known only from the western part of the Province of Formosa, Argentina, but may also occur in the areas contiguous to Salta and the Chaco, as well as in the southern Paraguayan Chaco; B. r. retusa in central and southern Bolivia extending south through the north of the Argentine Provinces of Jujuy and Salta (2).

POPULATION Unknown. Very little information exists concerning the status of this animal and the brief comments located tend to be contradictory. A status survey is urgently required to clarify the situation. Argentina: described in 1981 by the Argentinian Wildlife Dept. as 'vulnerable' (5) and in 1978 Grimwood reported that it was thought probably extinct in Argentina (6). However Tarak in 1980 described the species as not uncommon there (8). Dennler de la Tour (1965) believes that prior to European settlement it was probably fairly abundant in the country (4). Bolivia: Cabrera mentioned it as inhabiting Bolivia (2) but Professor Bejarano in 1981 reported that it had not been proved to occur in the country (1). Paraguay: Grimwood in 1978 noted that no information was available as to whether it in fact ever occured there (6). In general, Meritt believes the species was in all probability never common nor widely distributed, but that numbers were now (1980) probably stable (7).

HABITAT AND ECOLOGY   Inhabits areas with dry, well drained soils (3). Little is known of its ecology.

THREATS TO SURVIVAL   Portions of its habitat are good agricultural land and have been utilised for such purpose, however whether the species can persist in such modified areas is unknown. It continues to be sought after for museum collections (7).

CONSERVATION MEASURES TAKEN   None known. In 1980 IUCN's Species Survival Commission established an Edentate Specialist Group to initiate conservation efforts for this and other Edentates; its Chairman is D.A. Meritt Jr.

CONSERVATION MEASURES PROPOSED   Studies are urgently needed to determine its ecology, distribution and status, and if necessary to establish reserves for its protection.

CAPTIVE BREEDING   None known to have been kept in zoological collections.

REMARKS For description of animal see (2,3,9,10). This data sheet was compiled with assistance from D.A. Merrit Jr.

REFERENCES
1. Bejarano, G. (1981). In litt.
2. Cabrera, A. (1957-1961). Catalogo de los mamiferos de America del Sur. Vol. I and II. Revista del Museo Argentino de Ciencias Naturales "Bernardino Rivadavia", Ciencias Zoologicas, 4(1): 1-307; 4(2): 309-732. Buenos Aires.
3. Cabrera, A. and Yepes, J. (1940). Mamiferos Sud-Americanos. Compania Argentina de Editores, Buenos Aires.
4. Dennler de la Tour, G. (1965). The present situation of wildlife conservation in Argentina and the prospects for the future. Unpd. Report.
5. Gonzales Ruiz, E.O. (1981) In litt.
6. Grimwood, I.R. (1978). In litt.
7. Meritt, D.A. Jr. (1980). In litt.
8. Tarak, A. (1980). Pers. comm.
9. Walker, E.P. (1975). Mammals of the World. The Johns Hopkins Univ. Press, Baltimore and London.
10. Wetzel, R.M. (1980). Taxonomy and distribution of armadillos, Dasypodidae. In Montgomery, G.G. (Ed.), The Evolution and Ecology of Sloths, Anteaters and Armadillos (Mammalia, Xenarthra = Edentata). Smithsonian Institution Press, Washington, D.C.

VOLCANO RABBIT, TEPORINGO or ZACATUCHE   ENDANGERED

Romerolagus diazi (Ferrari-Pérez, 1893)

Order   LAGOMORPHA   Family   LEPORIDAE

SUMMARY   Limited distribution in subalpine areas on volcanoes in central Mexico. Numbers rapidly decreasing because of hunting for food and sport and habitat destruction. Nominally protected, though laws are not enforced, and part of its range is in a national park. Adequately guarded reserves are urgently needed. Captive breeding programmes are in progress in Europe and are proposed in Mexico.

DISTRIBUTION   Mexico; endemic to the Transverse Volcanic Axis, which lies between 18° and 22°N and runs west-east across the country from the states of Jalisco and Colima to Puebla and Veracruz. Presently known from three subalpine areas near Mexico City: the slopes of Iztaccihuatl and Popocatepetl, those of Ajusco, southwest of Mexico City, and a remnant population, discovered in 1977, on the Nevado de Toluca southwest of the Ajusco range (4,6). The combined area of the first two regions is about 150 sq. km. Granados in 1979 noted that no systematic surveys to determine the limits of the Teporingo's distribution had been carried out and he considered that it may also exist in other zones of the Volcanic Axis, possibly in close proximity to already established areas (4).

POPULATION   No recent reliable estimates. Granados in 1979 reported it to be relatively abundant in the Sierra de Ajusco and in decreasing order of abundance on the eastern slopes of Iztaccihuatl and Popocatepetl, the western slope of the same and the Nevado de Toluca where it had virtually disappeared (4). The populations in all these areas were said to be diminishing at an ever increasing rate (4). Curry-Lindahl visited the Iztaccihuatl-Popocatepetl National Park in 1974 and found the Teporingo to be very rare there, with considerably fewer than the 150-200 individuals per colony quoted in 1969 (1,2).

HABITAT AND ECOLOGY   Subalpine regions between 2800 and 4000 m in the tussocky 'zacaton' grass (mainly Epicampes and Festuca) herb-layer of open forest, consisting mainly of Pinus - Abies associations on the upper slopes and Quercus - Garrya on the middle and lower slopes (4,12). Lopez-Forment and Cervantes studied it on the eastern slopes of the Cerro Pelado in the Ajusco region in an area of Pinus montezumae forest with Alnus arguta and a herb layer principally of Muhlenbergia macroura and Festuca amplissima. Altitude averaged 3100 m, yearly rainfall 1222 mm and temperature 9.7°C (9). The Teporingo constructs elaborate burrows in sandy, loamy, deep soils, those examined having a length of 1.5 to 17 m and depths of 14.4 to 65 cm; entrances are hidden in the base of grass clumps. Abandoned pocket-gopher burrows, hollows between rocks and boulders and large boulder-strewn sinkholes are used as temporary daytime retreats and nesting chambers appear to be constructed in burrows up to 1.2 m long amongst boulders, in old tree stumps, holes left by fallen trees or even in shallow depressions beneath the 'zacaton' (4,9). An intricate system of surface runways is maintained for moving through the thick grass (8). Herbivorous, they have been observed feeding on forbs and grasses, especially Cyrsium, Rumex and Eryngium spp. along with Stipa ichu, Muhlenbergia macroura and Festuca amplissima. Chiefly diurnal with an activity peak between 1100 and 1300 hours, though some nocturnal activity also observed (9). Most reproduction appears to occur between January and April, with extremes from December to July, although previous studies reported the breeding season as from March to June (9,12). Litter sizes of 1 to 5 have been recorded, although Cervantes-Reza and Lopez-Forment found captive litters were always of two young, and gestation periods of 38 to 40 days have been measured in captivity (1,3,4,9,17). Felis (Lynx) rufus, Canis latrans and Buteo jamaicensis are all thought to predate on the Teporingo (9).

THREATS TO SURVIVAL Habitat destruction, from a variety of reasons, and hunting are identified threats (4,6). The Teporingo is relentlessly hunted for food in many areas, contrary to earlier reports which stated its flesh was unpalatable (4,6,8). This is believed to be the major cause of its decline in the Nevado de Toluca (4), and the inhabitants of some towns in the Sierra de Ajusco (e.g. Parres) are reported to hunt rabbits daily. The two larger sympatric species, Sylvilagus cunicularis and S. floridanus, are principally sought after but as these are shot out hunters are increasingly turning to the Teporingo (6). Rabbits are also wantonly killed for sport, and nesting habits make the young particularly vulnerable to predation by dogs and man (4,6). The least remote Teporingo population is now within 30 minutes of Mexico City, a rapidly growing conurbation of 15 million people. Access to formerly remote regions is continually increasing and new towns are being built between Mexico City and Cuernavaca, an area including the Sierra de Ajusco (6). Agriculture is rapidly expanding up the slopes of the volcanoes and in many areas large expanses of 'zacaton' are burned annually to improve grazing for sheep and cattle. 'Zacaton' is also of considerable commercial value for its roots which are dug up in great numbers to make household brooms and brushes (4).

CONSERVATION MEASURES TAKEN Listed in Appendix 1 of the 1973 Convention on International Trade in Endangered Species of Wild Fauna and Flora, trade in it or its products therefore being subject to strict regulation by ratifying nations, and trade for primarily commercial purposes banned. Nominally protected by law but most local inhabitants are unaware of this and there is no enforcement at all (6). 50 sq. km of the Iztaccihuatl-Popocatepetl area is a national park but hunting and grass-burning for livestock grazing still occurs within the boundaries (6). Studies on the animal both in the wild and in the laboratory have been carried out which should provide much-needed data for conservation plans (3,4,9,12,13,14,15,16).

CONSERVATION MEASURES PROPOSED The Teporingo should be designated a National Treasure by the Government of Mexico (5). There is an urgent need for an adequately protected reserve in at least one part of the present range, preferably in the Sierra de Ajusco, though it is considered by some that the Iztaccihuatl-Popocatepetl region offers the best prospect for the long term survival of the animal in view of the area's already nominally protected status (4,6). Translocation to other suitable areas has been suggested (6). Enforcement of laws against killing, and grass-burning in some areas, would greatly enhance chances of survival.

CAPTIVE BREEDING A captive breeding project was initiated at Jersey Wildlife Preservation Trust in 1968; the animals reportedly settled down rapidly and were easy to maintain (3). However the colony died out and a new colony, constituted of imported animals, was found to be difficult to maintain. In May 1981 it consisted of 2 males and 1 female (J. Mallinson 1981, Pers. comm.). Antwerp Zoo initiated a captive breeding project in 1978 (3,4); in 1979 it held 3 males and 5 females (11) which by May 1981 was down to 2 pairs (J. Mallinson 1981, Pers. comm.).

REMARKS For description see (8). The name Romerolagus diazi has been accepted for the Teporingo since 1911 (4,10). However the name of the describer cited is a matter of some controversy. The species was originally described under the name Lepus diazi by Ferrari-Pérez in 1893 and was independently named Romerolagus nelsoni by Merriam in 1896. Diaz de Leon proposed the combination

Romerolagus diazi in 1905 and this was upheld by Miller, since when the Teporingo has generally been known in full as Romerolagus diazi (Diaz, 1905). Granados following Rojas-Mendoza has concluded, however, the correct citation should be Romerolagus diazi (Ferrari-Pérez, 1893), as Diaz de Leon only introduced a new combination not a new specific name. Even if Diaz de Leon is accepted as describer, the correct citation should be Romerolagus diazi (Diaz de Leon, 1905) not Diaz, (1905) or even (Diaz, 1893) as it is sometimes known (4,10,12). Dr H. Granados very kindly provided information on which this data sheet was based and William Lopez-Forment commented on a draft in 1981.

REFERENCES
1. Curry-Lindahl, K. (1980). In litt.
2. Durrell, G. (1969). Pers. comm.
3. Durrell, G. and Mallinson, J. (1970). The Volcano Rabbit Romerolagus diazi, in the wild and at Jersey Zoo. In Lucas, J. (Ed.), International Zoo Yearbook 10. 118-122. Zool. Soc. London.
4. Granados, H. (1979). Basic information on the Volcano Rabbit (Romerolagus diazi). Paper presented to the 1st World Lagomorph Conference, Guelph, August 1979. 14pp.
5. IUCN. (1972). Volcano Rabbit. Sheet 9.59.3.1. In: Red Data Book Vol 1 Mammalia. IUCN, Switzerland.
6. Lagomorph Specialist Group, IUCN/SSC. (1979). Minutes of 1st meeting, Guelph, 15th Aug. 1979. 13pp.
7. Lagomorph Specialist Group, IUCN/SSC. (1980). Report presented at 53rd SSC meeting, Kilaguni Lodge, Kenya. 26 April-2nd May, 1980. 2pp.
8. Leopold, A.S. (1959). Wildlife of Mexico: the game birds and mammals. Univ. of California Press, Berkeley.
9. Lopez-Forment, W. and Cervantes, F. (1979). Preliminary observations on the ecology of Romerolagus diazi in Mexico. Unpd. Report. 9pp.
10. Miller, G.S. (1911). The Volcano Rabbit of Mount Iztaccihuatl. Proc. Biol. Soc. Washington 24: 228-229.
11. Olney, P.J.S. (Ed.) (1980). International Zoo Yearbook 20. Zool. Soc. London.
12. Rojas-Mendoza, P. (1951). Estudo biologico del Conejo de los Volcanes (Genero Romerolagus) (Mammalia, Lagomorpha). Tesis Profesional, Dpto. de Biologia, Facultad de Ciencias, U.N.A.M. Mexico 71pp.
13. Granados, H., Zulbaran, R. and Juarez, D. (1980). Studies on the biology of the Volcano Rabbit (Romerolagus diazi Ferrari-Perez, 1893). I. First observations on captured wild animals. XXXIII Internat. Congr. Physiol. Scie., Budapest, Abstracts (Vol. XIV) p.443, Abstract 1604.
14. Granados, H., Zulbaran, R. and Juarez, D. (1980). Estudios sobre la biologia del conejo de los volcanes II. Periodos de reproduccion de los animales silvestres en su habitat natural. XXIII Congr. Nat. Cienc. Fisiol., Queretaro, Qro., Resumenes, p. 88.
15. Granados, H., Juarez, D. and Zulbaran, R. (1980). Estudios sobre la biologia del conejo de los volcanes III. Presencia de un triangulo de pelo color amarillo dorado en la nuca. VIII Congr. Latinoamer. Zool., Mérida, Ven., Resumenes, p. 105.
16. Granados, H. (1981). Studies on the biology of the Volcano Rabbit (Romerolagus diazi Ferrari-Perez, 1893). IV. Preliminary report on the presence in the skin of some pigmented formations. Fed. Proc. 40(3) p 558. Abstract 1872.

17. Cervantes-Reza, F. and Lopez-Forment, W. (1981). Observations on the sexual behavior, gestation period, and description of young of captive Mexican Volcano Rabbits, Romerolagus diazi. J. Mammal. 62(3). In press.

DELMARVA FOX SQUIRREL   ENDANGERED

Sciurus niger cinereus Linnaeus, 1758

Order   RODENTIA   Family   SCIURIDAE

SUMMARY Extinct over most of its former range this subspecies is now confined to small, scattered populations on the Delmarva Peninsula, eastern U.S.A. Decline attributed to habitat destruction, hunting, and competition with the Grey Squirrel (Sciurus carolinensis). A Recovery Team was appointed in 1978 which has produced and begun implementation of a detailed Recovery Plan. Occurs in at least four wildlife refuges.

DISTRIBUTION U.S.A., where in 1971 was confined to disjunct areas on the Delmarva Peninsula - in parts of Dorchester, Kent, Queen Annes and Talbot counties on the eastern shore of Maryland State (11). There is also an introduced population on Chincoteague Island, Virginia (6,11). Formerly ranged through the Delmarva Peninsula (Delaware State, the eastern shore of Maryland and Northampton and Accomack counties in North Virginia) also Chester, Delaware and Lancaster counties in Pennsylvania, and perhaps southern New Jersey (7,8,9,12). Evidence suggests that distribution within its range was always patchy and discontinuous (11). For map see (2,6,12).

POPULATION Total numbers unknown. The most stable populations are thought to occur in the Blackwater and Eastern Neck National Wildlife Refuges in Dorchester county which in 1978 had estimated populations of 450 and 250 respectively (6). Chincoteaque island was believed to hold 80-100 individuals at that time (6). Detailed population trends are unknown though at least up to 1971 its numbers were considered to be rapidly declining and it was regarded by some authorities as in imminent danger of extinction (11). It appears to have always been less common than the largely sympatric Grey Squirrel and by the end of the 19th century it was already extremely rare in Pennsylvania and had been extirpated in New Jersey. It probably persisted in Delaware until the 1920s (8,9,11).

HABITAT AND ECOLOGY Shows a preference for mature, mixed timber with a minimum of undergrowth (2,6,7,11,12). Normally avoids large forest blocks with dense undergrowth and is most often found in savannah areas, oak openings, and in narrow belts of trees along streams and rivers (2,11). Formerly considered to be closely associated with the Loblolly Pine (Pinus taeda) though this has not been supported by recent work and much of the former range appears to be beyond the northern limit of the pine's distribution (3,11,12). Considerably more terrestrial than the Grey Squirrel, it will often forage in open agricultural areas exploiting cereal and fruit crops some distance away from tree cover (6,11). Diet otherwise consists of a large proportion of mast of trees such as oaks, hickorys, beech, walnut and Loblolly Pine, along with fungi, insects, fruit and occasionally birds' eggs and young. In spring it feeds extensively on tree buds and flowers (2,10). Fox squirrels have an extended breeding season with two peaks - in February-March and July-August. Average litter size is 3 (range 2-4), born after a gestation period of about 45 days; one or two litters a year are produced. Young open their eyes at approx. 5 weeks and are weaned after 9-12 weeks. Polygamous, the female raises the young alone, usually in a tree den though where these are not available leaf nests similar to those of Grey Squirrels may be constructed (2).

THREATS TO SURVIVAL The reasons for the decline are not fully understood though are believed to involve a combination of habitat destruction, competition with the Grey Squirrel and hunting (6,7,11). Lumbering and clearance for agriculture greatly increased in scale from 1860 onwards and removed much of the Fox Squirrel's preferred open mature woodland habitat (2,11). As forests regenerated or were replanted (often with pure Loblolly pine, itself a suboptimal habitat), dense undergrowth developed and relogging was carried out in most areas before the open park-like conditions of the Fox Squirrel's preferred habitat could develop or trees were sufficiently mature to provide adequate food or denning sites. In most marginal habitats the Fox Squirrel is thought to have been displaced by Grey Squirrels, which thrive in such regrowth areas and compete directly with it for food and nesting sites (7,11). Elsewhere in the U.S.A. the situation appears to be reversed and Fox Squirrels have increased in numbers and expanded their range, to the apparent detriment of the Grey Squirrel, in response to conversion of land for agriculture (11). Why this pattern has not been followed on the Delmarva Peninsula is unclear though it seems probable that hunting, logging and competition with Grey Squirrels, combined with a patchy initial distribution, caused local extinctions and, although much good Fox Squirrel habitat is thought to have now developed on the peninsula, there are no animals remaining in most areas to recolonise naturally (11). Despite legal protection some are probably still killed each year by hunters mistaking them for Grey Squirrels, but such mortality is not now believed significant. Natural predation and roadkills are also believed relatively unimportant (2). Mange (Cnemidoptes) is probably endemic and may cause heavy mortality in epidemic outbreaks in severe winters though the effect of this on long term population trends is not known (2).

CONSERVATION MEASURES TAKEN Listed as 'Endangered' on the United States Endangered Species List. Legally protected. Maryland State closed the hunting season on this species in 1971 (6,11). Occurs in the following protected areas: Blackwater National Wildlife Refuge, established in 1933; Eastern Neck National Wildlife Refuge, into which it is believed to have been introduced around 1920; Le Compte Wildlife Management Area, designated a refuge for this species in 1970; and Chincoteague National Wildlife Refuge where it was introduced in 1968 (6). Studies on Grey Squirrels have shown that provision of nest boxes can nearly double the population under some conditions and large numbers of nest boxes for the Fox Squirrel have been constructed and put out on Chincoteague Island and in parts of Maryland (1,6). Distribution surveys were conducted in 1971 (11,12) and a Recovery Team appointed in 1978 which has produced a detailed Recovery Plan (2). Part of the Plan -- the acquisition of approx. 1000 ha of additional squirrel habitat for the Blackwater Refuge -- had been accomplished by the end of the 1978 financial year (2).

CONSERVATION MEASURES PROPOSED The Recovery Plan aims to restore the squirrel to secure status throughout its former range. It considers this will have been achieved when the contraction of the present range has ceased and a minimum of 30 prospering colonies have been established outside this area. Action to achieve this includes: ecological and demographic studies, including radio-tracking; preservation and management of habitat within the existing range, possibly entailing control of Grey Squirrels, clearing of underbrush, provision of food and nest-boxes and acquisition of additional land for presently occupied refuges; re-establishment of colonies in suitable areas - many potential sites appear to be available, especially as the Fox Squirrel is tolerant of human activity and disturbance providing its basic habitat requirements are met; protection of squirrel populations through law enforcement; and promotion of public support and understanding (2). If the plan can be carried out in large measure, long term prospects are believed to be good as the taxon should respond well to management (2).

CAPTIVE BREEDING No information.

REMARKS For description see (4,5,6,11). This subspecies is variously known in the literature as Sciurus niger bryanti, S. n. neglectus or S. n. cinereus (6). Sciurus niger is widely distributed through eastern U.S.A., extending in the north through most of Michigan and Wisconsin and as far as eastern Texas in the west. It is absent from most of New England, with scattered populations in New York State (4). There can be great variation between individuals in the same locality and although several subspecies have been described the taxonomy of the group is sorely in need of revision (5). The species as a whole has expanded its range and numbers considerably in some areas this century and is not considered threatened (11). This data sheet was compiled with information very kindly supplied by Mr. G.J. Taylor, Leader of the Delmarva Fox Squirrel Recovery Team, and R.M. McKee of the Maryland Wildlife Administration.

REFERENCES
1. Burger, G.V. (1969). Response of Gray Squirrels to nest boxes at Remington Farms, Maryland. J. Wildl. Manage. 33: 796-801.
2. Delmarva Fox Squirrel Recovery Team. (1979). Recovery Plan for the Delmarva Fox Squirrel. 26pp.
3. Dozier, H.L. and Hall, H.E. (1944). Observations on the Bryant's Fox Squirrel, Sciurus niger bryantii (Bailey). Conserv. Maryland 21: 1-12.
4. Hall, E.R. and Kelson, K.R. (1959). Mammals of North America. Ronald Press, New York.
5. Hamilton, W.J. Jr. and Whitaker, J.O. Jr. (1979). Mammals of the Eastern United States. 2nd Ed. Cornell Univ. Press, Ithaca and London.
6. National Fish and Wildlife Laboratory. (1980). The Delmarva Peninsula Fox Squirrel. FSW/OBS-80/01.37. In Selected Vertebrate Endangered Species of the Seacoast of the United States. Biological Services Programme. U.S. Fish and Wildlife Service.
7. Paradiso, J.L. (1969). Mammals of Maryland. N. Am. Fauna. 66: 1-93.
8. Poole, E.L. (1944). The technical names of the northeastern fox squirrels. J. Mammal. 25: 315-317.
9. Rhoads, S.N. (1903). The mammals of Pennsylvania and New Jersey. Philadelphia.
10. Smith, C. and Follmer, D. (1972). Food preferences of squirrels. Ecology 53: 82-91.
11. Taylor, G.J. (1973). Present status and habitat survey of the Delmarva Fox Squirrel (Sciurus niger cinereus) with a discussion of reasons for its decline. Proc. 27th Ann. Conference of Southeastern Asscn. of Game and Fish Commissioners. 278-289.
12. Taylor, G.J. and Flyger, V. (1973). Distribution of the Delmarva Fox Squirrel (Sciurus niger cinereus) in Maryland. Chesapeake Sci. 14: 59-60.

VANCOUVER ISLAND MARMOT   ENDANGERED

Marmota vancouverensis Swarth, 1911

Order   RODENTIA   Family   SCIURIDAE

SUMMARY   Reduced to an estimated 50-100 individuals in isolated mountain colonies on Vancouver Island, Canada. Decline is believed to have been caused by hunting and habitat disturbance from logging and ski development. Legally protected but stringent habitat protection of all known colonies is urgently required. Surveys have been undertaken and future conservation plans include translocations to new colonies and captive breeding.

DISTRIBUTION   Endemic to Vancouver Island, British Columbia, Canada (4,5,7,10,12). An extensive survey in 1979 recorded eleven active colonies in eight areas, plus two additional possibly occupied colonies. Most of the colonies are in a small (ca 3000 ha) area between Green Mountain and Butler Peak in the southern part of the island with one further north on Mt. Washington (14,15). It is thought possible that further colonies exist although much apparently suitable habitat surveyed in 1979 and 1980 was found to be unoccupied (14). Historically there are records from about 13 different mountains, all on the central ridge south of the Gold River. The range has evidently contracted considerably since the species' discovery in 1910 (5,6,8,10,12); although even at that time it did not occur in all apparently suitable localities (12).

POPULATION   1980 counts recorded 51 adults, 11 subadults or yearlings, and 37 young of the year (13); the 1979 survey conducted before the young emerged recorded only 45 individuals and it is thought that juvenile mortality may be high (13,14). The percentage of animals not recorded is unknown though it has been suggested that the breeding population may number less than 70 animals (13). This is evidently fewer that occurred historically, as colony size is thought to be stable and the number of colonies has decreased (10). Present population trends are unknown though some indication should be gained if a proposed survey in 1981 is carried out. Classified as 'Endangered' by the Committee on the Status of Endangered Wildlife in Canada (10).

HABITAT AND ECOLOGY   Alpine and subalpine areas between 1000 and 2000 m characterised by steep slopes, talus debris and open meadows (8,10). Steep slopes, cleared of snow by avalanches, appear necessary to provide early foraging in spring. Avalanches also maintain the herbaceous plant communities favoured by the marmot by inhibiting or preventing tree growth (10). Existing colonies average about 8 individuals, excluding young of the year, and adults are usually paired. From studies of the closely related Hoary and Olympic Marmots (Marmota caligata and M. olympus), it seems likely that maturity is attained at three years and breeding occurs biennially thereafter. Mating probably occurs in April or May with young born a month later, the average litter size after young have emerged above ground being three. The marmot is only active above ground for about four months of the year, hibernating from September or early October until late April or early May. Although basically sedentary there is some movement between colonies on the same mountain and limited movement between those on different mountains. Diet is herbivorous, consisting especially of the flowering parts of alpine plants (7,10).

THREATS TO SURVIVAL   Decline during the present century is perhaps partly attributable to natural plant succession making some former colony sites unsuitable, but it is thought likely that the major factor has been direct or indirect interference by man (10). Ski developments have destroyed some suitable habitat and more is threatened - in particular construction of a large all-year ski resort was reported underway in spring 1981 on Mt. Washington in the immediate area of the colony there (13), and a smaller development was in progress on Green Mountain, an important area for the species (14). Logging may have removed important migration corridors to existing or potential colony sites, exposing dispersing marmots to predation and preventing natural establishment of further colonies, and logging up to the limits of colony areas may have altered the microclimate and made some sites unsuitable for marmots, though this has not been proven (10). Hunting and collecting for scientific purposes were probably important factors in the past and there is evidence that some wanton killing continues (1,3,10). Because of the isolation of many colony sites, once marmots are removed from a particular mountain they are highly unlikely to recolonise on their own even if the habitat remains suitable (10). Inbreeding may conceivably pose a long term threat in isolated colonies (10). The effect of human disturbance from hikers, mountaineers and photographers is unknown (10).

CONSERVATION MEASURES TAKEN Completely protected from exploitation (including collectors) under the British Columbia Wildlife Act since 1973 and in March 1980 was designated a 'Rare and Endangered Species' under the Act (9,10,13,15). The sites of all the colonies were reported in 1981 as privately owned, mainly by three logging companies (13). Some of the habitat has been protected by the companies with buffer zones left between logging areas and colonies (10). Such protection has no legal safeguard attached, however, and is regarded as inadequate in the long term (10). In March 1980 it was reported that one of the companies, McMillan Bloedel Ltd., had offered to exchange a tract of land occupied by marmots for a similar plot of the same size or value elsewhere, provided by the British Columbia provincial government (17). As of May 1981 this does not appear to have been acted upon. A preliminary study of the marmot has been carried out (8), and the Federation of British Columbia Naturalists has formed a Vancouver Island Marmot Preservation Committee which has carried out intensive field surveys and inventories of all known and much potential marmot habitat in 1979 and 1980 (13,14,15). It has also launched an extensive poster and publicity campaign to conserve the species (1,3,11).

CONSERVATION MEASURES PROPOSED The principal recommendation, which was submitted to the Provincial Cabinet of British Columbia in January 1981 (15), is the designation of the 3000 ha areas of mountain side above 3500 feet (approx. 2000 m) from Green Mountain south and west to Butler Peak, which contains the great majority of known marmot colonies, as an ecological reserve or nature conservancy area under the Park Act. This would afford the species permanent protection from further encroachment by the logging and mining industries and from any new recreational development (15). Establishment of colonies at formerly occupied or suitable new sites using captive bred animals or by translocation of surplus animals (probably two years old) from present colonies is a principal long-term conservation plan (10). The 1979 and 1980 surveys have located and examined many potential sites (14,15) and in 1981 a study was planned under the auspices of the University of British Columbia to provide detailed ecological information for such transplants (13). A further extensive survey was also planned by the Vancouver Island Marmot Preservation Committee for 1981 if funds and facilities were available (13).

CAPTIVE BREEDING As of May 1981, a pair were held in a semi-natural enclosure at Game Farm, on mainland British Columbia, as a nucleus for a captive breeding programme with funds for this provided by WWF (Canada) among others (13,16).

REMARKS For description see (4,7,12). J.D. Routledge of the Federation of

British Columbia Naturalists kindly provided much of the information on which this data sheet is based.

REFERENCES
1. Anon. (1979). Fight for rare Vancouver Island Marmot heats up. Fed. Brit. Columbia Naturalists, Vancouver Island Region. News release. 3pp.
2. Anon. (1979). Submission to Government of British Columbia. Fed. Brit. Columbia Naturalists. Unpd.
3. Anon. (1979). Vancouver Island naturalists fight to save Canada's only endangered endemic species of mammal. Federation Brit. Columbia Naturalists, Vancouver Island Region. 4pp.
4. Banfield, A.W.F. (1974). The Mammals of Canada. Univ. of Toronto Press.
5. Carl, G.C. (1944). The Vancouver Island Marmot. Victoria Nat. 1: 77-78.
6. Cowan, I. McT. and Guiguet, L.J. (1956). The mammals of British Columbia. Brit. Columbia Prov. Mus., Victoria.
7. Hawryzki, A.R. and Carpenter, M. (1978). Vancouver Island Marmot. Wildlife Review 8(8): 4-6.
8. Heard, D.C. (1977). The Behaviour of Vancouver Island Marmots (Marmota vancouverensis). M.Sc. Thesis. Univ. Brit. Columbia.
9. IUCN. (1974). Vancouver Island Marmot. Sheet code 10.61.29.2. In Red Data Book Vol 1 Mammalia. IUCN, Switzerland.
10. Munro, W.T. (1978). Status of the Vancouver Island Marmot (Marmota vancouverensis) in Canada. Status report to the Committee on the Status of Endangered Wildlife in Canada (COSEWIC). 9pp.
11. Routledge, J.D. (1979-80). In litt. to Sir Peter Scott.
12. Swarth, H. A. (1911). Two new species of marmots from British Columbia. Univ. of Calif. Pubns. Zool. 7(6): 201-204.
13. Routledge, J.D. (1981). In litt.
14. Routledge, J.D. and Merilees, W.J. (1980). Vancouver Island Marmot, Report No.1. Vancouver Island region of Federation of British Columbia Naturalists.
15. Vancouver Island Marmot Preservation Committee (1981). Submission to the Provincial Cabinet, Jan 22nd 1981. Unpd. 4pp.
16. WWF Canada. (1980). Project update - how we spend your dollar. Working for Wildlife. 1(4):1.
17. Evans, M. (1980). Marmot Misfortunes. New Scientist. 87(1198): 817.

UTAH PRAIRIE DOG

VULNERABLE

Cynomys parvidens J.A. Allen, 1905

Order   RODENTIA

Family   SCIURIDAE

SUMMARY Endemic to Utah, U.S.A., where numbers drastically declined this century as a result of habitat alteration and eradication programmes. Transplant attempts to publicly-owned land were begun in 1972 and the population has now apparently stabilised although colonies on private land are still at risk from habitat loss to development. A draft Recovery Plan has been produced.

DISTRIBUTION Southwestern Utah, U.S.A., where in 1980 was found in several disjunct areas in Beaver, Iron, Garfield and Wayne Counties, also extending just into Sevier and Kane Counties (10). Formerly ranged more widely, but still discontinuosly, in the same region from Pine and Buckskin Valleys in Beaver and Iron Counties in the west to Nephi in the north, Bryce Canyon National Park in the southeast, the eastern foothills of the Aquarius Plateau in the east and the northern borders of Kane and Washington counties in the south (10).

POPULATION In 1979 a spring (pre-breeding) census of all known sites gave a total of 2887 individuals distributed in 84 prairie dog towns, of which 6 had been founded by artificial transplants (9,10). Most of these (1697 individuals in 31 towns) occurred in Cedar Valley with 287 in Panguitch Valley (21 towns), 223 in John's Valley/Bryce (6 towns) and 452 at Parker Mountain (12 towns). Of the remainder, 68 were in 4 towns at Loa and the rest were in 4 scattered colonies (9). These numbers were actual counts and may account for less than 60 per cent of the individuals present at a colony at the time (4). Spring censuses have been carried out since 1976 when 2160 individuals were counted in 51 towns. The apparent increase is at least in part attributed to the discovery of several already existing towns though the population is now believed to be actually increasing (9,10). Population trends in 1979 were upward at Parker Mountain and in the transplant colonies, stable at Cedar Valley and Loa and downward elsewhere (9). The most successful colonies are those on privately owned agricultural land under active irrigation, where they also come into most conflict with farming interests (4). Estimates of former numbers are difficult to make though a figure of 95,000 has been approximated for the population before the instigation of control programmes in the 1920s (2). The population is noted to have drastically decreased in the 1960s and early 1970s, following which active conservation measures were initiated (2,10).

HABITAT AND ECOLOGY Lives in colonial towns, preferred habitat of which appears to be swale type formations at low elevation (up to 2200m) where moist herbage is available even during drought periods (10). Habitat requirements include well-drained soil deep enough to accommodate burrows to provide protection from predators and temperature extremes without risk of flooding. Soil colour may be important in camouflage against predators on the surface (10). Predominant vegetation height within the colony must be low enough to allow prairie dogs to scan the environment for predators and thus controlled grazing can be compatible with prairie dog towns (3). Principally herbivorous, alfalfa and grasses are preferred food items during all seasons although forbs may be critical to survival during drought. Preference is shown for flowers, seeds and young leaves. Dead vegetation and cattle faeces are also consumed and are preferred to shrub leaves and stems. Cicadas (Cicadidae) are eaten when available (10). Individuals gain most weight and colony expansion is greatest when alfalfa and other cool season palatable forage are available. This occurs most often in low elevation colonies (3). Breeding occurs in early spring with young reported born from early to late April after a gestation period of around 30 days. Litter size is variable (2-8 reported) and young appear above ground at an age of 5-7 weeks (10). A study reported in 1976 found an average of less than 4 young above-ground per successful female (10). Sexual maturity is reached at one year of age. Adult males cease surface activity some time from July to September, females follow some weeks later and juveniles remain above ground until about October. There is very little surface activity from the beginning of November until mid-February. Predation (primarily from badgers, coyotes and raptors) does not appear to control population density in established colonies but may have an effect on expanding or transplanted ones (1,10).

THREATS TO SURVIVAL The decline in numbers this century can be attributed chiefly to habitat disruption and deliberate elimination campaigns. Loss of suitable habitat is of immediate concern to the surviving populations (10). Part of the range contraction can be attributed to climatological changes. The prairie dog once occurred nearly to the Utah-Nevada state line in Beaver and Iron counties. Most of this region (once the major part of the range) has become less favourable due to higher temperatures, drier climate and the development of salt-shrub vegetation. Drought has been significant and has caused the elimination of several colonies (2). Much remaining available habitat has been taken for farms and houses and in 1977, 74% of towns and 76% of dogs were located on private land which is thus subject to development (10). Overgrazing has resulted in a great reduction in habitat quality in many areas by leading to a transition from grass to shrub dominated vegetation and reducing forage. It has also led to erosion of preferred swale areas, transforming them to gullies, consequently lowering the water table and thus eliminating succulent forage which supplied summer food (10). Poisoning campaigns have been periodically conducted to eliminate competition with agricultural and ranching interests (10). Population reductions following intensive campaigns occurred around 1933, 1950 and 1960. Recovery in numbers followed each of these though some colonies were completely eliminated (2). Physiographic barriers prevent expansion of the range eastward and southward and the prairie dog faces competition from the Uinta Ground Squirrel (Spermophilus armatus) in the north (10). Diseases, such as sylvatic plague, have been reported in dog towns but there is little evidence that this has had any long term effect on the population (1).

CONSERVATION MEASURES TAKEN Classified as 'Endangered' under the 1973 Endangered Species Act. Has been extensively studied, an ad hoc Recovery Team has been formed and a draft Recovery Plan drawn up (3,10). Conservation efforts so far have been centred on attempts to transplant animals from private agricultural lands, especially areas where they are causing damage, to suitable sites on public lands (4,6,9,10). Transplants were initiated in 1972 by the Utah Division of Wildlife Resources and up to 1979 a total of 4765 prairie dogs had been moved (9). Initial attempts met with only limited success due to a combination of factors - desertion of new colonies was very high and many suffered extensive predation, especially from badgers (9,10). Most animals were taken from low level sites and transplanted at considerably higher elevations which differed markedly in some aspects, particularly the composition of the grass community, and to which the individuals moved were probably not well adapted (4). By spring 1979, 6 colonies had been successfully established with an average of 16 prairie dogs in each. In that year, however, considerably improved transplant tehcniques and methods for evaluating and preparing transplant sites were tested and developed, leading to a markedly higher success rate which should be maintained in future years (4,6,9).

CONSERVATION MEASURES PROPOSED The primary objective of the draft Recovery Plan is the establishment of 40-50 self-sustaining towns on public lands

(6). In 1980 it was estimated that this could be reached in 3-5 years under the present reintroduction programme (6). There is at present some conflict with agricultural interests on private lands, particularly in Cedar City valley where in 1975 up to 100 bales of alfalfa were estimated to have been lost to prairie dogs in one town alone (6). Mound materials from burrows can be picked up by balers causing considerable equipment damage and there is some loss of irrigation water to burrows. There is also some fear of outbreaks of sylvatic plague if the animals expand into rural or residential areas (6). Proposals have been made to reclassify some populations on private land in Cedar City valley as 'Threatened' rather than 'Endangered', to allow control measures to be adopted in this area while maintaining stringent protection of other populations (6).

CAPTIVE BREEDING In 1979 Washington National Zoological park held 6 males and 1 female, all bred in captivity (7).

REMARKS For description see (5,10). Cynomys parvidens is one of the White-tailed prairie dogs (subgenus Leucocrossuromys) and is closely related to C. leucurus which also occurs in Utah, and which has been considered conspecific with it in the past though recent investigations have supported their classification as separate species (8,10). Mr. Robert Hasenyager of the Utah Prairie Dog Recovery Team very kindly assisted with the compilation of this data sheet.

REFERENCES   1. Collier, G.D. and Spillett, J.J. (1972). Status of the Utah prairie dog (Cynomys parvidens). Utah Acad. Sci. Arts and Letters 49: 27-39.
2. Collier, G.D. and Spillett, J.J. (1973). The Utah prairie dog--decline of a legend. Utah Sci. 34: 83-87.
3. Crocker-Bedford, D. (1975). Utah prairie dog habitat evaluation. Proc. Utah Wild. Tech. Mtg. 7pp.
4. Day, D.F. (1979). In litt. to L. Greenwalt
5. Hall, E.R. and Kelson, K.R. (1959). Mammals of North America. 2 vols. Ronald Press, New York.
6. Minnich, D.W. (1980). In litt to U.S. Fish and Wild. Service.
7. Olney, P.J.S. (Ed.) (1980). International Zoo Yearbook 20. Zool. Soc. London.
8. Pizzimenti, J.J. and Nadler, C.F. (1972). Chromosomes and serum proteins of the Utah prairie dog. Cynomys parvidens (Sciuridae). S.W. Natur. 17: 279-286.
9. Utah Division of Wildlife Resources. (1980). 1979 Annual Utah prairie dog progress report. Unpd. report 22pp.
10. Utah Prairie Dog Recovery Team. (1979/80). Utah prairie dog draft recovery plan (annotated). Unpd. report. 1-19.

Dipodomys heermanni morroensis (Merriam, 1907)

Order   RODENTIA   Family   HETEROMYIDAE

SUMMARY Confined to a very limited area (less than 1.5 sq. km) of Morro Bay, California, U.S.A., where probably fewer than 1500 remain. Principally threatened by habitat destruction for urban development, and seral changes in vegetation in the absence of fires or cutting. A small part of the habitat has been purchased to form an ecological reserve but further acquisitions of remaining land, to prevent building and allow effective management of vegetation, will be essential for the animal's survival. A Recovery Plan for the taxon was being reviewed in April 1981.

DISTRIBUTION California, U.S.A. A study in 1977 found it to occur in 5 separate parcels of land, totalling 93 ha, on the south and southeast sides of Morro Bay, San Luis Obispo County, California. It was thought possible, though unlikely, that it occurred in up to 40 ha of additional habitat (9,11). May possibly have originally occupied both north and south sides of the bay though evidence for this is tenuous (11). In 1922 the range was described as 'less than 4 miles square' (6,7). By 1971 it occupied only 4.5 sq. km of remaining habitat and this has since decreased further (2,3,9,11). The area is now bounded by coastal sand dunes, salt marsh, urban development, or mature, hard chaparral preventing natural range extension (7). For map see (14).

POPULATION In 1977 a live-trap sampling method produced an estimate for the total population of 1200-1500, conceivably as high as 2000 (9,11). In 1971 the population was estimated as 3000 while in 1957 it was thought to be about 8000 (2,11). Although sampling techniques differed on each occasion this is believed to certainly reflect a real decrease in the population (3,9). The 1977 study estimated a density varying from 42 per ha in optimal habitat to 5 per ha in marginal habitat (9,14).

HABITAT AND ECOLOGY Early seral stages of soft chaparral community on sandy loam where vegetation is low and sparse and shrubs are widely scattered (3,11,12). Open spaces are thought important for predator avoidance responses and breeding behaviour, and also to allow adequate growth of annual plants whose seeds are an important food source (10,12). Typical plants include Lotus scoparius, Eriogonum parvifolium, Salvia mellifera and scattered annual grasses (12). Nocturnal, it spends the day in shallow burrows up to 3 m long which are dug in rather loose soil and may have 3 or 4 entrances (10,12,14). Home range is estimated at around 0.07 ha (9,14). Exact composition of diet in the wild is unknown, though is probably similar to that of the closely related Tulare Kangaroo Rat (Dipodomys heermanni tularensis) in consisting primarily of seeds of grasses and shrubs during the dry season and grass and herb cuttings at other times, with occasional insects (5,13,14). Most young are probably born from February to August but breeding may continue through the year with a possible second peak in autumn (9,14). Average litter size is around 3, with a gestation period of about 30 days (10,12). Young first leave the burrow at about six weeks of age and reach adult size at 3.5 - 4 months (10). There appears to be considerable seasonality in activity, with little or none in January and February, increasing in early summer then falling again with a possible resurgence in autumn (9,14).

THREATS TO SURVIVAL Habitat changes, both by direct destruction for development and seral changes to unsuitable vegetation types, are implicated as major threats, with increased predation by domestic cats and road-kills probably additional factors (3,10,14). Suburban housing developments, principally Baywood Park and Los Osos, continue to expand rapidly and have already destroyed large areas of formerly suitable habitat especially in the eastern part of the range (11). Four of the five areas in which it is now known to occur are under private ownership and thus subject to future development (9,11). Of the remaining undeveloped habitat, only one-third was occupied by the Kangaroo Rats in 1977 (10). This is thought to be because fire-control has prevented the rejuvenation of the plant community to the preferred habitat of low, open scrub vegetation, and has allowed succession to unsuitable hard chaparral (e.g. Ceanothus, manzanita, scrub oak) to occur in many areas (3,10,11,14). Average height of vegetation in occupied areas in 1958 was 60 cm or less with considerable open space between plants, while by 1973 many of the same sites supported thick dense brush averaging 120-160 cm and were no longer occupied by Kangaroo Rats (3,12).

CONSERVATION MEASURES TAKEN Listed as 'Endangered' under the 1973 Endangered Species Act. Capture, possession or sale is prohibited by State and Federal Laws. The remaining range was determined 'Critical Habitat' in 1977 by the federal government so that federal funds of any sort cannot be used for development on the site (4,10). In 1978 a 20 ha tract of the westernmost part of the range adjacent to Montana de Oro State Park was acquired by the California Department of Fish and Game and has been designated an ecological reserve to preserve habitat for the Morro Bay Kangaroo Rat as well as for a rare banded dune snail and several rare plants (11,14). This area, however, contained the lowest density of Kangaroo Rats measured in any part of the range in 1977, though some habitat management was due to begin in late 1979 which may improve this (11,14). Kangaroo Rats have been observed to colonise almost immediately a site of formerly thick brush which was cleared, planted to grain for two years, and then allowed to lie fallow, indicating they may respond well to habitat manipulation (10). The extensive studies carried out on the taxon since 1958 should help in formulating effective management plans (2,3,9,11,12). In April 1981 it was reported that a Recovery Plan for the taxon was being reviewed (11).

CONSERVATION MEASURES PROPOSED Implementation of the Recovery Plan. If possible all further development on the remaining habitat should be stopped, preferably by acquisition of land for public ownership, though the need for adequate funding means this may not happen immediately (11). Vegetation could then be actively managed, either by controlled burning or hand clearing, to provide optimum Kangaroo Rat habitat.

CAPTIVE BREEDING Not known to have bred in captivity, though a three year project has successfully raised first generation young of the closely related Dipodomys heermani arenae, and management techniques developed should be applicable to D. h. morroensis if the need arises (11).

REMARKS For description see (1,6,8,14). Originally described as a separate species, Boulware classified it as a subspecies of Dipodomys heermanni in 1943, though found it to differ considerably from the geographically closest subspecies (D. h. jolonensis) and to be most similar to the more southern D. h. arenae (1). Its taxonomic position may thus repay examination (14). Dipodomys heermanni is widely distributed in arid regions of California, extending northwards roughly to the latitude of the San Francisco Bay area (6,11,15). It was formerly regarded as occurring as far north as Southern Oregon but recent studies have placed the northernmost three subspecies in a separate species, Dipodomys californicus (15). Several subspecies are recognised of which D. h. morroensis is the only one considered threatened at present. Dr. A.I. Roest who has studied this subspecies extensively very kindly supplied the information on which this data sheet is based.

<u>REFERENCES</u>

1. Boulware, J.T. (1943). Two new subspecies of Kangaroo Rat (genus <u>Dipodomys</u>) from southern California. <u>Univ. California Publ. Zool.</u> 46: 391-396.

2. Congdon, J.D. (1971). Population estimate and distribution of the Morro Bay Kangaroo Rat. <u>California Dept. Fish Game, Wildlife Mgmt. Br. Admin. Rpt.</u>, No. 71-11, Unpd. 16p.

3. Congdon, J. and Roest, A. (1975). Status of the endangered Morro Bay Kangaroo Rat. <u>J. Mammal.</u> 56: 679-683.

4. U.S. Fish and Wildlife Service. (1977). Critical habitat for six endangered species. News Release, August 17, 1977.

5. Fitch, H.S. (1948). Habits and economic relationships of the Tulare Kangaroo Rat. <u>J. Mammal.</u> 29: 5-35.

6. Grinnell, J. (1922). A geographical study of the Kangaroo Rats of California. <u>Univ. California Publ. Zool.</u> 24: 1-124.

7. IUCN. (1976). Morro Bay Kangaroo Rat. Sheet Code 10.63.3.2.1 In <u>Red Data Book, Vol. 1 Mammalia.</u> IUCN, Switzerland.

8. Merriam, C.H. (1907). Descriptions of ten new Kangaroo Rats. <u>Proc. Biol. Soc. Wash.</u> 20: 75-80.

9. Roest, A.I. (1977). Distribution and population estimate of the Morro Bay Kangaroo Rat. <u>California Dep. Fish Game Nongame Wildl. Invest Final Rep.</u> E-1-1. 19pp.

10. Roest, A.I. (1979). What's a nice Kangaroo Rat like you doing in a place like this? <u>Animal Kingdom</u> 82(3): 32-36.

11. Roest, A.I. (1976-81). In litt.

12. Stewart, G.R. and Roest, A.I. (1960). Distribution and habits of Kangaroo Rats at Morro Bay. <u>J. Mammal.</u> 41: 126-129.

13. Tappe, D.T. (1941). Natural history of the Tulare Kangaroo Rat. <u>J. Mammal.</u> 22: 117-148.

14. National Fish and Wildlife Laboratory (1980). Morro Bay Kangaroo Rat. In <u>Selected vertebrate endangered species of the Seacoast of the United States.</u> FWS/DBS-80/01.19. Biological Services Programme. U.S. Fish and Wildlife Service.

15. Patton, J.L., MacArthur, H.M. and Yang, S.Y. (1976). Systematic relationships of the four-toed populations of <u>Dipodomys heermanni.</u> <u>J. Mammal.</u> 57: 159-163.

TEXAS KANGAROO RAT   RARE

Dipodomys elator Merriam, 1894

Order   RODENTIA   Family   HETEROMYIDAE

SUMMARY Occupies a restricted range in south-central United States, where it apparently has somewhat specific habitat requirements, being confined to mesquite brushland on firm clay soils. Most of the range is on private land subject to uncontrolled habitat modification for agriculture. Although it can survive in cultivated areas as long as some Mesquite pastures or brushy fence rows are left, it does not apparently persist in areas treated with brush control chemicals. Studies are needed to determine critical habitat requirements and to ensure that land use practices do not conflict with these. Protected in Texas and is being considered (1981) for inclusion in the U.S. Endangered Species List.

DISTRIBUTION U.S.A, where has been recorded from a small area in north-central Texas and southwestern Oklahoma. Known distribution was mapped out in 1972 (5); records encompass an overall range of about 14,000 sq. km ranging over the following counties: Archer, Baylor, Clay, Foard, Hardeman, Motley, Wichita and Wilbarger, all in Texas, and Comanche County, Oklahoma (5). All records for Comanche and Clay County are prior to 1905 and surveys in the 1960s and 1970 failed to find it there; the range thus appears to have contracted over the present century (5). It is thought likely that the sand floodplain and dune areas along the Red River immediately north of the species' range, occupied by Dipodomys ordii, may prevent its northward spread into Oklahoma (5). A disjunct record from Corywell County, Texas, some 250 km south-southeast of the range in northern Texas, is questioned by some authors (5).

POPULATION Total numbers unknown. Although apparently locally abundant in suitable habitat (3,5), the species is considered at risk because of habitat modification within its limited range. Live-trap surveys in the region of Iowa Park, Wichita Co. in the early 1970s estimated densities of 8.6 to 24.7 per hectare (7). Dalquest in 1968 noted that numbers appeared to have increased since 1965 (2), although there is no information on more recent trends.

HABITAT AND ECOLOGY Inhabits Mesquite (Prosopis glandulosa) brushland with sparse short grasses in firm clay soils (3). Although the species will forage in agricultural areas, it appears to be always closely associated with Mesquite; extensive surveys by Martin and Matocha recorded no individuals further than half a mile (0.8 km) from Mesquite areas. A certain minimum clay content in the soil is apparently required for successful burrowing (3,7); burrows average 45 cm deep and are complex, with many interwoven tunnels, scattered food caches, and a single nest in the lowest part of the system (7). The tunnels are probably important in temperature control - air temperature 60 cm inside a burrow at Iowa Park only varied from 15.5 to 18°C over one week in May whilst the outside temperature at ground level ranged from 8 to 36°C (7). Home range size, as estimated by trapping at Iowa Park, was small (averaging around 0.08 ha for both sexes, with largest estimated at 0.19 ha) though individuals were recorded travelling longer distances (over 300 m) along roads at night (7). Grass seeds were the principal component of the diet, especially cultivated oats (Avena sativa) and Johnson Grass (Sorghum halepense) (1). Stems of Panicum spp. were taken, possibly for their moisture content; also annual weeds, leaves and immature fruits of the Cranesbill Erodium cicutarium being especially sought; perennial plants were not greatly utilised (1). Little known about reproductive biology. The effects of interspecific competition on populations of this species are unclear.

Roberts and Packard found seasonal decreases in the trapping rate of D. elator at Iowa Park, Wichita Co. to be associated with increases in the capture of other rodents though there was no actual evidence of interspecific competition (7). Martin and Matocha concluded on the basis of their study in Hardeman Co. that there would be minimal competition for food in typical D. elator habitat in years of normal food production (5). The species is, however, believed to avoid dense stands of grass inhabited by Cotton Rats Sigmodon hispidus (8).

THREATS TO SURVIVAL Restricted distribution and apparent dependence on Mesquite grasslands are considered to place the species at risk; most of the present range is on private land subject to uncontrolled habitat modification (1,5). Although the animal persists in agricultural areas provide Mesquite pastures or bushy fence rows are left, it does not appear to survive in areas treated with brush control chemicals (e.g. 2,4-D) (1). Here floristic composition considerably alters, with an absence of Mesquite and annual species such as Cranesbill. D. elator is also apparently absent from agricultural areas where bushy fence rows have been removed (1).

CONSERVATION MEASURES TAKEN A protected nongame species in Texas (8).

CONSERVATION MEASURES PROPOSED The species is being considered (1981) for inclusion in the U.S. Endangered Species List (9). There is an urgent need for ecological studies to more fully determine habitat requirements and population trends (5,8). In particular Martin and Matocha recommend that population studies be carried out in areas subject to various management practices (Mesquite controlled chemically, mechanically and uncontrolled) (5). The possible role of interspecific competition in limiting populations, especially in modified habitats, needs to be investigated. Once critical habitat requirements have been determined measures should be taken to ensure that management practices do not conflict with these.

CAPTIVE BREEDING Limited attempts at breeding this species in the laboratory have proved unsuccessful (6).

REMARKS For description of animal see (4). The species is also known as Loring's Kangeroo Rat. This data sheet was compiled from a draft kindly provided in May 1981 By Robert E. Martin, Departmant of Biology, University of Mary Hardin-Baylor, Texas.

REFERENCES
1. Chapman, B.R. (1972). Food habits of Loring's Kangaroo Rat, Dipodomys elator. J. Mammal. 53(4): 877-880.
2. Dalquest, W.W. (1968). Mammals of north-central Texas. Southwest. Nat. 13(1): 13-21.
3. Dalquest, W.W. and Collier, G. (1964). Notes on Dipodomys elator, a rare Kangaroo Rat. Southwest. Nat. 9(3): 146-150.
4. Davis, W.B. (1974). The mammals of Texas, rev. ed. Texas Parks and Wildlife Bull. 41: 1-294.
5. Martin, R.E. and Matocha, K.G. (1972). Distributional status of the Kangaroo Rat, Dipodomys elator. J. Mammal. 53(4): 873-877.
6. Packard, R.L. and Roberts, J.D. (1973). Observations on the behaviour of the Texas Kangaroo Rat, Dipodomys elator Merriam. Mammalia 37(4): 680-682.
7. Roberts, J.D. and Packard, R.L. (1973). Comments on movements, home range and ecology of the Texas Kangaroo Rat, Dipodomys elator Merriam. J. Mammal. 54(4): 957-962.
8. Martin, R.E. (1981). In litt.
9. Nowak, R.M. (1981). In litt.

SALT-MARSH HARVEST MOUSE

ENDANGERED

Reithrodontomys raviventris (Dixon, 1908)

Order RODENTIA   Family   CRICETIDAE

SUMMARY Restricted to salt marshes bordering San Francisco Bay, California, U.S.A. More than 80% of its former habitat has been lost due to filling, diking, vegetational changes and flooding following subsidence, consequently the species is considered endangered. Some marshes have been preserved in federal and state wildlife refuges while others are being considered for protection and are detailed in a Recovery Plan being prepared by the U.S. Fish and Wildlife Service.

DISTRIBUTION San Francisco Bay area of California, U.S.A. Main populations are in the Petalum and Napa marshes off the San Pablo Bay, the Contra Costa County coast of Suisun Bay and the marshes at the southern end of south San Francisco Bay. Scattered, small populations exist elsewhere around San Pablo and Suisun Bays but few remain between Richmond and the San Mateo Bridge in Central San Francisco Bay (1,5,7,9,13). For map see (4). Two distinct subspecies are recognised - Reithrodontomys raviventris raviventris in the southern part of the range as far north as Madera and Pt. San Pedro, and R. r. halicoetes further north (1). Overall limits of range are probably relatively unchanged but over 80% of the former habitat has been destroyed leading to a highly patchy and fragmented distribution (1,3,5).

POPULATION Numbers unknown. A few thousand may make up the summer maximum; however the once continuous distribution is now very fragmented and individual populations are small (7,8,11). The nominate southern subspecies is considered most at risk, being confined to areas with very high human populations (4), though the whole species is considered 'endangered' at both federal and state levels (10).

HABITAT AND ECOLOGY Restricted to salt and brackish marshes bordering the San Francisco Bay system. Salt marsh is characterised by Salicornia spp. with Spartina foliosa at lowest levels and Grindelia cuneifolia in higher areas, while brackish marshes are dominated by Typha latifolia and Scirpus spp. with Salicornia and Distichlis in depressed areas (1). Both habitats provide dense cover, ideally 0.2 to 1.0 m high, with a network of spaces beneath; the mice very rarely venture into the open. Adjacent grasslands are used to escape the highest summer tides as long as they provide sufficiently dense cover (1). Diet appears to consist mainly of salt marsh plant stems and leaves, with a low proportion of seeds and insects; in winter a high proportion of grasses is consumed (1). The two subspecies differ notably in several behavioural and physiological characteristics (e.g. tolerance to varying levels of salinity in drinking water and diet) and it has been suggested that they may be in the final stages of speciation (1,6). They are largely nocturnal and R. r. halicoetes constructs nests of dry grasses or sedges on the ground or in hummocks; these are often inhabited by several individuals. R. r. raviventris does not appear to build nests outside the breeding season, sheltering under vegetation or using the abandoned nests of other species (e.g. Song Sparrows Melospiza melodia) as temporary shelters (1,4). Breeding season is from March to November in R. r. raviventris and May to November in R. r. halicoetes with an average of just under four young per litter in both (1). Females of R. r. halicoetes may only produce one litter per year though population turnover rate is generally high with most mice surviving less than six months and very few more than a year (1,2,12).

THREATS TO SURVIVAL Habitat destruction. The species appears dependent on the dense cover provided by salt and brackish marshes; 80% of the original marshes in the area have been filled. Most that remain have been backfilled such that grasslands and the upper marsh zone have been destroyed, depriving the mice of vital refuges in periods of high tides. Others have been managed for waterfowl by growing monocultures of plant species unusable by the mice; still others have changed because of increased tidal coverage following subsidence or salinity changes or both. The average size and quality of tidal marshes has declined such that most populations are now very small (1,3,7). Most concern is expressed for the southern subspecies (R. r. raviventris) as the few marshes where it still survives are in areas of extensive development and very high human population density (10).

CONSERVATION MEASURES TAKEN Classified as 'Endangered' by the Department of the Interior and the California Dept. of Fish and Game (4). A number of marshes are protected within several federal wildlife refuges while others have been protected by the State (4,10). Few efforts have been made to reconstitute the upper edges of any of these marshes (10). A Recovery Plan for the species is being developed in 1981 by the U.S. Fish and Wildlife Service (11).

CONSERVATION MEASURES PROPOSED Numerous marshes are proposed for acquisition and upgrading in the Recovery Plan. Emphasis is placed on enlarging marshes, making them more contiguous and returning more of them to a natural state, particularly by restoring upper edges (11).

CAPTIVE BREEDING None at present (1981). Fisler maintained a captive colony for three years in the early 1960s, before the species was declared endangered (1).

REMARKS For description of animal see (8,9). It is difficult to distinguish from the Western Harvest Mouse (R. megalotis) in the field (8). Prof. Howard S. Shellhammer of the Department of Biological Sciences, San Jose State University, kindly provided a draft of this data sheet in May 1981.

REFERENCES 1. Fisler, G.F. (1965). Adaptations and speciation in Harvest Mice of the marshes of San Francisco Bay. Univ. of Calif. Pub. Zool. 77: 1-108.
2. Fisler, G.F. (1971). Age structure and sex ratio in populations of Reithrodontomys. J. Mammal. 52: 653-662.
3. Jones and Stokes et al. (1979). Protection and restoration of San Francisco Bay fish and wildlife habitat. Two volumes prepared for the U.S. Fish and Wildlife Service and the California Dept. of Fish and Game.
4. National Fish and Wildlife Laboratory (1980). Salt Marsh Harvest Mouse. FSW/OBS-80101.28. In Selected Vertebrate Endangered Species of the seacoast of the United States. Biological Services Program. U.S. Fish and Wildlife Service.
5. Pearson, O.O. (1960). Habitats of Harvest Mice revealed by automatic photographic recorders. J. Mammal. 41: 58-74.
6. Shellhammer, H.S. (1967). Cytotaxonomic studies of the Harvest Mice of the San Francisco Bay region. J. Mammal. 48: 549-555.
7. Shellhammer, H.S. (1977). Of mice and marshes. San Jose Studies, San Jose State University 3:23-35.
8. Shellhammer, H.S. (1981). Identification of Salt Marsh Harvest Mice, Reithrodontomys raviventris, in the field with cranial characteristics. California Department of Fish and Game, in press.
9. Shellhammer, H.S. (1981). Reithrodontomys raviventris. Mammalian Species, in press. American Society of

Mammalogists.

10. Shellhammer, H.S. (1981). In litt.

11. Shellhammer, H.S. and Harvey, T. (1981). Recovery Plan for the Salt Marsh Harvest Mouse and the California Clapper Rail. U.S. Fish and Wildlife Service, in prep.

12. Wondolleck, J.T., Zolan, W. and Sterens, G.L. (1976). A population study of the Harvest Mice (Reithrodontomys raviventris Dixon) in the Palo Alto Baylands Salt marsh. Wesmann J. Biol. 34: 52-64.

13. Zetterquist,, D. (1978). The Salt Marsh Harvest Mouse (Reithrodontomys raviventris raviventris) in marginal habitats. Wasmann J. of Biology 35: 68-76.

RABBIT-EARED TREE-RAT　　　　　　　　　　　　　　EXTINCT

Conilurus albipes (Lichtenstein, 1829)

Order　RODENTIA　　　　　　　　　　　Family　　MURIDAE

SUMMARY Probably extinct. Formerly occurred in eastern Australia but was last recorded in 1875. Any populations which may be discovered should be afforded immediate protection.

DISTRIBUTION Australia. Former distribution according to Gould was from the Darling Downs in southern Queensland to South Australia and the Port Phillip region of Victoria (1). Unrecorded since the last century, the last known specimen being about 1875 (2,3).

POPULATION Almost certainly extinct (3).

HABITAT AND ECOLOGY Little known. It was apparently always associated with trees and according to Gould's observations was strictly nocturnal, sleeping during the day in a nest of dried leaves in a hollow log or branch (1). A female sent to Sir George Gray when he was Governor of South Australia had three young clinging firmly to its teats and in this position they were carried along with the female as she moved (1).

THREATS TO SURVIVAL Unknown, though it seems likely that bush clearance during settlement and the introduction of feral predators, such as the cat in the 19th century and the fox in the early 1900s, were responsible for its presumed extinction.

CONSERVATION MEASURES TAKEN Included on the Official List of Endangered Australian Vertebrate Fauna.

CONSERVATION MEASURES PROPOSED Immediate protection of any areas where it is found to occur.

CAPTIVE BREEDING None.

REMARKS For description see (1,2,3). There are two specimens in Australian and a few in European Museums (2). Has also been known as the White-Footed Tree-rat or Rabbit-rat. The common name here used is that recommended in 1980 by the Australian Mammal Society.

REFERENCES　　1.　Gould, J. (1863). The Mammals of Australia. Taylor and Francis, London.
　　　　　　　　2.　Ride, W.D.L. (1970). A guide to the native mammals of Australia. Oxford Univ. Press, Melbourne.
　　　　　　　　3.　Troughton, E. (1941). Furred animals of Australia. Angus and Robertson Ltd., Sydney.

LESSER STICK-NEST RAT   EXTINCT

Leporillus apicalis (Gould, 1853)

Order   RODENTIA   Family   MURIDAE

SUMMARY Formerly widespread in Australia but not definitely recorded since 1933, though it may possibly still survive in arid inland regions such as the Gibson Desert. Surveys to try to locate this species would be desirable.

DISTRIBUTION Australia. Former limits of range not precisely known though was originally widespread in central and southern Australia from Victoria west to the Gibson Desert in Western Australia. Separation of the remains of this species from those of the congeneric L. conditor (also an IUCN Red Data Book species) has proved difficult though it is generally accepted that the latter occurred further south and east (it is now believed extinct on the mainland) (9). In New South Wales and Victoria L. apicalis was recorded as common along the Darling and Murray Rivers (from about Euston westwards) in 1856-57 but was evidently exterminated there soon afterwards (5). Further west, nests were observed in 1872-73 near Mt. Peculiar in the northwest MacDonnells, central Australia, and the capture of two specimens of L. apicalis at Alice Springs in 1895 indicated that this was the species involved (3). In 1941 Finlayson thought the species probably still persisted in the Mt. Peculiar region (3). In 1903 Stick-nest Rats were described as plentiful in an area south of the Mann Range and were probably of this species (3). The most recent specimens were two collected in 1933 8 km west of Mt. Crombie south of the Mann and Musgrove Ranges in South Australia (3,5). There have been several reports in the 1970s of nests with fresh material in them from the arid inland regions of Western Australia, particularly from rocky areas to the north of the Leonora to Warburton Road, in the southern Gibson Desert (2,4,7). Their location suggests that they probably belong to L. apicalis and not L. conditor and remains from similar constructions in Western Australia have been positively identified as L. apicalis (2). However no definite proof of its survival has been obtained to date.

POPULATION Unknown. If the species does indeed persist its population is likely to be very low.

HABITAT AND ECOLOGY Semi-arid shrubland in the southern portion of its distribution, and rocky ranges and dense mulga woodland in central Australia are described habitats (5,7). The genus Leporillus is notable for the construction of large, complex communal nests made from interwoven sticks. These are built in crevices and caves, or around bushes in the open, and may be up to 1 m high and 3 m across, though much larger nests were recorded in the 19th century (3,5,6,7,9). Krefft, who compiled habitat notes from the Murray plains in about 1864 stated that the rats were nocturnal and gregarious, living in hollow trees as well as in stick-nests (6). Watts and Eves analysed old faecal pellets found in northern South Australia, almost certainly from this species, and found a very high proportion (up to 70%) of remains of the succulent perennial Bassia eriacantha. Studies of captive L. conditor indicate that they cannot survive for long without free water and its is thought that Stick-nest Rats had to rely on a specialised diet of water-rich plants to survive in their arid or semi-arid habitat (9).

THREATS TO SURVIVAL Habitat alteration by stock-rearing and agriculture, and by introduced rabbits, was almost certainly a significant factor in New South Wales and Victoria. Their probable dependence on succulent perennials is likely to have brought them into direct competition with introduced animals such as rabbits, sheep and cattle leading to their rapid disappearance from areas as these invaders appeared, in contrast to other desert rodents (e.g. Rattus villosissimus, Pseudomys spp. and small Notomys spp.) whose less specialised diet allowed them to survive (9). However, in much of its range in central and possibly Western Australia the habitat remains largely undisturbed by these factors (2,3). Finlayson attributed its decline to hunting by aborigines, its communal and distinctive nesting habit making it especially susceptible (3), but this would not explain how it persisted in apparent abundance until the time of European settlement. The most likely cause outside areas of pastoralization would appear to be predation by feral cats and foxes, the former introduced in the nineteenth century, the latter in the early 1900s.

CONSERVATION MEASURES TAKEN Legally protected and appears on the Official List of Endangered Australian Vertebrate Fauna. At least some of the nests discovered in the Gibson Desert are in the proposed Baker Lake Conservation Area (2).

CONSERVATION MEASURES PROPOSED Any viable populations discovered should immediately be afforded full protection.

CAPTIVE BREEDING Krefft described the species as easily tamed at his camps in the bush (6), and experience with Leporillus conditor indicates that maintenance in captivity should be straightforward (1).

REMARKS For description see (5,6,8). This data sheet was compiled from a draft kindly provided in 1978 by Dr C.H.S. Watts.

REFERENCES
1. Aslin, H.J. (1972). Nest-building by Leporillus conditor in captivity. S. Austr. Naturalist 47: 43-46.
2. Burbidge, A.A., McKenzie, N.L., Chapman, A. and Lambert, P.M. (1976). The wildlife of some existing and proposed reserves in the Great Victoria and Gibson Deserts, Western Australia. Wildl. Res. Bull. West. Aust. 5: 1-16.
3. Finlayson, H.H. (1941). On Central Australian mammals: Part II. The Muridae. Trans. R. Soc. S. Aust. 63: 88-118.
4. Gratte, S. (1972). The Stick-nest Rat Leporillus conditor in the Gibson Desert. West. Australian Naturalist. 12(3): 50-51.
5. Ride, W.D.L. (1970). A guide to the native mammals of Australia. Oxford University Press, Melbourne.
6. Troughton, E. (1941). Furred animals of Australia. Angus and Robertson Ltd. Sydney.
7. Watts, C.H.S. (1979). The status of endangered Australian rodents. In Tyler, M.J. (Ed.), The status of endangered Australasian wildlife. Royal Zool. Soc. S. Aust.
8. Watts, C.H.S. and Aslin, H. (1981). The rodents of Australia. Angus and Robertson Ltd., Sydney.
9. Watts, C.H.S. and Eves, B.M. (1976). Notes on the nests and diet of the White-tailed Stick-nest Rat Leporillus apicalis, in northern South Australia. S. Aust. Naturalist 51(1): 9-12.

GREATER STICK-NEST RAT

RARE

Leporillus conditor (Sturt, 1848)

Order   RODENTIA

Family   MURIDAE

SUMMARY   Only known population is confined to Franklin Island off South Australia, though it may conceivably still exist on the Australian mainland. The Franklin Island population is fully protected and apparently stable but must be considered potentially vulnerable to fire, introduced predators and herbivores.

DISTRIBUTION   Australia, where now only occurs with certainty on Franklin Island (about 500 ha) in the Nuyts Archipelago off the South Australian coast (1,6,10). Extant limits of its former range on the mainland are unknown; it is known to have ranged over central southern Australia, probably from the south bank of the Murray River in Victoria as far west as the eastern part of the Nullarbor Plain in Western Australia. Its northern limit seems to have been around latitude 28°S in the north of the Lake Eyre Basin, South Australia (3,5,9,10).

POPULATION   Unknown. In 1978 the only available estimate for the Franklin Island population was 5000 although Watts questions the accuracy of this figure. The 1970 population there was estimated at 1500-2000 with no apparent decrease a year later despite a very dry summer intervening (1). On the mainland it was said to have originally been locally very plentiful but declined rapidly following settlement and by 1856-57 had become very rare in the River Darling area and extinct south of the Murray River (6). Further north and west it persisted longer; the last mainland museum specimens were caught at Ooldea on the eastern edge of the Nullarbor Plain in 1921 (7,8), though Finlayson stated it had persisted up to around 1931 in the Lake Eyre Basin and in 1961 he considered it still present near the southern margin of the Nullarbor Plain (15). If it does still exist there, numbers must be very low. There have been several reports in the 1970s of fresh-looking nests in the Gibson Desert area of Western Australia but their locality suggests the congeneric L. apicalis rather than L. conditor and remains from at least one (old) nest have been ascribed to the former species (2,4,10).

HABITAT AND ECOLOGY   The genus Leporillus is remarkable for the construction of elaborate stick-nests which are usually built in shallow caves or crevices or around the base of bushes. Sticks up to 50 cm long are used and nests can be up to 1m high and 3 m across with one or more interconnected nest chambers. The nests provide a refuge against predators and temperature extremes and may house several individuals (1,5,6,10,14,15). Habitat is semi-arid or arid shrubland, or low steppe (6,10). The diet of the Franklin Island population consists principally of succulents such as Tetragona implexicana, Carpobrotus rossii and Nitraria schoberi though in captivity the species is relatively unselective (1,6,15); captive specimens however cannot survive without free water for more than about six days and it is thought that the species is dependent in its arid natural environment on food plants with a high moisture content. Faecal pellets from northern South Australia, believed to be from L. apicalis, contained a very high proportion of the succulent perennial, Bassia eriacantha (14). The date of breeding appeared to vary throughout the species' range, probably being dependent on seasonal and climatic conditions (6). Gestation period is about 44 days and 1 to 4 well-developed young are born which are moved about attached to the nipples (6). On Franklin Island the rat is predated on by Barn Owls (Tyto alba) and Black Tiger Snakes (Notechis ater), though the intensity of such predation is not known (6).

THREATS TO SURVIVAL Reasons for decline on the mainland were probably habitat alteration by agriculture, stock raising and introduced herbivores, especially rabbits, and the introduction of predators such as foxes and feral cats. Watts and Eves have suggested that their apparent dependence on water-rich perennial plants may have brought the species into direct competition with cattle, sheep and rabbits and may have been an important factor in their rapid disappearance as the introduced species spread on the mainland in contrast to other desert rodents such as Rattus villosissimus, Pseudomys spp. and Notomys spp. whose less specialised diets may have allowed them to escape direct competition and thus persist (14). Wood-Jones additionally identified deliberate burning of nests, and trampling by cattle as important factors in settled areas (15). The small size of Franklin Island and of the population there makes it extremely vulnerable to fire and the introduction of rabbits or predators (10).

CONSERVATION MEASURES TAKEN Included in Appendix 1 of the 1973 Convention on International Trade in Endangered Species of Wild Fauna and Flora, trade in it or its products therefore being subject to strict regulation by ratifying nations, and trade for primarily commercial purposes banned. Legally protected and appears on the Official List of Endangered Australian Vertebrate Fauna. Since 1972 Franklin Island has been included in the Nuyts Archipelago Conservation Park. It is under the control of the South Australian National Parks and Wildlife Service and is classified as a Prohibited Area (6).

CONSERVATION MEASURES PROPOSED Any population discovered on the mainland should be immediately protected. Monitoring of the population and habitat on Franklin Island is considered of great importance and Watts has noted that at present (1981) this is not being carried out (12). Possible sites for the establishment of new populations should be investigated; this would guard against complete extinction should the Franklin Island population be wiped out.

CAPTIVE BREEDING The species has proved relatively easy to maintain in captivity (6). Watts succeeded in breeding from wild caught specimens in the 1970s but no captive-born females have raised litters (11).

REMARKS For description see (13). The Franklin Island population was originally named a separate species, Leporillus jonesi, but is now recognised as L. conditor (5,6,13). This data sheet was compiled from a draft provided in 1978 by Dr C.H.S. Watts, and he, Dr A.K. Lee of the IUCN/SSC Rodent Specialist Group and Dr. A.C. Robinson of the SSC Australian Mammal Specialist Group kindly commented on the final draft.

REFERENCES
1. Aslin, H.J. (1972). Nest-building by Leporillus conditor in captivity. S. Austr. Naturalist 47: 43-46.
2. Burbidge, A.A., McKenzie, N.L., Chapman, A. and Lambert, P.M. (1976). The wildlife of some existing and proposed reserves in the Great Victoria and Gibson Deserts, Western Australia. Wildl. Res. Bull. West. Aust. 5: 1-16.
3. Finlayson, H.H. (1961). On Central Australian mammals Part IV. The distribution and status of Central Australian species. Rec. S. Aust. Mus. 14: 141-191.
4. Gratte, S. (1972). The Stick-nest Rat Leporillus conditor in the Gibson Desert. West. Australian Naturalist. 12(3): 50-51.
5. Ride, W.D.L. (1970). A guide to the native mammals of Australia. Oxford University Press, Melbourne.
6. Robinson, A.C. (1975). The Stick-nest Rat Leporillus conditor, on Franklin Island, Nuyts Archipelago, South Australia. Austr. Mammal. 1(4): 319-327.
7. Troughton, E. le G. (1923). A revision of the rats of the

genus Leporillus and the status of Hapalotis personata Krefft. Rec. Aust. Mus. 14: 23-41.

8. Troughton, E. le G. (1924). The stick-nest building rat of Australia. Aust. Mus. Mag. 11: 18-23.

9. Troughton, E. le G. (1941). Furred animals of Australia. Angus and Robertson Ltd., Sydney.

10. Watts, C.H.S. (1979). The status of endangered Australian rodents. In Tyler, M.J. (Ed.), The status of endangered Australasian wildlife. Royal Zool. Soc. S. Aust.

11. Watts, C.H.S. (1980). Success rates in founding captive colonies of Australian rodents and marsupials. In Olney, P.J.S. (Ed.), International Zoo Yearbook 20. Zool. Soc. London.

12. Watts, C.H.S. (1981). In litt.

13. Watts, C.H.S. and Aslin, H.J. (1981). The Rodents of Australia. Angus and Robertson, Sydney.

14. Watts, C.H.S. and Eves, B.M. (1976). Notes on the nests and diet of the White-tailed Stick-nest Rat, Leporillus apicalis in Northern South Australia. S. Austr. Naturalist 51(1): 9-12.

15. Wood-Jones, F. (1923-25). The Mammals of South Australia. The Government Printer, Adelaide.

16. Robinson, A.C. (1981). In litt.

BEACH VOLE   RARE

Microtus breweri (Baird, 1857)

Order   RODENTIA   Family   MURIDAE

SUMMARY Endemic to the tiny island of Muskeget off the Massachusetts coast, U.S.A. A single population exists with a restricted habitat and is at risk to hurricanes and fires. No conservation measures have yet been taken but the rodent is the subject of studies by R.H. Tamarin.

DISTRIBUTION Muskeget Island, 2.6 sq. km, 32 km south of Cape Cod, Massachusetts, U.S.A. (2,5). Two-thirds of the island is privately owned and the remaining third belongs to the County of Nantucket. For map see (5).

POPULATION Apparently near extinction in the late 19th century (1,6), but R.H. Tamarin who has recently studied the species reported in 1981 that the population had recovered and was now relatively stable. He noted that lowest numbers occur in late winter and early spring, though some areas of more suitable habitat maintain a steady high density (3).

HABITAT AND ECOLOGY Muskeget lies just within the terminal moraine of the last glaciation (5) and is a tiny area of a vanished sandplain which once extended along the Atlantic coast of North America from New Jersey to Newfoundland. Muskeget separated from nearby islands (Nantucket, Martha's Vineyard) and Cape Cod between one and three thousand years ago, due to glacial melt (2). The dominant vegetation on the island is Beach Grass (Ammophila breviligulata) and Poison Ivy (Rhus radicans), although fresh and salt water marsh areas and open dunes also exist. The island is a major breeding ground for Herring Gulls (Larus argentatus) and Great Black-backed Gulls (L. marinus). The only other terrestrial mammal on the island is the White-footed Mouse, Peromyscus leucopus. Predators of the vole are Marsh Hawks (Circus cyaneus) and Short-eared Owls (Asio flammeus) (4). In habits, the Beach Vole closely resembles the Meadow Vole, Microtus pennsylvanicus. Runways are constructed above ground through the Beach Grass, and nests are built both above and below ground. If no shelter is available, short (30-60 cm), steeply sloping burrows are constructed terminating in a bulky nest (5). The voles appear to prefer low wet grassy areas and during periods of low abundance can only be found in this habitat (1). Miller in 1896 reported breeding to occur throughout the 'warm season' with litters of four or five (1). He also reported that the voles fed on the tender bases of Beach Grass stalks and stored caches of this in the autumn (1).

THREATS TO SURVIVAL According to Miller, M. breweri became extinct on Muskeget in 1891, probably because of feral cat predation (1). 26 voles were reintroduced in 1893 from Southwest Point Island which itself no longer exists (1,5). Tamarin reports the current principal threats to be hurricanes and fires (6), he does not mention the existence of feral cats on the island. Currently the isolated location of the island, its limited use and the abundance of Poison Ivy all contribute to minimal disturbance of the island's ecosystem.

CONSERVATION MEASURES TAKEN No specific conservation measures have been taken. R.H. Tamarin is currently (1981) studying this species (3,4,5). The Species Survival Commission of IUCN established a Rodent Specialist Group in 1980 and they will be reviewing the status of this taxon with a view to recommending appropriate conservation action. This species is not included on the U.S. Endangered Species List.

CONSERVATION MEASURES PROPOSED Continued monitoring of the status of this species and the implementation of appropriate conservation measures should they become necessary.

CAPTIVE BREEDING No information, but it would be advisable to establish a captive colony.

REMARKS For description see (5). Interestingly, the Beach Vole does not exhibit the population cycles of its mainland counterparts. It has also shown adaptations to island isolation of larger body size and reduced litter size as compared to the Meadow Vole, Microtus pennsylvanicus, from which it evolved; the two are sometimes considered conspecific (4). This data sheet was compiled from a draft kindly provided in 1981 by Robert H. Tamarin.

REFERENCES
1. Miller, G.S. Jr. (1896). The Beach Mouse of Muskeget Island. Proc. Boston Soc. Nat. Hist. 27: 75-87.
2. Starrett, A. (1958). Insular variation in mice of the Microtus pennsylvanicus group in southeastern Massachusetts. Ph. D. dissertation, Univ. Michigan, 137 pp.
3. Tamarin, R. (1977). Demography of the Beach Vole (Microtus breweri) and the Meadow Vole (Microtus pennsylvanicus) in southeastern Massachusetts. Ecology 58: 1310-1321.
4. Tamarin, R. (1978). Disperal, population regulation, and K-selection in field mice. Amer. Natur. 112: 545-555.
5. Tamarin, R.H. and Kunz, T.H. (1974). Microtus breweri. Mammal. Spec. 45: 1-3. The American Society of Mammalogists.
6. Wetherbee, D.K., Coppinger, R.P. and Walsh, R.E. (1972). Time lapse ecology, Muskeget Island, Nantucket, Massachusetts. MSS Educational Publ. Co., New York, 173 pp.

Notomys amplus Brazenor, 1936

Order   RODENTIA   Family   MURIDAE

SUMMARY Known from two specimens collected in 1894 and from remains in owl pellets, all from northern South Australia. May be extinct but could survive in remote areas.

DISTRIBUTION Australia. Limits of distribution unknown. Two specimens were collected by the Horn Expedition in 1894 in the Charlotte Waters district on the north central border of South Australia (2,3,5,6). Finlayson in 1961 noted that the Aborigines of the Musgrave Ranges, east of Charlotte Waters, had a name ('Arruja') for a species of Notomys much larger than N. alexis ('Dargawarra'), though it seemed almost legendary by that time. This could have been N. amplus (2). Remains of the species have also been identified in owl pellets dated at 100 to 200 years BP from the Flinders Range, northern South Australia (4,6).

POPULATION Unknown. Probably extinct.

HABITAT AND ECOLOGY Unknown. Notomys species in general are adapted to desert conditions. They are nocturnal, largely vegetarian and construct complex burrow systems (3,6).

THREATS TO SURVIVAL Unknown, though predation by feral cats and competitive displacement by introduced rabbits and rodents have been suggested as factors which threaten all Notomys species (1).

CONSERVATION MEASURES TAKEN All Notomys species are legally protected in Australia and are included in Appendix 2 of the 1973 Convention on International Trade in Endangered Species of Wild Fauna and Flora, trade in them or their products is thus subject to monitoring by ratifying nations. N. amplus is included on the Official List of Endangered Australian Vertebrate Fauna.

CONSERVATION MEASURES PROPOSED None, other than protection of any areas where a population may be discovered.

CAPTIVE BREEDING None.

REMARKS For description see (6). This is the largest of the genus Notomys, though is only very slightly larger than N. longicaudatus, another species listed in the IUCN Red Data Book, from which it differs in having a relatively shorter tail and longer ears (3). Dr. C.H.S. Watts kindly commented on a draft of this data sheet.

REFERENCES   1. Anon. (1980). Australian submission to CITES. No.18-19. Unpd. 3pp.
             2. Finlayson, H.H. (1961). On Central Australian mammals Part IV. The distribution and status of Central Australian species. Rec. S. Aust. Mus. 14: 141-191.
             3. Ride, W.D.L. (1970). A guide to the native mammals of Australia. Oxford University Press, Melbourne.
             4. Smith, M.J. (1977). The remains of mammals, including Notomys longicaudatus (Gould) (Rodentia: Muridae) in owl pellets from the Flinders Range, South Australia. Aust.

Wild. Res. 4: 159-170.

5. Troughton, E. (1941). Furred animals of Australia. Angus and Robertson Ltd., Sydney.

6. Watts, C.H.S. and Aslin, H.J. (1981). The Rodents of Australia. Angus and Robertson, Sydney.

NORTHERN HOPPING-MOUSE

INSUFFICIENTLY
KNOWN

Notomys aquilo Thomas,1921

Order   RODENTIA   Family   MURIDAE

SUMMARY   Recorded from Groote Eylandt off northern Australia and at two sites on the north coast of Australia. May be moderately common in suitable sand-dune habitat but little collecting has beeen carried out in much of its presumed range and surveys are needed to establish its status and distribution.

DISTRIBUTION   Northern Australia. Occurs on Groote Eylandt in the Gulf of Carpentaria, Northern Territory, where 13 were collected in 1948 from the region of Umbakumba (1,2). In 1975 it was reported as still present in sandy areas there (4). In addition one specimen was caught near the Calvert River in western Arnhem Land, Northern Territory in 1979 and one somewhere on Cape York Peninsula, in northern Queensland around 1860 (4), though the reliability of the latter record has been questioned (6).

POPULATION   Present status unknown, though in 1978 it was reported that it may be moderately common in some areas (4). The Umbakumba population was described as 'flourishing' when discovered by the Arnhem Land expedition of 1948. Failure to find the species on Cape York Peninsula since the first record, if correct, may be owing to lack of searching in the right habitats (6). It is probably a rare animal in western Arnhem Land although only limited collecting has been carried out in appropriate habitat (4).

HABITAT AND ECOLOGY   Found on light, sandy soils in coastal dunes, where it constructs complex burrows (2). Young were observed on Groote Eylandt in June in litters of 3 or 4 (2). Little else is known about its biology, though it is assumed to be similar to other Notomys species in being nocturnal and feeding principally on grass seeds and other vegetable matter supplemented by occasional insects (3).

THREATS TO SURVIVAL   Unknown. Much of Groote Eylandt is under mining leases (4), but the effect of this on the mouse's habitat is unknown.

CONSERVATION MEASURES TAKEN   All Notomys species are listed in Appendix 2 of the 1973 Convention on International Trade in Endangered Species of Wild Fauna and Flora, and trade in them or their products is thus subject to monitoring by ratifying nations. Fully protected by legislation in the Northern Territory (4) and appears on the Official List of Endangered Australian Vertebrate Fauna. Much of its presumed range is also within national parks or Aboriginal reserves (4).

CONSERVATION MEASURES PROPOSED   Assessment of its status on Groote Eylandt and appropriate measures to protect populations there are recommended. Surveys of the presumed range in Arnhem Land would also be desirable.

CAPTIVE BREEDING   As far as is known this species has never been kept in captivity.

REMARKS   For description see (2,4,5). The Groote Eylandt population was originally named Notomys carpentarius but is now included in N. aquilo, named in 1921 from the Cape York specimen (5). This data sheet was compiled from a draft provided in 1978 by Dr C.H.S. Watts, and G.W. Saunders, Director of the Queensland National Parks and Wildlife Service, kindly commented on the sheet.

REFERENCES

1. Johnson, D.H. (1959). Four new mammals from the Northern Territory of Australia. Proc. Biol. Soc. Wash. 72: 183-187.

2. Johnson, D.H. (1964). Mammals. In Specht, R.L. (Ed.), Records of the American-Australian Scientific Expedition to Arnhem Land 4: 427-515. Melbourne University Press.

3. Ride, W.D.L. (1970). A guide to the native mammals of Australia. Oxford University Press, Melbourne.

4. Watts, C.H.S. (1979). The status of endangered Australian rodents. In Tyler, M.J. (Ed.), The status of endangered Australasian wildlife. Royal Zool. Soc. S. Aust.

5. Watts, C.H.S. and Aslin, H.J. (1981). The Rodents of Australia. Angus and Robertson, Sydney.

6. Winter, J.W. and Allison, F.R. (1979). The native mammals of Cape York Peninsula - changes in status since the 1948 Archbold Expedition. In Stevens, N.C. and Bailey, A. (Eds), Contemporary Cape York Peninsula. Roy. Soc. Queensland.

Notomys longicaudatus (Gould, 1844)

Order   RODENTIA   Family   MURIDAE

SUMMARY Has been collected from two widely separate regions of Australia, most recently in 1901, though is also known from 'recent' owl pellet remains. Possibly extinct though may still survive in remote arid regions.

DISTRIBUTION Australia. Limits of range are unknown. Has been collected from widely separated areas: in the region of New Norcia on the Moore River north of Perth, Western Australia, where the type specimen was collected in 1843, and in central Australia where over 30 specimens were collected around 1900 - on Bert Plains north of Alice Springs, at Mt. Burrel (northwest of Idracowra), in 1894, at Barrow Creek in 1901 and in the Coonbaralba Range near Broken Hill (1,2,3,4,6). In 1973 it was reported that 'recent' owl pellets from a cave in the Highland Rocks area of the Northern Territory contained remains of either this species or of N. fuscus (5), and owl pellets dated 100-200 years BP from the Flinders Range, northern South Australia, contained remains positively identified as N. longicaudatus (7).

POPULATION Unknown; may be extinct, having not been definitely recorded for 80 years. In 1960 Finlayson stated that there were vague reports of the species in central Australia and it was possible that it still survived there (3) - Notomys species often show patchy and erratic, highly local distribution, occasionally becoming common in years following particularly favourable climatic conditions (as this species did in 1901), but being easily overlooked the rest of the time (3,6). N. longicaudatus was the fourth most abundant species identified in 3 owl pellet deposits from the Flinders Range (see above), after Rattus villosissimus, Notomys fuscus and Pseudomys gouldii, implying that some change of status may have occurred since the deposits were laid down (7).

HABITAT AND ECOLOGY Unknown. Notomys species in general are herbivorous, burrowing, nocturnal rodents well adapted to desert and semi-desert conditions (6,8,9). Gilbert noted that this species preferred to burrow in clay soil rather than sand in the Moore River region (8).

THREATS TO SURVIVAL Unknown, though presumably vulnerable to introduced predators such as foxes and feral cats, and to habitat modification by rabbits and domestic livestock.

CONSERVATION MEASURES TAKEN All Notomys species are legally protected and are included in Appendix 2 of the 1973 Convention on International Trade in Endangered Species of Wild Fauna and Flora, thus trade in them or their products is subject to monitoring by ratifying nations. N. longicaudatus is included on the Official List of Endangered Australian Vertebrate Fauna.

CONSERVATION MEASURES PROPOSED Immediate effective protection of any areas found to contain this species.

CAPTIVE BREEDING None.

REMARKS For description see (9). Dr. A.K. Lee of the IUCN/SSC Rodent Specialist Group and Dr. C.H.S. Watts kindly commented in 1981 on a draft of this data sheet.

REFERENCES   1.   Anon. (1973). Additional protection for rare fauna. State Wildlife Authority News Service (West. Australia) 4(2): 31-33.

2.   Brazenor, C.W. (1934). A revision of the Australian jerboa mice. Mem. Nat. Mus. Melb. 8: 74-89.

3.   Finlayson, H.H. (1961). On Central Australian mammals Part IV. The distribution and status of Central Australian species. Rec. S. Aust. Mus. 14: 141-191.

4.   Lee, A.K. (1981). In litt.

5.   Parker, S.A. (1973). An annotated checklist of the native land mammals of the Northern Territory. Rec. S. Aust. Mus. 16(11): 1-57.

6.   Ride, W.D.L. (1970). A guide to the native mammals of Australia. Oxford University Press, Melbourne.

7.   Smith, M.J. (1977). The remains of mammals, including Notomys longicaudatus (Gould) (Rodentia: Muridae) in owl pellets from the Flinders Range, South Australia. Aust. Wildl. Res. 4: 159-170.

8.   Troughton, E. (1941). Furred animals of Australia. Angus and Robertson Ltd. Sydney.

9.   Watts, C.H.S. and Aslin, H.J. (1981). The Rodents of Australia. Angus and Robertson, Sydney.

Notomys macrotis Thomas, 1921

Order   RODENTIA   Family   MURIDAE

SUMMARY Probably extinct; the only two specimens known were collected in Australia before 1850.

DISTRIBUTION Australia. Known only from two specimens; one obtained at the Moore River, in the vicinity of New Norcia, Western Australia in 1843 and the other, of unknown date and locality, purchased from Gould by the British Museum some time after 1840 (2).

POPULATION Unknown, probably extinct.

HABITAT AND ECOLOGY Unknown. Notomys species in general are herbivorous, burrowing, nocturnal rodents well adapted to desert and semi-desert conditions (3).

THREATS TO SURVIVAL Unknown.

CONSERVATION MEASURES TAKEN All Notomys species are listed in Appendix 2 of the 1973 Convention on International Trade in Endangered Species of Wild Fauna and Flora, and trade in them or their products is thus subject to monitoring by ratifying nations. N. macrotis is legally protected in Western Australia (1), and is included on the Official List of Endangered Australian Vertebrate Fauna as Notomys megalotis.

CONSERVATION MEASURES PROPOSED Effective protection of any areas found to hold populations of this species.

CAPTIVE BREEDING None.

REMARKS The only material available is in poor condition and external characteristics are not distinguishable (2). N. megalotis has been used in place of N. macrotis. Dr. C.H.S. Watts kindly commented on a draft of this data sheet.

REFERENCES   1.   Anon. (1973). Additional protection for rare fauna. State Wildlife Authority News Service (West. Australia) 4(2): 31-33.
             2.   Mahoney, J.A. (1975). Notomys macrotis Thomas, 1921, a poorly known Australian Hopping-mouse (Rodentia: Muridae). Aust. Mammal 1: 367-374.
             3.   Ride, W.D.L. (1970). A guide to the native mammals of Australia. Oxford University Press, Melbourne.

Notomys mordax Thomas, 1922

Order   RODENTIA   Family   MURIDAE

SUMMARY   Probably extinct; known from a single specimen collected in Queensland some time prior to 1846. May be an invalid species.

DISTRIBUTION   Australia. The only known specimen is a damaged skull, among material stated to have come from the Darling Downs in Queensland, registered in the British Museum collection in 1846 (1).

POPULATION   Probably extinct.

HABITAT AND ECOLOGY   Unknown; other Notomys species are burrowing, nocturnal and largely vegetarian. In general they are adapted to desert conditions (1).

THREATS TO SURVIVAL   Unknown.

CONSERVATION MEASURES TAKEN   All Notomys species are included in Appendix 2 of the 1973 Convention on International Trade in Endangered Species of Wild Fauna and Flora, and trade in them or their products is thus subject to monitoring by ratifying nations. N. mordax is on the Official List of Endangered Australian Vertebrate Fauna.

CONSERVATION MEASURES PROPOSED   Any area where the species may be found should be afforded immediate protection.

CAPTIVE BREEDING   None.

REMARKS   There are no details of external description (1).

REFERENCES   1.   Ride, W.D.L. (1970). A guide to the native mammals of Australia. Oxford Univ. Press, Melbourne.

Oryzomys argentatus Spitzer & Lazell, 1978

Order   RODENTIA   Family   MURIDAE

SUMMARY A recently described species, discovered in 1973 and known from very few specimens, apparently confined to freshwater marshes in the lower Florida Keys, U.S.A. Habitat is very vulnerable to destruction through drainage and filling in for development and only tiny remnants now remain. The species has been proposed for inclusion on the US. Endangered Species List.

DISTRIBUTION   U.S.A. where confined to the lower Florida Keys, Monroe County, Florida (1,2,3,4,7). By 1981 only 8 specimens had been collected, all since the winter of 1973 when 2 were collected from a small freshwater marsh (about 0.3 ha) on Cudjoe Key (5,7). A third specimen was rather close to the type locality in 1979 (7), and in winter 1980-81 five more were trapped in the Keys, though their precise locality is not given (5).

POPULATION Unknown. Trapping over a period of five years up to 1979 in suitable habitat (totalling only about 2 ha) on Cudjoe, Little Torch, Middle Torch, Sugarloaf and Big Pine Keys failed to produce any specimens and Humphrey and Barbour concluded that the species was extinct (2). Since then, however, six additional individuals have been obtained (5,7). Spitzer and Lazell conclude that the very low success rate of live trapping may be because the species is trap-shy, requiring a considerable time before it will enter any traps set, and most trapping has been carried out only for short periods at a time (4). Humphrey and Barbour have noted that the species' home range size is likely to be similar to that of the closely related and widespread Oryzomys palustris which exhibits an average of 0.33 ha for males and 0.21 ha for females. This is relatively large compared to the total area of apparently suitable remaining habitat and implies that the overall population is likely to be low (2).

HABITAT AND ECOLOGY The type locality is a small freshwater marsh (formed from a broad, shallow solution hole in the coral bedrock) in the centre of a 10 ha tropical hammock (1,2,3,4). It is bordered mostly by Red Mangrove (Rhizophora mangle) with Buttonwood (Conocarpus erecta), Black Mangrove (Avicennia germinans) and Sawgrass (Cladium jamaicense) and is dominated by Cattails (Typha domingensis) along its edge; at the centre, where water depth varies from 0.5 to 2 m according to season, Cattails become sparse and vegetation is principally Cordgrass (Spartina spp.) (1,2,3,4). The rat is also reported as venturing into adjacent salt savannah and mangrove swamps (6). Life history details are poorly known, though are likely to be similar to Oryzomys palustris (1,2). The latter species is markedly amphibious and swims and dives well; it is nocturnal and diet appears to consist primarily of seeds and the succulent parts of available plants, though a study in coastal Georgia found animal matter, particularly insects and small crabs, to be of considerable importance in summer and autumn (1). In Louisiana breeding season is from February to November and litters of one to five, born after a gestation period of 25 days, have been recorded (1). A pair of O. argentatus captured in the winter of 1980/81 were reported in April 1981 as having produced a litter of three young (5).

THREATS TO SURVIVAL Habitat destruction appears to be by far the most important threat (2,3,4,7). Freshwater marshes were once a common habitat on the lower Keys but have now mostly been destroyed either through drainage for development (which is rampant in the Keys) or road building, or for mosquito control - in the latter case ditches are dug through the limestone bedrock which allows the marshes to be inundated wth salt-water thus killing the natural vegetation. Only very small areas of freshwater marsh remain on the Keys (2,3,4,7). The type locality is immediately adjacent to U.S. Route 1. which was reported in March 1980 as being re-bedded and widened and in 1979 it was stated that a plan had been formulated to fill and develop those parts of the marsh on private property (2,7). Spitzer has noted that the species appears 'dependent on a very tenuous system affected by the weather which causes environmental fluctuations in the marsh, and the whim of the landowner', and also that in especially dry seasons Cotton Rats (Sigmodon hispidus) invade the inner marsh and may compete with Rice Rats for food and nesting sites (3). Persistent herbicidal spraying of the marsh which destroys Cattails and poisons food supplies may in part explain the apparent present rarity of O. argentatus (3,4) and will pose a continuing threat.

CONSERVATION MEASURES TAKEN The species is listed as State Endangered in Florida (3). In July 1980 the U.S. Fish and Wildlife Service accepted a petition to list the Silver Rice Rat in the U.S. list of Endangered and Threatened Wildlife under the 1973 Endangered Species Act (6,7) and in 1980/81 status surveys were being undertaken by the Service in connection with this (5,7).

CONSERVATION MEASURES PROPOSED Preservation of remaining habitat is the foremost requirement. In particular it is recommended that the type locality be purchased and set aside as a refuge; the area also harbours populations of Key Deer (Odocoileus virginianus clavium), Alligator (Alligator mississippiensis), Indigo Snake (Drymarchon corais cooperi), Key Mud Turtle (Kinosternon bauri bauri) and several other Florida State listed species (7). The whole of Cudjoe Key has been recommended as 'Critical Habitat' (7), which would legally require all Federal Agencies to ensure that actions authorized, funded or carried out by them do not result in the destruction or adverse modification of this habitat. Two federal agencies are immediately involved: the Department of Transportation which owns much of the marsh at the type locality and may threaten the habitat by improvement work to the highway (see above), and the U.S. Army Corps of Engineers which has authorization to prevent infill of freshwater wetlands dominated by Spartina, Juncus, Cladium and Typha (7). Much wetland on Cudjoe Key is within the Key Deer National Wildlife Refuge but construction of drainage ditches has led to most of it becoming brackish and is therefore considered likely to be unsuitable for this rodent (4). Spitzer and Lazell have suggested the filling of ditches on the Refuge which would thus allow large areas to eventually leach out and form fresh-water marshes again (4).

CAPTIVE BREEDING Has bred in captivity (see above).

REMARKS For description see (4). The status of this taxon as a full species has been questioned (2), though it is at present generally accepted as such.

REFERENCES   1.   Hamilton, W.J. Jr., and Whitaker, J.O. Jr. (1979). Mammals of the Eastern United States, 2nd Edition. Cornell University Press, Ithaca.
             2.   Humphrey, S.R. and Barbour, D.B. (1979). Status and habitat of eight kinds of endangered and threatened rodents in Florida. Special Sci. Rep. 2, Florida State Museum, Gainesville.
             3.   Spitzer, N. (1978). Cudjoe Key Rice Rat. In Layne, J. (Ed.), Rare and endangered biota of Florida, Vol 1: Mammals. University of Florida Presses, Gainesville.
             4.   Spitzer, N. and Lazell, J.D. Jr. (1978). A new rice rat (genus Oryzomys) from Florida Lower Keys. J. Mammal.

59(4): 787-792.

5. U.S. Fish and Wildlife Service. (1981). Regional briefs, 4. Endangered Species Technical Bulletin 6(4): 2.

6. U.S. Fish and Wildlife Service. (1980). Endangered and Threatened Wildlife and Plants; acceptance of petition and status review. Federal Register 45(136): 47365.

7. Wray, P., Lazell, J.D. Jr., and Spitzer, N. (1980). In litt to J.L. Spinks, Jr. Chief, Office of Endangered Species, U.S. Fish and Wildlife Service.

ALICE SPRINGS MOUSE   EXTINCT

Pseudomys fieldi (Waite, 1896)

Order   RODENTIA   Family   MURIDAE

SUMMARY Probably extinct. Known from one specimen collected in central Australia in 1895. May not be a valid species.

DISTRIBUTION Australia, known from one specimen collected at Alice Springs in the Northern Territory in 1895 (1,2,5).

POPULATION Unknown, but is probably very rare if it does still exist (1,2). The area where it was collected has apparently been intensively surveyed by biologists but no additional specimens have been recorded (6).

HABITAT AND ECOLOGY Unknown though the area where it was collected is arid or semi-arid (4).

THREATS TO SURVIVAL Unknown, though would presumably be vulnerable to introduced predators, and possibly to habitat modification by livestock and introduced rabbits.

CONSERVATION MEASURES TAKEN Included on the Offical List of Australian Endangered Vertebrate Fauna and is legally protected in the Northern Territory (6).

CONSERVATION MEASURES PROPOSED None other than protection of any populations which may be discovered.

CAPTIVE BREEDING None.

REMARKS There is some doubt if this species is valid - the only known specimen has a badly crushed skull making comparison with other material difficult. It may be an aberrant individual of another species (1,2,5). Troughton thought it most closely resembled the Plains Mouse (Pseudomys australis), though Watts has stated that he strongly suspects it to be a specimen of the Shark Bay Mouse (Pseudomys praeconis) from Western Australia (5), also an IUCN Red Data Book Species. If so, this would extend the latter's distribution some 2000 km to the east. Dr C.H.S. Watts kindly commented on a draft of this data sheet in 1981.

REFERENCES   1.   Ride, W.D.L. (1970). A guide to the native mammals of Australia. Oxford University Press, Melbourne.
             2.   Troughton, E. (1941). Furred animals of Australia. Angus and Robertson Ltd., Sydney.
             3.   Watts, C.H.S. (1979). The status of endangered Australian rodents. In Tyler, M.J. (Ed.), The status of endangered Australasian wildlife. Royal Zool. Soc. S. Aust. 75-83.
             4.   Watts, C.H.S. (1981). In litt.
             5.   Watts, C.H.S. and Aslin, H.J. (1981). The Rodents of Australia. Angus and Robertson, Sydney.
             6.   Anon. (1980). Australian submission to CITES. Unpd. 2pp.

SHARK BAY MOUSE   RARE

Pseudomys praeconis Thomas, 1910

Order   RODENTIA   Family   MURIDAE

SUMMARY   Recorded from Bernier Island, off Western Australia, and once on the adjacent mainland in 1858. Population on Bernier is probably secure as long as near-pristine conditions on the island can be maintained. Surveys are needed to establish whether the species still occurs on the mainland and steps should be taken to conserve any populations that may be found there.

DISTRIBUTION   Australia. Has only been recorded from Bernier Island (approx 5000 ha) in Shark Bay, Western Australia, and once from the mainland on Peron Peninsula, some 150 km south of Bernier, where the original specimen was collected in 1858 (5,7).

POPULATION   Unknown. In 1975 11 were trapped over two days in a small area of Bernier Island (5,7). The presence on the island of large areas of habitat similar to the trapping site implies the mouse is probably relatively common there (5,7). There are also large tracts of apparently suitable habitat on the adjacent Peron Peninsula where it could still exist (7). Up to 1975 only five specimens were known, all except one (qv) from Bernier, the most recent collected in 1959 (4).

HABITAT AND ECOLOGY   The mice trapped in 1975 were in sand dune areas with dense mats of Spinifex longifolius and Olearia axillaris with either scattered bushes of Atriplex paludosa and Rhagodia obovata or Zostera heaps and dead Salsola kali (5). Diet seems exclusively vegetarian, with most (about 60 per cent) comprising a dicotyledon flower, probably Olearia, and the rest principally leaves and stems, probably of a succulent (5). A pair sent to Adelaide produced two litters, one of four and the other of three young (5).

THREATS TO SURVIVAL   The population on Bernier appears to be reasonably secure under present conditions as long as cats or foxes do not become established on the island, and the risk of extensive fires is kept to a minimum (5,7). Feral goats are present but do not appear to cause much damage to the mouse's sandhill habitat (5) and their numbers were reported in 1978 as being reduced by an intensive eradication programme (7).

CONSERVATION MEASURES TAKEN   Listed in Appendix 1 of the 1973 Convention on International Trade in Endangered Species of Wild Fauna and Flora, trade in it or its products therefore being subject to strict regulation by ratifying nations, and trade for primarily commercial purposes banned. The species is protected under Western Australian legislation and appears on the Official List of Endangered Australian Vertebrate Fauna (1). Bernier Island is a Class 'A' faunal reserve with strictly controlled public access (4,7).

CONSERVATION MEASURES PROPOSED   Surveys of the mainland around Shark Bay, to determine whether the mouse is still present and, if so, the extent of its distribution, would be highly desirable (2). Any areas where the mouse is discovered should immediately be afforded rigorous protection (2). Continued protection of Bernier Island from any form of unnecessary disturbance is most important.

CAPTIVE BREEDING   Has bred in captivity (see above).

REMARKS For description see (2,3). Bernier and the adjacent Dorre Islands also hold viable populations of four other Red Data Book species, - the Boodie (Bettongia lesueur), Western Barred Bandicoot (Perameles bougainville) and Banded Hare Wallaby (Lagostrophus fasciatus), all probably extinct on the Australian mainland, and the Rufous Hare Wallaby (Lagorchestes hirsutus), which is now extremely rare elsewhere. Watts has stated that the he strongly suspects that the Alice Springs Mouse (Pseudomys fieldi, Waite) known from only one specimen (with a badly damaged skull) collected at Alice Springs in 1895, is in fact P. praeconis. If so, this would extend the distribution of the species over 2000 km to the east. P. fieldi at present is included in the IUCN Red Data Book as a separate species. This data sheet was compiled from a draft kindly provided in 1978 by Dr C.H.S. Watts.

REFERENCES   1.   Anon. (1973). Additional protection for rare fauna. State Wildlife Authority News Service (West. Australia) 4(2): 31-33.

2.   Anon. (1978). Shark Bay Mouse Pseudomys praeconis. Mammals No.11. In Australian Endangered Species. Australian National Parks and Wildlife Service.

3.   Ride, W.D.L. (1970). A guide to the native mammals of Australia. Oxford University Press, Melbourne.

4.   Ride, W.D.L. and Tyndale-Biscoe, C.H. (1962). Mammals. In Fraser, A.J. (Ed.), The results of an expedition to Bernier and Dorre Islands, Shark Bay, Western Australia in 1959. West. Australian Fisheries Dept. Fauna Bull. 2: 54-97.

5.   Robinson, A.C., Robinson, J.F., Watts, C.H.S. and Baverstock, P.R. (1976). The Shark Bay Mouse Pseudomys praeconis and other mammals on Bernier Island, Western Australia. Western Australian Naturalist. 13 (7): 149-155.

6.   Troughton, E. (1941). Furred animals of Australia. Angus and Robertson Ltd. Sydney.

7.   Watts, C.H.S. (1979). The status of endangered Australian rodents. In Tyler, M.J. (Ed.), The status of endangered Australasian wildlife. Royal Zool. Soc. S. Aust.

Pseudomys oralis (Thomas 1921)

Order RODENTIA   Family   MURIDAE

SUMMARY Recorded in the present century only from a small area of southeastern Queensland. Appears to be uncommon within its range and is expected to be at considerable risk from habitat modification as the area is good quality agricultural land subject to development. Not known to occur in any national park or reserve. Studies are needed to form the basis of conservation plans, which should include the setting aside of protected areas for the species.

DISTRIBUTION Australia; where all specimens this century have been collected since 1969 from a few scattered localities in small valleys on the Darling Downs in the Warwick area of southern Queensland (1,2,4,5,). Prior to this it was only known from two specimens collected in the first half of the 19th century: one from Hastings River, northern New South Wales, is in the Gould Collection in the City of Liverpool Museum, England; the second, in the British Museum, was purchased in, or prior to, 1847 and has no locality attached (3). Subfossil remains indicate the species to have been formerly common in the Great Dividing Range (4,5).

POPULATION Unknown. Extensive trapping since 1969 has revealed the presence of a few scattered, discrete colonies in suitable habitat in the Warwick district (2). Only a few specimens have been captured, indicating that the species is probably uncommon even within its limited range (4).

HABITAT AND ECOLOGY Recorded from areas of tall open eucalypt forest with a dense ground cover of False Bracken (2,4).

THREATS TO SURVIVAL The species is expected to be at considerable risk from habitat modification (1,4). Its known range is in good quality agricultural land subject to development and it is not known to occur in any national park or reserve (1,4).

CONSERVATION MEASURES TAKEN Legally protected since 1974 (4).

CONSERVATION MEASURES PROPOSED There is an urgent need for studies to determine the habitat requirements and present status of the species (4). Efforts should be made to ensure that land-use practices do not conflict with its conservation; these should include the setting up of reserves with an appropriate management regime to safeguard known populations.

CAPTIVE BREEDING No information.

REMARKS For description see (5).

REFERENCES   1. Calaby, J.H. (1981). In litt.
                2. Kirkpatrick, T.H. and Martin, J.H.D. (1971). Uncommon native fauna. Queensland Agric. J. 97: 114-115.
                3. Ride, W.D.L. (1970). A guide to the native mammals of Australia. Oxford Univ. Press, Melbourne.
                4. Watts, C.H.S. (1979). The status of endangered Australian rodents. In Tyler, M.J. (Ed.), The status of endangered

Australasian wildlife. Royal Zool. Soc. S. Aust. 75-83.

5. Watts, C.H.S. and Aslin, H.J. (1981). The Rodents of Australia. Angus and Robertson, Sydney.

FALSE WATER-RAT

INSUFFICIENTLY
KNOWN

Xeromys myoides Thomas, 1889.

Order   RODENTIA   Family   MURIDAE

SUMMARY Has been collected in swampy habitat and mangrove forest along streams at scattered localities in northern Australia, most recently in 1978. It may not be as rare as the paucity of records suggests and surveys are needed to determine its distribution and status.

DISTRIBUTION Australia. Limits of range unknown, but probably confined to coastal areas of Queensland and the Northern Territory. Seventeen specimens are known from widely scattered localities. Six are from the Mackay district on the central Queensland coast, collected in 1887 and 1935; three are from southeastern Queensland - two collected in 1975 in the Noosa River areas north of Brisbane, and one from Myora Spings on Stradbroke Island in Moreton Bay off Brisbane, collected in 1978; five are from the coast of the Arnhem Land region in the Northern Territory - two from the Tompkinson River collected in 1975, one from South Alligator River in 1903 and two from the Daly River in 1972; the remaining three are from the banks of Andranangoo Creek, Melville Island, off Arnhem Land, collected in 1975 (1,2,3,4,6,7). Much suitable habitat, most of it not yet surveyed by biologists, occurs along the coastline between southern Queensland and the Kimberley district of Western Australia and the species may well be more widespread and common than the paucity of records suggests (1).

POPULATION Unknown; very few specimens known but this may be indicative of lack of collecting rather than a threatened status.

HABITAT AND ECOLOGY All individuals have been obtained from swampy habitat of variable description, except the Beerwah specimen which was obtained in a five-year old stand of slash pine 25 m from a stream (2). The Mackay specimens were from a permanent reed swamp near the sea with thick cover of grass shrubs and Pandanus spp., those at Daly River from the margins of a freshwater lagoon encircled with Paperbark (Melaleuca nervosa) and Mangrove (Barringtonia acutangula); and the rest from closed canopy mangrove forest (e.g. Brugiera parviflora, Ceriops tagal), patches of salt-marsh grass in mangrove forest along tidal rivers (2,3,4,5,6), or in or near sedge swamps (2). Climbs well and seems well adapted to mangrove habitat, having a water-repellent pelage and a highly developed ritualised technique for capturing and consuming live crabs larger than itself (2). It does not appear to be aquatic, however, and is considered on the basis of morphological and behavioural evidence to be basically a terrestrial rat adapted for feeding on hard-shelled aquatic fauna (2,5). A Xeromys nest has been described, consisting of a mound of leaves and mud 60 cm high with a single opening near the apex leading to a nest chamber just below the surface with numerous interconnecting tunnels leading off, some extending up to 90 cm underground (2). Nothing is known of its reproductive biology.

THREATS TO SURVIVAL Habitat destruction appears to be the principal long-term threat. Cattle, feral buffalo, and pigs are reported as seriously damaging the edges of lagoons, swamps and rivers in the Northern Territory (1). In Queensland swamp and mangrove areas are being drained and reclaimed for sugar cane production and urban and recreational development (1); this is particularly the case on Stradbroke Island which is a major recreational centre for Brisbane and where sand mining poses an additional severe threat (6).

CONSERVATION MEASURES TAKEN Included in Appendix 1 of the 1973 Convention on International Trade in Endangered Species of Wild Fauna and Flora, trade in it or its products therefore being subject to strict regulation by ratifying nations, and trade for primarily commercial purposes banned. The species is fully protected under Queensland and Northern Territory legislation (1) and is on the official list of Endangered Australian Vertebrate Fauna. One of the specimens from southeast Queensland was trapped on the Cooloola Fauna Reserve (2).

CONSERVATION MEASURES PROPOSED Effective protection of areas of habitat where the species is found (1).

CAPTIVE BREEDING There are no known captive specimens at present (1981) and potential for breeding in captivity remains unknown.

REMARKS For description see (1,5). This data sheet was compiled from a draft provided in 1978 by Dr C.H.S. Watts, and G.W. Saunders, Director of the Queensland National Parks and Wildlife Service, kindly commented on the sheet.

REFERENCES   1.   Anon. (1978). False Water-rat Xeromys myoides. Mammals No.10. In Australian Endangered Species. Australian National Parks and Wildlife Service.
2.   Dwyer, P.D., Hockings, M. and Willmer, J. (1979). Mammals of Cooloola and Beerwah. Proc. R. Soc. Queensld. 90: 65-84.
3.   Magnusson, W.E., Webb, G.J.W. and Taylor, J.A. (1976). Two new locality records, a new habitat and a nest description for Xeromys myoides Thomas (Rodentia: Muridae). Aust. Wildl. Res. 3: 153-157.
4.   Redhead, T.D. and McKean, J.L. (1975). A new record of the False Water-rat, Xeromys myoides from the Northern Territory of Australia. Aust. Mammal. 1(4): 347-354.
5.   Troughton, E. (1941). Furred animals of Australia. Angus and Robertson Ltd. Sydney.
6.   Van Dyck, S., Baker, W.W. and Gillette, D.D. (1979). The False Water Rat Xeromy myoides on Stradbroke Island, a new locality in southeastern Queensland. Proc. R. Soc. Queensland. 90: 84.
7.   Watts, C.H.S. (1979). The status of endangered Australian rodents. In Tyler, M.J. (Ed.), The status of endangered Australasian wildlife. Royal Zool. Soc. S. Aust. Pp. 75-83.

Zyzomys pedunculatus (Waite, 1896)

Order   RODENTIA   Family   MURIDAE

SUMMARY Confined to rocky outcrops in mountain ranges in central Australia. Collected on very few occasions, most recently in 1960. Studies are needed to determine its status and distribution.

DISTRIBUTION Australia. Limits of range are unknown though all records are from the southern half of the Northern Territory. Six specimens were collected near Alice Springs and one from Illamurta on the south side of the James Range in 1894 (1,2). Finlayson has documented an unstated number of individuals (which he had not examined himself) at Hugh Creek in the MacDonnell Ranges in 1935, Napperby Hills in 1950 and the Davenport Range in 1953 (2). Recent records are from the Granites in the Tanami Desert (1952) and Haast's Bluff settlement in the MacDonnell Ranges (1960) (3).

POPULATION Unknown, though certainly rare. Watts and Aslin note, however, that little systematic collecting has been done in its habitat and it may be more abundant than presently appears (6). There is no obvious reason to believe that it has declined in recent years (6).

HABITAT AND ECOLOGY Dry rocky outcrops in mountain ranges (1). Nothing known of its breeding biology or diet.

THREATS TO SURVIVAL Unknown, though probably vulnerable to introduced predators such as cats and foxes (1). It may have been rare before European settlement (1).

CONSERVATION MEASURES TAKEN Listed in Appendix 1 of the 1973 Convention on International Trade in Endangered Species of Wild Fauna and Flora, trade in it or its products therefore being subject to strict regulation by ratifying nations, and trade for primarily commercial purposes banned. Legally protected, and appears on the Official List of Endangered Australian Vertebrate Fauna. Only small areas of suitable habitat are found within national parks (5).

CONSERVATION MEASURES PROPOSED The true status of this species should be established. The fact that rock-rats trap easily and are restricted to accessible rocky outcrops should make this task relatively easy (5). Appropriate steps should be taken to protect any areas where the species may be found (5).

CAPTIVE BREEDING Has never been kept in captivity as far as is known.

REMARKS For description see (6). The common name is that recommended by the Australian Mammal Society in 1980; the species is also known as the MacDonnell Range Rock-Rat. It is closely related to two other species, Zyzomys argurus and Z. woodwardi, which are found in rocky outcrops in mountain ranges in northern Australia (4); neither is considered threatened. This data sheet was compiled from a draft provided in 1978 by Dr C.H.S. Watts, and Dr. A.K. Lee of the IUCN/SSC Rodent Specialist Group kindly commented on the final version.

REFERENCES   1.   Anon. (1977). MacDonnell Range Rock-Rat, Central Thick-tailed Rat. Zyzomys pedunculatus. Mammals No.6. In Australian Endangered Species. Australian National

Parks and Wildlife Service.

2. Finlayson, H.H. (1961). On Central Australian mammals Part IV. The distribution and status of Central Australian species. Rec. S. Aust. Mus. 14: 141-191.
3. Parker, S.A. (1973). An annotated checklist of the native land mammals of the Northern Territory. Rec. S. Aust. Mus. 16(11): 1-57.
4. Ride, W.D.L. (1970). A guide to the native mammals of Australia. Oxford Univ. Press, Melbourne.
5. Watts, C.H.S. (1979). The status of endangered Australian rodents. In Tyler, M.J. (Ed.). The status of endangered Australasian wildlife. Royal Zool. Soc. S. Aust. 75-83.
6. Watts, C.H.S. and Aslin, H.J. (1981). The Rodents of Australia. Angus and Robertson, Sydney.

Chaetomys subspinosus (Olfers, 1818)

Order   RODENTIA   Family   ERITHIZONTIDAE

SUMMARY   Has a restricted range in southeastern Brazil where habitats are being destroyed or modified by deforestation. Protected by law and occurs in some parks and reserves. Status surveys and determination of habitat requirements are urgently needed as the basis of a conservation plan.

DISTRIBUTION   Southeastern Brazil; apparently confined to southeastern Bahia and northern Espirito Santo (1,3,5,7,8). Cabrera, however, gives a considerably wider range, including northern, northeastern and central Brazil, and giving the type locality as Cameta, Para (in Amazonia) (2). This is now thought most likely to have been in error as there are no other records outside southeastern Brazil (1,3). Coimbra-Filho has noted that before the extensive forest destruction in this region it was probably widely distributed through almost all Espirito Santo and eastern Bahia, though Moojen in 1952 reported it only from the smaller area delimited above (3). Definite records in the 1970s are from the same forests as the critically endangered Golden-headed Lion Tamarin, Leontopithecus chrysomelas, in Una, Bahia, and from the Santa Tereza region in Espirito Santo (3).

POPULATION   Numbers unknown but apparently rare and expected to become increasingly so due to the wholesale habitat destruction within its limited range (1,3,4). In 1965 it was already regarded as a likely candidate for extinction (1).

HABITAT AND ECOLOGY   Little known. Preferred habitat appears to be the edges of forests; Moojen recorded it as frequenting cocoa trees and feeding on their fruits while Ruschi noted it in granitic hills in Espirito Santo, almost always associated with Bombax (Bombaceae) trees. It is apparently nocturnal and, judging from other members of the family, can be expected to produce only one young at a time (3).

THREATS TO SURVIVAL   Its small range is within a region that has been subjected to considerable habitat destruction (4). Since the 1800s the Atlantic coastal forests of eastern Brazil have suffered a tremendous increase in human population and widespread, largely uncontrolled forest destruction to make way for coffee plantations, sugar cane, cocoa, eucalyptus, cattle pasture and above all lumber extraction and charcoal production. In recent years industrial development has also taken its toll. As a result the forests have been devastated, especially during the rapid development and economic expansion since the 1960s. Only a tiny fraction of the original forest cover remains (6). However if Chaetomys is indeed a forest-edge species which can survive in, for example, cocoa plantations, then its position may be somewhat less critical than that of other indigenous animals such as the Woolly Spider Monkey (Brachyteles arachnoides) and the Leontopithecus spp., which are completely tied to undisturbed, mature rainforest and are all listed as 'Endangered' in the IUCN Red Data Book. More research is required on this.

CONSERVATION MEASURES TAKEN   Protected by law. Occurs in Monte Pascoal National Park in Bahia and in the biological reserves of Corrego do Veado, Nova Lombardia and Sooretama, all in Espirito Santo (6). May also exist in Caparao National Park (Espirito Santo and Minas Gerais) (4). In 1976 the Brazilian Forestry Development Institute (IBDF) purchased 5268 ha in Una, where this species and Leontopithecus chrysomelas occur, as a reserve. However since then little has happened, the reserve covering an area of 11,400 ha was finally officially decreed in December 1980, but already approx. 3000 ha has been invaded by some 600 squatters who have clear-cut large areas in the west of the, and almost all the invaded sector is no longer suitable habitat for any forest animals. In May 1980 squatters were observed on the outskirts of the remaining forest (5).

CONSERVATION MEASURES PROPOSED Ecological study needed as a basis for conservation plan. Further reservation of suitable habitat and increasing effort to ensure adequate protection of these areas.

CAPTIVE BREEDING No information.

REMARKS For description of animal see (3,8,9). Chaetomys is a monospecific genus.

REFERENCES   1.   Avila-Pires, F.D. de. (1967). The type-locality of Chaetomys subspinosus (Olfers, 1818). Rev. Brasil Biol. 27(2): 177-179.
2.   Cabrera, A. (1957-1961). Catalogo de los mamiferos de America del Sur. Rev. Mus. Argent. de Cienc. Nat. 'Bernardino Rivadavia', Cienc. Zool. 4(1-2): 1-732.
3.   Coimbra-Filho, A.F. (1972). Mamiferos ameacados de extincao do Brasil. Especies da Fauna Brasileira Ameacadas de Extincao. Academia Brasileira de Ciencias: 13-98. Rio de Janeiro, Brazil.
4.   Coimbra-Filho, A.F and Mittermeier, R.A. (1974). In litt.
5.   Mittermeier, R.A., Coimbra-Filho, A.F. and Constable, I. (1980). Conservation of Eastern Brazilian Primates. WWF Project 1614. Report for the period 1979/80.
6.   Moojen, J. (1952). Os roedores do Brasil. MEC, Inst. Nac. Livro, Rio de Janeiro.
7.   Padua, M.T.J., Magnanini, A. and Mittermeier, R.A. (1974). Brazil's National Parks. Oryx 12(4): 452-464.
8.   Vieira, C.C. (1955). Lista remissiva dos mamiferos do Brasil. Arq. Zool. Sao Paulo 8: 341-474.
9.   Walker, E.P. (1975). Mammals of the World. The Johns Hopkins Univ. Press, Baltimore and London.

LONG-TAILED CHINCHILLA

INDETERMINATE

Chinchilla laniger (Molina, 1782)

Order   RODENTIA   Family   CHINCHILLIDAE

SUMMARY   Now confined as far as is known, to only one small area in the Coastal Cordillera of Chile. Numbers were severely depleted by hunting for the fur trade, especially around 1900, and illicit hunting continues although habitat destruction is now (1981) believed to be the most important threat. Legally protected and there is some active prevention of hunting, although establishment of a well-guarded reserve which would also protect habitat is of highest priority. IUCN/WWF Project 1297 aimed at the conservation and management of Chinchillas in Chile was approved in early 1981. The species was studies by C.K. Mohlis from 1975-1978.

DISTRIBUTION   Chile, where at present (1981) known to exist only in an area of around 4000 ha in the Coastal Cordillera between Illapel (31°40'S) and Combarbala (31°15'S) in Region IV (formerly Coquimbo Province) (2,6,7), though in 1977 Mohlis noted unconfirmed reports from the southern part of Region IV as far as the northern border of Chile (6). Formerly widespread from around 25° to 32°S in the Aracama desert region, along the foothills of the Andes and in the Coastal Cordillera, with records in the latter from near Taltal (25°25'S) to around the Rio Choapa (32°S) (2,6,7). Some references mention a much more extensive southern distribution (Talca, 35°30'S) (6).

POPULATION   Mohlis in 1977 (6) made a rough estimate of 7000 to 10,000 in the colonies she had observed, though Rottmann in 1981 stated that numbers in the wild at present were unknown (7). He did however note that in optimal habitat densities of over 10 animals per hectare might be attained (7).

HABITAT AND ECOLOGY   Altitudinal range quoted varies, with lower limits of from 400 to 800 m and upper limits of 1500 to 2500 m given (2,6,7). Colonial, inhabiting dry rocky areas, apparently favouring north-facing slopes and not found in valleys (7). Mohlis noted that shrub cover was dense and bunch grasses common in the immediate vicinity of many of the 'better' colonies (7). Live in dens in cracks and fissures in rocks or in nests under plants, especially the spiny 'chaguales' (Puya berteroana) (2,7). Several pairs of Chinchillas may apparently share a den (2,7). Diet varies seasonally, consisting mainly of leaves, seeds and fruits; in very dry years principal food items seem to be Puya berteroana and leaves of shrubs (7). Drinking water is apparently not required (7). Sexual maturity may be reached in six months but may depend on the season of birth (2,8). Breeding is seasonal, with a litter of 1 to 3 (usually 2), born in spring after a gestation period of around 110 days, and a second litter may be born in summer if conditions are good (2,7).

THREATS TO SURVIVAL   Hunting (now illegal) and habitat destruction (2,6,7). The near extinction of this species in the wild was brought about mainly by hunting for the fur trade in the late 19th and early 20th centuries. In 1899 over 400,000 Chinchilla pelts are believed to have been exported from Atacama Province alone (4), though what percentage of these were C. laniger as opposed to C. brevicaudata, the high altitude Andean species, is unknown. By 1915 this number had declined to around 3200 (4). The advent of large scale commercial captive breeding in the 1920s brought about an intense demand from fur farms for live wild animals. These could command very high prices and led to hunters pursuing Chinchillas in the most remote of areas. Despite legal protection (since 1929) the demand for live animals, and for wild-taken furs, still continues - in

1981 it was reported that wild Chinchilla coats were on sale in Japan priced at $US 48,950 (7). Rottman has stated, however, that habitat destruction is now (1981) by far the most important threat (7). Overgrazing, especially by goats, degrades habitat and reduces food supply as does collection of firewood - Puya beteroana in particular burns easily and may be wantonly destroyed as it is usually simply considered a weed (2,6,7). Mining activities also cause severe habitat degradation (6,7). Grau has noted that the area where the species is known to survive is now surrounded by railroads, mining centres, roads and towns (2).

CONSERVATION MEASURES TAKEN All South American Chinchilla populations are included on Appendix 1 of the 1973 Convention on International Trade in Endangered Species of Wild Fauna and Flora, trade in them between acceding nations being therefore subject to severe restriction, trade for primarily commercial purposes banned. Has been legally protected in Chile since 1929 but enforcement is extremely difficult, athough in 1981 it was reported that two CONAF (Corporacion Nacional Forestal) guards were actively protecting the known colonies from poaching, though with very limited resources at their disposal (6,7). Preliminary information on the biology and distribution of the species was obtained by Connie Mohlis who studied it in 1975-1978 (6,7). She noted in 1977 that one relatively isolated colony had begun to show signs of growth following the initiation of protection in 1975 (6).

CONSERVATION MEASURES PROPOSED The most urgent need is the establishment of an adequately protected reserve to cover the area where the species is known to occur, with habitat management to prevent overgrazing and desertification and effective control of hunting (2,7). However, the logistic problems involved are considerable as the land was reported in 1980 as owned by a cooperative of around 125 families (1), though Grau has stated that an attempt is being made to obtain the area by exchange (2). As of June 1981, IUCN/WWF Project No.1297 has been approved but not implemented (7). Its aim is to establish a national Chinchilla reserve and to develop a management programme for the species both in the reserve and elsewhere in the country (9). The need for further biological study, especially of reproduction and factors which limit population density, has been emphasised (7). Mohlis has stressed the need to develop and implement a public education programme in Chile on natural resource use and management that includes wildlife (6).

CAPTIVE BREEDING Chinchillas were kept in semi-captivity by the Incas in pre-Columbian times, though these are likely to have been the higher altitude Chinchilla brevicaudata which occurred further north (2). Modern domestication reportedly started in 1885 in Santiago, Chile, with the first captive birth in 1896. In 1923 eleven animals bred in Potrerillos, Chile, were transported to San Pedro in California, U.S.A.; this was the start of large scale captive breeding (2). The species involved is believed to be almost exclusively C. laniger, as C. brevicaudata has proved extremely difficult to breed under captive conditions outside of its original range, with hybridisation between the two also only very rarely achieved (2). About a dozen colour mutations have been developed since the 1920s and Grau has noted that generations of inbreeding have led to domestic Chinchillas being very badly adapted to survival under natural conditions; attempts to naturalise them, (e.g. in the Darvaz Mountains in Tajikstan in the U.S.S.R.) in the 1960s, have all apparently failed (2). Grau has reported, however, that several pairs of recently caught wild Chinchilla are being maintained in Chile at an experimental breeding station in preparation for reintroduction into the planned Chinchilla reserve (2).

REMARKS For description see (8). The other Chinchilla species now generally accepted (C. brevicaudata) has in the past often been regarded as a subspecies of C. laniger but is now considered separable on ecological and morphological grounds (2,7). Much of the information for this data sheet was kindly supplied by Connie K. Mohlis in 1977 and Dr. Jurgen Rottmann of CONAF, Chile, in 1981.

REFERENCES
1. Andrews, M. (1980). In litt. to J.A. Burton.
2. Grau, J. (no date). The extremely endangered wild Chinchilla. Unpd. report.
3. Grimwood, I.R. (1978). In litt.
4. Miller, S., Rottmann, J., Raedeke, K. and Taber, R.D. (1978). Endangered mammals of Chile. Status and conservation. Unpd. report prepared for II International Theriological Congress, Brno.
5. Milliken, T. (1981). Wildlife in commerce survey - Tokyo 1981. Unpd. report.
6. Mohlis, C. (1977). In litt.
7. Rottmann, J.S. (1981). In litt.
8. Walker, E.P. (1975). Mammals of the World. The Johns Hopkins University Press, Baltimore and London.
9. WWF/IUCN. (1981). List of approved projects. Gland, Switzerland.

Chinchilla brevicaudata Waterhouse, 1848

Order   RODENTIA   Family   CHINCHILLIDAE

SUMMARY A high altitude Andean species, brought to the brink of extinction by hunting for the fur trade. Reportedly still survives in isolated localities around 23°S and possibly in Lauca National Park in northern Chile. Protection of any viable colonies is essential for the survival of the species.

DISTRIBUTION Limits of former distribution unclear; Grau stated that it was recorded from the Andes at altitudes of over 3000 m between 7°5'S and 30°S in Peru, Bolivia, Argentina and Chile (2), while Rottman gives northern and southern limits as 10°S and 27°S (6), and Grimwood has noted that there appears to be no definite record for Argentina (3). According to Grau it still survives in very inaccessible localities near where the borders of Argentina, Bolivia and Chile meet (around 23°S) (2), while there have also been unconfirmed reports in the 1970s of a few individuals in Lauca National Park in Tarapaca Province in northern Chile (3). It could also conceivably survive in the contiguous Sajama National Park in Bolivia though there are no actual records (3). Pearson in 1951 reported it as extinct in Peru (5).

POPULATION Unknown, though presumably very rare.

HABITAT AND ECOLOGY Very little known, has been recorded from rocky hillsides (6), or desert areas between 3000 and 4500 m (2). In captivity, sexual maturity is reportedly attained at six months and breeding may occur biannually, gestation period is 128 days and mean litter size 1.45 young (2).

THREATS TO SURVIVAL Hunting for the fur trade, principally in the 19th and early 20th centuries, was responsible for the virtual extinction of Chinchillas in the wild. It has been estimated that 2 million Chinchilla pelts were exported from Chile to Europe between 1895 and 1900 (2,7), though what percentage of these were from C. brevicaudata is unknown. Despite protective legislation enacted in the early part of the century, hunting of Chinchillas still continues and it is noted that fur from C. brevicaudata is considerably more valuable, and hence sought after, than that from C. laniger (2,6). Rottmann has noted that habitat destruction does not seem a major threat for this species, collection of firewood seemed of no importance and there was little or no overgrazing in its habitat (6).

CONSERVATION MEASURES TAKEN All South American Chinchilla populations are included in Appendix 1 of the 1973 Convention on International Trade in Endangered Species of Wild Fauna and Flora, trade in them or their products therefore being subject to strict regulation by ratifying nations, and trade for primarily commercial purposes banned. Chinchillas are legally protected in Bolivia (since 1906), Chile (since 1929) and Peru (1,2,6); current legal status in Argentina unknown. In 1910 the Governments of Argentina, Bolivia, Chile and Peru subscribed to an agreement banning Chinchilla hunting and selling of fur (2). Enforcement of such legislation is very difficult, however, in the isolated inaccessible areas where Chinchillas occur (2,4,6,7).

CONSERVATION MEASURES PROPOSED Adequate protection of any viable colonies is of primary importance; this should be carried out by trained permanent guards (6). Studies of ecology and distribution would be desirable to formulate further conservation plans.

CAPTIVE BREEDING Breeding of Chinchilla brevicaudata has proved considerably more difficult than with C. laniger (2). Grau noted that many unsuccessful attempts have been made since the late 19th century, when modern captive breeding of Chinchillas began (the Incas are known to have kept them in their homes in Pre-columbian times); successful captive breeding has occurred, however, within the species' original range (2). Hybrids between C. brevicaudata and C. laniger have been produced with great difficulty, the resulting offspring have brevicaudata size and fur-type. Males were found to be sterile, though females were fertile and could be crossed with either of the parent species (2).

REMARKS For description see (2,7). Several species have been described, though the genus has also been considered monotypic, with this taxon a subspecies of Chinchilla laniger (7); two species are now generally recognised with C. brevicaudata distinguishable from C. laniger on ecological and morphological grounds (body weight 600 to 850 g as opposed to 400 to 450 g in C. laniger, smaller ears, shorter limbs and a shorter tail composed of 20 vertebrae compared to 23 in C. laniger) (2,6). Their karyotypes are identical (2n=64) (2).

REFERENCE
1. Bejarano, G. (1981). In litt.
2. Grau, J. (no date). The extremely endangered wild Chinchilla. Unpd. report.
3. Grimwood, I.R. (1978). In litt.
4. Miller, S., Rottmann, J., Raedeke, K. and Taber, R.D. (1978). Endangered mammals of Chile. Status and conservation. Unpd. report prepared for II International Theriological Congress, Brno.
5. Pearson, O.P. (1951). Mammals of the highlands of southern Peru. Bull. Harvard Mus. Comp. Zool. 106 (3): 117-174.
6. Rottmann S., J. (1981). In litt.
7. Walker, E.P. (1975). Mammals of the World. The Johns Hopkins University Press, Baltimore and London.

CABRERA'S HUTIA

ENDANGERED

Capromys angelcabrerai Varona, 1979

Order   RODENTIA   Family   CAPROMYIDAE

___

SUMMARY A recently described species, discovered in 1974 and apparently confined to a series of small islets and cays off southern Cuba. Numbers unknown, though believed to be very low, possibly even extinct. Legally protected. Surveys are needed to determine whether it still survives, and if so, to provide data as the basis for a conservation plan.

DISTRIBUTION Cuba, where it has been recorded on several small cays and islets of the Cayos de Ana Maria south of Jucaro, Camagüey Province (2). Its presence is also suspected in the Estero Las Characas, some 20 km west of Jucaro, and in the Estero Suavecito, both of which have suitable habitat but for which there are no actual records (2).

POPULATION Varona in 1981 stated it was probably extinct or at least highly endangered (3). The species was described in 1979 from a series of fifteen or so specimens collected by Dr Rivero de la Calle in the Gulf of Ana Maria in 1974 and 1975 (2). No other specimens appear to have been recorded.

HABITAT AND ECOLOGY Typical habitat is recorded as mangrove, with Red Mangrove (Rhizophora mangle) predominating. Varona considered it likely that the Hutia depends exclusively on this species for its survival although little definite is known of the animal's biology (2). Communal nests similar to those of Capromys auritus have been described; they are circular, approximately 1 metre in diameter and 30-40 cm high, and are constructed of mangrove twigs heaped together to form a platform-like structure which is covered with leaves and has four or five openings to the interior (2). Hutias in general are vegetarian and characteristically produce small litters (one to three) of highly developed young (1,3). C. angelcabrerai is sympatric with the common, adaptable, Conga Hutia Capromys pilorides (2).

THREATS TO SURVIVAL Principal threat to this and the three other recently described Cuban Hutias confined to small cays and islets (Capromys auritus, C. sanfelipensis and C. garridoi) appears to be hunting by fishermen, who land on the cays and can taken many hutias in a single raid (4). When disturbed C. angelcabrerai leaves the nest and takes refuge in the water, but being a slow and clumsy swimmer is easily caught (2). The slow reproductive rate of Hutias makes populations very vulnerable to disturbance (1).

CONSERVATION MEASURES TAKEN All Hutias are legally protected in Cuba, although enforcement has generally been inadequate in the past. Government Resolution No.21-79 was reported in 1980 as having recently forbidden all hunting in important wildlife areas, including all islets and cays in the Gulf of Ana Maria (4). It is hoped this will provide more effective protection (4).

CONSERVATION MEASURES PROPOSED Effective enforcement of existing legislation. More information is needed on the present status, distribution and biology of the species, in order to formulate detailed conservation plans.

CAPTIVE BREEDING Not known to have ever bred in captivity. Two of the specimens captured in 1974 were alive but only survived a few days in captivity (2).

REMARKS For description see (2). It is apparently closely related to the Dwarf Hutia (Capromys nanus) another IUCN Red Data Book species, and the two are now included in a new subgenus Pygmaeocapromys (2).

REFERENCES 1.   Oliver, W.L.R. (1977). The Hutias, Capromyidae, of the West Indies. In Olney, P.J.S. (Ed.), International Zoo Yearbook 17. Zool. Soc. London.
2.   Varona, L.S. (1979). Subgenero y especie nuevas de Capromys (Rodentia: Caviomorpha) para Cuba. Poeyana, Inst. Zool. Acad. Cienc. de Cuba 194: 1-33.
3.   Varona, L.S. (1980). Mamiferos de Cuba Editorial Gente Nueva, La Habana. Annotated by author, 1981.
4.   Varona, L.S. (1980). Protection in Cuba. Oryx 15(3): 282-284.

Capromys auritus   Varona, 1970

Order   RODENTIA   Family   CAPROMYIDAE

SUMMARY A species discovered in 1970 and known only from the type locality, a small area of mangroves on an island off northern Cuba. Population is expected to be very small by virtue of its limited distribution, and is subject to predation by visiting fishermen. Adequate enforcement of existing legal protection is regarded as essential for its survival.

DISTRIBUTION Cuba, where known only from one area of mangrove swamp on Cayo Fregoso, an island some 38 km long and 4 to 5 km wide at its broadest, off the central northern coast in the Sabana Archipelago, Las Villas Province. The population is apparently confined to the zone of shallow, mangrove-covered channels which traverse the centre of the island, known locally as El Bocoy, some 3 km northwest of Punta del Gallego which is on the south coast of the Cay (1). According to local fishermen the hutia is not found anywhere else (1).

POPULATION Numbers unknown; Varona in 1980 described it as endangered. The total population is expected to be small by virtue of its very limited range. The description is based on three animals that were captured in May 1970 (1).

HABITAT AND ECOLOGY Habitat is an area of almost pure Red Mangrove (Rhizophora mangle) growing over inundated areas, with virtually no dry land (1). The hutia is an adept climber and apparently feeds exclusively on the mangrove shoots, leaves, fruit and bark (1). Nests are built which are communal, according to local fishermen, and are comprised of large accumulations of small intertwined sticks with a number of access holes that connect to galleries or central chambers. The nests may be up to four sq. m in area, of a roughly semi-spherical shape, and are usually constructed between mangrove roots about 30 cm above high water level (1).

THREATS TO SURVIVAL Direct hunting by visiting fishermen is reported to be the major threat (1,3). The hutias are well known to the local fishermen as 'jutias ratas' (rat hutias) and are captured for food by disturbing the nest - either a sack is placed over the access holes or the animals are chased into the water where they are easily caught, being slow and clumsy swimmers. (1)

CONSERVATION MEASURES TAKEN All hutias in Cuba are legally protected, though enforcement in the past has generally been inadequate (3). In 1980 the Cuban government declared all the Cays of the Sabana Archipelago, including Cayo Fregoso, as well as several other regions, protected areas where all hunting was banned throughout the year (Resolution No.21-79) (3).

CONSERVATION MEASURES PROPOSED Better enforcement and more stringent control of hunting in the area is required. More information is needed on the status and biology of the species as a basis for detailed conservation plans.

CAPTIVE BREEDING No information.

REMARKS For description see (1). Varona has proposed a new subgenus (Mesocapromys) for this species and the Little Earth Hutia (Capromys sanfelipensis) also in the IUCN Red Data Book, and described by him in 1970 (1,2).

REFERENCES   1.   Varona, L.S. (1970). Neuva Especie y Neuvo Subgenero de Capromys (Rodentia: Caviomorpha) de Cuba. Poeyana, Instituto de Biologia, Cuba. Serie A. No.73.
2.   Varona, L.S. (1980). Mamiferos de Cuba. Editorial Gente Nueva, Habana, Annotated by author.
3.   Varona, L.S. (1980). Protection in Cuba. Oryx 15(3): 282-284.

GARRIDO'S HUTIA   INDETERMINATE

Capromys garridoi   Varona, 1970

Order   RODENTIA   Family   CAPROMYIDAE

___

SUMMARY A recently discovered species about which almost nothing is known; described from a single specimen collected in 1967. Apparently confined to a few small cays off southern Cuba and believed threatened because of hunting for food by fishermen. It is hoped that recent legislation will prevent this occurring in the future (3). More information is required on status and ecology.

DISTRIBUTION Cuba, where believed to occur on several islands and cays in the 'Banco de los Jardins y Jardinillos' which form part of the Archipelago de los Cannaroes east of Isla de Pinos and some 40 km south of Peninsula de Zapata (1). Type locality is a small islet (less than 1 km square) known as Cayo Maja, off the northwestern extremity of Cayo Largo. In 1969 evidence for its existence, in the form of readily identifiable faeces, was also found on Cayo Largo, the largest island in the Banco, Cayo de la Piedra just north of the type locality and on at least two of the three islets also known as Cayo Maja immediately west of the type locality (1).

POPULATION Unknown. The only known specimen consists of recent remains of a young adult collected in April 1967. An expedition in November 1969 failed to collect any further specimens but evidence of their continued existence was discovered in the localities listed above (1). Population is expected to be low and at risk by virtue of its very restricted distribution and the possible threat of hunting by fishermen, and Varona described it as 'highly endangered' in 1980 (2).

HABITAT AND ECOLOGY Cayo Maja is a small, dry, low-lying and sandy islet divided in two by a narrow sea channel. Channel and coast are densely covered with Red Mangrove Rhizophora mangle, 'yana' bushes Conocarpus erecta and 'yuraguanos' Thrinax sp. There is no permanent drinking water, small lagoons that form during the monsoons quickly disappear during the long dry season (1). Nothing is known of diet or breeding biology.

THREATS TO SURVIVAL Varona has noted that the principal threat to this and the other recently described Cuban hutias confined to islets and cays (Capromys sanfelipensis, C. auritus and C. angelcabrerai) is hunting by fishermen who land on the cays and can take many individuals in a single raid (3).

CONSERVATION MEASURES TAKEN All Cuban hutias are legally protected. In 1980 Varona reported that the government had recently passed a resolution (no. 21-79) declaring the presumed range of C. garridoi and several other threatened Cuban vertebrates as protected areas where all hunting was forbidden throughout the year (3).

CONSERVATION MEASURES PROPOSED Adequate enforcement of legal protection. Surveys are needed to determine its present status and distribution to formulate detailed conservation plans.

CAPTIVE BREEDING None.

REMARKS For description see (1). This species resembles the relatively common and widespread Conga Hutia (C. pilorides) which is sympatric with it over at least part of its range, but is smaller and has a relatively longer tail and lighter pelage

(1).

REFERENCES 1. Varona, L.S. (1970). Descripcion de una Neuva Especia de Capromys del Sur de Cuba. Poeyana Instituto de Biologia, Cuba. Serie A No.74.
2. Varona, L.S. (1980). Mamiferos de Cuba. Editorial Gente Nueva, Habana, Annotated by author.
3. Varona, L.S. (1980). Protection in Cuba. Oryx 15(3): 282-284.

BUSHY-TAILED HUTIA
or JURIA ANDARAZ

INDETERMINATE

Capromys melanurus (Poey in Peters, 1864)

Order   RODENTIA   Family   CAPROMYIDAE

SUMMARY Limited distribution in eastern Cuba. Protected by law and may occur in two existing and one planned reserve. Threatened by deforestation, its survival appears dependent on preservation of a suitable area of habitat.

DISTRIBUTION   Cuba; confined to scattered parts of the five easternmost Provinces (Oriente) (1,2,4).

POPULATION Unknown, but believed to be small in number (3); Varona in 1980 described it as 'rare' (4).

HABITAT AND ECOLOGY Dense forests. Gundlach in the 19th century noted that it was always found in the same areas as the Cuban Solenodon (Solenodon cubanus), which inhabits the humid primary montane forests of the eastern Provinces of Cuba (4). The hutia is nocturnal and arboreal, foraging in the tops of trees during the night and resting up by day in a hollow tree-trunk or other refuge (4). Gestation period in captivity has been measured as around three months (4).

THREATS TO SURVIVAL At risk mainly through deforestation (3). Some reports have suggested that hunting and the introduced mongoose (Herpestes auropunctatus) are also serious threats. The hutia's habitat, however, is dense and difficult to penetrate and those people in Cuba who eat hutias are reported to hunt mainly for the larger, relatively common, Conga Hutia (Capromys pilorides); also, the mongoose inhabits low-lying bush country and does not occur in the hutia's habitat (3).

CONSERVATION MEASURES TAKEN All hutias are legally protected in Cuba. A new Resolution (No.21-79), has forbidden all hunting in certain areas that are important for wildlife, including several parts of Oriente which may hold C. melanurus, and Varona in 1980 reported that efforts were being made to ensure that protection was enforced (5). The Cuban Academy of Sciences has established the Jaguani and Cupeyal Reserves for fauna and flora in eastern Oriente, near Toa Baracoa (3). Both the Solenodon and the Cuban Ivory-billed woodpecker (Campephilus principalis bairdii) occur here (3) and the area is likely to support C. melanurus. A third reserve in the area is planned at Duaba Arriba (3).

CONSERVATION MEASURES PROPOSED Adequate enforcement of legal protection. The survival of the species essentially depends on the preservation of an adequate area of its habitat; if the hutia does not occur in the reserves detailed above, there will be an urgent need to create further reserves in areas where it is still found.

REMARKS For description of animal see (1,4). Two subspecies have been described and sometimes recognized in the past, C. m. melanurus and C. m. rufescens. However, rufescens is now believed to be only an erythristic individual and not to represent a valid subspecies (2).

REFERENCES   1.   Hall, E.R. and Kelson, K.R. (1959). The Mammals of North America. Ronald Press, New York.
              2.   Varona, L.S. (1974). Catalogo de los mamiferos vivientes y

extinguidos de las Antillas. Academia de Ciencias de Cuba, Havana.

3.   Varona, L.S. (1969-81). In litt.
4.   Varona, L.S. (1980). Mamíferos de Cuba. Editorial Gente Nueva, Habana, Annotated by author.
5.   Varona, L.S. (1980). Protection in Cuba. Oryx 15(3): 282-284.

DWARF HUTIA or JUTIA ENANA   ENDANGERED

Capromys nanus (G.M. Allen, 1917)

Order   RODENTIA   Family   CAPROMYIDAE

SUMMARY   Confined to the Zapata Swamp in southern Cuba, where the last
specimen was taken in 1937, though evidence for its continued survival was
obtained in 1978. Habitat loss and hunting by fishermen are potential threats.
Legally protected and Zapata Swamp is a reserved area, though adequate
enforcement of laws will be necessary to safeguard the species.

DISTRIBUTION   Southern Cuba, where found only in the swampy jungle of the
Zapata Peninsula, Matanzas Province (formerly Las Villas Province) (1,2,4). Fossil
remains have been recorded from several localities throughout mainland Cuba and
on the Isla de Pinos, indicating a much wider former distribution (2,4).

POPULATION   Numbers unknown but population is likely to be very low and
Varona in 1980 described it as 'very endangered' (4). No specimens have been
taken since 1937, but in 1978 an intensive effort to locate the species found
evidence that it still survived in extremely remote areas near the centre of the
swamp where nests and faecal pellets were found and dogs chased a single
individual (6).

HABITAT AND ECOLOGY   Small, dry, bush-covered islands ('cayos de monte')
which are dotted about the marshes; also reported from the mangroves that
surround the swamp (4). Virtually nothing is known of its behaviour or ecology (4).

THREATS TO SURVIVAL   Agricultural development presents a potential menace
to the habitat (3); the species is also likely to be hunted for food by fishermen
visiting the swamps (5).

CONSERVATION MEASURES TAKEN   All hutias are legally protected in Cuba.
A reserved area has been established in the Zapata Swamp (3). Varona noted in
1980 that under a recent Resolution (No.21-79) several important wildlife areas in
Cuba, including the whole of the Zapata Peninsula, had been declared protected
areas where all hunting was forbidden throughout the year (5). Increased efforts
were being made to enforce new and existing protective legislation (5).

CONSERVATION MEASURES PROPOSED   Continued effective protection
against disturbance. Surveys of the area to ensure that the species does indeed
still survive and, if so, to determine distribution and ecology in more detail, are
recommended.

REMARKS   For description of animal see (1,4). This is the smallest Cuban hutia
(4). Charles A. Woods of Florida State Museum kindly provided a draft of this
data sheet in 1981.

REFERENCES   1.   Hall, E.R. and Kelson, K.R. (1959). The mammals of North
                  America. Ronald Press, New York.
             2.   Varona, L.S. (1974). Catalogo de los mamiferos vivientes y
                  extinguidos de las Antillas. Academia de Ciencias de Cuba,
                  Habana.
             3.   Varona, L.S. (1969). Pers. comm.
             4.   Varona, L.S. (1980). Mamiferos de Cuba. Editorial Gente
                  Nueva, Habana,; annotated by author.

5. Varona, L.S. (1980). Protection in Cuba. Oryx 15(3): 282-284.

6. Garrido, O.H. (1980). Los vertebratos terrestres de la Peninsula de Zapata. Poeyana 203: 1-49.

LITTLE EARTH HUTIA   ENDANGERED

Capromys sanfelipensis   Varona, 1970

Order   RODENTIA   Family   CAPROMYIDAE

SUMMARY A recently described species, discovered in 1970 on a small island off southern Cuba. May already be extinct and surveys are needed to determine whether it still survives. If so then effective prevention of (illegal) hunting will be necessary to ensure its survival.

DISTRIBUTION Cuba, where recorded only from the type locality, the very small but inhabited Juan Garcia Cay where the species was discovered in 1970. Also believed likely to occur on the larger neighbouring Cayo Real, separated from Juan Garcia by a narrow sea channel, although there were no actual records (4). Both islets are part of the Cayos de San Felipe, the most westerly of the Canarroes Archipelago, Pinar del Rio, southern Cuba.

POPULATION Varona in 1980 described it as probably extinct as a recent expedition to Juan Garcia had failed to record a single specimen (1,3). The 1970 expedition, which discovered the species, concluded that is was uncommon even within its very limited range (4). Four specimens were obtained (two captured alive) and only three or four others observed, despite frequent excursions with dogs into areas known to be inhabited (4).

HABITAT AND ECOLOGY All specimens recorded in areas of 'Yerba de Vidrio' or samphire Salicornia perennis which grow in abundance in dense clumps up to waist-height along a three km beach next to a zone of mangroves (Rhizophora mangle and Avincennia nitada) (4). The hutias were found to be nocturnal, sheltering during the day in the samphire but foraging widely at night, fresh footprints and faeces being found at considerable distance from this habitat (4). Diet is presumably vegetarian as in other hutias. Captive individuals ate samphire stems but despite extensive searches no evidence of this plant being eaten in the wild was found, nor did the hutia appear to feed on Rhizophora mangle, unlike the closely related Capromys auritus, also in the Red Data Book, which is believed to feed exclusively on the mangrove (4). No nests or burrows were found and nothing is known of its breeding biology (4).

THREATS TO SURVIVAL Principal threat to this, and the three other recently described Cuban hutias confined to small islets and cays (Capromys auritus, C. garridoi and C. angelcabrerai), appears to be hunting by fisherman and colonists (2,7). Although there are no actual records of hunting of C. sanfelipensis, fishermen were said to catch 'rats and mice' on Juan Garcia and adjacent cays by placing bait in fish traps (4). Hernandez and Garrido, who in 1970 captured the only recorded specimens, noted that the samphire clumps where they sheltered were virtually impenetrable and the hutias were only captured after being flushed out by dogs (4). True rats occurred in the houses and shacks on Juan Garcia, but there was no evidence of them in the mangroves or elsewhere in the cay (9).

CONSERVATION MEASURES TAKEN All hutias in Cuba are legally protected. In 1980 the government was reported as recently having declared all islets and cays of the Canarroes Archipelago a wildlife protection area where all hunting is forbidden throughout the year (2).

CONSERVATION MEASURES PROPOSED Further investigations to determine whether the species is extinct or not are required, especially surveys on Cayo Real and other islets and cays near Juan Garcia (4). Should any surviving population be found then effective enforcement of legal protection will be a prerequisite for its survival.

CAPTIVE BREEDING Two of the original four specimens were captured alive and were apparently very docile in captivity (4), though it is not known how long they survived.

REMARKS For description see (4). The species is similar to Capromys auritus, also described by Varona in 1970, differing in colouration and osteological characters, and a new subgenus (Mesocapromys) has been erected to contain the two (4).

REFERENCES   1.   Varona, L.S. (1980). Mamiferos de Cuba. Editorial Gente Nueva, Habana. Annotated by author.
              2.   Varona, L.S. (1980). Protection in Cuba. Oryx 15(3): 282-284.
              3.   Varona, L.S. (1980). In litt.
              4.   Varona, L.S. and Garrido, O.H. (1970). Vertebrados de los Cayos de San Felipe, Cuba, Incluyendo una Nueva Especie de Jutia. Poeyana, Instituto de Biologia, Cuba. Serie A No.75.

JAMAICAN HUTIA or INDIAN CONEY   INDETERMINATE

Geocapromys brownii (Fisher, 1830)

Order   RODENTIA   Family   CAPROMYIDAE

SUMMARY   A Caribbean rodent with two insular subspecies of which one, formerly on Little Swan Island, is almost certainly extinct and the other occurs in very reduced numbers in hilly areas of Jamaica. Hunting, habitat destruction and the effects of predators such as feral cats, dogs and the introduced Mongoose Herpestes auropunctatus, are chief threats. Effective enforcement of legal protection and the setting up of adequately guarded reserves are required.

DISTRIBUTION   Jamaica. Two subspecies are recognised, Geocapromys brownii brownii from Jamaica and the now almost certainly extinct G. brownii thoracatus which formerly occurred on Little Swan Island (ca 100 ha) 650 km southwest of Jamaica and 145 km northeast of the Honduras coast (1,2,3,10). Known range of the former at present is restricted to three areas: in the vicinity of Worthy Park, St. Catherine Parish in central Jamaica; the John Crow Mountains of St. Thomas and Portland Parishes in the east, and remote parts of the Hellshire Hills region west of Kingston in the southern section of St. Catherine Parish (1,2,6,9). There is a good possibility the animal survives in the heart of the Cockpit Country in Trelawny Parish in the north (12). From remains identified in kitchen middens it appears that Hutias occurred over most of the island in pre-Columbian times (6).

POPULATION   Unknown. Greatest numbers are believed to occur in the Worthy Park area, though even here the population was found to be apparently low in density in 1974 (2,13); however in 1972-73 Hutias were said to have caused considerable damage to Kola nut plantations in the region (verified by examination of stomach contents of captured individuals) and it was suggested that the animals involved represented an overspill from the resident population, thus in fact indicating an increase in numbers there at that time (6). In the John Crow Mountains the forest is being exploited and the population was reported in 1981 as rapidly diminishing (13), (although in 1976 Hutias were stated to be still well established there (9)). Information concerning the population in the Hellshire Hills is variable. The region is apparently arid and the animal has been said to be rare (13), though around 1973 it was reportedly abundant in one area near the south coast of this region (2). Also Mittermeier in 1973 reported that the species might be starting to make a comeback in some areas, for example around Great Salt Pond and Manatee Bay in the east and south of the Hellshire Hills, as records indicated their recent appearance in valley plantations as well as on hillsides (6,7). In general, however, it is now regarded as scarce in areas where it was common 30 years ago (1,2). On Little Swan Island Hutias were recorded as plentiful at least until the 1930s, and probably until the early 1950s. A survey in March 1960 failed to record any and in 1974 Clough and Howe found no evidence of its survival during a five day intensive search of the island (1,2).

HABITAT AND ECOLOGY   On Jamaica shows a preference for areas with limestone outcrops and numerous crevices. Predominantly terrestrial and does not build a nest, hiding in natural cavities and crevices under rocks or among roots of large trees. Diet is said to consist of grasses, leaves, twigs, bark, possibly fruit and fungi (4,9). Nocturnal or crepuscular and reportedly travels in pairs (male-female or female-young). Gestation period is about 123 days with usually two (range one to three) extremely precocial young in a litter; in captivity breeding occurs throughout the year with a minimum interbirth interval of about 132 days (9,11). Little Swan Island is a rugged, uplifted limestone reef with areas of dense vegetation. Clough on his visit to the island in 1974 noted that suitable food plants were abundant, notably Strumpfia maritima and Phyllanthus epiphyllanthus two of the most preferred food items of the similar Bahamian Hutia (Geocapromys ingrahami) (2).

THREATS TO SURVIVAL Hunting by man, depredation by introduced species, and habitat destruction are identified threats on Jamaica. Hutias were an important food source for the aboriginal Arawak Indians and hunting for food continued in some areas at least into the 1930s and was undoubtedly an important factor in the decline (2,6,7,9,10). Their present scarcity has meant that most hunting has ceased, though some continues (e.g. in the John Crow Mountains, and by pig-hunters in the Hellshire Hills), and domestic animals have taken over as the principal food supply (2,6,7,10). The impact of the Indian Mongoose Herpestes auropunctatus, introduced onto Jamaica in 1872 is not known for certain though it is believed to have adversely affected Hutia populations, probably by preying on the young (2,5,6,10). The two now appear to coexist however, and it has been suggested that an equilibrium has been reached between them (6). The most important threats at present appear to be predation by cats and dogs and habitat destruction through deforestation and the encroachment of agriculture as more of the slopes in the Hutia's hilly habitat are brought under cultivation (2,6,9,10). On Little Swan Island a very strong hurricane in 1955 may have caused an initial decrease in the population, the heavy rainfall drowning Hutias in their underground refuges, but the principal cause of their extinction is believed to have been predation by cats released from the adjacent Great Swan Island some time in the late 1950s or early 1960s. It has been suggested that rats may also have played a minor role, either in competition for food or predation on the young (1,2).

CONSERVATION MEASURES TAKEN Totally protected under the Wildlife Conservation Act though enforcement is generally inadequate (6).

CONSERVATION MEASURES PROPOSED Enforcement of all conservation laws in areas where Hutias occur. Special care should be taken to eliminate dogs and cats from these areas (1,2). The proposed Hellshire Hills National Park should benefit this species, as should the Cockpit Country National Park if the Hutia does occur in this area (1,2).

CAPTIVE BREEDING Births occurred at the Hope Zoo between 1962 and 1967. A successful breeding programme has been established at the Jersey Wildlife Preservation Trust (9). In 1979 this stood at 22 animals (10 males, 12 females) of which 17 had been bred in captivity (12). Animals have been distributed from this to form the nuclei of further breeding groups at West Berlin, Frankfurt, London and Philadelphia, U.S.A. (11).

REMARKS For description see (3). The Swan Island Hutia, Geocapromys brownii thoracatus may be a separate species (8) though is here retained as a subspecies of G. brownii. The genus Geocapromys has been regarded as a subgenus of Capromys but serological studies indicate the two genera are distinct (13). This data sheet was compiled from a draft kindly provided in 1981 by Charles A. Woods and James R. Bain, Florida State Museum, Gainesville.

REFERENCES
1. Clough, G.C. (1975). Project 1169 Hutia - Status survey on Little Swan Island and Jamaica. In Jackson, P. (Ed.), World Wildlife Yearbook 1974-75. WWF, Switzerland.
2. Clough, G.C. (1976). Current status of two endangered Caribbean rodents. Biol. Conserv. 10(1): 43-47.
3. Hall, E.R. (1981). The mammals of North America. John Wiley, New York.

4. Hayman, R.W. (1956). Mammals of the West Indies. Zoo Life 11(2): 41-45.
5. Lewis, C.B. (1953). Rats and mongoose in Jamaica. Oryx 2: 170-172.
6. Mittermeier, R.A. (1972). Jamaica's endangered species. Oryx 11(4): 258-262.
7. Mittermeier, R.A. (1972). In litt.
8. Morgan, G. (1981). Pers. comm. to C. Woods.
9. Oliver, W.L.R. (1976). The Jamaican Hutia, Geocapromys brownii brownii. Rep. Jersey Wildl. Presev. Trust 12: 10-17.
10. Oliver, W.L.R. (1980). In litt.
11. Oliver, W.L.R. (1977). The Hutias, Capromyidae, of the West Indies. In Olney, P.J.S. (Ed.), International Zoo Yearbook 17. Zool. Soc. Lond.
12. Olney, P.J.S. (Ed.) (1980). International Zoo Yearbook 20. Zool. Soc. London.
13. Woods, C.A. and Bain, J.R. (1981). In litt.

BAHAMIAN HUTIA or INGRAHAM's HUTIA   RARE

Geocapromys ingrahami (J.A. Allen, 1891)

Order   RODENTIA   Family   CAPROMYIDAE

___

SUMMARY Once occurred throughout most of the Bahama Islands, now confined to East Plana Cay, and possibly two other islands where animals were released in 1973 and 1981. Population on East Plana Cay is relatively large and apparently stable, though is potentially at great risk from hurricanes, fire, disease and the introduction of predators. Legally protected. Captive breeding colonies have been set up to help safeguard the species against any disaster on East Plana Cay.

DISTRIBUTION Bahama Islands. Occurs on East Plana Cay, a 465 ha coral island near the southeast end of the Bahamas Island chain (2,3,4,5); possibly also on two other cays where introductions were made in 1973 and 1981 (5). The 1973 introduction was to an island in the Exuma Cays Land and Sea Park where there was a reported sighting of Hutias in 1978 (2). Fossil and subfossil Geocapromys remains are known from many Bahama Islands, but Hutias are believed to have been exterminated from most of them in pre-Colombian times. The only other island from which there are records of live Hutias is Atwoods Cay (Samana Island) about 32 km north of Plana Cays and Crooked Island, where they were recorded some time before 1929, apparently becoming extinct there by 1934, possibly as a result of severe hurricanes in 1929 and 1932 (4).

POPULATION Clough estimated between 6000 and 12,000 animals on East Plana Cay in 1969 based on repeated counts of a measured area (4). The population appears stable as no significant change was detected between visits in 1973 and 1981 and it is possible that it has remained at this level since the first recorded visit to the island in 1891 (5). The animals are evenly distributed over the island at an estimated density of about 30 per ha; this is near the estimated maximum carrying capacity of the island (2).

HABITAT AND ECOLOGY The island is semi-arid with sparse shrub thickets and scattered cacti growing on the sandy soil and limestone terraces (4). The Hutia lives in caves and fissures (with which the whole island is undermined) and under loose slabs of weathered coral; it is nocturnal, highly social and gregarious with complex marking behaviour. Breeding occurs at all seasons of the year, with a gestation period of between 85 and 220 days and normally one highly precocial young born (4). Diet consists of leaves, small twigs, bark and fruits. Clough identified six food plant species, with highest preference shown for Strumpfia maritima. There is no permanent fresh water supply on the island and the Hutias do not seem to require free water (4).

THREATS TO SURVIVAL Although the population on East Plana Cay appears stable at present the small size of the island makes it potentially at great risk - hurricanes are the major threat and disease, which could be expected to spread rapidly through a dense population, is also a possibility. The introduction of cats or dogs could be disastrous - the former are believed to have been responsible for the extinction of the formerly abundant Swan Island Hutia (Geocapromys brownii thoracatus) on little Swan Island west of Jamaica within a few years of their arrival on the island in the early 1960s (6).

CONSERVATION MEASURES TAKEN The Bahamian Ministry of Agriculture and Fisheries has declared the entire island a protected area, and controls the study and collection of the Hutia. The species is specified in the Wild Animals

(Protection) Act of 1968 as an animal which may be captured only under licence, and such licences are not usually issued (8). Small colonies of Hutias from the island have been transplanted to two other small islands (see above). East Plana Cay was surveyed in early 1981 and animals were taken to establish captive breeding colonies (1).

CONSERVATION MEASURES PROPOSED Continued protection and surveillance of East Plana Cay as well as of each transplanted population is of vital importance; establishment of populations elsewhere should also be considered. It has been suggested that a single organisation in the Bahamas, such as the Bahamas National Trust, should coordinate and control all activities concerned with the Hutia (9).

CAPTIVE BREEDING Has bred at the Tacoma Zoo, the National Zoological Park and the University of Rhode Island, and appears to breed well in captivity. Animals were removed from the wild population in 1981 in order to establish two captive breeding colonies; one in the care of the Bahamas National Trust in Nassau and the second at the Florida State Museum in Gainesville (9). This should help safeguard the species in the event of disaster on East Plana Cay (9).

REMARKS For description see (4). This data sheet was compiled from a draft kindly provided in 1981 by Charles Woods and Lauri Wilkins, Florida State Museum, and Garrett C. Clough, Department of Biology, Nassau College, Maine.

REFERENCES
1. Bjorndal, K. (1981). In litt. to B. Groombridge.
2. Campbell, D.G. (1978). The Ephemeral Islands. A Natural History of the Bahamas. MacMillan, London.
3. Clough, G.C. (1969). The Bahamian Hutia; a rodent refound. Oryx 10: 106-108.
4. Clough, G.C. (1972). The biology of the Bahamian Hutia. J. Mammal. 53: 807-823.
5. Clough, G.C. (1974). Additional notes on the biology of the Bahamian Hutia, Geocapromys ingrahami. J. Mammal. 55(3): 670-672.
6. Clough, G.C. (1975). Project 1169. Hutia status survey on Little Swan Island and Jamaica. In Jackson, P. (Ed.), World Wildlife Yearbook 1974-75. WWF, Switzerland.
7. Howe, R. and Clough, G.C. (1971). The Bahamian Hutia in captivity. Int. Zoo Yearbook 11: 89-93.
8. Russel, O.S. (1971). In litt. to E. Baysinger.
9. Wood, C., Wilkins, L. and Clough, G.C. (1981). In litt.

Plagiodontia aedium (Cuvier, 1836)

Order   RODENTIA   Family   CAPROMYIDAE

SUMMARY   Confined to the island of Hispaniola in the Caribbean.   Two subspecies are recognized which have in the past been considered separate species.   In Haiti now extremely rare and threatened by hunting and destruction of the last few remnants of remaining habitat.   Status in the Dominican Republic apparentaly less critical though surveys are needed.   Occurs in two, possibly three, national parks in the Dominican Republic but reportedly unprotected in Haiti where there is an urgent need for reserves to be established.

DISTRIBUTION   Endemic to Hispaniola (7,10).   Haiti: now confined to scattered areas in mountains in the southern peninsula (5,8,9,11).   Dominican Republic: in 1981 said to occur in the southwest: the southwestern part of the Barahona peninsula, at moderate elevations of the Sierra de Bahoruco, Sierra de Neiba and Valley of San Juan in the foothills of the Cordillera Central.   In the east reported at the following localities: Boca de Yuma, Higuey, el Seibo, Hato Mayor, Los Haitises, Sabana de la Mar and Miches in the south, and on the Peninsula de Samana and around Nagua further north.   Other records suggest an additional population 45 kms north of Santo Domingo (5,6).   Two subspecies are recognised, P. aedium aedium and P. aedium hylaeum, which have been considered separate species in the past (2,7,10).   The distribution of the two forms is not precisely known, though it may reflect the boundaries of the old North and South Island masses of Hispaniola, with P. a. aedium found on the southern Peninsula of Haiti and the contiguous Barahona Peninsula of the Dominican Republic and P. a. hylaeum in the central and northern areas of the Dominican Republic (9).

POPULATION   Total numbers unknown, though everywhere rare.   Haiti: extirpated from most areas and 'extremely rare' in remaining habitat.   A few scattered breeding populations are believed to persist in isolated ravines and mountainous slopes, principally in the Massif de la Hotte and Massif de la Selle (5,8,9,11).   Dominican Republic: in 1981 said to be rare throughout its range; major populations were confined to two regions isolated by natural barriers and lowlands modified by agricultural activities (5).   Both subspecies have been little collected and the animal was considered rare even at the beginning of the nineteenth century, though P. a. hylaeum is generally better known (8).

HABITAT AND ECOLOGY   Occupies a variety of habitats from sea level to around 1800 m: mangrove, rain forest, subtropical dry forest, subtropical humid forest, low montane forest and a combination of conifers and hardwood.   Those at higher altitudes reportedly move to lower areas during December and January. They are largely nocturnal, remaining in burrows, limestone crevices or hollow trees during the day, and are predominantly terrestrial though capable of climbing trees (3,5,6,11).   Diet is presumably exclusively vegetarian as in other hutias; they are known to dig for root tubers and eat bark, leaves and garden crops, the most frequently eaten cultivated plants reportedly being stems and roots of Malanga (Xanthosoma sagittifolium), Mazumbella (Colocasia esculenta), cassava and yam (8).   Gestation period is somewhere between 125 and 150 days, with one young born (8).

THREATS TO SURVIVAL   Habitat destruction and hunting.   In Haiti the great majority of forest has been destroyed – in 1978 it was reported that the proportion of forest cover had dropped in the last 20 years from 80% to 9%, roughly half of which was second growth shrub. The clearance of forested mountain slopes for gardens is reportedly the most immediate threat to the hutias - large areas are burned over and planted to crops and many are apparently killed by the fires. Although the gardens are good sources of food, they are much frequented by people and hutias are killed whenever encountered; they are considered pests because they raid crops and are also hunted with dogs for food and sport. Woods in 1977 noted, however, that hutias were so rare by then that very few people had specially trained dogs to hunt them. The gardens generally have a short life and heavy rains soon wash the soil away, causing widespread erosion and leading to dry slopes virtually free of vegetation with the only remaining suitable habitat in steep ravines unsuitable for cultivation. Woods believes that hutias may persist in this habitat for a number of years but that populations will inevitably drift down to critically low levels from which they will not recover (5,8,9). In the Dominican Republic the situation is believed to be somewhat less critical, though the same threats can be expected to apply (5). Predation by the introduced mongoose Herpestes auropunctatus is believed to be relatively unimportant (5).

CONSERVATION MEASURES TAKEN Haiti: none at present (1981). Dominican Republic: fully protected by law with export forbidden. Occurs in the Parque Nacional del Este and Parque Los Haitises; may also exist in the Parque Nacional Jose del Carmen Ramirez (5).

CONSERVATION MEASURES PROPOSED Haiti has a large and widely distributed human population and can only afford minimal reserved areas; it has therefore been recommended that a careful evaluation of the minimum habitat requirements of the hutia be made and that all conservation efforts then be concentrated in a few carefully chosen lreas. Woods and Rosen have made detailed recommendations for possible reserves and have advocated the setting up of at least two in the south: one in the western region of the Southern Penisula (preferably at Pic de Macaya near La Hotte) and one southeast of Port au Prince in the Massif de la Selle (preferably along the ridge from the Morne d' Enfer to the Morne La Selle). Dominican Republic: a survey of the species' status and habitat requirements is required. Long-term studies of its general biology are recommended to develop a strategy for conservation and management of its habitat (5). The setting up of a national park in the Sierra de Bahoruco, where the species is found, is also advised (5).

CAPTIVE BREEDING In 1979 there were reported to be 15 in three zoos, of which nine had been bred in captivity (4). In 1981 there were proposals to establish a captive breeding colony at Florida State Museum and to transfer this to ZooDom in the Dominican Republic after 3-5 years (5).

REMARKS For description see (2,3). This data sheet was compiled from a draft kindly provided in 1981 by J.A. Ottenwalder, Museo Nacional de Historia Natural and ZooDom, Santo Domingo, and C.A. Woods, Florida State Museum, Gainesville.

REFERENCES   1.   Anon. (1978). Haitian desert. Oryx 14(3): 209.
             2.   Anderson, S. (1965). Conspecificity of Plagiodontia aedium and P. hylaeum (Rodentia). Proc. Biol. Soc. Washington 78: 95-98.
             3.   Hayman, R.W. (1956). Mammals of the West Indies. Zoo Life 11(2): 41-45.
             4.   Olney, P.J.S. (Ed.) (1980). International Zoo Yearbook 20. Zool. Soc. Lond.
             5.   Ottenwalder, J.A. and Woods, C.A. (1981). In litt.
             6.   Salazar, L (1977). Notas Generales Sobre Plagiodontia sp. con comentarios sobre los especimenes obtenidos por ZooDom. ZooDom 2: 16-23.

7. Varona, L.S. (1974). Catologo de los mamíferos vivientes y extinguidos de las Antillas. Academia de ciencias de Cuba.

8. Woods, C.A. (1977). The natural history of the Haitian Hutia. Unpd. report, 15pp.

9. Woods, C.A., and Rosen, R.C. (1977). Report on conservation work in southern Haiti. Unpd. report, 32pp.

10. Woods, C.A. and Howland, E.B. (9179). Adaptive Radiation of Capromyid Rodents. J. Mammal. 60: 95-116.

11. Woods, C.A. (In Press) Status of Plagiodontia and Solenodon in Hispaniola. Oryx.

Canis lupus Linnaeus, 1758

Order CARNIVORA   Family   CANIDAE

SUMMARY Formerly occurred in suitable habitats throughout much of the Northern Hemisphere, but now exterminated over large areas of its range and seriously depleted in much of the remainder. Numbers unknown. Habitat loss to human settlement and agriculture, stock predation, and a largely ungrounded fear of attacks upon humans have brought the Wolf into continual conflict with man. Recommendations of the IUCN/SSC Wolf Specialist Group for Wolf conservation are given.

DISTRIBUTION Circumpolar. At one time had a very extensive range throughout the Northern Hemisphere north of 20°N latitude, extending southwards into northern Mexico, Saudi Arabia, and peninsular India. Now sporadic or reduced to small scattered populations in much of North America and Europe, whilst precise data on its distribution over most of Asia are lacking, though its range is known to have contracted in many areas. The taxonomy of the Wolf is in considerable need of revision (35). Mech (1970) listed 24 New World and 8 Old World subspecies; at least 10 of the former are regarded as extinct as are 2 Old World subspecies, both from Japan (C. l. haltai and C. l. hadophilax) (1,21,32). However Corbet in 1978 noted with reference to the Old World Wolf that, although geographical variation was considerable, the continuity of distribution implied that discrete races were unlikely to be valid (18).

North America: Canada: the Wolf occupies significant portions of the north and west. Its presence in settled southern areas is generally sporadic, and it was eliminated from the southwest by the mid 1950s (11,60). In 1973 was reported as nearly extinct on Vancouver Island and absent from the Maritime Provinces (Novia Scotia, New Brunswick and Prince Edward Island)(60), and Newfoundland (32). Distribution and present status in Greenland unknown (29). U.S.A.: still occurs throughout Alaska with no apparent reduction in range (29). In the lower 48 States occurs as remnant populations in the northern third of Minnesota, adjacent Douglas Co. in Wisconsin, parts of Michigan (including Isle Royale in Lake Michigan), and in the Northern Rockies in western Montana and adjacent parts of Idaho and Wyoming, sightings being principally in Lewis and Clark and Glacier National Parks and in large tracts of National Forest (20,29,37,45,63,64,). In Minnesota about 26,000 sq. km in the north and northeast are considered 'primary range' with a larger (around 55,000 sq. km) peripheral area (20,63,64). Wolves occasionally wander from here into settled farming areas in the south and west, and are killed (63). The Mexican Wolf population (referred to the subspecies C. l. baileyi) was reported in 1979 as still extending into southwest New Mexico and southeast Arizona (10). Mexico: in 1980 only three areas, all in Chihuahua and Durango States, were known to harbour breeding populations – a large area south and southwest of Durango, one north and west of Durango and east of Tepehuanes, and a third north of Chihuahua and east of Casas Grandes in Chihuahua State. A fourth area which sometimes harboured Wolves and where they persisted at least until 1977 is the Sierra del Nido, extending southward to the mountains surrounding the Santa Clara Valley, Chihuahua. In 1976-77 there were creditable reports from other areas of Chihuahua and Durango and from southern Zacatecas and eastern Sonora, though these remain unconfirmed (10,31).

Europe: extinct in Austria, Belgium, Denmark, France, (though a Wolf, presumably wandering from northwest Spain was reported from the Basses Pyrenees in 1981 (3)), East Germany and West Germany (which occasionally receive wandering animals from eastern Europe), Great Britain, Ireland, the Netherlands, Luxembourg and Switzerland (47). In Iberia main area of concentration is in the northwest, principally in the inaccessible mountainous inland parts of Galicia, Asturias and Leon (especially the Cordillera Cantabrica and Montanas de Leon) in Spain, and contiguous parts of northeastern Portugal, where known to be permanently present in the districts of Bragança, Vila Real and Viseu. Remnant populations of very low density survive along the Spanish-Portuguese border mainly in Extremadura in Spain with individuals occasionally wandering into Portugal, along the Sierra Morena in northern Andalucia, in Galicia and possibly in the Alava/Logrono area of northeast Spain (13,14,41,42,43). Italy: restricted to approx. 8500 sq. km in the central and southern part of the Appenine Mountains where potentially suitable habitat covers about 70,000 sq. km (8). In Fennoscandia occurs in Finland, and persisted until 1977 at least in the southwest of Norway near the Swedish border, though by 1980 was reported as extinct in Sweden itself (26,40,58). In the Balkans it is still widespread in Yugoslavia in forested areas of Macedonia, Bosnia, Herzegovia and Croatia with wandering animals occasionally seen in other regions (9). Greece: bounties were claimed, at least up to 1972, from all regions of mainland Greece except the Peloponnese with most from Macedonia (53). Albania: unknown (29). Poland: occurs in the east, from Suałki in the north to Nowy Sącz in the south with occasional wandering individuals further west; it appears to have undergone a range expansion westwards in the 1970s (57,58). Czechoslovakia: in 1971 permanently present only in northeast Slovakia, an area continuous with its distribution in southern Poland (56,65). In Romania about 40,000 sq. km of forested hills and mountains, mainly in the Carpathians, were still occupied in 1973 (17). Distribution in European Russia in the early 1970s has been mapped as extensive but patchy. Main areas of absence are the lower Volga and central Russia around Moscow (5).

Asia: details generally poorly known. In the Middle East, was recorded in 1980 as still occurring in most of Anatolian Turkey, though mainly in the east (27); throughout Israel with concentrations in the north, near the Dead Sea and around Elat and also in Egyptian Sinai (67). Lebanon occasionally receives wandering animals from Syria or northern Israel, the most recent recorded being in 1974 (61). Distribution in Syria, Jordan, Iraq and the Arabian peninsula unknown (29). Iran was believed to hold a viable population in 1979, with Wolves occupying about 80% of their former range (29). Recorded in the 1970s as still widespread in Afghanistan (25,46) and Pakistan (13,51); in the latter mainly confined to remoter areas of extensive desert in the hilly regions, and in all mountainous districts from Baluchistan up to Gilgit and Chital in the north, being largely absent from the Indus plains (though a few survived in the Punjab at least up to 1972) (51). In the Indian subcontinent still persists in the northern uplands of Tibet, Ladakh and part of Nepal (where it is rare), and from Kashmir to Dharwar, thence eastwards to Bengal (48,62). Occurrence in the Luni Basin of the Great Indian Desert was reported in 1978 (55). Central and northern Asia, -- Russia, Mongolia, and China -- certainly hold significant populations though detailed distribution is not well known. Extinct in Japan (1).

POPULATION Total numbers unknown, though has undoubtedly declined and is continuing to do so throughout much of its range.

North America: still relatively abundant in Canada outside settled farming areas (10). A rough estimate for British Columbia and the Yukon in 1979 was 10,000 with unknown numbers elsewhere (29); all States were considered to hold viable populations (29), although in 1981 considerable concern was expressed for the future (see 'Threats to Survival'). U.S.A.: the 1979 estimate was 10,000-15,000 in Alaska with some 1200 in Minnesota although numbers in the latter fluctuate, probably due to changes in the deer population (20,29,34,64). In Michigan and Wisconsin there were about 60 of which 20-30 (increased to 50 by 1980 (45)) were on Isle Royale in Lake Superior (29). The Douglas County, Wisconsin, Wolves were believed in 1979 to comprise two packs with 4 to 8 animals in each and were thought to be immigrants from Minnesota; they are the first recorded in Wisconsin for nearly 20 years (64). In the northern Rockies, 10-20 were estimated in Glacier National Park, Montana, in 1978, with around 5 in Salmon National Forest, Idaho. No other estimates were available though there were reported sightings in several National Forests in Idaho, Montana and Wyoming and in the Lewis and Clark National Park, Montana (37). A recent search of Yellowstone National Park failed to confirm reported sightings there (16,37). In 1979 only the Alaskan and Minnesotan populations were considered fully viable, all others being regarded as highly threatened or endangered and, with the exception of Isle Royale, consisting of low density populations, lone Wolves or pairs (29). Mexico: Macbride in early 1980 estimated about 15 south of Durango, 6 east of Tepehuanes, possibly only 2 adults east of Casas Grandes, and probably less than 6 for the Sierra del Nido; extrapolating from these he estimated a total of 50 or so for the whole population, including several in southern U.S.A. (31).

Europe: numbers in Iberia unknown but thought unlikely to exceed 200 in 1980, and considered 'Threatened' or 'Endangered' in both Spain and Portugal (13,14,29,41,42). Italy: 1979 estimate of 100 and probably stable (8). Estimate of about 100 in late 1979 in Finland, all are migrants from the Soviet Union and numbers fluctuate; 73 were reported killed in 1977-79 (50); the last known Wolf-den was found in 1963 (50). In north Sweden numbers had increased gradually from fewer than 8 known before 1978 to at least 12 by December 1978, with the first known breeding since 1964 in that year (7); however by 1980 the pack had apparently been exterminated by illegal hunting (26). In Norway the remnant population in the southeast was thought to consist of about 6 animals in 1977 (40). Greece: bounty totals from 1969 to 1978 averaged 800 animals mostly from Macedonia (4,53). A tentative estimate for the whole country of around 2000 in total was made in 1979 and the population was considered viable (29). In Yugoslavia, 1979 estimate was 2000-2500 and thought to be declining (29); from 1954 to 1972 an average of 1000 were bountied annually (9). In Bulgaria an intensive eradication campaign led to about 15,000 being killed from 1954 to 1969, the pre-breeding population in 1970 being estimated at 110-120, rising to 240-250 after breeding (19). The 1979 estimate was 100 and the species considered highly threatened, although in 1971 it was noted that continual migration across borders into Bulgaria meant that complete extirpation was virtually impossible (19,29). Status in Albania is unknown though is thought likely to be threatened (29). Romania: a March 1973 census estimated about 2000, compared to about 4000 in 1950 (17). It was not considered endangered though a 1979 report categorized it as in a phase of steep decline, also giving 2000 as the estimate (29,57). Poland: estimate in March 1981 of 517, with the largest population (ca. 208) in the southeastern state of Krosno (70). This compares with a total of around 400 in 1979 of which about 60 were shot, and 360 in 1978 with at least 75 shot (58). In 1951 the population stood at round 800; by 1972 it had been reduced to approximately 60 (57), since then numbers have steadily increased though it is still regarded as in danger of extinction (29,58). Czechoslovakia: in 1973 estimated as under 100 and considered 'Endangered', with indications of a sharp decline in the early 1970s. A total of 426 were recorded as killed between 1945 and 1972 (56). U.S.S.R. (including Asian Republics): wolves are still relatively abundant in parts of the U.S.S.R. despite intensive control programmes since 1946 having greatly reduced numbers, particularly in livestock breeding areas. At the end of World War 2 there were an estimated 150,000-200,000; in 1946 62,700 were killed and for the next 15 years 40,000-50,000 were killed annually. In 1973 Soviet authorities estimated the total number to approach 50,000. Most of these (about 30,000) in the Asian Republic of Kazakhstan. Other centres of high Wolf density (30 animals or more per 1000 sq. km in some areas) were the Caucasian Republics (especially East Georgia, Dagestan and Azerbaijan), Central Asia (notably Kirghizia) and the mountain steppes of central Siberia. It was claimed at that time (1973) that no subspecies of Wolf in the U.S.S.R. was under threat of extinction though some concern was expressed for the Tundra Wolf (C. l. albus) whose numbers had been severely reduced by hunting from aircraft (5). Popular reports in 1978 and 1979 have spoken of a Wolf population 'explosion', with numbers approaching 100,000 and of an intensive campaign to reduce the population to around 18,000 (6,24).

Asia: Turkey: reported in 1980 as drastically reduced in numbers in west and northwest Anatolia, due to the increase in the human population and intensity of hunting (27). Still thought to be relatively abundant in the east, though an expedition in 1979 reported that here also numbers had been considerably reduced and remaining populations were almost certainly small and highly scattered (27,44). Israel: 1980 figure of 210 and increasing (67). Jordan: last reliable records were in 1968-69 from the Azraq desert in the north, however between 1975 and 1979 several reports were received from the extreme south and southwest (15,38). The 1979 report gave a tentative total of 200 but the basis of this is unknown (29). Iran: a 1979 tentative estimate of 1500 (29). Afghanistan: in 1977 still said to survive in good numbers in mountainous areas, especially in the northeast, though considered vulnerable because of intense hunting for its fur (25,46). Pakistan: unknown, believed to be nowhere very abundant though reasonable numbers are thought still to exist in mountainous areas, especially in the north (22,51). A 1976 survey estimated around 1000 in Chital (30). India: no more than 500 were thought to survive in 1981, with estimates of 35 in Rajasthan, 50 to 70 in Karnataka, 12 in Bihar, about 60 in the Little Rann of Kutch in Gujarat and unknown numbers in Maharasthra, Uttar Pradesh and Madhya Pradesh. It was thought likely that Wolves also survived elsewhere (54). Mongolia: in 1976 described as more or less stable in trend, though decreasing in steppe and semi-desert areas, with about 10,000 in total killed annually (47). U.S.S.R. see under Europe.

Virtually no information is available from elsewhere (Greenland, China and much of the Middle East).

HABITAT AND ECOLOGY Occurs in a wide range of habitats: tundra, forest and open plains, even to the edges of deserts, from the seashore to over 3000 m altitude. Preys primarily on wild mammals, often large ungulates (wild goats, mountain sheep, deer) but has also been known to rely heavily on smaller animals such as beavers, hares and rabbits and where hunting or human development has reduced natural prey, it will take almost any type of domestic animal. Some populations (e.g. in Italy, Mexico, Spain and India) are almost entirely dependent on man, scavenging from dumps as well as feeding on domestic animals (7,20,32,33,43,54). The Wolf is normally considered a group hunter but in areas of low population density it is often solitary or hunts in pairs (31,42). Elsewhere the unit of its society is a pack which is basically a family group. Packs usually contain 5-8 members, but packs of up to 36 have been reported. Within the pack there is a well-developed social system based on a dominance hierarchy. Like most other Wolf activities, breeding and raising of young involve the entire pack. Gestation period is 62-63 days. Average litter size is 4-6.5 pups. In populations unexploited by man, only about 60% of the adult females breed whereas in exploited populations 90% may breed. Wolves may live up to 16 years but 10 years is an old age for individuals in the wild (32,33).

THREATS TO SURVIVAL As forests have been cleared and plains ploughed up, the Wolf has been increasingly confined to inhospitable unsettled areas or exterminated. Stock depredations together with an unfounded fear of attacks upon humans have brought it into serious conflict with man throughout its range. It has been, and in many areas continues to be, subject to intensive eradication campaigns by bounties, poisoning and government control programmes. Hence extermination has occurred in more than 95% of the area of the 48 contiguous States of the U.S.A., in much of Mexico, in the settled farming areas of Canada, in most of western Europe, much of eastern Europe, and parts of the European Soviet Union. In many areas such as Alaska, Ontario in Canada, Fennoscandia and parts of Eastern Europe the Wolf is considered by hunters as a competitor for game species and thus there is considerable pressure from the hunting lobby to exterminate it in such areas (5,20,23,29,32,33,50,58,64). There has been very little detailed study of the effects Wolves have on prey populations and attempts to blame them e.g. for the decrease in the Alaskan and British Columbian Caribou (Rangifer tarandus) populations in the 1970s, have been the subject of fierce controversy (2,12,60); and in fact, in 1981 it was predicted that a high proportion of Canada's wolf population may have disappeared in another decade as a result of 'gross overharvest' of the Caribou, its primary prey species there (68). Wolf pelts are extensively used in the fur trade and in parts of Asia such as Turkey and Afghanistan large numbers are shot for this reason (25,44). Its status in much of Canada is that of a furbearer with fur royalties payable (29,60). Unlimited taking is apparently allowed in all Provinces (except perhaps Alberta), though there are controls on trapping techniques in some areas (e.g. leg-hold traps are banned in British Columbia) (60,64). In several areas, e.g. Alaska, British Columbia, Rumania and Iberia the Wolf is hunted for sport, and given the status of a game species (17,29,42,43,60); this is unlikely to affect population levels in areas with good numbers but in areas such as Iberia with small isolated populations this may be highly detrimental (42,43).

CONSERVATION MEASURES TAKEN The Wolf populations of Bhutan, India, Nepal and Pakistan are listed in Appendix 1 of the 1973 Convention on International Trade in Endangered Species of Wild Fauna and Flora, trade in them or their products therefore being subject to strict regulation by ratifying nations, and trade for primarily commercial purposes banned. All other populations are listed in Appendix 2, trade in them between acceding nations therefore being subject to regulation and monitoring of effects. Totally protected by law in Norway, Sweden, Italy, Israel, India and Mexico, although this protection is often minimally enforced, if at all (8,26,29,31,40). In the U.S.A. it is listed on the US Endangered Species List as 'Endangered', and thereby completely protected in all the lower 48 States except Minnesota where it is listed as 'Threatened'; this latter designation allows a limited kill by authorised State or Federal agents of Wolves which are preying on domestic animals. Approximately 26,000 sq. km in the northern part of Minnesota and Isle Royale National Park (544 sq. km) in Michigan have been declared 'Critical Habitat' for the species and thus all Federal Agencies are obliged by law to ensure that actions authorized, funded or carried out by them do not result in the destruction or adverse modification of this habitat. In about 11,500 sq. km of the range in Minnesota absolutely no killing of Wolves is allowed. Recovery Plans have been developed for the Northern Rocky Mountain Wolf (ascribed to the subspecies C. l. irremotus), and the Eastern Timber Wolf (C. l. lycaon) in Minnesota and adjacent States, and in 1979 a Recovery Team was appointed for the Mexican Wolf (C. l. baileyi) (20,36,63,64). The Alaskan Wolf population is not included on the U.S. Endangered Species List though there are enforced bag limits and closed seasons (29), healthy populations are thought to be capable of sustaining 50% annual harvests (32). It occurs in many national parks and reserves throughout its range and some, such as the Saruadih Wolf Sanctuary in Bihar State, India, have been established especially for it (5,8,45,30,62). The Italian Wolf has been the subject of a WWF research and conservation campaign, and in Spain an intensive publicity and public education campaign was in operation from 1967 to at least 1973 (52). It has been the subject of numerous studies (e.g. 8,14,23,45,67). In May 1981 a workshop on 'A conservation strategy for Wolves in Canada' was held at Edmonton, Alberta (68,69). An IUCN/SSC Wolf Specialist Group exists to coordinate and initiate conservation action, it meets regularly (29,49,56).

CONSERVATION MEASURES PROPOSED The Wolf Specialist Group of IUCN's Species Survival Commission, in Stockholm in September 1973, made recommendations for Wolf conservation that are still valid by 1981; they include the following: 1) full protection should be accorded to surviving populations that are endangered regionally, nationally, or internationally; 2) each country harbouring wolves should define areas suitable for their existence and enact suitable legislation to perpetuate the population or to facilitate reintroductions; 3) in Wolf management programmes, the use of poisons, bounty systems and sport hunting using mechanised vehicles should be prohibited; 4) consideration should be given to payment of compensation for damage caused by Wolves; 5) suitable Wolf habitats should be restored, including the reintroduction of large herbivores where necessary; 6) extensive economic development should be excluded from designated Wolf conservation areas; 7) national legislation should be enacted to require the registration of each Wolf killed. Additional recommendations were made on the need for widespread public education, scientific research and international co-operation in research, and management (28).

The Eastern Timber Wolf Recovery Plan in the United States calls for the maintenance and re-establishment of viable populations 'in as much of its former range as is feasible'. To this end it has specified ensuring the survival of the animal in Minnesota by highly regulated management and extensive improvement of the habitat of its prey, and also attempting re-establishment of at least one viable population outside Minnesota and Isle Royale (20,64). Attempts to reintroduce Wolves to the Upper Peninsula of Michigan in 1974 failed when all four individuals were killed either deliberately or accidentally in Coyote Traps (34). Reintroduction of the Woodland Caribou to the northern bogs of Minnesota (from where they were extirpated in about 1937), to provide an alternative food supply has been specifically advocated (20,64). The Northern Rocky Mountain Wolf Plan calls for the re-establishment and maintenance of at least two populations of the Wolf within its former range (64). The importance of adequate public understanding of Wolf ecology and management to the success of these plans has been stessed throughout (20,64). The 1980 report on the Mexican Wolf concluded that although very large areas of suitable habitat remained in Mexico and the U.S.A., illegal hunting (mostly predator control) had virtually eliminated it and the only prospect for long term survival was captive breeding and reintroduction, although the latter would almost certainly pose severe problems due to conflict with local people (31). Plans for captive breeding were well advanced in 1979 and the Arizona-Sonora Desert Museum has been designated the primary breeding centre, with San Diego as a back-up (36).

The IUCN/SSC Wolf Specialist Group recommended the following projects in order of priority in 1981: 1) continuation of the Wolf conservation programme in Italy; 2) initiation of a Wolf survey in India; 3) assistance to Wolf research in Poland; 4) study of Wolf ecology in Iberia; 5) research and conservation in Israel; 6) a survey of the Middle East (deferred because of political instability); and 7) review of Wolf taxonomy (35).

CAPTIVE BREEDING Breeds readily in captivity. Many hundreds are held in zoos around the world, and at least 260 were successfully reared in 1979 of which four were Mexican Wolves at the Arizona-Sonora Desert Museum in Tucson (39).

REMARKS For description of animal see (32,33). The Wolf Specialist Group of the IUCN/SSC provided much of the information on which this data sheet is based.

REFERENCES   1.   Anon. (1970). 'The Last Wolf of Japan'. A Short Story of Extermination. Selected Catalogue of the Harano Agricultural Museum. Osaka, Japan.

2. Anon. (1976). Lawsuit to save Wolves in Alaska. Animal Welfare Institute Info. Report.

3. Anon. (1981). The Times. Tues. 6th Jan. 1981.

4. Antipas, B. (1980). In litt.

5. Bibikov, D.I. (1976). The wolf in the U.S.S.R. In Pimlott, D.H. (Ed.), Wolves. Proc. of the First Working Meeting of Wolf Specialists and of the First International Conference on Conservation of the Wolf, 5-6 September 1973, Stockholm. IUCN Supplementary Paper No. 43.

6. Binyon, M. (1978). Big bad Wolf returns to menace Russians. The Times Tuesday, March 21. p. 7. London.

7. Bjarvall, A. (1980). In litt.

8. Boitani, L. (1978-80). The management of Wolves in areas of intensive land use in Italy. Paper presented to the Edinburgh Wolf Symposium, April 1978, and to the Portland Wolf Symposium, August 1979.

9. Bojovic, D. and Colic, D. (1976). Wolves in Yugoslavia. In Pimlott, D.H. (Ed.), Wolves. Proc. of the First Working Meeting of Wolf Specialists and of the First International Conference on Conservation of the Wolf, 5-6 September 1973, Stockholm. IUCN Supplementary Paper No. 43.

10. Carley, C.J. (1979). In litt.

11. Carlyn, L.N. (1979). In litt.

12. Carter, N. (1978). In litt. to S. Bawlf.

13. Castroviejo, J.B. (1980). In litt.

14. Castroviejo, J.B., Palacios, F., Garzon, J. and Cuesta, L. (no date). Sobre la alimentacion de los canidos Ibericos. 16pp.

15. Clarke, J.E. (1980). In litt.

16. Cole, G.F. (1971). Yellowstone Wolves (Canis lupus irremotus). Research Note No.4 Yellowstone National Park.

17. Commission on Nature Monuments, Academy of Romanian Socialist Republic. (1976). Data on the situation of the wolf in Romania. In Pimlott, D.H. (Ed.), Wolves. Proc. of the First Working Meeting of Wolf Specialists and of the First International Conference on Conservation of the Wolf, 5-6 September 1973, Stockholm. IUCN Supplementary Paper No. 43.

18. Corbet, G.B. (1978). The Mammals of the Palaearctic Region: A Taxonomic Review. British Museum (Nat. Hist.) and Cornell Univ. Press, London and Ithaca.

19. Dargoev, P. (1971). On the situation of Wolves (Canis lupus lupus L.) in Bulgaria. World Exhibition of Hunting. Scientific Conference, 16-18. Sept. 1971, Budapest.

20. Eastern Timber Wolf Recovery Team. (1978). Eastern Timber Wolf Recovery Plan. U.S. Fish and Wildlife Service Dept. of Interior.

21. Ellerman, J.R. and Morrison-Scott, T.C.S. (1951). Checklist of Palaearctic and Indian Mammals 1758 to 1946. British Museum (Nat. Hist.), London.

22. Ferguson, D.A. (1978). Protection, conservation and management of threatened and endangered species in Pakistan. Report of the US Fish and Wildlife Service, National Park Service Study Mission to Pakistan, February 5-16, 1978.

23. Fritts, S.H. (1980). Progress Report re expanded research and control/research programme, to agencies and individuals interested in wolf research and livestock depredation control work in Minnestoa. Unpd. 3pp.

24. Galass, C. and Schmidt, W.E. (1979). Russia's Wolf Bane. Newsweek Dec. 24 1979. p19.
25. Habibi, K. (1977). The mammals of Afghanistan. UNDP, FAO, and Dept. of Forests and Ranges, Ministry of Agriculture, Kabul, Afghanistan.
26. Hamdahl, B. (1980). Nature and the law. Sveriges Nat. 2:53.
27. Hus, S. (1980). In litt.
28. IUCN. (1974). Manifesto on Wolf conservation. IUCN Bulletin 5(5): 17-18.
29. IUCN/SSC Wolf Specialist Group. (1979). Appendix II to the report of the 1979 meeting, by L. David Mech.
30. Khan, Y.M. (1980). Development potential of wildlife in NWFP Pakistan. Paper presented at seminar in Organising Wildlife Management in Developing countries. Pakistan Forest Institute, Peshawar (Pakistan). Nov. 10-12 1980.
31. McBride, R.T. (1980). The Mexican Wolf (Canis lupus baileyi). Endangered Species Report 8. U.S. Fish and Wildlife Service, Albuquerque, New Mexico, 1980.
32. Mech, L.D. (1970). The Wolf. Natural History Press. Garden City, New York.
33. Mech, L.D. (1974). Canis lupus. Am. Soc. Mammalogists, Mammalian Species 37: 1-6.
34. Mech, L.D. (1979). Wolf management in the United States. Lecture at a Wolf Symposium, Edinburgh, April 1978.
35. Mech, L.D. Chairman IUCN/SSC Wolf Specialist Group. (1981). In litt. to R. Fitter.
36. Meritt, D. (1979). Mexican Wolf Recovery Team to be developed. AAZPA Newsletter 20(8): 13.
37. National Fish and Wildlife Laboratory (1980). Gray Wolf. FSW/OBS-80/01.53. In Selected Vertebrate Endangered Species of the Seacoast of the United States. Biological Services Program. Fish and Wildlife Service, U.S. Dept. of the Interior.
38. Nelson, J.B. (1973). Azraq Desert Oasis. Allen Lane, London.
39. Olney, P.J.S. (Ed.) (1980). International Zoo Yearbook 20. Zool. Soc. London.
40. Norderhaug, M. (1977). Status of the Wolf in Fennoscandia, at the beginning of 1977. Report to IUCN/SSC Meeting, April, 1977, Morges, Switzerland.
41. Paixao de Megalhaes, C.M. (1975). Aspectos do Lobo (Canis lupus signatus Cabrera) em Portugal. 12th Congress of the International Union of Game Biologists, Lisboa, Portugal.
42. Paixao de Megalhaes, C.M. (1979). In litt.
43. Paixao de Megalhaes, C.M. and Pettrucci da Fonesca, F. (1979). The wolf in Bragança County - Impact on cattle and game. 11p.
44. Peers, C. (1979). In litt.
45. Peterson, R.D. and Stephenson, P.W. (1980). Ecological studies of Wolves on Isle Royale. Annual Report 1979-80. Unpd. Report.
46. Petoçz, R.G. (1977). In litt.
47. Pimlott, D.H. (1976). The Wolf in Europe in 1973. In Pimlott, D.H. (Ed.), Wolves. Proc. of the First Working Meeting of Wolf Specialists and of the First International Conference on Conservation of the Wolf, 5-6 September 1973, Stockholm. IUCN Supplementary Paper No. 43.
48. Prater, S.H. (1971). The Book of Indian Animals. Bombay

Natural History Society, 3rd edition.

49. Pulliainen, E. (1978). In lecture given at a Wolf Symposium, Edinburgh, April 1978.

50. Pulliainen, E. (1979). In litt.

51. Roberts, T.J. (1977). The mammals of Pakistan. Ernest Benn Ltd., London.

52. Rodriquez de la Fuente, F. (1976). Protection of the Wolf in Spain - Notes on a public awareness campaign. In Pimlott, D.H. (Ed.), Wolves. Proc. of the First Working Meeting of Wolf Specialists and of the First International Conference on Conservation of the Wolf, 5-6 September 1973, Stockholm. IUCN Supplementary Paper No. 43.

53. Section of Game Economy, Ministry of National Economy (1976). The kill of Wolves in Greece, 1964-1972. In Pimlott, D.H. (Ed.), Wolves. Proc. of the First Working Meeting of Wolf Specialists and of the First International Conference on Conservation of the Wolf, 5-6 September 1973, Stockholm. IUCN Supplementary Paper No. 43.

54. Shahi, S.O. (1981). Indian Wolves. Report to the 55th IUCN/SSC Meeting, March 1981, New Delhi.

55. Sharma, I.K. (1978). Occurrence and survival of the Wolf in the Indian Desert. Tigerpaper 5(3): 32-33.

56. Slovak Institute for the case of Monuments and Nature Conservation (1976). Status, distribution and problems of protecting wolves in Slovakia. In Pimlott, D.H. (Ed.), Wolves. Proc. of the First Working Meeting of Wolf Specialists and of the First International Conference on Conservation of the Wolf, 5-6 September 1973, Stockholm. IUCN Supplementary Paper No. 43.

57. Suminski, P. (1976). The Wolf in Poland. In Pimlott, D.H. (Ed.), Wolves. Proc. of the First Working Meeting of Wolf Specialists and of the First International Conference on Conservation of the Wolf, 5-6 September 1973, Stockholm. IUCN Supplementary Paper No. 43.

58. Suminski, P. (1980). In litt.

59. Szaniawski, A. (1976). In litt.

60. Theberge, J.B. (1976). Wolf management in Canada through a decade of change. In Pimlott, D.H. (Ed.), Wolves. Proc. of the First Working Meeting of Wolf Specialists and of the First International Conference on Conservation of the Wolf, 5-6 September 1973, Stockholm. IUCN Supplementary Paper No. 43.

61. Tohme, G., Nahas-Zahreddine, G. and Neuschwander, J. (1975). Quelques nouvelles donneés sur le statut actuel du loup Canis lupus pallipes Sykes 1831 au Liban. Mammalia 39(3): 510-513.

62. Upreti, B.N. (1979). Conservation of Wildlife Resources in Nepal. National Parks and Wildlife Conservation Office, Katmandu, Nepal.

63. U.S. Fish and Wildlife Service. (1978). Grey Wolf reclassified to threatened list in Minnesota. News release.

64. U.S. Fish and Wildlife Service. (1977-80). Endangered Species Technical Bulletin. 2(3): 1,3,4,7; 3(8): 1,3,4; 4(4): 8; 4(7):1, 5(6): 3-4.

65. Voskar, J. (1971). In litt.

66. Wright, A. WWF (India). (1977). In litt.

67. Yoffe, A. (1980). In litt.

68. Mech, L.D. (1981). In litt. to Dr. L. Carbyn.

69. IUCN (1981). IUCN Bulletin, New Series 12(3-4): 19.
70. Gill, J. (1981). Report to 56th IUCN/SSC Meeting, June 1981, Switzerland.

RED WOLF   ENDANGERED

Canis rufus (Audubon & Bachman, 1851)

Order   CARNIVORA   Family   CANIDAE

SUMMARY Declared 'biologically' extinct in the wild in July 1980 by the Red
Wolf Field Recovery Programme. By the 1970s was restricted to a small area of
Texas and Louisiana coastlands. Decline due to habitat loss and persecution (it
was regarded as a threat to livestock), but recent main threat has been
hybridization with Coyotes. By 1980 less than 50 pure Red Wolves still existed in
the wild but all belonged to populations that included hybrids and Coyotes. 58
animals were held in captivity at the end of 1980 but not all had been certified as
genetically pure Red Wolves. Listed as 'Endangered' on the United States List of
Endangered and Threatened Wildlife. A captive breeding nucleus of pure stock
has been established and the U.S. Fish and Wildlife Service has devised a
conservation programme. Efforts must be continued to maintain pure stocks in
captivity and to restore the species to parts of its historic range.

DISTRIBUTION Southeast United States. Pure bred Red Wolves are virtually
extinct in the wild; in the late 1970s they survived only in Jefferson County, Texas
and adjacent parts of Cameron and Calcasieu Parishes, Louisiana (3,7). At the
time of the first European settlements in North America, the species ranged from
central Texas to the Atlantic coast and from the Gulf coast north to the Ohio
Valley and southern Pennsylvania. By 1900 it had disappeared from most of the
Atlantic seaboard and Ohio Valley and by 1920 from Florida, most other areas
east of the Mississippi, and much of central and northeastern Texas, central
Oklahoma and southeastern Kansas. By 1940 substantial numbers could only be
found in Louisiana and in the Big Thicket and coastlands of southeastern Texas.
Scattered populations also survived in extreme southeastern Oklahoma, southern
Arkansas, southern Mississippi and extreme western Alabama (6,8,9).

POPULATION Declared 'biologically' extinct in the wild in July 1980 (12) when
fewer than 50 pure Red Wolves still survived in the wild and all belonged to
populations that included hybrid animals and Coyotes, the species therefore being
essentially extinct in the wild. 58 animals existed in captivity at the end of 1980,
but not all of them had been certified as genetically pure Red Wolves (1,3,7,12).

HABITAT AND ECOLOGY Recently only coastal prairie and marshes but
formerly also eastern forests (1,2,3,10). Primarily nocturnal. Diet of small
mammals such as rabbits, squirrels and muskrats, supplemented with crayfish and
insects (1,3,5,10); deer also taken (4). Described as existing mainly in family
groups and not known to live in packs (1,3,10); mated pairs having a hunting
territory of 80-100 sq. km. (1,7). Dens usually above ground in heavy vegetation
in present habitat, occasionally in sand knolls. Underground den dug if habitat
allowed. A litter of 2-7 pups is born in April or May; most die before six months
of age due to parasites (1,3,8,10).

THREATS TO SURVIVAL Declined due to hunting, trapping and, later, poisoning
by settlers, who regarded it as a threat to livestock and possibly themselves, and
also to modification of its habitat and disappearance of natural prey species.
Major recent threat has been hybridization with Coyotes. Before the arrival of
white settlers the Red Wolf and Coyote had largely separate ranges; by the early
twentieth century man had altered much of the natural habitat, the clearing of
forests and development of agriculture creating conditions favourable to the
Coyote and enabling it to extend its range eastward to invade the remaining range
of the Red Wolf. The two species readily hybridized and both Coyotes and hybrids

now occupy all the coastal area of eastern Texas and adjacent Louisiana. Other current threats are habitat disruption, disease, parasites and flooding. The remaining wolf population is affected by heartworm, intestinal parasites and mange and cannot tolerate stress situations that would be of little consequence to healthy animals. The poor survival of pups is thought to be due to hookworms (1,3,7,8,10,11).

CONSERVATION MEASURES TAKEN The Red Wolf is listed as endangered on the United States List of Endangered and Threatened Wildlife and is therefore protected by law in all states of its present and former range. The Red Wolf Recovery Programme was established in October 1973 and has developed a conservation programme which involves public education, control of disease, maintenance of captive breeding stocks, and re-introduction into areas formerly occupied (1,3,7). A Red Wolf Recovery Team, an advisory board, was appointed in January 1975. The centre for the captive breeding group is Point Defiance Zoo, Tacoma, Washington. In 1980 a mated pair was sent from the centre to the Audubon Park and Zoological Garden, New Orleans, Louisiana and in autumn 1981 another mated pair will be sent to the Wild Canid Survival and Research Centre Wolf Sanctuary in St. Louis, Missouri (12). The first pups (13 in number) were born to the programme in 1977 (3). A pilot experiment to introduce the Red Wolf onto Bulls Island in the Cape Romain National Wildlife Refuge, South Carolina was successful (4). Re-establishment of the species within its historic range is being pursued. Both island and mainland sites are being considered; however mainland sites are preferred (2,3,4,5). The field recovery programme in Texas and Louisiana was concluded in September 1980 and the species was declared 'biologically' extinct in the wild. Programme emphasis has shifted to captive breeding and re-establishment (3,4,7).

CONSERVATION MEASURES PROPOSED Continuation of the established conservation programme.

CAPTIVE BREEDING In December 1980 the captive breeding programme held 58 animals, but not all of them have been certified as pure red wolves (12).

REMARKS For description of animal see (3,7). We are indebted to Curtis J. Carley who has extensively studied the Red Wolf and assisted in the compilation of this data sheet.

REFERENCES   1.   Carley, C.J. (1975). Activities and findings of the Red Wolf Field Recovery program from late 1973 to 1 July, 1975. U.S.F. & W. Report Pp. 215.
2.   Carley, C.J. (1979). Report and philosophy on Red Wolf translocations. In R. Lockwood (Ed.), Proc. of the 2nd symposium on endangered North American wildlife and habitat - June 1-5, 1977. The Wild Canid Survival and Research Center, Inc., St. Louis, Missouri, 76-80.
3.   Carley, C.J. (1979). Status summary: the Red Wolf (Canis rufus). U.S.F. & W. Endangered Species Report. No.7.
4.   Carley, C.J. (1979). Report on the successful translocation experiment of Red Wolves (Canis rufus) to Bulls Island, South Carolina. Paper presented at the Portland Wolf Symposium, Lewis and Clark College, Portland, Oregon, August, 13-17, 1979.
5.   Horan, J. (1977). Hope for the Red Wolf. Defenders 52(1): 16-19.
6.   McCarley, H. (1962). The taxonomic status of wild Canis (Canidae) in the south central United States. Southwestern Naturalist 7(3-4): 227-235.

7. McCarley, H. and Carley, C.J. (1979). Recent changes in distribution and status of Wild Red Wolves (Canis rufus). U.S.F. & W. Endangered Species Report No. 4.

8. Nowak, R. (1974). Red Wolf - our most endangered mammal. National Parks and Conservation Magazine 48(8): 9-12.

9. Paradiso, J. (1968). Canids recently collected in east Texas, with comments on the taxonomy of the Red Wolf. American Midland Naturalist. 80(2): 529-534.

10. Riley, G. and McBride, R. (1972). A survey of the Red Wolf (Canis rufus). Special Sci. Rep. Wildlife No. 162, USDI Washington, D.C.

11. USDI. (1973). Threatened Wildlife of the United States. Resource Publ. 14. USDI, Washington, D.C.

12. Carley, C.J. (1981). In litt.

Atelocynus microtis (Sclater, 1882)

Order   CARNIVORA   Family   CANIDAE

SUMMARY   A solitary, nocturnal and little known species with a sparse distribution in the Amazon and upper Orinoco river basins. Numbers and threats unknown but human disturbance may have a negative effect on its survival. Protected by law in Peru and Brazil. Distributional and ecological studies needed as the basis for a conservation plan, if required.

DISTRIBUTION   Amazon basin in Brazil, Peru, Ecuador and Colombia, thence into the upper Orinoco basin in Colombia and probably Venezuela (6,7). Carvalho states it is found only in the region between the Rios Madeira and Ucayali (3). Cabrera however, cites it from the entire region between the Rios Tapajos, Napo and Ucayali, and as far south as the Amazonian part of Mato Grosso and the Upper Parana Basin, also in the same state (3,7). The Peruvian range is usually given as that part of the Amazon region lying to the east of the Rios Napo and Ucayali (5). Grimwood found no record of its presence in northern Peru but saw specimens from the Rio Inuya (a tributary which joins the Rio Urubamba near its confluence with the Rio Apurimac), and from the Rio Curanja at approximately 71°50'W, 10°20'S (5). He was also reliably informed of its presence in the neighbourhood of Pucallpa, on the Rio Ucayali, and in the Manu Province of the Department of Madre de Dios (5). In 1981 David Macdonald, Chairman of the IUCN/SSC Canid Specialist Group received reports of additional records of this species from J. Patton (10): in 1968 six specimens were collected near the village of Balta on the Rio Curanja in southeastern Peru where the habitat is low tropical forest not subject to flooding. In thicker forest in northern Peru one was shot while killing chickens in an area of broken topography (between the Rio Santiago and Rio Cenepa) but this was believed to constitute poorer habitat for the species (9). In Ecuador this canid is known only from the area surrounding the foot of Mt. Sumaco in Napo Province; four records exist of which two are prior to 1941 (12). No detailed information has been located for its distribution in the rest of its range. For distribution maps see (1,7,14).

POPULATION   Numbers unknown. Peru: in 1969 reported as certainly very rare, with most inhabitants of the Amazon region unaware of its existence (5). However in 1981 Macdonald was informed by J. Patton that according to Indian lore Small-eared Dogs may not be so rare, but that their nocturnal and solitary habits made them very elusive (10). Hershkovitz reported similarly: 'the wild adult shuns man and cultivated areas and is rarely encountered by hunters' (6). Only four records are known from Ecuador, of which two were prior to 1941 (12). No information has been received from the rest of its range.

HABITAT AND ECOLOGY   Tropical forest ranging from near sea-level to an altitude of about 1000 m (7). Little is known of its life history and habits but its sleek pelage suggests that it has more than a casual aquatic habit, or else that it is specially adapted to regions of high rainfall (7). Food habits unknown (9), although a captive specimen at Brookfield Zoo, Chicago ate raw meat and occasionally the shoots of Kikuyo grass (Pennisetum clandestinum) (7). Said to be nocturnal and solitary (10). No information on breeding habits.

THREATS TO SURVIVAL   Unknown but possibly at risk from indirect influence of human intrusion throughout its range (9). Grimwood in 1968 reported that the skins of this species had no commercial value (a fact still true in 1981 (8)) although were occasionally bought as curiosities by fur dealers in Pucallpa (5).

CONSERVATION MEASURES TAKEN Protected by law in Peru and Brazil and is included in the Brazilian list of Endangered Species. Probably occurs in the Manu National Park in Peru (5) but is not found in any national park or reserve within its known range in Brazil (4). An IUCN/SSC Canid Specialist Group was established in 1980 and will be monitoring the status of this animal with a view to suggesting and implementing any appropriate conservation measures.

CONSERVATION MEASURES PROPOSED Legal protection in all countries of its range needed. Ecological and distributional studies to determine what conditions must be provided in parks and reserves to ensure its survival. Such a study would however be difficult given the sparse occurrence of this species in the wild.

CAPTIVE BREEDING In 1979 none were recorded in captivity (11). Brookfield Zoo, Chicago, at one time possessed three individuals but breeding was unsuccessful (13).

REMARKS For description of animal see (1,6,7,9,14,15). This is a monotypic genus.

REFERENCES   1. Bueler, L.E. (1973). Wild Dogs of the World. Constable, London.
2. Cabrera, A. (1957-1961). Catalogo de los mamiferos de America del Sur. Vols. I and II Revista del Museo Argentina de Ciencias Naturales 'Bernardino Rivadavia', Cienc. Zool., Buenos Aires.
3. Carvalho, C.T. (1957). Alguns mamiferos do Acre ocidental. Bol. Mus. Paraense E. Goeldi, N.S., Zool. 6: 1-22.
4. Coimbra-Filho, A.F. and Mittermeier, R.A. (1974). In litt.
5. Grimwood, I.R. (1969). Notes on the distribution and status of some Peruvian mammals, 1968. Special Pubn. No.21 American Committee for International Wild Life Protection and New York Zoological Society, New York. pp 86.
6. Hershkovitz, P. (1957). A synopsis of the wild dogs of Colombia. Novedades Colombianas Mus. Hist. Nat. Univ. del Cauca No.3: 157-161.
7. Hershkovitz, P. (1961). On the South American Small-eared Zorro: Atelocynus microtis Sclater (Canidae). Fieldiana: Zool. 39(44): 503-523.
8. IUCN Wildlife Trade Monitoring Unit. (1981). Pers. comm.
9. Langguth, A. (1975). Ecology and evolution in the South American Canids. In Fox, M.W. (Ed.), The Wild Canids. Their Systematics, Behavioural Ecology and Evolution. Van Nostrand Reinhold Co., New York.
10. Macdonald, D. (1981). In litt.
11. Olney, P.J.S. (Ed.) (1980). International Zoo Yearbook 20. Zool. Soc. London.
12. Ortiz-Crespo, F.I. (1981). In litt. Including information supplied by Prof. Gustavo Orces and Juan Black.
13. Rabb, G.B. (1979). In litt.
14. Stains, H.J. (1975). Distribution and taxonomy of the Canidae. In Fox, M.W. (Ed.), The Wild Canids. Their Systematics, Behavioural Ecology and Evolution. Van Nostrand Reinhold Co., New York.
15. Walker, E.P. (1975). Mammals of the World. The Johns Hopkins Univ. Press. Baltimore and London.

MANED WOLF   VULNERABLE

Chrysocyon brachyurus (Illiger, 1811)

Order   CARNIVORA   Family   CANIDAE

SUMMARY An inhabitant of grassland interspersed with open forest and swampy areas, mainly in Brazil but also reaching into neighbouring countries. Numbers unknown but the species is believed threatened by habitat loss and disturbance e.g. annual burning of grasslands to improve pasture, and by persecution because of its poultry stealing habits. Protected by law in Brazil and Argentina and occurs in a number of national parks and protected areas. Was the subject of an ecological study in Brazil by James Dietz from 1978-80 as the basis for recommending conservation measures. He suggests an educational campaign to promote awareness of the species threatened status, continued research to formulate specific conservation actions, coordination of captive breeding programmes, and increased documentation of its past and present distribution. An IUCN/SSC Canid Specialist Group was established in 1980 and will be suggesting and coordinating conservation action for this and other canids.

DISTRIBUTION Central and southeastern Brazil, from the State of Piaui as far as Rio Grande del Sul and Mato Grosso, extending into northeastern Argentina and the eastern extremity of Paraguay, and Bolivia in the savannas of the Departments of Beni and Santa Cruz (5,13,16,17,19,22,25). Within Argentina Schaller and Tarak, after a 22 day status survey in 1976, reported it to be confined to the northern part of the country, mainly in the Provinces of Formosa, Chaco and Corrientes, and perhaps a few penetrating into Santa Fe and the southwestern corner of Misiones (22). Macdonald who spent a month in Argentina in 1979 looking for the species believed that it had perhaps already disappeared from Corrientes (18); farmers in the vicinity of Esteros del Ibera said they had not seen any since the late 1960s (18). Macdonald found the greatest number of signs of wolf presence in the wet Chaco (confluence of the Paraguay and Parana rivers) where a small island (Isla del Cerrito) was reputedly optimal Maned Wolf habitat (18). The northern limit of its range appears to be the Parnaiba River in northern Brazil. Until the 19th century it also occurred south of the Rio de Plata in Argentina and in the interior of Uruguay (5).

POPULATION Total numbers unknown, but the species is believed to be declining because of habitat loss and disturbance, and persecution. Little detailed information is available and only the following brief comments have been located. Argentina: described in 1981 by the Director Nacional de Fauna Silvestre as vulnerable (12). Macdonald made no comment concerning status after his 1979 trip (18). In October 1976 Schaller and Tarak conducted a 22 day status survey of the Maned Wolf in Argentina. They drove through much of its range in Chaco, Formosa and Corrientes, interviewing various ranch owners, officials, farmhands and others, and whenever possible searched for spoor in marshes and grasslands (22). They found the species to be uncommon except in a small area of eastern Formosa and they made a guesstimate of possibly 1000-1500 in Argentina (22) and believed that its survival would depend upon protection afforded it on private ranches (22). Similarly in 1981 Tarak described the Maned Wolf as rare throughout Argentina being most numerous in Formosa (24). Brazil: Dietz who studied the species in Brazil from 1978-80 reported in 1979 that it existed at low density throughout much of the country and that when not molested could coexist with humans (9). He noted that the drier perimeter of the Pantanal region of Mato Grosso State seemed to harbour larger numbers than the swamplands of the interior Pantanal (9). In 1976 Schaller and Carvalho reviewed its status in Brazil and reported the species to be still widely distributed in Goias and Mato Grosso States and according to informants, to be often locally common (21). Also they were informed that good populations existed east of Paraiso do Norte in northern Goias, about 150 km north of Cuiabo in Mato Grosso, and on the higher ground bordering the northern Pantanal such as Fazenda Piquiri (21). They believed that the Maned Wolf was not yet endangered in Brazil but that its status would become increasingly vulnerable as its habitat was lost (21). The only estimate of numbers is a 1968 estimate by Silveira of 1500-2200 living in a total area of 650,000 sq. km, the main concentrations occurring in the central highlands and the Mato Grosso; 80-100 of these animals were believed to live in 125,600 sq. km round the towns of Luziania and Silvania and it was assumed that this population density was at least equalled in the other parts of the species' Brazilian range (8). However Coimbra-Filho and Mittermeier in 1974 considered 1500-2200 to be too low an estimate, having been based on a region already somewhat disturbed by man, so that densities were probably not quite as high as in less inhabited areas (6). They described Maned Wolves in Brazil as widely but sparsely distributed and to be fairly secure in the vast cerrados of the centre (6). Bolivia: in 1981 described as vulnerable (1). Peru: no data on status located but since its presence in Peru has only recently been documented it must presumably be very rare. Paraguay: no recent data; Meritt whilst investigating armadillos in Paraguay in 1974 noted that no reliable figures existed regarding numbers of Chrysocyon and that the species had a disjunct distribution. Despite several weeks spent in suitable habitat he did not observe any individuals, only several-day-old footprints (19). Mittermeier and Coimbra-Filho in 1974 thought it was fairly secure in the Chaco region (6).

HABITAT AND ECOLOGY   Savannas with open forest and swampy, marshy areas (15,17,21,22); avoids dense and continuous forest (22). The Maned Wolves in Dietz's study area in Brazil were monogamous but socially interacted very little with their partner except during the breeding season. Communication within and between pairs was accomplished by howling and by strategic deposition of scats and probably of urine. Each pair occupied a home range of about 25 sq. km in area, usually including a variety of vegetation types, and not overlapping with the ranges of neighbouring wolves (10,26). Diet consists of small prey such as birds, frogs, lizards, rodents, insects, eggs, armadillos, fruit and roots (8,10,11,15,16,17,19,21,22); domestic chickens are also taken (10). Nocturnal or crepuscular and very shy (6,10,15,26). Usually two young per litter (25), gestation period of 60-65 days (15), and in South America births occur from June to August (8,10,15,26). Dietz in his study area recorded litters of up to five pups but never more than two juveniles survived to leave their den sites, the reason was not discovered (10,26). Longevity is about 12-15 years (8). Kleiman found captive Maned Wolves to be rather timid and fearful in the presence of humans (15). Maned Wolves suffer from two serious disease problems: cystinuria, a hereditary disease, and infestation by giant kidney worms Dioctophyma renale (4,10,26). Six of eight individuals in Dietz's study area in Brazil tested positive for cystinuria (10,26).

THREATS TO SURVIVAL   Habitat loss and disturbance, and persecution as a chicken thief. In Brazil the main threat has been reported to be conversion of its habitat into fields (21), this has already happened west of Brasilia and around Goiania in Goias (although huge tracts still remain in the northern half of Goias and in central and southern Mato Grosso) (21). The annual burnings of the grassland to improve pasture (6,9) and capture of specimens for zoos (6) are also believed to constitute threats. Dietz believed that it was not known what effect large scale habitat modifications had on Maned wolves although he did mention that the annual burning did cause pup mortality (9). Within his study area the major cause of mortality was encounters between rural landowners and wolves which preyed on domestic chickens; 22 out of 25 wolves had died this way (26). Dietz felt that provided wolves were not persecuted they could survive well in areas of human habitation (9). In Argentina habitat modification has adversely affected the species by removing both cover and prey (22). Cattle ranching has had this effect, as has rice farming and draining of marshes (22). For Paraguay, Meritt cites disease as possibly the greatest detrimental force acting on wild populations (19). The species is neither hunted for its meat nor its fur (19,22). In Bolivia Bejarano reports it to be hunted by cattle farmers who accuse it of killing calves; also increased fencing of land limits its range (1).

CONSERVATION MEASURES TAKEN   Listed in Appendix 2 of the 1973 Convention on International Trade in Endangered Species of Wild Fauna and Flora, trade in it between acceding nations being therefore subject to regulation and monitoring of its effects. Protected by law in Argentina, (nevertheless Chaco promoted a hunt for this species, as well as for the protected Jaguar, Panthera onca, in 1975 (22)). Included on the Brazilian Endangered Species List, thus hunting, commercialization, transport, or export of this animal are prohibited by law (9). No information has been received concerning legal protection elsewhere. It occurs in a number of protected areas. In Argentina Tarak (1981) reported it to occur in the Parque Nacional Rio Pilcomayo in Formosa (24) although in 1975 this park was reported to be in a very bad state (22), and in Chaco National Park, but very rare in both (24). Given the Maned Wolf's propensity to travel widely and the fact that most land within its range is private property (22), there is no area large enough in Argentina to establish a park big enough to contain a viable population of Maned Wolves (22). The species survival in Argentina is thus dependent on the good will of private land owners, some of which (at least in 1975) already protected their wildlife (22). In Brazil it occurs in the national parks of Araguaia (6,21,22) and Tocantins (Goias) (6,16), Brasilia (Distrito Federal) (6,21,22), Emas (Goias, Matto Grosso) (6,21,22) and Serra da Canastra (Minas Gerais) (10,26). Also occurs in the Caracara Biological Reserve (6,21,22) and possibly in substantial numbers in Chapada dos Veadeiros Park (21). The species was the subject of an ecological study between 1978-80 by James Dietz in the Serra da Canastra National Park in Brazil (10,14,26). The objectives of the study were to identify major factors limiting population expansion, major problems associated with the species and to suggest solutions or necessary future studies to cope with these problems, and to evaluate necessary and essential criteria for the creation of a reserve for the species and its habitat (14). In 1980 an IUCN/SSC Canid Specialist Group was established to monitor the status of canids and to recommend and coordinate conservation measures.

CONSERVATION MEASURES PROPOSED   A species conservation plan is needed. For Argentina, Schaller states that its survival depends on protection afforded it on private ranches (22). The Caracara Biological Reserve (700 sq. km) in Brazil needs enlarging to include the higher ground outside the reserve -- an area which animals have to retreat to for the part of the year when the reserve is flooded (21). Dietz's two year study in Brazil resulted in the following recommendations: i) a campaign to educate the general public particularly in rural areas, about the threatened status of the Maned Wolf; ii) new research projects to collect the data necessary for the formulation of specific conservation - oriented programmes for this species; iii) documentation of the species distribution, both past and present; iv) coordination of captive breeding efforts (10,26).

CAPTIVE BREEDING   In 1979 at least 52 males and 50 females, 55 captive bred, were held in 30 zoo collections (20). Successful captive breeding is becoming more common (7). A possible serious threat facing specimens in zoological gardens is congenital cystinuria (4). Up to 1979 80% of zoo specimens tested were found positive for cystinuria (3).

REMARKS   For description of animal see (7,15,16,23,25). A monotypic genus. James Dietz very kindly supplied some of the information on which this data sheet it based, and David Macdonald, Chairman of the IUCN/SSC Canid Specialist Group commented on a draft in May 1981.

REFERENCES

1. Bejarano, G. (1981). In litt.
2. Brady, C.A. and Ditton, M.K. (1979). Management and breeding of Maned Wolves, Chrysocyon brachyurus at the National Zoological Park, Washington. Int. Zoo Yearb. 19: 171-176.
3. Bush, M. (1979). Pers. comm. to J. Dietz.
4. Bush, M. and Bovee, K.C. (1978). J. Amer. Vet. Med. Assn. 173 (9): 1159-1162.
5. Cabrera, A. (1957-1961). Catalogo de los mamiferos de America del Sur. Vols I and II. Rev. Mus. Argent. Cienc. Nat., 'Bernardino Rivadavia'. Cienc. Zool. 4(1) 1957: 1-307; 4(2) 1960: 309-732. Buenos Aires.
6. Coimbra-Filho, A.F. and Mittermeier, R.A. (1974). In litt.
7. Crotty, M.J. (1979). The Maned Wolf - South America's largest canine. Zoo View 13(3): 6-7.
8. Da Silveira, E.K.P. (1968). Notes on the care and breeding of the Maned wolf Chrysocyon brachyurus. Int. Zoo Yearb. 8: 21-23.
9. Dietz, J.M. (1979). In litt.
10. Dietz, J.M. (1980). Ecological studies of the Maned Wolf in the Serra da Canastra National Park, Minas Gerais State, Brazil, S.A. IUCN/WWF Project 1584. July 1978-June 1980. Final Report to IUCN/WWF.
11. Encke, W., Gandras, R. and Bieniek, H. (1970). Beobachtungen am Mahnenwolf (Chrysocyon brachyurus). Zool. Garten (NF) 38: 49-67.
12. Gonzalez Ruiz, E.O. (1981). In litt.
13. Hofmann, R.K., Ponce del Prado, C.F. and Otte, K.C. (1975-76). Revista Florestal del Peru. Vol. 6. (1-2). Ministerio de Agricultura, Lima.
14. IUCN/WWF Project 1584.
15. Kleiman, D.G. (1972). Social behaviour of the Maned Wolf (Chrysocyon brachyurus) and Bush Dog (Speothos venaticus): A study in contrast. J. Mammal. 53(4): 791-806.
16. Krieg, H. (1940-41). Im Lande des mahnenwolfes. Zool. Gart. 12: 257-269.
17. Langguth, A. (1975). Ecology and evolution in the South American Canids. In Fox, M.W. (Ed.), The Wild Canids. Their Systematics, Behavioural Ecology and Evolution. Van Nostrand Reinhold Company, New York. Pp. 192-206.
18. Macdonald, D. (1979-81). In litt.
19. Meritt, D.A. Jr. (1973). Some observations on the Maned Wolf, Chrysocyon brachyurus, in Paraguay. Zoologica (New York) 58: 53.
20. Olney, P.J.S. (Ed.) (1980). International Zoo Yearbook 20. Zool. Soc. London.
21. Schaller, G.B. and Carvalho de Vasconcelos, J.M. (1976). The status of some large mammals in Goias and Mato Grosso States of Brazil. Report to IBDF.
22. Schaller, G.B. and Tarak, A. (1976). The Maned Wolf in Argentina. Part 1 of a Report on a wildlife survey in northern Argentina and in the Emas National Park, Brazil. Unpd. Rep.
23. Stains, H.L. (1975). Distribution and taxonomy of the Canidae. In Fox, M.W. (Ed.), The Wild Canids. Their

Systematics, Behavioural Ecology and Evolution. Van Nostrand Reinhold Company, New York. Pp. 192-206.

24. Tarak, A. (1981). Pers. comm.
25. Walker, E.P. (1975). Mammals of the World. The Johns Hopkins Univ. Press, Baltimore and London.
26. WWF. (1980). The Wolf with the golden mane. WWF Project 1584. From a report by J.M. Dietz. WWF Monthly Report September 1980.

Speothos venaticus (Lund, 1842)

Order   CARNIVORA   Family   CANIDAE

SUMMARY   Occurs from eastern Panama to northern Argentina. Considered rare throughout its range, is absent from areas of human habitation and is possibly at risk as more and more forest is cleared and its range opened up. More information is required on distribution and ecological requirements before any sound conservation measures can be determined. An IUCN/SSC Canid Specialist Group was established in 1980 and will be suggesting and coordinating conservation action for this and other canids.

DISTRIBUTION   Eastern Panama south through Colombia and Ecuador to eastern Peru and northern Bolivia, and through Venezuela and the Guianas (Guyana, Suriname and French Guiana) to Brazil and northern Paraguay (1,9,11,13,19,20,22,26); recently discovered in northern Argentina (Misiones) (8). Within Ecuador it is found both west and east of the Andes in lowland rainforest. Prof. G. Orces is reported to have four records from the northern part of Manabi Province, one from the area north of the mouth of the Rio Santiago in Esmeraldas Province, and one from the 'Intag region'. A specimen obtained prior to 1933 came from San Jose de Sumaco in Napo Province (22). In Venezuela Mondolfi (1976) reports it to occur in the State of Amazonas (Rio Negro and Upper Rio Orinoco), in the State of Bolivar (la Gran Sabana), and in the Cordillera de la Costa (San Esteban, State of Carabobo, and El Guapo, State of Miranda) (20). For maps see (4,17). Cabrera mentions three subspecies (5): S. v. venaticus from the Guianas, north and central Brazil as far as the Mato Grosso, northeast Peru, Ecuador, eastern Bolivia and northern Paraguay; S. v. wingei from southeast Brazil; and S. v. panamensis from eastern Panama and probably northern Colombia (5). (Venezuela is not mentioned.) For map see (4,17).

POPULATION   A naturally rare species which appears to be adversely affected by forest clearance; total numbers unknown. Information on its status is extremely scanty; only the following brief comments have been located. Panama: reported in 1978 as in imminent danger of extinction (28). Peru and Colombia: said to have never been abundant (the native people have no name for it) and to have now entirely disappeared from areas of human habitation (I.R. Grimwood, 1967, In litt., 1,11). Bolivia: Bejarano in 1981 reported it to be rare, and becoming scarcer as more and more forest is destroyed (3). Ecuador: reported in 1981 to be 'rare everywhere' (22). Venezuela: described in 1976 as rare and threatened by habitat loss, and killed when encountered (20). Suriname: in 1979 reported to occur in all the interior forests and not considered endangered (H. Reichart, 1979. In litt.). French Guiana: rare in inhabited areas and generally only found in the interior forests (18). Brazil: widely but sparsely distributed, numbers unknown but thought probably to be fairly stable, except where habitat destruction is rampant (7). Best and Ayres in 1981 described it as threatened, principally by deforestation and agricultural practises (2). Argentina: described by the Director Nacional de Fauna Silvestre in 1981 as vulnerable (10). No data received concerning status in Guyana and Paraguay.

HABITAT AND ECOLOGY   Llanguth has reviewed the literature on this species and concludes that Speothos is primarily a forest dweller which also visits open country at the forest edge and is generally found close to watercourses (9,17,19,24). It is semi-aquatic and an excellent swimmer (1,17,25) and Tate reported that it was able to follow Pacas (Dasyprocta sp.) into the water and kill them there (27); and in 1977 two young males were reported captured whilst crossing the Rio Negro near Sao Gabriel da Cachoeira (2). Diet includes large rodents, birds and other small prey (16). Two held in captivity at the Lincoln Park Zoo, Chicago were observed to 'delight in attacking and eating live pigeons, chicks, rats and mice' (14). Kleiman describes it as a highly social species (2), and Hershkovitz (1957) mentions second-hand reports of it hunting in packs of up to 10-12 individuals and pursuing game as large as deer (12); Tate (1931) received reports from western Ecuador that Bush dogs hunt in packs of about 6 and that their principal prey was Paca (27). However Vanzolini, Director of the Museu de Zoologia of the Universidad de Sao Paulo states that he has never heard of this species hunting in packs and that on the contrary, it seems to be shy and solitary (29). Reported to be nocturnal (29), and Best and Ayres mention that it breeds in a burrow which is usually located under a fallen tree, or in the roots of a large tree (2). Gestation period is not precisely known; a pair at Lincoln Park Zoo produced a litter of three pups by Caesarian section 76 days from the last observed mating, 83 days from the first observed mating and even so the pups seem to have been born prematurely (14). It is perhaps unique among wild canids in having two oestrous cycles per year (15,16).

THREATS TO SURVIVAL   Like most other Amazon species it is adversely affected by habitat destruction (2,3,20). Although it is not especially hunted or sought as a pet (7), it is reported to be killed if encountered by hunters (7,20) and sometimes the pups are killed by hunter's dogs which enter the burrow (2). It is occasionally kept as a pet (1,7).

CONSERVATION MEASURES TAKEN   Listed in Appendix 1 of the 1973 Convention on International Trade in Endangered Species of Wild Fauna and Flora, trade in it or its products is therefore subject to strict regulation by ratifying nations, and trade for primarily commercial purposes is banned. Protected by law in Peru, and Brazil where it is on the Endangered Species List (7). Not protected by law in French Guiana (18). No information has been received concerning legal protection elsewhere in its range. In Brazil it occurs in the following national parks: Araguia and Tocantins (Goias), Brasilia (Distrito Federal), Emas (Goias and Mato Grosso), and Iguacu, and also in the Cara-Cara Biological Reserve (Mato Grosso) (7,23). In Peru it may occur in the Manu National Park (11). No field studies have yet been conducted, or specific conservation measures enacted. An IUCN/SSC Canid Specialist Group was established in 1980 to monitor the status of this and other canids and to suggest and assist implementation of appropriate conservation measures where required.

CONSERVATION MEASURES PROPOSED   Legal protection in all countries of its range is suggested plus ecological studies to determine what conditions must be provided in parks and reserves to ensure its survival (although such a study would be very difficult in view of its scarcity). More knowledge on its distribution would also be useful.

CAPTIVE BREEDING   In 1979 15 males and 8 females were held in 5 zoo collections (18 captive bred) (21). The Frankfurt Zoo has succeeded in breeding the species to the third generation. It is thought that the male needs to be present to assist in rearing the pups (6). Appears to be quite tame in captivity (1,14). A studbook of the species is maintained by Dr Peter Röben, Zoologisches Institut I der Universität Heidelberg, 6900 Heidelberg 1, im Neuenheimer Feld 230, W. Germany (21).

REMARKS   For description of animal see (4,12,13,16,26,30). A monotypic genus.

REFERENCES   1.   Bates, M. (1944). Notes on a captive Icticyon. J. Mammal. 25: 152-154.

2. Best, R. and Ayres, M. (1981). In litt.
3. Bejarano, G. (1981). In litt.
4. Bueler, L. (1973). Wild dogs of the world. Constable, London.
5. Cabrera, A. (1957-1961). Catalogo de los mamiferos de America del Sur. Vols. I and II Rev. Mus. Argent. Cienc. Nat., 'Bernardino Rivadavia'. Cienc. Zool. Buenos Aires.
6. Camp, V. (1976). Bushdog pair moves to Oklahoma City Zoo. Zoo Sounds 12(4):8.
7. Coimbra-Filho, A.F. and Mittermeier, R.A. (1974). In litt.
8. Crespo, J.A. (1974). Incorporacion de un genero de canidos a la fauna de Argentina. Com. Mus. Arg. de Cienc. Nat. Zoologica. 4:37-39.
9. Goldman, E.A. (1920). Mammals of Panama. Smith. Misc. Coll. 69(5): 1-309.
10. Gonzales Ruiz, E.O. (1981). In litt.
11. Grimwood, I.R. (1969). Notes on the distribution and status of some Peruvian mammals, 1968. Special Pubn. No.21 American Committee for International Wild Life Protection and New York Zoological Society, New York. pp 86.
12. Hershkovitz, P. (1957). A synopsis of the wild dogs of Colombia. Novedades Colombianas Mus. Hist. Nat. Univ. del Cauca No.3: 157-161.
13. Husson, A.M. (1978). The Mammals of Suriname. E.J. Brill, Leiden.
14. Kitchener, S.L. (1971). Observations on the breeding of the Bush Dog at Lincoln Park Zoo, Chicago. Int. Zoo Yb. 11: 99-101.
15. Kleiman, D. (1968). Reproduction in the Canidae. Int. Zoo Yb. 8: 3-8.
16. Kleiman, D.G. (1972). Social behaviour of the Maned Wolf (Chrysocyon brachyurus) and Bush Dog (Speothos venaticus): A study in contrast. J. Mammal. 53(4): 791-806.
17. Langguth, A. (1975). Ecology and evolution in the South American canids. In Fox, M.W. (Ed.), The Wild Canids. Their Systematics, Behavioural Ecology and Evolution. Van Nostrand Reinhold Co., New York.
18. Leclerc, J. (1976). In litt.
19. Linares, O.J. (1967). El perro de monte Speothos venaticus (Lund) en el norte de Venezuela (Canidae). Sociedad de Ciencias naturales "La Salle", Caracas Memoria 27: 83-86.
20. Mondolfi, E. (1976). Fauna silvestre de los bosques humedos de Venezuela. Assoc. Nacional para la defensa de la naturaleza.
21. Olney, P.J.S. (Ed.) (1980). International Zoo Yearbook 20. Zool. Soc. London.
22. Ortiz-Crespo, F.I. (1981). In litt. Including information from Prof. Gustavo Orces and Juan Black.
23. Padua, M.T.J., Magnanini, A. and Mittermeier, R.A. (1974). Brazil's National Parks. Oryx 12(4): 452-464.
24. Sanderson, I.T. (1949). A brief review of the mammals of Suriname (Dutch Guiana), based upon a collection made in 1938. Proc. Zool. Soc. London 119: 755-789.
25. Santos, E. (1945). Entre o Gamba e o Macaco, vida e costumes dos maniferos do Brasil, Briguiet, Rio de Janeiro.
26. Stains, H.J. (1975). Distribution and taxonomy of the Canidae. In Fox, M.W. (Ed.), The Wild Canids. Their Systematics, Behavioural Ecology and Evolution. Van

Nostrand Reinhold Co., New York.
27. Tate, G.H.H. (1931). Random observations on habits of South American mammals. J. Mammal. 12: 248-256.
28. Vallester, E. (1978). Informe de Panama sobre la situacion de la Fauna Silvestre. In Morales, R., Macfarland, C., Incer, J. and Hobbs, A. (Eds), Memorias de la Primera Reunion Regional Centroamerican sobre Via Silvestre. Matagalpa, Nicaragua 25-29 Julio 1978. Unidad de areas silvestres y cuencas del catie.
29. Vanzolini, P.E. (1977). In litt.
30. Walker, E.P. (1975). Mammals of the World. The Johns Hopkins Univ. Press, Baltimore and London.

SPECTACLED BEAR   VULNERABLE

Tremarctos ornatus (F. Cuvier, 1825)

Order   CARNIVORA   Family   URSIDAE

SUMMARY   The only bear native to South America, this species ranges from
western Venezuela to Bolivia. Declining throughout much of its range because of
habitat loss to agriculture as settlers invade once remote areas. Adapts readily to
feeding on farm crops and livestock as its natural foods disappear, thus bringing it
into conflict with farmers. Peyton studied the species in northern Peru from
1977-79 and an Ad hoc Spectacled Bear Group was formed in February 1980 which
aims to suggest and coordinate conservation measures. These will undoubtedly
include surveys to learn more of the bears distribution and the status of
populations, enforcement of game laws, and protection in large national parks and
reserves.

DISTRIBUTION   Western Venezuela, Colombia, Ecuador, Peru and Bolivia
(6,9,13,14,24,31). Small numbers may also exist in Panama (4,16), Brazil, and
Argentina (4), but confirmation needed. Northern Chile was said to be the type
locality but this is now believed unlikely (9). Hershkovitz (1957) gives its range as
extending from the Pacific slopes of the Andes in the west to the Amazonian and
Orinocoan slopes in the east; from the Caribbean and Lake Maracaibo drainages in
the north to southern Peru and southwestern Bolivia in the south. He also
mentions them occurring in the Cordillera Macarena, a low, isolated mountain
range east of the Colombian Cordillera Oriental (16). Peyton who studied the
species in Peru from 1977 to 1979 found it occurred in all three ranges of the
Andes, with the majority located between 1825-3320 m on the eastern slope of the
Cordillera Oriental, and above 1750 m in the Vilcabamba Range (25,27). For maps
see (25,27). From Ecuador there is a specimen record prior to 1941 from Calacali
on the western side of Mt. Pichincha, and footprints were still commonly seen
there in the early 1960s. However more recent records are from areas such as
Pinan west of Mt. Cotacachi, and 'Intag' southwest of this volcano in the western
Andes, and from the east side of Mt. Antisana (sight records in 1980 and 1981),
the east side of Mt. Cotopaxi, the eastern Andes at Pillaro and from the
neighbourhood of Amaluza in Azuay Province (21). Venezuela: occurs in the Andes
in the Cordillera de Merida and in the Sierra de Perija on the border with
Colombia (28). No detailed information on distribution elsewhere has been
located.

POPULATION   Total numbers unknown, and very little detailed information
available. A status survey throughout its range was conducted by Erickson in
1966, based on a literature review, contact with government officials, scientists,
and others familiar with South American wildlife, and two two-month field trips.
He found that the status of the bear varied in each of the five countries it was
definitely known to inhabit (details below) (12). Venezuela: Pedro J. Salinas of the
Universidad de Los Andes, Merida, Venezuela reported in 1981 that no more than
100 bears occur in the country (28). Erickson's comments were that the bear was
quite rare and probably always had been (12). For Colombia Jorgenson in 1981
reported that Tremarctos was now mainly confined to isolated patches of
mountainous forest and paramo (18); Erickson noted that the evidence indicated
that its distribution and abundance was markedly reduced from former times (12).
Ecuador: in 1981 described as still common in remote and inaccessible areas but
very intolerant of human activity and usually shot by peasants whenever
encountered. Orces (1981) believes it will survive in Ecuador 'for a long time'
because it inhabits the extremely rugged and inaccessible areas of the eastern

'Ceja de Montana' which is devoid of permanent human habitation (21). Erickson reported that its status seemed 'very good' with near pristine populations remaining throughout the country. Agricultural activities had encroached on the bear's range along the entire valley separating the east and west ranges, but it was considered unlikely to have appreciably affected numbers (12). Bolivia: in 1981 described by Professor Bejarano as vulnerable (7). Peyton reporting in the Ad hoc Spectacled Bear Newsletter of July 1981 noted that he had been informed that outside of the Ulla Ulla Reserve which still harbours bears, the 'best' populations occur due east of Lake Titicaca and in the Province of Cochabamba (5). However, in 1981 Hansen-Love noted that it had nearly completely disappeared from the area near Cochabamba (15). Erickson reported that a brief survey indicated that its status was 'quite good' though not as good as in Ecuador (12). Peru: Erickson noted that major reductions in distribution were apparent. However the species still had an extensive range, the 'best' residual populations being found in the southeast (12). However Peyton who conducted a two year (1977-79) survey of the species in northern Peru, which included hundreds of interviews with knowledgeable hunters and local farmers and 54 field trips to areas ranging in altitutde from 200 m to over 5200 m, reported the bear to have almost disappeared from the low subtropical desert, to be endangered on the peaks of the Occidental Andes, and to be rare but more secure in the Oriental Range (24,27). A major decline had occurred in the Occidental range along the Pampas, Apurimac, and Santo Thomas rivers where in the late 1950s hunters found the bear to be much more abundant (24). Based on his studies Peyton estimated about 850 bears in northern Peru (i.e. north of 10°30'S) (24); his estimate for the whole country was 2000-2400, based on sign observations and area and hunter reports (26). In 1968 Grimwood estimated 800-2000 for the total Peruvian population (14), however he was not able to get into such remote areas as Peyton and therefore the survey was not as extensive. Peyton found 'good' populations in remote areas, and existing in seemingly higher densities than was previously suspected, particularly in the humid forest and dry subtropical forest (26).

HABITAT AND ECOLOGY Adapted to a broad spectrum of habitat types: from near desert cactus and other plant associations at 200 m through dry-deciduous, rain, and cloud forests to treeless alpine-like associations exceeding 4000 m (6,8,12,14,16,21,25,27,30). In Peru, Peyton noted the best bear habitat to be the humid forest between 1800-2700 m with an annual precipitation of 1800-3000 mm (27). Tremarctos is primarily a vegetarian (22,23,24,25,27,30); Peyton lists 83 foods that were confirmed as eaten by Spectacled Bears, these included insects, rodents, livestock, corn, berries, tree wood, bamboo hearts, palm frond petioles, 22 species of Bromeliaceae, 11 species of Cactaceae, and the fruits of 31 species of tree (25). Litter size varies from one to three cubs and the mother remains with them in the den for several months (24). In Peru females were reported to give birth during the months of the heaviest rainfall, the cubs first 3-4 months then coinciding with the season of fruit abundance, this varying with altitude and slope aspect, and with yearly fluctuations in the weather pattern (25).

THREATS TO SURVIVAL Major threat is, and has been, habitat loss due to the rise in human numbers, the spread of agriculture, and the development of road systems, combined with the lack of effective conservation practices. The bear is also hunted for sport, as an alleged killer of livestock, and as a raider of cornfields (5,12,14,24,25,27). In Peru, overgrazing, agriculture and uncontrolled lumbering has endangered the species in all parts of the Andes except for the most remote areas of the eastern range (5,24); whilst hunting, although not the major factor in its decline, is responsible for its disappearance in the scrub desert and humid forests where highest densities were attained in the past (24). In 1977 Mittermeier et al reported that skins were sold in Peru for approx. US$15.00 each, and bear grease for US$7.50 per litre. Bear meat was highly esteemed and usually eaten by the hunter's family (19). Similarly the meat is eaten in Ecuador and the skin kept as a trophy (21). In Peru, large oil reserves have been found in the Madre de Dios basin and along the Ecuadorian border east of the Cordillera Central and Oriental and has meant the opening up of once remote areas as supplies, men, and forest clearing equipment has been flown in by helicopter e.g. to such areas as the Rio Las Piedras in the heartland of Manu National Park, Peru (5).

CONSERVATION MEASURES TAKEN Listed in Appendix 1 of the 1973 Convention on International Trade in Endangered Species of Wild Fauna and Flora, trade in it or its products therefore being subject to strict regulation by ratifying nations, and trade for primarily commercial purposes banned. Protected by law in Peru (24) and Colombia (1,5). In Peru it occurs in Manu National Park (5,11,14) but the highlands of this park are full of livestock and important bear food such as Ericaceae spp. are becoming increasingly scarce. In addition there is much corn depredation in the valleys of the Rio Paucartambo and Rio Queros and this has attracted bear hunters (5,27). The species also exists in Huascaran National Park (5,11,24,25,27) although this has marginal bear habitat and probably no permanent resident populations; in fact the bears are reported to use the park only during the rainy season (November-February) and permanently reside north of the park in the valley of the Rio Quitarascu and Cerro Alpamayo; also the important bear foods of this alpine area (Bromeliacea shinus molle, and orchid bulbs) are burned by goat herders to improve pasture (5,27). Tremarctos also resides in the parks of Tingo Maria and Cutervo, established 1963 and 1965 respectively, but these have yet (1981) to have their boundaries delineated, have no funding and few forestry police (5). Plans do exist to enlarge these parks but human settlements and activities have surrounded them and are encroaching rapidly (5). Bears also exist in the National Historical Sanctuary of Machu Picchu established 1980, but they inhabit less then 30,000 ha of its 50,500 ha area and the park is surrounded by land intensively farmed and burned annually. The park probably acts as a corridor for bear populations moving between the dry subtropical forest along the Apurimac, Santo Thomas, and Pampas rivers and the Ceja de Selva of the Cordillera Oriental (5). In Bolivia it occurs in the Ulla Ulla Reserve (2,5), and in Ecuador in the Sangay Park (3,5). In Colombia, Purace and Macarena National Parks comprise some of the best paramo and humid forest habitat for Tremarctos, but both are overrun by guerilla activity (5). Bears are also believed to inhabit the National Parks of Sierra Nevada de Santa Marta, Tama, El Cocuy, Las Orquideas, Sumapaz, Chingaza, Nevado del Huila, Munchique, Farallones and the Muscopan and Rio Piendamo areas (5). Erickson conducted a status survey in 1966 (12), and Peyton initiated studies in Peru in 1977 which are ongoing (24,25,27). Several studies planned for Colombia have never started or have had to be terminated prematurely because of logistic difficulties (5,18,29). At the 5th Bear Biology Association Conference in February 1980 an Ad Hoc Spectacled Bear Group (SBG) was formed and held its first meeting on February 12th 1980 in Madison, Wisconsin, U.S.A. The participants discussed the known status of T. ornatus and outlined topics of concern (4). By July 1981 they had published two newsletters (4,5), and in February 1981 the SBG became a recognised subgroup of the IUCN/SSC Bear Specialist Group (5).

CONSERVATION MEASURES PROPOSED Survival will depend on adequate protection in large national parks and reserves. Studies to determine the total extent of the bear's range and more about its behaviour and ecology are also needed. The IUCN/SSC Bear Specialist Group in 1981 recognised the following priority projects with respect to the Spectacled Bear (5): i) a survey throughout its range (essentially a follow up to Erickson's 1966 study); ii) a study in Venezuela, for which in May 1981 plans were progressing (5,26); and iii) a study in Peru of home ranges (5). The latter was originally planned for the valley of Quillabamba on the northeast boundary of the Historical Sanctuary of Machu Picchu, Dept. of Cuzco, by Peyton and Peruvian scientists. However early in 1981 logistic difficulties became so great that the study area has been changed to the Cordillera de Yanachaga near Oxapampa and Villa Rica; it is hoped the project will begin in 1982 and run for three years (5). For Peru, Peyton suggests that the national parks of Cutervo and Tingo Maria should have their boundaries delineated as soon as possible; that Huascaran Park should be extended to include Cerro Champara which contains a greater population of bears and Taruca (<u>Hippocamelus antisensis</u>) another threatened species, than found in the park; and that in the desert where the bears are in immediate danger of extinction, special attention should be given to enforcing forestry laws, controlling grazing practises, and protecting endangered watersheds (24). He adds that most of the bear inhabited territory in the parks is too small to preserve Spectacled Bears effectively. Furthermore the parks are surrounded by unsuitable habitat, or land in human usage. For instance cornfields are established right up to park boundaries, lumber is cut, cattle are sent into the parks to graze and firewood taken out. Although Spectacled Bears are adaptable in their habits and will readily eat crops, as natural foods become scarcer this inevitably leads to increased conflict between humans and bears. Peyton therefore believes buffer zones with controlled human usage should be established around the parks (26,27).

<u>CAPTIVE BREEDING</u> Captive propagation has occcurred in only a handful of zoos (10). In 1979 36 males, 42 females, and 4 unsexed animals were held in 31 zoological collections, 35 captive bred (20).

<u>REMARKS</u> For description of animal see (6,10,31).

<u>REFERENCES</u>   1.   Anon. (1974). New protective legislation around the world - Colombia. <u>Oryx</u> 12(4): 413.
2.   Anon. (1975). New measures in Bolivia. <u>Oryx</u> 13(1): 11.
3.   Anon. (1980). New parks in Ecuador. <u>Oryx</u> 15(3): 226.
4.   Ad Hoc Spectacled Bear Group Newsletter No.1 1980.
5.   Ad Hoc Spectacled Bear Group Newsletter No.2. July 1981.
6.   Allen, G.M. (1942). <u>Extinct and Vanishing Mammals of the Western Hemisphere.</u> Amer. Comm. for Int. Wild Life Protection. Special Publ. No.11.
7.   Bejarano, G. (1981). In litt.
8.   Brack Egg, A. (1961). El oso de anteojos. <u>Biota</u> 3: 345-350.
9.   Cabrera, A. (1957-1961). Catalogo de los mamiferos de America del Sur. <u>Rev. del Mus. Argent. de Cienc. Nat. 'Bernardino Rivadavia', Cienc. Zool.</u> 4(1,2): 1-731.
10. Crotty, M.J. (1977). The mysterious bear of the Andes. <u>Zoo News</u> 11(4): 7.
11. Dourojeanni, M.J. (1981). In litt.
12. Erickson, A.W. (1967). Spectacled Bear - Status survey in South America. In <u>The Ark Underway</u>: 2nd report of the World Wildlife Fund.
13. Festa, E. (1905). Osservazioni intorno agli Orsi Dell' Ecuador. <u>Academia Reale della Scienze di Torino</u> :3-12.
14. Grimwood, I.R. (1969). <u>Notes on the distribution and status of some Peruvian mammals, 1968</u>. Special Pubn. No.21 American Committee for International Wild Life Protection and New York Zoological Society, New York.
15. Hansen-Love, A. (1981). In litt.
16. Hershkovitz, P. (1957). On the possible occurrence of the Spectacled Bear, <u>Tremarctos ornatus</u> (F. Curvier, 1825), in Panama. <u>Säugetierk. Mitt.</u> 5: 122-123.
17. IUCN/SSC Bear Specialist Group. (1980). Report to the 53rd IUCN/SSC meeting, Kenya, April 1980.
18. Jorgenson, J. (1981). In litt.

19. Mittermeier, R.A., Macedo Ruiz, H. de, Luscombe, A. and Cassidy, J. (1977). Rediscovery and conservation of the Peruvian Yellow-tailed Woolly Monkey (Lagothrix flavicauda). In Prince Rainier and Bourne, G. (Eds). Primate Conservation. Academic Press, New York.

20. Olney, P.J.S. (Ed.) (1980). International Zoo Yearbook 20. Zool. Soc. London.

21. Ortiz-Crespo, F.I. (1981). In litt. incorporating information from Professor Gustavo Orces and Juan Black.

22. Osgood, W.H. (1912). Mammals from western Venezuela and eastern Colombia. Field Mus. Nat. Hist. Publ. (Chicago) 155 Vol.X (5): 33-66.

23. Osgood, W.H. (1914). Mammals of an expedition across northern Peru. Field Mus. Nat. Hist. Publ. (Chicago) 176 Vol.X (12): 143-185.

24. Peyton, B. (1979). Spectacled Bear status in northern Peru. Unpd. Report.

25. Peyton, B. (1980). Ecology, distribution, and food habits of Spectacled Bears, Tremarctos ornatus, in Peru. J. Mammal. 61(4): 639-652.

26. Peyton, B. (1981). In litt.

27. Peyton, B. (1981). Spectacled Bears in Peru. Oryx 16(1): 48-56.

28. Salinas, P.J. (1981). In litt.

29. Sanner, C.J. (1980). In litt.

30. Tate, G.H.H. (1931). Random observations of habits of South American mammals. J. Mammal. 12 (3): 248-256.

31. Thomas, O. (1902). On the bear of Ecuador. The Annals and Mag. Nat. Hist. Ser. 7 Vol. 9: 215-217.

NOTE: In the past many, many subspecies of Grizzly Bear were described from North America. For example the most commonly used Guide to North American Mammals, published in 1959, lists over 80 subspecies. Some of these subspecies were listed in previous editions of the Red Data Book e.g. the Mexican Grizzly Bear and the Barren Ground Grizzly Bear. However recent classifications (9) have placed all North American Grizzly bears and all Eurasian Brown bears in the single species, Ursus arctos, and in North America, with the exception of the Kodiak Bear (Ursus arctos middendorfi), all populations have been included in the subspecies U. a. horribilis. However the taxonomy of the species is again under review and it may be that additional subspecies will be recognised. Such a confusing taxonomic picture is difficult to accommodate within the usual Red Data Book structure which generally lists species or subspecies. The IUCN/SSC Bear Specialist Group has recommended that the species as a whole be included in the Red Data Book. The Group reports that numerous isolated and semi-isolated 'subpopulations' exist; such geographic subpopulations are often somewhat reproductively isolated and genetically distinct as well, even though they may not currently be granted subspecific status. However they are distinct entities and some are in danger of extinction. The high level of conflict between this species and humans for space and resources means that many, if not all, of these subpopulations must be managed. The Red Data Book and the Specialist Group are thus gathering data on the distribution and status of Ursus arctos throughout its range and this will appear in subsequent editions of the Red Data Book. In the meantime only information relating to the Mexican Grizzly is given below. Hall and Kelson (6) named this animal U. a. nelsoni although the existing classification would include it in the subspecies U. a. horribilis.

MEXICAN GRIZZLY BEAR   ENDANGERED

Ursus arctos nelsoni (Merriam, 1914)

Order   CARNIVORA   Family   URSIDAE

SUMMARY Probably extinct. Last definite record was in Mexico in the early 1960s; rumours of its continued existence have persisted but are all unverified. Declined because of relentless persecution as a threat to livestock and humans. If any population is found it should be given immediate effective protection.

DISTRIBUTION Mexico; no existing populations are known. U. a. nelsoni formerly ranged through Arizona and New Mexico, U.S.A. (where extinct by the 1920s/1930s), to Mexico - in Baja California, northeastern Sonora, most of Chihuahua and Coahuila, and south to northern Durango (3,5,6). By the 1960s it was known to exist only in the State of Chihuahua in the isolated 'mountain islands' of the Cerro Compana, Santa Clara, and Sierra del Nido about 80 km north of Chihuahua City (2,4,5).

POPULATION Probably extinct. A brief survey in 1975 in the Sierra del Nido area, where rumours of Grizzlies were strong, failed to find any evidence of them (5). The 1971 report of a remnant population on a cattle ranch in the upper Yaqui basin of Sonora has never been verified (5). Surveys from 1957-61 estimated that possibly 30 survived in the Sierra del Nida and adjoining Sierra Santa Clara and Cerro Campana, although the accuracy of this figure was in doubt (2,3,4,5). In 1961 a rancher in the area lost 16 head of cattle to an alleged Grizzly and began an all out campaign against them, using guns, traps and 1080 poison. The poison was used heavily in the winters of 1961-62 and 1963-64, and probably destroyed the last of the Mexican Grizzlies (2,4,5). A three month survey in 1968 by Dr. Carl Koford found no evidence that Grizzlies had survived after 1962, and concluded that the Mexican Grizzly was extinct, (2,5, C. Koford 1971, In litt.). Extensive studies by Fauna Silvestre and the University of Montana in 1977-79 failed to produce positive evidence that the Mexican Grizzly survives, but circumstantial evidence was found (7,8).

HABITAT AND ECOLOGY Leopold reports the preferred habitat to have been brush-covered foothills rather than the high, forested mountains. All the early reports he quotes mention Grizzlies in the scrub-oak belt or along the lower (xeric) fringe of the pine forest (3). The Sierra del Nido range consists of semi-desert plateau at 1500 m rising through grasslands and oak woodland to pine forest at approximately 3000 m (2). Diet was omnivorous, including acorns, walnuts, pinons (the fruit of Pinus edulis), manzanillas, carrion, insects, honey, all kinds of fruits and berries, ground squirrels and other rodents, and occasionally livestock and such big game as they could catch. Adults were usually solitary; first mating was believed to be at 4 or 5 years old and thereafter the female gave birth to young only every second or third year. A litter consisted usually of 1 or 2 cubs, rarely of triplets (3).

THREATS TO SURVIVAL Was relentlessly persecuted as a threat to livestock and humans, and for sport (2,5). Koford reported that it appeared that from the 1930s the remnant population in central Chihuahua diminished rapidly because of shooting by loggers, miners, ranchmen, and Mexican and American sportsmen (2,5). In 1981 Jonkel reported that there was now less pressure from the ranchers, but that if the animal still survived, numbers might be too low for recovery (7).

CONSERVATION MEASURES TAKEN The Mexican Grizzly Bear is listed in Appendix 1 of the 1973 Convention on International Trade in Endangered Species of Wild Fauna and Flora, trade in it or its products therefore being subject to strict regulation by ratifying nations, and trade for primarily commercial purposes banned. In 1959 Mexico officially placed the Grizzly Bear on the list of protected mammals (1,5), followed in 1960 by an even more formal presidential proclamation of protection (5). However regulations were not enforced (1), and according to Johnson, the protection never extended to the mountains and thus in practice never really existed (5).

CONSERVATION MEASURES PROPOSED If a population of this animal should be found to survive, it must be given immediate, effective protection from killing, and its habitat declared a reserve with adequate guards.

CAPTIVE BREEDING No Mexican Grizzlies occur in captivity.

REMARKS For a description of this animal see (3,6).

REFERENCES 1. McTaggart Cowan, I. (1964). Threatened species of mammals in North America. In Moore, J.A. (Ed.), Proceedings 16th International Congress of Zoology 8: The protection of vanishing species 17-21. Washington: 16th International Congress of Zoology.
2. Koford, C.B. (1969). The last of the Mexican Grizzly Bear. IUCN Bulletin 2 (12): 94.
3. Leopold, A.S. (1959). Wildlife of Mexico: the game birds and mammals. Univ. California Press, Berkeley.
4. Leopold, A.S. (1967). Grizzlies of the Sierra del Nido. Pacific Discovery 20 (5): 30-32.
5. Johnson, A.S. (1975). Donde Esta el Oso Plateado: Search

for the Mexican Grizzly. <u>Defenders of Wildlife</u> 50 (3): 242-245 and 50 (5): 436-439.

6. Hall, E.R. and Kelson, K.R. (1959). <u>The Mammals of North America</u>. The Ronald Press Co., New York.

7. Jonkel, C., Kisen, S., Rockwell, D., Dominguey, P. (1977). Status of the Mexican Grizzly. Univ. of Montana BGP Spec. Report No. 6.

8. Lee, L.C. and Thier, T.J. (1979). Mexican Grizzly Bear studies. Univ. of Montana BGP Spec. Report No. 32.

9. Rausch, R.L. (1963). Geographic variation in size in North American Brown bears <u>Ursus</u> <u>arctos</u> L., as indicated by condylobasal length. <u>Can. J. Zool.</u> 41: 33-45.

POLAR BEAR   VULNERABLE

Ursus maritimus (Phipps, 1774)

Order   CARNIVORA   Family   URSIDAE

SUMMARY Circumpolar distribution in the Arctic in association with the sea ice in coastal regions. World population in 1981 thought to be about 20,000 or more. Population declines could result from over-hunting or environmental degradation associated wth non-renewable resource exploration e.g. for oil. Recovery of populations would be slow because of the low reproductive rate. Polar bears are protected under an International Agreement which restricts hunting and requires research on the species and its environment. The main conservation need is for better analysis and modelling of field data to improve understanding of population dynamics and ecological relationships.

DISTRIBUTION Northern hemisphere, circumpolar, in association with polar sea ice, i.e. U.S.A., U.S.S.R., Canada, Norway and Denmark (including Greenland). Polar Bears occur throughout most of the polar basin, as far north as 88°N (40) and about as far south as 52°N (14,30,46), but closely associated with coastal regions. In some areas, they undertake extensive movements related to seasonal movements and changes in the distribution of sea ice (7,42,56). For map see (4).

POPULATION Estimates as low as 10,000 have been proposed (51), but a rough estimate of 20,000 was derived by Larsen in 1972 by summing the regional estimates of Polar Bear populations (17). The population trend is not known but is thought to be stable or increasing. Polar bears were all once thought to be part of one circumpolar population (28). However, the results of recent tagging studies indicate that they are divisible into relatively discrete populations (17,21,42,44,49,51). The sizes of the areas in which these populations exist vary from relatively small areas in the Canadian Arctic to relatively large areas in the Chukchi Sea. The relative discreteness of populations is greatly influenced by the distribution and movements of the sea ice (20,42,44,56). No information is currently available on hereditary or genetic differences between the various sub-populations, some data indicate a cline of increasing size from Svalbard west to the Bering Straits (26).

The following rough estimates have been made of numbers in several areas where studies have been conducted. These give a range of about 18,500 to 27,000 total. However considerable variability exists in the methods used, and in the statistical reliability of the methods of analysis, furthermore to date there are no estimates for several large and significant areas (1). Barents and Greenland Sea, Svalbard, Franz Josef Land, Novaya Zemla: 4779-5750, based on ship survey and observed harvest (1,19); Central East Greenland (resident): approximately 100, from mark-recapture studies (1,5,57,58); Northeast Greenland (resident): approximately 100, from aerial survey (1); Ellesmere, Jones Sound, Thule area (resident): 300+ based on sustained harvest (1); Canadian Arctic, Zone Al and A2: 1750, based on estimated cub production (1,14,45); Zone A3: 254, from mark-recapture (14); Zone B: (Labrador Coast): 60-90 from mark-recapture (46), (Ungava Bay): unknown; Zone C: unknown; Zone D: (south): 700, from mark-recapture (44), (north): unknown; Zone E: 1100, from mark-recapture (49); Zone F: 2008, from mark-recapture (33); Zone G: unknown; Zone H: 1800, from mark-recapture (2). Alaskan north slope: 1200-2500, from computer simulation of harvest and mark-recapture (1,23); Chukchi Sea: 2500-7000, from computer simulation of harvest and mark-recapture (1,23); Soviet Union (central): 1800-3600, from aerial survey (53).

HABITAT AND ECOLOGY The Arctic Ocean, from the ice edge to the permanent polar pack, and along its shores and islands. The preferred habitat is ice that is periodically active, where wind and sea currents cause movements and fracturing of the ice followed by refreezing. This process creates intermittent lanes or patches of recently refrozen ice (4,42). This may occur at the interface between landfast ice and drifting pack ice, across the mouths of bays, or in tidal zones along coastlines. It is in this habitat that hunting success is highest (43). In the polar basin and adjacent areas, Polar Bears spend the summer along the edge of the pack ice. Near islands or the mainland, they concentrate in bays that retain shore-fast ice. After breakup, most of the bears that are near islands spend the summer along the coastlines of these islands. Occasionally, adult males have been observed to climb snow-covered glaciers and ice caps (32). In Hudson Bay, bears go inland and endure the warmer weather by digging caves or pits down into the permafrost (13,45). In winter, Polar Bears move to the southern edge of the drift ice, to the coastlines of islands, and to the northern edges of the continents after the annual ice forms in these areas. On the basis of available data, it appears that most pregnant females do not winter along the ice edge, but return in October or November to coastlines where suitable habitat exists to make dens for bearing their young (4). Polar Bears feed primarily on Ringed seals (Phoca hispida) (43,50), but also prey on Bearded seals (Erignathus barbatus), Harp seals (Pagophilus groenlandicus), and Hooded seals (Cystophora cristata), and scavenge on whale, walrus, and seal carcasses (10,31). Occasional references (8,10) have been made to Polar Bears attacking Beluga whales (Delphinapterus leucas) and Walruses (Odobenus rosmarus), but Polar Bear mortalities have also been attributed to the latter (15). Polar Bears occasionally eat small mammals, birds, eggs, and vegetation when other food is unavailable (31). Breeding takes place from February to May, and possibly into June (6,24,25). Implantation is delayed (29,51) and the cubs are born in dens in December and January (9,24,54,55). Litter size and reproductive rates vary geographically, but usually females attain maturity at 4 to 6 years, and have a mean litter size of about 1.6 to 2.0 every 3 to 4 years (3,14,24,25,42,44,45,49). The cubs usually stay with the female for 2-2.5 years (24,42,44). Other than family groups, and occasional groupings on the Hudson Bay shore while waiting for ice to form, Polar Bears are solitary.

THREATS TO SURVIVAL Overexploitation, and habitat deterioration and disturbance. Recent analyses using a mathematical model indicate that sustained yield may be less than 2% of the total population (unpubl. data), but, for example, the Canadian harvest levels in some areas may exceed 5% (1). Hides taken in Canada and Greenland can be sold legally. The trade in Polar Bear hides in Canada 1972-78 has been summarized (34,35,36,37,38,39). In the case of a harvest, the number of bears that could be harvested from a population is variable depending on the age and sex composition of the bear in both the total population and the harvest (1). The variability in these calculations points out the urgency of continued work on population estimates and modelling of Polar Bear populations. Non-harvested portions of some populations may serve as reservoirs for replenishing subpopulations that have declined. The impact of harvesting immigrant animals should be evaluated. Without immigration, recovery time for depleted populations will be slow because of the low intrinsic rate of increase of Polar Bear populations. Similarly, it appears from the modelling done to date that Polar Bear populations may decline more slowly than can be readily detected by monitoring harvest (1).

Although more difficult to evaluate than harvest, losses of animals and declines in productivity may result from environmental degradation (1) associated with the exploitation of minerals and fossil fuels, especially in offshore areas. Heavy metals and toxic chemicals have been found in tissue samples from bears checked for these contaminants. Their effect on the survival of Polar Bears is unknown.

CONSERVATION MEASURES TAKEN   The Polar Bear is listed in Appendix 2 of the 1973 Convention on International Trade in Endangered Species of Wild Fauna and Flora, and trade in it or its products is thus subject to monitoring by ratifying nations. Since 1976, Polar Bears have also been protected under an International Agreement (22) that restricts their taking and directs the signatory nations (U.S.A., U.S.S.R, Canada, Norway, and Denmark) to conduct research to identify the status of populations and to protect those areas critical for survival and reproduction. The Polar Bear Specialist Group of the Species Survival Commission of IUCN meets every two years to discuss Polar Bear research and management on an international basis. In 1972, the U.S. Marine Mammal Protection Act banned the harvesting of Polar Bears in the U.S.A. but allowed native subsistence hunters an unlimited take (subject to the condition that populations do not become depleted). In Canada only Inuit and Indians are allowed to hunt Polar Bears. The total harvest (726 for 1980-81) is made up of individual quotas allocated to specific villages. In Greenland, only residents are allowed to hunt Polar Bears; the annual take is estimated to be between 125 and 150 bears. In the Soviet Union and Norway, moratoria on taking Polar Bears were initiated in 1955 and 1973, respectively (4). There have been several ongoing research programmes on the population dynamics, behaviour, and movements of the species (16,17,18,24,41,44,45,47,52,58) and recently, population modelling with computers has proven useful in evaluating the effect of harvesting different age and sex classes (48 and unpubl. data).

CONSERVATION MEASURES PROPOSED   Continuation of current research and conservation efforts (e.g. protection of major denning and feeding areas as they are identified). Recent developments in population modelling indicate that changes in quotas should be made with extreme caution. Further research into methods of analysis and modelling of each Polar Bear population requires the following information as soon as possible to reduce the chance of overharvesting: estimates of population size, mortality rate and reproductive parameters; delineation of the geographical boundaries of the populations; degree of immigration and emigration from the population; and bias in the sex and age composition of the harvest. Other major conservation points include identification and protection from disturbance or destruction of critical denning and feeding areas, and protection of the marine ecosystem as a whole from the detrimental effects of human industrial activities (1).

CAPTIVE BREEDING   A total of 53 institutions world-wide reported the holding of 169 Polar Bears in captivity at the end of 1979 (11). Although there is a preponderance of females over 3 years of age, the number of captive births remains low and cub mortality high. Polar bears have been successfully bred and reared in captivity (12,27,59), but success depends on such factors as security, solitude, confinement to a small area, and a heated den. In 1979, only 7 cubs were born and, of these, 3 died within 30 days of birth.

REMARKS   For description of animal see (4,51). The draft of this data sheet was researched and written in May 1981 by Dr Ian Stirling, Chairman of the IUCN/SSC Polar Bear Specialist Group and Wendy Calvert. The Red Data Book is greatly indebted to them.

REFERENCES   1.   Consultative Meeting of the Contracting Parties to the Agreement on the Conservation of Polar Bears. (1981). Report of the Meeting: Summary and Conclusions. Oslo, 20-22 January 1981.
2.   DeMaster, D.P., Kingsley, M.C.S. and Stirling, I. (1980). A multiple mark and recapture estimate applied to Polar Bears (Ursus martimus) in the Western Canadian Arctic. Can. J. Zool. 58: 633-638.

3. DeMaster, D.P. and Stirling, I. (In press). The estimation of annual survivorship and mean litter size of Polar Bear cubs. In Meslow, C. (Ed.), Bears - Their Biology and Management. IUCN New Series.

4. DeMaster, D.P. and Stirling, I. (1981). Ursus maritimus. Mammalian Species 145: 1-7. American Society of Mammalogists.

5. Erikson, E. (1976). Capture and investigation of 42 Polar Bears, North East Greenland, April-May 1974. In Proc. Fifth Working Meeting of the Polar Bear Specialist Group. IUCN Publ. New Series. Supp. Paper 42. 37-48.

6. Erickson, A.W. (1972). Bear studies. Alaska Fed. Aid Wildl. Restoration. Seg. Report, Project W-6R3. 9 pp.

7. Frame, G.W. (1972). Occurrence of Polar Bears in the Chuckchi and Beaufort Seas, Summer, 1969. J. Mammal. 53: 187-189.

8. Freeman, M.M. R. (1973). Polar Bear predation on beluga in the Canadian Arctic. Arctic 26: 163-164.

9. Harington, C.P. (1968). Denning habits of the Polar Bear. Canadian Wildl. Service Report Ser. 5: 1-30.

10. Heyland, J.D. and Hay, K. (1976). An attack by a Polar Bear on a juvenile beluga. Arctic 29: 56-57.

11. ISIS Species distribution summary. (1979).

12. Jacobi, E.F. (1968). Breeding facilities for Polar Bears, (Thalarctos maritimus) (Phipps, 1774), in captivity. Bijdr. Dierk. 38: 39-46.

13. Jonkel, C.J., Kolenosky, G.B., Robertson, R.J. and Russell, R.H. (1972). Further notes on Polar Bear denning habits. In Herrero, S. (Ed.), Bears - Their Biology and Management. IUCN New Series 23: 142-158.

14. Jonkel, C., Smith, P., Stirling, I. and Kolenosky, G.B. (1976). Notes on the present status of the Polar Bear in James Bay and the Belcher Islands. Canadian Wildl. Service Occas. Paper 26: 1-40.

15. Kiliaan, H.P.L. and Stirling, I. (1978). Observations on overwintering walruses in the eastern Canadian high arctic. J. Mammal 59: 197-200.

16. Larsen, T. (1968). Ecological investigations of the Polar Bear in Svalbard. Norsk Polarinst. Arbok 1966: 92-98.

17. Larsen, T. (1972). Air and ship census of Polar Bears in Svalbard. J. Wildl. Mgmt. 36: 562-570.

18. Larsen, T. (1976). Polar Bear den surveys in Svalbard, 1972 and 1973. In Pelton, M.R., Lentfer, J.W. and Folk, G.E. (Eds), Bears - Their Biology and Management. IUCN New Series 40: 199-208.

19. Larsen, T. (1981). Distribution, numbers, and population characteristics of Polar Bears in Svalbard. Report to the 8th meeting of the IUCN Polar Bear Specialist Group, Oslo, January 1981.

20. Lentfer, J.W. (1972). Polar bear - sea ice relationships. In Herrero, S. (Ed.), Bears - Their Biology and Management. IUCN New Series 23: 165-171.

21. Lentfer, J.W. (1974). Discreteness of Alaskan Polar Bear population. International Game Biol. 11: 323-329.

22. Lentfer, J.W. (1974). Agreement on conservation of Polar Bears. Polar Record 17: 327-330.

23. Lentfer, J.W. (1976). Polar Bear reproductive biology and denning. Final Report 5.4R. Alaska Dept. Fish and Game.

22pp.

24. Lentfer, J.W., Hensel, R.J., Gilbert, J.R. and Sorensen, F.E. (1980). Population characteristics of Alaskan Polar Bears. In Martinka, C.J. and McArthur K.L. (Eds), Proc. of the Fourth Int. Conf. on Bear Res. and Manag. Kalispell, Mont. February 1977.

25. Lono, O. (1970). The Polar bear in the Svalbard area. Norsk Polarinst. Skrifter 149: 1-103.

26. Manning, T.H. (1971). Geographical variation in the Polar Bear, Ursus maritimus Phipps. Canadian Wildl. Service Report Ser. 13: 1-27.

27. Nunley, L. (1977). Successful rearing of Polar Bears. Internat. Zoo Yearbook 17: 161-164.

28. Pederson, A. (1945). Der Eisbar; Verbreitung und Lebenweise. E. Bruun and Co., Copenhagen. 166pp.

29. Ramsay, M.A. and Stirling, I. (In press). Reproductive biology and ecology of female Polar Bears in western Hudson Bay. Naturaliste Canadien.

30. Ray, C.E. (1971). Polar Bear and mammoth on the Pribilof Islands. Arctic 24: 9-19.

31. Russell, R.H. (1975). The food habits of Polar Bears of James Bay and southwest Hudson Bay in summer and autumn. Arctic 28: 117-129.

32. Schweinsburg, R.E. (1979). Summer snow dens used by Polar Bears in the Canadian High Arctic. Arctic 32: 165-169.

33. Schweinsburg, R.E., Lee, J. and Latour, P. (1980). Polar Bear studies in eastern Lancaster Sound and Baffin Bay. NWTWS Final Report No. 6. 91 pp.

34. Smith, P.A. (1977). Resume of the trade in Polar Bear hides in Canada, 1975-76. Canadian Wildl. Service Prog. Note 82: 1-8.

35. Smith, P.A. (1978). Resume of the trade in Polar Bear hides in Canada, 1976-77. Canadian Wildl. Service Prog. Note 89: 1-5.

36. Smith, P.A. (1979). Resume of the trade of Polar Bear hides in Canada, 1977-1978. Canadian Wildl. Service Prog. Note 103: 1-6.

37. Smith, P.A. and Jonkel, C.J. (1975). Resume of the trade in Polar Bear hides in Canada 1972-73. Canadian Wildl. Serv. Prog. Note 43: 1-9.

38. Smith, P.A. and Jonkel, C.J. (1975). Resume of the trade of Polar Bear hides in Canada, 1973-74. Canadian Wild. Service Prog. Note 48: 1-5.

39. Smith, P.A. and Stirling, I. (1976). Resume of the trade in Polar Bear hides in Canada, 1974-75. Canadian Wild. Service Prog. Note 66: 1-7.

40. Stefannson, V. (1921). The Friendly Arctic MacMillan, New York. 361 pp.

41. Stirling, I. (1980). The biological importance of polynyas in the Canadian Arctic. Arctic 33: 303-315.

42. Stirling, I., Andriashek, D., Latour, P. and Calvert, W. (1975). The distribution and abundance of Polar Bears in the eastern Beaufort Sea. A final report to the Beaufort Sea Project. Fisheries and Marine Service, Dept. of the Environment, Victoria, B.C. 59 pp.

43. Stirling, I. and Archibald, W.R. (1977). Aspects of predation of seals by Polar Bears. J. Fish. Res. Bd. Canada 34: 1126-1129.

44. Stirling, I., Calvert, W. and Andriashek, D. (1980). Population ecology studies of the Polar Bears in the area of southeastern Baffin Island. Canadian Wildlife Service Occ. Pap. No.44. 33pp.

45. Stirling, I., Jonkel, C., Smith, P., Robertson, R. and Cross, D. (1977). The ecology of Polar Bears (Ursus maritimus) along the western coast of Hudson Bay. Canadian Wildlife Service Occ. Pap. No.33. 64pp.

46. Stirling, I. and Kiliaan, H.P.L. (1980). Population ecology studies of the Polar Bear in northern Labrador. Canadian Wildlife Service Occ. Pap. No.42. 18pp.

47. Stirling, I. and Latour, P. (1978). Comparative hunting abilities of Polar Bear cubs of different ages. Canadian J. Zool. 56: 1768-1772.

48. Stirling, I., Pearson, A.M. and Bunnell, F.L. (1976). Population ecology studies of Polar and Grizzly Bears in northern Canada. Trans. 41st N. Amer. Wildl. Nat. Res. Conf. 41: 421-430.

49. Stirling, I., Schweinsburg, R.E., Calvert, W. and Kiliaan, H.P.L. (1978). Population ecology of the Polar Bear along the proposed Arctic Islands Gas Pipeline Route. Final Rep. Environ. Mgmt. Service, Dept. Environ. Edmonton, Alberta. 93pp.

50. Stirling, I. and Smith, T.G. (1975). Inter-relationships of arctic ocean mammals in the sea ice habitat. Proc. Circumpolar Conf. North. Ecol., (Ottawa, Canada) 2: 129-136.

51. Uspenskii, S.M. (1977). The Polar Bear. Nauka, Moscow. 107 pp. (English translation by Canadian Wild. Service, 1978).

52. Uspenskii, S.M. and Belikov, S.E. (1980). Data on the winter ecology of the Polar Bear in Wrangel Island. In Martinka, C.J. and McArthur, K.L. (Ed.), Proc. of the Fourth Int. Conf. on Bear Res. and Manag. Kalispell, Mont. February 1977.

53. Uspenskii, S.M. and Shilnikov, V.I. (1969). Distribution and the numbers of Polar Bears in the Arctic according to data aerial ice surveys. pp. 89-102. In The Polar Bear and its Conservation in the Soviet Arctic. Hydrometeriological Publishing House, Leningrad. 184 pp.

54. Van de Velde, F. (1957). Nanuk, king of the arctic beasts. Eskimo 45: 4-15.

55. Van de Velde, F. (1971). Bear stories. Eskimo, new ser. 1: 7-11.

56. Vibe, C. (1967). Arctic animals in relation to climatic fluctuations. Meddelelser om Gronland. 227 pp.

57. Vibe, C. (1976). Preliminary report on the first Danish Polar Bear expedition to North East Greenland, 1973. In Proc. Fifth Working Meeting of the Polar Bear Specialist Group. IUCN New Series Supp. Paper 42: 74-81.

58. Vibe, C. (1976). Preliminary report on the second Danish Polar Bear expedition to North East Greenland, 1974. In Proc. Fifth Working Meeting of the Polar Bear Specialist Group. IUCN New Series Supp. Paper 42: 91-98.

59. Wemmer, C. (1974). Design for Polar Bear maternity dens. Int. Zoo Yearbook 14: 222-223.

BLACK-FOOTED FERRET

ENDANGERED

Mustela nigripes (Audubon & Bachman, 1851)

Order   CARNIVORA   Family   MUSTELIDAE

SUMMARY   Now thought to be restricted to no more than a handful of localities within its former North American range. Total numbers are unknown and sightings are very infrequent. Depleted directly, or indirectly, by the poisoning of prairie dogs (its natural prey) and the destruction of its grassland habitat. Listed as endangered on the United States List of Endangered and Threatened Wildlife and a Recovery Team exists to promote conservation of the species. Has been the subject of extensive studies.

DISTRIBUTION   United States of America. During the century following its discovery its range has contracted considerably (11,14) and the Ferret is now believed to survive only in western North and South Dakota, eastern Montana, Wyoming and Colorado (being found up to altitudes of 3200 m in the Rockies)(13,16), in Nebraska, and possibly south to Oklahoma and New Mexico (13). Most of the recent records have been from western South Dakota, Wyoming and Montana (about 20 in total since 1970) (5,11,12), and the most recent sightings have been in Wyoming in September and October 1981 (19,20). Before colonization of the prairies the Ferret occurred throughout the Great Plains of North America from Alberta and Saskatchewan in southern Canada to Texas and Arizona in the United States, usually in association with prairie dog towns (9,11,14). It has not been recorded in Canada since 1937 and is now believed to be extinct there (1,17). For map see (14).

POPULATION   No figures available; last reported sightings were in September and October 1981 (19,20) (prior to that in 1979 (16) and prior to that in 1974 (16)). A Ferret was killed by dogs on September 25 1981 on a ranch near Cody (19). As a result of this kill investigations led to the finding of a live individual on October 29, 1981, it was later captured and radio-tagged (20). Seven to eight skulls have been located in the past two years, none probably more than 20 years old (2,16,18). The Ferret has never been considered a common species, (8,11), is rarely seen (11,13), and since its discovery in 1851 only about 1000 sightings have been made. However, at the turn of the century the prairie dog population was estimated at 5000 million and it seems likely, but only a guess, that the Ferret must have existed in good numbers amidst such an abundance of its prey (4).

HABITAT AND ECOLOGY   Short and mid grass prairies, in which prairie dog towns are the principal habitat; the Ferret has also been found living in ground squirrel colonies, haystacks and under buildings. Prairie dogs are undoubtedly its principal food. Very secretive and mainly nocturnal but also active during daylight hours, especially in summertime (11,14). Captive females enter breeding condition in late February to early March, proestrus lasts 21-28 days, copulation occurs in March and early April, and gestation of the female in two breeding seasons has been noted as 42-45 days. Litter size of wild females ranges from one to five (14). Longest recorded lifespan is at least nine years, in a captive specimen at the Patuxent Wildlife Research Centre (7).

THREATS TO SURVIVAL   Habitat destruction as a result of the prairies being ploughed and planted with domestic grasses. Poisoning campaigns directed at prairie dogs, which are regarded as pests by farmers and ranchers (4,11,14,15), have deprived the Ferret of its shelter and food supply and it may die from secondary poisoning (10,11,14). Prairie dog populations have increased in recent years but Ferret sightings have been fewer (18). Vehicular traffic accounts for some losses each year and Ferrets are occasionally shot by people hunting prairie dogs for sport. Other predators may include the domestic dog and cat, coyote, badger, owls, hawks and eagles (11,14), and in some localities the surviving Ferrets may be too scattered to breed successfully (8).

CONSERVATION MEASURES TAKEN   Listed in Appendix 1 of the 1973 Convention on International Trade in Endangered Species of Wild Fauna and Flora, trade in it or its products is therefore subject to strict regulation by ratifying nations, and trade for primarily commercial purposes is banned. It is also listed as endangered by the United States Department of the Interior under the Endangered Species Act of 1973, and therefore protected in all States of its former and present range. Studies have been undertaken by the U.S. Fish and Wildlife Service and South Dakota Cooperative Wildlife Research Unit, and a Recovery Team has been established to develop plans for the restoration of the Ferret (18). A full-time biologist at the Patuxent Wildlife Research Centre studied the species from 1965 to 1980 (7,18) and several other federal and state agencies are cooperating in surveys to determine its presence. Search dogs have been trained, scent lures developed, and in Wyoming a reward for sightings is offered (5,16). At Patuxent, specimens of the closely related Siberian Polecat (Mustela e. eversmanni) are being used for studies of captive propagation and radio tagging (18). Prairie dog towns must be determined to be 'Ferret-free' before a federal agency may undertake 'damage suppression' measures against the dog, but it is extremely difficult to make certain whether or not the Ferret is present. Several ten-year easements (payments to ranchers to leave prairie dog towns along) have been obtained on private lands in western South Dakota. There are also large prairie dog towns in three National Parks, all in the Dakotas -- Badlands, Wind Cave and Theodore Roosevelt -- and many more on Bureau of Land Management and United States Forest Service lands, where management programmes are being developed for the prairie dog and Ferret (13).

CONSERVATION MEASURES PROPOSED   Since survival of the Ferret depends on preservation of prairie dog towns, establishment of additional sanctuaries in which such towns occur, through easement or purchase, is necessary. Steps should also be taken to ensure that Ferrets captured on private lands where prairie dog control is contemplated are released in suitable natural habitats in one of the several areas of federally-owned land where habitat preservation can be assured (3,6,11,13).

CAPTIVE BREEDING   In 1977, two wild-caught male and two female Black-footed Ferrets were held in captivity at the Patuxent Wildlife Research Centre, Laurel, Maryland, but all have since died (R.Nowak 1981,Pers.Comm.)

REMARKS   For description of animal see (8,11,14). This data sheet was compiled with the assistance of C.N. Hillman, T.W. Clark, R.C. Erickson, F.R. Henderson, R.L. Linder and P.F. Springer, to whom we are most grateful.

REFERENCES   1.   Banfield, A.W.F. (1974). The Mammals of Canada. Univ. of Toronto Press.
2.   Boggess, E.K., Henderson, F.R. and Choate, J.R. (1980). A Black-footed Ferret from Kansas. J. Mammal. 61(3): 571.
3.   Cahalane, V.H. (1954). Status of the Black-footed Ferret. J. Mammal. 33: 418-424.
4.   Clark, T.W. (1976). The Black-footed Ferret. Oryx 13(3): 275-280.
5.   Clark, T.W. and Dorn, R.D. (1981). Rare and endangered vascular plants and vertebrates of Wyoming. In press.
6.   Erickson, R.C. (1973). Some Black-footed Ferret Research

Needs. In Proceedings of the Black-footed Ferret and Prairie Dog Workshop, Sept. 4-6, 1973. South Dakota State Univ., Brookings.

7. Erickson, R.C. (1977). In litt.

8. Fortenberry, D.K. (1972). Characteristics of the Black-footed Ferret. Resource Publication 109. U.S. Dept. of the Interior, Bureau of Sport Fisheries and Wildlife, Washington, D.C. 8 pp.

9. Hall, E.R. and Kelson, K.R. (1959). The Mammals of North America. Ronald Press, New York.

10. Henderson, F.R. (1977-81). In litt.

11. Henderson, F.R., Springer, P.F. and Adrian, R. (1974). The Black-footed Ferret in South Dakota. Technical Bulletin No. 4. South Dakota Department of Game, Fish and Parks.

12. Hillman, C.N. and Linder, R.L. (1973). The Black-footed Ferret. In Proceedings of the Black-footed Ferret and Prairie Dog Workshop, Sept. 4-6, 1973. South Dakota State Univ., Brookings.

13. Hillman, C.N. (1977). In litt.

14. Hillman, C.N. and Clark, T.W. (1980). Mustela nigripes. Mammalian Species No. 126: 1-3. American Society of Mammalogists.

15. Homolka, C.L. (1964). Our Rarest Mammal? Audubon 66(4): 244-256.

16. Linder, R.L. (1980-81). In litt.

17. Saskatchewan Department of Tourism and Renewable Resources. (1978). The status of the Black-footed Ferret Mustela nigripes (Audubon and Bachman) in Canada. Committee on the status of Endangered Wildlife in Canada. Status reports and evaluations Vol 1.

18. Springer, P.F. (1977). In litt.

19. Anon. (1981). Positive sighting of a Ferret is first in more than 2 years. The New York Times Thursday, October 15th.

20. Anon. (1981). Ferret, feared extinct, is found in Wyoming. New York Times Saturday, November 7th.

MARINE OTTER or CHINGUNGO   VULNERABLE

Lutra felina (Molina, 1782)

Order   CARNIVORA   Family   MUSTELIDAE

SUMMARY Extensively but sparsely distributed along coasts of Peru and Chile. Numbers unknown. Persecuted for its fur in Chile, and because of alleged damage to freshwater prawn stocks in Peru. Fully protected by law in both countries but enforcement difficult. Occurs in the Paracas Nature Reserve, and the proposed conservation area of Morro de Sama in Peru and in Chepu Forest Reserve in Chile. Some studies have been carried out but more data is needed regarding ecology and seasonal distribution. Conservation will depend on effective protection from persecution.

DISTRIBUTION Pacific coastline of Peru and Chile from at least 9°S, and possibly 6°S, to Cape Horn at approx. 56°S (3,4,5,6). In Chile it was reported in 1978 as virtually absent in the region from the Chile-Peru border south to the Canal de Chacao, though still known from isolated, inaccessible areas north of Coquimbo (around 29°S) and of Valparaiso (32°-33°S) (5). South of the Canal de Chacao, its range is believed to be more continuous though is not accurately known (5,6). Originally occurred more or less continously from northern Peru to Cape Horn, and possibly also in Argentinian waters (6,7).

POPULATION No recent reliable estimates though a 1976 FAO report noted that 'South American marine otters, once abundant, have been reduced to scattered remnant populations; unconfirmed estimates total less than 1000' (1). The basis of this estimate is unknown. Peru: there has been no detailed census though Grimwood estimated 200-300 in 1967/68 (8). A general assessment in 1977 indicated that it had become very scarce along the coast, the most important remaining areas being the Paracas Peninsula and Morro de Sama (3). In 1975 it was also said to be seen regularly off the town of Ancon, north of Lima (14). In 1977 it was included among the 25 most endangered animals in Peru (3). Chile: no overall figures are available. A survey in progress in 1979 reported an apparently stable population on the Taitao peninsula in Aysen Province, an area considered secure because of its inaccessibility to hunters (12). Cabello in 1977 noted densities of one otter per 100m of shore on Chiloe Island, though he stressed that this was a purely provisional figure (5). By 1967/68 it had been virtually exterminated in the Cape Horn and southern Tierra del Fuego region where Darwin in the 1830's had found it to be very abundant in the Chonos Archipelago and the islands off southwest Tierra del Fuego (8,9,11,14).

HABITAT AND ECOLOGY Mainly littoral, occupying rocky coastal areas, secluded bays and inlets near estuaries, although Hernandez recorded that it sometimes ascended rivers in search of fresh-water prawns to their upper limit of distribution, given as 650m above sea level (4,6,8,10,14). Studied on the north end of Chiloe Island, Chile, in an area characterised by a rocky shore of irregular topography with a heavy swell and constant strong northeasterly, westerly or south westerly winds (5,6) a tidal range of 2-2.5m, and a dense cover of shrubs and small trees stunted by wind and poor soil extending down to the high-water-mark; below this there is heavy growth of seaweed and algae. The high productivity of the area leads to very high numbers and diversity of shellfish (bivalves, gastropods, crustaceans, echinoderms etc.) (5,6). Faecal analysis and direct observation indicate that diet consists mainly of crustaceans and molluscs with lesser amounts of fish. 72% of remains identified in spraints collected at Chiloe over 17 months were crustacean (mainly Homalapsis plana and Taliepus dentatus), and 27% molluscan, (mainly Concholepas concholepas) (6). Fruits of the seashore bromeliads Greigia sphacelata and Fascicularia tricolor are also believed to be deliberately taken although small amounts of seaweed identified in spraints are probably accidentally ingested with shellfish (5,6). In Peru diet is said to include the freshwater prawn Criphiops caementarius and a specimen collected near the Paracas Peninsula contained remains of a toadfish (Aphos porosus) (4,8,14). Most observations are of single individuals, though occasionally seen in groups of three or more. The extent of nocturnal activity is unknown though most reports note it as chiefly diurnal (6,8). Preliminary observations indicate that breeding at Chiloe occurs in summer with matings observed in December-January. Gestation period lasts somewhere between 60 and 120 days with young born in autumn and winter. It is not known if delayed implantation occurs as has been observed in other Lutrinae nor is there any evidence for more than one litter per year (6). Normal litter size appears to be two although a figure of 4-5 has been quoted for populations in the Magallanes area (5,6,13). The Killer whale (Orcinus orca) is thought to be a likely predator and there may be competition for food with gulls Larus spp. and the Southern sea-lion (Otaria flavescens) (5). Nothing is known of any seasonal movements, though it is reportedly largely sedentary in Chile (15).

THREATS TO SURVIVAL In Chile persecuted for its fur and in Peru because of alleged damage to prawn fisheries. In Peru there is very little hunting for its fur, which is not considered to have any commercial value, though it is persecuted by fishermen, especially in the Majes and Ocona Rivers, for the damage it is alleged to do to freshwater prawn stocks (3,8,14). It is also often shot by fishermen and owners of firearms as a convenient living target (8). In Chile considerable hunting occurs for its pelt, which is highly valued there; most is carried out from boats 9-10 m long (Chalupas) which have sails or oars and a crew of 4 men. These remain afloat for up to 5 months at a time, sailing up and down the coast harvesting whatever is available. The Chingungo is the most sought after prize and is shot, or hunted on the shore by dogs which are carried in the boats. In one voyage 30 or 40 pelts may be obtained. The value of a pelt to a hunter fluctuated around US$37 in 1979, over twice the figure quoted in 1977. At that time a local dealer would expect US$75 per skin. Most pelts are destined for Argentina and the principle centres for this (illegal) trade are Pto. Montt, Castro, Melinka, Pto. Aysen and Pta. Arenas (5,6). No damage to freshwater prawn stocks is known in Chile (5).

CONSERVATION MEASURES TAKEN Listed in Appendix 1 of the 1973 Convention on International Trade in Endangered Species of Wild Fauna and Flora, trade in it or its products therefore being subject to strict regulation by ratifying nations, and trade for primarily commercial purposes banned. Legally protected in Peru since 1977, before which there was an annual closed-season from 15 December to 31 March (3,14). Present in Paracas National Reserve, Peru (3,4). Nominally protected in Chile, under law No. 4601 of 1929, but enforcement is hampered by a lack of trained and equipped officials, by the inaccessibility and complexity of the terrain in southern Chile, and by the largely nomadic nature of the hunters (6). Occurs in the Chepu Forest Reserve on Chiloe Island, where an 18 month study of the species finished in 1979 (6). A further study of this and Lutra provocax was underway in Chile in 1979 (12).

CONSERVATION MEASURES PROPOSED Effective enforcement of protection throughout its range, especially clamping down on illicit export of pelts to Argentina, would be of great benefit. The proposed conservation area of Morro de Sama in Peru harbours the species. It is not known whether populations remain within present or proposed conservation areas throughout the year and investigations are needed to determine any seasonal movements, so that marine parks can be established that would provide permanent protection for at least some populations. Re-establishment in parts of northern central Chile where it has been exterminated is also advocated (6).

CAPTIVE BREEDING   None known in captivity.

REMARKS   For description see (6,9). Two subspecies are said to be described --
one from southern Chile which is reportedly slightly darker brown than that from
northern Chile and Peru (2). However, elsewhere subspecific classification is
described as 'not clear and external characteristics cannot be used for subspecific
separation' (1). Cabello also notes that differences between northern and southern
specimens are more likely to represent clinal variation over the species extensive
distribution (more than 5000km) rather than subspeciation (6).

REFERENCES   1.   Anon. (1976). Marine Otters. Scientific Consultation on
Marine   Mammals.   Bergen,   Norway,   31   August   -   9
September, 1976. ACMRR/MM/SC/WG Rep 5.
2.   Anon. (1978). Marine Otter included under the Marine
Mammal Protection Act of 1972. U.S. Dept. of the
Interior. Fish and Wildlife Service News Release, Levitt
202/343-5634.
3.   Brack Egg, A. (1978). Situacion actual de las nutrias
(Lutrinae, Mustelidae) en el Peru. In Duplaix, N. (Ed.).
Otters - Proceedings of the First Working Meeting of the
IUCN/SSC Otter Specialist Group, Paramaribo, Suriname
27-29 March 1977. 76-84.
4.   Brownell, R.L. Jr. (1978). Ecology and conservation of the
Marine Otter (Lutra felina). In Duplaix, N. (Ed.). Otters -
Proceedings of the First Working Meeting of the IUCN/SSC
Otter Specialist Group, Paramaribo, Suriname 27-29 March
1977. 104-106.
5.   Cabello, C.C. (1978). La Nutria de Mar (Lutra felina) en la
Isla de Chiloe, Chile. In Duplaix, N. (Ed.). Otters -
Proceedings of the First Working Meeting of the IUCN/SSC
Otter Specialist Group, Paramaribo, Suriname 27-29 March
1977. 108-118.
6.   Cabello, C.C. (1979). La Nutria de Mar Lutra felina Mol.
1782, en la Isla de Chiloe (II). Corporacion Nacional
Forestal, Ministerio de Agricultura, Chile.
7.   Cabrera, A. (1957-1961). Catalogo de los mamiferos de
America del Sur. Rev. Mus. Argent. Cienc. Nat. 'Bernardino
Rivadavia'. Cienc. Zool. 4(1,2): 1-731.
8.   Grimwood, I.R. (1969). Notes on the distribution and status
of some Peruvian mammals 1968. Spec. Pub. 21. Am.
Comm. Int. Wildlife Protec. and New York Zool. Soc.
9.   Harris, C.J. (1968). Otters: A study of the recent Lutrinae.
Weidenfeld and Nicolson, London.
10.   Hernandez, J.E. (1960). Contribucion al conocimiento de
camarois de rio. Pesca y Caza. Ministeria de Agricultura,
Lima. 10: 84-106.
11.   Osgood, W.H. (1943). The mammals of Chile. Field Mus.
Nat. Hist. Zool. Ser. 30: 1-268.
12.   Otter Specialist Group, IUCN/SSC. (1979). Report to SSC
Meeting, Cambridge, Sept. 1979. Unpd.
13.   Sielfeld,   W.,   Venegas,   C.   and   Atalah,   A.   (1977).
Consideraciones acerca del estado de los mamiferos marinos
en Chile. An Inst. Patagonia 8: 297-315.
14.   South American Otter Sub-Group of IUCN Otter Specialist
Group (1976). A report prepared by N. Duplaix-Hall. Ms.
15.   Rottman, J. (1977). In litt.

LA PLATA OTTER or LOBITO DE RIO　　　　VULNERABLE

Lutra platensis (Waterhouse, 1838)

Order　CARNIVORA　　　　　　　Family　MUSTELIDAE

SUMMARY　Eastern South America. Numbers unknown but reportedly has declined because of over exploitation, and in some regions river pollution adversely affecting its main prey species. National and international controls on the otter skin trade have improved of late but continuing restrictions are required. Surveys needed as basis for effective conservation plan which must include establishment of further reserves and controls on river pollution.

DISTRIBUTION　Southern Brazil, Paraguay, northern Argentina and Uruguay (1). Also Grimwood believes this is the species that occurs in the Pilcomayo/Paraguay drainage of S.E. Bolivia (8); if true, this considerably extends its range. Argentina: a 1979 report noted three concentrations: the Parana river basin in Santa Fe between latitudes 28° and 31°5', an area of many small tributaries, streams and islands; the delta region at the confluence of the Rios Parana and Uruguay near the mouth of the Rio de la Plata (though not in that river itself (14)), between 32° and 34°5'S, in particular on the eastern bank of the Parana in Entre Rios; and along lake shores (especially Galaza and Ibera) in the Ibera Basin, Corrientes Province. Also small numbers in Formosa, Chaco and Misiones Provinces (6). Range has evidently contracted this century and a 1973 survey of Santa Fe found it absent in many areas, e.g. the Salado, Coronda and Carcarana Rivers, where it was known to have formerly occurred (7). Uruguay: still present though has been exterminated in the larger rivers (14). Grimwood in 1978 noted it as reportedly still occurring in a wide variety of habitats, especially in coastal lakes (8). Little detailed information available from Brazil and Paraguay.

POPULATION　Numbers unknown. In Argentina has decreased markedly since the 1930s (6,7). A 1973 field survey in Santa Fe classified it as 'scarce' in the Parana River basin; 36 records were noted, of which 20 were captures, along about 700 km of river (7). In Brazil it is on the Endangered Species List, and in Uruguay has disappeared from many areas (14). No information obtained for Paraguay. Cabrera and Yepes in 1940 noted it as a rare species even then, with numbers considerably reduced compared to its original abundance (2).

HABITAT AND ECOLOGY　Poorly known. Inhabits large rivers, smaller tributaries and lakes (2). Usually solitary, quiet and primarily nocturnal, though is sometimes active in daylight (3).

THREATS TO SURVIVAL　The most immediate cause of decline is hunting for its valuable fur (2,7,14,16). In 1977 the value of a skin to a hunter in Santa Fe, Argentina was around US$40, nearly three-quarters of the average monthly income of a rural peasant (7); consequently the otter has been exterminated from areas near human settlements. However the incentive to hunt is strong and hunters are prepared to go to great lengths to obtain skins (7,16). Hunters mostly subsist by trapping Coypus (Myocastor coypus), but will move traps to any area where signs of otters are detected, using the traps by day and hunting the otter with lights by night; they are reputedly prepared to dedicate weeks to obtaining a single skin (7). Habitat destruction from increased agricultural exploitation is also said to be important, especially in Entre Rios and Corrientes Provinces, Argentina (6). Pollution of rivers in some areas has affected the fish on which it is believed to chiefly subsist (13).

CONSERVATION MEASURES TAKEN Listed (within Lutra longicaudis) in Appendix 1 of the 1973 Convention on International Trade in Endangered Species of Wild Fauna and Flora, and trade in it or its products is therefore subject to strict regulation by ratifying nations, and trade for primarily commercial purposes is banned. Protected by law in Argentina, Paraguay, Uruguay and Brazil and on the Brazilian Endangered Species List. A notable decrease in the illegal hide trade in Argentina was observed between 1975-79, a fact attributed to stricter regulations and enforcement by official wildlife and conservation inspectors rather than to a further decline in otter numbers (6). Hunting in Paraguay is said to be difficult due to the terrain (16). Attempts are being made in Uruguay to control the skin trade (14). In Argentina said to be present (or present in recent times) in Iguazu , Pilcomayo, El Rey, Baritu and El Palmar National Parks, but records not always reliable (7). In Brazil reportedly occurs in the National Parks of Emas, Iguaçu, Itatiaia, Serra da Bicaina, Serra dos Orgaos, Monte Pascoal, San Joaquim and Aparados da Serra, also in the Biological Reserve of Cara-Cara (11,12,15). In Paraguay almost certainly occurs in Tinfunque National Park and possibly others (8). In Uruguay said to occur in Cabo Polonio, Arequita and possibly Santa Teresa National Parks but again records may not be reliable (8).

CONSERVATION MEASURES PROPOSED In 1977 the IUCN/SSC Otter Specialist Group recommended the following actions: urge the governments of Paraguay, Argentina, Brazil, and Uruguay to enforce existing protection and trade laws; ban the export and re-export of skins; establish reserves where it can be better protected; support status surveys; control river pollution (5,12).

CAPTIVE BREEDING In 1979, there was 1 male in Sao Paulo Zoo, Brazil (10). In Argentina a research programme on this species in captivity was begun in 1973 at the Wildlife Reproduction Centre (12). Breeding has taken place though mortality, especially in pre-weaned young, was reportedly high (7,14). Recommendations for any further captive breeding programmes have been made (7).

REMARKS For description of animal see (1,2,8). Six species of neotropical Lutra have been recognised - the river otters Lutra annectens, L. enudris, L. incarum, L. provocax and L. platensis, and the Marine Otter Lutra felina. However, van Zyll de Jong in his review of the nearctic and neotropical Lutrinae in 1972 lumped four of these (excepting Lutra provocax and L. felina) together as one species, L. longicaudis (17). Davis, following Hershkovitz, has gone further and considers these four, and also Lutra provocax, to be conspecific with the nearctic L. canadensis, this name having priority over L. longicaudis (19,20). Full agreement over this has not yet been reached (18), and Lutra platensis is here retained as a species.

REFERENCES 1. Cabrera, A. (1957-1961). Catalogo de los mamiferos de America del Sur. Rev. Mus. Argent. Cienc. Nat. 'Bernardino Rivadavia'. Cienc. Zool. 4(1,2): 1-731.
2. Cabrera, A. and Yepes, J. (1940). Mamiferos Sud-Americanos. Vols. 1 and 2. Buenos Aires.
3. Coimbra-Filho, A.F. and Mittermeier, R.A. (1974). In litt.
4. Dennler de La Tour, G. (1965). The present situation of wildlife conservation in Argentina and the prospects for the future. Unpd. report.
5. Duplaix, N. (Ed.) (1978). Otters - Proceedings of the First Working Meeting of the IUCN/SSC Otter Specialist Group, Paramaribo, Suriname 27-29 March 1977. IUCN, Switzerland.
6. Garcia-Mata, R. (1979). Report on Lutra platensis and Lutra provocax in Argentina. In: Otter Specialist Group

Report to SSC Meeting, Cambridge, Sept. 1979.

7. Griva, E.E. (1978). El Programa de Cria y Preservacion de Lutra platensis en Argentina. In Duplaix, N. (Ed.), Otters - Proceedings of the First Working Meeting of the IUCN/SSC Otter Specialist Group, Paramaribo, Suriname 27-29 March 1977. IUCN, Switzerland.
8. Grimwood, I.R. (1978). In litt.
9. Harris, C.J. (1968). Otters: a study of the recent Lutrinae. Weidenfeld and Nicolson, London.
10. Olney, P.J.S. (Ed.) (1980). International Zoo Yearbook 20. Zool. Soc. London.
11. Padua, M.T.J. (no date). Parques nacionais e reservas equivalentes. Instituto Brasiliero de Desonvolvimento Florestal.
12. Padua, M.T.J., Magnanini, A. and Mittermeier, R.A. (1974). Brazil's National Parks. Oryx 12(5): 452-464.
13. Pires, F.D.A. (1968). In litt.
14. Praderi, R. (1981). In litt.
15. Schaller, G.B. (1976). Report on a Wildlife Survey in northern Argentina and in the Emas National Park, Brazil. Unpd. report.
16. South American Sub-Group of IUCN Otter Specialist Group. (1976). Report prepared by N. Duplaix-Hall. Unpd. report.
17. Zyll de Jong, C.G. van (1972). A systematic review of the nearctic and neotropical river otters (genus Lutra). Contr. Life Sci. Div. R. Ontario Mus. 80: 1-104.
18. Duplaix, N. (1979). In litt.
19. Davis, J.A. (1978). A classification of the otters. In Duplaix, N. (Ed.), Otters - Proceedings of the First Working Meeting of the IUCN/SSC Otter Specialist Group, Paramaribo, Suriname 27-29 March 1977. IUCN, Switzerland.
20. Hershkovitz, P. (1972). The recent mammals of the Neotropical region: a zoogeographical and ecological review. In Keast, A., Erk, F.O. and Glass, B. (Eds), Evolution, mammals and southern continents. State Univ. Press, New York.

SOUTHERN RIVER OTTER or HUILLIN INDETERMINATE

Lutra provocax (Thomas, 1908)

Order   CARNIVORA   Family   MUSTELIDAE

SUMMARY Occurs in Chile and Argentina. Numbers unknown but reportedly drastically reduced due to overhunting for its fur. Protected by law in both countries but requires effective legal action. Studies also needed to determine ecology and distribution as basis of a conservation management plan which must include establishment of adequately protected reserves.

DISTRIBUTION Central and southern Chile and western Argentina. Chile: in rivers and estuaries from Temuco in Cuatin Province (39°S) south to the Magallan straits (6). Northern limit in the 19th century was established as the Cauquenes and Cachapoal rivers (approx. 36°S). Argentina: recorded in the Andes in a north-south strip about 100km wide from 38°S to the border (2). Garcia-Mata noted in 1977 that it possibly occurred in rivers and lakes between Lake Alumine and the Barrancas River up to about 36°S in northern Nequen Province, but that as yet no detailed surveys had been conducted (4). No recent reliable records exist south of Los Alerces National Park (42°S), though again there have been no surveys. Over the last two centuries there have also been numerous reports from parts of Patagonia; this is well outside its normal range and up to 100km away from the Andes. At the beginning of this century specimens were hunted at the mouth of the Rio Negro on the Atlantic coast; these however are considered to have been vagrants washed down by flood waters (4).

POPULATION Numbers unknown and information on its status is often conflicting. Chile: Grimwood (1978) considered it very rare in rivers and lakes in the Andes though much commoner along the coast from Chiloe Island south (6). In the late 1970s it was reported to have disappeared from most of its range (11), and was said to be less common than Lutra felina, itself a 'Vulnerable' species, and with which it is sympatric in coastal areas (6,12). Hawke, however, conducting a field survey in 1979 reported signs and trails of L. provocax in almost all the areas he surveyed, even near the busy port of Puerto Aguirre. He estimated it to be common in the Aysen area and sighted five individuals which showed little fear of man (10). Argentina: although it has been reported as extinct it is now known that reasonable numbers exist in remote and inaccessible areas, especially in some of the Andean national parks (4,14).

HABITAT AND ECOLOGY Poorly known. Found in estuaries, rivers and lakes i.e. fresh and brackish waters (12). Preliminary investigations indicate it feeds almost entirely on crayfish and freshwater mussels (11). Local reports in Chile suggest that it breeds throughout the year (10).

THREATS TO SURVIVAL Main cause of decline is hunting for its valuable fur (2,5). Water pollution may have been an additional factor (captive otters are very susceptible to bacillary enteritis) although by the time human populations are sufficiently high to cause serious pollution the otters would probably have already been hunted out (13).

CONSERVATION MEASURES TAKEN Listed in Appendix 1 of the 1973 Convention on International Trade in Endangered Species of Wild Fauna and Flora, and trade in it or its products is therefore subject to strict regulation by ratifying nations, and trade for primarily commercial purposes is banned. Fully protected by law in Chile since 1972 and almost certainly occurs in Bernardo O'Higgins,

361

Alberto M. de Agustino and Hernando de Magallanes National Parks in southern Chile, and could occur in 9-10 parks further north, however enforcement of protection is usually minimal (6). Hunting, trade and export of skins has been forbidden in Argentina since 1950 (4), though again enforcement is difficult and up to at least 1977 pelts were smuggled from Chile into Argentina for export (12). Most of the areas where it is known to occur in Argentina are in national parks though here increased tourist pressure appears to have forced it into the more remote and inaccessible areas (4). The total area of national parks within the delimited range in Argentina is 2,086,000 ha (4).

CONSERVATION MEASURES PROPOSED Effective legal protection throughout its range. Surveys needed to determine status, distribution and ecology as the basis of a sound management plan including establishment of suitable reserves (13).

CAPTIVE BREEDING No information.

REMARKS For description of animal see (7,9). Van Zyll de Jong reviewed the systematics of neartic and neotropical Lutra in 1972 and lumped four of the six previously recognised species (Lutra annectens, L. enudris, L. incarum and L. platensis) together as L. longicaudis. He considered L. provocax and the Marine Otter, L. felina, to be distinct species, the former principally on the basis of its isolated distribution (15). Davis, however, following Hershkovitz, considers all the American Lutra excepting L. felina, but including L. provocax and the nearctic L. canadensis, to be conspecific, the name L. canadensis having priority. Full agreement over this has not yet been reached (3), and L. provocax is here retained as a full species.

REFERENCES

1. Davis, J.A. (1978). A classification of the otters. In Duplaix, N. (Ed.), Otters - Proceedings of the First Working Meeting of the IUCN/SSC Otter Specialist Group, Paramaribo, Suriname 27-29 March 1977. IUCN, Switzerland.
2. Dennler de La Tour, G. (1965). The present situation of wildlife conservation in Argentina and the prospects for the future. Unpd. report.
3. Duplaix, N. (1979). In litt.
4. Garcia-Mata, R. (1978). Nota sobre el status de L. provocax en la Argentina. In Duplaix, N. (Ed.), Otters - Proceedings of the First Working Meeting of the IUCN/SSC Otter Specialist Group, Paramaribo, Suriname 27-29 March 1977. IUCN, Switzerland.
5. Grimwood, I.R. (1967). In litt.
6. Grimwood, I.R. (1978). In litt.
7. Harris, C.J. (1968). Otters: A study of the recent Lutrinae. Weidenfeld and Nicolson, London.
8. Hershkovitz, P. (1972). The recent mammals of the Neotropical region: a zoogeographical and ecological review. In Keast, A., Erk, F.O. and Glass, B. (Eds), Evolution, mammals and southern continents. State Univ. Press, New York.
9. Osgood, W.H. (1943). The mammals of Chile. Field Mus. Nat. Hist. Zool. Ser. 30. 268pp.
10. Otter Specialist Group, IUCN/SSC. (1979). Report to SSC Meeting, Cambridge, Sept. 1979. Unpd.
11. Rageot, R. de (1978). In litt.
12. Rottman, J. (1977). In litt.
13. South American Otter Sub-Group of IUCN Otter Specialist Group. (1976). A report prepared by N. Duplaix. Unpd.

14. Tarak, A. (1980). Pers. comm.
15. Zyll de Jong, C.G. van (1972). A systematic review of the nearctic and neotropical river otters (genus _Lutra_). _Contr. Life Sci. Div. R. Ontario Mus._ 80: 1-104.

Pteronura brasiliensis (Gmelin, 1788)

Order   CARNIVORA   Family   MUSTELIDAE

SUMMARY Inhabits rivers and creeks of the greater Amazon basin. Distribution now discontinuous due to local extinction caused by overhunting for its skin which commands a high price; the species is particularly susceptible to poaching because of its diurnality, social habits and curiosity. Numbers unknown but declining in all countries except perhaps the Guianas. Trade bans and protection exist almost everywhere but enforcement is difficult and illegal trade continues. Occurs in a number of national parks and reserves. Protection from hunting is of primary importance plus studies to learn more of its distribution, numbers and ecology.

DISTRIBUTION South America. Formerly ranged in Colombia, Venezuela and the Guianas south to northern Argentina, and west to the foothills of the Andes. Now has a sporadic distribution within this range, still occurring in reasonable numbers in the Guianas, but only remnant populations in Brazil (inhabiting the eastern rivers but also the northern and central areas of Brazilian Amazonia (25)), Bolivia, Colombia, Ecuador, Peru, Paraguay and Venezuela (3,7,9,12,13,17,18). May be extinct in Uruguay, and Argentina (with the exception of the Iguazu Falls area (10,12,20)). Two subspecies are described: P. b. paranensis (of doubtful taxonomic validity) from the Paraguay and Parana rivers and in Brazil, northern Argentina and Uruguay, and P. b. brasiliensis elsewhere (7).

POPULATION Total numbers unknown but has undoubtedly declined over much of its range. Colombia: seriously endangered (4), numbers very low and has disappeared from many areas where it once occurred (4,8,12). Reasonably common in a few areas, notably the Tuparro National Park in the Orinoco drainage in the Comisaria del Vichada, on the Rio Mesay in Dpto. del Caqueta, and along the Rio Apaya which is to become a national park in 1981 (12). Elsewhere only a few local populations still survive in inaccessible areas (12). Ecuador: endangered (17); extremely rare, Professor Orces knows of only two records, one from the Sarayacu area of the Rio Pastaza and the other from the confluence of the Rio Aguarico and the Rio Napo (24). Suriname: a study conducted by N. Duplaix from July 1976 to April 1978 found them to be still common along most of the rivers of the interior (7). She estimated a total of about 1000 animals and considered the population to be probably stable (5,7). French Guiana: no information. Guyana: preliminary investigations by E. Laidler in 1979 learnt that Giant Otters were fairly widespread, including occurring close to Georgetown and to the coast. The only place they seemed depleted was in the Rupununi Savannah next to the Brazilian border where they were severely persecuted (15,16). Venezuela: in 1978 described (along with the manatee, Trichechus manatus) as the 'most endangered species of Venezuela's wildlife' (18). Little detailed information available but without doubt has declined drastically in recent years (18). Bolivia: unknown, probably very low (8). Paraguay: unknown, probably very low (G. Schaller, 1980 Pers. comm. to N. Duplaix). Brazil: has disappeared from large areas; isolated groups still remain in the southwest (10). Now virtually absent from all larger tributaries of the Amazon with the possible exception of the Xingu river (G. Shaller, 1980. Pers. comm. to N. Duplaix). Peru: exterminated from large areas of its former range (2,9). Argentina: virtually extinct except in the Iguazu Falls National Park area bordering Brazil (12,14). Uruguay: either extinct or virtually so (10,20), a few may still occur on the upper Rio Negro on the border with Brazil (20).

HABITAT AND ECOLOGY Inhabits large rivers and narrow forest creeks in seasonally flooded and high forest areas, apparently favouring blackwater areas and oxbow lakes. Two key factors in habitat choice are i) abundance of prey species in relatively shallow waters; ii) low sloping banks with good cover, and preferably easy access to small forest creeks or swampy areas and, in broader rivers, access to shallower areas such as rapids or waterfalls, with pools and ponds between boulders and sandbars (7). In Suriname Pteronura's seasonal movements were observed to be in accord with those of its preferred prey (Characoid fish) which move into flooded forest to spawn at the onset of the rainy season. Diurnal and gregarious, the otter's social system is based on an extended family unit with a well-defined pair bond; groups are therefore usually of 4-6 animals, although congregations of 8-15 have been noted. Clearly delineated territories are exhibited, during the dry season at least (7). 2-5 cubs are born once a year, with a second litter produced should the first one fail (noted in captive situations); gestation period is about 70 days (1,7,23).

THREATS TO SURVIVAL Poaching for its skin, and disturbance/destruction of riverine habitat. The main reason for Pteronura's disappearance over large portions of its range has been hunting for the fur tade. Giant Otters are shot on sight and are particularly easy targets because of their group social structure and curiosity (they can be enticed to approach boats by imitating the territoral 'snorting' call). A skin is very valuable, apparently approaching the same price as that of a Jaguar (Panthera onca). Smith reported in 1980-81 that a hunter would receive the equivalent of US$50 for a single skin, as much as he could expect to make clearing forest for 10 arduous days. By the time it reached Europe or the U.S.A. the skin would be worth about US$250 (22). Almost 20,000 Giant Otter skins were officially exported from the Brazilian Amazon between 1960 and 1969. The Peruvian Amazon, of smaller area, exported 23,980 skins between 1946 and 1973 (2,22). The trade declined significantly at the beginning of the 1970s when bans first came into effect (2,4,7,8,9), however illegal trade still continues and shipments were seized by Bolivia and Brazil in 1979-80 (8). The demand for skins has centred in Western Europe, mainly West Germany (8). The increasing invasion by man of once remote areas destroys the otter's habitat and exacerbates the hunting problem. For instance in Brazil Pteronura was once not uncommon on the Rios Aripuana and Canuma but the penetration of these areas by roads has heralded the otter's disappearance (25).

CONSERVATION MEASURES TAKEN Listed in Appendix 1 of the 1973 Convention on International Trade in Endangered Species of Wild Fauna and Flora (CITES), trade in it or its products therefore being subject to strict regulation by ratifying nations, and trade for primarily commercial purposes banned. Legally protected throughout its range and all countries involved have ratified the CITES (with the exception of Colombia) (4). However enforcement is patchy at best and handicapped by the extent of unpatrolled borders (8). Occurs in a number of national parks and reserves, notably in Venezuela, Suriname and Peru. It may occur in some parks in Brazil but confirmation is needed in most cases (25). Largely unstudied in the wild until recently; research is ongoing in Suriname, Peru and Guyana. This species was declared the top priority of the IUCN/SSC Otter Specialist Group in 1977 and 1980 (21). Preliminary findings on its ecology and behaviour were detailed by N. Duplaix in 1980 based on a study conducted in Suriname (6,7).

CONSERVATION MEASURES PROPOSED Protection from poaching is the greatest requirement. Increased protection in existing national parks and reserves is necessary and the creation of new reserves in areas where it still occurs is desirable. More detailed information is needed on distribution and numbers, particularly in Brazil, Paraguay, and Bolivia if conservation and management policies are to be properly planned and implemented in future (8).

CAPTIVE BREEDING In 1979 there were at least 14 males and 11 females (4 females bred in captivity) held in 7 zoological collections (6). The Sao Paulo and Brazilia zoos (Brazil) (1) and the Caracas Zoo (Venezuela) (7) have had success in breeding this species which requires ample space and burrowing facilities. It would appear possible to launch a broad-scale breeding programme in countries within its range and elsewhere if funds are made available.

REMARKS For description see (3,4,5,17). Dr. Nicole Duplaix, Chairman of the IUCN/SSC Otter Specialist Group very kindly assisted with the compilation of this data sheet.

REFERENCES 1. Autuori, M.P. and Deutsch, L.A. (1977). Contribution to the knowledge of the Giant Brazilian Otter Pteronura brasiliensis. Zool. Garten. 47: 1-8.

2. Brack Egg, A. (1978). Situacion actual de las nutrias (Lutrinae, Mustelidae) en el Peru. In Duplaix, N. (Ed.), Otters - Proceedings of the First Working Meeting of the IUCN/SSC Otter Specialist Group, Paramaribo, Suriname 27-29 March 1977. IUCN, Switzerland.

3. Cabrera, A. and Yepes, I. (1940). Mamiferos sud-americanos. Comp. Arg. Editores, Buenos Aires, Argentina.

4. Donadio, A. (1978). Some comments on otter trade and legislation in Colombia. In Duplaix, N. (Ed.), Otters - Proceedings of the First Working Meeting of the IUCN/SSC Otter Specialist Group, Paramaribo, Suriname 27-29 March 1977. IUCN, Switzerland.

5. Duplaix, N. (1978). Synopsis of the status and ecology of the Giant Otter in Suriname. In Duplaix, N. (Ed.), Otters - Proceedings of the First Working Meeting of the IUCN/SSC Otter Specialist Group, Paramaribo, Suriname 27-29 March 1977. IUCN, Switzerland.

6. Duplaix, N. (1980). Giant Otters: "Big Water Dogs" in Peril. National Geographic 158(1): 13-142.

7. Duplaix, N. (1980). Observation on the Ecology and Behaviour of the Giant River Otter Pteronura brasiliensis in Suriname. Rev. Ecol. (Terre Vie) 34: 495-620.

8. Duplaix, N. (1980). In litt.

9. Grimwood, I.R. (1969). Notes on the distribution and status of some Peruvian mammals 1968. Spec. Pub. 21. Am. Comm. Int. Wildlife Protec. and New York Zool. Soc. Bronx, New York.

10. Gudynas E. (1980). In litt.

11. Harris, C.J. (1968). Otters, a study of the Recent Lutrinae. Weidenfeld and Nicolson, London.

12. Hernandez-Camacho, J. (1980). Pers. comm.

13. Husson, A.M. (1978). The Mammals of Suriname. E.J. Brill, Leiden.

14. IUCN/SSC Otter Specialist Group (1979). Report SSC Meeting, Cambridge, Sept. 1979. Unpd.

15. Laidler, E. (1979). Giant Otter Expedition to Guyana. Unpd. report.

16. Laidler, E. (1979). In litt.

17. Melendres, A.P. (1978). Notas sobre las Nutrias de Rio del Ecuador. In Duplaix, N. (Ed.), Otters - Proceedings of the First Working Meeting of the IUCN/SSC Otter Specialist Group, Paramaribo, Suriname 27-29 March 1977. IUCN,

Switzerland.
18. Mondolfi, E. and Trebbau, P. (1978). Distribution and Status of the Giant Otter (Pteronura brasiliensis in Venezuela. In Duplaix, N. (Ed.), Otters - Proceedings of the First Working Meeting of the IUCN/SSC Otter Specialist Group, Paramaribo, Suriname 27-29 March 1977. IUCN, Switzerland.
19. Olney P.J.S. (Ed.) (1980). International Zoo Yearbook 20. Zool. Soc. London.
20. Praderi, R., Museo Nacional de Historia Natural Uruguay, (1981). In litt.
21. Recommendations of the Otter Specialist Group to the IUCN. Survival Service Commission arising from the first working meeting, Paramaribo, Suriname. In Duplaix, N. (Ed.), Otters - Proceedings of the First Working Meeting of the IUCN/SSC Otter Specialist Group, Paramaribo, Suriname 27-29 March 1977. IUCN, Switzerland.
22. Smith, N.J.H. (1980-81). Caimans, Capybaras, Otters, Manatees, and Man in Amazonia. Biological Conservation 19: 177-187.
23. Trebbau, P. (1978). Some observations on the mating behaviour of the Giant Brazilian Otter Pteronura brasiliensis. Zool. Garten 48(2-3): 187-188.
24. Ortiz-Crespo, F.I. (1981). In litt. Including information supplied by Prof. Gustavo Orcés and Juan Black.
25. Best, R. and Ayres, M. (1981). In litt.

Felis pardalis Linnaeus, 1758

Order   CARNIVORA   Family   FELIDAE

SUMMARY   Wide distribution from southern Texas to northern Argentina, but has disappeared from many areas because of hunting for its pelt, and habitat loss. Protected by law in most countries but adequate enforcement needed. Whilst illegal hunting should be controlled, the future of the species will ultimately depend on habitat preservation.

DISTRIBUTION   Southern Texas, U.S.A., south through Central and South America to northern Argentina (2,4,8,9,14,16,18,22,24,37), but not Chile (9), or Uruguay (10). Many subspecies have been described (16,18) but data on their distribution and status are scanty and the validity of many seems dubious and requires further study. The endangered F. p. albescens is now restricted to the Texas/Mexico border region south of a line between Eagle Pass and Corpus Christi, Texas, as far as the coastal lowlands of southeastern Tamaulipas, about 32 km north of Tampico (2,4,35), with one record each from the Trans-Pecos (12) and northern Texas (13), but these are believed to be released or escaped captives (35). F. p. mearnsi from Panama, Costa Rica and Nicaragua, and F. p. mitis from central and eastern Brazil (south of the lower Amazon), Paraguay and northern Argentina (8,18), are both listed in Appendix 1 of the 1973 Convention on International Trade in Endangered Species of Wild Fauna and Flora.

POPULATION   Koford who in 1972 conducted a seven month investigation into the status of the Ocelot (and Jaguar, Panthera onca) in Central and South America reported that although no precise estimates existed the species was known to be rare and threatened in parts of its range but not in others such as large areas of the Amazon rainforest. Its populations near settlements, roads and waterways had been everywhere seriously reduced (22,23). Very little specific data is available from the South American countries and only the following brief conjectural comments have been located. Bolivia: described in 1981 as endangered (5). Uruguay: Caviglia Tahier reports there to be no evidence that the Jaguar ever existed in Uruguay (10), though if it did, it disappeared at least a century ago (28). Brazil: vulnerable; hunted throughout Amazonia (3). Paraguay: field scientists have noted a reduction in Ocelot numbers in the Chaco region in the 1970s due to the rapid destruction of native vegetation in favour of introduced pasture grass and the great increase in the number of roads which allow easier access by hunters and settlers to once remote areas (38). Argentina: exact status reported as unknown in 1980 but Tarak considered it threatened (33); in 1976 described as rare to uncommon (20). Suriname: described in 1977 as not endangered (29). In Central America the Ocelot seems greatly diminished in number. El Salvador: included as endangered in a 1978 list of threatened species (31). Boursot (1979) reported it as rare and confined to two forests - Montecristo and El Imposible (6). In 1978 also considered endangered in Nicaragua (30), Costa Rica (25) and Panama (36), and all Felidae in Honduras were considered 'threatened or endangered' (1). No recent information has been located from Mexico. Numbers in the U.S.A. are unknown; preliminary findings of a survey in Texas in the late 1970s indicated about 35 at Santa Ana National Wildlife Refuge and 24 at Laguna Atascosa National Wildlife Refuge (35). However others claim that there are only 12-15 Ocelots at Laguna Atascosa and none at Santa Ana (35). A 1976 survey of southern Texas estimated 30-40 in Willacy County, 0-2 in Hidalgo Co., 12-20 in Cameron Co., and an unknown number in Kennedy Co. (35). Koford in 1977 suggested that less than 1000 adults of albescens possibly survived

(23). Ocelots occur rarely in southern Arizona (F. p. sonoriensis) (11,35).

HABITAT AND ECOLOGY   Humid tropical and subtropical forests, coastal mangroves, swampy savannas and even semi-arid thorn scrub (9,18,22). The Texas race inhabits scrub vegetation along waterways and in mountainous areas (24), and brushy coastal lowlands of Tamaulipas (23). The Ocelot is more adaptable than the Jaguar and may persist in partly-cleared forests, dense cover near large towns, second growth woodland, and abandoned cultivation which has gone back to bush (22,23). Solitary, nocturnal, an expert climber and hunts for food both in trees and on the ground (18,37). The varied diet includes fish and reptiles as well as small mammals and birds (18,23). Its cubs, usually two in number, are born between September and January (18).

THREATS TO SURVIVAL   Hunting and habitat loss. The Ocelot is in great demand for the fur trade. It is widespread, easily trapped or shot, and is therefore the most frequently hunted cat in Latin America. Demand for Latin American spotted cat skins increased substantially in the mid-1960s but known exports dropped after 1969, with new conservation restrictions and probably because accessible populations had been depleted (19,22,23,24,32). In the late 1960s it was estimated that 80,000 Ocelots were killed annually in Brazilian Amazonas, but implementation of conservation legislation in 1967 is thought to have halved the number. Nonetheless, in 1968, 128,966 Ocelot skins and in 1969, 133,069 were imported into the USA (27). In 1975, Britain imported 76,838 (7). Panama, Honduras, Guyana and a few other countries still allow hunting and commerce in Ocelot pelts. In the mid-1970s and late 1980 the price paid to a hunter for a crude pelt was about U.S. $40 (3,32). Such conditions invite smuggling from countries now trying to protect their cats (23). In 1980 a West German fur and leather trader was discovered to have used false permits issued in Paraguay authorizing the export of more than 40,000 Ocelot skins; in W. Germany an Ocelot coat sells for up to U.S. $40,000 (21). Ocelots are also reported to be much in demand as pets, selling for U.S. $800 (15); in 1977 the trade was still flourishing in Nicaragua, where the method is to kill the mother in order to capture the cubs (S. Ryan 1977, In litt.). The new roads being built in the Amazonian region are not considered by Smith as likely to threaten the status of wild cats for decades; as yet the Trans-Amazonian highway has had little impact on the rainforest ecosystem, only 1 km of the 20 km wide strip along the road allocated by the government for agricultural development having been effectively taken up; poor soils, ill-chosen crops and other factors having slowed down the human colonisation (22,32); although in 1980 Best and Ayres reported that the poor returns from agricultural ventures had forced many settlers to turn to subsistence hunting, including the trapping of cats for their furs (3). Clearing of forest for cattle raising is posing a bigger threat (22,32). Elsewhere, clearing of land for plantation crops e.g. cotton, cane and bananas, has eliminated vast belts of the Ocelot's lowland habitat (22). If protected from hunting the Ocelot would survive but adequate woody cover is essential (23).

CONSERVATION MEASURES TAKEN   The species as a whole is listed in Appendix 2 of the 1973 Convention on International Trade in Endangered Species of Wild Fauna and Flora (CITES), trade in it or its products therefore being subject to regulation and monitoring by ratifying nations. Two subspecies, F. p. mearnsi and F. p. mitis are listed in Appendix 1, trade in them therefore being subject to much stricter regulations and trade for primarily commercial purposes banned. The species is also listed as endangered in the U.S.A., which makes hunting and importation illegal (34), and is protected by law in Mexico (23). In fact, Ocelot hunting and trading are prohibited in most countries of its range (in Colombia and Peru, for example, from 1973). Unfortunately, enforcement is difficult because hunters are so numerous and Ocelot skins easy to conceal. Several national parks, reserves and private ranches give the species protection

370

(22,23), the Texas race, for example, in the National Wildlife Refuges of the lower Rio Grande Valley, where river-bottom brush is not cleared for agriculture (23,35).

CONSERVATION MEASURES PROPOSED Field surveys are needed to more accurately determine distribution and current status of populations throughout its range in order to provide a sound basis for the creation of effective conservation measures. These will include the establishment of adequately protected reserves and more effective suppression of illegal hunting and international commerce in illicit skins. Koford mentions that studies are needed to determine the extent to which wild populations could supply a sustainable yield for the fur industry (23).

CAPTIVE BREEDING In 1979, 85 males, 99 females and five of unknown sex were held in 81 collections, 77 captive bred (26).

REMARKS For description see (2,9,16,18). The Ocelot, Margay (F. wiedii) and Little Spotted Cat (F. tigrina) are all included in the subgenus Leopardus which some authors elevate to generic status. Donna L. Mayers is studying the phylogeny and distribution of Latin American Spotted Cats (including F. pardalis) (38). Dr. C.B. Koford and Dr. R.H. Baker assisted with the original draft of this data sheet.

REFERENCES 1. Aguilar, W. (1978). El manejo de la Vida Silvestre en Honduras. In Morales, R., Macfarland, C., Incer, J. and Hobbs, A. (Eds), Memorias de la Primera Reunion Regional Centroamerican sobre Vida Silvestre. Matagalpa, Nicaragua 25-29 Julio 1978. Unidad de areas silvestres y cuencas del catie.

2. Alvarez, T. (1963). The recent mammals of Tamaulipas, Mexico. Univ. Kansas Publ. Mus. Nat. Hist. 14(15): 363-473.

3. Ayres, M. and Best, R. (1981). In litt.

4. Baker, R. (1956). Mammals of Coahuila, Mexico. Univ. Kansas Publ. Mus. Nat. Hist. 9(7): 125-335.

5. Bejarano, G. (1981). In litt.

6. Boursot, J. (1979). In litt.

7. Burton, J.A. (1976). Wildlife imports in Britain 1975. Oryx 13(4): 330-331.

8. Cabrera, A. (1957). Catalogo de los mamiferos de America del Sur. Rev. del Mus. Argent. de Cienc. Nat. 'Bernardino Rivadavia', Cienc. Zool. 4(1,2): 1-731.

9. Cabrera, A. and Yepes, J. (1940). Mamiferos Sud-Americanos. Comp. Arg. Edit., Buenos Aires.

10. Caviglia Tahier, L. (1981). In litt.

11. Cockrum, W.L. (1960). The recent mammals of Arizona: their taxonomy and distribution. Univ. Arizona Press.

12. Culbertson, K. and Schmidly, D.J. (1974). Summary of statements on the status of the rare, endangered, and peripheral mammals in Texas. Texas Organization for Endangered Species. Temple. 8pp.

13. Davis, W.B. (1951). Unusual occurrence of the Ocelot in Texas. J. Mammal. 32: 363-364.

14. Davis, W.B. (1974). The Mammals of Texas. Texas Parks Wildl. Dep. Bull. 41: 1-294.

15. Domalain, J.-Y. (1977). Confessions of an animal trafficker. Natural History 86(5): 54-66.

16. Goldman, E.A. (1943). The races of the Ocelot and Margay in middle America. J. Mammal. 24(3): 372-385.

17. Guggisberg, C.A.W. (1975). Wild Cats of the World. David

and Charles, Newton Abbot and London.

18. Hall, E.R. and Kelson, K.R. (1959). The Mammals of North America. The Ronald Press Co., New York.
19. Hanson Love, A. (1981). In litt.
20. IUCN/SSC Cat Group Newsletter No.2, 1976.
21. IUCN. (1980). Multi-million forgeries in fur trade documents uncovered. IUCN/WWF News Release No. 8/80.
22. Koford, C.B. (1973). Project 694. Status survey of Jaguar and Ocelot in tropical America. World Wildlife Yearbook 1972-73: 215-219.
23. Koford, C.B. (1977). In litt.
24. Leopold, A.S. (1959). Wildlife of Mexico: the game birds and mammals. Univ. of California Press, Berkeley.
25. Lopez, E. (1978). Informe sobre las actividades de la Direccion General de Recursos Pesqueros y Vida Silvestre de Costa Rica. In Morales, R., Macfarland, C., Incer, J. and Hobbs, A. (Eds), Memorias de la Primera Reunion Regional Centroamerican sobre Vida Silvestre. Matagalpa, Nicaragua 25-29 Julio 1978. Unidad de areas silvestres y cuencas del catie.
26. Olney, P.J.S. (Ed.) (1980). International Zoo Yearbook 20. Zool. Soc. London.
27. Paradiso, J.L. (1972). Status Report on Cats (Felidae) of the World, 1971. Spec. Sci. Report 157, U.S. Dept. of the Interior, Fish and Wildlife Service (Bureau of Sport Fisheries and Wildlife), Washington, D.C.
28. Praderi, R. (1981). In litt.
29. Reichart, H. (1979). In litt.
30. Salas, J.B. (1978). Informe sobre las actividades que desarrolla el Departamento de Vida silvestre en Nicaragua. In Morales, R., Macfarland, C., Incer, J. and Hobbs, A. (Eds), Memorias de la Primera Reunion Regional Centroamerican sobre Vida Silvestre. Matagalpa, Nicaragua 25-29 Julio 1978. Unidad de areas silvestres y cuencas del catie.
31. Serrano, F. (1978). Informe de actividades de la Unidad de Parques Nacionales y Vida Silvestre en El Salvador. In Morales, R., Macfarland, C., Incer, J. and Hobbs, A. (Eds), Memorias de la Primera Reunion Regional Centroamerican sobre Vida Silvestre. Matagalpa, Nicaragua 25-29 Julio 1978. Unidad de areas silvestres y cuencas del catie.
32. Smith, N.J.H. (1976). Spotted cats and the Amazon skin trade. Oryx 13(4): 362-371.
33. Tarak, A. (1980). Pers. comm.
34. USFWS. (1980). Endangered and threatened wildlife and plants; U.S. populations of seven endangered species. Federal Register 44 (144): 43705.
35. USFWS. (1980). The Ocelot. In Selected vertebrate endangered species of the seacoast of the United States. Fish and Wildlife Service. U.S.Dept. of the Interior.
36. Vallester, E. (1978). Informe de Panama sobre la situacion de la Fauna Silvestre. In Morales, R., Macfarland, C., Incer, J. and Hobbs, A. (Eds), Memorias de la Primera Reunion Regional Centroamerican sobre Vida Silvestre. Matagalpa, Nicaragua 25-29 Julio 1978. Unidad de areas silvestres y cuencas del catie.
37. Walker, E.P. (1975). Mammals of the World. The Johns Hopkins Univ. Press, Baltimore and London.
38. Wetzel, R.M. (1980). In litt.

EASTERN COUGAR or EASTERN PUMA   ENDANGERED

Felis concolor cougar (Kerr, 1792)

Order   CARNIVORA   Family   FELIDAE

SUMMARY Remnant populations may survive in former range in eastern North America, but conclusive evidence lacking. Decline due to hunting, decreasing prey abundance and habitat loss. Classified as 'Endangered' in the U.S. Endangered and Threatened Wildlife listing, similarly in Canada.

DISTRIBUTION United States and Canada. Range extended from southern Ontario, Quebec and New Brunswick to the Carolinas where it intergraded with another subspecies, coryi; and from the eastern seaboard across to the Great Plains (2,3,9,10). Its present distribution is uncertain and it may be extinct but sightings throughout its range suggest that a remnant population may still survive. It was reported in 1972 to have re-established itself in southeastern Canada, particularly New Brunswick (8), and a 1978 report mentions recent sightings in Nova Scotia, Quebec and Ontario, as well as in New Brunswick (10). It is unknown whether those sighted in the eastern United States are natives or belong to western subspecies and have escaped from zoos (4). There is probably a scattering of cougars along the Appalachians, at least from Tennessee up to Virginia; in the lowlands from South Carolina to Alabama; and another group in New Brunswick to New England (5).

POPULATION The subspecies cougar was first stated to be extinct as long ago as 1946 (9). However, there have since been repeated sightings throughout its range, notably in Virginia, on the North Carolina-Tennessee State Line, and in South Carolina (5,6). In Canada, Wright put the 1972 population in New Brunswick alone at 25-50 (8). However van Zyll de Jong and van Ingen report that no reliable estimates of cougar numbers in eastern Canada exist or can be made, but numbers are probably very low (10). The number of reported sightings increased in the 1940s and since then has levelled off or decreased slightly (10).

HABITAT AND ECOLOGY Forested areas where game is abundant (8). Deer are the preferred food (7). Little is known of the life history of this subspecies but it is presumably much the same as that of the western form. Litters of 1-6, usually two; gestation 92 to 104 days (4).

THREATS TO SURVIVAL Would still probably be shot by those who consider the cougar a threat to themselves and their livestock. Continuing loss of habitat, and decline in prey, notably deer, are other adverse factors (4).

CONSERVATION MEASURES TAKEN Listed in Appendix 1 of the 1973 Convention on International Trade in Endangered Species of Wild Fauna and Flora, trade in it or its products therefore being subject to strict regulation by ratifying nations, and trade for primarily commercial purposes banned. Listed as 'Endangered' by the United States Department of the Interior and therefore protected in all states of its former and present range (4). Protected by law in Nova Scotia, New Brunswick and Ontario, but not in Quebec (10). Numerous protected areas exist within its former range. No official Eastern Cougar Recovery Team exists in the U.S.A. but Robert L. Downing coordinates efforts to locate cougars in the Eastern States. This is done by encouraging, receiving, screening, investigating, and filing reports of sightings and sign. He is also writing a Recovery Plan for the subspecies, the initial aim of which must be to devise a practical search strategy for the eastern U.S.A. (11).

CONSERVATION MEASURES PROPOSED Creation of a reserve in any area where this subspecies may be found to survive.

CAPTIVE BREEDING None.

REMARKS Described as a medium to large-sized dark subspecies similar to coryi of the southeastern states but differing in cranial characters (anteriorly more convergent zygomata and narrower flatter nasals); also similar to hippolestes of Wyoming but smaller and skull differing in detail (1,9). The generic name Profelis is sometimes used.

The species ranges from southern Yukon and British Columbia through North and Central America to Patagonia, and from the Atlantic to the Pacific coast and has the widest distribution of any terrestrial mammal in the Western Hemisphere. Many subspecies are described, Young and Goldman listing 15 in North and Central America, and about 30 being recognized altogether (3,5,9). In addition to the present subspecies, the Florida cougar coryi, likewise considered as 'Endangered' (see separate data sheet), and F. c. costaricensis (eastern Panama to Costa Rica and probably Nicaragua) are all listed in Appendix 1 of CITES; the species as a whole is listed in Appendix 2. This data sheet was compiled with the assistance of the Fish and Wildlife Service of the United States Department of the Interior and the Committee on the Status of Endangered Wildlife in Canada.

REFERENCES 1. Allen, G.M. (1942). Extinct and vanishing mammals of the western hemisphere with the marine species of all the oceans. Spec. Publ. Amer. Comm. Int. Wildlife Protection No.11.
2. Cahalane, V.H. (1964) A preliminary study of distribution and numbers of cougar, grizzly and wolf in North America. New York Zool. Soc.
3. Hall, E.R. and Kelson, K.R. (1959). The Mammals of North America. The Ronald Press Co., New York.
4. Horan, J. (1975-76). Eastern cats. The Predator 11(4).
5. Nowak, R. (1975). The Cougar in the United States and Canada. Unpd. Report.
6. Pritchard, P.C.H. (1976). Endangered Species: Florida Panther. The Florida Naturalist 49(4): 15-22.
7. Wright, B.S. (1959). The Ghost of North America. Vantage Press, New York.
8. Wright, B.S. (1972). The eastern panther: a question of survival. Clarke, Irwin and Co., Toronto and Vancouver.
9. Young, S.P. and Goldman, E.A. (1946). The Puma, Mysterious American Cat. The American Wildlife Institute, Washington D.C.
10. van Zyll de Jong, C.G. and van Ingen, E. (1978). Status of the eastern Cougar (Felis concolor cougar) in Canada. In Committee on the Status of Endangered Wildlife in Canada: Status Reports and Evaluations. Vol.1 1976-1979.
11. Downing, R.L. (1981). Eastern Cougar Newsletter, January 1981.

FLORIDA COUGAR or PANTHER

ENDANGERED

Felis concolor coryi (Bangs, 1896)

Order   CARNIVORA

Family   FELIDAE

SUMMARY   Occurs in southern Florida and possibly other southeastern States of the United States. Estimated numbers vary between 30 and 300 but no in depth census has been conducted. Decline due to hunting, decrease of prey populations and habitat loss. Listed as 'Endangered' on the United States List of Endangered and Threatened Wildlife. A Florida Panther Recovery Team was established in July 1976, and has developed a Recovery Plan for the animal.

DISTRIBUTION   United States. Formerly ranged from eastern Texas or western Louisiana and the Lower Mississippi River Valley to the southeastern States, including Arkansas, Mississippi, Alabama, Georgia, Florida and parts of Tennessee and South Carolina (4,5,12,15). Present distribution uncertain, but consistently documented evidence of its presence is available only from Collier, Dade and Monroe Counties in southern Florida - in the Fakahatchee Strand, the Big Cypress National Preserve, the Everglades National Park, and Collier - Seminole State Park (18). Questionable whether it survives outside Florida but recent reports over much of its historical range suggest such a possibility. Consistent groupings of sighting reports may indicate its presence in Arkansas and Louisiana (5,6,12,13,14,18), and the Chief of Game Management in Alabama was reported in 1976 to believe it still survived in that State (10). For map see (4,15,18). Intergrades in the north with F. concolor cougar and to the west and northwest with F. c. stanleyana and F. c. hippolestes (15).

POPULATION   No detailed census. The present status of the Florida panther over most of its historical range is poorly known and depends to a large extent upon the reliability of sighting reports, most of which are questionable (18). One population is definitely known to exist in the vicinity of the Fakahatchee Strand, Big Cypress Swamp and the Everglades National Park (16,18). Estimated numbers for Florida range from 30 to 300. The number of alleged Cougar sightings in the State over the past 20 years has steadily increased. Reports in other southeastern States have also become more frequent (5). The Florida population has declined drastically since the colonization of America, having probably been relatively abundant at the turn of the century, although apparently already reduced in northern Florida but surviving in good numbers in parts of southern Florida until the 1930s (5,7). At one time it seemed uncertain whether those now occurring within the former range of coryi were of that subspecies (5), however two illegally killed in Florida in 1974 and 1976, and examined by R.M. Nowak, exhibited characters in close agreement with those of coryi (R.M. Nowak, 1977. In litt.) and a third taken in the Big Cypress Preserve in 1978 was also attributed to coryi (2).

HABITAT AND ECOLOGY   Because of its scarcity and secretive nature, little is known of this Cougar. In Florida its habitats include savanna, hardwood, button-wood, dune and coastal hammocks, mangrove thicket, cypress and mangrove swamps, and open pinelands (5). Requirements seem simply to be a large area with adequate food supply and some dense vegetation for cover (1,5). Home range unknown but putatively anything from 130 sq. km to 1000 or 2000 sq. km (5,12). Prey includes deer, hogs, racoons and other small mammals, insects and reptiles. Solitary. The few records suggest an average litter size of two with a range of 1-3 (5).

THREATS TO SURVIVAL   Layne and McCauley consider excessive hunting as the primary cause of decline, with illegal killing and highway mortality now the major forces depressing the population below carrying capacity, and habitat loss and decline in prey populations of secondary importance except perhaps in the late 1930s and early 1940s when the Texas cattle tick eradication programme involved the slaughter of thousands of deer (5). Nowak believes increased human access and activity within its range is probably the greatest threat (7). The construction of 'Alligator Alley' and other roads and the popularity of swamp buggies and all-terrain vehicles resulted in much of the Big Cypress and adjoining lands being dotted with hunting camps and criss-crossed by trails (7,9). The Cougar is vulnerable to all the long term threats to the southern Florida ecosystems, including large-scale diversion of fresh water, intensification of oil exploration and exploitation, potential upgrading of access roads, and continued use of a training runway at the proposed Big Cypress Jetport site (7).

CONSERVATION MEASURES TAKEN The Florida cougar is listed in Appendix 1 of the 1973 Convention on International Trade in Endangered Species of Wild Fauna and Flora, trade in it or its products therefore being subject to strict regulation by ratifying nations, and trade for primarily commercial purposes banned. Being also listed as 'Endangered' by the United States Department of the Interior, it is protected in all states of its former and present range as well as in National Parks and Wildlife Refuges. A month-long investigation was undertaken in 1973 by Nowak and McBride for WWF (8) and by McBride again in 1974 (9). In March 1976 The Florida Audubon Society held a 2 day Florida Panther Conference in Orlando, Florida in an attempt to develop some consensus on the status of the subspecies and the most desirable strategy for its conservation (19). A Florida Panther Recovery Team was established in July 1976 and has developed a Recovery Plan for the cat (19). Because the first factor limiting the conservation and management of the Florida Panther is lack of information on status and distribution a 'Florida Panther Record Clearinghouse' consisting of a central filing system for reports of panthers was established in October 1978 (16,17,19). In the period 1 July 1979 through 30 June 1980 it received, categorized and filed 139 panther records from within Florida. These included a 68 pound roadkilled adult female and 11 pound roadkilled young adult male, both hit on Highway 29; the hides and skeletons are in the Florida State Museum (20). The Everglades National Park consists of about 525,000 ha which is totally protected. Acquisition of the Big Cypress National Preserve is in progress and eventually 220,000 ha will come into public ownership The Fakahatchee Strand is also being acquired for a State preserve; by 1981 about 17,000 ha of an approximate 24,000 ha preserve had come into public ownership (18).

CONSERVATION MEASURES PROPOSED Implementation of the Recovery Plan, which aims at: 1) finding and maintaining any existing populations; 2) a captive breeding programme for possible restocking in the future; 3) a public education programme; and 4) evaluating existing rules and regulations applying to the subspecies and formulating any necessary new ones (12,18). In particular the plan mentions that it is vital to acquire the remainder of the Fakahatchee Strand and the prairies and cypress forests adjacent to it to ensure a unified management strategy which will take into consideration the needs of the Florida Panther, and which will also provide an extremely important permanent corridor of natural habitat between the Strand, the Big Cypress National Preserve and the Everglades National Park (19). The Strand and the Big Cypress are heavily hunted and the Recovery Team recommends its cessation in light of the illegal killing of a panther in the Big Cypress in 1978 (2,19).

CAPTIVE BREEDING A captive group at the Everglades Wonder Gardens, Bonita Springs, Florida, comprised 4 males and 4 females in 1976 (10).

REMARKS For description of animal see (1,3,4,14,15): it is a medium-sized, dark subspecies, closely allied to nominate cougar but distinguished by a broader, high skull with more inflated nasals and more evenly spreading zygomata. The species as a whole is found from southern Yukon and British Columbia to Patagonia and from the Atlantic to the Pacific Coast (5,7,15), thus having the greatest natural range of any terrestrial mammal in the Western Hemisphere (4). Young and Goldman list 15 subspecies in North and Central America and about 30 are recognized altogether (4,6,10). The eastern F. c. cougar is also considered 'Endangered' (see separate data sheet) and with F. c. costaricensis also in Appendix 1 of the Washington Convention, the species as a whole being included in Appendix 2. This data sheet benefited greatly from information supplied by Robert C. Belden, Leader of the Florida Panther Recovery Team.

REFERENCES

1. Bangs, O. (1899). The Florida Puma. Proc. Biol. Soc. Wash. 13: 15-17.

2. Belden, R.C. and Forrester, D.J. (1980). A Specimen of Felis concolor coryi from Florida. J. Mammal. 61(1): 160-161.

3. Cory, C.B. (1896). Hunting and fishing in Florida. Estes and Lauriat, Boston.

4. Hall, E.R. and Kelson, K.R. (1959). The Mammals of North America. The Ronald Press Co., New York.

5. Layne, J.N. and McCauley, M.N. (1976). Biological Overview of the Florida Panther. Revised version of paper presented at Florida Panther Conference, Orlando, 17-18 March 1976.

6. Lowman, G.E. (1975). A survey of endangered, threatened, rare, status undertermined, peripheral and unique mammals of the southeastern national forests and grasslands. U.S. Dept. Agric. Forest. Serv., Southern Region.

7. Nowak, R. (1975). The Cougar in the United States and Canada. Report.

8. Nowak, R.M. and McBride, R. (1974). WWF Project 973. Status survey of the Florida Panther. WWF Yearbook 1973-74: 237-242.

9. Nowak, R.M. and McBride, R. (1975). WWF Project 973. Status of the Florida Panther. WWF Yearbook 1974-75: 244-246.

10. Pritchard, P.C.H. (1976). Endangered Species: Florida Panther. The Florida Naturalist 49(4): 15-22.

11. Tinsley, J.B. (1970). The Florida Panther. Great Outdoors Publishing Co., St. Petersburg, Florida.

12. USDI, National Fish and Wildlife Laboratory, U.S. Fish and Wildlife Service, (1977). Draft data sheet, Florida panther.

13. Williams, L.E. Jr. (1976). Florida panther. In Inventory of rare and endangered biota of Florida. Interim Microfiche ed. prepared by Fla. Comm. on Rare and Endangered Plants and Animals. Pp. 1019-1024.

14. Williams, L.E. Jr. (1978). Florida Panther. In Layne, J.N. (Ed.), Rare and Endangered Biota of Florida. Vol.1 Mammals. Univ. Presses of Florida.

15. Young, S.P. and Goldman, E.A. (1964). The puma, mysterious American cat. The American Wildlife Institute, Washington D.C. 358pp.

16. Belden, R.C. (1979). Florida Panther Investigation - A 1978 Progress Report. In Odom, R.R. and Landers, L. (Eds), Proc. of the Rare and Endangered Wildlife Symposium. Georgia Dept. Nat. Resour. Tech. Bull. WL4, Athens, Ga. pp.123-133.

17. Belden, R.C. (1978). How to recognise Panther Tracks. Proc. Ann. Conf. S.E. Assoc. Fish and Wildlife Agencies 32: 112-115.

18. Belden, R.C. (1978-1981). Florida panther (Felis concolor coryi Bangs) Recovery Plan. Report. 29pp.

19. Pritchard, P.C.H. (Ed.) (1976). Proceedings of a Florida Panther Conference. March 1976. Florida Audubon Society and Florida Game and Fresh Water Comm. 121pp.

20. Belden, R.C. (1980). Florida Panther. Project Number E-1-04. Annual Performance Report.

ANDEAN or MOUNTAIN CAT   RARE

Felis jacobita (Cornalia, 1865)

Order   CARNIVORA   Family   FELIDAE

SUMMARY   The range of this little known species is limited to the sector of the high Andes between 14° and 24°S. There is no knowledge of whether or not numbers are declining or the amount of suitable habitat decreasing, and there appears to be no commercial exploitation.

DISTRIBUTION   The high Andes of northern Chile, southern Peru, southwestern Bolivia and northwestern Argentina (1,4).

POPULATION   No estimates have been made of numbers, but the species seems to be naturally very rare (4,7).

HABITAT AND ECOLOGY   Apparently the treeless, rocky arid and semi-arid zone of the high Andes to at least 5000 m elevation (4,6). Presumably feeds on the birds, Mountain Viscacha (Lagidium peruanum) and other rodents of the sierra (1,4).

THREATS TO SURVIVAL   Unknown. The amount of suitable habitat is not obviously decreasing (4) and there is no evidence of commercial exploitation (5,8).

CONSERVATION MEASURES TAKEN   Listed in Appendix 1 of the 1973 Convention on International Trade in Endangered Species of Wild Fauna and Flora, trade in it or its products therefore being subject to severe restriction by ratifying nations, and trade for primarily commercial purposes banned. Protected by law in Peru, but apparently not specifically listed as protected in any of the other countries of its range (4). Possibly occurs in the 400,000 ha Lauca National Park, Chile, and in the 300,000 ha Pampa Galeras Nature Reserve in Peru (4).

CONSERVATION MEASURES PROPOSED   Studies to learn more of this species. Because of its rarity and limited distribution, protection in all countries of its range is highly desirable.

CAPTIVE BREEDING   There is no record of any captive breeding and hardly any references to it being kept in captivity (Mrs A. Hansen Love maintained two young animals for a while (8)). Otherwise all recorded captive specimens have proved on examination to be Felis (Lynchailurus) pajeros garleppi, the northern subspecies of the Pampas Cat (9).

REMARKS   For description of animal see (2). This species is about twice the size of a domestic cat, with long soft pelage, dark spots and a long, thick, ringed tail. Skins are often misidentified (4). Some authorities place it in a genus to itself: Oreailurus.

REFERENCES   1.   Cabrera, A. (1957-1961). Catalogo de los mamiferos de America del Sur. Rev. del Mus. Argent. de Cienc. Nat. 'Bernardino Rivadavia', Cienc. Zool., 4(1-2): 1 - 731.
2.   Cabrera, A. and Yepes, J. (1940). Mamiferos Sud-Americanos. Vols. 1 and 2. Compania Argent. Edit., Buenos Aires.
3.   Grimwood, I.R. (1969). Notes on the distribution and status of some Peruvian mammals, 1968. Spec. Publ. 21, Am.

Comm. Int. Wildlife Protec. and New York Zool. Soc. Bronx, New York.

4. Koford, C. (1977). In litt.
5. Paradiso, J.L. (1977). Status Report on Cats (Felidae) of the World, 1971. Spec. Sci. Report 157, U.S. Dept. of the Interior Fish and Wildlife Service (Bureau of Sport Fisheries and Wildlife), Washington D.C.
6. Pearson, O.P. (1957). Additions to the mammalian fauna of Peru and notes on some other Peruvian mammals. Breviora Mus. Comp. Zool., Cambridge, Mass. 6 pp.
7. Bejarano, G. (1981). In litt.
8. Hansen Love, A. (1981). In litt.
9. Leyhausen, P. (1981). In litt.

LITTLE SPOTTED CAT, TIGER CAT   VULNERABLE
or ONCILLA

Felis tigrina (Schreber 1777)

Order   CARNIVORA   Family   FELIDAE

SUMMARY   Widely distributed from southern Central America to northern Argentina. Appears to be naturally rare and is subject to intense hunting pressure for the fur trade. Also threatened throughout much of its range by habitat loss. Studies are urgently needed to allow the formulation and implementation of conservation measures.

DISTRIBUTION   Poorly known, the species being little observed and easily confused with the Margay (F. wiedii) (1,7,10). Occurs possibly as far north as Nicaragua, and certainly from Costa Rica south through Panama and into South America as far as northern Argentina. Unrecorded in Chile, Bolivia and Uruguay, and not definitely known to occur in Peru, though thought likely (6). Hall and Kelson and Cabrera recognise four subspecies (1,8): F. t. oncilla inhabits Costa Rica, where it is found throughout except for part of the Atlantic zone, and northern Panama. The species is also included in a 1978 list of endangered mammals of Nicaragua but is not recorded by Hall and Kelson as occurring in that country (4,5,8,20,21). F. t. pardinoides the Andean zone from western Venezuela, (where locally distributed in tropical and subtropical cloud forest regions in the Coastal Cordillera and the Andes (26)), Colombia, Ecuador and possibly as far as northern Peru, also extending into southern Panama (1,4). Absent from central Panama (4). F. t. tigrina in northeast Brazil and from French Guiana to eastern Venezuela where recorded from Bolivar and the Amazon Territory (1,9) and F. t. guttula in eastern and southern Brazil, Paraguay and northern Argentina from Misiones to the Chaco of Salta Province (1,2).

POPULATION   No estimates available. In 1973 reported as rare in most areas and common in none (14) Based on the number of skins obtained or exported, Grimwood in 1978 considered it to be either much rarer or more restricted in habitat than the Ocelot (F. pardalis) (7), itself a 'Vulnerable' species (13). Considered 'Endangered' in Nicaragua (see above) and Costa Rica (19,21). Not included in a 1978 report of threatened mammals of Panama (23), but this is almost certainly because it was not distinguished from the Margay. Noted as 'rare to uncommon' in Argentina in 1976 (3). There is no specific information from the rest of its range.

HABITAT AND ECOLOGY   In common with most Latin American felids this species remains unstudied and its habits virtually unknown in the wild (15). Apparently favours subtropical forests, ranging up into montane forest in the highlands of eastern Brazil (14). It is considerably less arboreal than the Margay (17). Gestation period averages 75 days (18).

THREATS TO SURVIVAL   Principle threats are uncontrolled hunting and habitat destruction. It is subject to intense hunting pressure for the fur trade (12,14,15). In 1971 28,000 pelts were counted in Brazilian warehouses alone (12). Recorded trade in 1977 comprised at least 13,000 skins but the actual trade was certainly far greater (11). Pelts are considerably less valuable than those of the Ocelot (14), but as the latter are hunted out from accessible areas, pressure on the smaller and rarer spotted cats such as F. tigrina and F. wiedii will doubtless increase. In Brazil, however, in 1973 it was reported that in general known exports of spotted cats dropped after 1969, partially as a result of the new conservation laws enacted at the time, though probably also through depletion of accessible populations (12). Much of the species' subtropical forest habitat in Brazil has been converted to coffee plantations (14). F. t. oncilla in Costa Rica is in an area suffering heavily from forest depletion (16).

CONSERVATION MEASURES TAKEN The species as a whole is listed in Appendix 2 of the 1973 Convention on International Trade in Endangered Species of Wild Fauna and Flora, therefore any trade in it or its products is subject to regulation and monitoring by ratifying nations. The Central American subspecies, F. t. oncilla, is listed in Appendix 1, trade in it being subject to much stricter regulations, trade for primarily commercial purposes being banned. Protected in Costa Rica (19) and in Ecuador (12). Its legal status elsewhere is unknown, though it is certainly included in general wildlife legislation in other countries, e.g. bans on hunting and trade in Paraguay and the Peruvian Amazon (7), on trade in Brazil, and on exports of untanned wildlife skins in Colombia (12). However, such laws are very difficult to enforce and their real impact difficult to assess since much of the trade goes unrecorded. Known to occur in Iguazu National Park in Misiones, Argentina (22) and doubtless occurs in other national parks and reserves throughout its range, though in many of these protection is perhaps only nominal. However strict protection is enforced on several large private ranches in the Venezuelan Llanos and Brazilian Pantanal regions, some of which almost certainly hold populations of this species (15).

CONSERVATION MEASURES PROPOSED Koford in a 1975 report makes extensive recommendations for the management and conservation of Latin American felids including their controlled exploitation as a resource for tourism and licensed hunting, though in the latter context it is noted that other than in northeastern Brazil where it may be a valuable source of income to the campesinos, there is little justification for hunting this cat (14,15). Before detailed recommendations can be formulated, extensive ecological studies are needed (15). Adoption of uniform wildlife regulations or cooperative enforcement agreements between adjacent countries would reduce illegal trade in market centres such as Leticia and Buenos Aires (15). Enforcement of a minimum size regulation would limit the proportion of exports of the smaller species, such as F. tigrina (14).

CAPTIVE BREEDING Has been bred in captivity on a number of occasions (18).

REMARKS For description see (8). The taxonomy and distribution of the subgenus Leopardus, including Felis tigrina is the subject of a study by Donna L. Mayers begun in 1980 (24). Some authorities consider Leopardus to be a genus rather than a subgenus, the Tiger Cat thus having the name Leopardus tigrinus. Leyhausen, based on the fact that some specimens have a regular gestation period of 63-65 days, believes this argues in favour of the idea that L. tigrinus may cover two or even three species (25).

REFERENCES   1.   Cabrera, A. (1957-61). Catalogo de los mamiferos de America del Sur. Revista del Museo Argentina de Ciencias Naturales 'Bernardino Rivadavia', Cienc. Zool., 4(1-2): 1-731.

2.   Cabrera, A. (1963). Los Felidos Vivientes de la Republica Argentina. Revista del Museo Argentina de Ciencias Naturales 'Bernardino Rivadavia' e Instituto Nacional de Investigacion de las Ciencias Naturales. 6 (5): 161-247.

3.   Cat Specialist Group, Newsletter No.2 (1976). IUCN Survival Service Commission. Unpd. Report. 12 pp.

4.   Gardner, A.L. (1971). Notes on the Little Spotted Cat, Felis tigrina oncilla Thomas, in Costa Rica. J. Mammal. 52

(2): 464-465.

5. Goodwin, G.C. (1946). Mammals of Costa Rica. Bull. Am. Mus. Nat. Hist. 87 (5): 275-478.
6. Grimwood, I.R. (1969). Notes on the Distribution and status of some Peruvian Mammals in 1968. Special Pubn. No.21 Am. Comm. Int. Wildlife Protec. and New York Zoological Society, Bronx, New York.
7. Grimwood, I.R. (1978). In litt.
8. Hall, E.R. and Kelson, K.R. (1959). The Mammals of North America. The Ronald Press Company, New York.
9. Handley, C.O. (1976). Mammals of the Smithsonian Venezuelan Project. Brigham Young Univ. Sci. Bull. Biol. Ser. 20 (5): 1-89.
10. Husson, A.M. (1978). The Mammals of Suriname. E.J. Brill, Leiden. Zoologische Monographieën van het Rijkmuseum van Natuurlijke Historie No.2.
11. The International Trade in Felidae 1977. In Convention on International trade in endangered species of wild fauna and flora. Proceedings of the second meeting of the conference of the parties. San José, Costa Rica, 19 to 30 March 1978. Vol.1. Secretariat of the Convention, IUCN, Gland, Switzerland, 1980. 264-293.
12. IUCN. (1973). Jaguar and Ocelot Survey. IUCN Bulletin New Series 4 (2): 6-7.
13. IUCN. (1978). Ocelot (Felis pardalis). Sheet Code 12.108.1.16. Red Data Book Vol. 1. Mammalia. IUCN, Switzerland.
14. Koford, C.B. (1973). Spotted cats in Latin America: an Interim Report. Oryx 12 (1): 37-39.
15. Koford, C.B. (1975). Felids of Latin America: Importance and Future Prospects. In Symposium on 'Wildlife and its Environments in the Americas' June 25th 1973. Publicaciones Biologicas Instituto de Investigaciones Cientifcas O.A.N.L. Vol 1. No.7 Julio 10 1975.
16. Koford, C.B. (1977). In litt.
17. Leyhausen, P. (1963). Über Sudamerikanische Pardelkatzen. Zeit. Tierpsychol. 20: 627-640.
18. Leyhausen, P. and Falkena, M. (1966). Breeding the Brazilian Ocelot-cat Leopardus tigrinus in captivity. In Olney, P.J.S. (Ed.), The International Zoo Yearbook 6. Zool. Soc. London.
19. Lopez, E. (1978). Informe Sobre las actividades de la Direccion General de Recursos Pesqueros y Vida Silvestre de Costa Rica. In Morales, R., Macfarland, C., Incer, J. and Hobbs, A. (Eds), Memorias de la Primera Reunion Regional Centroamerican sobre Vida Silvestre. Matagalpa, Nicaragua 25-29 Julio 1978. Unidad de areas silvestres y cuencas del catie. 90-96.
20. Mena Moya, R.A. (1978). Fauna y caza en Costa Rica. R.M. Costa Rica.
21. Salas, J.B. (1978). Informe sobre las actividades que desarrolla el Departamento de Vida silvestre en Nicaragua. In Morales, R., Macfarland, C., Incer, J. and Hobbs, A. (Eds), Memorias de la Primera Reunion Regional Centroamerican sobre Vida Silvestre. Matagalpa, Nicaragua 25-29 Julio 1978. Unidad de areas silvestres y cuencas del catie. 99-110.
22. Tarak, A. (1980). Pers. comm.
23. Vallester, E. (1978). Informé de Panama sobre la situacion

de la Fauna Silvestre. In Morales, R., Macfarland, C., Incer, J. and Hobbs, A. (Eds), Memorias de la Primera Reunion Regional Centroamerican sobre Vida Silvestre. Matagalpa, Nicaragua 25-29 Julio 1978. Unidad de areas silvestres y cuencas del catie. 44-65.

24. Wetzel, R.M. (1980). In litt.
25. Leyhausen, P. (1981). In litt.
26. Mondolfi, E. (1976). Fauna silvestre de los bosques humedos de Venezuela. Asociacion Nacional Para la Defensa de la Naturaleza, Venezuela.

Felis yagouaroundi Geoffroy, 1803

Order   CARNIVORA   Family   FELIDAE

SUMMARY Widely distributed from southern U.S.A. through Central America to South America. Virtually nothing known of status and ecology. Studies urgently required to determine population levels and the effects of habitat change and hunting.

DISTRIBUTION Widely distributed from extreme southern U.S.A. through Central and South America to northern Patagonia in Argentina. Not recorded from Chile and if occurred in Uruguay probably now extinct (8,13,20,45,46). Little information available about the species as a whole, and the ranges of many of the eight recognised subspecies are based on old records and a few museum specimens. F. y. tolteca inhabits a limited area of southern Arizona, U.S.A. in Cochise, Pima and Santa Cruz Counties, thence southwards in a narrow strip along the Pacific Coast of Mexico to Guerrero state (20,34). F. y. cacomitli from extreme southern Texas in Cameron, Hidalgo, Starr and Wilacy Counties southwards along the eastern coast of Mexico to Veracruz (20,34). F. y. fossata in Mexico, south and east from Oaxaca (tropical regions in east and probably southwest) and Veracruz; Guatemala, where it has been recorded from Dptoes. Peten, Izabal, Progresso, Mazatenango and Suchitepéquez; also in El Salvador, Honduras, Belize, and Nicaragua (7,17,20,22,25). F. y. panamensis in Costa Rica, Panama, western Colombia, and Ecuador where definitely recorded from Esmeraldas on the coast (2,6,8,16,20). F. y. yagouaroundi in eastern Venezuela, the Guianas and northeast Brazil (8). The Smithsonian Venezuelan project recorded the cat from scattered lowland localities throughout Venezuela but did not specify the subspecies (21). F. y. melantho: Andean valleys of Peru; reliably reported from Dptoes. Loreto, La Libertad, Huanuco, Madre de Dios and Puno (8,18). F. y. eyra: southern Brazil (as far north as Sao Paulo), Paraguay, and northeast Argentina in Misiones and the Mesopotamian and Chaquenan zones, extending south at least as far as northern Entre-Rios and northeast Cordoba, and west to western Salta and Tucuman where it may intergrade with F. y. ameghinoi (9,44). F. y. ameghinoi: sub-Andean low mountain zone in western Argentina from Jujuy south to northern Patagonia (west of Viedma at approx. 41°S) (9,44).

POPULATION No estimates available and the status of the Jaguarundi in most of its range is almost totally unknown, there having been virtually no studies of the animal in the wild. The following comments have been located for different countries. U.S.A.: extremely rare in Arizona by 1960 (11). Repeated sightings of escaped or released captive individuals tend to lead to inaccurate distribution and population data, and are probably the basis of reports of range extension in Texas (34). Mexico: most frequently recorded from the Tamaulipas plains and from northern Yucatan (31), though also recorded in 1969 as common in Oaxaca Province (17). In the early 1950s it was evidently sufficiently common to be considered something of a poultry pest in Yucatan and Chiapas (3). Guatemala: a wildlife survey in 1950 found it to be common in drier areas on both sides of the Sierra, and probably most common in the Pacific lowlands (40). Reportedly 'fairly frequent' on some estancias in the Dpto. del Progesso in the 1930s (25). Honduras: no specific data available but in 1978 all felidae were reported severely reduced or threatened (1). El Salvador: reported as vulnerable in 1978 (41). Nicaragua: included in a 1978 list of endangered mammals (39). Costa Rica: classed as endangered in 1978 (33). Panama: reported in 1978 as in imminent danger of extinction (43).

Data on its status in South America are similarly scanty: Suriname: considered rare even in the nineteenth century (24). Peru: Grimwood in 1969 stated that it was probably not as rare as the paucity of records would suggest as it was known by name in a wide variety of localities; it was, however, nowhere common (18). Argentina: in 1980 all felidae except F. concolor and perhaps some races of F. geoffroyi were reported as rare (42), though in 1976 the Jaguarundi was said to be still common (10), and it persisted in Corrientes at least until 1978 (19). Uruguay: in 1935, Devincenzi reported it from the Sierra de Minas and that furthermore considering the infrequency with which it was encountered compared to other cats, it seemed very likely to soon become extinct (13). It was not included in a 1972 list of Uruguayan mammals (45). Dr. Caviglia Tahier (1981, In litt.) writes that although numerous authors have in the past listed this species as occurring in Uruguay, there is in fact no actual evidence for this in museum collections. He believes that the references are based on melanic specimens of Felis geoffroyi which is common enough and exhibits certain similarites in colouration to the Jaguarundi. Bolivia: in 1981 described by Professor Bejarano (1981, In litt.) as endangered. Brazil: described by Ayres and Best (1981, In litt.) as vulnerable because of habitat loss, but not specifically hunted for its skin, although trapping is indiscriminate as to species.

HABITAT AND ECOLOGY Its habitat requirements have not been well-defined. Normally considered a lowland species, being unrecorded from above 1500m in Guatemala and 2200m in Peru and apparently absent from the high Sierra of Mexico and from high mountains within its range in Argentina (9,18,20,31,40). Generally appears to inhabit areas of thick undergrowth, preferably near water and is reputedly a good swimmer (20,34,35,38). Although referred to as a deep forest animal (15,24) it also seems to favour clearings and forest edges (30). In Texas and Mexico it has been recorded from dense thorny brushlands and areas of low timber (mesquite) with impenetrable underbrush of catsclaw and granjeno which may be interspersed with more open areas (5,12); similarly in Guatemala where it was most commonly recorded in dense thickets and wooded areas in broken, semi-open country (40). Rengger in the 19th century in Paraguay mostly encountered it along forest edges in thickets and hedgelike strips of scrub but never in open country (38). In El Salvador specimens were taken in swampy forest regions as well as better-drained areas and in Venezuela in dry pasture or thorn forest (7,21). Climbs well, foraging arboreally as well as taking refuge in trees when hunted (5,12,31,40), (though Hall and Kelson state that it seems more cursorial and less arboreal than other small cats in Central America (20)). Primarily nocturnal but also freqently active by day (5,12,20,34,40). Preferred food is thought to be birds, though small mammals and, in captivity, some fish are also taken (20,23,37). Mating in Paraguay was recorded in September-November, and in Mexico in November-December, though kittens have been seen there in March and August; there may thus be a possibility of two litters per year (5,15,38). Gestation period in captivity is 72-75 days, and 2-3, sometimes 4 young are the norm (15,23). Usually considered solitary though Rengger encountered pairs which occasionally shared their territory with others - this is unusual for cats and Hulley noted that their complex vocal repetoire might imply a fairly high degree of sociality (23).

THREATS TO SURVIVAL Its pelt has little commercial value and the species does not appear to be subjected to the same overall intense hunting pressure as the spotted cats e.g. F. pardalis, F. wiedii and F. tigrina (30,31,40). In 1977 the only recorded licensed skin trade was of 2 garments (approx. 65 skins) imported into Switzerland (26). The pelt, however, is not immediately recognisable, resembling that of a monkey and would usually be listed under 'any other skins' in import statistics so the actual extent of trade is unknown (14). There is a limited trade in live animals (4) principally for zoos, though there has been some demand from the pet trade, particularly in the U.S.A. (37). In Central America it is subject to the same generalised threats as most other species, -- uncontrolled hunting and habitat destruction -- and is considered threatened in at least five countries (1,33,39,41,43). Koford considered it to be the least affected by loss of primary vegetation cover of all the New World cats, and that it possibly even increased on farmland (29), though this needs further study. In the U.S.A. and northern Mexico, human persecution and habitat loss due to intense habitat alteration, particularly brush-clearing operations in the Rio Grande Valley are responsible for the population decline (12,34).

CONSERVATION MEASURES TAKEN The species as a whole is listed in Appendix 2 of the 1973 Convention on International Trade in Endangered Species of Wild Fauna and Flora, therefore any trade in it or its products is subject to regulation and monitoring by ratifying nations. The four subspecies which occur in Central and North America: F. y. cacomitli, F. y. fossata, F. y. panamensis and F. y. tolteca are listed in Appendix 1, trade in them therefore being subject to much stricter regulations and trade for primarily commercial purposes being banned. These four subspecies are also listed as 'Endangered' on the U.S. Endangered Species List, making importation and hunting in the U.S. illegal (34). Also protected in Panama, Costa Rica and probably Nicaragua (33,34,39,43); legal status elsewhere unknown, though it is almost certainly included in wildlife legislation, especially that governing export, in other countries such as Suriname and Guyana. Known to occur in the following national parks and reserves - Santa Ana and Laguna Atascosa National Wildlife Refuges in the Rio Grande Valley, Texas, U.S.A. (brush is no longer cleared in these refuges so as to maintain brush habitat in its natural state (34)); in the Pipeline Biological Reserve, Panama; Cabo Blanco National Reserve, Costa Rica; Henri Pittier N.P., Venezuela; and Sete Cidades N.P., Brazil (27,43); doubtless occurs in other parks and reserves.

CONSERVATION MEASURES PROPOSED Studies are needed throughout its range to provide accurate information on distribution, population sizes and trends, habitat requirements, and the effects of hunting and environmental disturbance.

CAPTIVE BREEDING An unknown number are kept in captivity. Appears to breed fairly readily (23). In 1977 six young were recorded born in 3 zoos (36).

REMARKS For description see (20,31,34). Three colour phases are recorded, -- reddish brown, grey and dusky black -- all of which can occur in the same litter although they were originally ascribed to different species (31, Leyhausen, P. 1981 In litt.).

REFERENCES 1. Aguilar, W. (1978). El manejo de la Vida Silvestre en Honduras. In Morales, R., Macfarland, C., Incer, J. and Hobbs, A. (Eds), Memorias de la Primera Reunion Regional Centroamerican sobre Vida Silvestre. Matagalpa, Nicaragua 25-29 Julio 1978. Unidad de areas silvestres y cuencas del catie.

2. Allen, J.A. (1912). Mammals from Western Colombia. Bull Amer. Mus. Nat. Hist. 31: 71-95.

3. Alvarez del Toro, M. (1952). Los animales silvestres de Chiapas. Ediciones del Gobierno del Estado, Tuxtla Gutierrez, Chiapas.

4. Antram, F.B.S., Wildlife Trade Monitoring Unit, Cambridge. (1980). Pers. comm.

5. Bailey, V. (1905). Biological Survey of Texas. N. American Fauna. No.25.

6. Baker, H.R. (1974). Records of Mammals from Ecuador. Pubns. of Michigan State Univ. Museum 5(2): 1-142.

7. Burt, W.H. and Stirton, R.A. (1961). The Mammals of El Salvador. Misc. Publ. Mus. Zool. Univ. Michigan. No.117.

8. Cabrera, A. (1957-61). Catalogo de los mamiferos de America del Sur. Revista del Museo Argentina de Ciencias Naturales 'Bernardino Rivadavia', Cienc. Zool., 4(1-2): 1-731.

9. Cabrera, A. (1963). Los Felidos Vivientes de la Republica Argentina. Revista del Museo Argentina de Ciencias Naturales 'Bernardino Rivadavia' e Instituto Nacional de Investigacion de las Ciencias Naturales. 6 (5): 161-247.

10. Cat Specialist Group Newsletter No.2 (1976). IUCN Survival Service Commission. Unpd. Report. pp 12.

11. Cockrum, E.L. (1960). The recent mammals of Arizona: Their taxonomy and distribution. Univ. Arizona Press, Tucson.

12. Davis, W.B. (1974). The mammals of Texas. Texas Parks Wildl. Dep. Bull. 41: 1-294.

13. Devincenzi, G.J. (1935). Mamiferos del Uruguay. Anal. Mus. Hist. Nat. Montevideo, Ser. 2, Vol. 4, No. 10.

14. Ford, M.J. (1979). Notes on meeting of the ad hoc cat group held at the British Museum (Nat. Hist.), on 15 February 1979. Unpd. Report. pp7.

15. Gaumer, G.F. (1917). Mamiferos de Yucatan. Dept. Talleres Graficos, Secretaria de Fomento, Mexico.

16. Goldman, E.A. (1920). Mammals of Panama. Smithsonian Misc. Coll. 69 (5): 1-309.

17. Goodwin, G.C. (1969). Mammals from the State of Oaxaca, Mexico, in the American Museum of Natural History. Bull. Am. Mus. Nat. Hist. 141: 1-269.

18. Grimwood, I.R. (1969). Notes on the distribution and status of some Peruvian Mammals in 1968. Special Pubn. 21. Am. Comm. Int. Wildl. Protec. and New York Zool. Soc., Bronx, New York.

19. Grimwood, I.R. (1978). In litt.

20. Hall, E.R. and Kelson, K.R. (1959). The Mammals of North America. The Ronald Press Co., New York.

21. Handley, C.O. (1976). Mammals of the Smithsonian Venezuelan Project. Brigham Young Univ. Sci. Bull. Biol. Ser. 20 (5): 1-89.

22. Hershkovitz, P. (1951). Mongrafia de los mamiferos de Yucatan. Dep. de Talleres Graficos de la Secretaria de Fomento, Mexico. Fieldiana, Zool. 31: 547-569.

23. Hulley, J.T. (1976). Maintenance and breeding of captive Jaguarundis (Felis yagouaroundi) at Chester Zoo and Toronto. In Olney, P.J.S. (Ed.), The International Zoo Yearbook 16. Zool. Soc. London.

24. Husson, A.M. (1978). The Mammals of Suriname. E.J. Brill, Leiden. Zoologische Monographieën van het Rijkmuseum van Natuurlijke Historie No.2.

25. Ibarra, J.A. (1959). Apuntes de Historia Natural y Mamiferos de Guatemala. Editorial del Ministerio de Educacion Publica.

26. The International Trade in Felidae 1977. In Convention on international trade in endangered species of wild fauna and flora. Proceedings of the second meeting of the Conference of the Parties. San José, Costa Rica, 19 to 30 March 1978. Vol.1 Secretariat of the Convention, IUCN, Gland, Switzerland, 1980, pp. 264-293.

27. IUCN. (1979). World Directory of National Parks and other protected areas. IUCN, Switzerland.

28. Kirkpatrick, R.D. and Cartwright, A.M. (1975). List of Mammals known to occur in Belize. Biotropica 7(2): 136-140.

29. Koford, C.B. (1975). Felids of Latin America: Importance and future prospects. In Symposium on Wildlife and its Environments in the Americas, June 25th 1973. Publicaciones Biologicas Instituto de Investigaciones Cientifcas O.A.N.L. Vol 1. No.7 Julio 10 1975.

30. Koford, C.B. (1977). In litt.

31. Leopold, A.S. (1959). Wildlife of Mexico. Univ. of Calfornia Press, Berkeley and Los Angeles.

33. Lopez, E. (1978). Informe sobre las actividades de la Direccion General de Recursos Pesqueros y Vida Silvestre de Costa Rica. In Morales, R., Macfarland, C., Incer, J. and Hobbs, A. (Eds), Memorias de la Primera Reunion Regional Centroamerican sobre Vida Silvestre. Matagalpa, Nicaragua 25-29 Julio 1978. Unidad de areas silvestres y cuencas del catie.

34. National Fish and Wildlife Laboratory. (1980). The Jaguarundi. FWS/OBS-80/01.45. In Biological Services Program. Selected Vertebrate Endangered Species of the Seacoast of the United States. U.S. Fish and Wildlife Service.

35. Nelson, E.W. (1930). Wild Animals of North America. National Geographic Society, Washington, DC.

36. Olney, P.J.S. (Ed.) (1979). International Zoo Yearbook 19. Zool. Soc. London.

37. Price, E.A. (1959). Jagouaroundi - the new look in pets. In 'All Pets' June: 24.

38. Rengger, J.R. (1830). Naturgeschichte der Saeugethiere von Paraguay. Basel.

39. Salas, J.B. (1978). Informe sobre las actividades que desarrolla el Departamento de Vida silvestre en Nicaragua. In Morales, R., Macfarland, C., Incer, J. and Hobbs, A. (Eds), Memorias de la Primera Reunion Regional Centroamerican sobre Vida Silvestre. Matagalpa, Nicaragua 25-29 Julio 1978. Unidad de areas silvestres y cuencas del catie.

40. Saunders, G.B., Holloway, A.D. and Handley, C.O. (1950). A Fish and Wildlife Survey of Guatemala. U.S. Dept. Interior, Fish and Wildlife Service, Spec. Scient. Rep. Wild. No.5.

41. Serrano, F. (1978). Informe de actividades de la Unidad de Parques Nacionales y Vida Silvestre en El Salvador. In Morales, R., Macfarland, C., Incer, J. and Hobbs, A. (Eds), Memorias de la Primera Reunion Regional Centroamerican sobre Vida Silvestre. Matagalpa, Nicaragua 25-29 Julio 1978. Unidad de areas silvestres y cuencas del catie.

42. Tarak, A. (1980). Pers. comm.

43. Vallester, E. (1978). Informé de Panama sobre la situacion de la Fauna Silvestre. In Morales, R., Macfarland, C., Incer, J. and Hobbs, A. (Eds), Memorias de la Primera Reunion Regional Centroamerican sobre Vida Silvestre. Matagalpa, Nicaragua 25-29 Julio 1978. Unidad de areas silvestres y cuencas del catie.

44. Ximenez, A. (1973). Nueva amlicacion de la distribucion del gato eiro en Patagonia. Comunicacciones Zoologias del Museo de Historia Naturel de Montevideo 10 (135): 1-3.

45. Ximenez, A., Langguth, A. and Praderi, R. (1972). Lista

Sistematica de los Mamiferos del Uruguay. Anales Mus. Nac. Hist. Nat. Montevideo 7 (5): 1-49.

46. Caviglia Tahier, L. (1981). In litt.

MARGAY   VULNERABLE

Felis wiedii (Schinz, 1821)

Order   CARNIVORA   Family   FELIDAE

SUMMARY Widely distributed from Mexico to northern Argentina. Under intense hunting pressure for the fur trade and probably suffers considerably from habitat loss. Nominally protected throughout much of its range but greater enforcement of existing laws needed. Little known in the wild, studies are urgently required to formulate and implement conservation measures.

DISTRIBUTION From Mexico through Central and South America to Argentina; not recorded in Chile. Following Cabrera (6) and Goldman (10), eleven subspecies are described; their ranges are in general poorly defined. F. w. cooperi is known only from a single specimen taken at Eagle Pass, Texas prior to 1852 (10); this constitutes the sole record and is considerably north of the rest of the species' described range. The individual is now considered an aberrant vagrant and the subspecies is almost certainly invalid (24,25). F. w. glaucula occurs in western Mexico from southern Sinaloa south to Jalisco; the limits of its range are unknown (10,15). F. w. oaxacensis is found in eastern Mexico from Tamaulipas south through Veracruz to the interior of Oaxaca (10,12,15). F. w. yucatanica: Mexico - Yucatan Peninsula, northern Chiapas and the Isthmus of Tehauntepec in Oaxaca (10,12); Belize, where recorded near Uaxactun; and northern Guatemala where in 1950 reported as recently recorded only in Peten though thought likely to occur elsewhere (21,29,32). F. w. salvinia: in Guatemala where in 1950 known only from Vera Paz but also old records in the highlands (32). Specimens taken in 1961 from Mt. Cocaguatique and Colinas de Jucuaran in El Salvador were tentatively ascribed to this subspecies (9). F. w. nicaraguae: Honduras, Nicaragua, and Costa Rica other than the Sixaola region (10,28). F. w. pirrensis: the Sixaola region of Costa Rica, eastern Panama, thence through the Andean zone of northern Colombia, and Ecuador where specimens are recorded from the coastal areas of Esmereldas, Manabi, Los Rios and Pichincha, to San Juan in Sandia Province, of Dpto. Puno, Peru (3,6,10,13,15,28). F. w. vigens: northeastern South America from the Orinoco River basin to the lower Amazon (6). In Venezuela has been collected from scattered lowland localities in the north and south - in Bolivar, Falcon, T.F. Amazonas and Yaracuy (16). F. w. amazonica: inhabits the upper Amazon in the basins of the Solimoes and Maranon Rivers and their tributaries (6). F. w. boliviae: is described from Dpto. de Santa Cruz in Bolivia, Mato Grosso State in Brazil and probably northern Paraguay (6). F. w. wiedii: southern and eastern Brazil, Uruguay, where recorded from Dptoes. Tacuarembo, Durazno, Laralleja, and Cerro Largo, eastern Paraguay and northern Argentina from Misiones to Tucuman; its northern limit is not well defined (6,7,37).

POPULATION No estimates available, status throughout its range is very poorly known, though in most areas it is considered much rarer than the Ocelot (Felis pardalis), itself a 'Vulnerable' species (3,20), and to be nowhere common (14,25,36). Mexico: known from very few specimens (25). Goldman noted that in a general collection of over 15,000 mammals taken in Mexico by himself and E.W. Nelson in the first half of the century only 2 were Margay, though he thought it possible that the species may be less rare than this would suggest (10). Guatemala: has apparently always been very rare (32). Nicaragua: recorded as endangered in 1978 (31). Honduras: no specific information though in 1978 all felidae were reported as reduced in number or threatened (1). El Salvador: in 1979 said to be much commoner that the Ocelot (4), though still vulnerable (33). Costa Rica: endangered (27). Panama: reported as rare in 1920 (9) and by 1978 as in imminent danger of extinction (35). Little information exists for South America. Ecuador: in 1981 it was reported that the best habitats for this species had virtually disappeared because of massive deforestation, this being particularly the case in the Costa region, less so in Oriente, though the latter was increasingly the source of illegal skins (38). Uruguay: described in 1981 as endangered and the least abundant Uruguayan cat, deforestation and illegal hunting threatening its existence (39,43). Bolivia: reported endangered in 1981 (40). Brazil: considered vulnerable in 1981 because of habitat loss and hunting (41). Peru: in 1969 reported as rare (13). Argentina: in 1976 reported as rare (8) and in 1963 Cabrera considered it the rarest of the subgenus Leopardus (7). No information obtained from elsewhere in its South American range.

HABITAT AND ECOLOGY Little known. Considerably more arboreal than the Ocelot Felis pardalis, or Tiger Cat Felis tigrina, and thus is probably more restricted to forest habitat (22,26). It has been described from arid regions - e.g. Oaxaca, Mexico, the Yucatan Peninsula, and El Salvador as well as from humid forest (5,11,12). Thought to be primarily nocturnal and diet is presumed to consist mainly of small mammals and birds (2).

THREATS TO SURVIVAL The Margay is under intense hunting pressure for the fur trade throughout it range. The pelt is less highly regarded than that of the Ocelot, though is often difficult to distinguish from it. Up to 1961 it had no commercial value. Trade increased rapidly in the 1960s; recorded annual exports from Iquitos in Peru increasing from 42 in 1961 to 4061 in 1966 (13). By 1976 the top price for a Brazilian Margay skin was US$10, less than a quarter the value of an Ocelot's (34). Even so in 1971, 56,000 Margay skins were counted in Brazilian warehouses (18), and in 1977 trade in Margays involved at least 33,000 skins though the precise number is impossible to estimate due to the large amount of unrecorded trade and smuggling and the lack of correlation between import and export figures for the countries involved (17). However recorded trade in South American cats has decreased somewhat since the late 1960s, probably in part due to new conservation legislation at that time but also because accessible populations were largely hunted out (18,22). There is heavy demand for the zoo and pet trade, though this is probably insignificant compared to the numbers taken for pelts. It is undoubtedly affected by the massive destruction of lowland forest throughout Latin America, principally for cattle grazing and agriculture (23). It probably suffers more than the Ocelot from deforestation, being more arboreal, though Koford considers that the smaller Latin America felids can re-establish themselves in secondary forest and can maintain populations in small forest patches left in areas unsuitable for clearance (22,23).

CONSERVATION MEASURES TAKEN Listed in Appendix 2 of the 1973 Convention on International Trade in Endangered Species of Wild Fauna and Flora, and trade in it or its products is therefore subject to regulation and monitoring by ratifying nations Two of the Central American subspecies, F. w. nicaraguae and F. w. salvinia are listed in Appendix 1 hence trade in them or their products is subject to strict regulation by ratifying nations, and trade for primarily commercial purposes is banned. Protected by law in Panama, Costa Rica, Nicaragua and Ecuador (18,27,31,35). Included in wildlife legislation in most countries of its range; e.g. in bans on hunting and trade in Paraguay and the Peruvian Amazon, on trade in Brazil, and on the export of untanned skins from Colombia (18). Effective enforcement of these laws is very difficult as hunters are very numerous, skins are easy to conceal, and smuggling operations are often highly organised and efficient. Known to occur in the following national parks and reserves: Cahuita N.P. and Capo Blanco National Reserve, Costa Rica; Cabo Polonia and Santa Teresa N.P.s, Uruguay; Guatopo N.P., Venezuela (19). Doubtless occurs in other protected areas though in many of these protection from habitat destruction and hunting is likely to be only nominal. Wildlife is probably more effectively protected on several large private ranches in Brazil and Venezuela, some of which may hold good Margay populations (23).

CONSERVATION MEASURES PROPOSED Koford in a 1975 report makes extensive recommendations for the management and conservation of Latin American felids including their controlled exploitation as a resource for tourism and licensed hunting, though with respect to the Margay he considers there is no economic justification for allowing hunting of the species (22,23). Before detailed recommendations can be formulated extensive field studies are needed (23). Adoption of uniform wildlife regulations or cooperative enforcment agreements between adjacent countries would reduce illegal trade in such market centres as Leticia and Buenos Aires (23). Enforcement of a minimum size regulation would limit the proportion of exports of the smaller species, such as F. wiedii (22).

CAPTIVE BREEDING Breeds readily in captivity. In 1978 a total of nine young were reported as reared in six zoos (30).

REMARKS For description see (15,25,28). The taxonomy of the subgenus Leopardus, including Felis wiedii, is complex, having been a subject of considerable confusion and controversy and is now (1981) under study by Donna L. Mayers (36). Leopardus is sometimes regarded as a full genus (42).

REFERENCES
1. Aguilar, W. (1978). El manejo de la vida silvestre en Honduras. In Morales, R., Macfarland, C., Incer, J. and Hobbs, A. (Eds), Memorias de la Primera Reunion Regional Centroamerican sobre Vida Silvestre. Matagalpa, Nicaragua 25-29 Julio 1978. Unidad de areas silvestres y cuencas del catie.
2. Alvarez del Toro, M. (1952). Los animales silvestres de Chiapas. Ediciones del Gobierno del Estado, Tuxtla Gutierrez, Chiapas.
3. Baker, H.R. (1974). Records of Mammals from Ecuador. Pubns. of Michigan State University Museum 5(2): 1-142.
4. Boursot, J. (1979). In litt.
5. Burt, W.H. and Stirton, R.A. (1961). The Mammals of El Salvador. Misc. Publ. Mus of Zool. Univ. of Michigan. No.117.
6. Cabrera, A. (1957-61). Catalogo de los mamiferos de America del Sur. Revista del Museo Argentina de Ciencias Naturales 'Bernardino Rivadavia', Cienc. Zool., 4(1-2): 1-731.
7. Cabrera, A. (1963). Los Felidos Vivientes de la Republica Argentina. Revista del Museo Argentina de Ciencias Naturales 'Bernardino Rivadavia' e Instituto nacional de Investigacion de las Ciencias Naturales 6 (5): 161-247.
8. Cat Specialist Group Newsletter No.2 (1976). IUCN Survival Service Commission. Unpd. Report. pp 12.
9. Goldman, E.A. (1920). Mammals of Panama. Smithsonian Misc. Coll. 69 (5): 1-309.
10. Goldman, E.A. (1943). The races of the Ocelot and Margay in Middle America. J. Mammal. 24 (1): 372-385.
11. Goodwin, G.C. (1942). Mammals of Honduras. Bull. Amer. Mus. Nat. Hist. 79 (2): 107-195.
12. Goodwin, G.C. (1969). Mammals from the State of Oaxaca, Mexico, in the American Museum of Natural History. Bull. Am. Mus. Nat. Hist. 141: 1-269.
13. Grimwood, I.R. (1969). Notes on the distribution and status of some Peruvian Mammals in 1968. Special Pubn. 21. Am.

Comm. Int. Wildl. Protec. and New York Zool. Soc., Bronx, New York.

14. Grimwood, I.R. (1978). In litt.
15. Hall, E.R. and Kelson, K.R. (1959). The Mammals of North America. The Ronald Press Company, New York.
16. Handley, C.O. (1976). Mammals of the Smithsonian Venezuelan Project. Brigham Young Univ. Sci. Bull. Biol. Ser. 20 (5): 1-89.
17. Inskipp, T. (1977). The International Trade in Felidae. In Convention on International Trade in Endangered Species of Wild Fauna and Flora. Proceedings of the second meeting of the Conference of the Parties. San Jose, Costa Rica 19 to 30 March 1979. Vol. 1 Secretariat of the Convention, IUCN, Gland, Switzerland.
18. IUCN. (1973). Jaguar and Ocelot Survey. Bulletin IUCN New Series 4 (2): 6-7.
19. IUCN. (1978). World Directory of National Parks and other protected areas. IUCN, Switzerland.
20. IUCN. (1981). Ocelot (Felis pardalis). Red Data Book Vol. 1. Mammalia. IUCN, Switzerland.
21. Kirkpatrick, R.D. and Cartwright, A.M. (1975). List of Mammals known to occur in Belize. Biotropica 7(2): 136-140.
22. Koford, C.B. (1973). Spotted cats in Latin America: an Interim Report. Oryx 12 (1): 37-39.
23. Koford, C.B. (1975). Felids of Latin America: Importance and Future Prospects. In Symposium on 'Wildlife and its Environments in the Americas'. June 25th 1973. Publicaciones Biologicas Instituto de Investigaciones Cientifcas O.A.N.L. Vol 1. No.7 Julio 10. 1975.
24. Koford, C.B. (1977). In litt.
25. Leopold, A.S. (1959). Wildlife of Mexico. Univ. of Calfornia Press, Berkeley and Los Angeles.
26. Leyhausen, P. (1963). Über Sudamerikanische Pardelkatzen. Zeit. Tierpsychol. 20: 627-640.
27. Lopez, E. (1978). Informe Sobre las actividades de la Direccion General de Recursos Pesqueros y vida silvestre de Costa Rica. In Morales, R., Macfarland, C., Incer, J. and Hobbs, A. (Eds), Memorias de la Primera Reunion Regional Centroamerican sobre Vida Silvestre. Matagalpa, Nicaragua 25-29 Julio 1978. Unidad de areas silvestres y cuancas del catie.
28. Mena Moya, R.A. (1978). Fauna y caza en Costa Rica. R.M. Costa Rica.
29. Murie, A. (1935). Mammals from Guatemala and British Honduras. Univ. Mich. Mus. Zool. Publ. 26: 1-30.
30. Olney, P.J.S. (Ed.) (1980). International Zoo Yearbook 20. Zool. Soc. London.
31. Salas, J.B. (1978). Informe sobre las actividades que desarrolla el Departamento de Vida silvestre en Nicaragua. In Morales, R., Macfarland, C., Incer, J. and Hobbs, A. (Eds), Memorias de la Primera Reunion Regional Centroamerican sobre Vida Silvestre. Matagalpa, Nicaragua 25-29 Julio 1978. Unidad de areas silvestres y cuencas del catie.
32. Saunders, G.B., Holloway, A.D. and Handley, C.O. (1950). A Fish and Wildlife Survey of Guatemala. U.S. Dept. Interior, Fish and Wildlife Service, Spec. Scient. Rep. Wild. No.5.
33. Serrano, F. (1978). Informe de actividades de la unidad de Parques nacionales y vida silvestre en El Salvador. In

Morales, R., Macfarland, C., Incer, J. and Hobbs, A. (Eds), Memorias de la Primera Reunion Regional Centroamerican sobre Vida Silvestre. Matagalpa, Nicaragua 25-29 Julio 1978. Unidad de areas silvestres y cuencas del catie.

34. Smith, N.J.H. (1976). Spotted cats and the American skin trade. Oryx 8(4): 362-370.

35. Vallester, E. (1978). Informé de Panama sobre la situacion de la Fauna Silvestre. In Morales, R., Macfarland, C., Incer, J. and Hobbs, A. (Eds), Memorias de la Primera Reunion Regional Centroamerican sobre Vida Silvestre. Matagalpa, Nicaragua 25-29 Julio 1978. Unidad de areas silvestres y cuancas del catie.

36. Wetzel, R.M. (1980). In litt.

37. Ximenez, A., Langguth, A. and Praderi, R. (1972). Lista sistematica de los mamiferos del Uruguay. Anales Mus. Nac. Hist. Nat. Montevideo 7 (5): 1-49.

38. Ortiz-Crespo, F.I. (1981). In litt. Including information supplied by Prof. Gustavo Orces and Juan Black.

39. Caviglia Tahier, L. (1981). In litt.

40. Bejarano, G. (1981). In litt.

41. Ayres, M. and Best, R. (1981). In litt.

42. Leyhausen, P. (1981). In litt.

43. Gudynas, E. (1981). In litt.

Panthera onca (Linnaeus, 1758)

Order   CARNIVORA   Family   FELIDAE

SUMMARY   Once fairly common from Mexico to northern Argentina, but exterminated in much of its former range and in most of the remainder greatly reduced in number. Hunting and habitat loss are the prime causes. The Jaguar is now protected in most countries in which it occurs though enforcement is difficult. Whilst illegal hunting must be halted, its future largely depends on habitat preservation. Surprisingly the Jaguar remains largely unstudied.

DISTRIBUTION   Formerly southern United States (California, Arizona, New Mexico, Texas and possibly lower Louisiana) through Central America to Venezuela, the Guianas and Brazil, and through Colombia, eastern Peru and Bolivia (east of the Andean foothills), to Paraguay, Uruguay, and northern Argentina but not Chile (5,6,10,11,15,18,19). It is now extinct in Uruguay (7,9,20), and virtually extinct in the United States, most of Mexico and Argentina, and developed areas of Central and South America (8,12,13,15,18). Eight subspecies are recognized: P. o. palustris -- southern Brazil from Sao Paulo to Mato Grosso, southern Bolivia east of the Andes, Paraguay and Argentina as far south as Chaco and northern Corrientes and, earlier on in the century, the Provinces of San Luis and La Pampa, though now extinct there; P. o. onca -- Venezuela, the Guianas and central Brazil east to the State of Espirito Santo; P. o. peruvianus -- basins of the upper Solimoes (Amazon), Maranon and Ucayali rivers in northeastern Peru; P. o. centralis -- northwestern South America, through the mountainous region of Colombia and Central America to El Salvador (5); P. o. goldmani -- Yucatan peninsula; P. o. hernandesii -- western coastlands of Mexico; P. o. veraecrucis -- from Chiapas up the east coast to Texas and Louisiana; and P. o. arizonensis -- Sonora to the southwestern United States (11).

POPULATION   Hornocker who in 1970 conducted a brief investigation into the status of the Jaguar in Central and South America (12), states that, 'It is extremely difficult, at best, to determine population status of the Jaguar throughout its varied habitat. The animal is highly secretive, largely nocturnal, and it frequents dense cover'. Koford who did a followup investigation in 1972 (13,14), and Ellis in 1979 (8) found likewise. All three studies involved a review of available literature, contact with government officials, scientists and others knowledgeable about wildlife in their respective countries, and some limited fieldwork. All three reached a similar conclusion, namely that although no precise estimates exist the species is known to be severely reduced in numbers or absent from large areas of its former range (8,12,13). The largest remaining population is in the Amazon rainforest. Highest densities formerly occurred in the Orinoco 'llanos' of Venezuela and the 'pantanal' or swampy savannas of the Mato Grosso in Brazil, but both were heavily hunted from the 1930s to 1960s and according to Koford Jaguars now only survive on large cattle ranches there (15). For Brazil Ayres and Best (1981 In litt.) report it as particularly rare in areas where agriculture predominates, such as northeastern Para, Mato Grosso, Rondonia and Acre (2). However a 1979 report received by Ellis mentioned Jaguars to be still common in the upper Orinoco River Basin including the 'llanos' area (8). Hunting has eliminated them from the Brazilian coastal forests, and although fair numbers may survive in the Paraguayan Chaco and adjacent areas of Bolivia and Brazil (3,15), recent rapid destruction of native habitat in favour of cattle pasture, and the large increase in the numbers of roads in the area has undoubtedly adversely affected the species (28). In 1981 Bejarano (In litt.) described it as endangered in Bolivia. In Argentina Jaguars have steadily retreated and are now confined to a few forest or scrubland areas near the northern border. Ellis in 1979 quoted a total for the whole country of 200+, with an estimated density of adults of 1 per 100 sq. km in favourable areas; Tarak (1980, Pers. comm) believes total numbers are probably less than 100 and that the species is endangered. At the northern end of its range, the Jaguar was once widespread in the lowlands but is now largely restricted to rainforests, palm thickets and coastal mangroves in southern Mexico and the savannas of northwestern Guatemala. In 1978 it was considered endangered in Panama (26), Costa Rica (17) and Honduras (1); extinct in El Salvador (4,24) and not mentioned as occurring in Nicaragua (22). In the U.S.A. it is considered endangered with only the occasional stray individual entering from Mexico, no viable breeding populations are known to exist (18). Generally throughout its range where the Jaguar was common 10 to 30 years ago, it is now rare (3,8,12,13,14,15,18).

HABITAT AND ECOLOGY   Tropical and sub-tropical forests, sometimes more open woodland, also mangroves, swamps and scrub thickets (15,27), particularly along watercourses (10,13). The Jaguar rarely occurs at altitudes over 1000 m or in waterless zones (15). It is an excellent swimmer and climbs trees easily, hunting mainly at dawn or dusk or during moonlit nights (10). Its food consists largely of aquatic animals such as capybaras, turtles, iguanas and fish, often scavenged as carrion. Peccaries, both collared and white-lipped, are also taken (15). Gestation varies from 93 to 105 days and litters range from one to four (10).

THREATS TO SURVIVAL   Hunting and habitat loss (2,8,12,13,18). The Jaguar is the largest Neotropical cat and the richest prize for fur hunters, who pursue it with guns or traps, the latter baited with monkeys (often of threatened species) (8,25,27). Demand for Latin American spotted cat skins increased substantially in the mid-1960s, but known exports dropped after 1969, thanks to new conservation restrictions and probably because accessible populations had been depleted (15,25). In the mid-1960s an estimated 15,000 Jaguars were killed annually in the Brazilian Amazon, but the number is thought to have been halved after the enactment of conservation legislation in 1967 (25). The price of a crude pelt varies between US $65 and $130 (14,25,27), and in Brazilian Amazonia in 1979 it was about $40 (2). Near cattle ranches it is still treated as vermin, (12) owners paying bounties equivalent to the price of two cattle (roughly US $250 in Paraguay) and the hide going to the successful hunter as a bonus (3). The U.S.A. officially imported 13,516 Jaguar skins in 1968; 9,831 in 1969 (25). Hunting and export is still allowed in some Central American countries and restrictions in other countries are poorly enforced; even if hunting is prohibited, the import, manufacture or transit of skins originating from elsewhere is sometimes allowed. The situation generally favours bribery, smuggling and other illicit trade (15). The new roads criss-crossing the Amazon basin, such as the Trans-Amazonian Highway, constitute a continuing threat to fur-bearing cats (12). Although up till now the highway itself has had little impact on the rainforest ecosystem, and of the 20 km-wide strip set aside by the government for farming, only one km has yet been taken up, the biggest danger is now conversion of forest into cattle pasture (13,25). Clearing, whether for timber, firewood, cropland, grazing, or pine and eucalyptus plantations (notoriously poor habitats for wildlife) together with construction of airstrips for mining and oil exploration, have made once remote areas accessible to hunters and developers. Huge areas of savanna are also burned annually during the dry season (as in Venezuela and Colombia), thus further reducing the woody cover and prey needed by the Jaguar (15).

CONSERVATION MEASURES TAKEN   The Jaguar is listed in Appendix 1 of the 1973 Convention on International Trade in Endangered Species of Wild Fauna and Flora, trade in it or its products therefore being subject to strict regulation by ratifying nations, and trade for primarily commercial purposes banned. Legal protection in most countries of its range is difficult to enforce but a gradual improvement has been noted in this respect (15). A few large national parks in Colombia, Peru, Bolivia and Brazil protect limited populations of Jaguars. Several small reserves protect isolated pairs or families and a number of vast private ranches in Brazilian and Venezuelan savannas are de facto reserves (15).

CONSERVATION MEASURES PROPOSED Stamping out of illegal hunting and illegal trade in skins. Studies of population densities and dynamics and the ecology of the species. Its survival depends largely on preservation of habitat and a few suitable savanna reserves have been proposed but have met with opposition because of their high value as potential pasture (8,12,13,15). Koford argues that conservation based on safeguarding isolated remnants within the boundaries of a park or reserve is insufficient and that the cat must be recognized as an essential part of the lowland tropical ecosystem as well as of a wildlife heritage which is being squandered (15).

CAPTIVE BREEDING Breeds readily in zoos throughout the world, although little attention has been given to breeding subspecies apart (16).

REMARKS For description of animal see (6,10,21). Dr. C. Koford, a member of the IUCN/SSC Cat Specialist Group, kindly assisted with the initial draft of this data sheet.

REFERENCES
1. Aguilar, W. (1978). El manejo de la Vida Silvestre en Honduras. In Morales, R., Macfarland, C., Incer, J. and Hobbs, A. (Eds), Memorias de la Primera Reunion Regional Centroamerican sobre Vida Silvestre. Matagalpa, Nicaragua 25-29 Julio 1978. Unidad de areas silvestres y cuencas del catie.
2. Ayres, M. and Best, R. (1981). In litt.
3. Berrie, P.M. (1977). In litt.
4. Boursot, J. (1979). In litt.
5. Cabrera, A. (1957-61). Catalogo de los mamiferos de America del Sur. Rev. del Mus. Argent. de Cienc. Nat. 'Bernardino Rivadavia', Cienc. Zool. 4(1,2): 1-732.
6. Cabrera, A. and Yepes, J. (1940). Mamiferos Sud-Americanos. Comp. Argent. Edit., Buenos Aires, Argentina.
7. Caviglia Tahier, L.(1981). In litt.
8. Ellis, D.H. (1979). Report of the 1979 Institute for Raptor Studies Jaguar survey expedition to South America. Unpd. Report.
9. Gudynas, E. (1981). In litt.
10. Guggisberg, C.A.W. (1975). Wild Cats of the World. David & Charles, Newton Abbot and London.
11. Hall, E.R. and Kelson, K.R. (1959). The Mammals of North America. The Ronald Press Co., New York.
12. Hornocker, M.G. (1971). Project 526. Jaguar - Status survey in Central and South America. World Wildlife Yearbook 1970-71: 149-150.
13. Koford, C.B. (1973). Project 694. Status survey of Jaguar and Ocelot in Tropical America. World Wildlife Yearbook 1972-73: 215-219.
14. Koford, C.B. (1973). Spotted Cats in Latin America: an Interim Report. Oryx 12(1): 37-39.
15. Koford, C. (1977). In litt.
16. Leyhausen, P. (1981). In litt.
17. Lopez, E. (1978). Informe sobre las actividades de la Direccion General de Recursos Pesqueros y Vida Silvestre de

Costa Rica. In Morales, R., Macfarland, C., Incer, J. and Hobbs, A. (Eds), Memorias de la Primera Reunion Regional Centroamerican sobre Vida Silvestre. Matagalpa, Nicaragua 25-29 Julio 1978. Unidad de areas silvestres y cuencas del catie.

18. National Fish and Wildlife Laboratory. (1980). The Jaguar. FWS/OBS-80/01.41. In Biological Services Program. Selected Vertebrate Endangered Species of the Seacoast of the United States. Fish and Wildlife Service. U.S. Dept. of the Interior. 6pp.

19. Nowak, R.M. (1973). A possible occurrence of the Jaguar in Louisiana. Southwest Natur. 17: 430-432.

20. Praderi, R. (1981). In litt.

21. Rick, M.S. (1976). The Jaguar. Zoonooz 49(9): 14.

22. Salas, J.B. (1978). Informe sobre las actividades que desarrolla el Departamento de Vida silvestre en Nicaragua. In Morales, R., Macfarland, C., Incer, J. and Hobbs, A. (Eds), Memorias de la Primera Reunion Regional Centroamerican sobre Vida Silvestre. Matagalpa, Nicaragua 25-29 Julio 1978. Unidad de areas silvestres y cuencas del catie.

23. Schaller, G.B. and Carvalho de Vasconcelos, J.M. (1976). The status of some large mammals in Goias and Mato Grosso States of Brazil. Unpd. Report. 9 pp.

24. Serrano, F. (1978). Informe de actividades de la Unidad de Parques Nacionales y Vida Silvestre en El Salvador. In Morales, R., Macfarland, C., Incer, J. and Hobbs, A. (Eds), Memorias de la Primera Reunion Regional Centroamerican sobre Vida Silvestre. Matagalpa, Nicaragua 25-29 Julio 1978. Unidad de areas silvestres y cuencas del catie.

25. Smith, N.J.H. (1976). Spotted cats and the Amazon skin trade. Oryx 13(4): 362-371.

26. Vallester, E. (1978). Informé de Panama sobre la situacion de la Fauna Silvestre. In Morales, R., Macfarland, C., Incer, J. and Hobbs, A. (Eds), Memorias de la Primera Reunion Regional Centroamerican sobre Vida Silvestre. Matagalpa, Nicaragua 25-29 Julio 1978. Unidad de areas silvestres y cuencas del catie.

27. Vanzolini, P.E. (1977). In litt.

28. Wetzel, R.M. and Mayers, D.L. (1980). In litt.

GALAPAGOS FUR SEAL

Arctocephalus galapagoensis (Heller, 1904)

Order   PINNIPEDIA   Family   OTARIIDAE

SUMMARY   Once common throughout the Galapagos Islands, was reduced to near extinction by sealing expeditions, and by the early 1900s was thought extinct. A small colony was discovered on Isla Genovesa in 1932-33 and another on Isla Santiago in 1957. Today, as a result of absolute protection the species numbers probably at least 40,000 animals. Provided hunting and capture remain prohibited this fur seal's future seems secure. However disturbance from increased tourism and a possible threat to breeding colonies from predation by introduced feral dogs will need constant monitoring.

DISTRIBUTION   Ecuador. Restricted to the Galapagos Islands (1,2,3,4,5,6,7). Of the larger islands only Espanola, and Santa Fe apparently have no breeding colonies. Colonies are most numerous on the south and west coast of Fernandina, the north coast of Isabela and on the west of Santiago (or San Salvador) (8).

POPULATION   A 1978 population census by Fritz Trillmich gave a provisional total of about 40,000 fur seals (8,9), and he considered this probably a minimum estimate (8). Breeding colonies occurred on at least 15 islands (Islas Culpepper (Darwin), Wenman (Wolf), Isabela, Fernandina, Santa Maria (Santiago), Pinta, Marchena, Baltra, Rabida, Genovesa, Pinzon, Seymour Norte, Santa Cruz. Very small breeding colonies may exist on Floreana and San Cristobal). Numbers have increased from near extinction and are apparently still increasing. Once common throughout the archipelago, this species was thought extinct by the early 1900s and it was not until 1932-33 that Captain G. Allan Hancock discovered a small group of the seals on Genovesa. In 1957, another colony, at that time estimated at about 100 animals, was found on Santiago, followed in the 1960s by the much larger colonies on Fernandina and northern Isabela. Presumably the species had been slowly recovering and extending its range since the 1930s but due to its rather inaccessible habitat tended to be overlooked by the scientific community although local fishermen knew of its presence (8,9).

HABITAT AND ECOLOGY   Steep, rocky coastlines with caves or boulders providing shade from the sun. Young migrating males are occasionally seen in other habitats. Colonies are always close to deep water (200 fathoms or more). Local upwelling of colder water from the deep, besides lowering water temperature may be necessary for the nourishment of a sizeable fur seal colony. The seals feed mostly during the night. The reproductive season lasts from August through November; a female has one pup and stays with it until entering oestrus and copulating with the territorial male, usually about a week after parturition. She then leaves the pup to feed, returning to it every day or every other day. Young seals are dependent on their mothers for about 2 years (8,9).

THREATS TO SURVIVAL   The decline of the species to near extinction is attributed almost entirely to sealing expeditions. Trillmich mentions the possible new threat of predation by introduced feral dogs; around Cerro Azul on Isabela such predation has resulted in confinement of fur seal breeding colonies to areas not accessible by land because of steep cliffs (9). If the dogs are able to penetrate the Perry Isthmus and thus settle on northern Isabela as well, then about one third of the fur seal population will be seriously threatened (8).

CONSERVATION MEASURES TAKEN   Listed in Appendix 2 of the 1973

Convention on International Trade in Endangered Species of Wild Fauna and Flora, and trade in it or its products is therefore subject to regulation and monitoring by ratifying nations. Hunting and catching of Galapagos Fur Seals has been prohibited by Ecuadorian law since 1959 (Decreto Ley de Emergencia No. 17 of 20 July 1959, Art. 2) (8). The Galapagos Islands were declared a National Park in 1935 and in 1980 the Galapagos were formally declared a World Natural Heritage Area. The species has been the subject of studies by Fritz Trillmich for a number of years (8,9).

CONSERVATION MEASURES PROPOSED The future of the Galapagos Fur Seal will depend on continued protection. The influence of tourism -- at present apparently negligible -- needs to be regularly checked as does the possible threat of predation by feral dogs (8,9).

CAPTIVE BREEDING No information.

REMARKS For description of the species, which is the smallest of the fur seals, see (4,5,9). It has evolved from Arctocephalus australis, of which in the past it has been considered to be a subspecies (4,5). This data sheet was compiled with the assistance of Dr. F. Trillmich, who has been making a special study of the species.

REFERENCES
1. Heller, E. (1904). Mammals of the Galapagos Archipelago, exclusive of the Cetacea. Papers of the Hopkins Stanford Galapagos Expedition, 1898-1899. Proc. Calif. Acad. Sci. 3(3): 233-250.
2. King, J.E. (1954). The Otariid seals of the Pacific coast of America. Bull. Brit. Mus. Nat. Hist., Zool. 2: 309-337.
3. Kramer, P. and Willa, R.J. (1971). Conservation and scientific Report from the Charles Darwin Research Station No. 23, p.4.
4. Orr, R.T. (1973). Galapagos Fur Seal (Arctocephalus galapagoensis). In Holloway, C.W. (Ed.), Seals. Pp. 124-128. IUCN Supp. Paper No. 39, Morges, Switzerland.
5. Repenning, C.A., Peterson, R.S. and Hubbs, C.L. (1971). Contributions to the systematics of the southern fur seals, with particular reference to the Juan Fernandez and Guadalupe species. In Burt, W.H. (Ed.), Antarctic Research Series 18: Antarctic Pinnipedia. Am. Geophys Union, Nat. Acad. Sci., Nat. Res. Council, Washington, D.C.
6. Scheffer, V.B. (1958). Seals, sea lions and walruses: a Review of the Pinnipedia. Stanford Univ. Press, Stanford, Calif. and Oxford Univ. Press, London.
7. Townsend, C.H. (1930). The Astor Expedition to the Galapagos Islands. Bull. New York Zool. Soc. 33: 135-155.
8. Trillmich, F. (1977-80). In litt.
9. Trillmich, F. (1979). Galapagos Sea Lions and Fur Seals. Noticias de Galapagos No. 29: 8-14.

JUAN FERNANDEZ FUR SEAL   VULNERABLE

Arctocephalus philippii (Peters, 1866)

Order   PINNIPEDIA   Family   OTARIIDAE

SUMMARY Restricted to the Juan Fernandez archipelago off Chile. Censuses in 1978/79 counted a total of 2416 animals; numbers are increasing. Severely depleted by sealing expeditions in the 17th, 18th and 19th centuries and believed extinct by the early 1960s until rediscovered in 1965. Totally protected by Chilean law. An expedition to Isla Alejandro Selkirk (as Mas Afuera is now called) in 1975 found that protection in the Juan Fernandez National Park was inadequate, with poaching and other harassment of the adult seals occurring; a preliminary management plan was consequently presented to the authorities. WWF/IUCN Project 1410 initiated in 1981 under the direction of Prof. D. Torres N. aims to continue studies, begun in 1978, implement appropriate recommendations from the 1975 plan, and suggest additional conservation measures.

DISTRIBUTION Chile; restricted to the islands of the Archipelago Juan Fernandez (Isla Alejandro Selkirk - formerly Mas Afuera -, Isla Robinson Crusoe - formerly Mas a Tierra - and Santa Clara), about 600 km off the coast of central Chile at 34°S (1,2,3,4,11,17). Former distribution generally assumed to have included the Islas de los Desventuradas at 26°S (San Felix and San Ambrosio) (1,2,3,17) and although Schürholz could find no supporting evidence (11), two specimens were recorded on San Ambrosio in 1970 (4,5,6).

POPULATION A 1978/79 census conducted by counting seals from both land and sea arrived at a total of 2416 for the whole archipelago: 820 for Alejandro Selkirk I., 512 for Robinson Crusoe I. and 84 for Santa Clara (17). However, numbers are almost certainly higher than this since the very rugged terrain limits observations (17). Torres et al assumed that at least 20% of the animals could not be seen from the boats, and many caves which undoubtedly housed seals were totally inaccessible (17). 1969 and 1970 censuses gave figures of about 700, the majority on Alejandro Selkirk, the least disturbed island (1,2,3,4,11). Schürholz on his 1975 expedition to Alejandro Selkirk I. estimated the population at 360-400 but noted that an accurate count was extremely difficult (12). Mann who visited the Archipelago in 1976, reported sightings as increasingly frequent on Robinson Crusoe I. and was told by fishermen that the same applied to Alejandro Selkirk I. (G. Schürholz 1977, in litt.). In the 16th and 17th centuries the species was abundant and although no precise figures are available, several million were said to have been slaughtered up to 1824 (1,6) when it became commercially extinct (7). Torres et al quote the example that between 1797 and 1804, 14 ships loaded 3 million furs at Alejandro Selkirk (17). By the early 1960s scientists thought it totally extinct (6,7,10,11) but local fishermen always considered the so-called 'Lobo Fino' to be still present in small numbers (4,6). In 1965, the species was rediscovered on Alejandro Selkirk I. by Dr. Nibaldo Bahamonde of the Chilean National Museum of Natural History and in 1968, 50 were found on Robinson Crusoe I. (1,2,3,4,17).

HABITAT AND ECOLOGY Rocky shorelines and caves in isolated localities in summer and autumn, possibly at sea in cold waters of the Humboldt current in winter and spring (17, A. Aguayo, 1977, In litt.). Stomach contents of one specimen contained fish bones and cephalopod beaks identified as from Dosidicus gigas, Octopoteuthis sp., and Tremoctopus violaceus (14). Breeding period is between November and January (17).

THREATS TO SURVIVAL Nearly exterminated by sealing during the 17th, 18th and 19th centuries. The 1975 expedition considered poaching and natural accidents the main threats. Robinson Crusoe I. has about 300 permanent inhabitants depending for their livelihood on lobster fishing and, in summer, some limited tourism. About 20 families (45 persons) move annually from September to May to Alejandro Selkirk I. to set their lobster traps. The 1975 expedition found evidence of poaching of seal pups, about 30 having been taken in the 1974/75 calving season (11,12,14,17). A temporary change from total to partial protection between August 1976 and June 1978 resulted in some fishermen believing that seal hunting was unrestricted (14). No National Parks Branch guards are posted to Alejandro Selkirk I. and, because of its remoteness, the island is seldom visited by wildlife conservation officials. A limiting factor on the build-up of stocks may be that the only major calving ground is accessible by land, whilst the two others, to which the seals are forced to retreat by human harassment, are located on very rugged parts of the coast where infant mortality by drowning could well be high. Better wardening on Santa Clara and Robinson Crusoe I. makes the seals less exposed to poaching and disturbance there (11,12).

CONSERVATION MEASURES TAKEN Listed in Appendix 2 of the 1973 Convention on International Trade in Endangered Species of Wild Fauna and Flora, and trade in it or its products is therefore subject to regulation and monitoring by ratifying nations. The seal was given partial protection in August 1976 by Decree No. 183; however, total protection was again restored in June 1978, by Decree No. 182. In recognition of the interest of its endemic flora and fauna, the archipelago was declared a National Park in 1970 (12) but the 1974 master plan for the Park paid no attention to Alejandro Selkirk I. and excluded definite management proposals for the seals. The 1975 expedition therefore collected much information on the seals, preparing a preliminary management plan which was presented to the local authorities for implementation (11). The 1978/79 study not only conducted a census but also initiated a tagging plan for pups in an attempt to discover whether movement between the islands occurred (17). IUCN/WWF Project 1410 begun in 1981 aims to continue studies of the seal and thereby to establish a conservation plan (15,16). The project will include additional census and tagging programmes, navigation around the island and land exploration to detect breeding areas, mapping of such sites, behaviour and reproductive studies, and an educational campaign (16).

CONSERVATION MEASURES PROPOSED Recommendations from WWF/IUCN Project 1410. The project also hopes to put into effect the recommendations from the 1975 preliminary management plan, which were: construction of a guard house on Alejandro Selkirk I.; posting of a guard during the eight months of the lobster season; intensive protection of the calving grounds; marking and censusing of pups and adults for life history and movement studies (11). A survey of San Ambrosio to determine whether it supports a population of the seals would also be desirable.

CAPTIVE BREEDING No information.

REMARKS For description of animal see (8,10). The Guadalupe fur seal, A, townsendii, also in the Red Data Book, was formerly classified as a race of A. philippii but is now tentatively recognized as a distinct species (6,9,10,13). Professor D. Torres N. who is studying this seal very kindly assisted with the compilation of this data sheet.

REFERENCES   1.   Aguayo L., A. (1971). The present status of the Juan Fernandez Fur Seal. K. Norske Vidensk. Selsk. Skr. 1: 1-4
2.   Aguayo L., A. (1973). The Juan Fernandez Fur Seal. In

Holloway, C.W. (Ed.), Seals. IUCN New Ser. Suppl. Pap. 39: 140-143. Morges, Switzerland.

3. Aguayo L., A. and Maturana, R. (1970). Primer censo de Lobos Finos en el Archipielago de Juan Fernandez. Biol. Pesq. Chile 4: 3-15.

4. Aguayo L., A., Maturana, R. and Torres, D. (1971). El Lobo Fino de Juan Fernandez. Rev. Biol. Mar. Valparaiso 14(30): 135-149.

5. Gilmore, R.M. (1971). Observations on marine mammals and birds off the coast of southern and central Chile, early winter 1970. Antarct. Journal of the U.S. 6(1): 10-11.

6. Hubbs, C.L. and Norris, K.S. (1971). Original teeming abundance, supposed extinction and survival of the Juan Fernandez fur seal. In Burt, W.H. (Ed.), Antartic Res. Ser. 18: 35-52.

7. King, J.E. (1954). The Otariid seals of the Pacific coast of America. Bull. Brit. Mus. (Nat. Hist.), Zool. 2: 311-337.

8. Peters, W.C.H. (1866). Uber die Ohrenrobben (Seelowen und Seebaren), Otariae, insbesondere über die in den Sammlungen zu Berlin befindlichen Arten. Monatsber., K.P. Akad. Wissensch., Berlin.

9. Repenning, C.A., Peterson, R.S. and Hubbs, C.L. (1971). Contribution to the systematics of the southern fur seals, with particular reference to the Juan Fernandez and Guadalupe species. In Burt, W.H. (Ed.), Antarct. Res. Ser. 18: Antartic Pinnipedia, 1-34. Am. Geophys. Union, Nat. Acad. Sci., Nat. Res. Council, Washington, D.C.

10. Scheffer, V.B. (1958). Seals, sealions, and walruses: a review of the Pinnipedia. Stanford. 179 pp.

11. Schürholz, G. (1976). The conservation of the Juan Fernandez Fur Seal. CONAF Report. Unpd. 9 pp.

12. Schürholz, G. and Mann, G. (1977). Comments on the population of the Juan Fernandez Fur Seal (Arctocephalus philippii). In Proc. of International Game Biology Conference. Atlanta.

13. Sievertsen, E. (1954). A Survey of the eared seals with remarks on the Antartic seals collected by M/K Norwegia in 1928-29. In Det. Norske Videnskaps-Akademi i Oslo. Sci. Res. Norw. Antarct. Exp. 1927-1928 et seq. 36: 1-76.

14. Torres N., D. (1977-80). In. litt. and Pers. comm.

15. WWF/IUCN. (1981). List of Approved Projects. February 1981.

16. Torres N., D., Cattan, P.E. and Yanez V., J.L. (1978). Ecological studies for the conservation of the Juan Fernandez Fur Seal Arctocephalus philippii and its environment. WWF/IUCN Project 1410 proposal.

17. Torres N.,D., Cattan, P.E. and Yanez V., J.L. (1979). Ecological studies on the Fur seal of the Juan Fernandez Archipelago. Arctocephalus philippii (Peters). Report on the Expedition 1978-1979. Unpd.

GUADALUPE FUR SEAL   VULNERABLE

Arctocephalus townsendi (Merriam, 1897)

Order   PINNIPEDIA   Family   OTARIIDAE

SUMMARY Only known breeding colony is on Guadalupe Island off northwest Baja California. Commercial sealing drastically reduced the species and by the 1920s it was thought extinct. A colony was found in 1954. A 1977 population estimate gave 1300-1500 animals and censuses indicate a gradual increase. Only probable threat is increased human disturbance from a fishermen's camp but the impact of tourism also needs monitoring.

DISTRIBUTION Mexico. The one known breeding colony is on the east coast of Guadalupe (28°53'N and 118°18'W), 256 km west of the Baja California mainland (2,3,4). Has been recorded in United States waters, specimens being regularly reported on San Miguel Island southwest of Santa Barbara, California (7). In 1965, three individuals were seen off Cedros Island 300 km southeast of Guadalupe (11). Fleischer states that before exploitation of the seal began, the Channel Islands off Los Angeles were probably the northern breeding limit. It is also reported to have occurred on a nearby small volcanic islet, Islote Negro (5,7,9).

POPULATION Estimated at between 1300 and 1500 and increasing, on the basis of the 1073 counted by Fleischer on an expedition to Guadalupe in June and July of 1977 (4,5). Accurate counting is however very difficult due to the inaccessibility of the habitat. Little information is available on numbers prior to commercial sealing, but the population is thought to have been large, Hubbs thinks possibly as many as 200,000 on Guadalupe Island alone (6), while Fleischer estimates 20,000 for the unexploited population (4). By 1928 it was believed to be extinct, but in 1949 Bartholomew found a single bull on one of the Channel Islands, San Nicolas (1). In 1954, C.L. Hubbs discovered a small breeding colony of 14 seals on Guadalupe (6). Since then, several censuses have been taken and indicate that the population is slowly increasing and the area occupied along the east coast of the island continually extending (2,7).

HABITAT AND ECOLOGY Rocky shorelines. Although the species seems to range widely, the smallness of its numbers means that it is seldom seen in the open ocean (2,4,7). Copulation and the birth of young occur in May, June and July, caves being favoured for the purpose (5). Males are territorial and usually have harems of 2 or 3 females, but occasionally as many as 6-8 (7).

THREATS TO SURVIVAL Commercial sealing reduced the species to supposed extinction by the 1920s. Because of its innate tameness, it is exceedingly vulnerable to illegal hunting. A fishermen's camp was established on the west coast of Guadalupe in 1976 and in 1977 was moved to the east coast. Although the fishermen respect the fur seal, human activities with boats constantly coming to shore during the fishing season will almost certainly interfere with the seals' breeding (5). Cruise ships visit the island to observe the northern elephant seal in winter and the fur seal rookery in summer, with effects at present unknown but needing to be carefully monitored (2). Feral goats may also be having an adverse effect on breeding seals. In parts of the rookery goats continually wandering across the territories of breeding males have certainly reduced their number (5). However, the habitat remains relatively undisturbed and the presence of several Mexican families and a garrison of marines at the southwest tip of Guadalupe do not pose a threat (2,7).

CONSERVATION MEASURES TAKEN Listed in Appendix 1 of the 1973 Convention on International Trade in Endangered Species of Wild Fauna and Flora, and trade in it or its products is therefore subject to strict regulation by ratifying nations and trade for primarily commercial purposes is banned. Legally protected in Mexican waters and in United States waters by the Fur Seal Act of 1966 (80 stat. 1091) and the Marine Mammal Protection Act of 1972, which prohibited taking of the seal by American citizens in any waters anywhere. Guadalupe Island was declared a wildlife sanctuary by President Obregon of Mexico in 1922 (4,7), confirmed by a new presidential decree in 1971 (5), and in May 1978 Mexico declared all the islands of the Baja California Peninsula and adjacent Sonoran Desert coast as wildlife reserve, this includes Guadalupe (12). Luis Fleischer studied this species between 1975 and 1977 (2,3,4,5).

CONSERVATION MEASURES PROPOSED Regular patrols to enforce legal protection. Resiting of the fishermen's camp. Prohibition of too close an approach to the shore by cruise ships and, in particular, of landing except under permit for scientific purposes. Regular population censuses and research into life history parameters and ecology.

CAPTIVE BREEDING No information.

REMARKS For description see (4,6,10). Some authorities regard A. townsendi as a synonym or subspecies of A. philippii of the Juan Fernandez Islands off the coast of Chile. Repenning et al. considers both to be good species though closely related (10). This data sheet has been compiled with the assistance of L. Fleischer.

REFERENCES
1. Bartholomew, G.A. (1950). A male Guadalupe Fur Seal on San Nicolas Island, California. J. Mammal. 3(2): 60-71.
2. Fleischer, L. (1977). A Preliminary Report on the Expedition to the Guadalupe Island, Baja California, Mexico, Summer 1976. Unpd. Report. 21pp.
3. Fleischer, L. (1977). Guadalupe Fur Seal. In Marine Mammals in Eastern North Pacific and Arctic. Pacific Search Books, Seattle.
4. Fleischer, L. (1978). The distribution, abundance, and population characteristics of the Guadalupe Fur Seal, (Arctocephalus townsendi) (Merriam 1897). Master's degree thesis, College of Fisheries, Univ. of Washington, Seattle.
5. Fleischer, L. (1977). In litt.
6. Hubbs, C.L. (1956). Back from oblivion, Guadalupe Fur Seal: still a living species. Pacific Discovery 9: 14-21.
7. Kenyon, K.W. (1973). The Guadalupe fur seal (Arctocephalus townsendi). In Holloway, C.W. (Ed.), Seals. IUCN New Series Suppl. Paper 39: 82-87
8. Merriam, C.H. (1897). A New Fur Seal or Sea Bear (Arctocephalus townsendi) from Guadalupe Island, off Lower California. Proc. Biol. Soc. Washington 11: 175-178.
9. Peterson, R.S., Hubbs, C.L., Gentry, R.L. and DeLong, R.I. (1968). The Guadalupe Fur Seal: habitat, behaviour, population size and field identification. J. Mammal. 49: 665-675.
10. Repenning, C.A., Peterson, R.S. and Hubbs, C.L. (1971). Contributions to the systematics of the southen fur seals, with particular reference to the Juan Fernandez and Guadalupe species. In Burt, W.H. (Ed.), Antartic Research Series 18: Antartic Pinnipedia. Am. Geophys. Union, Nat. Acad. Sci., Nat. Res. Council, Washington, D.C.

11. Rice, D.W., Kenyon, K.W. and Lluch, B.D. (1965). Pinniped populations of Islas Guadalupe, San Benito, and Cedros, Baja California, in 1965. Trans., San Diego Soc. of Nat. Hist. 14(7): 73-84.
12. Anon. (1979). New Parks and Reserves. Oryx 15(1): 24.

CARIBBEAN MONK SEAL   ENDANGERED

Monachus tropicalis (Gray, 1850)

Order   PINNIPEDIA   Family   PHOCIDAE

SUMMARY   Probably extinct. Inhabiting shores and islands of the Caribbean and Gulf of Mexico, was decimated by an 18th century seal fishery. The survivors were persecuted by local fishermen and their habitat became subject to increasing human pressure. A 1973 survey of the less disturbed parts of the former range was negative, as was a 1980 expedition to the southeast Bahamas where two seals were seen in 1974 although were not certainly identified as M. tropicalis. If a population is rediscovered it will require immediate, strictly enforced protection and observational study by an experienced pinniped biologist.

DISTRIBUTION   Caribbean Sea, Gulf of Mexico. Formerly ranged from the Bahamas west to Yucatan, thence along the east coast of Central America through the western Caribbean Sea and eastwards to the northern Lesser Antilles. Records being based on secondhand accounts of explorers and fishermen make it difficult to define its original range precisely and it doubtless included many unrecorded localities; Rice (1973), who reviewed all available data concluded that the 1952 record of a small colony on Serranilla Bank off the coast of Mexico's Yucatan peninsula was the last reliable sighting and that post-1952 reports from that locality and from Yucatan Channel (1964), Chinchorro Reef, Quintana Roo (1969) and Rockport, Texas (1957) could not be confirmed (8). However, Luis Varona (1976, In litt.) reports that at least two seals were sighted by fishermen in international waters near Cay Verde and Cay Burro, southeast Bahamas (approximately 22°N, 75°W) in 1974 (2). Whether they were in fact M. tropicalis is not known; escaped California sealions (Zalophus californianus) have been found in the Gulf of Mexico on several occasions (8).

POPULATION   Probably extinct. A 2-week expedition to the southeast Bahamas where the 1974 sightings were reported was undertaken in April 1980. All beaches, rocky coasts and shallows round them were searched but no monk seals were sighted, nor were any bones found. Five possible sightings in the area were recorded, referring to the 1960s and 1970s. The expedition felt that it was not yet appropriate to regard the species as extinct because of the number of recent records (7). An aerial survey that covered the main parts of the seal's former range, with particular attention to likely localities, was undertaken by experienced observers in March 1973, but produced no evidence of the seal's existence (1,6). A little earlier, the International Society for Protection of Animals had issued a circular in English and Spanish offering a $500 reward for information on recent sightings, but elicited no response (J.C. Walsh 1972, Pers. comm.). This species was encountered by Columbus in 1494; and early travellers speak of its abundance; H. Sloane in 1707 wrote that 'The Bahama Islands are filled with seals'. By the time it was described in 1850, it was already scarce and in 1887 was referred to as an 'almost mythical species'. Few modern biologists have seen it in the wild and there are fewer than 50 skulls in museums (4,8).

HABITAT AND ECOLOGY   Very little known. Probably similar to those of the Hawaiian monk seal -- shallow lagoons and reefs for feeding; sandy beaches for hauling-out; and islets or beaches, above high tide and adjacent to shallows protected from wave action, for pupping. Latter is believed to have reached its peak in December and probably never in two successive years for any one female (8). Diet presumably fish but no evidence available.

THREATS TO SURVIVAL Uncontrolled hunting in the past, increasing human disturbance today. The seal was very seriously over-exploited in the 18th century and already rare by 1850, large numbers being killed without difficulty due to their sluggish and unsuspicious nature (3,4). Within the historical range, there are doubtless still many areas that satisfy its habitat requirements, but they are being penetrated by a large, rapidly growing and mostly indigent human population and more recently, by tourists and yachtsmen. Monk seals are particularly vulnerable to human exploitation and generally intolerant of human disturbance. As the diet was no doubt largely composed of fish, the people within its range who mostly live by fishing or catching turtles, would probably kill any seal encountered (8).

CONSERVATION MEASURES TAKEN The Caribbean Monk Seal is listed in Appendix I of the 1973 Convention on International Trade in Endangered Species of Wild Fauna and Flora, and trade in it or its products is therefore subject to strict regulation by ratifying nations, trade for primarily commerical purposes being banned. Although legally protected in Jamaica, no effective conservation measures have ever been applied to any part of its range (8).

CONSERVATION MEASURES PROPOSED If a viable colony of seals were to be located, the following urgent steps are advocated: a) complete legal protection of the species by the government concerned, hauling-out grounds and adjacent waters being declared an inviolate refuge; b) posting of a full-time warden to ensure that the seals are not molested; and c) initiation by an experienced pinniped biologist of a detailed observational study of the colony. This species should not be captured and kept in captivity, most individuals in zoos and aquaria have not lived very long. If it were essential to capture animals, they should be kept under as near natural conditions as possible - preferably a portion of natural habitat enclosed by nets and fences (8). The 1980 expedition suggested that a search of the southeast Bahamas should be made in December/January when any surviving animals would most likely be on the beaches (7).

CAPTIVE BREEDING None.

REMARKS For description of animal see (3,5).

REFERENCES
1. Anon. (1976). End of the Caribbean Monk Seal. Oryx 13(3): 225-226.
2. Anon. (1977). 1974 Report of Caribbean Monk Seals. Oryx 14(1): 50.
3. Allen, G.M. (1942). Extinct and vanishing mammals of the western hemisphere with the marine species of all the oceans. Spec. Publ. Amer. Comm. Int. Wildlife Protection No. 11.
4. Campbell, D.G. (1978). The Ephemeral Islands. A Natural History of the Bahamas. MacMillan. Pp. 28-31.
5. Gray, J.E. (1850). Catalogue of the specimens of mammalia in the collection of the British Museum. Pt. 2, Seals. Brit. Mus. (Nat. Hist.), London.
6. Kenyon, K.W. (1977). Caribbean Monk Seal extinct. J. Mammal. 58(1): 97-98.
7. Nichols, G., Campbell, D. and Sergeant, D. (1980). Expedition of R/V Regina Maris to Search for Caribbean Monk Seals in the southeast Bahamas Islands, April 13 to 26, 1980. Report to World Wildlife Fund, U.S.A. and People's Trust for Endangered Species.
8. Rice, D.W. (1973). Caribbean Monk Seal (Monachus tropicalis). In Holloway, C.W. (Ed.), Seals. IUCN New Ser. Suppl. Pap. 39: 98-112. Morges, Switzerland.

HAWAIIAN MONK SEAL   ENDANGERED

Monachus schauinslandi (Matschie, 1905)

Order   PINNIPEDIA   Family   PHOCIDAE

SUMMARY Regular breeding colonies restricted to seven atolls of the Leeward Hawaiian Chain. 700 to 1500 estimated to survive. Numbers believed greatly reduced during the 19th and early 20th centuries. Present threats include human disturbance which forces seals to abandon preferred haul-out and pupping beaches probably resulting in increased juvenile mortality, and possibly ciguatera poisoning from certain reef fishes which may have killed at least 50 seals at Laysan Island in 1978. Listed as 'Endangered' in the United States with (in 1981) government designation of a 'critical habitat' zone pending. Six of its breeding atolls are included in the Hawaiian Islands National Wildlife Refuge. Protection of its habitat from human disturbance is essential to recovery.

DISTRIBUTION Hawaiian Islands, U.S.A. (1,4,9,10,12,17); pupping occurs regularly only on seven of the northwestern Islands -- French Frigate Shoals, Laysan Island, Lisianski Island, Pearl and Hermes Reef, and Kure Atoll, and in recent years also at Nihoa and Necker Islands (4,6). Breeding activity at Midway Islands has not been confirmed in recent years. Animals are occasionally seen in waters around Maro Reef, Gardner Pinnacles, and the main Hawaiian Islands and there are a few reports of monk seals hauled out on Niihau, Kauai, and Oahu (4,6). It is possible that monk seals bred in the main Hawaiian Islands before the arrival of the Polynesians, but firm evidence is lacking (10).

POPULATION The 1957-58 counts of monk seals were 1013 and 1206 respectively, in 1969-70 they were 683 and 551 (13,14,16). During the following ten years, total counts have ranged between a high of 695 in 1976 and a low of 502 in 1978 (1,4). A study at Laysan in 1978 demonstrated that the number of seals using that island was three times the average number of animals counted on the beach (7). Since the 1950s, there has been a major decline in the population at the far western end of the chain (Kure Atoll, Midway Islands, and Pearl and Hermes Reef), and a less dramatic decline at Lisianski and Laysan Islands in the centre of the chain, however, there has been a pronounced increase in numbers at French Frigate Shoals and Necker and Nihoa Islands (6,20).

HABITAT AND ECOLOGY Available data indicate only a low level of movement between the main breeding islands; however, seals are occasionally seen in the main Hawaiian Islands and may dive to at least 60 fathoms to feed (2). They do not congregate in large numbers on breeding grounds, but are found hauled out in scattered small groups along beaches providing easy access from the water. Mating has only been observed in the nearshore water. Pups are born from December through August with the peak in April-May; and are weaned at about 5 weeks. Births may occur high on the beach in dry sand, at the water line, and on rough lava ledges or cobble beaches as at Necker and Nihoa Islands. If undisturbed, females tend to return to the same location to give birth (8). However frequent human disturbance may force females to give birth at less preferred sites including isolated shifting sandspits where the potential of pup loss is greater. Feeds principally on octopuses, eels and bottom and reef fishes (17).

THREATS TO SURVIVAL Believed to have been greatly reduced by sealers, feather hunters and guano diggers in the 19th and early 20th centuries (10,11,17). Since the 1950s human disturbance has been responsible for reductions in seals at Midway Islands and Kure Atoll (9). During U.S. Coast Guard occupation of Tern

Island in French Frigate Shoals, monk seals rarely frequented the beach; however since the departure of the 20-man Coast Guard complement and the arrival of a small U.S. Fish and Wildlife Service maintenance staff more conscious of disturbance, beach counts one year later averaged 15 seals and the numbers continue to increase (19). Beaches constantly disturbed are abandoned by the seal even if they are preferred pupping grounds. The less preferred sites for pupping include shifting sandspits with greater exposure and potential inundation by high tides and rough seas (3,9,10,13). Use of these sites may lead to pup mortality by separation of mother and pup, by shark predation, or because of inadequate nursing to prepare the pup for the time in which it must learn to feed for itself. Another major threat may be ciguatera poisoning from certain reef fishes which may have killed at least 50 seals at Laysan Island in 1978 (5). Entanglement in fishing nets and lines has been observed with some frequency, but mortality as a result has not been reported (2,12). Shark predation may be an important mortality factor (2,9,10,12,21).

CONSERVATION MEASURES TAKEN Listed in Appendix 1 of the 1973 Convention on International Trade in Endangered Species of Wild Fauna and Flora, any trade in it or its products therefore being subject to strict regulation by ratifying nations, and trade for primarily commercial purposes banned. It is also classified as Endangered in the United States list of 'Endangered' and Threatened Wildlife, so receives protection throughout its present and former range. Protection from harassment is also afforded by the U.S. Marine Mammal Protection Act (1972). Under provisions of the Endangered Species Act (1973), a Hawaiian Monk Seal Recovery Team was established in 1980 and charged with development of a Recovery Plan for the species; but the plan has not yet (May 1981) received final approval. The Hawaiian Islands National Wildlife Refuge includes all the seal's current breeding islands except Kure Atoll which is a U.S. Coast Guard station and a State of Hawaii seabird sanctuary. Entry into all these areas requires special permits and is discouraged or prohibited except for certain scientific and government work (23).

CONSERVATION MEASURES PROPOSED Under the U.S. Endangered Species Act, a 'Critical Habitat' has been proposed, and thus all Federal Agencies are obliged by law to ensure that actions authorized, funded or carried out by them do not result in the destruction or adverse modification of this habitat. This area should receive final approval and implementation as soon as possible. Enforcement of regulations prohibiting harassment should be increased at Midway Islands and Kure Atoll (23).

CAPTIVE BREEDING None.

REMARKS For description of animal see (9,18). A bibliography of the species was published in 1978 (22). William G. Gilmartin, Leader of the Hawaiian Monk Seal Recovery Team was extremely helpful in providing new information and a draft script, upon which this data sheet is based.

REFERENCES   1. DeLong, R.L. (1976). Current information on Hawaiian monk seals. Conference on Marine Mammals of the Sea, Group III, Seals and Marine Otters, Advisory Committee on Marine Resources Research, Bergen, Norway, 31 August - 9 Septmber 1976. 4p.
              2. DeLong, R.L. (1980). Pers. comm.
              3. FAO. (1976). Advisory Committee on Marine Resources Research. Mammals in the Seas. Unpd. Report.
              4. Fiscus, C.H., Johnson, A.M. and Kenyon, K.W. (1978). Hawaiian monk seal (Monachus schauinslandi) survey of the Northwestern (Leeward) Hawaiian Islands. Northwest and

Alaska Fish. Cent., Natl. Mar. Fish. Serv., NOAA, Seattle, WA 98112, Processed Report, 27p.

5. Gilmartin, W.G., DeLong, R.L., Smith, A.W., Griner, L.A. and Dailey, M.D. (1980). An investigation into unusual mortality in the Hawaiian monk seal, Monachus schauinslandi. In Grigg, R.W. and Pfund, R.T. (Eds), Proceedings of the Symposium on Status of Resource Investigations in the Northwestern Hawaiian Islands, April 24-25, 1980, University of Hawaii, Honolulu, Hawaii. Sea Grant Misc. Rep. UNIHI-SEAGRANT-MR-80-04, p. 32-41.

6. Johnson, A.M., DeLong, R.L., Fiscus, C.H. and Kenyon, K.W. (1980). Population status of the Hawaiian monk seal (Monachus schauinslandi), 1978. Unpd. Report.

7. Johnson, B.W. and Johnson, P.A. (1981). Estimating the Hawaiian monk seal population on Laysan Island. Final Report to U.S. Marine Mammal Commission, Wash. D.C. in fulfillment of Contract MM1533701-4. 25p.

8. Johnson, P.A. (1980). Pers. comm.

9. Kenyon, K.W. (1972). Man versus the Monk Seal. J. Mammal. 53(4): 687-696.

10. Kenyon, K.W. (1973). Hawaiian Monk Seal (Monachus schauinslandi). In Holloway, C.W. (Ed.), Seals. IUCN New Ser. Suppl. Paper 39: 88-97. Morges, Switzerland.

11. Kenyon, K.W. (1975). The Monk Seal's Cloistered Life. Defenders of Wildlife 50(6): 497-499.

12. Kenyon, K.W. (1980). No man is benign. The endangered monk seal. Oceans, May 1980: 48-54.

13. Kenyon, K.W. and Rice, D.W. (1959). Life history of the Hawaiian monk seal. Pac. Sci. 13: 215-252.

14. Kridler, E. (1969-70). Unpd. reports.

15. Matschie, P. (1905). Eine Robbe von Laysan. S.B. Ges. Naturfr. Fr. Berl. 254-262.

16. Rice, D.W. (1960). Population dynamics of the Hawaiian monk seal. J. Mammal. 41(3): 376-385.

17. Rice, D.W. (1964). The Hawaiian Monk Seal. Nat. Hist. 73(2): 48-55.

18. Scheffer, V.B. (1958). Seals, Sea lions and Walruses. A review of the Pinnipedia. Stanford Univ. Press, California; Oxford Univ. Press, London.

19. Schulmeister, S. (1981). Hawaiian monk seal numbers increase on Tern Island. 'Elepaio 41(7): 62-63.

20. U.S.National Marine Fisheries Service. (1980). Narrative Report, Townsend Cromwell, cruise 80-03 (TC-89) Part I, Table 2. Southwest Fish. Cent., Natl. Mar. Fish. Serv., NOAA, Honolulu, HI 96812.

21. Wirtz, W.O., II (1968). Reproduction, growth and development, and juvenile mortality in the Hawaiian monk seal. J. Mammal. 49(2): 229-238.

22. Balazs, G.H. and Whittow, G.C. (1978). Bibliography of the Hawaiian Monk Seal Monachus schauinslandi Matschie 1905. Univ. of Hawaii, Hawaii Inst. of Marine Biology Technical Report No.35.

23. Gilmartin, W.G. (1981). In litt.

DUGONG   VULNERABLE

Dugong dugon (Müller, 1776)

Order   SIRENIA   Family   DUGONGIDAE

SUMMARY Uncontrolled exploitation and incidental take has seriously depleted populations throughout most of its wide range along mainland and island coasts of the Indo-Pacific region. Local extinctions have occurred and may be occurring in coastal and island waters off Africa and Asia and in some western Pacific Island regions. The largest known populations occur in northern Australia. The main immediate threat is from direct hunting for food and other products, and from accidental capture in shark and fish nets. The Dugong has a low reproductive rate and therefore cannot recover easily from overexploitation. Long term threats may result from destruction of coastal habitats and pollution. Studies are required to determine numbers and distributions over most of its range and to monitor changes in abundance so that management plans can be formulated. Large sanctuaries, e.g. marine national parks, in which habitats are protected and net fishing excluded, need to be established in important Dugong areas. Hunting by indigenous peoples should be monitored and managed. Losses from illegal hunting and incidental catches in net fishing have to be reduced and habitats protected against destruction and pollution.

DISTRIBUTION The shallow coastal and island waters of the Indian and western Pacific Oceans from Mozambique, Madagascar and the Comoro Islands north along the east African coast to the northernmost reaches of the Red Sea including the Gulfs of Suez and Aqaba; east along the southern coast of Asia (Arabian Peninsula, Persian Gulf, India, Sri Lanka, Bangladesh, Burma, Andaman Islands, Mergui Archipelago, Thailand, Malaysia, Kampuchea, Viet Nam, and southern China), as far north as Taiwan and the Ryukyu Islands; south, west and east through the Philippines, Indonesia, Palau and Yap Islands, Guam, New Guinea, the Solomon Islands, New Hebrides, New Caledonia and Loyalty Islands; south and west to the northern, western and eastern coasts of Australia (from Shark Bay in Western Australia to Moreton Bay and occasionally as far south as Sydney in eastern Australia) (9,10,11,18,20,22,32,38,44,46,48,49,54,62,64,73). There is very little or no information on present distribution in China, Taiwan, the Philippines, the Santa Cruz Islands, Pakistan, Iran and Madagascar. The precise extent to which the range has contracted is unknown, but over much of it the species is now represented by relict populations with large intervening areas where it is close to extinction or in which there may be local extinctions, e.g. Red Sea, Arabian Gulf, Philippines, Ryukyu Islands, Palau, Yap, Guam (10,11,22,44,46,62,64). There have been unconfirmed reports from Kyushu in Japan and Gunsan in Korea (39). Dugongs are extinct in the Mascarene, Laccadive and Maldive Islands (44,46,49).

POPULATION Total population size unknown, but now rare over most of its range, approaching extinction in some regions, and extinct in others. On the basis of local interviews and literature reports a very rough estimate has been made that there may be about 30,000 Dugongs left in the entire Indo-Pacific region, with those populations ranging from India and Sri Lanka westward along the west coast of India, Persian Gulf, Arabian Peninsula, Red Sea, East Africa and Madagascar being the most endangered. Herds of several hundred were reported in the past (e.g. Moreton Bay in Queensland, Australia, and Gulf of Mannar and Palk Bay, India, and Sri Lanka) and also occasionally in recent years (e.g. Somalia and Queensland) (9,10,11,18,22,25,32,44,46,48,49,62,64).

Australia: relatively large populations are still found in northern waters

(Queensland, Northern Territory and Western Australia) (5,8,9,10, 17,21,25,26,34,35,51,60,62,66). The estimated total number in Queensland is probably only a few thousand (26,51); and populations in the south may be increasing (37); a composite of maximum counts obtained by aerial surveys of sections of the coast (between 1974 and 1980) totals 2325 (26). During the surveys, a single herd of more than 200 was observed in Moreton Bay and a herd of 500 to 600 along a 13 km stretch of coast on Cape York north of Cooktown (25,30,32). The most important Dugong areas in the State, where more than 100 have been seen in single aerial surveys, are: Moreton Bay, Great Sandy Strait and Hervey Bay, Port Clinton and Shoalwater Bay, Townsville to Cardwell area, eastern Cape York (Cape Flattery to Shelburne Bay), Torres Strait, the Gulf of Carpentaria (particularly between Archer Bay and Karumba), and the Wellesley Islands (25,26,60). Almost 60 hours of aerial survey covering virtually the entire Northern Territory coastline in November 1977 counted a total of 557 Dugongs. This was less than 1 per 27 sq. km of area surveyed. Group sizes were usually small with the largest being 27 (17). In Western Australia aerial surveys of Shark Bay in 1979 yielded a count of 496 with a minimum population estimate of 900; a maximum count of 152 was obtained for the coastal waters between Exmouth Gulf and the De Gray River with 138 of these being seen in Exmouth Gulf (5,66). Papua New Guinea: still present along the coasts and reported to be abundant in some regions (40,53). In 1976, 186 were counted during an aerial survey covering 1207 km of coastline and coral reefs. Two concentrations, of 28 and 39, were seen in the Warrior Reef area south of Daru (53). Southwestern Pacific: small numbers are thought to occur in the waters off New Caledonia, Vanuatu (formerly the New Hebrides) and the Solomon Islands (10,64). In Palau, a minimum of 15 were seen during an aerial survey in December 1977, and 34 in December 1978; the total population was estimated to be about 50 with an estimated 20 taken annually by poachers (11). They are very rare on Yap and Guam Islands (64). Small numbers occur throughout the Philippines including Luzon, Palawan, Panay, Cebu, and Mindanao (64). Japan: only known from the Ryukyus where it is very rare,(10,64), with about 10 captured over the last 30 years as far north as Anami Oshima (M. Nishiwaki, pers. comm., in Heinsohn, 1976). One young female was caught in 1979 (69,72). Occurs in at least small numbers off southern China and Taiwan (73). No recent information for Viet Nam and Kampuchea. Indonesia: scattered in small numbers throughout suitable habitat. Live catches of between 1 and 7 were made in several places between 1975 and 1978. Small numbers are confirmed from south Sulawesi, south Bali, west Java, Kalimantan, and Bangka Islands, and many Dugongs are known to occur off Timor (38). No information for western and northern Sumatra or Irian Jaya. Malaysia: small numbers occur in East Malaysia (northern Borneo); rare in West Malaysia (10). Rare in Singapore (10). Thailand: scarce (49,64). Burma: present in at least small numbers along the coast (49,64). Bangladesh: a resident population does not seem to exist although there are reports of Dugongs straying into the region from the northern coast of Burma (49). Indian Ocean: present in the Andaman and Nicobar Islands; present, but declining in the Gulf of Mannar and Palk Bay between India and Sri Lanka. India: the Gulf of Kutch in the northwest has a small population (49); probabaly rare along the west coast and none recorded along the east coast (64). The Pakistan coast extending from the Qatter Gulf at the Iranian border to the Rann of Kutch in India does not provide suitable habitat. However, individual Dugongs may stray into Pakistan waters from the Gulf of Kutch (49). Persian Gulf: seemingly very rare (10) but known at Bahrain (19). Apparently absent from Muscat and the south coast of the Arabian Peninsula (10). Present, but rare, in the Gulfs of Suez and Aqaba and the rest of the Red Sea (10,20,54). Generally scarce in East Africa and Madagascar, although there is one recent report of a large herd numbering in the hundreds off the south coast of Somalia (10,64). A total of 27 were observed during two hours of aerial surveys over the large estuary and mangrove lined channels at Antionio Enes, northern Mozambique in July 1970 (43). In October and November 1975, a 12.2 hour aerial survey was flown in a grid pattern giving 25% coverage of the entire shallow water area along the 482 km long Kenya coast, only 8 Dugongs (4 individuals plus 2 cows with calves) were seen (52).

HABITAT AND ECOLOGY   A strictly marine species inhabiting sheltered, shallow, warm (18°C and above), tropical and subtropical coastal mainland and island waters chiefly between latitudes 30°N and 30°S in areas where fine bottom sediments support extensive beds of seagrasses.   Most abundant in the nutrient-rich inshore shoals and in the vicinity of inshore continental islands but also occurs on coral reefs and island fringing reefs and present in both turbid and clear water (4,27,32,37).   Diet is almost exclusively seagrasses (Family Potamogetonaceae and Hydrocharitaceae), with little apparent selectivity for species.   Dugongs usually uproot sparsely distributed seagrass to feed on the rhizomes and roots as well as on the stems and leaves (4,7,27,37), but in dense beds will graze on leaves (4,6).   Marine algae are occasionally eaten, particularly when seagrasses are scarce.   Invertebrates are sometimes consumed but are probably taken incidentally with seagrasses rather than being specifically sought after (25,29,37,54,59,67).   Where undisturbed and not hunted Dugongs will feed at any hour of the day or night, with their daily movements and activities largely determined by tides and to a lesser extent by weather.   They feed on intertidal seagrasses when the tide is high enough (over 1 meter deep) to allow them to swim.   During calm weather they will move from protected into exposed water (7,32,37).   Where hunted and where seagrass biomasses are high (e.g. Palau) Dugongs feed at night (4) and daytime resting areas are in locations isolated from human activities (4).   Deeper water resting areas are utilized at low tide.   Also where they are hunted, Dugongs seem to require calving areas (i.e. shallow water protected by sand bars) where they are safe from large sharks and other predators (32).   Aerial surveys indicate considerable daily movements of up to 25 km as well as longer seasonal ones of up to 100 km or more (4,7,32).   Long distance movements resulting in colonization of remote island groups are considered to be a rare event (4).   Seemingly gregarious, although solitary individuals can often be seen.   Herds of up to several hundred can be found in areas where they have not been disturbed or extensively hunted (25,30,32).   Man is the most important predator, others being large sharks, the Estuarine Crocodile (Crocodylus porosus) and the Killer Whale (Orcinus orca) (4,32,37).   Cyclones and typhoons may also cause mortality (28,48).   A very low reproductive rate makes the species very vulnerable to extinction.   Both males and females are at least 9 to 10 years old before reaching reproductive maturity (32,55,57), and in some areas, 15 to 17 years (58).   Males have a complex seasonal cycle of sexual activity with only about one third of mature males producing sperm at any one time during the May to November period of sexual activity, suggesting that there are behavioural or social factors suppressing sexual activity in some males (32,55,57).   In females, the gestation period is believed to be about 12 months (58).   A single young is usually born, but twins have been reported.   Calves apparently stay with their mothers for at least a year and possibly up to two years.   In addition to suckling milk calves start feeding on seagrasses a few weeks after birth.   Birth interval is likely to be a minimum of 2 years (32), and the mean calving interval of several Queensland populations has been variously estimated to range from 3 to 6 years (58).   Most births in the Townsville (Queensland) population are between September and December (58), and in Daru (Papua New Guinea), between October and April (42).   The pregnancy rate is very low (13%) with only 23 of 174 females presumed to be mature from Daru (Papua New Guinea) being pregnant (42).   Sixteen of 23 parous females (70%) examined from northern Australia were neither pregnant nor lactating, again suggesting a calving interval of several years (55,57).   Individual Dugongs can be long-lived with a life span of 50 years or more (32,55,57).

THREATS TO SURVIVAL   Uncontrolled hunting, and netting primarily for meat and oil has been conducted by local subsistence hunters, fishermen and small scale commercial fishermen throughout its range. A Dugong oil industry previously flourished in Queensland. Hides have been utilized and various parts of the body have been used for aphrodisiac and medicinal purposes (10,18,22,32,37,62). Dugongs are still hunted and fished for food over most of their range, with much of the hunting being illegal; only very limited data is available on numbers taken. In Australia, Dugongs are legally hunted by Aboriginals (17,26). For example at Numbulwar (Rose River), Northern Territory, a community of 250 Aboriginals killed at least 433 Dugongs for food between 1963 and 1969 (10); in the Wellesley Islands, Queensland, Aboriginals kill an estimated 40 annually, this being about one-tenth of the maximum number of 374 counted during aerial surveys (60); at Lockhart River Aboriginal Community on northeastern Cape York, Queensland, with 300 people, 18 Dugongs were taken during a highly favourable three month period (14); it is estimated that about 25 to 30 are killed every year by Aboriginal hunters at Hopevale Community near Cooktown, Queensland (28); it was suggested that about 500 are killed for food every year by Torres Strait Islanders and Papuans in the Torres Strait Region (64); and in this area Torres Strait Islanders at Mabuiag Island killed 47 for food from September 19, 1976 to February 6, 1977; and between 1978 and 1981 more than 330 were brought into Daru, Papua New Guinea, 200 being taken in one year (41,71).

Dugongs are also hunted illegally. In Palau, it is estimated that about 20 per year are poached out of a total of about 50, explosives sometimes being used; this number exceeds the recruitment rate and Dugongs will have disappeared from these islands by the year 2000 if poaching is not stopped (11). In Indonesia Dugongs are protected by law and many fishermen consider them to be sacred and avoid deliberate hunting. However some are taken incidently by fishermen who will eat the meat, and Dugong meat is sold on Bangka Island (38). Dugongs are netted along the coast of Kwangsi, China, north of Hainan Island (73). Between 1957 and 1970, it was estimated that 225 to 325 per year were taken for food from Palk Bay and the Gulf of Mannar between India and Sri Lanka; since 1979 the number caught per year has been declining (49). About 25 to 30 are netted for food every year in southern India (62) and they are still being taken by fishermen in this region (47).

Netting is a major threat (33). Accidental deaths in nets employed in some tropical fisheries (e.g. Sri Lanka, India, Kenya and northern Australia) and in shark nets used to reduce shark numbers near swimming beaches in Queensland have significantly reduced numbers locally (10,18,21,22,28,33,34,37,44,62,65).

Pollution, sedimentation, dredging, cyclones and typhoons, and excessive freshwater runoff from land are major threats to the vital seagrass beds (18,21,22,34,36,37). The species is also subject to a wide range of diseases (e.g. pneumonia), and parasitic infections (e.g. enteritis from heavy trematode infections) (12). Iron and zinc occur naturally in exceptionally high concentrations in Dugong liver, and haemosiderosis in wild Dugongs is associated with a high natural intake of iron from seagrasses (15,16). Pollution from additional heavy metals and other toxic substances in even small concentrations in Dugong habitat may threaten animals already possibly under some physiological stress from naturally occurring heavy metals consumed with their food. Other threats may result from disturbance by human activities (e.g. use of power boats, seismic exploration and military activities) (22,36).

CONSERVATION MEASURES TAKEN Except for Australian populations, the Dugong is listed in Appendix 1 of the 1973 Convention on International Trade in Endangered Species of Wild Fauna and Flora, with any trade in it or its products being subject to strict regulation by ratifying nations and trade for primarily commerical purposes being banned. Australian populations are listed in Appendix

2 of the Convention with commercial trade being subject to approval. The species is also included in Class A of the African Convention (1969), i.e. it may be hunted or collected only on the authorization of the highest competent authority, if required in the national interest or for scientific purposes. Totally protected by law in many of the countries in which it occurs, but with a few exceptions, protection is inadequately enforced (10,38,44,49,62). In some countries limited hunting is allowed, e.g. hunting by Aboriginal and Torres Strait Islanders in Australia, and traditional hunting by local people in Papua New Guinea (10,17,26,41). Dugongs are protected in the Paradise Island National Park in Mozambique which seems to be the only park in Africa in which they occur 944). Portions of some important habitat areas in Morteton Bay, Great Sandy Strait, Tin Can Bay and Hinchinbrook Channel in Queensland, Australia, are protected as 'Fish Habitat Reserves'. However net fishing which threatens Dugongs with accidental death is still permitted (28). In Papua New Guinea, Wildlife Management Areas are being established for the management and conservation of Dugongs and other marine life. The local inhabitants make rules, which become gazetted as laws, and they enforce these laws. Two 'Management Areas', one near Daru and the other in west New Britain, have been established (41).

Established research programmes are presently being carried out at the following locations: James Cook University, Queensland, supported by the Australian Government (13,56); Wildlife Division, Papua New Guinea supported by the Papua New Guinea Government and the World Wildlife Fund (41,71), and Jaya Ancol Oceanarium, Jakarta, Indonesia (38,68). Considerable work is also being done in India (49,62) and various projects are being supported by the Japanese, United States, and Canadian governments, the Western Australian State Government and the World Wildlife Fund (5,6,11,66,70). In 1979 a Seminar/Workshop on Dugongs was held at James Cook University, Queensland (13,56), and a Symposium on Dugongs, at the University of Tokyo, Japan (70).

CONSERVATION MEASURES PROPOSED There should be no commercial exploitation at present as all populations are too small. Where subsistence hunting is an important part of the traditional way of life of indigenous peoples, e.g. Australian Aboriginals, Torres Strait Islanders and Papuans, conservation measures including legislation and establishment of Dugong reserves should be discussed by wildlife and fisheries administrators with local communities likely to be affected, to ensure that the greatest possible agreement is achieved (2,17). Existing legislation with regard to the Dugong needs to be reviewed in relation to their status in the enforcement areas in which they occur (1). Protective legislation should have sufficient power and penalties to provide deterrents to poaching, disturbance and habitat destruction, and laws need to be rigorously enforced (1). Aircraft should be used for surveillance to apprehend poachers as well as to monitor Dugong numbers, distributions and habitats (25,32). An extensive series of marine reserves (marine national parks and management areas) based on a knowledge of numbers, distribution, movements and habits of Dugongs, that would include both resident populations and serve as refugia for migrating ones should be identified and established over the species' entire range. Reserves need to provide all of the habitat required and thus include feeding grounds, resting areas and breeding and calving areas. Sanctuaries and management areas including important areas in which all net fishing is excluded need establishing (1,18). In Australia many of the important Dugong areas have been identified, and include parts of Moreton Bay, Shoalwater Bay and Port Clinton, parts of eastern Cape York (Cape Flattery to Shelburne Bay) and western Cape York (Archer Bay to Karumba), Torres Strait, and the Wellesley Islands in Queensland; Port Arthur and the Coburg Peninsula in the Northern Territory; and Shark Bay and Exmouth Gulf in Western Australia (1,17,26,66). Joint Dugong conservation efforts should be established between India and Sri Lanka including the establishment of a major Dugong sanctuary in the Palk Bay and Gulf of Mannar region (49).

Continued and expanded research on its biology and conservation is required. The most pressing research needs are: the determination of present distributions and abundance and levels of exploitation and accidental killing in relation to recruitment; assessment of the extents and periodicities of movements; the determination of basic habitat requirements for the maintenance and increase of present populations; and the determination of factors limiting or adversely affecting population sizes and distributions (e.g. siltation, pollution, various human activities). Important techniques to be used, and to be improved, are aerial survey, marking and tagging, behaviour studies, carcass studies (where carcasses are available from subsistence hunters or accidental killings), and historical studies (1,18). Public awareness and education on the biology, significance and conservation of the Dugong should be fostered, especially in regions of particular importance (1).

CAPTIVE BREEDING Dugongs have not bred in captivity and are very difficult and expensive to maintain in zoos and oceanaria. Two were successfully maintained in captivity at Mandapam Camp, India, for 11 years (49,62) and in 1981 two were held at the Toba Aquarium, Japan, and two in the Jaya Ancol Oceanarium, Indonesia. One of the Dugongs in the Toba Aquarium has been in captivity for more than 2.5 years, and the two in the Jaya Ancol Oceanarium for more than 469 days. Elsewhere they have been kept unsuccessfully for short periods of time (50,68). The Dugong is not suitable for farming as has been suggested, it being difficult to keep and breed in captivity and having a very low reproductive rate.

REMARKS For description of the species see (3,10,23,24,31,32, 37,44,45,46,61,62). Dugongs are of importance to indigenous subsistence hunters as sources of high quality meat and other products. Also in many societies (e.g. Australian Aboriginal, Torres Stait Islander and Papua New Guinean), the Dugong is of important traditional significance in terms of ceremony, religion, economy and culture and has a highly important co-ordinating role, (2,13,14,18,40,60). Dugongs are of educational, scientific, and tourist value (18,22). They are active but gentle animals and, if not hunted or harrassed, show curiosity toward swimmers and divers and can be readily photographed (3,4,18,32). Dr. G.E. Heinsohn of the IUCN Marine Mammal Committee very kindly researched and wrote the draft of this data sheet in May 1981, the Red Data Book is greatly indebted to him.

REFERENCES 1. Anon. (1981). Recommendations of the Seminar/Workshop on the biology and conservation of the Dugong. In Marsh, H. (Ed.), The Dugong. Proceedings of a Seminar/Workshop held at James Cook University, 8-13 May 1979. James Cook University, Queensland. pp. 205-214.
2. Anon. (1981). Additional recommendations relating to the involvement of Aboriginal and Torres Strait Islander communities in information gathering and conservation programs. In Marsh, H. (Ed.), The Dugong. Proceedings of a Seminar/Workshop held at James Cook University, 8-13 May 1979. James Cook University, Queensland. pp. 215-216.
3. Anderson, P.K. (1979). Dugong behaviour: On being a marine mammalian grazer. The Biologist 61(4): 113-144.
4. Anderson, P.K. (1981). Dugong behaviour: Observations, extrapolations, and speculations. In Marsh, H. (Ed.), The Dugong. Proceedings of a Seminar/Workshop held at James Cook University, 8-13 May 1979. James Cook University, Queensland. pp. 91-111.
5. Anderson, P.K. (In press). Studies of Dugongs at Shark Bay,

Western Australia. I. Analysis of population size, composition, dispersion, and habitat use on the basis of aerial survey. Australian Wildlife Research.

6. Anderson, P.K. (In press). Studies of Dugongs at Shark Bay, Western Australia. II. Surface and subsurface observations. Australian Wildlife Research.

7. Anderson, P.K. and Birtles, A. (1978). Behaviour and ecology of the Dugong Dugong dugon (Sirenia). Observations in Shoalwater and Cleveland Bays, Queensland. Australian Wildlife Research 5: 1-23.

8. Anderson, P.K. and Heinsohn, G.E. (1978). The status of the Dugong and Dugong hunting in Australian waters: A survey of local perceptions. Biol. Conserv. 13: 13-26.

9. Bertram, G.C.L. (1974). Conservation of Sirenia. IUCN Occ. Paper 12. 20 pp.

10. Bertram, G.C.L. and Ricardo Bertram, C.K. (1973). The modern Sirenia: their distribution and status. Biol. J. Linnean Soc. 5(4): 297-338.

11. Brownell, R.L. Jr., Anderson, P.K., Owen, R.P. and Ralls, K. (1981). The status of Dugongs at Palau, an isolated island group. In Marsh, H. (Ed.), The Dugong. Proceedings of a Seminar/Workshop held at James Cook University, 8-13 May 1979. James Cook University, Queensland. pp. 19-42.

12. Campbell, R.S.F. and Ladds, P.W. (1981). Diseases of the Dugong in northeastern Australia: A preliminary report. In Marsh, H. (Ed.), The Dugong. Proceedings of a Seminar/Workshop held at James Cook University, 8-13 May 1979. James Cook University, Queensland. pp. 176-181.

13. Caton, A. (1979). Dugong, like mermaids, are scarce but northern Australian population may be increasing. Australian Fisheries 38(7): 13, 15-17.

14. Chase, A. (1981). Dugongs and Australian indigenous cultural systems, some introductory remarks. In Marsh, H. (Ed.), The Dugong. Proceedings of a Seminar/Workshop held at James Cook University, 8-13 May 1979. James Cook University, Queensland. pp. 112-122.

15. Denton, G.R.W. (1981). The effect of diet on the unusual metal status of the Dugong (Dugong dugon (Müller)). In Marsh, H. (Ed.), The Dugong. Proceedings of a Seminar/Workshop held at James Cook University, 8-13 May 1979. James Cook University, Queensland. pp. 169-174.

16. Denton, G.R.W., Marsh, H., Heinsohn, G.E. and Burdon-Jones, C. (1980). The unusual metal status of the Dugong Dugong dugon. Marine Biology 57(3): 201-219.

17. Elliott, M.A. (1981). Distribution and status of the Dugong in Northern Territory waters. In Marsh, H. (Ed.), The Dugong. Proceedings of a Seminar/Workshop held at James Cook University, 8-13 May 1979. James Cook University, Queensland. pp. 57-66.

18. FAO. (1978). Annex B - Proceedings of the Scientific Consultation on the Conservation and Management of Marine Mammals and their Environment 6. Sirenians. In Mammals in the Seas. Volume 1. FAO Fisheries Series. pp.136-138.

19. Gallagher, M.D. (1976). The Dugong Dugong dugon (Sirenia) at Bahrain, Persian (Arabian) gulf. J. Bombay Natural History Society 73(1): 211-212.

20. Gohar, H.A.F. (1979). Notes on the Red Sea Dugong.

Unpublished paper given at Symposium on Biology of the Dugong, Ocean Research Institute, University of Tokyo, Japan, 6-7 Dec. 1979. 8pp.

21. Heinsohn, G.E. (1972). A study of Dugongs (Dugong dugon) in northern Queensland, Australia. Biol. Conserv. 4(3): 205-213.

22. Heinsohn, G.E. (1976). WG4 Sirenians - Draft Report. FAO ACMRR/MM/SC/WG4-1 (Scientific Consultation on Marine Mammals, Bergen, Norway, 31 August - 9 September 1981). 21pp.

23. Heinsohn, G. (1977). Dugongs and turtles. Part 1. Wildlife in Australia 14(4): 134-138.

24. Heinsohn, G. (1978). Dugongs and turtles. Part 2. Wildlife in Australia 15(1): 26-30.

25. Heinsohn, G.E. (1978). Marine mammals of the northern Great Barrier Reef Region. In Workshop on the Northern Sector of the The Great Barrier Reef. Papers and Proceedings of a Workshop held in Townsville, Australia, 20 and 21 April, 1978. Great Barrier Reef Marine Park Authority Workshop Series No.1. pp.315-335.

26. Heinsohn, G.E. (1981). Status and distribution of Dugongs in Queensland. In Marsh, H. (Ed.), The Dugong. Proceedings of a Seminar/Workshop held at James Cook University, 8-13 May 1979. James Cook University, Queensland. pp. 55-56.

27. Heinsohn, G.E. (1981). The Dugong in the seagrass ecosystem. In Marsh, H. (Ed.), The Dugong. Proceedings of a Seminar/Workshop held at James Cook University, 8-13 May 1979. James Cook University, Queensland. pp. 162-163.

28. Heinsohn, G.E. (1981). Pers. comm.

29. Heinsohn, G.E. and Birch, W.R. (1972). Foods and feeding habits of the Dugong, Dugong dugon (Erxleben), in northern Queensland. Mammalia 36(3): 414-422.

30. Heinsohn, G.E., Lear, R.J., Bryden, M.M., Marsh, H. and Gardner, B.R. (1978). Discovery of a large population of Dugongs off Brisbane, Australia. Environmental Conservation 5: 91-92.

31. Heinsohn, G. and Marsh, H. (1977). Sirens of tropical Australia. Australian Natural History 19(4): 106-111.

32. Heinsohn, G., Marsh, H. and Anderson, P. (1979). Australian Dugong. Oceans 12(3): 48-52.

33. Heinsohn, G.E., Marsh, H. and Spain, A.V. (1976). Extreme risk of mortality to Dugongs (Mammalia: Sirenia) from netting operations. Aust. J. Wildl. Res. 3: 117-121.

34. Heinsohn, G.E. and Spain, A.V. (1974). Effects of a tropical cyclone on littoral and sub-littoral biotic communities and on a population of Dugongs (Dugong dugon (Müller)). Biol. Conserv. 6(2): 143-152.

35. Heinsohn, G.E., Spain, A.V. and Anderson, P.K. (1976). Populations of Dugongs (Mammalia: Sirenia): Aerial survey over the inshore waters of tropical Australia. Biol. Conserv. 9(1): 21-23.

36. Heinsohn, G.E. and Wake, J.A. (1976). The importance of the Fraser Island region to Dugongs. Operculum 5: 15-18.

37. Heinsohn, G.E., Wake, J., Marsh, H. and Spain, A.V. (1977). The Dugong (Dugong dugon (Müller)) in the seagrass system. Aquaculture 12: 235-248.

38. Hendrokusumo, S., Sumitro, D. and Tas'an. (1981). The distribution of the Dugong in Indonesian waters. In Marsh,

H. (Ed.), The Dugong. Proceedings of a Seminar/Workshop held at James Cook University, 8-13 May 1979. James Cook University, Queensland. pp. 10-18.

39. Hirasaka, K. (1934). On the distribution of sirenians in the Pacific. Proc. 5th Pac. Sci. Congr. 5: 4221-2.

40. Hudson, B.E.T. (1976). Dugongs: Distribution, hunting, protective legislation and cultural significance in Papua New Guinea. FAO ACMRR/MM/SC/86 (Scientific Consultation on Marine Mammals, Bergen, Norway, 31 August - 9 September 1976). 30pp.

41. Hudson, B.E.T. (1981). The Dugong conservation, management and public education programme in Papua New Guinea: Working with people to conserve their Dugong resources. In Marsh, H. (Ed.), The Dugong. Proceedings of a Seminar/Workshop held at James Cook University, 8-13 May 1979. James Cook University, Queensland. pp. 123-140.

42. Hudson, B.E.T. (1981). Pers. comm.

43. Hughes, G.R. and Oxley-Oxland, R. (1971). A survey of Dugong (Dugong dugon) in and around Antonio Enes, northern Mozambique. Biol. Conserv. 3(4): 299-301.

44. Husar, S.L. (1975). A review of the literature of the Dugong (Dugong dugon). United States Dept. of the Interior, Fish and Wildlife Service Wildlife Research Report 4. 30pp.

45. Husar, S.L. (1975). The Dugong: endangered siren of the south seas. Nat. Parks and Conserv. Magazine 49(2): 15-18.

46. Husar, S.L. (1978). Dugong dugon. Mammalian Species No.88. The American Society of Mammalogists. 7pp.

47. IUCN. (1980). Dugong killing. IUCN Bulletin 11(12): 103.

48. Jones, S. (1976). The present status of the Dugong, Dugong dugon (Müller) in the Indo-Pacific and problems of its conservation. FAO ACMRR/MM/SC/26 (Scientific Consultation on Marine Mammals Bergen, Norway, 31 August - 9 September 1976). 47pp.

49. Jones, S. (1981). Distribution and status of the Dugong Dugong dugon (Müller) in the Indian region. In Marsh, H. (Ed.), The Dugong. Proceedings of a Seminar/Workshop held at James Cook University, 8-13 May 1979. James Cook University, Queensland. pp. 43-54.

50. Kataoka, T. and Asano, S. (1981). On the keeping of Dugong (Dugong dugon) in Toba Aquarium. In Marsh, H. (Ed.), The Dugong. Proceedings of a Seminar/Workshop held at James Cook University, 8-13 May 1979. James Cook University, Queensland. pp. 199-203.

51. Ligon, S.H. (1976). A survey of Dugongs (Dugong dugon) in Queensland. J. Mammal. 57: 280-282.

52. Ligon, S. (1976). Aerial survey of the Dugong in Kenya. FAO ACMRR/MM/SC/107 (Scientific Consultation on Marine Mammals, Bergen, Norway, 31 August - 9 Septemebr 1976). 2pp.

53. Ligon, S.H. and Hudson, B.E.T. (1976). Aerial survey of the Dugong (Dugong dugon) in Papua New Guinea. FAO ACMRR/MM/SC/89 (Scientific Consultation on Marine Mammals, Bergen, Norway, 31 August - 9 September 1976). 5pp.

54. Lipkin, Y. (1975). Food of the Red Sea Dugong (Mammalia: Sirenia) from Sinai. Israel J. of Zoology 24: 81-98.

55. Marsh, H. (1980). Age determination of the Dugong (Dugong dugon (Müller)) in northern Australia and its biological

implications. In Perrin, W.R. and Myrick, A.C. (Eds), <u>Age Determination of Toothed Cetaceans and Sirenians</u>. Rep. Int. Whal. Commn. (Special Issue 3). pp. 181-201.

56. Marsh, H. (Ed.) (1981). <u>The Dugong</u>. Proceedings of a Seminar/Workshop held at James Cook University, 8-13 May 1973. James Cook University, Queensland. 400pp.

57. Marsh, H. (1981). The life history parameters of the Dugong and their implications for conservation. In Marsh, H. (Ed.), <u>The Dugong</u>. Proceedings of a Seminar/Workshop held at James Cook University, 8-13 May 1979. James Cook University, Queensland. pp. 88-90.

58. Marsh, H. (1981). Pers. comm.

59. Marsh, H., Channells, P.W., Heinsohn, G.E. and Morrissey, J. (In press). Analysis of stomach contents of Dugongs from Queensland, Australia. <u>Australian Wildlife Research</u>.

60. Marsh, H., Gardner, B.R. and Heinsohn, G.E. (1981). Present-day hunting and distribution of Dugongs in the Wellesley Islands (Queensland): implications for conservation. <u>Biol. Conserv</u>. 19(4): 255-267.

61. Marsh, H., Spain, A.V. and Heinsohn, G.E. (1978). Minireview. Physiology of the Dugong. <u>Comp Biochem. Physiol</u>. 61A: 159-168.

62. Nair, R.V., Lal Mohan, R.S. and Satyanarayana Rao, K. (1975). The Dugong <u>Dugong dugon</u>. <u>ICAR Bulletin of the Central Marine Fisheries Research Institute (Cochin, India)</u> No.26. 44pp.

63. Nietschmann, B. (1977). Torres Strait Islander hunters and environment. Work-in-Progress Seminar, Dept. of Human Geography, Research School of Pacific Studies, Australian National University. 18pp.

64. Nishiwaki, M., Kasuya, T., Miyazaki, N., Tobayama, T. and Kataoka, T. (1979). Present distribution of the Dugong in the world. <u>Sci. Rep. Whales Res. Inst</u>., No.31 pp. 133-141.

65. Paterson, R. (1979). Shark meshing takes a heavy toll of harmless marine animals. <u>Australian Fisheries</u> 38(10): 17-19, 21-23.

66. Prince, R.I.T., Anderson, P.K. and Blackman, D. (1981). Status and distribution of dugongs in Western Australia. In Marsh, H. (Ed.), <u>The Dugong</u>. Proceedings of a Seminar/Workshop held at James Cook University, 8-13 May 1979. James Cook University, Queensland. pp. 67-87.

67. Spain, A.V. and Heinsohn, G.E. (1973). Cyclone associated feeding changes in the Dugong (Mammalia: Sirenia). <u>Mammalia</u> 37(4): 678-680.

68. Tas'an, Sumitro, D. and Hendrokusumo, S. (1979). Some biological notes on two male Dugongs in captivity at the Jaya Ancol Oceanarium, Jakarta. Gelanggang Samudra, Jaya Ancol (Oceanarium), Jakarta, Indonesia. 30pp. (To be published in <u>Oceanol. Indonesia</u>).

69. Uchida, S. (1979). Dugongs kept in Okinawa. Abstract 2-1. Abstracts of the Symposium on Biology of the Dugong (<u>Dugong dugon</u>). Ocean Research Institute, University of Tokyo, Japan, 6-7 December 1979. pp 8-11.

70. University of Tokyo. (1979). <u>Abstracts of the Symposium on Biology of the Dugong (Dugong dugon)</u>. Ocean Research Institute, University of Tokyo, 6-7 December 1979. 46pp.

71. World Wildlife Fund Australia. (1981). Project 19: Dugong conservation, management and public education programme

in Papua New Guinea. World Wildlife Fund Australia Newsletter No.6. p.4-5.

72. Yamaguchi, M. (1979). Distribution of sea-grass meadows in the Ryukyu Islands. Abstract 3-2. Abstracts of the Symposium on Biology of the Dugong (Dugong dugon). Ocean Research Institute, University of Tokyo, Japan, 6-7 December 1979. pp.25-26.

73. Zhang, Zhou Man. (1979). About Dugong. The secret of mermaids. Natural History. (Shanghai Natural History Museum) 1: 33-36. (In Chinese).

CARIBBEAN MANATEE   VULNERABLE

Trichechus manatus (Linnaeus, 1758)

Order   SIRENIA   Family   TRICHECHIDAE

SUMMARY   A widely ranging species occurring in the coastal waters and rivers of the Caribbean and Atlantic regions of the Americas, in tropical and subtropical latitudes. Populations everywhere have been severely reduced by hunting, mainly for meat, over the last three centuries. Numbers are now so low that commercial hunting has virtually ceased though in many countries animals are still killed for local consumption whenever encountered. This and the low reproductive rate have meant that populations have remained at very depressed levels and are probably still decreasing in most areas, despite legal protection in almost all countries of its range. Reasonable populations still exist in Florida, Belize, Guyana and Suriname. Occurs in a few national parks and reserves and status surveys have been carried out in several countries since 1973. In the United States, where principal causes of mortality are collisions with boats and drowning in floodgates, a Manatee Recovery Plan, aimed principally at controlling these factors, was produced in 1980 and several Manatee sanctuaries have been created. Effective enforcement of legal protection throughout its range would allow populations to start recovering though long term threats of habitat destruction through water pollution, drainage and development would remain. This species has been used for weed-control under semi-captive conditions and could conceivably be managed as a food resource, though the latter is not considered practicable at present.

DISTRIBUTION   Coastal waters, estuaries and rivers of the Americas in the Atlantic and Caribbean regions from northern Florida in the U.S.A. to Brazil at about 12°S.

In the U.S.A. year-round distribution is largely confined to peninsular Florida but seasonal variation occurs. Manatees in northern and central Florida congregate around natural and industrial warm-water sources in winter. Winter distribution limits were reported in 1978 as having extended northward during the last few decades, from around 27°52'N (Sebastian Creek) to around 30°12'N (Duval County) on the east coast, and from 26°45'N (Charlotte Harbor) to around 28°59'N (Crystal River) on the west coast, probably as a result of proliferation of industrial warm-water discharge sites (14,23,37). Inland, Manatees occur in St. Johns River from Jacksonville south to at least Lake Monroe, with winter concentrations at Blue Spring, also moving along the Caloosahatchee River and St. Lucia Canal into Lake Okeechobee in summer (23,37,38,59). In spring animals disperse throughout Florida, some moving further north, in the east into Georgia and occasionally beyond - the most northerly documented individual is a dead male found in Chesapeake Bay, Virginia in October 1980 (39) - and in the west into the Florida Panhandle, generally up to the Aucilla and Port St. Joe Rivers, with sightings as far west as Louisiana (37). Occasional records from extreme southern Texas are probably representatives of a remnant population which occurs along the northern Mexican Gulf coast (22,37). Mexico: although they do occur along the coast in the Gulf of Mexico, Manatees were reported in 1978 as most commonly recorded south of Tamaulipas or Veracruz, within the Bay of Campeche, and on both sides of the Yucatan Peninsula (37). In Belize distribution in 1974 was reported as apparently continuous, with concentrations in or near the mouths of rivers as well as on offshore islands such as the Drowned Cayes near Belize City (16). 1977 aerial surveys noted little change, although additionally recorded its occurrence in New River up to 100 km upstream; none were seen in the 5 southernmost rivers although here visibility was severely hampered by a high sediment load in the water (4). Guatemala: a 1976-77 survey encountered them in Lake Izabal, the Rio Dulce, along the Caribbean Coast and also in the Rio Sarstun and other minor rivers north of Puerto Barrios (24). No data are available for distribution in Nicaragua. Honduras: surveys in Feb/March 1979 indicated that the two main areas frequented by Manatees were the lagoons and rivers of the La Mosquitia in the east and the lagoons and creeks in the region of the Rio Curero in the west, particularly the Rio Salado - Laguna de Boca Cerrada area (33). Manatees in Costa Rica in the 1970s were believed to be confined to a few isolated areas such as the lagoons at Tortuguero National Park and perhaps some of the less inhabited areas of the Rio San Juan and its tributaries (Rios Colorado, Sarapaqui and San Carlos). It was also presumed to occur on the Atlantic coast near the border with Panama (44), while in Panama itself only isolated populations were thought to remain, probably in Chiriqui Bay, the Rios Changuinola, Sicaola and possibly Cocle, and Gatun Lake (37).

In Colombia Hernandez-Camacho described it in 1973 as present in the Orinoco as far as the Tabaje and Borje rapids below Puerto Carreno; also in the Rio Meta and possibly in rivers draining into the south and west of Lake Maracaibo, although this was unconfirmed. On the Caribbean coast it was found in the Rio Atrato and its delta and also in the deltas of the Rios Leon and Suriqui in the Gulf of Uraba (12). In the Magdalena basin it still survived between the mouth of the Cauca and the Salto de Honda rapids, mainly in cienagas (shallow lagoons or lakes connected with rivers or the sea). It was also found in the Canal del Dique, between Magdalena and Pta. Barbacoas (although a 1978 report described it as extinct there (37)), and in the system of channels and swamps of south and west Cienaga Grande between Barranquilla and Santa Marta, also being still occasionally caught by fishermen in Transmallo in Cienaga Grande. There was no evidence of it ever having occurred in the Rio Sino or the Rio Rancheria in Dpt. Gajira, although the latter apparently contained suitable habitat (12). Venezuela: Mondolfi in 1974 summarised available information (27): at that time the Manatee was said to still occur in the middle and lower Orinoco and some of its tributaries - Cuchivero, Meta, Cinaruco, Capanaparo, Arauca, Payara, Arichuna, Claro, Apure and Manapire. It still frequented the canals, 'cagnos', lagoons and 'rebalses' (overflows) of the Orinoco delta, in the dry season seeking refuge in lagoons near the 'barras' (estuarine streams) of Macareo, Mariusa, Mariusita and Güinikina where these enter the sea. It also still occurred in the Lago de Maracaibo, with records in the southwest from the vicinity of Ensenada Zulia between Punta Palisada and Boca Escalante (27). The Manatee in the Orinoco drainage basin has in the past often been referred to Trichechus inunguis, the Amazonian Manatee. Mondolfi, however, has noted that this appears to stem from a misidentification by Humboldt, based on observations made in 1800, and he himself has identified as Trichechus manatus three specimens from the Apure and Orinoco Rivers at least 500 km from the coast (27). Guyana: reported in 1974 as occurring throughout the coastal reaches of rivers and had also been deliberately introduced as a weed control agency to several canals and water conservancies, totalling over 1000 sq. km in area (29). In Suriname distribution in the 1970s has been mapped (19); reports were received from coastal reaches and lower stretches of all major rivers except the Marowijne. Areas of apparent highest densities were the Nanni Creek, (a tributary of the Corantijn), the Coesewijne and Tibiti Rivers (tributaries of the Coppename), and the Perica, part of the Cottica River system (19). Distribution in northern French Guiana unknown, though in the south Best received reports in 1978 that it was present in the mouth of the Rivers Approuage, Mhury, Laughan and Ouanari as well as in the smaller rivers in these areas (11). In Brazil in 1978, Manatees appeared distributed throughout the coastal areas of the State of Amapa, with specific reference to the mouth of the Rio Oiapoque, Rio Uaca (as far as Rio Urucawa) and the Larispore in the northern part and Cunani, Marrecal, the mouth of the Rio Araguari and Ilhas Maraca and Bailique further south (11).

Around the mouth of the Amazon, Domning in 1981 reported that T. manatus probably occurred north of Cabo Norte in Amapa, its place in the Amazon mouth being taken over by the Amazonian Manatee T. inunguis, with a possible zone of sympatry near Cabo Norte and in some of the interior lakes of eastern Amapa (especially Novo and Comprido) (18). South of the Amazon mouth, T. manatus was recorded from the Rio Mearim in Maranhao, though had apparently been exterminated from the Atlantic Coast of Para, assuming that it, not T. inunguis, formerly occurred there (18). Modern records extend along the coast as far south as Sergipe and possibly Salvador, whilst historical references extend to Espirito Santo (9,43).

Widely though sparsely distributed in the Caribbean Sea in coastal regions near rivers and away from population centres. They occur along both coasts of Cuba and in 1978 were said to be most frequently seen in the Hatiguanic River in the Zapata Swamp and in the Ensenda de la Bara (37). In Jamaica they were most frequently reported from the Black River area in the southwest and in the Portland Point area of the south-central coast (37). A 1977 survey of the Dominican Republic found them concentrated in coastal waters near Monte Cristi in the northwest, Samana Bay in the northeast and in Ocoa and Neiba Bays in the southwest with additional sightings and reports from elsewhere along the coast (3). Very little is known of Manatees in Haiti, although there may be some interchange with the Dominican population, especially along the north coast (3,37). In Puerto Rico, although accurate distribution is not well known, small groups were reported in 1978 as frequently sighted near Guanajibo on the west coast, the mouth of the Fajardo River on the east coast and near Guanica, Guayanilla, La Parguerra, Jobas Bay and Roosevelt Roads Naval Station on the south coast (37). In 1975 two individuals were recorded from Grand Bahama Island (30) and in 1978 a 'recent' sighting was reported from Trinidad (37). Mondolfi considers it likely that Manatees may travel from the Orinoco delta to the estuaries of the east coast rivers of Trinidad (27). The species is thought likely to be extinct in the Lesser Antilles (34).

POPULATION   Total numbers unknown though certainly considerably reduced everywhere compared to its former abundance.

U.S.A.: aerial surveys of Florida coasts and rivers from 1972 to 1976 and interview data in 1975-76 indicated a population of about 1000. 738 were counted in a concentrated aerial survey in early 1976 but the percentage of the population not observed is unknown. Current (1981) estimate is still of around 1000 animals (2). Present population trends are the subject of some controversy; it has been stated that on the basis of mortality figures the population must be decreasing although others argue that the figures imply a larger population than has been hitherto estimated (13,14). Mexico: in 1978 it was noted that interviews with fishermen indicated that numbers had drastically declined from past population levels (37). Reports of sightings were rare and its present status unknown (37). Belize: aerial surveys in 1977 gave 101 sightings though some may have been duplicates and the percentage of the population unrecorded is unknown (4). In 1974 it was noted that there had been no obvious change in abundance for at least 7 years and that the population was possibly increasing as a result of decreased persecution. It was described as plentiful, although numbers were reduced compared to historic levels (16). Guatemala: a 1976-77 study estimated numbers to be as low as 100, with data indicating a rapid decline since the early 1960s (24). Honduras: on the basis of a 1979 survey it was estimated that there were probably 20 to 50 Manatees in the Rio Salado - Laguna de Boca Cerrada area and perhaps 15 in each of the five larger freshwater lagoons (Laguna Tansin, L. Warunta, L. Tilbalaka, L. de Brus and L. de Ibans) in the La Mosquita (33). Based on these it was estimated that there were perhaps 100-200 Manatees in Honduras, though it was noted that as there were no reliable methods for determining the proportion of a Manatee population seen during an aerial census, such estimates would be largely speculative (33). It was considered likely that the population was decreasing due to human hunting and fishing activities (33). The species was included on a national endangered species list in 1978 (1). Estimates for Nicaragua in the 1970s varied from the mid-tens to several hundred (37); it was included on a 1978 list of endangered mammals (35).

Panama: numbers low (37); considered in imminent danger of extinction in 1978 (41). Costa Rica also regarded as endangered in 1978 (26).

Colombia: Hernandez-Camacho in 1973 reported it as much reduced throughout, though still relatively common in the Rio Atrato (12). It was very scarce in the Magdalena Basin and had been exterminated from the Upper Rio Magdalena in the 1930s. It was also now scarce in the lower Rio Cauca and the Rio San Gorge, areas of former abundance (12). Suriname: a 1978 estimate of 500-600 and considered the most endangered mammal in Suriname, although as it was no longer relentlessly hunted, its status was considered unlikely to change in the forseeable future (19,35). Venezuela: Mondolfi in 1974 noted that no survey or census had been carried out, though reports indicated it was now very scarce throughout those parts of the Orinoco drainage basin where it still occurred, except perhaps in some areas of the delta, where it could be found in relative abundance during the dry season (June to October). It was almost extinct in the Lago de Maracaibo and very few individuals had been seen there recently (27). Guyana: estimates in the 1970s of some thousands but reduced compared with original abundance (37). In 1974 Bertram considered this to be the largest remaining population anywhere, though probably of lower density than in Belize (7). French Guiana: Best in 1978 received reports from fishermen that it was common in river estuaries at least in the south (11). Brazil: populations said to be seriously reduced though in 1978 reportedly still common along much of the virtually uninhabited coastline of Amapa. Actual numbers and current population trends unknown (9,11,18).

Said to be uncommon to rare throughout the Caribbean. Numbers seriously reduced in Cuba (40) and reported as extremely rare in Haiti in 1977 (42). Puerto Rico: a survey in 1978 indicated a total of less than 100; the current trend was unclear, though a small number were reportedly still taken each year in fishing nets (14,32) An aerial survey, also in 1978, of Vicques Island off eastern Puerto Rico indicated that part of Vicques may serve as a nursery and important feeding ground with around 15 Manatees concentrated in two small areas of Thalassia (sea-grass) meadow in the northwest of the island and calves constituting some 25% of total sightings compared to 9 to 18% in other parts of the species' range (45). Aerial surveys of the Dominican Republic in 1977 recorded a maximum of 30 along the north coast and 11 on the south coast in any one survey; the population level was apparently considerably reduced compared with former abundance. Present trends were unknown, though it was reportedly still hunted (3). It is not known whether individuals reported from the Bahamas represent part of a small resident population or are vagrants from Florida (30). They have reportedly been exterminated in the Virgin Islands (20) and there is no recent evidence of survival in the rest of the Lesser Antilles, though it is thought possible (34).

HABITAT AND ECOLOGY Shallow coastal waters, bays, estuaries, lagoons and rivers - in the Orinoco basin being recorded at least 800 km upstream. Feed on a very wide variety of available vegetation; studies in Florida (where almost all research on T. manatus has been carried out) indicate they eat almost all species of submergents, emergents and floating vegetation encountered, but that the order of preference may differ between populations (46,54). It is believed that Manatees also ingest considerable quantities of aufwuchs such as diatoms, algae and crustacea which adhere to aquatic macrophytes and these may be an

432

important additional nutrient source (8,21). Captive Manatees will also take fish, and wild individuals in Jamaica have been seen occasionally feeding on dead fish in gill nets (31). Daily food consumption is reported to be 7-80 kg (53) or 5-11% of body weight for captives (8), and is estimated to vary seasonally between 21-44 kg for wild Manatees in the St. Johns River (15). There is not believed to be a specific breeding season, though in Florida most young appear to be born in spring and early summer (38,46,54). Gestation period is estimated at 385-400 days with parturition thought to occur in secluded shallows (14,37,46). Three females calved in protected creeks with access to deep channels in April, May, and August 1980 along the St. Johns River system (54,55). Usually a single offspring is produced but twins and a case of fostering have been reported (14,37,46). Calves may begin grazing immediately after birth but suckle and remain with the female for one to two years (14,37,55). Individuals are thought to breed every 2 to 5 years and sexual maturity is reached at 7 to 10 years of age (14,37,46,47,54). Two tagged females in the St. Johns River exhibited a two-year calving interval (54). Longevity in the wild is unknown though a captive has lived in Florida for at least 29 years (13,38). Manatees have been considered only slightly social, with the only prolonged association believed to be between cow and calf (14,46). A recent study in Florida, however, has indicated that Manatees may have a more complex social structure, with individuals associating during feeding and travelling, in addition to reproductive behaviour (54). Radio-tracking showed that whereas females had relatively small home ranges, adult males patrolled large areas searching for sexually receptive females. Males congregrate around oestrous females and attempt to copulate; such mating groups may persist for several weeks (14,46,54). Although the large aggregations at warm water refugia during winter in Florida (14,46) are caused by Manatees' need to escape cold water, the tendency to use such sites may be influenced by social aspects within groups; behavioural tradition may serve an important role in transmitting information on the location and reliability of resources such as winter refugia (54). Seasonal movements occur in the Florida populations (see Distribution) and animals in the Orinoco basin are reported to move out into flooded savannah to feed in the rainy season, returning to the main rivers or taking refuge in lagoons as the water level recedes (27); in Florida, radio-tagged individuals have been observed travelling to points up to 350 km away from their winter refuge before returning the following winter (54). There is some indication of predation by sharks (3).

THREATS TO SURVIVAL Hunting for meat and, to a lesser extent, for other products such as leather, oil, and bones (used for carvings), has been the principal cause of decline in most of its range (6,9,11,19,29,37). Large scale slaughter began in the late 16th century with Spanish colonisation of the Caribbean - the flavour of the meat was highly esteemed and its excellent keeping qualities made it especially valuable for extended voyages and expeditions; later on it was also used to provide meat for slaves in sugar plantations in the Caribbean (19,29). Antonio Vieira remarked in 1660 that each year more than 20 Dutch ships were loaded with Manatee meat obtained from the Nheengaiba Indians near Cabo do Norte in northern Brazil for export to the Caribbean Islands (11). In Suriname it is thought that the heaviest toll was taken between 1600 and 1800, although Duplaix and Reichart report that the first mention of decline in numbers there appears to have been in 1887 when trade had virtually ended (19). Recent protective legislation throughout most of its range and very low remaining population densities has led to a virtual cessation of commercial hunting although subsistence hunting, much of it doubtless opportunistic, still reportedly occurs in most areas outside the United States and continues to pose a substantial threat (3,11,27,37). In 1978 it was reported that meat was still occasionally sold in local markets of Colombia, Brazil and Venezuela, although in Mexico only one sale of Manatee meat was reported within the previous ten years in 23 major markets visited (37). Mondolfi in 1974 noted that is was still very much sought after in the Orinoco basin, despite its scarcity and the difficulty of capture (27). It was

433

mainly hunted for its meat, though there was also demand for live individuals for zoos and for weed control in dams (27). Best, who visited the north Brazilian coast in 1978, encountered 3 Manatee hunters in Oiapoque and Tapereba near the border with French Guiana (8). They were stated to have killed altogether around 660 Manatees in their lifetimes although all but one had now ceased hunting. South of Oiapoque the Amapa coastline was reported to be virtually uninhabited due to seasonal flooding, mangrove swamps and shallow, silt-laden waters hampering navigation, and Best noted the species here did not seem in any particular danger (8). Elsewhere even in areas where they are not deliberately hunted, many undoubtedly drown each year through being trapped in fishing nets. In Florida a study conducted jointly by the University of Miami and the National Fish and Wildlife Laboratory indicated that human activities were by far the greatest identifiable cause of Manatee mortality in the area (14). Of 305 dead Manatees salvaged from April 1974 to June 1979, 103 were identified as human-related mortalities, comprising 62 attributed to boat/barge collisions, 24 to being crushed or drowned in flood gates or canal locks and 17 to other activities (vandalism, shooting, poaching, entrapment in fishing nets or lines) (14). The presence of artifical warm-water refugia leading to Manatees overwintering outside their historic range has also been implicated as a cause of mortality - in the extremely cold winter of 1976-77, susbtantial die-offs were reported in areas north of the historic winter range - it being thought that the artificial warmth provided by the industrial outlets was inadequate due to a combination of partial industrial shutdown and the severe winter, and the animals apparently died of cold related causes (14,48). Other possible, though as yet undocumented, causes of mortality are oil spills, herbicides (e.g. to control water hyacinths, Eichornia crassipes and Hydrilla spp.) and other chronic chemical contaminants which could act directly or by destroying food supply (14,37). Dredging operations and excess boat use of shallow areas can increase turbidity and kill submerged food plants (14). Best notes that oil exploration off the Brazilian coast could threaten populations through oils spills destroying estuarine food plants such as Montricardia and Rhizophora (11). In Venezuela, Mondolfi stated that intensive pollution in the Lago de Maracaibo could be harmful to the few Manatees remaining there and that extensive land reclamation in the Orinoco delta was leading to a reduction of Manatee foraging grounds in the swamps (27).

CONSERVATION MEASURES TAKEN Listed in Appendix 1 of the 1973 Convention on International Trade in Endangered Species of Wild Fauna and Flora, trade in it or its products therefore being subject to strict regulation by ratifying nations, and trade for primarily commercial purposes banned. Protected in most countries of its range, including the U.S.A. (under the 1972 Marine Mammals Protection Act, and by Florida State law since 1893), Mexico, Jamaica, Belize, Honduras, Guatemala, Colombia, Costa Rica, Panama, Venezuela Guyana, Suriname, French Guiana, Haiti, Brazil, Dominican Republic, Puerto Rico, Trinidad and Cuba (3,16,19,25,27,29,33,37,38,44). No official status in Nicaragua. In most areas, however, prevention of local subsistence hunting is virtually impossible. Known to occur in the Everglades (U.S.A), Rio Dulce (Guatemala), Tortuguero (Costa Rica), and Salamaca (Colombia) National Parks and the 10,000 ha Coppename Rivermouth Nature Reserve in Suriname (14,19,37,44). Status surveys have been carried out in several areas since 1975, including Guatemala, Puerto Rico, Suriname, Honduras, Dominican Republic, Mexico, Belize and Brazil (3,4,11,17,19,24,32,33). In the United States, the 1980 Annual Report of the Marine Mammal Commission (49) noted that after several years of what they considered a 'distressingly low level of activity with respect to efforts to protect and encourage the recovery of this species', they were pleased to report considerable progress during the year with a marked intensification of effort and increased cooperation amongst the various agencies and organisations involved - $100,000 had been allocated for Manatee conservation and the Commission developed a plan to use this to maximum effect with the emphasis on increased protection and coordination of recovery efforts rather than on further research, and a West Indian Manatee Recovery Plan was finalised in April 1980 (14,49). In Florida, as of April 1981, 13 sanctuaries in which boat speeds are restricted have been established and three Manatee protection areas prohibiting all waterborne traffic, including skin divers, have been delimited at Crystal River, an important wintering area (2). It was also to be hoped that modifications to the operation of floodgates would decrease the considerable mortality caused by them (2). Active research is being undertaken (1981) at the U.S. Fish and Wildlife Laboratory in Gainesville and the Rosensteil School of Oceanic and Atmospheric Sciences, Florida (10). A workshop on Manatees was held in Georgetown, Guyana in February 1974 and another in Orlando, Florida in March 1978 (13,29). Robin Best in 1980/81 has undertaken a questionnaire survey to determine the status of Manatees in Latin America (10). A proposed International Centre for Manatee Research at Georgetown, Guyana (29) has not materialized.

CONSERVATION MEASURES PROPOSED Adequate enforcement of protective laws throughout its range. The establishment of well-guarded marine or freshwater reserves is advocated to safeguard particular populations though studies are needed to determine the extent of seasonal movements to ensure that areas large enough to give year-round protection are set aside. As a result of the 1978 survey of the northern (Amapa) Brazilian Coast, the setting up of the 5260 sq. km Cabo Orange National Park and the 5705 sq. km Lago Piratuba Biological Reserve has been advocated - both these areas, and the already proposed ecological station of Ilha Maracea, also in Amapa, are believed to hold Manatee populations (11). Best has advocated a co-ordinated approach to Manatee research and conservation in the Americas, with a team of experienced researchers initiating surveys and conservation programmes in countries where Manatees still exist but are not sufficiently protected (10). Training of Latin American personnel in research techniques could possibly be carried out using the infra-structure of the already established Brazilian Manatee Project in Manaus (which is principally concerned with T. inunguis) (10). Active management of Manatees for weed control and possibly for meat production has frequently been advocated (5,6,7,29,37). Semi-captive Manatees have been used as weed-control agents, often with considerable success, in canals and water conservancies in Guyana since 1916 (29), and also on a smaller scale in Mexico and Panama, where in 1964-65 eight T. manatus (5 males, and 3 females) and one T. inunguis were introduced into Gatun Lake in the Panama Canal (50). Recent reports indicate the population is still present there and may even be increasing (51). Breeding success in confined conditions has, however, generally been poor and most semi-captive populations have not been self sustaining (29). The Bertrams have additionally noted that Sirenians are the only large mammals which feed almost exclusively on aquatic vegetation and are thus capable of turning an otherwise virtually unexploited food source into meat utilisable by man. Rational and managed harvesting of rebuilt populations could thus potentially be of real value in providing protein for man over a wide area (5,6,7). It has been pointed out, however, that very low reproductive rates and the current very reduced population levels make large-scale exploitation of Manatees unrealistic in the forseeable future (37). The primary objective of the West Indian Manatee Recovery Plan in the U.S.A. is 'to re-establish and maintain optimum sustainable populations of West Indian Manatees in natural habitats throughout their historical range in the United States'. It states that this can be done most effectively by minimising human-associated injury and mortality (particularly from boat collision and floodgates) and protecting natural habitat within all significant portions of the historic range (14).

CAPTIVE BREEDING In 1979 there were at least 19 in 8 collections (52); in May 1975 the first T. manatus conceived in captivity was born at Miami Seaquarium, Florida; this was followed by a second at Artis Zoo, Netherlands on 8th August

1977 (10).

REMARKS   For description see (22). We are very grateful to the many correspondents who have provided information for this data sheet.

REFERENCES   1.   Aguilar, W. (1978). El manejo de la Vida Silvestre en Honduras. In Morales, R., Macfarland, C., Incer, J. and Hobbs, A. (Eds), Memorias de la Primera Reunion Regional Centroamerican sobre Vida Silvestre. Matagalpa, Nicaragua 25-29 Julio 1978. Unidad de areas silvestres y cuencas del catie.
2.   Baker, J.L. (1981). In litt.
3.   Belitsky, D.W. and Belitsky, C.L. (1980). Distribution and abundance of Manatees, Trichechus manatus in the Dominican Republic. Biol. Cons. 17: 313-319.
4.   Bengtson, J.L. and Magor, D. (1979). A survey of Manatees in Belize. J. Mammal. 60(1): 230-232.
5.   Bertram, G.L.C. and Ricardo Bertram, C.K. (1968). The Sirenia as aquatic meat-producing herbivores. Symp. Zool. Soc. Lond. 21: 385-391.
6.   Bertram, G.L.C. and Ricardo Bertram, C.K. (1973). The modern Sirenia: their distribution and status. Biol. Journ. Linn. Soc. 5(4): 297-338.
7.   Bertram, G.L.C. (1974). Conservation of Sirenia - current status and perspective for action. Occasional paper No.12. IUCN, Switzerland.
8.   Best, R.C. (1981). Food and feeding habits of wild and captive Sirenia. Mammal Review. 11(1): 3-29.
9.   Best, R.C. (1981). Pers. comm.
10.   Best, R.C. (1981). In litt.
11.   Best, R.C. (1979). Preliminary report on the distribution and apparent status of Manatees (Mammalia: Sirenia) on the northern coast of Brazil. Unpd. Report. 9pp.
12.   Blaine, A. (1973). Report on endangered species of S. America. Colombia - information furnished by Prof. J. Hernandez-Camacho. Unpd. Report.
13.   Brownell, R.L. Jr., Ralls, K. and Reeves, R. (1978). Report of the West Indian Manatee Workshop, Orlando, Florida, 27-29 March 1978. Unpd. Report.
14.   Brownell, R.L. Jr. in cooperation with the West Indian Manatee Recovery Team. (1980). West Indian Manatee Recovery Plan. 35pp.
15.   Bengtson, J.L. (1981). Estimating food consumption of wild Manatees in the St. Johns River, Florida. Unpd. Report. 20 pp.
16.   Charnock-Wilson, J.P., Bertram, C.K.R. and Bertram, G.L.C. (1974). The Manatee in Belize. Belize Audubon Soc. Bull. 6(1): 1-4.
17.   Campbell, H.W. and Villa, D.W. (In press). Resena preliminar del estado en Mexico, Serie Zool. Anales del Inst. Biol. Univ. Nac. Anton. Mexico.
18.   Domning, A. (1981). Distribution and status of Manatees Trichechus spp. near the mouth of the Amazon River, Brazil. Biol. Cons. 19(2): 85-97.
19.   Duplaix, N. and Reichart, H.A. (1978). History, status and protection of the Caribbean Manatee Trichechus. m. manatus in Suriname. Unpd. Report. 32pp.
20.   Erdman, D.S. (1970). Marine mammals from Puerto Rico to

Antigua. J. Mammal. 51: 636-639.

21. Hartman, D.S. (1971). Behaviour and ecology of the Florida Manatee, Trichechus manatus latirostris (Harlan), at Crystal River, Citrus County. Ph. D. Dissert. Cornell Univ. Ithaca, New York.

22. Husar, S.L. (1978). Trichechus manatus. Mamm. Species. 93: 1-5. American Society of Mammalogists.

23. Irvine, A.B. and Campbell, H.W. (1978). Aerial census of the West Indian Manatee, Trichechus manatus in the southeastern United States. J. Mammal. 59: 6.

24. Jansen, T. (1978). Ecology and conservation of the Guatemalan Manatee. Abstract. In Mate, B.R. (Ed.), Marine Mammal Information. Oregon State University, Sea Grant College Program. December 1978.

25. Leclerc, J. (no date). In litt.

26. Lopez, E. (1978). Informe sobre las actividades de la Direccion General de Recursos Pesqueros y Vida Silvestre de Costa Rica. In Morales, R., Macfarland, C., Incer, J. and Hobbs, A. (Eds), Memorias de la Primera Reunion Regional Centroamerican sobre Vida Silvestre. Matagalpa, Nicaragua 25-29 Julio 1978. Unidad de areas silvestres y cuencas del catie.

27. Mondolfi, E. (1974). Taxonomy, distribution and status of the Manatee of Venezuela. Mem. Soc. Cienc. Nat. La Salle 34(97): 5-23.

28. Moore, J.C. (1951). The range of the Florida Manatee. Q.J. Florida Acad. Sci. 19(1): 1-19.

29. National Science Research Council (Guyana). (1974). An international centre for Manatee research. Report of a Workshop held 7-13 February 1974, Georgetown, Guyana.

30. Odell, D.K., Reynolds, J.E. and Waugh, G. (1978). New records of the West Indian Manatee (Trichechus manatus) from the Bahamas Islands. Biol. Cons. 14: 289-291.

31. Powell, J.A., Jr. (1978). Evidence of carnivory in Manatees (Trichectus manatus). J. Mammal. 59: 442.

32. Powell, J.A. and Rathburn, G. (1978). Puerto Rico Manatee survey, 21-29 June 1978. Unpd. trip report, Nat. Fish and Wild. Lab, Gainesville, Florida.

33. Rathburn, G. and Powell, J.A. (no date). Honduras Manatee Survey, 28 February - 15 March 1979. Unpd. Trip report.

34. Ray, C.E. (1960). The Manatee in the Lesser Antilles. J. Mammal. 40(3): 412-413.

35. Reichart, H.A. (1979). Pers. comm.

36. Salas, J.B. (1978). Informe sobre las actividades que desarrolla el Departamento de Vida silvestre en Nicaragua. In Morales, R., Macfarland, C., Incer, J. and Hobbs, A. (Eds), Memorias de la Primera Reunion Regional Centroamerican sobre Vida Silvestre. Matagalpa, Nicaragua 25-29 Julio 1978. Unidad de areas silvestres y cuencas del catie.

37. U.S. Fish and Wildlife Service. (1978). Administration of the Marine Mammal Protection Act of 1972. June 22, 1977 to March 31, 1978. Report of the Department of the Interior. Washington D.C.

38. U.S. Fish and Wildlife Service. (1980). West Indian Manatee. FSW/OBS-80/01-35. In Selected Vertebrate Endangered Species of the Seacoast of the United States. Biological Services Program. U.S. Dept of the Interior.

39. Gill, W. (1981). Manatee found in Chesapeake Bay,

Virginia. Endangered Species Technical Bulletin 6(1): 6-7.

40. Varona, L. (1979). Pers. comm to R.C. Best.

41. Vallester, E. (1978). Informe de Panama sobre la situacion de la Fauna Silvestre. In Morales, R., Macfarland, C., Incer, J. and Hobbs, A. (Eds), Memorias de la Primera Reunion Regional Centroamerican sobre Vida Silvestre. Matagalpa, Nicaragua 25-29 Julio 1978. Unidad de areas silvestres y cuencas del catie.

42. Woods, C. (1977). In litt.

43. Whitehead, P.J.P. (1978). Registros antigos da presenca do peixe-boi do Caribe (Trichechus manatus) no Brasil. Acta Amazonica 8(3): 497-506.

44. Vaughan, C. (1975). In litt.

45. Magor, D., Rainey, W. and Hoover, A. (1979). Impact of feeding by Manatees on a seagrass meadow in eastern Puerto Rico. Abstract. In Mate, B.R. (Ed.), Marine Mammal Information. Oregon State University Sea Grant College Program. December 1979.

46. Hartman, D.S. (1979). Ecology and behaviour of the Manatee (Trichechus manatus) in Florida. Am Soc. Mamm. Spec. Publ. Ser. 5: 1-153.

47. Odell, D.K., Forrester, D.J., and Asper, E.D. (1978). A preliminary analysis of organ weights and sexual maturity in the West Indian Manatee (Trichechus manatus). Proc. West Indian Manatee Workshop, 27-29 March 1978, Orlando, Florida.

48. Campbell, H.W. and Irvine, A.B. (1978). Manatee mortality during the unusually cold winter of 1976-77. Proc. West Indian Manatee Workshop, 27-29 March 1978, Orlando, Florida.

49. Marine Mammal Commission. (1980). Annual Report to Congress, Calendar Year 1980. Washington D.C.

50. Mclaren, J.P. (1969). Manatees as a naturalistic biological mosquito control method. Mosquito News 27(3): 387-393.

51. Montgomery, G.G. (1980). Pers. comm. to R.C. Best.

52. Olney, P.J.S. (Ed.) (1980). International Zoo Yearbook 20. Zool. Soc. London.

53. Packard, J.M. (1981). Abundance, distribution, and feeding habits of Manatees (Trichechus manatus) wintering between St. Lucie and Palm Beach Inlets, Florida. Report for U.S. Fish and Wildlife Service Contract No. 14-16-0004-80-105. 127pp.

54. Bengtson, J.L. (1981). Ecology of Manatees (Trichechus manatus) in the St. Johns River, Florida. Ph.D. Dissertation, Univ. of Minnesota, Minneapolis, MN. 126 pp.

55. Bengtson, J.L. (1981). In litt.

Trichechus inunguis (Natterer, 1883)

Order   SIRENIA   Family   TRICHECHIDAE

SUMMARY Confined to rivers of the Amazon drainage basin where populations have been seriously depleted by subsistence and commercial hunting. The latter has considerably decreased since the early 1960s, however low reproductive rates and continued poaching for local consumption have led to populations remaining at considerably depressed levels. Enforcement of laws which protect the species throughout its range is generally inadequate and there is a need for well guarded reserves to cover areas of high population density, particularly those large freshwater lakes ('pocos') which are important refugia in the dry season and where Manatees are very vulnerable to hunting. A long-term study of the species is in progress in Brazil.

DISTRIBUTION Amazon drainage basin in Brazil, Colombia, Peru, Guyana and possibly Ecuador. Colombia: recorded by Hernandez in 1973 as occurring in the Rio Putumayo, the lower Caqueta to the Araracaura rapids, tributaries of the Amazon, and possibly the lower Rio Apaporis (17). Peru: in 1978 said to occur in the lower and middle reaches of the main Amazon tributaries including: Putumayo, Napo, Tigre, Pastaza, Nanay, Orosa, Maranon, Ucayali and also the Samiria and Huallago (13,18). Grimwood in 1969 noted that is was absent from the Madre de Dios and Purus river systems within Peru and probably did not occur south of 7°S (19). Its upper limit in the Maranon basin was said to be the junction of the Rio Pataza (19). Guyana: presence confirmed in 1980 in the Takutov River on the Brazil/Guyana border (6). Brazil: Solimoes - Amazon and tributaries (e.g. Rios Negro, Branco, Jurua, Purus, Madeira, Tapajos, Xingu, Tocantins, Nhamunda) (5,12,18). Found in the Amazon estuary, including Ilha de Marajo out to its Atlantic coast, around coastal islands (Ilhas Caviana, das Pacas, Mexicana) and the northern (Amapa) and southern (Para) sides of the estuary. In Amapa it appears to extend as far as Cabo Norte where there may be a zone of sympatry with the Caribbean Manatee (Trichechus manatus). In Para recorded in 1978 from the Belem region of the Bahia de Marajo. Manatees appear to have been exterminated from the Atlantic coast of Para where they probably persisted until the 1950s, though it is not known if they were T. inunguis or T. manatus (11). Occurrence in Venezuela very doubtful, its reported presence in the Orinoco drainage, although repeatedly asserted in the literature, remains unconfirmed and appears to be based on a misidentification of T. manatus by Humboldt in the early nineteenth century and its distribution in the upper Rio Negro is limited by rapids (14). In 1980 believed to probably persist throughout most of its former range, though considerably depleted in numbers (5,10).

POPULATION No estimates exist but numbers appear considerably reduced compared with early reports (5). The decline in numbers taken in the early 1960s is thought likely to represent a real decrease in the population and Domning in 1981 noted that the habitat could probably support considerably greater numbers (10). He also stated, however, that there was no solid evidence that the population was still diminishing (10). In Peru, it was noted in 1978 that subsistence hunting was no longer significant and the species appeared to be abundant (13); although Dourojeanni in 1981 stated that it was still considerably rarer than it had been despite legal protection (20) and Grimwood in 1969 considered it very rare and possibly the most endangered Amazonian mammal in Peru (19).

HABITAT AND ECOLOGY   Occurs exclusively in freshwater, in all river types of the Amazon ('black', 'white' and clean water) where it feeds on aquatic and semi-aquatic vegetation (4,16).   Seasonal movements occur and are synchronized with the annual rise and fall of the water level, which in the central Amazon Basin has an amplitude of 10-15 m, with high water usually in June and lowest levels in November, though this differs for individual rivers (7).   In the dry season Manatees migrate to deeper water lakes ('pocos') where food is severely limited and animals may fast for long periods or possibly consume deposits of dead vegetation, a low quality food source (7).   Up to 1000 animals may be present in some of the larger lakes and if the dry season is unduly prolonged or severe, considerable natural mortality may result (7).   With the rise in water level they move into seasonally inundated grasslands ('varzeas') or forest ('igapo') to feed on rapidly growing vegetation (7).   Gestation period is estimated at 12-14 months and calving and conception appear timed to coincide with this period of high productivity and an optimal nutritional regime (3).

THREATS TO SURVIVAL   Heavily exploited for both subsistence and commercial purposes from at least 1780 until 1962 when a sharp drop in recorded trade occurred.   Until then an estimated annual total of 7000-10,000 were killed, at least between 1935 and 1954 (5,10).   Up to around 1925 the only Manatee product common in Amazonian commerce was mixira (fried meat packed in lard), but from 1935 to 1954 the hide trade became of great importance - Manatee leather is very tough and was used for a variety of heavy-duty purposes (10).   Around 1954 synthetic substitutes became widely available and the hide industry collapsed, but Manatees continued to be hunted at much the same level for meat, and meat products, until the recorded catch (excluding subsistence hunting) fell off to 1000-2000 per year in the early 1960s and continued to decline until hunting was banned in 1973 and official records ceased (10).   This is thought likely to be a result of over-exploitation leading to a real decline in numbers (10).   Despite legal protection subsistence hunting continues, as does local commercial hunting near towns or cities where the meat is regarded as a delicacy although is less expensive than beef (2).   Manatees are particularly vulnerable during the prolonged dry season when the normally deep 'pocos' dry out, leaving the animals exposed (5,6).   Very large numbers may be indiscriminately killed at such times as occurred in 1963 in the lakes of Coari, Tefé and Manacapuru in Brazilian Amazon (5,6).   They are also susceptible when travelling out of the 'pocos' along the principal migration ('arribacao') routes at the start of the wet season (5,6).   In the mouth of the Amazon, Domning in 1978 found hunting pressure to vary from light to fairly heavy, the most intensive being in the Canal Perigoso on Ilha de Marajo where at least 13 were caught in 1977 and 3 in early 1978 (11).   Hunting here is often (illegally) carried out by enclosing up to several hundred metres of tidally-flooded shore with a fence of wooden stakes or camboa which is submerged at high tide when Manatees and other aquatic animals pass over it to feed in the intertidal zone, becoming trapped as the tide recedes.   Large numbers of animals can be easily caught in this way, which can thus have a significant impact on the population.   Use of this method seems to be declining, however, and had apparently ceased altogether on the coast of Amapa (11).   Subsistence hunting in general was reported in 1980 as possibly decreasing as there is a trend to urbanisation and the use of nets instead of the traditional harpoon for fishing, resulting in fewer people capable of practising the specialised techniques needed to capture the species (5).   However, the importance of Manatees as a food source to the inhabitants of the Amazon (mainly 'caboclos' or river-people) is expected to increase dramatically as terrestrial game animals disappear due to overhunting and habitat destruction, leaving only fish and Manatees as natural protein sources - the cost of beef was described in 1979 as already too great for the 'caboclos' to afford (1,8).   At present animals are occasionally caught during commercial fishing operations and young calves often drown through becoming entangled in gill nets (5).   Reproductive rates are probably low as in other Sirenia (estimates in

440

T. manatus of one calf per female only every 3-5 years, and maturity not attained until 7-10 years (18)), hence past over-exploitation may have long term effects (5). A long term threat may be increased mortality due to climatic changes, recent models of evapotranspiration in the Amazon region predict that large-scale deforestation will reduce the annual rainfall possibly considerably prolonging the dry season and increasing natural mortality of the species through starvation (5).

CONSERVATION MEASURES TAKEN Included in Appendix 1 of the 1973 Convention on International Trade in Endangered Species of Wild Fauna and Flora, trade in it or its products therefore being subject to strict regulation by ratifying nations, and trade for primarily commercial purposes banned. Legally protected in Peru, Colombia, Guyana, Brazil and possibly Ecuador, but enforcement difficult due to large and remote areas with few wardens. Occurs in the Pacaya-Samiria National Reserve, which is situated between the Ucayali and Maranon rivers in Peru as well as in the Ecological Station of the Anvilhanas Archipelago near Manaus and the recently created Biological Reserves of Rio Trombetas and Jau in Brazil (5). This species is the subject of an active research programme at the Instituto Nacional de Pesquisas da Amazonia in Manaus, Brazil including studies on metabolism, nutrition, husbandry, behaviour, physiology etc., on captive animals, as well as field studies of the distribution, food habits and general ecology (4,5,8). A radio-tracking study is in progress to evaluate the effectiveness of this species in aquatic weed control using 29 Manatees introduced into the hydroelectric reservoir of Curua-Una, Para, in the central Brazilian Amazon (5,8).

CONSERVATION MEASURES PROPOSED Sanctuaries and national parks should be set aside to preserve existing populations. It is still unknown what area is necessary to contain a viable population of Manatees and radio-tracking studies need to be employed to determine 'critical habitat' as well as home ranges and seasonal movements. Concentration on enforcement in the rivers that are used as principal migration ('arribacao') routes as well as in the deeper water areas used during the dry-season and the adjacent feeding areas would be very desirable. Increased control of the commercial trade boats ('regatoes') as well as commercial fish boats, and in the market places in the local towns and cities would considerably reduce the illicit commercial trade in Manatee conserve (mixira) (2,5). In extremely dry years, mobile enforcement teams should be available to prevent mass slaughters in the larger lakes (5).

CAPTIVE BREEDING In 1980 there were 20 Amazonian Manatees in captivity: 14 at the Instituto Nacional de Pesquisas de Amazonia (INPA), Manaus, Brazil; 2 at Museu Goeldi, Belem, Brazil; 2 at Yomiuri Land Aquarium, Tokyo, Japan; and one each at Atagawa Tropical and Alligator Garden, Higashi Izu-Machi, Japan, and Steinhart Aquarium, San Francisco, U.S.A. (6).

REMARKS For description see (12). This data sheet was compiled from information kindly provided in 1978 by Dr. Daryl P. Domning, then of the Brazilian Manatee Project, Instituto Nacional de Pesquisas da Amazonia, and in 1981 by Robin C. Best, also of the Brazilian Manatee Project.

REFERENCES 1. Ayres, J.M. and Ayres, C. (1979). Aspectos de caca no alto rio Aripauna. Acta Amazonica 9(2): 287-298.
2. Ayres, J.M. and Best, R.C. (1979). Estrategias para a conservacao da fauna amazonica. Acta Amazonica 9(4), Suppl.: 81-101.
3. Best, R.C. (1981a). Seasonal breeding in the Amazonian manatee Trichechus inunguis (Mammalia: Sirenia). Biotropica (in press).
4. Best, R.C. (1981b). Food and feeding habits of wild and

captive Sirenia. Mammal Review (in press).
5. Best, R.C. (1981). In litt.
6. Best, R.C. (1981). Pers. comm.
7. Best, R.C. (in prep.). Apparent dry season fasting in Amazonian Manatees. Unpd.
8. Best, R.C. and Magnusson, W.E. (1979). Status report of the Brazilian Manatee Project 1975-1979. Instituto Nacional de Pesquisas da Amazonia (I.N.P.A.), Manaus.
9. Carvalho, J.C. (1967). A conservacao da natureza e recursos naturais no Amazonia Brasileira. Atas Simp. Biota Amazonica 7: 1-47.
10. Domning, D.P. (in press). Commercial exploitation ofmanatees (Trichechus) in Brazil ca. 1785-1973. Biol. Cons.
11. Domning, D.P. (1980). Distribution and status of manatees (Trichechus spp.) near the mouth of the Amazon river, Brasil. Biol. Cons. 19(2): 85-98.
12. Husar, S.L. (1977). Trichechus inunguis. Mammalian Species 72: 1-4.
13. Marmol, A. (1978). Pers. comm.
14. Mondolfi, E. (1974). Taxonomy, distribution and status of the manatee in Venezuela. Mem. Soc. Cienc. Nat. La Salle, 97(34): 5-23.
15. Montgomery, G.G., Best, R.C. and Yamakoshi, M. (in press). A preliminary radio-tracking study of an Amazonian manatee. Biotropica.
16. Pereira, M.N. (1944). O peixe-boi da Amazonia. Bol. Minist. Agric. (Rio de Janeiro), 33(5): 21-95.
17. Blaine, A. (1973). Report on endangered species of South America - Colombia. Information supplied by Prof. J. Hernandez-Camacho.
18. U.S. Fish and Wildlife Service (1978). Administration of the Marine Mammal Protection Act of 1972. June 22, 1977 to March 31, 1978. Report of the Department of the Interior. Washington D.C.
19. Grimwood, I.R. (1969). Notes on the distribution and status of some Peruvian mammals, 1968. Special Pubn. No.21. Am. Comm. for Int. Wildl. Protec. and New York Zool. Soc., New York.
20. Dourojeanni, R.M. (1981). In litt.

Tapirus pinchaque (Roulin, 1829)

Order   PERISSODACTYLA   Family   TAPIRIDAE

SUMMARY   Restricted range, mostly in the Andean region of Colombia and Ecuador. Numbers unknown. Threatened mainly by modification of habitat for cattle grazing and the penetration of remote areas by man. Protected by law in Colombia, Ecuador and Peru but laws poorly enforced. A conservation action plan is needed and to this end in 1980 IUCN's Species Survival Commission established a Tapir Specialist Group to initiate conservation efforts.

DISTRIBUTION   Upper subtropical and temperate zones in the Andes of Colombia, and Ecuador; also northern Peru and western Venezuela (Sierra de Mérida) (9). For map see (9,13). Ecuador: in 1981 known to survive in a few localised areas in the eastern chain of the Andes; in particular from the Llanganati mountains north on the eastern slopes at least as far as Mt. Saraurco where an adult male was shot by a hunter in December 1980. Fresh footprints are also often seen on the eastern slopes of Mt. Antisana (15). Although none have been observed in the western Cordilleras (11,13), recent evidence suggests it may in fact exist there (15). Colombia: actual specimens recorded in the scientific literature were taken only in the eastern and central Cordilleras to a northern limit of 5°N., in the temperate and cold zones surrounding Mount Tolima; although there is a 1942 report of tapirs being rather common in the southern part of the Department of Santander near the Venezuelan border at about 7°N. (2,9). The species is unknown in the western Cordillera (9). Peru: although its presence is unconfirmed by museum specimens it does occur in Peru (2,8,10,12), being probably restricted to the Ayabaca and Huancabamba Provinces of the Department of Piura and the Jaen Province of the Department of Cajamarca, where it occurs on high ground from the Ecuadorian border to about 6°S. (8). Venezuela: no data. The present distribution of T. pinchaque suggests that it arrived in South America when a temperate climate prevailed at sea level in equatorial latitudes. It now inhabits an area representing part of the original Colombian Central Land Mass and this restriction is probably the result of a need for a cool climate, this forcing it to retreat to higher altitudes as temperatures at sea level rose. Newly established tropical zone habitats at the base of the Andes were invaded subsequently by other kinds of tapirs (9).

POPULATION   Very little up-to-date information but has undoubtedly disappeared from many areas since the 1950's (13). Colombia: no recent data. Schauenberg (1969) reported that it had certainly become rarer and might even have disappeared completely in some areas where it was hunted 20 years previously (13). Ecuador: no recent estimates (15). Schauenberg who studied its distribution and status in 1968 reported it to survive only in a few localised zones in the east. Although censusing the population was impossible because of the dense vegetation and the extreme steepness of the land he doubted whether numbers could possibly exceed a few hundred, and that even if 2000 still survived they would be no less endangered (12). Peru: in 1968 Grimwood reported it to be rare, numbering not more than one or two hundred animals (8). Venezuela: no data.

HABITAT AND ECOLOGY   Between 2000-4400 m in a vegetative zone of stunted trees and shrubs (Polylepis and Hypericum) dwarfed by low temperatures and wind exposure and almost constantly enshrouded and saturated in mist. Higher up, the trees are replaced by impenetrable 'chaparrales' scrub so dense that the tapir carves out a tunnel network for thoroughfare. Its tracks have been observed at 4,700 m altitude in permanent snow (8,9,12,13,14). The bulk of the diet consists of green shoots of browsing plants (9); stomach contents examined contained mostly ferns and shoots of 'chusque', a trailing bamboo of the genus Chusquea. These are the dominant plants of the steeper, more sterile wooded slopes of the Andean temperate zone. It also consumes colca (Micronia crocea) and regularly visits natural salt and mineral licks (14). In the grassland zones an 1843 report stated Woolly tapirs ate the tender shoots of "frailejon" (Espeletia) as well as those of rough grasses (9,13). The species is most active at dawn and dusk (13). Tapirs usually have a single young after a gestation of about 400 days (5).

THREATS TO SURVIVAL Modification of habitat and general disturbance are the main threats. The tapir has receded before the progressive invasion of its habitat by man. Since the 1930-40s the stunted woodland and the 'chaparrales' scrub have been progressively destroyed by cattle which are grazed at altitudes up to 4000 m. This timid species is intolerant of disturbance and abandons a habitat in which it has been disturbed several times. The mountain peoples have always hunted it for its meat, however this has had very little effect on the decline compared to that caused by habitat alteration. Roads are penetrating deeper into the Andes facilitating human colonization of once remote areas. Between 1966-1970 organised hunting of the species for live capture and export to zoos caused considerable losses (almost a hundred animals died) in parts of Ecuador (8,12,13).

CONSERVATION MEASURES TAKEN Listed in Appendix 1 of the 1973 Convention on International Trade in Endangered Species of Wild Fauna and Flora, trade in the species between acceding nations being therefore subject to severe restriction, and trade for primarily commercial purposes banned. Protected by law in Colombia, Ecuador and Peru although laws are not enforced. Unknown whether legally protected in Venezuela. Restrictions exist on export of live animals from Ecuador and Colombia and it occurs in protected areas in both countries (1,3). This species was the subject of a WWF project to define its distribution and status in Ecuador in July 1968 (12,13). In 1980 IUCN's Species Survival Commission established a Tapir Specialist Group to initiate and coordinate conservation efforts for this and other Tapirs.

CONSERVATION MEASURES PROPOSED Adequately protected reserves are urgently required, as is much additional information on population, distribution and ecology as the basis of an effective conservation plan. Mittermeier et al report that a sanctuary to ensure the survival of Peru's endangered endemic monkey Lagothrix flavicauda would also include the Mountain tapir which is thought to survive in the same region (10).

CAPTIVE BREEDING In 1979 3 males and 4 females (one female captive bred) were held in 3 zoo collections (11). The first captive live birth occurred at the Los Angeles Zoo in 1977 (4,6).

REMARKS For description of animal see (2,5,6,7,9,13). T. roulinii has been used instead of T. pinchaque (2). Keith Williams, Chairman of the IUCN/SSC Tapir Specialist Group assisted with the compilation of this data sheet.

REFERENCES   1. Anon. (1980). New parks in Ecuador. Oryx 15(3): 226.
             2. Allen, G.M. (1942). Extinct and Vanishing Mammals of the Western Hemisphere. American Committee for International Wild Life Protection. Special Publication No. 11.
             3. Blaine, A. (1970). Report on endangered species of South America: Colombia. Information supplied by Prof. J. Hernandez Camacho. Unpd. Report.
             4. Bonney, S. and Crotty, M.J. (1979). Breeding the Mountain Tapir Tapirus pinchaque at the Los Angeles Zoo. Int. Zoo

Yb. 19: 198-200.

5. Crandall, L.S. (1964). The Management of Wild Mammals in Captivity. Univ. Chicago Press.

6. Crotty, M.J. (1977). The Year of the Tapir. Zoo View 12(1): 10.

7. Gale, N.B. and Sedgwick, C.J. (1968). A note on the Woolly tapirs Tapirus pinchaque at Los Angeles Zoo. Int. Zoo. Yearbook 8: 211-212. Zool. Soc. London.

8. Grimwood, I.R. (1969). Notes on the distribution and status of some Peruvian mammals 1968. Spec. Pub. 21. Am. Comm. Int. Wildlife Protec. and New York Zool. Soc. Bronx, New York.

9. Hershkovitz, P. (1954). Mammals of Northern Colombia. Preliminary report no. 7: Tapirs (genus Tapirus), with a Systematic Review of American Species. Proc. US. Nat. Mus. 103 (3329): 465-496.

10. Mittermeier, R.A., Macedo Ruiz, H. de and Luscombe, A. (1975). A Woolly Monkey Rediscovered in Peru. Oryx 13 (1): 41-46.

11. Olney, P.J.S. (Ed.) (1980). International Zoo Yearbook 20. Zool. Soc. London.

12. Schauenberg, P. (1969). No. 380. Mountain Tapir - Status Survey in Ecuador. World Wildlife Yearbook 1969. World Wildlife Fund, Switzerland Pp 182-184.

13. Schauenberg, P. (1969). Contribution a l'Etude du Tapir pinchaque. Tapirus pinchaque Roulin 1829. Revue Suisse de Zoologie. 76: (8) 211-256.

14. Stummer, M. (1971). The Woolly Tapir, Tapirus pinchaque (Roulin), in Ecuador. Zool. Garten N.F., Leipzig 40(3): 148-159.

15. Ortiz-Crespo, F.I. (1981). In litt. Including information supplied by Prof. Gustavo Orcés and Juan Black.

CENTRAL AMERICAN or BAIRD'S TAPIR   VULNERABLE

Tapirus bairdii (Gill, 1865)

Order   PERISSODACTYLA   Family   TAPIRIDAE

SUMMARY Ranges from southern Mexico to northern South America. Numbers unknown and ecological requirements not clarified. Threatened primarily by forest clearance for agricultural use, and excessive hunting. Legally protected throughout its range but laws generally poorly enforced. Present in reserves in Honduras, Costa Rica, Panama, Nicaragua and possibly Colombia. Studies needed as the basis of a conservation management programme. IUCN's Species Survival Commission established a Tapir Specialist Group in 1980 to initiate conservation action.

DISTRIBUTION Central America to northern South America. Mexico: in the south in southern Veracruz and eastern Oaxaca Provinces (8,15). Guatemala: in 1950 reported to be restricted to the larger swamps of the Caribbean and Pacific lowlands and Peten and in montane cloud forests of Quiche and Alta Vera Paz (11,20). Range continues through Belize (6,14), Honduras, and Nicaragua to Costa Rica where in 1978 potentially suitable habitat (with a large proportion of woody cover) was estimated at 2,700,000ha or 52% of the national territory, mainly in the northwest and southern parts of the country. Preliminary observations indicated it was still present in most areas of uncleared habitat where excessive hunting did not occur (25,26). Continues through Panama to the west coast of Colombia, extending eastwards as far as the Sinu River in the north (4,5,7,10). May also occur on the coast of Ecuador somewhere between Babahoyo in the north and Ponce Enriquez in the south (Los Rios and Azuay Provinces), east of Guayaquil (30).

POPULATION Numbers unknown but decreasing throughout most of its range (27). Mexico: no recent data; in 1959 Leopold wrote that there remained no secure and assured population anywhere. By 1947 it was already virtually extinct in Quintana Roo with only a few known to remain in a marshy and sparsely inhabited area south of Dzula. Several were observed in the mid-1950s along the Rio Chalchijatapa near the Oaxaca/Veracruz border, with a scattered handful along the Pacific slope of the Sierra de Chiapas, and records at several localities in mountains in eastern and northern Chiapas (15). Honduras: reported as 'Endangered' in 1978 (1); El Salvador: extinct (3,21); Costa Rica: in 1978 reported as most abundant in woods and marshes in humid lowland areas, especially on the Peninsula de Osa where the 36,000ha Corcovado National Park is thought to contain one of the highest densities of the species anywhere (26). Panama: in 1978 recorded as in imminent danger of extinction (24). In 1966 was apparently very rare or absent on the Pacific side though still relatively common at all elevations in the east and along the Caribbean coast (9). Colombia: in 1970 reported as not immediately endangered, though likely to become so in the near future due to forest clearance (2). Ecuador: in 1981 it was believed a 'small population' might survive (30). No data located for Guatemala, Belize or Nicaragua.

HABITAT AND ECOLOGY A variety of mostly humid habitats from sea-level to at least 3350m, including marshes, mangrove swamps, tropical rain forest, riparian woodland, monsoonal deciduous forests, montane cloud forest and 'paramo' above the tree line (about 3200m in Costa Rica) (6,8,15,17,25). An excellent swimmer, it is essentially solitary and nocturnal and spends most of its active hours foraging in a zig-zag pattern. Eats fallen fruits (acting as a seed disperser for some plant species), twigs, flowers, sedges and grasses, though leaves form the bulk of the diet (12,13,15,23). Gestation period of 390-405 days;

a single young is the norm and is weaned after one year (23). Sympatric with Tapirus terrestris colombianus east of the western cordillera in northwestern Colombia (10).

THREATS TO SURVIVAL Habitat destruction and hunting. Highly intolerant of disturbance and rarely occurs in cleared or cultivated areas although will move into plantations and fields to feed at night. Most of its range has already been cut over and it is now largely confined to disjunct areas of suitable secondary forest (10,15,17,25,27). It is also hunted whenever possible as its meat is highly prized (15,17,27).

CONSERVATION MEASURES TAKEN Listed in Appendix 1 of the 1973 Convention on International Trade in Endangered Species of Wild Fauna and Flora, trade in it or its products therefore being subject to strict regulation by ratifying nations, and trade for primarily commercial purposes banned. Protected by law throughout its range though enforcement is generally inadequate. Occurs in reserves in Honduras, Costa Rica, Panama and Nicaragua and possibly in Los Farallones National Park, Colombia (2,24,25,26,27,28,29). A project to study the species began in Costa Rica in 1980 funded by the New York Zoological Society. IUCN's Species Survival Commission established a Tapir Specialist Group in 1980 to coordinate and initiate Tapir conservation efforts.

CONSERVATION MEASURES PROPOSED Adequate legal protection throughout its range. Population and range surveys, ecological studies and investigations as a basis for conservation management plans including establishment of reserves.

CAPTIVE BREEDING In 1979 there were 11 males and 8 females (5 bred in captivity) held in 8 zoo collections (18).

REMARKS For description of animal see (4). Reports that separate subspecies are identifiable have not yet been substantiated (27). Keith Williams who is conducting the Costa Rican tapir study and is also Chairman of the IUCN/SSC Tapir Specialist Group very kindly assisted with the compilation of this data sheet.

REFERENCES 1. Aguilar, W. (1978). El manejo de la Vida Silvestre en Honduras. In Morales, R., Macfarland, C., Incer, J. and Hobbs, A. (Eds), Memorias de la Primera Reunion Regional Centroamerican sobre Vida Silvestre. Matagalpa, Nicaragua 25-29 Julio 1978. Unidad de areas silvestres y cuencas del catie. 111-114.
2. Blaine, A. (1970). Report on endangered species of South America: Colombia. Information supplied by Prof. J. Hernandez Camacho. Unpd. Report.
3. Boursot, J. (1979). In litt.
4. Cabrera, A. (1957-1961). Catalogo de los mamiferos de America del Sur. Rev. Mus. Argent. Cienc. Nat. 'Bernardino Rivadavia'. Cienc. Zool. 4(1-2): 1-731.
5. Eigener, W. (1954). Bergtagire. Z. Säugetierke. 19(3): 179-180.
6. Gaumer, G.F. (1917). Mamiferos de Yucatan. Dept. Talleres Graficos, Secretaria de Fomento, Mexico.
7. Goldman, E.A. (1920). Mammals of Panama. Smithsonian Misc. Coll. 69 (5): 1-309.
8. Goodwin, G.C. (1969). Mammals from the State of Oaxaca, Mexico, in the American Museum of Natural History. Bull. Am. Mus. Nat. Hist. 141: 1-269.
9. Handley, C.O. Jr. (1966). Checklist of the Mammals of Panama. In Wenzel, R.L. and Tipton, V.J. (Eds),

Ectoparasites of Panama. Field Museum of Natural History, Chicago.

10. Hershkovitz, P. (1954). Mammals of Northern Colombia. Preliminary report no. 7: Tapirs (genus Tapirus), with a Systematic Review of American Species. Proc. U.S. Nat. Mus. 103 (3329):465-496.

11. Ibarra, J.A. (1959). Apuntes de Historia Natural y Mamiferos de Guatemala. Editorial del Ministerio de Educacion Publica.

12. Janzen, D. (1981). Wild plant acceptability to a captive Costa Rican Baird's tapir. Brenesia. 19. In press.

13. Janzen, D. (1981). Digestive seed predation by Baird's tapir (Tapirus bairdii). Biotropica. In press.

14. Kirkpatrick, R.D. and Cartwright, A.M. (1975). List of Mammals known to occur in Belize. Biotropica 7(2): 136-140.

15. Leopold, A. (1959). Wildlife of Mexico: The game birds and mammals. Univ. of California Press, Berkeley.

16. Lopez, E. (1978). Informe sobre las actividades de la Direccion General de Recursos Pesqueros y Vida Silvestre de Costa Rica. In Morales, R., Macfarland, C., Incer, J. and Hobbs, A. (Eds), Memorias de la Primera Reunion Regional Centroamerican sobre Vida Silvestre. Matagalpa, Nicaragua 25-29 Julio 1978. Unidad de areas silvestres y cuencas del catie. 90-96.

17. Mena Moya, R.A. (1978). Fauna y Caza en Costa Rica. R.M. Costa Rica.

18. Olney, P.J.S. (Ed.) (1980). International Zoo Yearbook 20. Zool. Soc. London.

19. Salas, J.B. (1978). Informe sobre las actividades que desarrolla el Departamento de Vida silvestre en Nicaragua. In Morales, R., Macfarland, C., Incer, J. and Hobbs, A. (Eds), Memorias de la Primera Reunion Regional Centroamerican sobre Vida Silvestre. Matagalpa, Nicaragua 25-29 Julio 1978. Unidad de areas silvestres y cuencas del catie. 99-110.

20. Saunders, G.B., Holloway, A.D. and Handley, C.O. (1950). A Fish and Wildlife Survey of Guatemala. U.S. Dept. Interior, Fish and Wildlife Service, Spec. Scient. Rep. Wild. No.5.

21. Serrano, F. (1978). Informe de actividades de la Unidad de Parques Nacionales y Vida Silvestre en El Salvador. In Morales, R., Macfarland, C., Incer, J. and Hobbs, A. (Eds), Memorias de la Primera Reunion Regional Centroamerican sobre Vida Silvestre. Matagalpa, Nicaragua 25-29 Julio 1978. Unidad de areas silvestres y cuencas del catie. 119-125.

22. Stummer, M. (1971). The Woolly Tapir, Tapirus pinchaque (Roulin), in Ecuador. Zool. Garten N.F., Leipzig 40 (3): 148-159.

23. Terwilliger, V.J. (1978). Natural history of Baird's tapir on Barro Colorado Island, Panama Canal Zone. Biotropica 10(3): 211-220.

24. Vallester, E. (1978). Informé de Panama sobre la situacion de la Fauna Silvestre. In Morales, R., Macfarland, C., Incer, J. and Hobbs, A. (Eds), Memorias de la Primera Reunion Regional Centroamerican sobre Vida Silvestre. Matagalpa, Nicaragua 25-29 Julio 1978. Unidad de areas silvestres y cuencas del catie. 44-65.

25. Vaughan, C. (1978). Una metodologia para determinar la distribucion actual y datos sobre el etado actual de especies

de la fauna silvestre con enfasis en aquellas en vias de extinction. In Morales, R., Macfarland, C., Incer, J. and Hobbs, A. (Eds), Memorias de la Primera Reunion Regional Centroamerican sobre Vida Silvestre. Matagalpa, Nicaragua 25-29 Julio 1978. Unidad de areas silvestres y cuencas del catie. 212-230.

26. Vaughan, C. (1978). Pilot study on the population status of Bairds Tapir, Taprius bairdii, a Costa Rican endangered species. OTS. San Jose, Costa Rica.

27. Williams, K.D. (1979-81). In litt.

28. WWF. (1980). Honduras establishes first Biosphere Reserve in Central America. WWF Monthly Report November. Project 1648.

29. WWF. (1980). Vast tropical forest park spans Panama Isthmus. WWF Monthly Report November. Project 1648.

30. Ortiz-Crespo, F. I. (1981). In litt. Including information supplied by Prof. Gustavo Orcés and Juan Black.

CHACOAN PECCARY or TAGUA   VULNERABLE

Catagonus wagneri (Rusconi, 1930)

Order   ARTIODACTYLA   Family   TAYASSUIDAE

SUMMARY   Confined to the Gran Chaco region of South America. Previously
known only as a Pleistocene fossil, this 'extinct' peccary was found living in
Paraguay in 1974. Total numbers are unknown but are considered to be declining.
Habitat is increasingly being cleared for cattle ranching. Diurnal activity,
curiosity and strong social cohesion make them particularly vulnerable to hunting,
and hunting pressure is mounting as the Chaco is opened up by roads and
settlements. Hunted for food, hide and sport. Conservation measures still under
study.

DISTRIBUTION   Bolivia, Argentina and Paraguay. Found only in the Gran Chaco:
in Bolivia probably in the Departments of eastern Tarija, Chuquisaca and
southeastern Santa Cruz, all in the southeast; in Paraguay in the western
Departments of Boqueron, Chaco and Nueva Asuncion, the west of Presidente
Hayes and Alto Paraguay; and in Argentina in the northern Provinces of Formosa,
Chaco and western Salta and northern Santiago del Estero (3,4). When
rediscovered the Tagua's range was believed to possibly extend to parts of the
Brazilian Mato Grosso adjoining southeastern Santa Cruz (Bolivia) (5), but Schaller
who worked in this area in the late 1970s found no trace of it and it's presence
there now seems unlikely (6). However it may possibly occur in northeastern Alto
Paraguay (5).

POPULATION   Field surveys in the Gran Chaco of Bolivia in 1979 and 1980 by the
American Museum of Natural History, and in the Chaco of Argentina by the
Pittsburgh Carnegie Museum of Natural History, found Tagua to be rare in both
countries (6). Similarly, in 1981 Professor Gaston Bejarano described this peccary
as vulnerable in Bolivia because of hunting, mainly for its hide but also for meat
(1). The remainder of its range -- in the Chaco of Paraguay -- is being rapidly
altered for beef cattle pasture, or in areas not so disturbed, new roads for oil
exploration or for military use have opened up much of the species range to
uncontrolled hunting, and because of its vulnerability to such activity the Tagua is
rapidly declining (6). Verschuren who visited the Chaco for two months in 1979
described the species as common in parts of the northern Chaco, but
indiscriminate hunting necessitated that it be protected (2).

HABITAT AND ECOLOGY   Semi-arid Chaco. Precise data is not available but
seems to prefer the thorn forest, but with excursions into the grass-carandy palm
or pantanal and thorn steppe. Travels in small herds of about six animals, bound
together by strong social ties: the survivors will stay for a time with one of their
members injured or killed by hunters. Noted for its curiosity, being readily
attracted by strange sounds, and is most frequently seen during the middle of the
day. Cacti and seeds of leguminous trees are the main food (3,4,5).

THREATS TO SURVIVAL   Habitat destruction (5) and hunting (1,5). The main
threat is the replacement of native vegetation by grass to provide pasture for
cattle. In Paraguay this is being promoted by the government, under the heading
of 'land improvement', as a condition of land tenure. This peccary is the chief
source of meat, even more so than brocket (Mazama spp.) or other kinds of
peccary (Tayassu spp.) for hunters, trappers, army personnel in the numerous
outposts, and ranchers during the initial stage of land clearance. Its hide,
although thinner and not as valuable as that of other peccaries, is included in the
large numbers of peccary hides exported for leather goods manufacture and it has

become the quarry of the increasing number of travellers through the Chaco -- truck drivers, sportsmen and tourists (5). In Bolivia Bejarano describes hunting for its hide as the main threat (1).

CONSERVATION MEASURES TAKEN Paraguay has declared a ban on all wildlife hunting. While enforcement is sporadic, by 1977 hunting pressure on game populations had definitely decreased during the previous few years in most parts of the country (P. Myers, 1977. In litt.). Within Paraguay Tagua occur in the Defensores del Chaco National Park which protects 900,000 ha of intact typical Chaco habitat (2), and it is here that studies of Catagonus by a team of scientists are being undertaken (5,6). The species also occurs, and is apparently more common, in the proposed Taniento Enciso National Park, also in Parguay (2). No information has been received concerning protection in Argentina and Bolivia.

CONSERVATION MEASURES PROPOSED In Paraguay it is hoped that studies will provide a basis for conservation measures, which will probably include better protection of the national park, inspection and limitation of Tagua hides for export, enforcement of hunting regulations and incorporation of a policy of green belts or forest refugia in all future land clearance projects (5). An IUCN/SSC Pigs and Peccaries Specialist Group was established in 1980 and is considering appropriate conservation measures for the species.

CAPTIVE BREEDING No information.

REMARKS For description of animal see (4,5,7). This data sheet was compiled with the assistance for Dr. Ralph M. Wetzel and Dr. Philip Myers. Mr Lyle K. Sowls also very kindly reviewed the draft of this account.

REFERENCES
1. Bejarano, G. (1981). In litt.
2. Verschuren, J. (1980). Saving Paraguay's Wilderness. Oryx 15(5): 465-470.
3. Wetzel, R.M., Dubos, R.E., Martin, R.L. and Myers, P. (1975). Catagonus, an "extinct" peccary, alive in Paraguay. Science 189: 379-381.
4. Wetzel, R.M. (1977). The Chacoan Peccary Catagonus wagneri (Rusconi). Carnegie Mus. Nat. Hist. Bull. No. 3. 36 pp.
5. Wetzel, R.M., Brandt, P.N. and Mayer II, J.J. (Unpublished). Studies on Catagonus wagneri. Supported by World Wildlife Fund, National Geographic Soc., Univ. Connecticut Research Foundation, and Carnegie Museum of Nat. Hist.
6. Wetzel, R.M. (1980). In litt.
7. Wetzel, R.M. (1981). Comparison of the Pecarries. Report to the First Meeting of the IUCN/SSC Pigs and Peccaries Specialist Group, New Delhi, Feb. 1981.

VICUNA   VULNERABLE

Vicugna vicugna (Molina, 1782)

Order   ARTIODACTYLA   Family   CAMELIDAE

SUMMARY An inhabitant of the rangeland (puna) of the Central Andes of South America. Extremely abundant (probably several million) in pre-Columbian times but subjected to mass slaughter for its wool, reputedly the finest in the world, ever since the arrival of the Spanish Conquistadors in South America and by 1965 reduced to a mere 6000 animals. Conservation measures, principally protection in newly established reserves, enacted at that time have resulted in steadily increasing numbers, and by May 1981 the estimated total was 80,000-85,000 and increasing. By far the largest concentration occurs in Peru in the Pampa Galeras National Vicuna Reserve and surrounding areas which in late 1980 harboured an estimated 48,000 Vicuna. Conservation measures in the reserve initially concentrated on protecting the species and building up numbers, but since the late 1970s have included translocation and culling of animals to investigate the potential of using hides, wool and meat for the benefit of the local community. In addition, in 1978 there were reports that drought combined with the increased number of Vicuna, had decreased available forage in the central part of the reserve, that Vicuna were dying of starvation and that numbers would have to be rapidly reduced. The authorities therefore believed that not only had numbers increased sufficiently to allow the population to sustain a harvest but also that a cull was essential if the rangeland was to be preserved. Translocation of animals to other areas was considered but was deemed both too expensive and too slow. This culling sparked an international controversy. The appropriateness and necessity of the cull was challenged by various conservation groups who expressed doubt as to the the need for a cull, the method of harvesting, and the true extent of the rise in numbers. A November 1979 report which found no evidence of drought or unhealthy animals and an April 1980 aerial survey which concluded that only about 15,000 Vicuna inhabited Pampa Galeras added to the controversy. To clarify the situation the Government of Peru with financial support from the German Agency for Technical Cooperation (GTZ) invited IUCN and WWF to organise an independent evaluation mission to coincide with their September/October 1980 census. The IUCN/WWF mission concluded that the high estimates were correct, the census technique possibly even slightly under-estimating the total number of Vicuna, that numbers were increasing at an average annual rate of 19%, and that no factual basis could be found for the view of a substantially degraded or overgrazed rangeland; though this has been contested. IUCN and WWF then issued a 'Position Statement on Vicuna' in which they recommended that 'if there was to be a cull that it be carefully controlled, humane, scientifically based and kept at a very conservative level, pending the accumulation of the essential, additional scientific information on which any large cull can be planned and implemented.' Vicuna are protected by law in all countries of their range and occur in many reserves. They are also protected by a 'Convention on the Conservation and Management of Vicuna' signed in 1979 and adhered to by the Governments of Peru, Bolivia, Chile and Ecuador, and open for the signature of Argentina. This treaty replaced an earlier 'La Paz' agreement which banned for ten years the hunting of Vicuna and trade in their wool. Trade in wool is also banned internationally by parties to the Convention on International Trade in Endangered Species of Wild Fauna and Flora (CITES).

DISTRIBUTION Argentina, Bolivia, Chile and Peru where now found only in widely separated areas. Current distribution spans the punas (flat or rolling range land) of the high Andes from the Department of Ancash, Peru at 9°S through

Bolivia and Chile to 30°S in Argentina. Major population concentrations are in the Peruvian Departments of Junin, Huancavelica, Ayacucho, Apurimac, Cuzco, Puno and Arequipa. Formerly the species probably ranged from the puna of Cajamarca, Peru at 7°S to beyond 30°S latitude in both Chile and Argentina (4,8,9,10,25,31,32,36). The past existence of Vicuna in Ecuador is frequently mentioned in the literature but has not yet been confirmed by reliable evidence (36).

POPULATION   Total in May 1981 according to a meeting of Vicuna specialists, was 80,000-85,000 and increasing (38); this compares with an estimate of 6000 in 1965 (29). When the Spaniards arrived in South America, it is believed that Peru alone possessed perhaps as many as 1-2 million Vicuna (6,36). By far the greatest number occur in Peru which in May 1981 was estimated to possess almost 62,000 (38) compared with 10,000 in 1970 (23,31) and 5000 in 1965. Within Peru the largest concentration inhabits the Pampa Galeras National Vicuna Reserve and its surrounds in the Province of Lucanas, Department of Ayacucho. On the basis of ground counts conducted in September/October 1980 the reserve was estimated to hold about 48,000 Vicuna (34), a tremendous increase from the 5000-10,000 it was thought to contain in 1970 (29). Ground counts in the reserve have been conducted every year since 1969 and record a steady rise in numbers (6) (though these are not comparable from year-to-year since the area of survey has not always been the same, see Norton-Griffiths and Torres Santibanez for comments (34)). The annual rate of increase is 19% (34). Within the reserve area itself the rise in numbers has shown a pattern of rapid population increase at a time of abundant resources, gradually slowing down, and then reversing, as resources have become more and more scarce (34). Based on the annual census counts it was felt in 1977 that the status of the Vicuna in Pampa Galeras was so improved that experimental cropping for meat and wool (a long term aim of the conservation programme) could begin. In addition there were reports in 1978 that a severe drought in the nuclear zone of the reserve, combined with the increased Vicuna numbers, was causing a large reduction of ground cover, and therefore forage, and thus a large dieoff of Vicuna through starvation (6). The authorities therefore felt that a cull was not only appropriate for experimental purposes but was also essential for the recovery of the range and the continued survival of the Vicuna in Pampa Galeras (6). Brack Egg recommended a reduction of 10,000 animals - 5000 bachelor group members to be slaughtered, and 5000 family groups members preferably to be translocated if international funding was forthcoming, if not, then also for slaughtering (6). Hofmann and Otte, the scientists on the reserve, also suggested a reduction of 10,000 but of different segments and proportions of the population, causing in their view less social disturbance (27). However in 1979/80 doubts over the accuracy of the ground counts, and the existence and effect of drought on the rangeland and Vicuna, were voiced by various conservation groups. They believed that Vicuna numbers were much lower than the 40,000+ figure estimated by the ground counts and that the rangeland and Vicuna were not in jeopardy because of drought; both opinions militating against the appropriateness and need for a cull (3,28,33,41,42,46,47,48). In November 1979 the International Fund for Animal Welfare (IFAW) had invited the veterinary surgeon W.J. Jordan to visit Pampa Galeras and report on the condition of Vicuna. He reported that the animals were in healthy condition, were grazing successfully, and that there was no evidence that severe drought and overgrazing were causing a die off of animals (28,33). Then in April 1980 IFAW sponsored a 2-day aerial survey which concluded that contrary to the 1979 ground count of 43,000 Vicuna, the reserve in fact held only about 15,000 Vicuna (range 11,480-18,496) (18). The ensuing controversy (3,28,33,41,42,46,47,48) resulted in the Government of Peru with financial support from the German Agency for Technical Cooperation (GTZ) inviting IUCN and WWF to organise an independent evaluation mission of the September/October 1980 ground count (34). Dr. M. Norton-Griffiths and Mr. H. Torres Santibanez undertook this task on behalf of

IUCN and WWF (34). Their findings confirmed the high numbers of Vicuna inhabiting the reserve, the two scientists even suggesting that the ground counts underestimate total Vicuna numbers (34). The possibility that drought, and/or high Vicuna numbers, had caused the rangeland to be substantially overgrazed or degraded and a consequent die off of large numbers of Vicuna by starvation (6) was not found to have substance (29,34). IUCN and WWF have issued a 'Position Statement on the Vicuna' outlining the findings of the Sept./Oct. mission and their recommendations (29).

1981 estimates of Vicuna numbers elsewhere are given in a report of a meeting of the Technical/Administrative Committee associated with the 1979 Convention on the Conservation and Management of Vicuna, which met in Arica, Chile, and La Paz, Bolivia, from 1st to 6th May 1981 (38). For Bolivia the meeting reported a 1981 total of almost 4500 Vicuna plus just over 30 in captivity (38); most are concentrated in the Ulla-Ulla Nature Reserve where numbers increased from 97 to 1139 between 1965 and 1979 (13), the Huancaroma National Park, and south of Ocuri (17,36). Previous estimates for Bolivia were of 2000 in 1977 (37), and 1000 in 1970 (30,31,37). Chile: the May 1981 meeting reported a total of almost 8200 animals (38), the vast majority occurring in the Lauca National Park (38), which Rottmann reports was estimated to possess 7980 based on a 1980 census (40). In 1973 the estimated number in the park was just over 1000 (43). Rottmann also mentions that in 1980 51 animals were seen in the Norte Chico (27°S) (40), however the May 1981 meeting mentions 200 Vicuna in this area (38) (the latter is perhaps an extrapolation from the 51 seen, but the RDB requires further information about this). Argentina: in April 1981 the Red Data Book received the following detailed information concerning Vicuna numbers in Argentina from the Director Nacional de Fauna Silvestre (22). Based on censuses conducted in 1979 and 1980 in areas of Vicuna concentration it is estimated that a total of about 8000, possibly as many as 10,000 Vicuna occur in Argentina, distributed as follows: San Juan Province: only found in the Reserva Provincial de San Guillermo where a 1979 direct count totalled 4200, allowing for unseen animals it is believed the reserve holds about 5000 Vicuna; La Rioja Province: a 1979 count of 300 in the Reserva Provincial de Vicunas y de Proteccion del Ecosistema Laguna Brava extrapolating to an estimated 1500 for the whole reserve; Catamarca Province: 520 counted in February 1979 in the central zone of the Reserva Provincial Natural de Vida Silvestre Laguna Blanca; Salta Province: nine localities visited in May 1980 in the Reserva Natural de Fauna Silvestre Los Andes yielded 225 Vicuna, extrapolating to 450 for the whole reserve and 575 total for the Department of Los Andes; Jujuy Province: 560 censused in 8 localities. An additional 330 are held in captivity at the Estacion Zootecnica de Abra Pampa (22).

HABITAT AND ECOLOGY Vicuna inhabit the semi-arid rolling grasslands and barren plains of the Central Andes at altitudes above 3500 m (20.31,32). Social grouping consists largely of family parties composed of an adult male with several females and their young, bachelor groups of non-breeding males, and solitary males (20,32). Family groups in preferred habitat will occupy a feeding territory where most of the day is spent, and a sleeping territory located on higher terrain where they spend the night (19). Franklin found these two areas to be connected by an undefended neutral corridor. Territories were observed to be exclusively occupied by the resident family group and defended against all intruding Vicuna. Territorial boundaries were discrete and well-defined; the size and shape of feeding territories sometimes changed slightly from one season to the next but usually remained in the same basic location for the entire year, and included a permanent supply of water. The family group was noted to be a stable unit with essentially the same adult females remaining throughout the year. Bachelor groups were precluded from utilizing occupied and preferred habitat by resident territorial males (19). Diet consists largely of perennial bunch grasses and forbs

(19). Most females produce their first offspring as three-year-olds although some may produce a year earlier; one young is the usual and gestation lasts about 11 months (19). Predators of Vicuna include the Puma (Felis concolor) and the Andean Fox (Dusicyon culpaeus), the latter is believed to cause heavy mortality of the newborn (19).

THREATS TO SURVIVAL Persecution for its wool, reputedly the finest in the world. The Vicuna has never been domesticated unlike its relative the Guanaco (Lama guanicoe) from which the domestic Llama (Lama glama) and Alpaca (Lama pacos) originated. Vicuna have thus generally been killed to obtain their wool, although the Incas did manage to harvest this valuable product by rounding up and shearing Vicuna once every 3-5 years, killing some for meat, but releasing the vast majority (10). Such roundups or 'chacos' required considerable numbers of people and are not considered feasible in the present age. After the Spanish conquest Vicuna were subjected to uncontrolled hunting. Wool from about three Vicuna is needed to knit a sweater, from one animal to produce a scarf, and a 'colcha' (a blanket made from the skins) can utilize pieces from 150-250 animals (31). Jungius (1972) found one colcha in a Bolivian tourist shop which was made from the heads of 168 animals, and another made from the necks of 60 lambs (31). Sixteenth century reports tell of 80,000 animals being killed annually in Peru and northern Chile (9,31,32). Mass slaughter continued during the next four centuries, and by 1957 it was estimated that only 400,000 Vicuna were left (32), reduced to 6000 by 1965 (29). The reasons for this catastrophic decline can be summarised as: abandonment of the Inca system of management; importation and subsequent use of firearms; increasing hunting efficiency; indiscriminate shooting by foreigners as well as by the local inhabitants; lack of enforcement of existing laws; lack of control of Vicuna products in international trade; and competition for forage and space with domestic livestock (23,31,36).

CONSERVATION MEASURES TAKEN The Vicuna is listed in Appendix 1 of the 1973 Convention on International Trade in Endangered Species of Wild Fauna and Flora, thus trade in it or its products is subject to strict regulation by ratifying nations, and trade for primarily commercial purposes is banned. All countries harbouring Vicuna are signatories to this Convention. The species is also protected by the Convention for the Conservation and Management of Vicuna, signed in Lima on 20 December 1979 and adhered to by the Governments of Bolivia, Chile, Peru and Ecuador (39). The treaty is open for the signature of Argentina. This agreement replaces an earlier one, commonly called the 'La Paz Agreement' signed in August 1969 (to which Argentina was a signatory but Ecuador was not) which forbade for ten years the hunting of Vicuna and trade in their products (6). A bilateral agreement for the protection of Vicuna has recently been signed by Bolivia and Argentina (49). All the above Governments have taken measures nationally to protect Vicuna, not only by national protection laws (39) but especially by the creation of reserves. In Peru Vicuna occur in the Pampa Galeras National Vicuna Reserve established May 18th, 1967, the Huascaran National Park, and the Salinas Aguada Blanca National Reserve (6,45); in Argentina in the Reserva Provincial de San Guillermo decreed in 1972 (San Juan Province), the Reserva Provincial de Vicunas y de Proteccion Ecosistema del Laguna Brava, decreed 1980 (La Rioja Province,), the Reserva Provincial Natural de Vida Silvestre Laguna Blanca decreed in 1979 (Catamarca Province), the Reserva Natural de Fauna Silvestre Los Andes, decreed 1980 (Salta Province), and in Jujuy Province where it is protected in a binational reserve with Bolivia (1,22); in Bolivia in the Reserva National de Fauna Ulla-Ulla (23,31) and in the Huancaroma National Park created a Refuge for Vicuna on 26 August 1975 (13); and in Chile Vicuna inhabit the Lauca National Park established in 1970 (23).

Vicuna have been the subject of several ecological studies (1,20,32), conservation oriented studies concerned mainly with the establishment of reserves and the protection of Vicuna within them, and an intensive public education programme (6,21,25,44). In Peru the Project 'Rational Utilization of the Vicugna in Peru' was initiated in 1965 in Pampa Galeras and neighbouring areas (6). Since 1972 the Federal Republic of Germany has been contributing to this project under a technical cooperation (GTZ) programme (6,26). The stated aim of the project is to 'repopulate the plain with a native species of great economic potential and to increase the economic value of the outer regions of the Andes by utilizing the Vicugna and other wild animals for the benefit of the community and agricultural enterprises' (26). In its initial stages, the programme concentrated on protecting Vicuna and building up their numbers, but since 1977 has included the culling of animals, mainly bachelor group members, to investigate the potential of using hides, wool and meat for the benefit of the local community (29,34). This killing was authorized by Ministerial Resolution No.01155-77-AG of June 28 1977 (6). In 1977 a total of 210 Vicuna (34) (Brack Egg reports 120 (6)) were shot, increasing to 400 in 1978 (6,34), 1352 in 1979, and to 2100 in 1980 (34)). A total of 34.4 metric tonnes of meat were produced and marketed, the hides and wool being stored at Pampa Galeras pending international agreements as to their disposal (34). Translocation of animals was also begun - in 1979, a total of 67 animals were captured, and in 1980 a further 736 Vicuna were translocated, the majority going to Huancavelica (34). It was the culling that sparked off the recent controversy (as mentioned above) (29). The IUCN/WWF Position Statement explains their viewpoint on Vicuna conservation in general and the Pampa Galeras Project in particular (29). An IUCN/Species Survival Commission South American Camelid Specialist Group exists to monitor the status of these animals, including the Vicuna, and to suggest appropriate conservation measures when necessary.

CONSERVATION MEASURES PROPOSED Continuation of the measures that have resulted in a dramatic increase in Vicuna numbers since 1965. However, border controls between Peru, Bolivia, Chile and Argentina and international controls generally should be strengthened to prevent illegal smuggling of, or dealing in, Vicuna products (2,36). The standard of protection provided in the reserves in which Vicuna occur needs to be maintained and made increasingly effective, and educational campaigns in favour of its conservation should likewise be continued and intensified (2,36). Brack Egg has produced an analysis of the possibility of (re)introducing Vicuna into Ecuador (7). With regard to the Pampa Galeras Project, the IUCN/WWF Position Statement states:

'IUCN and WWF appreciate that it may be necessary that some Vicuna continue to be harvested in order to provide essential scientific data to achieve the original objectives of the Pampa Galeras Project. Nevertheless, IUCN and WWF consider it essential, if there is to be a cull, that it be carefully controlled, humane, scientifically based and kept at a very conservative level pending the accumulation of the essential, additional scientific information on which any larger cull can be planned and implemented. Additionally, IUCN and WWF believe that any such cull should be associated with an expanded programme for re-location of the Vicuna from Pampa Galeras to other areas, experimental shearing of wool from live Vicuna, proper monitoring of the effects of the management programme (including effective control over the marketing of wool) and continued efforts to protect and manage the area, including strong protection against poaching. In short, a cull, if conducted, should be placed on a sound, scientific footing. A cull conducted in such a manner, would be consistent with the World Conservation Strategy and with the original objectives of the Pampa Galeras Project, thus enabling the Government of Peru to honour the Agreement it reached with the local people in the area that - when Vicuna populations would allow - they would receive the benefits from any legal trade in Vicuna products' (29).

The IUCN/WWF mission also found that important scientific data upon which a cull should be based were lacking (29), consequently these two organisations have made the following recommendations to the Government of Peru:

'a) a programme to gather these data, e.g. on the population dynamics of Vicuna and their relationship with the range condition, is essential; b) any culling operations should be integrated with this scientific programme guided by its findings, strictly controlled and implemented for the benefit of local communities; c) if there is a cull, it should be held at a minimum level, pending the accumulation of scientific data' (29).

Detailed recommendations are given by Norton-Griffiths and Torres Santibanez (34).

CAPTIVE BREEDING In 1979 there were at least 28 males and 22 females (47 captive bred) held in 14 zoological collections (35), plus the 330 held in captivity at the Estacion Zootecnica de Abra Pampa (22).

REMARKS For description of animal see (9,10,32). The generic name Lama is occasionally used instead of Vicugna. Cardozo has published an extensive bibliography of the South American Camelids including the Vicuna (12).

REFERENCES 1. Anon. (1979). The Vicuna in Argentina. In Reunion de los paises signatarios del convenio para la conservacion de la Vicuna. La Paz (Bolivia) - Lima (Peru), 9-19 Oct. 1979. Documento Final.
2. Advance Report Technical Meeting, Tacna-Arica. 20-24 Feb. 1980. April 1980. 5pp.
3. Asheshov, N. and Jackman, B. (1980). One angry man and his 40,000 Vicunas. The Sunday Times (London). Feb. 24. 1980. p.50.
4. Boswall, J. (1972). Vicuna in Argentina. Oryx 19(6): 448-453.
5. Brack Egg, A. (1979). La situacion actual de la Vicuna en el Peru. In Reunion de los paises signatarios del convenio para la conservacion de la Vicuna. La Paz (Bolivia) - Lima (Peru), 9-19 Oct. 1979. Documento Final.
6. Brack Egg, A. (1979). The Vicuna's present situation in Peru and the alternatives for their management. Report of the Ministry of Food and Agriculture. Special Project on rational use of the Vicuna. 16pp.
7. Brack Egg, A. (1980). Estudio de viabilidad tecnica para la reintroduccion de la Vicuna en el Ecuador. Estudio preparado para la Organizacion de las Naciones Unidas para la Agricultura y la Alimentacion (FAO).
8. Cabrera, A. (1957-61). Catalogo de los mamiferos de America del Sur. Revista del Museo Argentina de Ciencias Naturales 'Bernardino Rivadavia', Cienc. Zool. 4(1-2): 1-732.
9. Cabrera, A. and Yepes, J. (1940). Mamiferos Sud-Americanos (Vida, costumbres y descripcion) Compania Argent. Edit., Buenos Aires.
10. Cardozo G., A. (1954). Auquenidos. La Paz, Bolivia.
11. Cardozo G., A. (1976). Legislacion International sobre Camelidos Sudamericanos. Instituto Colombiano Agropecuario, Bogota. 113 pp.
12. Cardozo, A. (1977). Bibliografia de los camelidos sudamericanos. Universidad Nacional de Jujuy, Argentina.
13. Cardozo, A. and Lopez, S.J. (1979). Situacion de la Vicuna en Bolivia. In Reunion de los paises signatarios del convenio para la conservacion de la Vicuna. La Paz (Bolivia) - Lima

(Peru), 9-19 Oct. 1979. Documento Final.

14. Cardozo, A. and Nogales O., J. (1979). Evolucion de la poblacion de Vicunas en Ulla Ulla (Bolivia). In Reunion de los paises signatarios del convenio para la conservacion de la Vicuna. La Paz (Bolivia) - Lima (Peru), 9-19 Oct. 1979. Documento Final.

15. Direccion General Forestal y de Fauna. (1977). Plan Nacional para la Utilizacion Racional de la Vicuna (1977-1981). Lima.

16. Dourojeanni R., M. (1973). La Vicuna. Flora et Fauna del Peru vol. 7, El Serrano No. 278.

17. Dourojeanni R., M. (1978). Report of the South American Neotropical Camelid Group to the 49th Survival Service Commission Meeting, Portugal.

18. Eltringham, S.K. (1980). An aerial count of Vicuna in the Pampa Galeras National Reserve and surrounding regions, Ayacucho, Peru in April 1980. Final Report to the International Fund for Animal Welfare. 25pp+.

19. Franklin, W.L. (1974). The social behaviour of the Vicuna. In Geist, V. and Walther, F. (Eds), The Behaviour of Ungulates and its relation to management. IUCN PUbl. N.S. 24: 477-487.

20. Franklin, W.L. (1976). Socioecology of the Vicuna. Utah State University, Logan, Utah. 172 pp.

21. Godoy, J.C. (1975). Conservacion de la vicuna en la Republica Argentina. Jornada Tecnica Multinacional sobre Manejo de Vicunas, Arica (Chile): 15-99.

22. Gonzalez Ruiz, E.O. (1981). In litt.

23. Grimwood, I.R. (1969). Notes on the distribution and status of some Peruvian mammals, 1968. Special Pubn. No.21 American Committee for International Wild Life Protection and New York Zoological Society, New York. pp 86.

24. Grimwood, I.R. (1979). Report concerning South American Camelids. In Summarised minutes of the 52nd meeting of the Survival Service Commission of IUCN, Kings College, Cambridge. 11-12th September 1979. p.14.

25. Hofmann, R. (1971). Stado Actual de la Vicuna y Recomendaciones para su Manejo. Conferencia Internacional sobre Conservacion y Manejo Racional de la Vicuna, Lima, 6-11 Sept. 1971.

26. Hofmann, R. and Otte, K-C. (1977). Utilization of Vicugnas in Peru. German Agency for Technical Cooperation, Ltd. (GTZ), Eschborn, Federal Republic of Germany.

27. Hofmann, R. and Otte, K-C. (1979). Observaciones y recomendaciones para el manejo de la Vicuna en Pampa Galeras durante el ano de 1979. Proyecto para la utilizacion racional de la Vicuna silvestre, Pampa Galeras, May 1979.

28. IFAW. (1981). New Vicuna population figures suggest mis-management of an endangered animal. Press Release. International Fund for Animal Welfare.

29. IUCN/WWF Position Statement on Vicuna. (1981). IUCN Bulletin New Series 12 No.3-4: 12-13.

30. Jungius, H. (1971). The Vicuna in Bolivia: the status of an endangered species and recommendations for its conservation. Z. Saugetierk. 36(3): 129-146.

31. Jungius, H. (1972). Bolivia and the Vicuna. Oryx 11(5): 335-346.

32. Koford, C. (1957). The Vicuna and the Puna. Ecol. Mon. 27:

153-219.

33. Letters to the Sunday Times. (1980). Let's save our animals for their own sake. The Sunday Times (London). March 2. 1980.

34. Norton-Griffiths, M. and Torres Santibanez, H. (1980). Evaluation of ground and aerial census work on Vicuna in Pampa Galeras, Peru. Results of a WWF/IUCN evaluation mission 17 September - 7 October 1980. Undertaken with the financial assistance of the German Agency for Technical Cooperation (GTZ). Report of WWF and IUCN. 96pp.

35. Olney, P.J.S. (Ed.) (1980). International Zoo Yearbook 20. Zoo. Soc. London.

36. Ponce del Prado, C. (1977). Draft data sheet submitted to the IUCN Red Data Book. In litt.

37. Red Data Book vol. 1, Mammalia. Vicuna. Sheet code 19.123.2.1 (1972-76). IUCN, Switzerland.

38. Report of the Technical/Administrative Commission Meeting, 16th May 1981, of the Convention for the Conservation and Management of Vicuna.

39. Reunion de los paises signatarios del convenio para la conservacion de la Vicuna. La Paz (Bolivia) - Lima (Peru), 9-19 Oct. 1979. Documento Final.

40. Rottmann R., J. (1981). In litt.

41. Sitwell, N. (1981). Go shoot a Vicuna. New Scientist 89 (1240): 413-415.

42. Telander, R. (1981). Riding herd on Peru's Vicunas. International Wildlife 11(3): 36-43.

43. Torres Santibanez, H. (1979). La conservacion de la Vicuna en Chile. In Reunion de los paises signatarios del convenio para la conservacion de la Vicuna. La Paz (Bolivia) - Lima (Peru), 9-19 Oct. 1979. Documento Final.

44. World Wildlife Yearbook, 1974-75, South America: Vicuna projects, pp. 247-249, 252, 261; 1975-76, pp. 187, 195-196; 1976-77, pp. 203, 208, 217-219, 222. 1977-78, pp WWF, Morges.

45. WWF. (1979). Peru announces national reserve for Vicuna. WWF Press Release No. 16/1979. WWF, Switzerland.

46. WWF. (1980). WWF calls for reassessment of Vicuna population. WWF Press Release No.5/1980. May.

47. WWF. (1980). WWF and IUCN request the Peruvian Government to suspend Vicuna harvesting. WWF Press Release No.7/1980. May.

48. WWF-U.S. (1980). World Wildlife Fund calls for halt to culling of Vicuna. WWF-U.S. Press Release No.12-80. May 22, 1980.

49. Zentilli, B. (1981). In litt.

Cervus elaphus nannodes (Merriam, 1905)

Order   ARTIODACTYLA   Family   CERVIDAE

SUMMARY Endemic to California, U.S.A. In 1980 numbered around 870 in 13 widely scattered, artificially established populations; the largest (c. 500 in 1980) in Owens Valley, outside the elk's original range. Now considered 'Out of Danger' though individual herds will remain at risk because of their low numbers and small ranges. Continued management and protection is neccessary to safeguard the taxon.

DISTRIBUTION United States; endemic to California where by 1980 herds had been artificially established in 13 areas, the largest, founded in 1933-35, inhabiting Owens Valley, Inyo County. Others are at Cache Creek (established 1922), in the coastal range northeast of Sacramento; Tupman Tule Elk Reserve (est. 1930) near Bakersfield and San Luis Island (est. 1974) near Los Banos, both in the San Joaquin Valley; Concord Naval Weapons Station (est. 1971), and Grizzly Island (est. 1977), both near Richmond in the San Francisco Bay area; Mt. Hamilton in northeast Santa Clara Co.; Lake Pillsbury in Lake Co.; Point Reyes National Seashore in Marin Co.; Camp Roberts in San Luis Obispo Co.; Jawbone Canyon, Kern Co; and Fort Hunter Ligget, Monterey Co; (all est. in 1978). Attempts to found a herd on a ranch at Laytonville, Mendocino Co., were begun in late 1979 (8). Total area occupied, or available for occupancy, by elk in early 1980 comprised just over 157,000 ha, most of this (approx. 85,000 ha) in Owens Valley, about 23,500 ha at Cache Creek and 14,000 ha at Mt. Hamilton, the remainder comprising areas of from 300 ha at San Luis Island to 10,000 ha at Camp Roberts (8). All except Laytonville, Owens Valley and Jawbone Canyon are within the elk's original range in coastal and inland valleys (principally San Joaquin and Sacramento) from near Santa Barbara north to Cow Creek in Shasta County (8). It was noted in March 1980 that only three of the areas (Owens Valley, Cache Creek and Grizzly Island) had well established herds, the rest occupying fenced enclosures or, although free-roaming, had not yet established definite herd boundaries (8).

POPULATION Estimated total in March 1980 of 872, consisting of: Owens Valley 487 (divided into 6 herds); Cache Creek, 120; Tupman, 40; San Luis Island, 37; Concord Naval Weapons Station, 35; Grizzly Island, 21; Mt. Hamilton, 40; Lake Pillsbury 33; Point Reyes, 13; Jawbone Canyon, 4; Camp Roberts, 14; Fort Hunter Ligget, 16; Laytonville, 12 (8). This compares with a total of around 785 in 1977 and about 450 in 1965. Originally the population numbered hundreds of thousands but crashed following the Gold Rush of 1849, and by the late 1860s the elk was thought extinct. However in 1874 a small remnant, possibly only two animals, was discovered in tule marshes at Buena Vista Lake, Kern Co. in the southern San Joaquin Valley. Following careful protection numbers increased markedly. Persistent agricultural damage by the elk led to repeated transplants between 1904 and 1934, resulting in the herds at Owens Valley, Tupman Refuge and Cache Creek; these have formed the nucleus for the establishment of the other herds (4,6).

HABITAT AND ECOLOGY Formerly occupied a fairly wide variety of habitat types and climatic areas, though principally the marshland and perennial bunchgrass plains of the open valley bottoms with some seasonal utilisation of foothills (4,8). The Owens Valley population has been studied in detail by McCullough (4). The elk are well adapted to the semi-arid conditions in the valley. Most precipitation occurs in winter but the valley is primarily watered by spring and summer runoff from snowmelt in the surrounding Sierra. The elk eat a wide variety of plants - mainly forbs and ditch-bank vegetation including willow leaves and twigs in spring and summer, and browse supplemented with dry grasses in winter. Important species are Bassia (<u>Bassia hyssopifolia</u>), Bitterbrush (<u>Purshia tridentata</u>) and Globe Mallow (<u>Sphaeralcea ambigua</u>). Forage conditions vary considerably between years, being largely determined by the amount of precipitation, and are especially critical during the summer months. The population is divided into six herds which are largely segregated except for stags wandering during the rut. The timing of the rut and subsequent calving season varies from year to year depending on forage conditions but is usually in August-September, good conditions leading to an early rut. Most females breed as yearlings, with calves born in April-May after a gestation of about 250 days. About 90% of females carry a foetus in the autumn but only about 33% have calves at foot when the young join the herd. It is not known if mortality occurs <u>in utero</u> or after birth, but coyotes take some newborn calves. Recruitment of calves is about 18-20% of the herd per year, the typical rate of increase being about 14-15%. Illegal shooting and accidents, excluding legal hunts, are responsible for 4-5% mortality of adults. Competition between elk and domestic stock is generally small, athough some occurs with <u>Odocoileus hemionus</u> in the Goodale area (4). Habitat at other sites is variable but generally consists of some combination of rolling grassland, oak woodland, riparian willow woodland, low chaparral and marshland (8). In 1980 the habitat condition in 81% of the range was described as 'good' or 'fair', 3% as 'excellent'; whilst that at Cache Creek, Tupman and Point Reyes was considered 'poor' due mainly to overgrazing (8). The Tupman Refuge herd is, however, intensively managed and maintained on a high quality diet; recruitment was 36% of the herd in 1979 and the unit provides stock for transplant attempts (8).

THREATS TO SURVIVAL Although the Tule Elk was undoubtedly affected by competition with introduced stock and replacement of the dominant perennial bunchgrasses with introduced annuals following Spanish colonisation, its near extinction appears to have been brought about almost entirely by heavy and persistent market hunting especially following the Gold Rush of 1849 (4,6,8). It is however no longer regarded as immediately threatened. In Owens Valley there is some conflict with farmers over fence destruction and damage to alfalfa fields, the latter especially in years of poor natural forage, but the amount of illegal killing is small (4). The principal danger is of a population crash if a succession of poor forage years follows high population levels, or if there is an uncontrollable outbreak of disease. To mitigate against this the population size is controlled, it being considered that if numbers are kept low there is likely to be less contact between herds and hence disease will not be so easily transmitted (6). In 1980 the City of Los Angeles Department of Water and Power was reported to have had developed plans to increase the amount of ground water pumping from Owens Valley. This is expected to be detrimental to the elk as it would reduce the amount of riparian vegetation. Environmental Impact Reports have been prepared and mitigating measures proposed, including reducing the amount of livestock grazing and periodic diversion of water from the aqueducts to produce meadow type habitat (8). Elsewhere (e.g. Camp Roberts, Fort Hunter Ligget) roadkills and suspected poaching have caused some mortality, and at three sites at least (Camp Roberts, Laytonville and Cache Creek) excess livestock grazing may pose a threat to habitat quality (8). At Point Reyes National Seashore an excess of molybdenum in the diet (molybdenosis), causing a deficiency in copper uptake, has led to some mortality, and supplemental feeding to compensate for this was begun in late 1979. Farmland depredation caused by the elk may cause conflict at some sites and some herds (e.g. Jawbone Canyon) may have to be relocated if this continues. Most of the critical habitat at Cache Creek is in private ownership and the herd may be threatened by future land development (8).

CONSERVATION MEASURES TAKEN Following the establishment of the Owens Valley herd in 1933-34 the population increased to the point that local farmers began to complain of excessive crop damage. The California Dept. of Fish and Game which managed the populations at Cache Creek and Owens Valley therefore licensed intermittent hunts to control numbers. The numbers taken, and losses by crippling during these hunts, were sufficiently high to provoke increasing public outcry throughout the 1960s, and in 1971 the State Legislature enacted Senate Bill 722 (the 'Peter Behr' Bill), prohibiting the taking of Tule Elk until the total Statewide population exceeded 2000 animals, or until it is determined by the Legislature that suitable habitat to maintain a population of that size cannot be found. The bill also limited the total number of elk inhabiting Owens Valley to 490, or any greater number determined to be the Valley's carrying capacity. In 1976 Federal legislation in the form of Public Law 94-389 provided for Federal participation in preserving Tule Elk populations in California. This legislation, while agreeing to the 490 elk carrying capacity of the Owens Valley, stated that the conservation and restoration of at least 2000 Tule Elk was an appropriate national goal. At the same time it directed the Secretaries of Agriculture, Defence, and Interior to cooperate with the State of California in making Federal lands reasonably available for the preservation and grazings of Tule Elk in such a manner as may be consistent with Federal law (8). This legislation led to the establishment of herds at the sites listed above. Each herd has had a management plan formulated for it and an estimated carrying capacity calculated, ranging from 30 at Grizzly Island to 300 at Point Reyes and 490 in Owens Valley. Management at the different sites is under the auspices of a variety of agencies, including the Bureau of Land Management, the Fish and Wildlife Service, the Forest Service, National Park Service, Army and Navy, the California Depts. of Fish and Game and Parks and Recreation (8). To coordinate conservation efforts for the elk a Statewide management plan was completed in June 1979 (8).

CONSERVATION MEASURES PROPOSED The overall goal of the management plan is 'to ensure the continued growth of healthy, free-roaming Tule Elk herds of sizes that are ecologically compatible with the suitable habitats of California'. Objectives include: identification of additional public and private lands to support elk (it is considered that the long-term stability of populations will require public ownership and/or management authority over most of the suitable habitat); development and implementation of detailed management plans for each herd; provision for public use of the Tule Elk, eventually including controlled harvesting. The elk are to be maintained in as natural conditions as possible and are only to be relocated to areas within their historic range (8). It was estimated in March 1980 that the legislated goal of 2000 elk could be reached by 1985-87. Four potential relocation sites had been identified and surveyed, the largest of which, Cottonwood Creek, consists of 56,000 ha with an estimated carrying capacity of 300 elk. Total estimated capacity of all occupied and assessed potential sites was 2045 animals. It was considered that the largest long-term problem would be finding additional suitable relocation sites, although it was reported that several additional areas were being considered, especially on United States Forest Service and Military land. Funding was also required to develop some of the new sites and to allow full implementation of management plans at existing sites, in particular to acquire or manage private lands to preserve the existing Cache Creek herd but also to allow provision of water, construction of retaining-fences and extensive habitat management elsewhere (8).

CAPTIVE BREEDING In 1978 at least 6 young were reared in 2 zoos outside California (7). An unknown number is held in captivity, - in 1980 a total of 15 were held in zoos in California alone (8).

REMARKS For description see (4). Over its range in North America, Europe and

Asia 25 subspecies of Cervus elaphus (Cervus canadensis now being considered conspecific with C. elaphus) are generally recognized. Of these C. e. canadensis (eastern America) and C. e. merriami (Arizona and north Mexico) are extinct; C. e. wallichi (Tibet/Bhutan) may be extinct; at least 4 are in the 'Endangered' category, namely C. e. hanglu (Kashmir), C. e. corsicanus (Corsica and Sardinia), C. e. barbarus (North Africa), C. e. bactrianus (northern Afghanistan and Russian Turkestan) and C. e. yarkandensis (Chinese Turkestan); C. e. macneilli (Tibetan/Chinese border) is in the 'Indeterminate' category.

REFERENCES

1. Anon. (1977). Tule Elk to be Culled. Oryx 14(3): 207-208.
2. Hunt, E.G. (1971). In litt.
3. Hunt, E.G. (1977). In litt to D.R. McCullough.
4. McCullough, D.R. (1969). The Tule elk: its history, behavior, and ecology. Univ. Calif. Publ. Zool. 88: 1-209.
5. McCullough, D.R. (1977). In litt.
6. McCullough, D.R. (1978). Case histories - The Tule elk (Cervus canadensis nannodes). In Threatened Deer. Proceedings of a Working Meeting of the SSC Deer Specialist Group, Longview, Washington State, U.S.A., 26 Sept - 1 Oct 1977. IUCN, Switzerland.
7. Olney, P.J.S. (Ed.) (1980). International Zoo Yearbook 20. Zool. Soc. London.
8. Bureau of Land Management. (1980). The Tule Elk in California. 4th Annual Report to Congress. 50pp.

Odocoileus virginianus clavium Barbour and Allen, 1922

Order   ARTIODACTYLA   Family   CERVIDAE

SUMMARY Restricted to islands off the lower Florida Keys, U.S.A. where in 1979 the population was estimated at 300-400, possibly up to 600, and stable, having increased from near extinction in the 1950s. Most now occur in the 1764 ha National Key Deer Wildlife Refuge established in 1954 on Big Pine Key which includes most of the suitable remaining habitat. Principal cause of decline was loss of habitat but most mortality is now through roadkills. Management consists mainly of protection and controlled burning of habitat. In 1980 a Recovery Plan was approved by the U.S. Fish and Wildlife Service. The deer seems to be at the carrying capacity of its available habitat and provided it receives continual protection, its future seems secure.

DISTRIBUTION Florida, USA. Once inhabited islands from Key West to Key Vaca in the lower Florida Keys, but now restricted to islands in the vicinity of Big Pine Key, Monroe Co. Florida. The western boundary is Sugarloaf Key, the eastern the Little Pine - Johnson Key complex (5). Within this area deer are resident only on Keys with permanent freshwater: Big Pine, Big Torch, Cudjoe, Howe, Little Pine, Little Torch, Middle Torch, No Name, Sugarloaf and Summerland Keys, but are also found on at least ten other islands during the wet season (7).

POPULATION In 1979 estimated at 350-400 and appears relatively stable due to high mortality, low reproductive rate, and a large proportion of male fawns (5,7,11). The 1980 official estimate for the National Key Deer Wildlife Refuge was 600 deer but this may be revised downward as monthly census data are analysed (7). Big Pine Key is estimated to hold about two-thirds of the total population (5,7). Three population concentrations can be discerned and there is probably little exchange of animals between them (5). Although the population has apparently stablized, the relatively low numbers and limited range continue to make this an animal of concern. The Recovery Plan aims to maintain a stablized population as opposed to increasing it (8). Numbers began to increase around 1950 in response to protection from hunting and disturbance. The estimated total in 1955 was 25-80 (2,5,7).

HABITAT AND ECOLOGY The ecology and behaviour of the Key deer has been extensively studied (3,4,5,7). Five habitat types have been noted in descending order of preference: pinelands, hardwood hammock, buttonwood - scrub mangrove, mangrove swamp, and developed areas. Habitat selection varies with season, time of day, and age and sex of the individual (6,7). Pinelands, recent clearings, roadsides, grassy areas and hardwood hammocks are used for feeding while hammocks and Red Mangrove act as daytime retreats (5). Red Mangrove (Rhizophora mangle) also constitutes an important food source, with 63 per cent occurrence in pellet analysis (2,7). Food plant utilization changes seasonally, probably reflecting availability and nutritional needs and virtually no plant species is immune from deer use at one time or another (6,7,8). The deer are strongly attracted to newly burned areas, and will feed extensively on new woody and herbaceous growth for up to 6-9 months (8). A fresh water supply is essential (10) although there is a limited tolerance for salt (11). Adult females form loose matriarchal groups with one or two generations of offspring, while bucks feed and bed together only in the non-breeding season (5). Adult males maintain ranges of about 120 ha., adult females of about 52 ha. (5). Most breeding occurs in

September and October with fawns born in April/May. Reproductive rate is low (av. 1.08 fawns per adult doe annually) (7). Male fawns outnumber females, but differential mortality leads to adult females outnumbering males by 2.38 to 1. Longevity records are 8 years for males and 9 years for females and few males breed at less than three years of age (6,7,11).

THREATS TO SURVIVAL Loss of habitat to development was the primary reason for the original population decline and continues to be a major threat. Big Pine Key, the main stronghold for deer, had 37 per cent of it cleared for development by 1973 (an average of 46 ha per year between 1969 and 1973) (6,7). Most mortality on Big Pine Key is now caused by roadkills which comprised 76 per cent of known mortalities between 1968-73 (8). Another significant factor is the drowning of fawns in drainage ditches. Overhunting with dogs and jacklights was probably an important factor in the 1940s and 1950s and poaching was reported as still rather frequent in 1974 (7).

CONSERVATION MEASURES TAKEN Afforded full legal protection in the U.S.A (5,7). The National Key Deer Wildlife Refuge was established in 1954, and by 1980 comprised 1764 ha of which 300 ha were leased; it includes most of the suitable remaining deer habitat. Management consists mainly of protection and some controlled burning (5,7). In 1980 the United States Fish and Wildlife Service approved a Key Deer Recovery Plan (8). The animal has been the subject of a study by Southern Illinois University since 1967 (3,4,6,10).

CONSERVATION MEASURES PROPOSED Klimstra recommends: continued protection from illegal hunting, and of the refuge lands from development and major changes; acquisition of additional deer habitat, especially on Big Pine, No Name and Cudjoe Keys; use of controlled burning to maintain pinewoods; maintenance of existing fresh water holes on refuge lands; possible fencing of islands where refuge lands and privately owned housing subdivisions adjoin; and continued research on all aspects of the deers' biology (5). The Key Deer Recovery Plan additionally recommends: restriction of dogs from refuge lands; lower speed limits; the posting of deer warning signs; fencing of highways except at trail crossing points; and increased public awareness (8).

CAPTIVE BREEDING According to the Recovery Plan, because the Key Deer are the product of a unique selective system (a restrictive insular environment with no natural predators), management should involve the retention of those natural selection factors that influenced their evolution and thus under no circumstances should a captive, zoo-bred herd be used for re-stocking purposes (8).

REMARKS For description of animal see (1). In recent years it has been noted that Key Deer appear to be growing to a larger size, perhaps due to improved nutrition. The taxonomic status of the animal has been questioned and is now under investigation by Klimstra and others (7). The full species has a very wide distribution in North America being resident in practically every state in the U.S.A. except Alaska, and possibly Utah. Northwards its range extends into southern Canada and southwards it occurs through Mexico and Central America into the northern half of South America. At present at least 38 subspecies are recognised, of these two are listed in the Red Data Book, the above mentioned taxon and the Columbian White-tailed Deer O. v. leucurus (9). Dr. W.D. Klimstra, Director of the Cooperative Wildlife Research Laboratory, Southern Illinois University, kindly assisted with the compilation of this data sheet.

REFERENCES   1.   Barbour, T. and Allen, G.M. (1922). The White-tailed Deer of eastern United States. J. Mammal. 3: 65-78.
              2.   Dickson, J.D. III (1955). An ecological study of the Key Deer. Fla. Game Fresh Water Fish Comm. Tech. Bull. No.3.

104pp.
3. Dooley, A. (1975). Food of the Florida Key Deer. MA Thesis. S. Illinois Univ., Carbondale. 80pp.
4. Hardin, J.W. (1974). Behaviour, socio-biology, and reproductive life history of the Florida Key deer, Odocoileus virginianus clavium. Ph.D. Thesis. So. Illinois Univ., Carbondale.
5. Klimstra, W.D. and Hardin, J.W. (1978). Key Deer. In Layne, J.N. (Ed.) Rare and Endangered Biota of Florida. Vol. 1 Mammals. Univ. Presses of Florida, Gainesville. Pp. 15-17.
6. Klimstra, W.D., Hardin, J.W., Silva, N.J., Jacobson, B.W. and Terpening, V.A. (1974). Key Deer Investigations. Final Report to the U.S. Dept. of Interior, Bur. Sports Fish. Wildl., Coop. Wild. Res. Lab., S. Illinois Univ., Carbondale. 184pp.
7. National Fish and Wildlife Laboratory, Gainesville. (1980). The Key Deer. FWS/OBS-80/01.48. In Selected Vertebrate Endangered Species of the Seacoast of the United States. Biological Services Program, Fish and Wildlife Service. U.S. Department of the Interior.
8. U.S. Fish and Wildlife Service. (1980). Endangered Species Technical Bulletin 5 (7): 9.
9. Whitehead, G.K. (1972). Deer of the World. Constable, London.
10. Jacobson, B.N. (1974). Effects of drinking water on habitat utilization by Key Deer. MS Research Paper, S. Illinois Univ. Carbondale.
11. Klimstra, W.D. (1981). In litt.

467

Odocoileus virginianus leucurus (Douglas, 1829)

Order   ARTIODACTYLA   Family   CERVIDAE

SUMMARY   Occurs on floodplains and islands along the Lower Columbia River in Washington and Oregon States, and in southern Oregon, U.S.A. In 1977 was thought to number around 2400 including about 1900 head whose integrity as pure-bred O. v. leucurus was in doubt until recently. A secure population of at least 260 survives on the Columbian White-tailed Deer National Wildlife Refuge on the lower Columbia River which is under constant management, though hybridisation with sympatric Columbian Black-tailed Deer (Odocoileus hemionus columbianus) may become a problem there. Habitat loss to agriculture and cattle ranching was the main reason for the original population decline and habitat deterioration continues outside the Refuge. A Recovery Team was appointed in 1975 to monitor the deer's status and to formulate management and conservation plans.

DISTRIBUTION   U.S.A. where now survives in scattered populations on islands and floodplains along the lower Columbia River in Oregon and Washington States, from Tenas Illahee Island, Clatsop Co., Oregon to Little Wallace and Kinnunen Cut Islands, north of Clatskanie, Columbia Co., Oregon, and in southern Oregon in the Roseburg Co. region where they inhabit the area around Roseburg, Glide and Sutherlin (3,5). Formerly inhabited a narrow north-south strip between the Pacific Ocean and the Cascade Mountains from southern Puget Sound south to the Roseburg-Winston area (4,5,9). Other small isolated populations may persist within the deer's former range, possibly as far north as the Willapa Bay area, Washington Co.; claimed sightings of which need to be investigated (5).

POPULATION   A 1977 estimated total of about 2400, most of which belong to the Roseburg herd which in 1975 numbered about 1900 head (4,5,8). In 1975 the population along the lower Columbia River as far east as Brown Island, off Puget Island in Clark Co. Washington was estimated at a minimum of 307 with at least 260 of these in the Columbia White-tailed Deer National Wildlife Refuge; this compares with estimates in 1939 of 507-710 for the same area (11). However the recent estimates are known to be conservative and the decrease may therefore not be as serious as would seem; less conservative estimates in 1976 were of 400-500 for this area (5,8). Greatest changes have occurred on Puget Island which in 1940 was a population stronghold with at least 150 deer; in 1977 it held about 30. On Tenas Illahee Island numbers rose from 2-5 in 1939 to more than 50 in 1975, though in 1976 dropped to an estimated 20 following floods due to dyke breakage (5). In 1976 an estimate of 25 was given for the Oregon (south) bank of the river between Rainier and Knappa (5). Some authorities reported estimates of 100-200 here in 1975 but this is possibly based on a 1936 estimate (4). The Columbia River from Wallace Island as far as the The Dalles was extensively surveyed for White-tailed Deer in 1978-79. Populations were discovered on five adjacent islands: Wallace, Little Wallace, Skull, Anundes and Kinnunen Cut. Total numbers were estimated as at minimum 68, probably 70-80, most of these (around 50) on Wallace Island (3). Historical accounts show the deer to have been relatively common throughout its range in the early nineteenth century; settlement then led to considerable decreases in number and by the early 1930s it was generally considered extinct (2,5). In 1939 Scheffer rediscovered the Columbia River population which was well known to local farmers and fishermen but it was not until the mid-1960s that attempts to conserve the population were initiated (2,11).

HABITAT AND ECOLOGY The original habitat is thought to have been forested swamps characterized by dense, tall shrub communities with scattered Picea sitchensis and, less frequently, other trees such as Alnus rubra, Populus trichocarpa and Salix spp. (3). The deer on Wallace and adjacent islands occupy habitat very similar to this, however on the Refuge only 17 per cent of the mainland area remains wooded (3) and preferred habitat appears to be pasture interspersed with cover (4,5). Large tracts of open area (improved pasture) or heavily wooded cover without interspersion appear much less favoured and deer densities are much reduced (4). The Roseburg herd occurs at higher elevations on hills 30-100 m above the Umpqua River, its place on the floodplain being occupied by Black-tailed Deer (4). The deer are good swimmers, resulting in noticeable mixing of subpopulations in the lower Columbia River area (4). Until recently it was believed to be principally a grazer, however preliminary results of a dietary study suggest that deer on the Refuge also utilize a wide variety of browse species throughout the year (2,3,4). This is borne out by the maintenance of a population of relatively high density on Wallace Island where large areas of pasture are unavailable (3). The predominantly grazing habit of deer on the mainland Refuge may reflect accommodation to a sparsely wooded habitat rather than actual dietary preference (3).

THREATS TO SURVIVAL Principal threats at present (1981) appear to be habitat destruction, hybridisation with sympatric Columbia Black-tailed Deer and, in the case of the Columbia River population, vulnerability to extensive flooding and outbreaks of epidemic diseases (3). The original decline was due to drainage of swamps and conversion of riverside woodland to pasture for livestock and hay production (2,3,4,11). Woodland cover on the mainland (Washington State) portion of the Refuge decreased from 66 per cent to 17 per cent between 1938 and 1972 and on Puget Island from 43 per cent to 1 per cent between 1938 and 1978, with a corresponding decrease in deer numbers (3,6). Wallace Island stills retains much optimal woodland habitat but is scheduled as a site for future development by its present owners (3). The 1978-79 survey disclosed a growing economic interest in the development of Columbia River Islands, particularly for beef production, timber harvesting (cottonwood and alder species) and marina development (3). Habitat deterioration is thus certain to continue on land outside the Refuge (3,8). Originally improvement of pastures led to local population increases if sufficient woodland was left, however such increases in turn led to conflict with cattle graziers and farmers (2,4,11). In 1940 deer were accused of destroying garden crops and this resulted in retaliatory killing (2). The belief that the deer carried and transmitted cattle diseases also led to much poisoning and killing at that time (4,11). Some authorities, however, neither consider that this, nor subsistence poaching and sport hunting have been significant factors in the decline (4). Although the deer may benefit indirectly from the presence of cattle, by the latter maintaining pasture in optimal condition, they will not tolerate crowding by them and deer numbers are found to be negatively correlated with the presence of livestock (4,9). The genetic integrity of some of the deer has been the subject of controversy (1,3,5); the Roseburg herd was considered by some to be hybridised with Black-tailed Deer, though a recent study has indicated that they are in fact O. v. leucurus (3). This population was protected (though with intermittent open hunting seasons) until 1972 when protection was lifted. In 1972-73 hunting was noted as intense and uncontrollable in a 850 ha area of the range near Winston (4). However reports indicate that hunting has not significantly affected the population, though habitat disturbance through urbanisation and clearing may become of increasing importance (8). The 1978-79 survey discovered that 31 per cent of presumed O. v. leucurus observed on the mainland Refuge displayed hybrid tendencies, principally in the colouration and structure of the tail, though many deviated only slightly from typical O. v. leucurus (3). No deer showing hybrid characteristics were observed on Puget or Wallace Islands (3). A captive hybridisation study carried out by the Oregon Department of Fish and Wildlife from 1969-72 showed that O. v. leucurus and O. h. columbianus were capable of interbreeding and producing fertile offspring with the characteristics of the male parent predominating in the young (3). The Refuge deer are relatively safe from habitat deterioration and hunting but being confined to an area of approx. 2000 ha are considered vulnerable to outbreaks of disease and serious flooding (3). The latter is thought by some authorities to have been a factor in the original population decline and although construction of dykes and dams has decreased the probability of major flooding, the possibility still exists (3).

CONSERVATION MEASURES TAKEN The deer is protected in its lower Columbia River range by the U.S. Fish and Wildlife Service and the Washington and Oregon State Wildlife Authorities (2,5). In 1972 the U.S. Fish and Wildlife Service began land acquisition for the Columbian White-tailed Deer National Wildlife Refuge which by 1976 comprised 2105 ha; 790 ha on the Washington shore of the Columbia River near Cathlament, and the adjacent Prince (119 ha), Tenas Illahee (830 ha) and Hunting Islands (390 ha) (1). Some of the land is leased (1,2,5). Management of habitat includes retention of cattle to optimise pasture quality. The deer has been extensively studied and in 1975 the U.S. Fish and Wildlife Service appointed a Recovery Team to formulate and implement conservation plans and to continually monitor the status of the deer (3,4,5,6,8,9,12).

CONSERVATION MEASURES PROPOSED The Recovery Plan has the stated aim of maintaining a minimum of 400 deer, distributed in at least four sub-populations as the basic requirement for safeguarding the taxon (3). The populations on Tenas Illahee Island and the Refuge mainland are considered viable and their habitats safe, though the importance of hybridisation in the latter needs further investigation (3). The acquisition of Wallace Island for the Refuge would secure a further population in what is considered to be nearly pristine habitat and is strongly recommended, as is the addition of land on Puget Island to safeguard the remaining deer there (3,7). Other islands on the Columbia River (e.g. Cottonwood, 344 ha and Crims, 295 ha) are potential reintroduction sites for captive-bred or excess refuge stock so long as habitat can be made secure by the acquisition of land for the Refuge, or by land-use agreements with current owners (3,5). The verification of the Roseburg deer as O. v. leucurus makes this latter measure somewhat less urgent, however, although it is now important that effective conservation and management plans for this population be drawn up. Continued studies of all aspects of the deer's biology, and management of the Refuge lands are both important for the long-term conservation of the deer.

CAPTIVE BREEDING Antwerp Zoo, Belgium bred four males and one female in 1977, at least some of which were second or subsequent generation captive-bred stock (10). The total captive population is unknown; in 1976 Tacoma Zoological Society reportedly held one individual (4).

REMARKS For description see (13). The full species has a very wide distribution in North America being resident in practically every state in the U.S.A. except Alaska, and possibly Utah. Northwards its range extends into southern Canada and southwards it occurs through Mexico and Central America into the northern half of South America. At least 38 subspecies are recognised; the validity of many of these, however, is questioned (14). Two are currrently listed in the Red Data Book, the taxon mentioned above and the Key Deer O. v. clavium (13). C.F. Martinsen, Leader of the Columbian White-tailed Deer Recovery Team provided information for this data sheet and Dr. E. Charles Meslow, Leader of the Oregon Cooperative Wildlife Research Unit, kindly commented on a draft.

REFERENCES 1. Buechner, H.K. and Marshall, D.B. (1975). Threatened

Ungulates of North America. In Proceedings of the Symposium on Endangered and Threatened Species of North America, 11-14 June 1974, Washington, D.C. The Wolf Sanctuary, St. Louis, Mo.

2. Davis, R. (1976). Hope for Western White-tail. Defenders of Wildlife 51(6): 373-377.

3. Davison, M.A. (1979). Columbian White-tailed Deer Status and Potential on Off Refuge Habitat. Completion Report, Project E1, Study 2. Washington Game Department.

4. Eaton, R.L. (1978). Status of the Columbian White-tailed deer (O. v. leucurus). Unpd. report. 10pp.

5. Gavin, T. (1978). Status of Columbia White-tailed Deer Odocoileus virginianus leucurus: some quantitative uses of biogeographic data. In Threatened Deer. Proceedings of a Working Meeting of the SSC Deer Specialist Group, Longview, Washington State, U.S.A., 26 Sept - 1 Oct 1977. IUCN, Switzerland. Pp. 185-202.

6. Gavin, T.A. (1979). Population ecology of the Columbian White-tailed Deer. Ph.D. Thesis. Oregon State Univ., Corvallis.

7. IUCN. (1976). Columbia White-tailed Deer. Sheet code 19.125.8.1.2. Red Data Book Vol. 1 Mammalia. IUCN, Switzerland.

8. Martinsen, C.F. (1980). In litt.

9. Minutes of Columbian White-tailed Deer Recovery Team Meeting. Roseburg, Oregon, 7 May 1980. Unpublished. 2pp.

10. Olney, P.J.S. (Ed.) (1979). International Zoo Yearbook 19. Zool. Soc. London.

11. Scheffer, V.B. (1940). A newly located herd of Pacific White-tailed Deer. J. Mammal. 21(3): 271-282.

12. Suring, L.H. (1974). Habitat use and activity patterns of the Columbian White-tailed Deer along the lower Columbia River. M.S. Thesis. Oregon State Univ., Corvallis.

13. Whitehead, G.K. (1972). Deer of the World Constable, London.

14. Whitehead, G.K. (1981). In litt.

CEDROS ISLAND MULE DEER
or VENADO DE CEDROS

RARE

Odocoileus hemionus cerrosensis (Merriam, 1898)

Order   ARTIODACTYLA   Family   CERVIDAE

SUMMARY Confined to Cedros Island off Baja California, Mexico. A 1980 survey found the deer's status to be considerably better than previously thought, with a population possibly numbering several hundreds. Principal threat is believed to have been poaching, although this has apparently declined in recent years and outlook for the deer appears good, though human population pressure on the island is expected to increase in the future. A 4-month field study of the deer was completed in 1980.

DISTRIBUTION Mexico; endemic to Cedros Island (approx. 350 sq. km in area) off the western coast of Baja California. Deer are absent from the extremely hot and dry southeastern region and from the southwest tip of the island (7,9). They appear to be scattered throughout the rest, though there are thought to be three areas of relatively high concentration with larger areas of moderate to low density (4).

POPULATION An extensive survey in 1980 found the population to be substantially greater than previously thought, possibly numbering several hundreds (4). 42 deer were directly observed comprising 13 males, 23 does, and 6 fawns (9). More accurate population estimates are expected following analysis of survey results (4,9). Up to 1979 it was thought that fewer than 50 deer survived with estimates as low as a dozen in 1975 (3), and believed extinct in 1977 (11), though a survey by the Mexican Wildlife Service around that time estimated 69 on the basis of tracks and droppings (5).

HABITAT AND ECOLOGY The island is very rugged and mountainous and is mostly covered with open desert scrub, the most conspicuous components of which are Copalquin (Pachycormus discolor) and the Century Plant, Agave shawii var sebastiana. At middle and high elevations the desert scrub occasionally gives way to other vegetation types, notably pine forest, chaparral and sage scrub and, on wet north facing slopes and cliffs in the centre and north of the island, pure stands of the Closed-cone Pine, Pinus muricata var. cedrosensis. The California Juniper (Juniperus californica) is abundant on higher peaks and ridges and extends well down in some canyons (9). The deer do not seem restricted to any particular habitat type (5,9). There is very little fresh water; a scattering of small springs is known in the northern hills and there is at least one major spring in the south (5). Average temperature is 18-20°C (range 15-22°C over a 20 year period) with mean rainfall of about 80 mm and a rainy season from late November to mid-February (9). Calving takes place in April (9).

THREATS TO SURVIVAL Poaching has been generally considered the major threat, though by 1980 it had apparently been reduced to negligible proportions. Predation by feral dogs has been mentioned in the past as an important factor, though the 1980 study found them to be few in number and to occur in the southern part of the island, outside the deer's range (3,9). Fire is thought unlikely to have had any significant impact on the deer's habitat (6). Virtually all poaching was previously by lobster fishermen living in isolated camps at the north end of the island which is currently undergoing an economic boom due to thriving fishing and salt industries. Red meat is more widely available and affordable than previously and travel round the island by boat easier. There is thus less incentive for the fishermen to supplement their seafood diet by poaching in the inhospitable hinterlands which constitute the deer's principal terrain (5). Commercial hunting seems non-existent and such killing as does occur at present appears to mainly involve young men who hunt for sport (5). However human pressure is predicted to increase in the near future as both the fish cannery and salt company have further expansion plans (9). Feral goats do not flourish on the island and have had no perceivable impact on the vegetation and the only feral asses present are restricted to lowland areas near villages (9).

CONSERVATION MEASURES TAKEN Protected by law; the penalty for poaching is severe (5), and a recent increase in visits to the island by Mexican Wildlife Service personnel may have discouraged it (5). In May 1978 Mexico declared all the islands (including Cedros) off the Baja California Peninsula and the adjacent Sonoran Desert coast to be wildlife reserves (1). A January 1980 field trip was undertaken to determine the feasibility of a study and conservation project. It concluded that the prognosis for survival of the deer had improved in recent years (5). Following this IUCN/WWF funded a 4-month field project on the deer (Project No.1646) which was completed in 1980; it included an extensive survey of the island and more detailed study at chosen sites to determine habitat use, demography, behaviour and general ecology (5).

CONSERVATION MEASURES PROPOSED The 1980 study should provide data to allow detailed conservation plans to be drawn up. Pérez Gil Salcido strongly advocates a campaign to encourage public awareness of the desirability of conserving the deer and its habitat. He reports that the island's inhabitants are keen to learn more about 'their' deer and local officials and enterprises are willing to co-operate in conservation (9).

CAPTIVE BREEDING Not known to have ever been kept in captivity.

REMARKS For description of animal see (2,9,12). The taxonomic rank of the Cedros Island Mule Deer is open to question - it is still a matter of doubt whether it is a subspecies of the Mule Deer (Odocoileus hemionus) or a full species, though it is usually considered the former (7). The Mule Deer occurs in western Canada and western United States southward into northern Mexico (2) and as a species is not considered threatened. Dr. D.R. McCullough of the IUCN/SSC Deer Specialist Group, very kindly provided information on which this data sheet was based.

REFERENCES
1. Anon. (1978). New Parks and Reserves. Oryx 15(1): 24.
2. Hall, E.R. and Kelson, K.R. (1959). The Mammals of North America. The Ronald Press Co., New York.
3. IUCN. (1973). Cedros Island Deer. Sheet Code: 19.125.8.1.3. Red Data Book. Vol. 1 Mammalia. IUCN, Switzerland.
4. McCullough, D.R. (1980). In litt. to S. Guignard, IUCN.
5. McCullough, D.R. (1980). Report on the feasibility of a study of the Cedros Island Mule Deer. Berkeley, California. Ms 8pp.
6. McCullough, D.R. (1981). In litt.
7. McTaggart Cowan, I. (1980). In litt.
8. McTaggart Cowan, I. and Holloway, C.W. (1978). Geographical location and current conservation status of the threatened deer of the world. In Threatened Deer. Proceedings of a Working Meeting of the SSC Deer Specialist Group, Longview, Washington State, U.S.A., 26 Sept - 1 Oct, 1977. IUCN, Switzerland.
9. Perez-Gil Salcido, R. (1980). Cedros Island Deer, Project

No. 1646 Mexico. Annual Report 1980 to IUCN/WWF, Switzerland. Unpd. 13pp.

10. U.S. Fish. and Wildlife Service. (1975). In Federal Register Vol. 40 (187): 44149-44150.

11. Villa Ramirez, B. (1977). In litt.

12. Whitehead, G.K. (1972). <u>Deer of the World</u>. Constable, London.

SOUTH ANDEAN HUEMUL   ENDANGERED

Hippocamelus bisulcus (Molina, 1782)

Order   ARTIODACTYLA   Family   CERVIDAE

SUMMARY   Found in scattered localities in the southern part of the Andes chain
in Chile and Argentina, where the total population is almost certainly less than
2000.   Threatened by poaching, dogs, disease, and loss of habitat to fire and
domestic stock.   Known to occur in five national parks.   Legally protected in both
countries but enforcement generally inadequate.   A conservation programme was
begun in Chile in 1975, and in 1980 the Argentine National Parks Service was said
to be seriously considering initiating one.

DISTRIBUTION   Chile and Argentina where inhabits the southern part of the
Andes chain (3,12,21).   Chile: known to occur with certainty only in the Nevados
de Chillan area of Nuble Province (approx. 37°S) and in the southern Provinces of
Aysen and Magallanes (45-47°S) (12,13).   In Magallanes, a 1973 report mentions it
also occurring on some of the large mountainous islands, such as Wellington and
Riesco (9).   While field confirmation is lacking, small groups may persist at other
sites along the 1800 km stretch of the Andes between approx. 34° and 52°S,
particularly in the Provinces of Colchagua (34°-35°S), Linares (36°S) and
continental Chiloe (43°-44°S) (12,15).   There are no reports from the entire Lake
District (39-41°S), and none were recorded during a 1965 survey of mammals in
Malleco Province (38°S) (12).   Argentina: in 1980 definitely recorded only from
Santa Cruz and Chubut Provinces.   In the former known from the region of Los
Glaciares National Park (approx. 49°15'-50°S, 73°W) - in the Pampa del Desierto
just north of the park and near Glacier Viedma within the park boundaries; and
also Perito Moreno N.P. (47°30'S, 77°W) where Huemul are thought to persist
despite lack of recent sightings.   In Chubut there have been recent sightings in the
Rio Grande and Lago Menendes areas of Los Alerces N.P. (42°10'-42°20'S,
71°35'-72°10'W).   Contrary to earlier reports there are no Huemuls in Nahuel
Huapi or Lanin N.P.'s in Nequen and Rio Negro Provinces (20).   Formerly found
from about 35°S through Santa Cruz to the Atlantic Coast (3,7).   In 1961 said to
persist within this range but to have disappeared from much of the Santa Cruz
region (3).

POPULATION   Total numbers unknown, though Tarak in 1980 gave 2000 as the
likely maximum estimate (20).   Chile: in 1976 said to number 375-1000, with
possibly about 40 (min. 26, max. 59) at Nevados de Chillan (12), and 1980 censuses
suggest little overall change.   1981 surveys of the Rio Claro in Aysen estimated a
minimum of 32 deer, but probably over 50 (14,15).   A 1977 Aysen survey estimated
60-160 in 7000 sq. km of the Puerto Aysen - Coyhaique area (12); this extrapolated
to 350-900 for the total 40,000 sq. km of mountainous environment in Aysen and
Magallanes (12).   Hernandez and Rosas gave 11 and Colomes listed 19 sites in
Aysen where Huemuls have been reported in recent years.   Inspection of some of
these suggests that at most sites numbers are low (4,5,15).   Argentina: small,
scattered populations.   In 1975 was considered less threatened than in Chile,
especially in some high areas of Rio Negro, Chubut and Santa Cruz (though see
Distribution) (7).   In 1973 a population of less than 100 was reported at Cerros
Huemeles, an upland area of 45,000 ha. in Los Glaciares National Park, Santa
Cruz (2).

HABITAT AND ECOLOGY   Principally at higher elevations in temperate forests,
shrubland and open areas above and below timberline (12,13).   Although reported
from relatively level areas along valleys and in the alpine zone, evidence suggests

it has always inhabited areas in proximity to rugged, steep topography (12,13). In the Nevados de Chillan study, Huemuls were typically found between 1450-1700 m, on slopes of 30°-40°, along northern and western exposures, and at localities with diversified and irregular terrain (12,13). Shrubland of Nothofagus and Chusquea spp. was the preferred vegetation type (12,13,15). They foraged principally on forbs but also consumed woody browse, particularly during winter. Small groups ranged within an average annual 340 ha minimum home range (13,15). In winter they moved lower, sometimes travelling up to 6.5 km to areas at 1100-1500 m, or lower if snows were heavy, where they occupied the steepest and rockiest localities available (12,13,15). During the driest summer months they sought shade, food and water in tall forests of lenga or roble (Nothofagus spp.), which comprise a small fraction of their total annual range (12). These special winter and summer habitats afford protection during unfavourable periods and seem essential for the Huemul's survival. Other environmental zones may be important as dispersion and colonisation routes or serve as corridors between winter and summer localities (16). Miller et al record that only those southern populations inhabiting dense cover have survived, making characterisation of their optimal habitat difficult, though they considered Huemuls, originally foraged in subclimax shrubs and adjacent meadows (9), and results of a Jan. 1981 survey at Rio Claro indicate they use a broad range of habitats including alpine grasslands, shrub (in areas recovering from fire), climax forest, and early and mid-successional forests created by periodic natural disturbances such as rock movements and high winds (15). Historical accounts imply a polygamous social structure of small groups, occasionally up to six or more animals, with larger aggregations being reported in winter, or when population density was especially high (10,12). However the Nevados de Chillan study found most Huemuls solitary or, more rarely, in groups of two or three (male-female pairs with or without fawns, or female-fawn pairs), with some indication of a male-biased sex ratio (12). This apparent change in social behaviour is thought to be a response to increased human predation, both indirectly in reflecting a greater reliance on dense cover (which normally leads to decrease in group size), and directly since solitary individuals are less conspicuous than larger groups (12). At Rio Claro during the 1980 rut, individual male and female Huemuls were seen in pair associations for up to 7 days, and it has been observed that male - female associations in general are more common for the Huemul than for most other deer (15).

THREATS TO SURVIVAL Believed to be a combination of poaching, attacks by dogs, disease, and loss of habitat through fire and displacement by domestic stock (5,6,7,8,13). Despite legal protection the law is obscure and virtually impossible to enforce in the isolated areas where Huemuls, occur (8). Early reports stated it was very unwary of humans and thus an easy target for hunters with dogs and lassoos or guns (8,15). The Nevados de Chillan animals, at least, are now very wary - indication of past persecution (8). Röttmann states that hunting is not very important but that dogs can be a serious problem (10). Povilitis, who has observed dogs harassing Huemuls, notes that those observed in Huemul habitat were clearly associated with people and considers the Andean environment too harsh to support truly feral dogs (15). Habitat changes caused by fire, often to improve accessibility for domestic stock, pose a serious threat. Native vegetation (especially lenga) is destroyed leading to soil erosion and a more arid environment (11,12). In Aysen Province extensive areas of forest were burnt in the 1930s during initial colonization and natural reforestation has been severely retarded because of widespread soil erosion (11). Logging and unregulated recreational use of some areas in Nuble also pose a threat (11,12). Habitat destruction seems to be particularly important in the lower and more vulnerable winter habitats (17). The threat from livestock (principally free-ranging cows, goats, sheep and horses) includes competition for forage and alteration of vegetation and soils (in post-burn areas, domestic stock may retard the recovery of vegetation and accelerate soil erosion) as well as actual displacement of Huemuls from preferred localities (12,17,19). Competition with introduced Red Deer (Cervus elaphus) may be an additional factor in the deer's disappearance from lower elevations (7). Huemuls are susceptible to foot-and-mouth disease, coccidosis, nematodes of strongyloida, and tapeworm (Moniezia), all of which are transmitted by domestic bovids (12). Foot-and-mouth is said to be present on the Argentinian side of the border with Nuble and could easily re-enter Chile. Many other domestic livestock diseases (such as anthrax, foot rot and contagious echtyma) may infect them, and at Aysen autopsied Huemuls had the bladderworm Cysticerous tenuicollis which can weaken or kill, and is spread by faecal contamination of the environment by dogs (12). Röttmann considers foot-and-mouth and cysticercosis to be especially important factors in the Huemul decline in Chile (17).

CONSERVATION MEASURES TAKEN Listed in Appendix 1 of the 1973 Convention on International Trade in Endangered Species of Wild Fauna and Flora, trade in it or its products therefore being subject to strict regulation by ratifying nations, and trade for primarily commercial purposes banned. Chile: protected by law but enforcement very difficult (8,12). At Nevados de Chillan four wildlife guards had been assigned by 1981 to patrol portions of existing Huemul habitat. In Aysen, a forestry technician has been placed in charge of Huemul protection at the Rio Claro; both sites currently (1981) have informal reserve status, i.e. land use directives affecting them take into account the Huemul's presence. As the Rio Claro population occurs just beyond Rio Simpson National Park (45° 30'S) (which itself probably contains small numbers of Huemuls), expansion of the Park to include this site was being considered. Habitat over portions of Rio Claro is less than optimal because of degradation from livestock by soil erosion; however, livestock have been excluded from a small section of the site, and Huemuls have ample access to fresh water (the latter may be a limiting factor at Nevados de Chillan). Reintroduced to the 'Torres del Paine' National Park near Puerto Natales in Magallanes Province, where it occurs in very small numbers (16). In 1975 IUCN/WWF project 1218, concerned with the biology and conservation of the Huemul in Chile, was initiated; its first phase was an intensive study of the populations in Nevados de Chillan and the relations between Huemul, Pudu (Pudu pudu) and introduced Red Deer (12,19). In 1980 IUCN/WWF Project 1639 began, its aim being to conserve a viable population of Huemul by protection of its habitat (6). At the same time a Huemul conservation education programme was initiated, although as of 1981 this was reportedly of very limited extent due to lack of funds (15). Argentina: protected by law but only enforced in Los Alerces, Perito Moreno and Los Glaciares National Parks, outside these areas protection is said to be ineffective (7,8,20).

CONSERVATION MEASURES PROPOSED Povilitis, on the basis of his study in Chile, proposed the following measures in 1979: 1) Identification of surviving Huemul populations of significant size, evaluation of their habitat requirements (as was done at Nevados de Chillan), and development of administrative programmes to protect them. 2) Establishment of Huemul/Ecosystem reserves along northern, central and southern portions of the deer's former range. 3) Creation of national and regional Huemul conservation teams and local public involvement groups (13). More recently, and after consultation with Chilean conservationists, he has proposed a Huemul Recovery Team to help implement the above measures (15). He concludes that the only areas where Huemuls can survive in the long term must be: free from poaching, uncontrolled use of fire, over-exploitation of vegetation and range, and the hazards posed to Huemuls by domestic animals; large and varied enough in habitat to support a sizeable Huemul population that is resistant to extinction by local catastrophes (natural or man-caused) or by chance; and contiguous in the sense that Huemuls can disperse, breed with other groups, and (re)colonize vacant sites. As well as preservation of populations in existing sites, he suggests reintroduction into large, well managed parks in southern Chile, such as Puyehue (1170 sq. km), Vicente Perez Rosales (1362 sq. km) and Torres del Paine (110 sq. km) but only after research has selected suitable habitat in the parks, established that potential donor populations are stable and secure, and determined the means of successful capture, transportation and establishment (12,15). The reintroduction attempt to Torres del Paine is believed to have been carried out after these suggestions were made but it is noted that numbers of Huemuls were killed in the process (1,15). In Argentina in 1980 a breeding/reintroduction programme was being seriously considered by the National Parks Service (19).

CAPTIVE BREEDING In 1981 there were four females, one male, and a fawn in a private zoo in Chile. The fawn was born there but it is not known whether it was conceived in the wild or in captivity (15).

REMARKS For description see (3). The Huemul is a national symbol appearing on the Chilean Coat-of-Arms (12). Dr. Anthony Povilitis extensively assisted in the compilation of this data sheet.

REFERENCES
1. Astorga, R. (1980). Safari tras el Huemul. Revista del Domingo (El Mercurio). 7 Sept.
2. Boswell, J. (1973). A Park in the Andes. Oryx 12(2): 243-251.
3. Cabrera, A. (1957-1961). Catalogo de los mamiferos de America del Sur. Revista del Museo Argentina de Ciencias Naturales 'Bernardino Rivadavia', Cienc. Zool., Buenos Aires. 4(1-2): 1-732.
4. Colomes, A. (1978). Biologia y ecologia del Huemul Chileno. Estudios de sus habitos alimentos. Thesis. Univ. de Chile, Santiago.
5. Hernandez, M. and Rosas, H. (1979). Aisen, paraiso del Huemul. Trapananda. Ano 1, Numero 2. pp. 2-10.
6. IUCN. (1980). List of approved projects, September 1980. IUCN, Switzerland.
7. Jungius, H. (1976). Project 960. Deer - International programme for conservation of threatened species. In Jackson, P. (Ed.), World Wildlife Yearbook 1975-76. WWF, Switzerland. pp 201-217.
8. McTaggart Cowan, I. and Holloway, C.W. (1978). Geographical location and current conservation status of the threatened deer of the world. In Threatened Deer. Proceedings of a Working Meeting of the SSC Deer Specialist Group, Longview, Washington, U.S.A., 26 Sept - 1 Oct, 1977. IUCN, Switzerland.
9. Miller, S., Röttman, J. and Taber, R.D. (1973). Dwindling and Endangered Ungulates of Chile - Vicuna, Lama, Hippocamelus and Pudu. Transactions N. Amer. Wildl. Nat. Res. Conf. 38.
10. Osgood, W.H. (1943). The mammals of Chile. Field Mus. Nat. Hist. Zool. Ser. 30. 268 pp.
11. Povilitis, T. (1976). A progress report on the Huemul project, Huemul biology and conservation. Unpd. Report.
12. Povilitis, T. (1978). The Chilean Huemul Project - a case history (1975-76). In Threatened Deer. Proceedings of a Working Meeting of the SSC Deer Specialist Group, Longview, Washington, U.S.A., 26 Sept - 1 Oct, 1977. IUCN, Switzerland. pp 109-129.
13. Povilitis, A. (1979). The Chilean Huemul project (1975-76):

Huemul ecology and conservation. Report to Corporacion Nacional Forestal de Chile. Ph. D. Dissertation, Colorado State Univ., Fort Collins.

14. Povilitis, A. (1981). In search of the Huemul, Field Report. Unpd. 4pp.
15. Povilitis, A. (1981). In litt.
16. Rau, J. (1978). Las especies en peligro de extinction que sobreviven en 'Torres del Paine'. Nandu 1(2): 22-24.
17. Röttmann, J. (1977). In litt.
18. Stutzin, G. (1977). Protection for a rare deer in Chile. Oryx 14(2): 104-5.
19. Taber, R.D. (1975). Project 1218. The Huemul of Chile - biology and conservation. In Jackson, P. (Ed.), World Wildlife Yearbook 1974-75. WWF, Switzerland. pp. 250-251.
20. Tarak, A. (1980). Pers. comm.
21. Whitehead, G.K. (1972). Deer of the World. Constable, London.

Hippocamelus antisensis (d'Orbigny, 1834)

Order   ARTIODACTYLA   Family   CERVIDAE

SUMMARY Widely but sparsely distributed at high altitudes in the northern Andes. Numbers unknown but declining, principally because of hunting, habitat destruction especially at lower altitudes, and competition with domestic livestock. Legally protected but enforcement usually inadequate, although in some areas increased protection of the Vicuna (Vicugna vicugna) appears to be directly benefitting the species. Occurs in several national parks and reserves. Field studies are required to formulate detailed conservation plans.

DISTRIBUTION Northern Andes: in Peru, western Bolivia, northeastern Chile and northwestern Argentina (3). Only scattered populations now survive within this range. Argentina: in 1980 known to occur in Catamarca, Jujuy and Salta Provinces (16). Bolivia: a 1975 report mentions isolated populations throughout the eastern Cordillera, some known localities being: north of La Paz, around Pelechuco (Cordillera de Apolobamba), Altura de Araca (Cordillera de Tres Cruzes), and around Cochabambe. Believed exterminated in the Altiplano. No data located for the western Cordillera (9). Chile: reportedly confined to the Cordillera de Arica, Province Tarapaca, mainly around Socoroma Zapahuira and Putre (18°15'S) (7). Peru: in 1969 recorded by Grimwood in the following areas: Dpto. de Puno, especially Azangaro, Carabaya, Melgar and Lampa Provinces, and almost certainly in the southwest; Dpto. de Cuzco on high ground in the south of Quispicanchis, Paucartambo and Calca Provinces, in many parts of Canchis, Canas and Urubamba Provinces, and almost certainly in Chumivilcas and Espinar in the south; Dpto. de Arequipa in suitable localities in the north and east; Dpto. de Apurimac in part of every Province; Dpto. Ayachucho - well known in Parinarochas and Lucanas Provinces; Dpto. de Huancavalica; Dptoes. de Junin and Pasco - several localities in the west; Dpto. de Lima - eastern part extending north as far as the Cordillera Blanca in Dpto. Ancash, to high ground both east and west of the Rio Maranon, Huamachuco Province in Dpto. de la Libertad (5). Ecuador: contrary to a 1977 report (12), there is no evidence of its present survival in Ecuador, if it ever existed there at all (18).

POPULATION Total numbers unknown though certainly declining throughout much of its range. Argentina: rare; greatest numbers exist in Catamarca Province, principally in the Sierra de Ambarto, with small numbers in Jujuy and Salta Provinces (16). Bolivia: in 1981 considered rare and declining (19), and to have virtually disappeared from the area near Cochabamba (20). Some stable populations were reported in 1975 in isolated inaccessible localities (9). Chile: in 1977 400 were reported in Lauca National Park (17). Rottmann notes (1981) that Taruca seem to have recently become more numerous and tamer in this area (21). Peru: in 1969 Grimwood stated that although widespread, total numbers were small (5), however Jungius noted in 1975 that estimates varied from 10,000-15,000 (9). In 1977 the highest known concentrations occurred on the western slopes of the Andes in Ayacucho Department (2).

HABITAT AND ECOLOGY A high altitude species although there is disagreement as to its preferred (or typical) habitat. Roe and Rees observed Taruca in an area 50 km northwest of Lake Titicaca in Puno Province, Peru in a semi-arid area with broad, flat, frequently marshy valley bottoms separating steep-sided, round-topped mountains (15). Taruca were observed there between 3950 and 4200 m on the tops and slopes of the mountains in areas of bare rocks and small cliff-like outcroppings interspersed with dry grassland vegetation. Deer also utilised Polylepis thickets in some areas (15). However, in Bolivia Jungius observed Taruca in wet montane forest fringes and alpine grasslands, principally at elevations of 2500-5000 m, and concentrating in areas of low vegetation such as bramble ('matorrales'), high altitude swamps ('bofedales'), and grasslands ('hajios') (8). Tarak reported Taruca in Argentina to be confined to regions of rocky, wet grasslands ('puna') above 3500 m, and not known as a forest fringe species (16). For Peru Grimwood stated it was found above 4300 m, its presence being largely determined by the availability of cover (usually Polylepis spp.). He did not consider it a 'puna' species (5). Rottman reports that in Chile it is only known from the western slope of the Andes between 3500 and 4600 m, sometimes being found in lower valleys. The area has dry pastures, shrubs and some small Polylepis trees and the deer live on steep sided mountains and in deep canyons, and are not seen in swamps or 'bofedales' (21). Roe and Rees observed groups of 3-14 individuals, usually one adult male, one yearling male and several adult and yearling females. Taruca appear to graze on small, ground-hugging plants rather than on the taller grasses and hedges (15).

THREATS TO SURVIVAL Principal causes of decline are hunting, habitat destruction and loss to agriculture especially at lower altitudes, and increased competition from domestic livestock (5,7,8,9,10,11,14). Reportedly a relatively easy animal to hunt, it has almost been eliminated from lower altitudes in Peru (5), and in Bolivia is subject to intense hunting pressure for local commercial meat markets (sold as 'Charque' - salted meat dried in the sun) (7,8). In Chile its liking for lucerne brings it into conflict with local Indians who readily kill it (7,11). In Dpto. Ayacucho, Peru, a 1977 report mentioned that increased mining activities had increased poaching pressure and was also destroying the deer's habitat (2). Miller et al stress that in Chile destruction of cover by charcoal burners is an important threat, with conversion of stream bottom habitat to agriculture, and competition from sheep, cattle, llamas etc. probably also playing a part (11). Contagious livestock diseases may also affect the species (14).

CONSERVATION MEASURES TAKEN Listed in Appendix 1 of the 1973 Convention on International Trade in Endangered Species of Wild Fauna and Flora, trade in it or its products therefore being subject to strict regulation by ratifying nations, and trade for primarily commercial purposes banned. Reportedly protected by law in all countries in which it occurs but enforcement is virtually non-existent in most areas (9,11). Argentina: plans were well advanced in 1980 for a national park of 300,000 ha of 'puna' upland at Sierra de Ambarto in Catamarca Province to protect the largest concentration of Taruca left in the country (16). Bolivia: protected on the 200,000 ha Ulla Ulla National Faunal Reserve (which also protects the threatened Vicuna), though in 1975 Taruca were still subject to some poaching within the reserve (9). Chile: occurs in Lauca National Park in Tarapaca Province (7,21). Rottmann reports (1981) that increased protection of Vicuna in this area has definitely benefitted Taruca (21). Peru: occurs in Huascaran (Dpto. de Ancash) and Manu (Deptoes. de Madre Dios and Cusco) National Parks. Also in the Pampa Galeras National Reserve (Dpto. de Ica) (9,14,22), the Salinas Aguada Blanca National Reserve in Dpto. Arequipa, founded in 1977 (1,22), the conservation area of Projecto Lago de Junin (Dpto. de Junin), and the projected Andean Nature Reserve in Lucanas and Parinacochas Provinces, Dpto. de Ayacucho (2,6,14,22). In 1978 the Peruvian Government installed guards to counteract increased poaching in the last named area, with financial support from IUCN/WWF Project 1609 (6).

CONSERVATION MEASURES PROPOSED Principal need is effective enforcement of legal protection (5,7). In Chile increased interest in the conservation of the Vicuna has apparently benefitted the Taruca and it is hoped this will also be the case elsewhere as the two species are sympatric over much of their range (4,11,21). A Peruvian report mentions that Taruca should be included in any management plans for the Altiplano (4).

CAPTIVE BREEDING There is no record of Taruca ever having been successfully maintained in captivity. Establishment of a captive breeding herd would, however, be a valuable safeguard for the species.

REMARKS For description of animal see (3,12).

REFERENCES
1. Anon. (1976). New national parks. Oryx 15(2): 128.
2. Anon. (1978). Peru - Guanaco and Andean Deer. WWF Monthly Report, December 1977, p. 5
3. Cabrera, A. (1957-1961). Catalogo de los mamiferos de America del Sur. Revista del Museo Argentina de Ciencias Naturales 'Bernardino Rivadavia', Cienc. Zool. 4(1-2): 1-731.
4. Dourojeanni Ricordi, M. (1977). Utilization of Vicunas in Peru. GTZ, Eschbom Pp. 48.
5. Grimwood, I.R. (1969). Notes on the distribution and status of some Peruvian mammals, 1968. Special Pubn. No.21 Am. Comm. Int. Wildl. Protec. and New York Zool. Soc., New York.
6. Hofmann, R. (1978). Project 1609 - Guanaco and Andean Deer. In Jackson, P. (Ed.), World Wildlife Yearbook 1977-78. WWF, Switzerland. p. 193.
7. IUCN. (1976). North Andean Huemul or Taruca. Sheet code 19.125.10.2. Red Data Book Vol 1 Mammalia. IUCN, Switzerland.
8. Jungius, H. (1974). Beobachtungen am Weisswedehirsh und Anderen Cerviden in Bolivien. Zeit. für Säugetierkunde 39 (6): 373-383.
9. Jungius, H. (1976). Project 960. Deer - International programme for conservation of threatened species. In Jackson P. (Ed.), World Wildlife Yearbook 1975-76. WWF, Switzerland. Pp 201-217.
10. McTaggart Cowan, I. and Holloway, C.W. (1978). Geographical location and current conservation status of the threatened deer of the world. In Threatened Deer. Proceedings of a Working Meeting of the SSC Deer Specialist Group, Longview, Washington State, U.S.A., 26 Sept - 1 Oct 1977. IUCN, Switzerland.
11. Miller, S., Rottmann, J. and Taber, R.D. (1973). Dwindling and endangered ungulates of Chile - Vicuna, Lama, Hippocamelus and Pudu. Trans. N. Amer. Wildl. Nat. Res. Conf. 38.
12. Perry, R. (1977). Lonely world of the Huemul. Wildlife 19(6): 256-257.
13. Povilitis, T. (1976). A progress report on the Huemul project, Huemul biology and conservation. Unpd. report. pp.7.
14. Roe, N.A. and Rees, W.E. (1976). The status and ecology of the Taruca (Hippocamelus antisensis) in Peru. Final Project proposal. Unpd. report pp.12.
15. Roe, N.A. and Rees, W.E. (1976). Preliminary observations of the Taruca in southern Peru. J. Mammal. 57 (4): 722-730.
16. Tarak, A. (1980). Pers comm.
17. Anon. (1977). Vicuna in Chile. Oryx 13 (5): 437.
18. Ortiz-Crespo, F.I. (1981). In litt., including information supplied by Prof. Gustavo Orcés and Juan Black.

19. Bejarano, G. (1981). In litt.
20. Hansen Love, A. (1981). In litt.
21. Rottman, J. (1981). In litt.
22. Dourojeanni Ricordi, M. (1981). In litt.

MARSH DEER or GUASU PUCU   VULNERABLE

Blastocerus dichotomus (Illiger, 1815)

Order   ARTIODACTYLA   Family   CERVIDAE

SUMMARY   Occurs in or near swampy habitat in central South America
(northeast Argentina, Bolivia, Brazil south of the Amazon, Paraguay, southeast
Peru and possibly western Uruguay). Total numbers unknown but certainly
declining in all areas as a result of poaching, disease transmitted by domestic
stock, and habitat loss to cattle ranching and agriculture. Legally protected
throughout its range and occurs in several national parks and reserves but
protection is almost always inadequate and no sizeable population appears to be
secure. Highest numbers occur in the Pantanal marshland region in southwest
Mato Grosso, Brazil, where a census in 1977 estimated a maximum of 7000.
However recruitment to this population in 1975-1977 was nonexistent, possibly as
a result of brucellosis following severe floods in 1974, which also caused many
deer to die of starvation and drowning. Well protected reserves are essential for
the survival of the species.

DISTRIBUTION Central South America where only scattered populations now
survive throughout its former range. Argentina: mainly in the northeast where it
occurs as far south as the Parana Delta 80 km north of Buenos Aires (4). A three
week survey by Schaller and Tarak in 1975 (8) recorded Marsh Deer in the
following Provinces: Formosa: in a few isolated large marshes on ranches in the
south, possibly also along the lower Pilcomayo River and in areas south of
Clorinda. Salta: a few possibly in the northeast along the Pilcomayo River and
adjoining marshes. Chaco: Jungius (1975) thought it might exist in the western
Chaco (4) but Schaller and Tarak could find no evidence for this and the habitat
seemed unsuitable, being very arid (8). Corrientes: populations scattered
throughout, mainly in marshlands of the del Batelito and adjoining Esteros del
Ibera in the north. Misiones: a few possibly along the Parana River in the
southwest adjoining Corrientes. Santa Fe: small numbers perhaps survive in the
northeast where they were once common. Entre-Rios and Buenos Aires: a small
population was said to exist north of Gualequaychu; and there were fair numbers
in the vast marshy region along the Rio Parana between Santa Fe and Buenos
Aires City particularly near the towns of Rosano and San Pedro and in the delta
along the Parana de las Palmas (8). Bolivia: Jungius (1975) recorded it throughout
eastern Bolivia in seasonally flooded savannah country from the foot of the Andes
(from Punto Heath to Santa Cruz), southeast through wet savanna lowlands as far
as the Brazilian border (4). It has been recorded as far north as the transit zone
with the Amazon forest, the most northerly records being from Punto Heath
(although a 1977 survey between Rios Beni and Marmore found no evidence of its
existence there (11)) and Rio Madre de Dios. No deer were encountered in the
northern part of the 1977 survey area (around Lakes Rogagua, Rogaguado,
Huatunas, Grande and Aguas Claras) (11). Brazil: occurs south of the Amazon
forest where largest aggregations are in the flood plains and swamps along the
branches and tributaries of major rivers, such as Tocantins, Araguaia (Bananal
Island), Paramaiba, Sao Francisco and Paraguay; especially in the huge Pantanal
marshlands east of the Rio Paraguay in southwest Mato Grosso (4,12). A small
population also exists along the Rio Uruguay, north of the Uruguayan border (4). A
1978 survey of Mato Grosso received reports of deer along the banks of the
Parana and Araguaia Rivers; also along the Rio Guaporé, a tributary of the
Madeira, particularly in a 10,000 sq. km area of marshlands along the north bank
in the territory of Rondonia. Deer were recorded along tributaries of the Rio
Xingu in northwest Mato Grosso and along the upper Rio Verde, a tributary of the

Tapajos west of the Xingu. Additional populations may exist in northern Mato Grosso between Cuiaba and the southern limit of the rainforest but are as yet unconfirmed (9). Paraguay: scattered distribution, main centres reported as Isla Yacyreta in the Rio Parana, around Lago Ypoa and Lago Vera (south of Asuncion) and along the Rio Pilcomayo (mainly the Estero Patino) (4). Also reported from the Rio Paraguay e.g. along the Brazilian border as far as Fuerte Olimpo (4). Peru: reported only from Pampa Heath near the Bolivian border (4,16). Uruguay: the last museum specimen is from Depto. Rocha in the southeast of the country dated 1958 and the Marsh Deer is thought by some to be extinct in Uruguay (13), though in 1981 it was reported that a few still persisted in the marsh of India Muerta and Esteros de Santa Teresa in Rocha (18,19), and in 1971 there were unconfirmed reports of about 80 deer on a private ranch in the province of Treinta-y-Tres and about 8-10 possibly in the Cabo Polonio National Park in Rocha (5).

POPULATION Total numbers unknown. Argentina: populations very vulnerable, being small and scattered (8). Very few in Santa Fe, Misiones, Salta, Formosa and Chaco (8). In Corrientes which in the 1960s was considered a stronghold, an aerial survey in 1973 recorded very low population densities (8). In Entre Rios and Buenos Aires, 'fair numbers' were thought to exist in 1975 (8). In 1980 Tarak considered the deer to be 'faring badly' in Argentina; the situation not having improved since 1975 (14). Brazil: a 1977 aerial survey of the Pantanal produced an estimate of 5000-6000, possibly 7000 for the whole region, with most (about 4000) in the northern part, north and east of the Rio Sao Lourenço (9). There is no accurate information on the size of other populations, though it may be relatively common in the 10,000 sq. km marshy area on the northern bank of the Rio Guaporé (9). Bolivia: rare, with a very marked decline over recent years. Very small populations exist in a few isolated areas with difficult access, and on private landholdings of conservation-oriented owners (10,11). The 1977 survey recorded a total of only 12 specimens in nearly four weeks spent in the field and five hours aerial survey, covering most of the wet savanna (except Ixiamas) between the Beni and Marmore Rivers in the northwest, indicating that deer density was extremely low, with the highest believed to be between the Mattos and Diabolo Rivers. However the survey was carried out at a time when the high seasonal vegetation offered good cover to the deer and thus any conclusions about actual numbers are considered tenuous (11). Schuerholz and Mann nevertheless predicted in 1977 that the Marsh Deer was likely to become extinct in Bolivia in another decade, or sooner if steps to conserve it were not immediately taken (11). Peru: size of population at Pampa Heath unknown but thought unlikely to exceed 150-200 animals in 1976 (2). Paraguay: unknown but considered rare; most populations apparently declining although in 1975 said to be stable around Lago Ypoa and Isla Yacyreta (4). Uruguay: regarded as almost extinct in 1981 (18,19).

HABITAT AND ECOLOGY Swampy habitat - marshes and seasonally flooded areas along rivers. Prefer to be in or near standing water not more than 60 cm deep, with low cover such as reeds or bunch-grasses nearby; avoid dense forest (9). Constantly change their range in accordance with their preferred water level (9). In Formosa (Argentina) they concentrate in dense Cyperus, 2m or more high, from where they spread into surrounding grasslands during the annual flooding (8). In Corrientes they were seen near the edges of large marshes, foraging and resting in standing water with a sparse reed cover. Here the deer preferred a habitat similar to that of nesting Maguari Storks (Euxenura maguari). On some of the Parana islands the deer occupied a mosaic of tall, dense marsh vegetation and scrubby forest (8). In the Pantanal of Brazil the calving season was noted to last at least four months (May to September), while in Bolivia evidence for a specific calving season was conflicting (9,11). One fawn only is normally produced (11). Deer tended to be solitary or in groups of 2-4 unless forced into aggregations on islands during floods (9). Both a browser and grazer (9).

THREATS TO SURVIVAL Principal threats are poaching (for meat, trophies, hides and sport), habitat loss through drainage of marshland, seasonal competition with domestic stock for food and space, and disease transmitted by domestic bovids (4,8). The deer's rather limited habitat preference severely restricts its distribution and as more and more swamps are drained, its range will inevitably decrease; also its occurrence in small, scattered populations make it prone to local extinction. Marsh deer are particularly vulnerable during the rainy season when floods force them to take refuge on higher patches of ground from where cattle are likely to displace them and will outcompete them for limited forage, causing mortality if the floods are unusually prolonged, or the islands too small (4,9). At other times of year competition for food is thought unlikely to be important and Marsh Deer are considered generally better adapted to wet savanna than livestock (11). Deer are particularly vulnerable to human predation during the floods e.g. in the Parana delta in Buenos Aires Province, Argentina, where they are forced to the populated periphery of the marshes, and in the Esteros del Ibera in Corrientes, Argentina where they are excluded from the only dry land in the area by fishermen and poachers (8). Grass burning, carried out in many areas in the dry season deprives deer of the cover on which they are highly dependent and exposes them to hunters and predators (4,8). Habitat loss due to marsh drainage is also particularly important in areas such as the Parana Delta and along the lagoon zone of the southern Brazilian coast (e.g. Lago dos Patu, Taim Marsh) (4) and is reported to threaten the last few Marsh Deer in Uruguay (19). Deer in the Parana Delta near Ituzaingo are threatened by a dam (8), as are those on Isla Yacyreta in southern Paraguay (17). In Bolivia the preferred habitat of wet grassland interspersed with open forests is much favoured for cattle production and most is now ranched. Indiscriminate hunting by Indians (e.g. in Formosa, Argentina), or by ranch-hands poses a severe threat in many areas (8,10); in Bolivia the Marsh Deer is the principal source of meat for labourers on many of the cattle ranches (10). Schaller and Vasconcelos discovered virtually no recruitment in the Pantanal population in 1977, the years 1975-77 being effectively reproductive failures (9). This is attributed to brucellosis (spontaneous abortion) which is common in the Pantanal cattle, and particularly increased in frequency after heavy floods in 1974 which themselves also caused extensive mortality amongst the deer (9). There is evidence that the population is also affected by foot and mouth or a babesiosis-like disease, both of which are prevalent in local cattle (9), and two young animals examined in Bolivia in 1977 both had foot and mouth (11). Hunting is considered to be the single most immediate threat in Argentina (8), whereas habitat loss is thought to be the major factor in Bolivia (10). In the Pantanal, as outlined above, disease has almost certainly been the principle factor in the population decrease, though poaching may become increasingly important with the construction of the Transpantanal Highway opening the area up to motorised poachers; up to 1977 the deer were little hunted in this area (9).

CONSERVATION MEASURES TAKEN Listed in Appendix 1 of the 1973 Convention on International Trade in Endangered Species of Wild Fauna and Flora, trade in it or its products therefore being subject to strict regulation by ratifying nations, and trade for primarily commercial purposes banned. Legally protected in all countries of its range but enforcement is generally lacking (4). Argentina: although federally protected there is very little enforcement in most areas (8). In Formosa where many private landowners would like to protect the deer they are hampered by the large Indian population which is legally able to hunt on the ranches (8); though in 1975 it was stated that a population was protected in a provincial reserve (4). An attempt to establish a herd on an island in the Parana delta was made some years ago but failed, the four surviving deer out of the original ten being transferred to a 4000 ha island near Santa Fe where the provincial Recursos Naturales hoped to reestablish the deer (8). Bolivia:

IUCN/WWF Project No.1587 initiated in 1977 to examine the feasibility of establishing a Marsh deer reserve near Lake Rogaguado had disappointing results, most of the area being already colonised and used for grazing under the Reforma Agraria (11). A few deer were reported as protected on some private ranches (11), and in 1975 they were said to occur in very low numbers in Isilboro Secure National Park (4). Brazil: in 1980 the principal reserves containing Marsh Deer were reported as: Emas (100,000 ha) and Araguaia (560,000 ha) National Parks in Goias State, the Guapore Reserve (ca. 15,000 ha) and Caracara Biological Reserve (ca. 70,000 ha) in Mato Grosso, the Jaru Reserve in Rondonia (350,000 ha), and the Sema Island reserve in the Pantanel (15). There was no real knowledge of deer numbers or distribution in any of these, although they have been reported as very scarce in Emas and as leaving Caracara seasonally (9,15). In 1977 there was reported to be a small but viable population in Araguaia N.P. but the park is beset with problems (ranches, Indian claims, poachers) and long term prospects are not good (9). In 1980 the Caracara, Sema Island and Jaru Reserves were noted as unguarded and possibly heavily hunted (15). Contrary to earlier reports, no deer are believed to exist in Chapada dos Veadeiros National Park, though they have been reported as occurring in Sierra Canastra National Park in Minas Gerais State (4), and in the 3000 ha Poco das Antas Federal Biological Reserve in the coastal foothills of Sierra do Mar (3). Paraguay: protected on some private ranches (e.g. west of Lago Ypoa, Isla Yacyreta on the Parana River though the latter is threatened with inundation (17)) (4). Peru: in 1976 said to be moderately secure in Pampa Heath, the area being inaccessible and little inhabited (4).

CONSERVATION MEASURES PROPOSED Adequate enforcement of the laws protecting the species are needed plus the establishment of well guarded reserves in suitable areas, preferably as free as possible of foot and mouth and other introduced ungulate diseases. Unfortunately the deer's apparent need for a specific water regime means that it is liable to range over extensive areas following seasonal changes in water level, and protection of suitably large areas is therefore made especially difficult. The cooperation of ranchers on land surrounding any such reserves would have to be sought (9). Continued monitoring and ecological study of the deer is needed throughout its range especially in its Pantanal stronghold to try to accurately determine immediate causes of the population decline. Argentina: in 1976 the Servico Nacional de Parques Nacionales proposed a 9000 ha national park in the little disturbed southwestern part of the Estero del Ibera (8); some of the large undisturbed islands in the Parana delta were considered ideal for deer reserves (8). However by 1980 no specific habitat had been reserved for the species and no definite plans had been made (14). Brazil: in 1980 the government planned to extend the Caracara Biological Reserve by acquiring 200,000 ha of adjoining higher land to make it a suitable deer reserve and a further 200,000 ha was to be added to Sema Island Reserve (15). Bolivia: Schuerholz and Mann state that, despite the largely negative results of their 1977 survey, the search for a suitable area of at least 20,000 ha for a Marsh Deer reserve has to be continued as the only means to ensure its survival in the country. Logistic problems are great, however, and there is minimal governmental input into any form of conservation. They consider the best prospects to be to try to coordinate conservation efforts by private land-owners, with the possibility of establishing a reserve open to tourism, or to attempt to obtain land which has been registered under the Reforma Agraria but which has not been used according to the requirements of the act and thus returns to the possession of the Reforma after two years (11). Paraguay: in 1980 rescue projects had reportedly been proposed to try to save those deer on the threatened Isla Yacyreta (17). Peru: in 1981 it was reported that the Ministry of Agriculture had just evaluated a proposal to establish a conservation unit in the pampas of the Rio Heath which would encompass virtually the whole of the Marsh Deer's distribution in Peru (16).

CAPTIVE BREEDING A breeding colony at Sao Paulo Zoo, Brazil, had dwindled to one female by 1978; in 1979 a pair was held at Berlin Zoo, West Germany; also there are recent reports of specimens at Bahia Blanca Zoo (Argentina) and Hellenthal in West Germany (4,6). Neto is quoted by Jungius as strongly advising against reintroduction programmes and capture of wild animals for captive breeding until more is known of the species' ecology (4).

REMARKS For description of animal see (1); it is the largest deer in South America (8).

REFERENCES 1. Cabrera, A. (1957-1961). Catalogo de los mamiferos de America del Sur. Revista del Museo Argentina de Ciencias Naturales 'Bernardino Rivadavia', Cienc. Zool., Buenos Aires. 4(1,2): 1-731.
2. IUCN. (1976). Marsh Deer. Sheet code: 19.125.11.1 Red Data Book Vol 1 Mammalia. IUCN, Switzerland.
3. IUCN. (1977). World Directory of National Parks and other Protected Areas. IUCN, Switzerland.
4. Jungius, H. (1976). Project 960 Deer - International programme for conservation of threatened species. In Jackson, P. (Ed.), World Wildlife Yearbook 1975-76. WWF, Switzerland. Pp 201-217.
5. Mittermeier, R.A. (1977). Notes on some endangered and potentially endangered species of South American mammals. Unpd. Report. 10 pp.
6. Olney, P.J.S. (Ed.) (1980). International Zoo Yearbook 20. Zool. Soc. London.
7. Padua, M. (no date). Parques nacionais e reservas equivalentes. Instituto Brasileiro de Desenvolvimento Florestal, Brasilia. 35 pp.
8. Schaller, G.B. and Tarak, A. (1976). The Marsh Deer in Argentina. In Schaller, G.B. Report on a wildlife survey in northern Argentina and in the Emas National Park, Brazil. Unpd. Report. 17 pp.
9. Schaller, G.B. and Vasconcelos, J.M.C. (1978). A Marsh Deer census in Brazil. Oryx 14 (4): 345-351.
10. Schuerholz, G. (1978). Project 1587. Marsh Deer, Rogaguado Reserve. In Jackson, P. (Ed.), World Wildlife Yearbook 1977-78. WWF, Switzerland. Pp. 172-173.
11. Schuerholz, G. and Mann, G. (1977). Draft Final Report on IUCN/WWF Project No.1587/1977. Marsh Deer in Rogaguado Reserve. Unpd. Report to IUCN/WWF.
12. Autori, M.P (1972). Biological data and growth of the first horns of the Marsh Deer (Blastocerus dichotomus). Der Zool. Garten 42: 225-235.
13. Ximenez, A., Langguth, A. and Praderi, R. (1972). Lista sistematica de los mammiferos del Uruguay. Anal. Mus. Nac. Hist. Nat. de Montevideo 7(5): 1-49.
14. Tarak, A. (1980). Pers. comm.
15. Clutton-Brock, T.H. (1981). In litt.
16. Dourojeanni Ricordi, M. (1981). In litt.
17. Vershuren, J. (1980). Saving Paraguay's wilderness. Oryx 15(5): 465-470.
18. Praderi, R. (1981). In litt.
19. Gudynas, E. (1981). In litt.

ARGENTINIAN PAMPAS DEER, VENADO   ENDANGERED
or GAMA

Ozotoceros bezoarticus celer (Cabrera, 1940)

Order   ARTIODACTYLA   Family   CERVIDAE

SUMMARY   Reduced to two small populations on the coast of Buenos Aires Province and scattered groups in San Luis Province, Argentina. Severely depleted by hunting, habitat loss, and possibly disease. Following a 4 year IUCN/WWF project, the 1980 estimate was 400 and increasing; with most populations afforded some protection on reserves or private estancias. Recommendations for future management include reintroduction of captive-bred stock, or translocation of threatened populations to suitable protected sites. One captive herd is known in Buenos Aires Province.

DISTRIBUTION   Argentina where it occurs in scattered groups on private estancias in the Province of San Luis in western Argentina and in two areas in the Province of Buenos Aires (3,4,5). The latter are in a narrow coastal strip along the Bahia de Samborombon - one in the north of the bay between canals 1 and 15, just south of the Rio Salado, and the second further south at Campos del Tuyu near General Lavalle. A single relict group occurred 250 km further south at Punta Médanos near General Madariaga until around 1980 (3,4,5). Formerly abundant throughout the Argentine pampas region from the Atlantic Coast to the Andean foothills (southeast of Mendoza) and south to Rio Negro (1). A captive herd exists at 'La Corona' a private estancia south of Buenos Aires City (3,4,5). Unconfirmed reports had suggested that Pampas Deer in Uruguay may be O. b. celer but recent examination has shown them to correspond to Cabrera's subspecies O. b. leucogaster (3,7).

POPULATION   In 1980 estimated at about 400 in the wild and increasing (5), compared with less than 100 in 1975 (8). In San Luis numbers in 1980 estimated at about 300 head, most (about 200) on one estancia ('La Travesya') with smaller isolated groups on at least 7 others. In Buenos Aires estimates were about 30 at Campos del Tuyu and 60 in the Rio Salado region (5). However the difference in the 1980 and 1975 estimates does not soley reflect a real increase, as many of the San Luis groups were not known to exist in 1975. The years 1977-78 were, however, noted as exceptionally good climatic years in San Luis and the populations there were genuinely increasing. This subspecies was extremely abundant in the early nineteenth century but declined under a variety of pressures until it was considered critically endangered in the early 1970s (5).

HABITAT AND ECOLOGY   The Bahia de Samborombon deer live in areas of tall grasses, marismas and tidal rivers. Islands of higher ground with trees and shrubs (Montes de tala) are preferred habitat and act as refuges during floods. This is, however, probably a marginal environment, the original habitat being pampas and wooded grassland (2). In San Luis, areas still inhabited by Venado were characterised as: (a) near-natural, semi-arid tussock grassland with small copses of chanar scrub, notably centred on the large fixed dunes or 'huecas' rather than on the plains; (b) properties with low cattle stocking rate which were never overgrazed; (c) remote zones with difficult or restricted access; (d) estancias where hunting by the sparse human population was discouraged by the landowner (5). Where it is not harassed, the Venado feeds at intervals throughout the day and normally occurs in groups of less than 5, larger groups being rarely seen even when there are sufficient numbers to do so (7). Most calving occurs in October-November (12).

THREATS TO SURVIVAL   Hunting for the commercial skin trade and habitat loss to ranching and agriculture were probably the main factors in original decline (3,5). In the 18th and 19th centuries vast numbers of Venado pelts were exported (an estimated 2,130,000 between 1860 and 1870) and the deer were killed for a variety of other reasons (sport, food, medicinal purposes) (3,5). Habitat loss has been such that in 1980 it was reported that, excepting lagoons and small pockets of agriculturally marginal land, practically no large areas of its ancestral habitat remain and there is no appreciable protected stretch representative of the former pampas which once covered some 647,000 sq. km (5). Competition for food and space with domestic and feral stock and introduced exotic herbivores such as Axis deer (Axis axis), Fallow deer (Dama dama) and the European hare (Lepus capensis) was probably also an important factor (5). Various livestock diseases, notably foot and mouth, and some gut parasites have been transmitted to, and have periodically drastically reduced, populations of O. b. celer (5). Poaching is still considered a serious problem. In 1980 it was reported that a provincial road was planned in San Luis which would facilitate access to the principle Venado population and greatly increase the risk of poaching. The deer's habitat in San Luis is also threatened by the conversion of many areas to short coverless pastures of exotic Gramineae species. Periodic die-offs of the deer population which occur in San Luis are often attributed to disease but normally seem to occur after years of low productivity (e.g. 1971) when the deer are weakened by a poor food supply, accentuated by competition with livestock (5). Fawns are sometimes kept locally or sold as pets, and skins are occasionally used in tack but are not openly sold (7). The population at Punta Medanos had by 1981 been wiped out by a combination of extensive habitat destruction through road and deep-water port construction, afforestation with softwoods, and poaching which accounted for at least 10 out of 16 or 17 known individuals in 1975-79 (4,5).

CONSERVATION MEASURES TAKEN   The entire species is listed in Appendix 1 of the 1973 Convention on International Trade in Endangered Species of Wild Fauna and Flora, trade in it or its products therefore being subject to strict regulation by ratifying nations, and trade for primarily commercial purposes banned. Legally protected in Argentina. In 1976 IUCN/WWF Project 1303 was initiated jointly with the Province of Buenos Aires, specifically for the conservation of the Venado. As a result a private reserve of 3500 ha with a buffer zone of 4000 ha was established at Campos del Tuyu in 1979 in conjunction with the Fundacion Vida Silvestre Argentina (FVSA), and with financial backing from WWF and the Banco de la Provincia de Buenos Aires. This will safeguard the Venado and other representatives of the humid pampean biota which are now scarce or extinct elsewhere (4,5,6). A federal reserve of 9000 ha has been established in the Rio Salado area, jointly administered by the FVSA and the provincial authorities of Buenos Aires (4,5,7,11). In areas safeguarded against poaching, there has inevitably been an almost immediate increase in deer numbers without the need for other forms of intervention, illustrating the Venado's capacity for rapid natural recovery in numbers (5). In San Luis a provincial decree (No. 3860) was passed in Sept. 1978 to provide a legal framework to protect both the deer and its habitat, and substantial funds were promised for 1980 to purchase equipment for inspectors and guards to live and work in the deer zone, however in 1981 it was reported that none of the facilities promised had materialised, nor were they apparently likely to in the forseeable future (7). However the project is reported to have helped stimulate public interest in the preservation and management of the Venado and other threatened Argentinian species, helping to modify attitudes to conservation (4,5).

CONSERVATION MEASURES PROPOSED   Jackson in the final report of IUCN/WWF Project 1303 recommends the following: in San Luis: habitat protection from ploughing, reseeding, scrub clearance, burning and overgrazing, although he stresses this may be difficult to enforce extensively, but 'core' Venado habitats are areas probably unsuitable for anything other than the light grazing currently practised and may be left intact without official protection; supplementary feeding or pasture management in years when food appears limiting; predator control and fence-line modifications to be experimented with; continued biological studies; control of road building; increased conservation education. He stresses the need for expert guidance and leadership to consolidate recent advances, and notes that: 'because of the rich autochthonous fauna and flora still present, the large extensions of neo-natural ecosystems, the compartively low agricultural value of the land and the lack of any reserve typical of the dry pampas, the zone might be considered for the creation of a national reserve or park (although this would be a long term policy due to the logistic complexities involved)' (5). Apart from continued management of the reserves at Bahia de Samborombon, the principle recommendation is reintroduction of captive-bred animals to suitable parks and reserves, or translocation of wild populations from areas where they become seriously threatened. O. b. leucogaster has bred well in captivity and breeding of O. b. celer would appear to present no inherent problems. Criteria for suitable reintroduction sites have been evaluated and sites identified (5). In 1980 the Argentinian National Parks Service was developing plans for reintroduction of the Venado into El Palmar National Park in Entre Rios Province (11). The captive herd at La Corona could provide a nucleus for such reintroductions but there are difficulties involved (5). Other sites which may still have Venados should be investigated (5).

CAPTIVE BREEDING The captive herd in a 28 ha. enclosure at 'La Corona', Buenos Aires Province numbered 22 in May 1978, having been founded with 19 Venado in 1968/69 mostly from the Bahia de Samborombon stocks. The deer have bred well but management problems have led to deterioration in range quality and resultant high mortality, especially of pre-reproductive individuals, and the potential of this stock for reintroduction remains untapped. It would be very advisable to split this herd to minimize the risk of epidemics exterminating it completely (4,5). In 1979 there were 8 male and 10 female Ozotoceros bezoarticus in 6 collections, of which 9 were bred in captivity (9). Some, at least, are known to be O. b. leucogaster and the rest are this or O. b. bezoarticus (7,8).

REMARKS For description of animal see (1,9). Two other subspecies of Pampas Deer are usually recognised: O. b. leucogaster inhabits southwestern Brazil, southeast and east Bolivia, Paraguay the extreme north of Argentina and Uruguay; and O. b. bezoarticus occurs over much of eastern and central Brazil extending down to the Uruguayan borderlands (1,7,9). Neither are considered threatened at the present time. Dr. J.E. Jackson very kindly commented on a draft of this data sheet.

REFERENCES   1.   Cabrera, A. (1957-1961). Catalogo de los mamiferos de America del Sur. Revista del Museo Argentina de Ciencias Naturales 'Bernardino Rivadavia', Cienc. Zool., Buenos Aires 4(1-2): 1-731.
2.   IUCN. (1976). Argentine Pampas Deer. Sheet Code 19.125.12.1.1 Red Data Book Vol. 1 Mammalia IUCN, Switzerland.
3.   Jackson, J.E. (1978). The Argentine Pampas Deer or Venado (Ozotoceros bezoarticus celer). In Threatened Deer. Proceedings of a Working Meeting of the SSC Deer Specialist Group, Longview, Washington State, U.S.A., 26 Sept - 1 Oct 1977. IUCN, Switzerland.
4.   Jackson, J.E. (1980). Pampas Deer, Argentina - ecology and conservation in Buenos Aires Province. WWF Monthly Report, March 1980.

5. Jackson, J.E. (1980). Final Report on IUCN/WWF project 1303. - Pampas Deer, Argentina - 'Conservation of a critically endangered species in Argentina.' Unpd. Report. 37 pp.

6. Jackson, J.E. (1980). Project 1303. Pampas Deer. In Jackson, P. (Ed.), World Wildlife Yearbook 1979-80. WWF, Switzerland. 177-178.

7. Jackson, J.E. (1981). In litt.

8. Jungius, H. (1976). Project 960 Deer - International programme for conservation of threatened species. In Jackson P., (Ed.), World Wildlife Yearbook 1975-76. WWF, Switzerland. 201-217.

9. Olney, P.J.S. (Ed.) (1980). International Zoo Yearbook 20. Zool. Soc. London.

10. Schaller, G.B. (No date). In litt.

11. Tarak, A. (1980). In litt.

12. Whitehead, G.K. (1972). Deer of the World. Constable, London.

Pudu mephistophiles (de Winton, 1896)

Order   ARTIODACTYLA   Family   CERVIDAE

SUMMARY Probably disjunct distribution in the Andes in Colombia, Ecuador and Peru. Very few specimens have been collected; possibly declining but more data required. Habitat destruction and hunting believed important. Protected in a few reserves in Colombia and possibly in Ecuador. Further reserved areas are needed, especially in Peru, along with more information on status and ecology.

DISTRIBUTION Colombia, Ecuador, and central Peru (12). In Colombia reportedly restricted to the southwestern central Andean Cordillera in the Departments of Valle, Cauca, Narino and Huila, where the paramos of San Rafael, Sotora, Puracé, Moras, Las Hermosas, Guanacas and Delicias (headwaters of the Rio Palacé), perhaps Leirero and Barragan (east of Pulua and possibly the northern limit), and the savannas of Paletarà, have been reported as important habitats, though there appear to be no recent data on distribution (4,6). Ecuador: known from few specimens; from the eastern slopes of the Andes from Mt. Antisana northwards, extending into the western side in the area around Volcan Chiles near the border with Colombia (14); the type specimen was collected from Paramo de Papallacta, Dpto Napo. Peru: reported by Grimwood in 1969 from limited areas of the Dptos de Huanuco and Junin in isolated forest patches in the Upper Huallaga valley above the town of Huanuco and in the area of Carpish Summit with reports also from forested areas above San Ramon, in the valley of the Rio Hausanausi and from the upper Rio Paucartambo. The Peruvian population is apparently totally isolated from those in Ecuador and Colombia (2). Two races are currently recognized (1) but may not be valid: P. m. mephistophiles from Ecuador and Peru and P m. wetmorei from Colombia.

POPULATION Total numbers unknown. Few specimens of either race have been collected (4,5,6,14). Colombia: rare and has been reported as declining rapidly (4,5,6,13). Ecuador: overall status unknown, very few specimens are known as it is both inconspicuous and apparently sparsely distributed and thus easily overlooked (8,14). However, in 1976 it was reportedly frequently seen in the Mt. Antisana region, in paramos east and west of the mountain, though an eight day survey by a National Parks and Wildlife Dept. officer on the northern side of the mountain around that time found no strong evidence of its presence (8). A local naturalist, Juan Black, did not sight any himself while living in the area from 1979 to 1981 but considers that they are almost impossible to see unless pursued with specially trained dogs (14). Its presents status there thus remains conjectural. In 1976 Orcés reported it as apparently very common in the paramo of Volcan Chiles (8). Peru: Grimwood in 1969 reported it as apparently common in very limited areas where it did occur but subject to hunting pressure and habitat destruction and not expected to persist for much longer in some areas (e.g. Huallaga) (2).

HABITAT AND ECOLOGY In Colombia paramos, dense thickets and swampy savannas covered with tall grass and frailejon (Espeletia sp.), in cold areas at altitudes of 3000-4000 m (4,5,6). In Ecuador, thickets surrounded by grass vegetation (8), also at altitudes between 3000-4000 m (10). In Peru, forest areas between 2000-3300 m, dominated by Alnus jorulensis, and isolated patches of forest in drier habitats of high valleys rather than the cold and damp woods and thickets at the highest elevations (2). Its small size and dark colouration allow it to be easily missed among the patches of vegetation (8). Pudu are reported to live in small groups though in Peru at least, P. mephistophiles is said to be solitary (15). The does are believed to normally produce one fawn, occasionally twins (12);

the breeding season is unknown though Grimwood has records of full-term foetuses in April and November (2).

THREATS TO SURVIVAL Habitat destruction and hunting, mainly for its flesh (2,4,5,6,8,13,15). Because of its secretive nature and preference for thick cover, dogs are reportedly necessary to hunt it. However the extent of this threat is unknown; Grimwood (1969) noted that in Peru at least, it had outlasted the sympatric White-tailed Deer (Odocoileus virginianus) in some areas because, unlike the latter, it does not break cover when pursued and is thus harder to capture (14,15). In Colombia it is hunted for sport (13) and in Ecuador in 1976 it was said to be taken by peasants (8), although in 1981 Ortiz-Crespo noted that it was not hunted there to any great extent (14). Grimwood (1969) stated that in Peru habitat destruction was the most important threat in most areas - the small isolated forest patches (5 to 25 sq. km) which it mainly inhabited were rapidly being encroached on for agriculture, firewood and timber, and grazing (2,15). In Colombia burning of grass and shrubs on the paramos during the dry season destroys habitat and also kills some Pudu directly (13), while in Ecuador growing exploitation of the bush for firewood and charcoal was said in 1976 to be limiting the amount of habitat available (8).

CONSERVATION MEASURES TAKEN The Northern Pudu is listed in Appendix 2 of the 1973 Convention on International Trade in Endangered Species of Wild Fauna and Flora, trade in it or its products therefore being subject to regulation and monitoring by ratifying nations. It is protected by law in Colombia and Ecuador (3,9,16)) but not for sure in Peru . The Puracé and Las Farallones de Cali National Parks of Colombia protect a few (11), possibly also the Condor Fauna Sanctuary (N.A. Roe 1976. In litt). In Ecuador, it may occur in areas covered by the Reserva Nacional Ecuatorial and Reserva Cotopaxi (although legislation for these areas was reported in 1977 as still not definite or approved) (7) and also by the Angel Param Reserve (11), and the Sangay Park, though there are no definite records (14).

CONSERVATION MEASURES PROPOSED Resolution No.25, First World Conference on National Parks, Seattle, U.S.A., 1962, called for special protective measures for the species. Creation of further reserves within its range is necessary (8), especially in Peru, where it does not occur in any existing or projected national park or reserve; the San Ramon gorge, Dpto. Junin, would be a good site for such a special sanctuary backed by legislation to control hunting of the Pudu (2). A general survey of its status and ecology would also be desirable.

CAPTIVE BREEDING No information.

REMARKS For description of animal see (12). This data sheet was compiled with the assistance of information supplied by Nicholas A. Roe and Dr. F. Ortiz-Crespo in conjunction with Professor G. Orcés and Juan Black.

REFERENCES   1. Cabrera, A. (1961). Catalogo de los mamiferos de America del Sur, Vol. 2. Revista del Museo Argentina de Ciencias Naturales 'Bernardino Rivadavia', Cienc. Zool. Buenos Aires. 4(1,2): 1-731.
2. Grimwood, I.R. (1969). Notes on the distribution and status of some Peruvian mammals 1968. Spec. Publ. No.21, Am. Comm. Int. Wildl. Protec. and New York Zool. Soc., Bronx, New York.
3. Hunsaker, D. (1972). National Parks in Colombia. Oryx 11(6): 441-448.
4. Lehmann V., F.C. (1945). Un venado del subgenero Pudella nuevo para la ciencia. Revista del Universidad Cauca,

Popayan, Colombia, No.6: 76-79.

5. Lehmann V., F.C. (1959). Pudu mephistophiles wetmorei Lehmann: venado conejo. Novedades Colombianas 1(4): 202-204.

6. Lehmann V., F.C. (1960). Notas adicionales sobre Pudu mephistophiles wetmorei Lehmann. Novedades Colombianas 1(5): 280-283.

7. MacBryde, B. (1971). Setbacks to conservation in Ecuador. Biol. Conserv. 4(5): 387-488.

8. Ortiz-Crespo, F. (1976). In litt., including information supplied by Professor Gustav Orcés and Juan Black.

9. Perry, R. (1972). Parks and problems in Colombia. Oryx 11(6): 433-440.

10. Schauenberg, P. (1973). Le mystérieux cerf nain des Andes. Musées de Genève 14(134): 12-16.

11. Harroy, J-P. (Ed.), United Nations List of National Parks and Equivalent Reserves, 1971, 2nd Ed. and Addendum - Corrigendum, 1972. Hayez, Brussels.

12. Whitehead, G.K. (1972). Deer of the World. Constable, London.

13. Medem, F. (1977). In litt.

14. Ortiz-Crespo, F. (1981). In litt., including information supplied by Prof. Gustavo Orces and Juan Black.

15. Grimwood, I. (1968). In litt.

16. Figueroa S., S. (1980). Revision de especies faunisticas silvestres registradas en el Ecuador, que deben constar en los anexos de la ley vigente. Unpd. Report.

Antilocapra americana peninsularis (Nelson, 1912)

Order   ARTIODACTYLA   Family   ANTILOCAPRIDAE

SUMMARY   Reduced to a few scattered herds in the Vizcaino region of Baja California, Mexico. Threatened by hunting, and habitat deterioration through overgrazing by livestock. Legally protected though enforcement is generally inadequate. Studies are needed, and the co-operation of local people in its protection should be encouraged.

DISTRIBUTION   Southern Baja California, Mexico; where by the 1970s was confined to the region of the Sierra Vizcaino and Desierto de Vizcaino (3). Principal areas of distribution are the Arroyo San Jose, Rancho San Jose de Castro, and Los Voladores south of the Ojo de Liebra lagoon (3). Formerly appears to have ranged from the Magdalena Desert region in the south along the Pacific (West) side of Baja California to the region of San Antonia, about 200 km from the border with the U.S.A. (5). Distribution in northern Baja California was probably once continuous with that of the Sonoran Pronghorn (Antilocapra americana sonoriensis) also listed in the IUCN Red Data Book (5).

POPULATION   A survey in June 1978, using a transect census method, counted 80 individuals, - 45 does, 27 bucks and 8 juveniles; this compared with 83 counted in February 1977 - 30 does, 29 bucks, 13 juveniles and a group of 11 unclassified; the percentage of the population not observed is unknown (3). In 1925 500 were estimated to exist in Baja California and there are records of bands of up to 30 seen in the Vizcaino plains (4). Guzman characterised the Pronghorn as 'abundant' in the Magdalena Desert in early 1958, though neither specimens nor sight records are cited (1,5).

HABITAT AND ECOLOGY   The taxon is said to be ecologically very similar to the Sonoran Pronghorn, (5). They occur in flat, open, arid or semi-desert areas ('llanos') with widely scattered, xerophytic vegetation and dry washes and dunes (3,5). Observations around 1917 in northeastern Baja California indicated that they fed throughout most of the year on a variety of sun-cured vegetation, though showing a preference for tender new growth during spring. Abronia villosa the 'Four O'Clock Plant' was reportedly a preferred food plant and flower heads of the parasitic Desert Broom-rape Orobanche multiflora were chewed, apparently for their moisture. They are believed not to require free water (5). Calving in northern Baja California was reported as occurring in February (5,6), and Pronghorn gestation period is estimated at around 240 days, with 1 or 2 kids produced (8).

THREATS TO SURVIVAL   Hunting, now illegal, has undoubtedly been the major factor in the decline. Much of it used to be in the form of trophy hunting by Americans; though by 1968 this was said to have been largely curtailed, but subsistence hunting by local people has certainly continued (4,5). Competition for forage with domestic livestock (notably sheep and goats) is also thought likely to be important especially during the drier parts of the year, and cattle fences may have a detrimental effect by impeding seasonal movements (4,5).

CONSERVATION MEASURES TAKEN   Listed in Appendix 1 of the 1973 Convention on International Trade in Endangered Species of Wild Fauna and Flora, trade in it or its products therefore being subject to strict regulation by ratifying nations, and trade for primarily commercial purposes banned. Legally protected in Mexico since 1922 (3). Enforcement is generally inadequate though some private ranches in Mexico afford Pronghorns a degree of protection (4,5); however, it is not known if this specifically applies to A. a. peninsularis.

CONSERVATION MEASURES PROPOSED Enforcement of legal protection. Refuges for the animal should be established and studies are needed to determine ecological requirements as the basis for more detailed conservation plans. It has been suggested that an education programme be initiated to seek the support of local people (4). Leopold has stated that, once restored in numbers, the Pronghorn in Mexico could yield a substantial annual harvest as it does in the Western United States (4), though it is unlikely that the inhospitable environment of the Baja California deserts could ever support sufficient numbers to make this feasible there .

CAPTIVE BREEDING Pronghorn are kept in several North American zoos, though no captive individuals at present are believed to be A. a. peninsularis (7).

REMARKS For description see (2). The validity of this taxon as a separate subspecies has been questioned; it has been considered identical with A. a. sonoriensis, though recent study has shown the two to be well separable on morphometric grounds (2,8). Three other subspecies are also currently recognised: A. a. americana, A. a. mexicana and A. a. oregano (2). The species as a whole is not considered threatened; in 1975 it was reported to number over 300,000 (9).

REFERENCES   1.   Guzman, H., G. (1961). Vegetation zones of the Territory of Baja California in relation to wildlife. In 1961 Transactions of the Desert Bighorn Council.

2.   Hall, E.R. (1981). The Mammals of North America. Wiley Interscience.

3.   Hernandez G., M.A. (1979). The Pronghorn Antelope in Mexico. Unpd. report.

4.   Leopold, A. (1954). Wildlife of Mexico. University of California Press, Berkeley.

5.   Monson, G. (1968). The Sonoran Pronghorn. In 1968 Transactions of the Desert Bighorn Council.

6.   Murphy, R.C. (1917). Natural history observations from the Mexican portion of the Colorado Desert. Abst. Proc. Linnaean Soc. New York for years ending March 14, 1916 and March 13, 1917, Nos. 23-29: 43-101.

7.   Olney, P.J.S. (Ed.) (1980). International Zoo Yearbook 20. Zool. Soc. London.

8.   Paradiso, J.L. and Nowak, R.M. (1971). Taxonomic status of the Sonoran Pronghorn. J. Mammal 52 (4): 855-858.

9.   U.S. Fish and Wildlife Service. (1975). Sonoran Pronghorn Antelope Team Established. U.S.A.F. News Release.

SONORAN PRONGHORN   ENDANGERED

Antilocapra americana sonoriensis (Goldman, 1945)

Order   ARTIODACTYLA   Family   ANTILOCAPRIDAE

SUMMARY   Reduced to an estimated 300-450 animals in the Sonoran Desert of
Arizona, U.S.A., and Mexico. Decline associated with hunting, which still
continues in Mexico despite legal protection, and habitat destruction mainly from
overgrazing by domestic stock. Habitat is protected in most of its Arizonan
range and in one area in Mexico. A Recovery Team has been established in the
U.S.A. and a Recovery Plan is in draft form.

DISTRIBUTION U.S.A. and Mexico. Present range is in a portion of the Sonoran
desert in southwest Arizona, U.S.A., roughly between Yuma and Ajo, extending
south and eastwards into Sonora, Mexico to northwest of Carborca with a further
outlying region south of this between Cerro Viejos and Punto de Lobos.
Historically found throughout the Sonoran Desert - from the region of Bahia Kino,
southwest of Hermosillo in Sonora, almost as far as Tucson and Phoenix in
Arizona, and extending westward into California to the Salton Sea and south into
Baja California to around Punta Estrella (2,3,5,9,10).

POPULATION 1980 estimate, derived from aerial and ground surveys, of 300-450
in total, comprising 100-150 in the U.S.A.and 200-300 in Mexico. The U.S.A.
population is stable at present and has been so for over 40 years, while that in
Mexico is decreasing (9). A survey in the late 1950s estimated 1000 remaining in
Mexico (1).

HABITAT AND ECOLOGY Although originally occurring throughout the Sonoran
Desert, it is now confined to undeveloped and lightly grazed areas of small,
scattered patches of grassland, generally in regions with less than 12 cm rainfall
per year, from sea level to 600 m (10). Diet is poorly known, though is believed to
consist largely of dried and withered remains of annual and biennial plants, the
animals also browsing to some extent on the perennials Palo Verde (Cercidium
spp.), Mesquite (Prosopis juliflora), Ironwood (Olneya tesota) and the Chain Cholla
(Opuntia fulgida) (7). Monson has stated that they do not require free water and
that there is no good evidence that they ever drink water when it is available (7).
Rutting season is in July and females give birth to 1 or 2 fawns in early March,
following a gestation period of around 240 days. Fawn mortality is high with only
about 20% survival to sexual maturity (about 18 months) (9). Pronghorns
characteristically roam in small scattered groups throughout the summer,
congregating in larger herds in the winter. Old bucks are occasionally solitary
(10).

THREATS TO SURVIVAL The Sonoran pronghorn occupies marginal pronghorn
habitat; the environment where it persists being of the most severe in North
America (8) and cattle and horse grazing has further reduced the quality of the
habitat in most areas (6,9). In Mexico agrarian reform programmes and unlawful
hunting continue to have a deleterious effect on the population. Most hunting is
in the form of subsistence poaching for food rather than sport shooting for
trophies and is very difficult to control (8). Cattle fences may pose an additionl
problem in impeding seasonal movements (7).

CONSERVATION MEASURES TAKEN   Listed in Appendix 1 of the 1973
Convention on International Trade in Endangered Species of Wild Fauna and Flora,
trade in it or its products therefore being subject to strict regulation by ratifying

nations, and trade for primarily commercial purposes banned. There is no evidence of any international trade. Hunting has been banned in Mexico since 1922 and in Arizona since about 1927 and the taxon is listed as 'Endangered' under the 1973 U.S. Endangered Species Act (9). The Arizona habitat is reasonably secure, being contained within the Cabeza Prieta Game Range, the Organ Pipe Cactus National Monument and an Airforce gunnery range (9). In the first two, predator control is applied when needed to protect kids, livestock has been removed from areas used by the pronghorns, and waterholes have been provided where possible (although this may not be necessary for the species) (6). A Recovery Team formed by the US Fish and Wildlife Service began a study of the taxon in 1975 (10,11). In Mexico one of the areas inhabited by the pronghorn, the Sierra del Pinacate, has been declared a national park and biologists have been collecting data to help formulate conservation plans (5). Some private ranches in Mexico offer the pronghorn a degree of protection (5).

CONSERVATION MEASURES PROPOSED A Sonoran Pronghorn Recovery Plan, concerned principally with the Arizona portion of the population, is in review draft form (9). Adequate enforcement of hunting laws and protection of remaining habitat in Mexico would greatly benefit the animal.

CAPTIVE BREEDING Pronghorn are kept in several North American Zoos. In 1979 56 individuals in 13 collections were registered, of which 30 had been bred in captivity; none of these, however, were believed to be A. a. sonoriensis (4,8).

REMARKS For description see (3,10). Originally described by Goldman in 1945 (2), the validity of this taxon has been questioned, though it has now been shown to be well separable as a subspecies on morphometric grounds (12). Hall (1981) also recognises 4 other subspecies : A. a. americana, A. a. mexicana, A. a. oregano, and A. a. peninsularis (3). The last is also included in the IUCN Red Data Book. The species as a whole is not considered threatened, in 1975 it was reported to number more than 3000,000 (11). This data sheet was compiled from a draft provided in 1981 by John S. Phelps of the Sonoran Pronghorn Recovery Team.

REFERENCES
1. Bernardo Villa, A. (1958). Informal report on studies of Bighorns and Antelope in northern Mexico. Instituto de Biologica, Mexico, D.F.
2. Goldman, E.A. (1945). A new pronghorn antelope from Sonora. Proc. Biol. Soc. Washington 58: 3.
3. Hall, E.R. (1981). Mammals of North America. Wiley Interscience.
4. Hanson, C.L. (1976). In litt to R.S.R. Fitter.
5. Hernandez G., M.A. (No date). The Pronghorn Antelope in Mexico. Unpd. report 8pp.
6. IUCN (1976). Sonoran Pronghorn, Sheet Code 19.127.1.1.2. In Red Data Book Vol.1 Mammalia. IUCN, Switzerland.
7. Monson, G. (1968). The Sonoran Pronghorn. In 1968 Transactions of the Desert Bighorn Council.
8. Olney, P.J.S. (Ed.) (1980). International Zoo Yearbook 20. Zool. Soc. London.
9. Phelps, J.S. (1981). In litt.
10. U.S. Bur. Sport Fisheries and Wildlife (1975). News release, 16.6.75.
11. U.S. Fish and Wildlife Sevice (1975). Sonoran Pronghorn Antelope Team Established. USDI News Release. McGarvey 202/343-5634.
12. Paradiso, J.L. and Nowak, R.M. (1971). Taxonomic status of the Sonoran Pronghorn. J. Mammal. 52(4): 855-858.

INDEX

Taxa in brackets are no longer regarded as valid